Research Methods for Education

Research Methods for Education

Gregory J. Privitera
St. Bonaventure University

Lynn Ahlgrim-Delzell
The University of North Carolina at Charlotte

Los Angeles | London | New Delhi
Singapore | Washington DC | Melbourne

FOR INFORMATION:

SAGE Publications, Inc.
2455 Teller Road
Thousand Oaks, California 91320
E-mail: order@sagepub.com

SAGE Publications Ltd.
1 Oliver's Yard
55 City Road
London EC1Y 1SP
United Kingdom

SAGE Publications India Pvt. Ltd.
B 1/I 1 Mohan Cooperative Industrial Area
Mathura Road, New Delhi 110 044
India

SAGE Publications Asia-Pacific Pte. Ltd.
3 Church Street
#10-04 Samsung Hub
Singapore 049483

Acquisitions Editor: Karen Omer
Content Development Editors: Lucy Berbeo/
Jennifer Jovin
Editorial Assistants: Elizabeth You/Sarah Dillard
Production Editor: Kelly DeRosa
Copy Editor: Gillian Dickens
Typesetter: C&M Digitals (P) Ltd.
Proofreader: Lawrence Baker
Indexer: Will Ragsdale
Cover Designer: Michael Dubowe
Marketing Manager: Jill Oelson

Printed in the United States of America

ISBN 978-1-5063-0332-1

This book is printed on acid-free paper.

18 19 20 21 22 10 9 8 7 6 5 4 3 2 1

BRIEF CONTENTS

DETAILED CONTENTS

ABOUT THE AUTHORS

St. Bonaventure University

Gregory J. Privitera is a professor and chair of the Department of Psychology at St. Bonaventure University, where he is a recipient of its highest teaching honor, the Award for Professional Excellence in Teaching, and its highest honor for scholarship, the Award for Professional Excellence in Research and Publication. Dr. Privitera received his PhD in behavioral neuroscience in the field of psychology at the State University of New York at Buffalo and continued his postdoctoral research at Arizona State University. He is an author of multiple books on statistics, research methods, and health psychology, in addition to authoring more than three dozen peer-reviewed scientific articles aimed at advancing our understanding of health and well-being. For his work developing a literacy strategy to promote health education for children that has implications for public policy, he was awarded an early career presentation award from the American Psychological Association at its 2015 conference in Toronto, Canada. For his work with students and fruitful record of academic and research advisement, Dr. Privitera was honored as Advisor of the Year by St. Bonaventure University in 2013. He is the award-winning author of *Research Methods for the Behavioral Sciences* (2nd ed.), from which this book is adapted and for which he received the Most Promising New Textbook Award from the Text and Academic Authors Association. In addition to his teaching, research, and advisement, Dr. Privitera is a veteran of the U.S. Marine Corps and is married with two children: a daughter, Grace Ann, and a son, Aiden Andrew.

Florence Martin

Lynn Ahlgrim-Delzell is an associate professor of research at the University of North Carolina at Charlotte with 25 years of experience conducting research on issues pertinent to individuals with moderate to severe developmental disability. She earned her BS in psychology and MS in school psychology from Illinois State University in Normal, Illinois. She earned her PhD in educational research methodology at the University of North Carolina at Greensboro. She has more than 40 peer-reviewed articles and book chapters on literacy instruction and assessment and access to academic content for individuals with moderate to severe developmental disability. She teaches master's and doctoral-level courses on research methods and statistics and serves as an external consultant on U.S. Department of Education–funded research grants on reading instruction for this population. She is coauthor of the Early Literacy Skills Builder (ELSB), Early Reading Skills Builder (ERSB), and the Nonverbal Literacy Assessment (NVLA). She was awarded Fellow status by the American Association on Intellectual and Developmental Disabilities and received the 2017 Excellence in Research Award from the College of Education at the University of North Carolina at Charlotte.

ACKNOWLEDGMENTS

From Gregory J. Privitera:

I want to take a moment to thank all those who have been supportive and endearing throughout my career. To my family, friends, acquaintances, and colleagues—thank you for contributing to my perspective in a way that is indubitably recognized and appreciated. In particular to my son, Aiden Andrew, and daughter, Grace Ann—every moment I am with you I am reminded of what is truly important in my life. As a veteran, I also want to thank all those who serve and have served—there is truly no greater honor than to serve something greater than yourself.

From Lynn Ahlgrim-Delzell:

I would like to thank the many friends, teachers, colleagues, and mentors in my life who have supported me in so many ways. I extend special acknowledgment to Drs. Daniel Graybill and James Dudley for empowering me to find my way. I would also like to thank the thousands of students and their parents, teachers and school administrators, graduate students, and everyone else who have allowed me the opportunity to learn from them through my research over the past 25 years. I would also like to thank my husband, Pete Delzell, and my children, Lindsey and Samantha. To all of you, thank you for making my life rich, meaningful, and fun!

***

Importantly, to the thousands of methodology students and educators across the country who will use this book—thank you! It is your pursuit of education that has inspired this contribution. Our hope is that you take away as much from reading this book as we have from writing it.

Last, but certainly not least, we would also like to thank the many reviewers who gave us feedback during the development process:

Steven R. Aragon, Texas State University

Kenneth R. Austin, Stephen F. Austin State University

Charletta H. Barringer-Brown, Fayetteville State University

James A. Bernauer, Robert Morris University

Blanche S. Brownley, Trinity DC University

Tyrone Bynoe, University of Michigan-Flint

Alex D. Colvin, Prairie View A&M University

Ginevra Courtade, University of Louisville

Jacqueline S. Craven, Delta State University

Travis Crone, University of Houston-Downtown

Diana R. Dansereau

Maryann Dudzinski, Valparaiso University

Octavio J. Esqueda, Biola University

Claire B. Gallagher, Georgian Court University

Ramona A. Hall, Cameron University

Leslie Huling, Texas State University

Stacey L. Kite, Johnson & Wales University

Jamie Branam Kridler, East Tennessee State University

Lydia Kyei-Blankson, Illinois State University

Hsuehi (Martin) Lo, Saint Cloud State University

Amu Magaya, Georgian Court University

Mabel CPO Okojie, Mississippi State University

James Pann, Nova Southeastern University

Gary Reglin, Nova Southeastern University

Tammy Shutt, Lipscomb University

Eric Shyman, St. Joseph's College, New York

Theresa Van Lith, Florida State University

Lisa LM Welling, Oakland University

Carol Winkle, Aquinas College

Lea Witta, University of Central Florida

Jennifer R. Wolgemuth, University of South Florida

Jiyoon Yoon, University of Texas Arlington

Jingshun Zhang, Florida Gulf Coast University

Laurence G. Zoeckler, Utica College

PREFACE

Research Methods for Education uses a problem-focused approach to introduce research methods in a way that fully integrates the decision tree—from identifying a research question to choosing an appropriate analysis and sharing results. This book begins with an introduction to the general research process, ethics, identifying and measuring variables, conducting literature reviews, selecting participants, and more. Research designs across education are introduced, from designs that are nonexperimental, quasi-experimental, and experimental to those that are qualitative and quantitative. Throughout each chapter, students are shown how to structure a study to answer a research question (design) and are navigated through the challenging process of choosing an appropriate analysis to make a decision (analysis). This book integrates methodology with a particular focus on methodology and design for education. The following are unique features in this book to facilitate student learning:

- **Strengthened organization of research design:**
  - ○ **Follows a problem-focused organization.** This book is organized into five main sections. Each section builds upon the last to give a full picture of the scientific process. In Section I, "Scientific Inquiry," students are introduced to the process and ethics of engaging in the scientific method. In Section II, "Defining and Measuring Variables, Selecting Samples, and Choosing an Appropriate Research Design," students are shown how to define and measure scientific variables, and methods used to select samples and choose an appropriate research design are described. Sections III and IV fully introduce each type of research design, from "Nonexperimental Research Designs" (Chapters 8–12) to "Quasi-Experimental, Experimental, and Mixed-Methods Research Designs" (Chapters 13–15), respectively. Section V, "Applied Research Designs" (Chapters 16–17), introduces students to action research and program evaluation, which engage in systematic inquiry to evaluate instructional changes and their implementation within a specific context. In Section VI,

"Analyzing, Interpreting, and Communicating Research Data" (Chapters 18–21), students are shown how to summarize and describe outcomes (using American Psychological Association [APA] style) for both quantitative and qualitative studies. Also included is a full chapter that introduces how to use APA style to write manuscripts and gives an introduction to creating posters and giving talks. The organization of this book is "problem focused" in that it introduces the scientific process as it would be applied from setting up a study, to conducting a study, to communicating the outcomes observed in that study—all while applying the decision tree to engage further the critical thinking skills of students.

- **Ethics in Focus sections in each chapter.** Ethical considerations are often specific to a particular research design or methodology. For this reason, the topic of ethics is not only covered in Chapter 3, but at least one Ethics in Focus section is also included in each chapter. These sections review important ethical issues related to the topics in each chapter. This allows professors the flexibility to teach ethics as a separate section and integrate discussions of ethics throughout the semester. This level of organization for ethics is simply absent from most comparable research methods textbooks.

- **Introduces three broad categories of research design.** In truth, research design is complex. Many designs are hybrids that cannot be neatly fit into a single type of category or research design. This is especially true for education where research designs are often dynamic depending on the educational environment being studied. For this reason, we simplify research designs into nonexperimental, quasi-experimental, and experimental categories, then identify the strengths and limitations of these designs for education.

- **Reduced bias in language across research designs:**
  - **Research design is introduced without bias.** Research designs are introduced as being used to answer different types of questions. We avoid referring to all studies as "experiments." In that spirit, experiments are instead introduced as answering different types of research questions. It is emphasized throughout this book that the ability to demonstrate cause does not make a design superior to other designs; it simply allows researchers to answer different types of questions (i.e., research questions pertaining to cause).
  - **The qualitative research design and perspective is given fair coverage.** While many textbooks appropriately focus on quantitative methods that make up most of the research conducted in the education sciences, many omit or even are dismissive of qualitative methodology. This bias can mislead students into thinking that all research is quantitative. This book includes a fair balance of qualitative methods throughout the book in addition to quantitative methods. All of these methods contribute to the peer-review literature, and many robust qualitative methodologies are used often by educational researchers.

- Engages student learning and interest:
  - Conversational writing style. We write in a conversational tone that speaks to the reader as if he or she is the researcher. It empowers students to view research methods as something they are capable of understanding and applying. It is a positive psychology approach to writing that involves students in the process and decisions made using the scientific process. The goal is to motivate and excite students by making the book easy to read and follow without "dumbing down" the information they need to be successful.
  - Written with student learning in mind. There are many features in this book to help students succeed. Many figures and tables are given in each chapter to facilitate student learning and break up the readings to make the material less intimidating. Key terms are bolded and defined on a separate text line, as they are introduced. Each defined term is included in a glossary, and these terms are also restated at the end of each chapter to make it easier for students to search for key terms while studying. In addition, margin notes are included in each chapter to summarize key material, and many reviews and activities are included at the end of each chapter to test learning and give students an opportunity to apply the knowledge they have learned.
  - Learning objectives and learning objective summaries. Learning objectives are stated in each chapter to get students focused and thinking about the material they will learn, as well as to organize each chapter and to allow students to review content by focusing on those learning objectives they struggle with the most. In addition, a chapter summary organized by learning objective is provided at the end of each chapter. In this summary, each learning objective is stated and answered. Hence, not only are learning objectives identified in each chapter, but they are also answered at the end of each chapter.
  - Connecting to the Classroom sections take an idea from the chapter and illustrate how it can be applied to educational research. These sections, included in most chapters in the book, are aimed at helping students see how the ideas from the book can be used to evaluate common classroom educational practices. We believe the inclusion of classroom examples will also make research more approachable and understandable to students.
  - Learning Checks are inserted throughout each chapter for students to review what they learn, as they learn it. Many research methods textbooks give learning check questions, with no answer. How can students "check" their learning without the answers? Instead, in this book, all learning checks have questions with answer keys to allow students to actually "check" their learning before continuing their reading of the chapter.
  - Making Sense sections support critical and difficult material. A research methods course can have many areas where students can struggle, and the Making Sense sections are included to break down the most difficult concepts and material in the book—to make sense of them. These sections, included

in most chapters in the book, are aimed at easing student stress and making research methods more approachable to students. Again, this book was written with student learning in mind.

- **APA Appendices** support student learning of APA style. The appendices include an essential APA writing guide (A.1); a guide to grammar, punctuation, and spelling (A.2); a full-sample APA-style manuscript from a study that was published in a peer-reviewed scientific journal (A.3); and instructions for creating posters using Microsoft PowerPoint, with a sample poster and poster template given (A.4). Also included are instructions for using randomization (B.1) and constructing a Latin square (B.2). Hence, this book provides the necessary support for students who are asked to complete a research project and an APA-style paper, poster, or talk. Few books provide this level of comprehensive supportive materials.

In addition, there is one more overarching feature that we refer to as *teachability*. Although this book is comprehensive and a great reference for any undergraduate student, it sometimes can be difficult to cover every topic in this book. For this reason, the chapters are organized into sections, each of which can largely stand alone, to give professors the ability to more easily manage course content by assigning students particular sections in each chapter when they cannot teach all topics covered in a chapter. Hence, this book was written with both the student and the professor in mind. Here are some brief highlights of what you will find in each chapter:

Chapter 1 is a traditional chapter opener that features examples that are relevant to those in education (e.g., American Educational Research Association, American Association of School Administrators, Council for Exceptional Children). The importance of the scientific method to research in education is described.

Chapter 2 largely features examples drawn from education research to reflect the "need-driven" basis of much education research as opposed to the pure inquiry-driven basis of some behavioral research. In this section, the role of publication of research will emphasize the practice- or need-driven applications of research in education (e.g., oftentimes our research in education is driven by a need to address a particular applied problem). In addition to querying the reader regarding interesting and novel research ideas, readers are asked to reflect on problems of relevance in their classrooms or areas of specialization as the impetus for developing and cultivating their research agenda.

Chapter 3 introduces the APA code of ethics, as well as a brief history of the role of ethics in research, and the need for institutional review boards. Examples from education research are emphasized, as well as commonly accepted protocols for conducting research in schools. In addition to discussing anonymity and confidentiality, a discussion of parental consent for education research is included.

Chapter 4 explores the types, uses, and ways of measuring variables. Particular emphasis is given to providing substantial examples to help students work through how to identify variables as qualitative/quantitative, continuous, or discrete and by scale of measurement. Discussions of reliability and validity are emphasized to reflect the most common application of those terms in education in reference to the use of tests and other measures.

Chapter 5 introduces the diversity of assessment tools that exist within the domain of education and education research as a whole. Descriptions of each of the different tools, including advantages and disadvantages, and how they can be used are provided.

Chapter 6 details contemporary issues in sampling with an emphasis on commonly used school-based approaches. Readers will be provided with school-based research sampling issues (e.g., use of convenience samples) and introduced to probability sampling methods. Links will be made between types of sampling and sampling error as related to the development of commonly used educational tests (e.g., norm-referenced standardized tests) to solidify concepts in this chapter, as well as some psychometric concepts presented earlier in Chapter 5.

Chapter 7 is an introduction to the various categories of research design, with a general framework provided for how each design can address common issues of internal and external validity. Steps involved in choosing a research design are presented and couched in a framework that illuminates the constraints faced by school personnel in the design selection process. Threats to the generalizability of research results are explored, with particular emphasis placed on limitations that may be present due to the nature of accessible population data.

Chapter 8 introduces two common nonexperimental research designs. Naturalistic observation and existing data designs are described, and illustrations on how these designs and the techniques are used in educational settings are presented. Examples from educational settings are provided.

Chapter 9 discusses survey designs as a commonly used approach in education research when attempting to assess attitudinal variables or perceptions regarding school-based initiatives. Correlational designs will be presented with an emphasis on the utility of such designs when exploring the relationship between variables such as demographic characteristics and achievement data or other performance data. These designs are introduced as nonexperimental in that each demonstrates the extent to which variables arc related (not causal).

Chapter 10 introduces the foundation of qualitative research designs and compares them to quantitative designs. This chapter provides qualitative perspectives and general processes that will "set up" Chapters 11 and 12 and lead to qualitative data analysis in Chapter 20.

Chapter 11 introduces phenomenology, ethnographic research, and grounded theory designs. Particular nuances of data collection for the different designs are presented. Examples from published research will be presented for each type of qualitative research design.

Chapter 12 introduces narrative, case study, and critical theory research with an emphasis on describing them from an educational research perspective and the special challenges associated with each design. Examples from published research in educational settings will be presented for each type of design.

Chapter 13 introduces quasi-experimental designs as they relate to research in education, with a particular emphasis placed on examples in school settings. The discussion of single-case designs is expanded to feature extended discussions of classroom-based experimental designs linked to applied behavior analysis and behavior intervention planning, common in education research.

Chapter 14 introduces common experimental designs to include between-subjects, within-subjects (repeated measures), and factorial designs, as well as designs in which more than one factor is manipulated. Common statistical analysis approaches used with these designs are also discussed. In addition, a particular emphasis will be placed on explaining how cause is demonstrated in an experiment, with examples applied to research in education throughout the chapter.

Chapter 15 introduces mixed-methods designs as one of the most rapidly growing research types within the field of education. Readers will be informed about the conditions under which mixed-methods designs are most appropriate, types of basic and advanced mixed-methods designs, and how to conduct such designs. Caveats of conducting mixed-methods studies will be presented via the Ethics in Focus feature.

Chapter 16 introduces participatory action research and practical action research as methods of addressing common educational problems (classroom based or systems based) while concurrently evaluating the impact of program changes made as a result of the action research. An emphasis is placed on the notion of action research as an opportunity for "real-time" evaluation of instructional changes made in the school setting. In essence, content related to action research is couched as a vehicle to monitor educational practices.

Chapter 17 describes the need for and purpose of program evaluation and presents it in the context of increased federal and state demand for evidence of the efficacy of educational practices. Like action research, program evaluation is discussed using both classroom-based and district-wide applications.

Chapter 18 introduces standard approaches to the presentation of descriptive statistics. Educational examples illustrate how to take raw data and apply them to the descriptive statistic. The approaches are presented to strengthen the skills of students both as consumers of educational research to understand the use of these statistics and as practitioners who may need to use the statistic in their own research.

Chapter 19 introduces keystone aspects of analyzing quantitative data using inferential statistics with an emphasis on how quantitative data are used in education. Commonly encountered analyses are presented in a framework assisting the readers to strengthen their skills as consumers of inferential statistics, as well as practitioners who may need to use the statistic in their own research.

Chapter 20 describes how qualitative data are used in a meaningful way. Given the diversity of the types of qualitative data that may be collected, a general process, with illustrations, of content analysis is presented. How qualitative data analysis differs from the qualitative designs presented in Chapters 11 and 12 is included. Coding tools from low-tech (manual coding) to high-tech (computer software) options are presented.

Chapter 21 introduces communicating research, whether small-scale action research or large-scale program evaluations, which is most certainly an increasingly important element in the role of the contemporary educator. For those who wish to pursue advanced study in education or who are consumers of research, dissemination of research findings via scholarly means, including manuscript writing and professional presentations, is presented.

Appendix A fully supports the content covered in Chapter 21. It includes an essential APA writing guide (A.1); a guide to grammar, punctuation, and spelling (A.2); a full-sample APA-style manuscript from a study that was published in a peer-reviewed scientific journal (A.3); and instructions for creating posters using Microsoft PowerPoint, with a sample poster and poster template given (A.4). These resources give students guidelines to support their APA writing.

Appendix B includes a random numbers table (B.1) with directions for using this table to randomly sample or randomly select participants in a study. The random numbers table supports concepts taught in Chapter 6 (random sampling) and Chapter 7 (random assignment).

Also given are directions for constructing a Latin square (B.2) to support concepts taught in Chapter 14 (repeated measures designs).

Digital Resources

SAGE edge offers a robust online environment featuring an impressive array of free tools and resources for review, study, and further exploration, keeping both instructors and students on the cutting edge of teaching and learning.

SAGE edge for Students provides a personalized approach to help you accomplish your coursework goals in an easy-to-use learning environment.

- Mobile-friendly eFlashcards and quizzes strengthen your understanding of key terms and concepts.

- Learning objectives reinforce the most important material.

- EXCLUSIVE! Access to full-text SAGE journal articles provides support and expands on the concepts presented in each chapter.

SAGE edge for Instructors supports your teaching by making it easy to integrate quality content and create a rich learning environment for students. Sage edge includes the following:

- Test banks with a diverse range of prewritten and editable options, helping you assess students' progress and understanding

- Sample course syllabi for semester and quarter courses that assist in structuring your course

- Editable, chapter-specific PowerPoint slides that offer you flexibility in creating multimedia presentations

- EXCLUSIVE! Access to carefully selected SAGE journal articles, which support and expand on concepts presented in each chapter

- Video and multimedia links that appeal to students with different learning styles.

- An Instructor's Manual that includes brief chapter outlines, learning objectives, and lecture suggestions to help you prepare for class

- An Answer Key for all of the review questions in the textbook

Thank you for choosing *Research Methods for Education*, and best wishes for a successful semester.

Gregory J. Privitera, St. Bonaventure, New York
Lynn Ahlgrim-Delzell, Charlotte, North Carolina

SCIENTIFIC INQUIRY

Identify a problem

- Determine an area of interest.
- Review the literature.
- Identify new ideas in your area of interest.
- Develop a research hypothesis.

Develop a research plan

- Define the variables being tested.
- Identify participants or subjects and determine how to sample them.
- Select a research strategy and design.
- Evaluate ethics and obtain institutional approval to conduct research.

Conduct the study

- Execute the research plan and measure or record the data.

Analyze and evaluate the data

- Analyze and evaluate the data as they relate to the research hypothesis.
- Summarize data and research results.

Communicate the results

- Method of communication: oral, written, or in a poster.
- Style of communication: APA guidelines are provided to help prepare style and format.

Generate more new ideas

- Results support your hypothesis—refine or expand on your ideas.
- Results do not support your hypothesis—reformulate a new idea or start over.

After reading this chapter, you should be able to:

1. Define science and the scientific method.

2. Describe six steps for engaging in the scientific method.

3. Describe five nonscientific methods of acquiring knowledge.

4. Identify the four goals of science.

5. Distinguish between basic and applied research.

6. Distinguish between quantitative and qualitative research.

7. Delineate science from pseudoscience.

INTRODUCTION TO SCIENTIFIC THINKING

Are you curious about the world around you? Do you think that seeing is believing? When something seems too good to be true, are you critical of the claims? If you answered yes to any of these questions, the next step in your quest for knowledge is to learn about the methods used to understand events and behaviors—specifically, the methods used by scientists. Much of what you think you know is based on the methods that scientists use to answer questions.

For example, on a typical morning, you may eat breakfast because it is "the most important meal of the day." If you drive to school, you may put away your cellphone because "it is unsafe to use cellphones while driving." At school, you may attend an exam review session because "students are twice as likely to do well if they attend the session." In your downtime, you may watch commercials or read articles that make sensational claims like "scientifically tested" and "clinically proven." At night, you may try to get your "recommended 8 hours of sleep" so that you have the energy you need to start a new day. All of these decisions and experiences are related in one way or another to the science of human behavior.

Teaching is also a scientific endeavor. Have you ever wondered if collaborative student groups, graphic organizers, or project-based teaching strategies can improve student learning? Have you tried to use different incentives to encourage students to complete homework assignments, increase student engagement, or decrease inappropriate behavior during class? Are you curious about the prevalence of bullying in your school? Teachers frequently ask these types of questions. The practice of teaching is also based on decisions and experiences that are related to the science of human behavior. This book reveals the scientific process, which will allow you to be a more critical consumer of knowledge, inasmuch as you will be

edge.sagepub.com/
priviterarme

- Take the chapter quiz
- Review key terms with eFlashcards
- Explore multimedia links and SAGE articles

$SAGE edge™

able to critically review the methods that lead to the claims you come across each day. Understanding the various strengths and limitations of using science can empower you to make educated decisions and confidently negotiate the many supposed truths in nature. The idea here is that you do not need to be a scientist to appreciate what you learn in this book. *Science* is all around you—for this reason, being a critical consumer of the information you come across each day is useful and necessary across professions.

1.1 Science as a Method of Knowing

This book is a formal introduction to the scientific method. Science is one way of knowing about the world. The word *science* comes from the Latin *scientia*, meaning knowledge. From a broad view, science is any systematic method of acquiring knowledge apart from ignorance. From a stricter view, though, science is specifically the acquisition of knowledge using the scientific method, also called the research method.

> Science is the acquisition of knowledge through observation, evaluation, interpretation, and theoretical explanation.
>
> The scientific method, or research method, is a set of systematic techniques used to acquire, modify, and integrate knowledge concerning observable and measurable phenomena.

To use the scientific method, we make observations that can be measured. An observation can be direct or indirect. For example, we can directly observe how well a student performs on a test by counting the number of correct answers on the test. However, learning, for example, cannot be directly observed. We cannot "see" learning. Instead, we can indirectly observe learning by administering tests of knowledge before and after instruction or by recording the number of correct responses when applying the knowledge to a new situation. In both cases, we indirectly observe learning by defining how we measure learning. The number of correct responses when applying the knowledge, for example, is not learning, but we can infer that more correct responses are associated with greater learning. Hence, we can make direct or indirect observations of behavior by defining how we exactly measure that behavior.

> Science is one way of knowing about the world by making use of the scientific method to acquire knowledge.

The scientific method requires the use of systematic techniques, many of which are introduced and discussed in this book. Each method or design comes with a specific set of assumptions and rules that make it *scientific*. Think of this as a game. A game, such as a card game or sport, only makes sense if players follow the rules. The rules, in essence, define the game. The scientific method is very much the same. It is defined by rules that scientists must follow, and this book is largely written to identify those rules for engaging in science. To begin this chapter, we introduce the scientific method and then introduce other nonscientific ways of knowing to distinguish them from the scientific method.

1. Define the scientific method.

2. Engaging in the scientific method is like a game. Explain.

1.2 The Scientific Method: Relevance in Educational Research

To engage in the scientific method, we need to organize the process we use to acquire knowledge. This section provides an overview of this process. The remainder of this book will elaborate on the details of this process. The scientific method is composed of six general steps, which are shown in Figure 1.1. The steps are as follows:

Identify a problem

Develop a research plan

Conduct the study

Analyze and evaluate the data

Communicate the results

Generate more new ideas

Step 1: Identify a Problem

The research process begins when you identify the problem to be investigated or a problem that can be resolved in some way by making observations. For example, Browder, Wakeman, Spooner, Ahlgrim-Delzell, and Algozzine (2006) found that students with intellectual disability received very little reading instruction other than memorization of sight words. From this study, Allor, Mathes, Roberts, Jones, and Champlin (2010) identified a problem to be investigated. Specifically, they asked if students with intellectual disability could learn to read. For example, could students with intellectual disability learn to read if provided with phonics instruction? This was the problem to be investigated that could be resolved by observing how well participants read words before and after phonics instruction.

Figure 1.1 The Six Steps of the Scientific Method

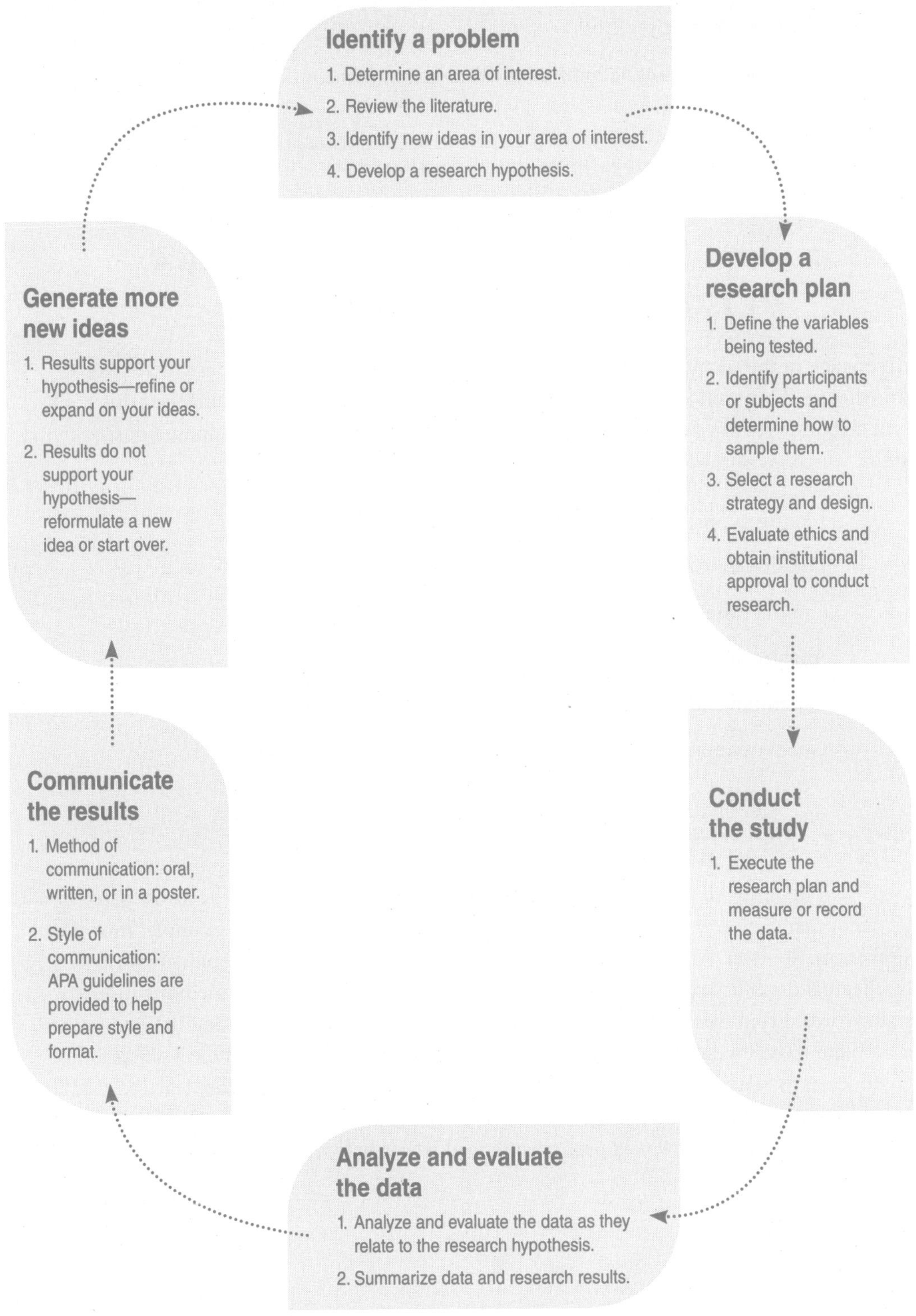

Identify a problem

1. Determine an area of interest.
2. Review the literature.
3. Identify new ideas in your area of interest.
4. Develop a research hypothesis.

Develop a research plan

1. Define the variables being tested.
2. Identify participants or subjects and determine how to sample them.
3. Select a research strategy and design.
4. Evaluate ethics and obtain institutional approval to conduct research.

Generate more new ideas

1. Results support your hypothesis—refine or expand on your ideas.
2. Results do not support your hypothesis—reformulate a new idea or start over.

Communicate the results

1. Method of communication: oral, written, or in a poster.
2. Style of communication: APA guidelines are provided to help prepare style and format.

Conduct the study

1. Execute the research plan and measure or record the data.

Analyze and evaluate the data

1. Analyze and evaluate the data as they relate to the research hypothesis.
2. Summarize data and research results.

In Step 1, we determine what to observe in a way that will allow us to answer questions about the problem we are investigating. In the education sciences, we often investigate problems related to human learning (e.g., instructional practices): processes and mechanisms of learning (e.g., cognition, memory, motivation) or other factors that influence learning (e.g., mental health, socioeconomic, school structure, resources). Step 1 is discussed in greater detail in Chapter 2.

(1) DETERMINE AN AREA OF INTEREST.

The scientific process can take anywhere from a few days to a few years to complete, so it is important to select a topic of research that interests you. Certainly, you can identify one or more educational issues that interest you.

(2) REVIEW THE LITERATURE.

The literature refers to the full database of scientific articles, most of which are now accessible using online search engines. Reviewing the scientific literature is important because it allows you to identify what is known and what can still be learned about an educational issue that interests you. It will be difficult to identify a problem without first reviewing the literature.

(3) IDENTIFY NEW IDEAS IN YOUR AREA OF INTEREST.

Reviewing the literature allows you to identify new ideas that can be tested using the scientific method. The new ideas can then be restated as predictions or expectations based on what is known. For example, below are two outcomes identified in a literature review. From these outcomes, we then identify a new (or *novel*) idea that is given as a statement of prediction, called a **research hypothesis**:

> A **research hypothesis** or **hypothesis** is a specific, testable claim or prediction about what you expect to observe given a set of circumstances.

> *Scientific Outcome 1:* Grade school children make food choices influenced by images on packaging.

> *Scientific Outcome 2:* Grade school children can readily understand expressions of emotion displayed as emoticons.

> *Research hypothesis:* Using expressions of emotion using emoticons on foods to indicate health (happy = healthy, sad = not healthy) will increase healthy food choices among grade school children.

(4) DEVELOP A RESEARCH HYPOTHESIS.

The research hypothesis is a specific, testable claim or prediction about what you expect to observe given a set of circumstances. We identified the research hypothesis that placing emoticons on food packaging to indicate health (happy = healthy, sad = not healthy) will increase healthy food choices among grade school children, similar to a hypothesis tested by Privitera, Phillips, Zuraikat, and Paque (2015)—we will revisit this study at the end of this section. In their study, they identified "healthy" foods as low-calorie foods (i.e., vegetables and fruits), so we will likewise use this criterion. We use Steps 2 to 6 of the scientific process to test this hypothesis. Note also that we used the literature review to develop our research hypothesis, which is why we must review the literature before stating a research hypothesis.

Step 2: Develop a Research Plan

Once a research hypothesis is stated, we need a plan to test that hypothesis. The development of a *research plan*, or a strategy for testing a research hypothesis, is needed to be able to complete Steps 3 and 4 of the scientific process. The chapters in Sections II, III, and IV of this book discuss Steps 2 to 4 in greater detail. Here, we will develop a research plan so that we can determine whether our hypothesis is likely to be correct or incorrect.

To make a testable claim, or hypothesis, it is appropriate to then develop a plan to test that claim.

(1) DEFINE THE VARIABLES BEING TESTED.

A variable, or any value that can change or vary across observations, is typically measured as a number in science. The initial task in developing a research plan is to define or *operationalize* each variable stated in a research hypothesis in terms of how each variable is measured. The resulting definition is called an operational definition. For example, we can define the variable identified in the research hypothesis we developed: Placing emoticons on food packaging to indicate health (happy = healthy, sad = not healthy) will increase healthy food choices among grade school children.

A variable is any value or characteristic that can change or vary from one person to another or from one situation to another.

An operational definition is a description of some observable event in terms of the specific process or manner by which it was observed or measured.

In our research hypothesis, we state that healthy food choices will increase if emoticons are placed on the packaging. The term *choice*, however, is really a decision made when faced with two or more options. We need a way to measure this phenomenon in such a way that it is numeric and others could also observe or measure food choice in the same way. How we measure food choice will be the operational definition we use. The following are two ways we could measure or operationalize liking:

Operational Definition 1: The number of healthy/low-calorie food options chosen.

Operational Definition 2: The difference in the number of healthy foods chosen with versus without the emoticons added.

To operationally define a variable, you define it in terms of how you will measure it.

Each operational definition clearly identifies how *choice* will be measured—either as a count (i.e., the number of healthy/low-calorie foods chosen) or as a difference (in choices made with vs. without emoticons). Both operational definitions make *choice* a suitable variable for scientific study because we have identified how it will be objectively measured. We typically need to choose one operational definition, which can be influenced by the type of study we conduct in Step 3.

MAKING SENSE—OBSERVATION AS A CRITERION FOR "SCIENTIFIC"

In science, only observable behaviors and events can be tested using the scientific method. Figure 1.2 shows the steps to determine whether a phenomenon can be tested using the scientific method. Notice in the figure that we must be able to observe and measure behaviors and events. Behaviors and events of interest (such as liking a food) must be observable because we must make observations to conduct the study (Step 3). Behaviors and events must be measurable because we must analyze the observations we make in a study (Step 4)—and to analyze observations, we must have defined the specific way in which we measured those observations.

The scientific method provides a systematic way to test the claims of researchers by limiting science to only phenomena that can be observed and measured. In this way, we can ensure that the behaviors and events we study truly exist and can be observed or measured by others in the same way we observed them by defining our observations operationally.

Figure 1.2 A Decision Tree for Identifying Scientific Variables

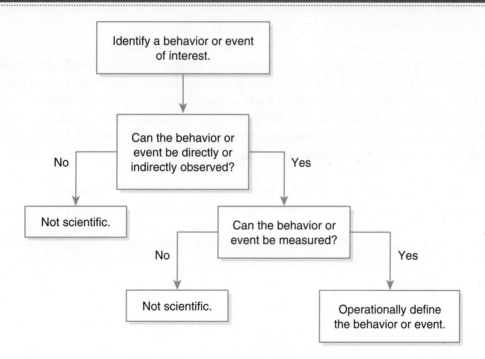

Note: A behavior or event must be observable and measurable to be tested using the scientific method.

(2) IDENTIFY PARTICIPANTS OR SUBJECTS AND DETERMINE HOW TO SAMPLE THEM.

Next we need to consider the population of interest, which is the group that is the subject of our hypothesis. A **population** can be any group of interest. In our research hypothesis, we identify how grade school children make food choices (i.e., using images on the foods). The population of interest to us, then, is grade school children. We need to define this population further so that we can define the exact group of children of interest to us. For example, we could define this group by an age range. In this case, we can define the population as children between 5 and 11 years of age, which is roughly kindergarten through fifth grade in U.S. schools.

> A **population** is a set of *all* individuals, items, or data of interest about which scientists will generalize.
>
> A **sample** is a set of *selected* individuals, items, or data taken from a population of interest.

Of course, we cannot readily observe every 5- to 11-year-old child. For this reason, we need to identify a sample of 5- to 11-year-old children that we will actually observe in our study. A **sample** is a subset or portion of individuals selected from the larger group of interest. Observing samples instead of entire populations is more realistic. It also requires less time, money, and resources than observing entire populations. Indeed, most scientific research is conducted with samples and not populations. There are many strategies used for appropriately selecting samples, as introduced in Chapter 5.

(3) SELECT A RESEARCH STRATEGY AND DESIGN.

After defining the variables and determining the type of sample for the research study, we need a plan to test the research hypothesis. The plan we use will largely depend on how we defined the variable being measured. For example, Figure 1.3 illustrates two research plans—one using Operational Definition 1 and a second using Operational Definition 2. Using Operational Definition 1, we predict that children in the Emoticon Group will choose more healthy food options than those in the No Emoticon Group. To test this prediction, we set up a two-group design to compare the number of healthy food choices between the two groups.

Using Operational Definition 2, we predict that children will choose more healthy food options when emoticons are added compared to when they are not added. To test this prediction, we set up a one-group design in which we take the difference in the number of healthy foods chosen with versus without the emoticons added. Selecting an appropriate research strategy and design is important, so Chapters 6 to 12 in this book are devoted to describing this step.

(4) EVALUATE ETHICS AND OBTAIN INSTITUTIONAL APPROVAL TO CONDUCT RESEARCH.

While a research design can be used to test a hypothesis, it is always important to make considerations for how you plan to treat participants in a research study. It is not acceptable to use unethical procedures to test a hypothesis. For example, we cannot force children to choose any foods. Hence, participation in a study must be voluntary. Because the ethical treatment of participants can often be difficult to assess, research institutions

Figure 1.3 Two Research Plans to Test the Same Hypothesis

Research Plan 1 (Two-Group Study)

Groups	*Emoticons Group*: Children choose foods from a list with emoticons added to inform them about health.	vs.	*No Emoticons Group*: Children choose foods from a list without emoticons added to inform them about health.

Measurements — Operational Definition 1: The number of healthy/low-calorie food options chosen.

Prediction from research hypothesis — Children in the Emoticon Group will choose more healthy food options than those in the No Emoticon Group.

Research Plan 2 (One-Group Study)

Groups — *Choice Group:* Children are shown two identical lists of foods, one with and one without emoticons added to inform them about health.

Measurements — Operational Definition 2: The difference in the number of healthy/low-calorie foods chosen with versus without the emoticons added.

Prediction from research hypothesis — More healthy food options will be chosen with versus without emoticons added to inform the children about health.

Note: These are two ways that scientists could design a study to test the same research hypothesis. The type of design we implement influences how the dependent variable will be defined and measured.

have created ethics committees to which a researcher submits a proposal that describes how participants will be treated in a study. Upon approval from such a committee, a researcher can then conduct his or her study. Because ethics is so important to the research process, this topic is covered in each chapter in the Ethics in Focus sections in subsequent chapters, and it is also specifically described in detail in Chapter 3.

LEARNING CHECK 2 ✓

1. What three tasks should a researcher perform before stating a research hypothesis?

2. A researcher studying attention measured the time (in seconds) that students spent working continuously on some task. Longer times indicated greater attention. In this study, what is the variable being measured, and what is the operational definition for the variable?

3. A psychologist wants to study a small population of 40 students in a local private school. If the researcher is interested in selecting the entire population of students for this study, then how many students must the psychologist include?

A. None, because it is not possible to study an entire population in this case.

B. At least half, because 21 or more students would constitute most of the population.

C. All 40 students, because all students constitute the population.

Step 3: Conduct the Study

The goal of Step 3 is to execute a research plan by actually conducting the study. In Step 2, we developed a plan that led to two ways we could conduct a study to test our hypothesis, as illustrated in Figure 1.3. Now we pick one. In other words, we will execute only one of the plans shown in Figure 1.3. For example, let us execute Research Plan 2. Using this plan, we would select a sample of 5- to 11-year-old children, show the children an identical list of foods (one with and one without emoticons added), and record the difference in the number of healthy foods chosen between the two lists. By doing so, we have conducted the study.

Step 4: Analyze and Evaluate the Data

(1) ANALYZE AND EVALUATE THE DATA AS THEY RELATE TO THE RESEARCH HYPOTHESIS.

Data are typically analyzed in numeric units, such as the counts we analyzed for Research Plan 2 (i.e., the difference in the number of healthy foods chosen between the two lists). In Step 4, we analyze the data to specifically determine if the pattern of data we observed in our study shows support for the research hypothesis. In Research Plan 2, we start by assuming that there will be 0 difference in healthy food choices between the two lists if emoticons do not influence food choice, and then we test this assumption. To make this test,

> **Data** (plural) are measurements or observations that are typically numeric. A datum (singular) is a single measurement or observation, usually called a **score** or **raw score.**

we use *statistics*, which will be introduced throughout this book to provide a more complete understanding of how researchers make decisions using the scientific method.

(2) SUMMARIZE DATA AND REPORT THE RESEARCH RESULTS.

Once the data are evaluated and analyzed, we need to concisely report the data. Data are often reported in tables graphically as shown in Figure 1.4 later in this chapter. Also, statistical outcomes are reported by specifically using guidelines identified by the American Psychological Association (APA). The exposition of data and the reporting of statistical analyses are described throughout the book beginning in Chapter 5 and also specifically reviewed in Chapters 13 and 14.

Step 5: Communicate the Results

To share the results of a study, we must decide how to make our work available to others as identified by the APA.

(1) METHOD OF COMMUNICATION.

Communicating your work allows other professionals to review your work to learn about what you did, test whether they can replicate your results, or use your study to generate their own new ideas and hypotheses. The most typical ways of sharing the results of a study are orally, in written form, or as a poster.

Oral and poster presentations are often given at professional conferences, such as national conferences held by the American Educational Research Association (AERA), the National Council of Teachers of English (NCTE), the National Council of Teachers of Mathematics (NCTM), the American Association of School Administrators (AASA), and the Council for Exceptional Children (CEC). The strongest method for communication, however, is through publication in a peer-reviewed journal. To publish in these journals, researchers describe their studies in a manuscript and have it reviewed by their peers (i.e., other professionals in their field of study). Only after their peers agree that their study reflects high-quality scientific research can they publish their manuscript in the journal. Chapter 15 provides guidelines for writing manuscripts using APA style, as well as for writing posters and giving talks. Several examples of posters and an APA manuscript that has been published are given in Appendix A.

(2) STYLE OF COMMUNICATION.

Written research reports often must conform to the style and formatting guidelines provided in the *Publication Manual of the American Psychological Association* (APA, 2009), also called the *Publication Manual*. The *Publication Manual* is a comprehensive guide for using ethics and reducing bias, writing manuscripts and research reports, and understanding the publication process. It is essential that you refer to this manual when choosing a method of communication. After all, most educational researchers across the education sciences follow these guidelines.

For our research hypothesis, we chose Research Plan 2. Privitera et al. (2015) also used a plan similar to Research Plan 2 except that children in their study chose from actual foods displayed on shelves and not from a list of choices. These researchers published their results in the peer-reviewed journal *Appetite*. Their results, a portion of which is shown in Figure 1.4, show support for the hypothesis—children at each grade level chose more healthy/low-calorie food options with versus without emoticons on the food packaging. The researchers call this strategy *emolabeling*, and it is one of the first efforts to develop a strategy that can effectively communicate information about health (and influence healthy food choices) to early literacy children.

Figure 1.4   A Portion of the Results Reported by Privitera et al. (2015)

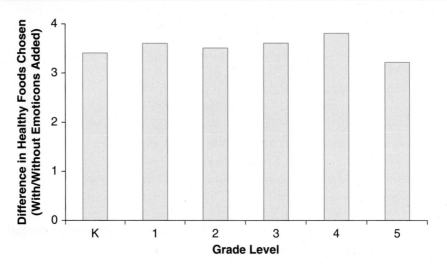

Note: Children chose more healthy/low-calorie food options with versus without emoticons on the food packaging at each grade level. The healthy/low-calorie foods were fruits and vegetables; the less healthy/high-calorie foods were cakes, cookies, and chips. The results are adapted from those reported by Privitera, Phillips, Zuraikat, and Paque (2015).

Step 6: Generate More New Ideas

When your study is complete, you can publish your work and allow other researchers the opportunity to review and evaluate your findings. You have also learned something from your work. If you found support for your research hypothesis, you can use it to refine and expand on existing knowledge. If the results do not support your research hypothesis, then you propose a new idea and begin again.

Steps 1 to 6 of the scientific process are cyclic, not linear, meaning that even when a study answers a question, this usually leads to more questions and more testing. For this reason, Step 6 typically leads back to Step 1, and we begin again. More important, it allows other researchers to refute scientific claims and question what we think we know. It allows researchers to ask, "If your claim is correct, then we should also observe this," or "If your claim is correct, then this should not be observed." A subsequent study would then allow other researchers to determine how confident we can be about what we think we know of that particular behavior or event of interest.

The scientific process is cyclic, not linear; it is open to criticism and review.

Joyful Middle School is a neighborhood school located in a large, urban city with a magnet program that attracts a diverse body of students from across the area. The faculty and staff noticed an increase of student bullying incidents. After searching the Internet and local university library, they found some research that indicated that school uniforms might help in reducing the number of bullying incidents. They also found that school uniforms might have other advantages such as improved school spirit. They developed the hypothesis that school uniforms would reduce the number of bullying incidents. (Step 1: Identify a problem.)

The school faculty, staff, and several parents formulated a plan to study how school uniforms affected bullying and school spirit. They decided to collect information about the bullying incidents and a survey on school spirit before implementing the school uniform policy for all of the students and again 1 year later. (Step 2: Develop a research plan.)

The research team collected information on school bullying incidents for the year before the school uniform policy was implemented and the year during the school uniform policy was implemented. They disseminated the survey about school spirit in the spring before and during the school uniform policy was implemented. (Step 3: Conduct the study.)

The data on bullying incidents and school spirit survey were analyzed. They found that the number of bullying incidents decreased and school spirit increased. (Step 4: Analyze and evaluate the data.)

The results were shared with students during the end-of-the-year pep rally and at the spring parent-teacher meeting. The results were also shared on the school webpage. A manuscript of the study was published in the *Journal of School Violence* to share with other educators. (Step 5: Communicate the results.)

The principal decided to continue to collect data on bullying incidents and the school spirit survey to see if the effect of the school uniform was maintained over time. She also decided to disseminate a parent survey to investigate other effects of the school uniform policy. (Step 6: Generate more new ideas.)

LEARNING CHECK 3 ✓

1. A researcher reviews the pattern of data in a study to see if there is support for the research hypothesis. Which step in the scientific method does this describe?

2. State three methods of communication. What style of communication is used in the education sciences?

Answers: 1. Step 4: analyze and evaluate the data; 2. Oral, written, and as a poster. APA style is used in psychology and much of the behavioral sciences.

Other Methods of Knowing

[The scientific] method is one way of knowing about the world. There are also many other methods, and each has its advantages and disadvantages. Five other methods of knowing that do not use the scientific process are collectively referred to as nonscientific methods. Although not an exhaustive list, the five nonscientific ways of knowing in this section are tenacity, intuition, authority, rationalism, and empiricism. Yet, at some level, each of these methods can be used with the scientific method.

[Handwritten note: ✳ There are 5 nonscientific ways of knowing but each of these can be used with the scientific method.]

Tenacity is a method of knowing based largely on habit or superstition; it is a belief that exists simply because it has always been accepted. Advertising companies, for example, use this method by creating catchphrases such as Budweiser's slogan "King of Beers," Nike's slogan "Just Do It," or Geico's much longer slogan "15 minutes could save you 15% or more on car insurance." In each case, tenacity was used to gauge public belief in a company's product or service. A belief in superstitions, such as finding a penny heads up bringing good luck or a black cat crossing your path being bad luck, also reflects tenacity. Tenacity may also reflect tradition. The 9-month school calendar providing a 3-month summer vacation originated in the late 1800s to meet the needs of communities at the time (mostly due to heat, not farming). While the needs of our society have changed, the school calendar has not. The key disadvantage of using tenacity, however, is that the knowledge acquired can often be inaccurate, partly because tenacity is mostly assumed knowledge. Hence, there is no basis in fact for beliefs using tenacity.

> **Tenacity** is a method of knowing based largely on habit or superstition.

Intuition

Intuition is an individual's subjective hunch or feeling that something is correct. Intuition is sometimes used synonymously with instincts. For example, stock traders said to have great instincts may use their intuition to purchase a stock that then increases in value, or gamblers said to have great instincts may use their intuition to place a bet that then wins. Parents often use their intuition when they suspect their child is getting into trouble at school, or students may use their intuition to choose a major that best fits their interests. The disadvantage of using intuition as a sole method of knowing is that there is no definitive basis for the belief. Hence, without acting on the intuition, it is difficult to determine its accuracy.

> **Intuition** is a method of knowing based largely on an individual's hunch or feeling that something is correct.

Intuition also has some value in science in that researchers can use their intuition to some extent when they develop a research hypothesis, particularly when there is little to no information available concerning their area of interest. In science, however, the

researchers' intuition is then tested using the scientific method. Keep in mind [...]
the scientific method to differentiate between hypotheses that do and do not [...]
describe phenomena, regardless of how we initially developed our hypothese[...]
scientific method, and not intuition, that ultimately determines what we kno[...]

Our intuition may guide us to develop a hypothesis or recognize an issue but it's the scientific method that leads us to determine results + what we know.

Authority

Authority is knowledge accepted as fact because it was stated by an e[...]
respected source in a particular subject area. In faith-based practices, it is the [...]
the Torah, or another text that is the authority in a given faith-based practice. [...]
pastors, rabbis, and other religious leaders teach
about God using the authority of those texts, and the
teachings in those texts are accepted based solely on
the authority of those texts. Education agencies such as
the National Education Association (NEA) often lobby

> **Authority** is a method of knowing accepted as fact because it was stated by an expert or respected source in a particular subject area.

for regulations that many educators will trust as benefiting them without reviewing in detail
the policies being lobbied for. The U.S. Food and Drug Administration (FDA) was the second
most trusted government agency behind only the Supreme Court around the turn of the 21st
century (Hadfield, Howse, & Trebilcock, 1998), and the FDA likewise makes policy decisions
that many Americans trust without detailed vetting. The disadvantage of using authority as
a sole method of knowing is that, in many cases, there is little effort to challenge this type of
knowledge, often leaving authoritative knowledge unchecked.

Like intuition, authority has value in science. Einstein's general theory of relativity,
for example, requires an understanding of mathematics shared by perhaps a few hundred
scientists. The rest of us simply accept this theory as accurate based on the authority of the
few scientists who tell us it is. Likewise, many scientists will selectively submit their research
for publication in only the most authoritative journals—those with a reputation for being
the most selective and publishing only the highest-quality research compared to other
presumably less selective journals. In this way, authority is certainly valued to some extent in
the scientific community.

Rationalism

Rationalism is any source of knowledge that requires the use of reasoning or logic.
Rationalism is often used to understand human behavior. For example, if a spouse is unfaithful
to a partner, the partner may reason that the spouse does not love him or her; if a student

receives a poor grade on a homework assignment,
the professor may reason that the student did not
put much effort into the assignment. Here, the
spouse and professor rationalized the meaning of

> **Rationalism** is a method of knowing that requires the use of reasoning and logic.

a behavior they observed—and in both cases, they could be wrong. This is a disadvantage of
using rationalism as a sole method of knowing in that it often leads to erroneous conclusions.

Even some of the most rational ideas can be wrong. For example, it would be
completely rational to believe that heavier objects fall at a faster rate than lighter objects. This

was, in fact, the rational explanation for falling objects prior to the mid-1500s until Galileo Galilei proposed a theory and showed evidence that refuted this view.

Rationalism certainly has some value in science as well inasmuch as researchers can use rationalism to develop their research hypotheses—in fact, we used reasoning to develop our research hypothesis about food packaging. Still, all research hypotheses are tested using the scientific method, so it is the scientific method that ultimately sorts out the rationally sound from the rationally flawed hypotheses.

Empiricism

Empiricism is knowledge acquired through observation. This method of knowing reflects the adage "seeing is believing." While making observations is essential when using the scientific method, it can be biased when used apart from the scientific method. In other words, not everyone experiences or observes the world in the same way—from this view, empiricism alone is fundamentally flawed. One way that the scientific method handles this problem is to ensure that all variables observed in a study are *operationally defined*—defined in terms of how the observed variable is measured such that other researchers could observe that variable in the same way. An operational definition has the advantage of being more objective because it states exactly how the variable was observed or measured.

> **Empiricism** is a method of knowing based on one's experiences or observations.

Many factors bias our perception of the behaviors and events we observe. The first among them is the fact that human perception can be biased. To illustrate, Figure 1.5 depicts the Poggendorff illusion, named after the physicist who discovered it in a drawing published by German astrophysicist Johann Zöllner in 1860. The rectangles in Parts A and B are the same, except that the rectangle in Part A is not transparent. The lines going through the rectangle in Part A appear to be continuous, but this is an illusion. Viewing them through the transparent rectangle, we observe at once that they are not. There are many instances in which we do not see the world as it really is, many of which we still may not recognize or fully understand.

Human memory is also inherently biased. Many people are prone to forgetting and to inaccurate recollections. Memory is not a bank of recordings to be replayed; rather, it is a collection of representations for the behaviors and events we observe. Memory is an active process, and you are unlikely to accurately recall what you observed unless you make a conscious effort to do so. If you have ever entered a room and forgot why you wanted to go there in the first place, or you forgot someone's name only minutes (often seconds) after being introduced, then you have experienced some of the vagaries of memory. Many factors influence what we attend to and remember, and many of these factors work against our efforts to make accurate observations.

> The nonscientific ways of knowing are ways of acquiring knowledge that are commonly applied but not based in science.

In all, tenacity, intuition, authority, rationalism, and empiricism are called the nonscientific methods of knowing. While some of these methods may be used during the scientific process, they are only used in conjunction with the scientific method. Using the scientific method ultimately ensures that only the most accurate hypotheses emerge from the observations we make.

Figure 1.5 The Poggendorff Illusion

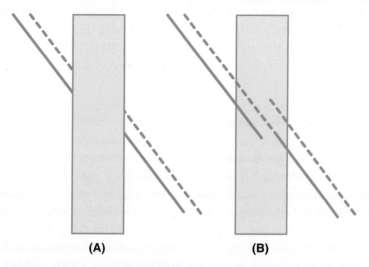

(A)   (B)

Note: In Part A, both lines appear to be continuous. In Part B, the rectangle is transparent, which shows that the lines are, in fact, not continuous.

LEARNING CHECK 4 ✓

1. State the five nonscientific methods of knowing.

2. State the method of knowing illustrated in each of these examples.

   A. Your friend tells you that he likes fried foods because he saw someone enjoying them at a buffet.

   B. You close up the store at exactly midnight because that is when the store always closes.

   C. A teacher states that students do not care about being in school because they are not paying attention in class.

   D. Your mother locks up all the alcohol in the house because she has a feeling you may throw a party while she is at work.

   E. You believe that if you do not read your textbook, you will fail your research methods class because your professor said so.

Answers: 1. The five methods of knowing are tenacity, intuition, authority, rationalism, and empiricism; 2. A. empiricism, B. tenacity, C. rationalism, D. intuition, E. authority.

1.4 The Goals of Science

Many people will seek only as much knowledge as they feel will satisfy their curiosity. For instance, people may conclude that they know about love because they have experienced it themselves (empiricism) or listened to stories that others tell about their experiences with love (authority). Yet science is a stricter way of knowing about the world. In science, we do not make observations for the sake of making observations. Instead, we make observations with the ultimate goal to describe, explain, predict, and control the behaviors and events we observe. Each goal is described in this section and listed in Table 1.1.

Describe

To understand the behaviors and events we study, we must describe or define them. Often, these descriptions are in the literature. We can even find descriptions for behaviors and events quite by accident, particularly for those that are not yet described in the literature or not fully understood. For example, a young boy named John Garcia had his first taste of licorice when he was 10 years old. Hours later, he became ill with the flu. Afterward, he no longer liked the taste of licorice, although he was fully aware that the licorice did not cause his illness. As a scientist, Garcia tried to describe his experience, which eventually led him to conduct a landmark study showing the first scientific evidence that we learn to dislike tastes associated with illness, known as *taste aversion learning* (Garcia, Kimeldorf, & Koelling, 1955). Scientific knowledge begins by describing the behaviors and events we study, even if that description originates from a childhood experience.

> The first goal of science is to describe or define the variables we observe and measure.

Explain

To understand the behaviors and events we study, we must also identify the conditions within which they operate. In other words, we identify what causes a behavior or event to occur. Identifying cause can be a challenging goal in that human behavior is complex and often caused by many factors in different situations. Suppose, for example, that we want to understand what makes people view someone as being *competent*, which we describe as the ability to successfully master some task or action. Some obvious causes for being viewed as competent are someone's rank or position at work, as well as education and income level. Less obvious, though, is that an individual will be viewed as more competent if he or she is simply more attractive (see Langlois et al., 2000). Imagine now how many less obvious factors exist

Goal	Question Asked to Meet the Goal
Describe	What is the behavior or event?
Explain	What are the causes of the behavior or event?
Predict	Can we anticipate when the behavior or event will occur in the future?
Control	Can we manipulate the conditions necessary to make a behavior or event occur and not occur?

Table 1.1 The Four Goals of Science

but have not yet been considered. Explaining behavior is a cautious goal in science because there are so many variables to consider.

Predict

Once we can describe and explain a particular behavior or event, we can use that knowledge to predict when it will occur in the future. Knowing how to predict behavior can be quite useful. For example, if a parent wants a child to take a long nap, the parent may take the child to the park for an hour before naptime to tire the child out. In this case, the parent predicts that greater activity increases sleepiness (for review, see Horne, 1988). However, as with most behaviors, sleep is caused by many factors, so parents often find that this strategy does not always work. Predicting behavior, then, can be challenging because to predict when a behavior will occur depends on our ability to isolate the causes of that behavior.

> The second goal in science is to explain the conditions or causes for the behaviors or events we study.

> The third goal of science is to predict when a behavior or event will occur.

Control

The central, and often most essential, goal for a scientist is control. Control means that we can make a behavior occur and not occur. To establish control, we must be able to describe the behavior, explain the causes, and predict when it will occur and not occur. Hence, control is only possible once the first three goals of science are met.

The ability to control behavior is important because teachers can use this knowledge to provide interventions that can help students learn and use knowledge to improve their lives. For example, Maynard, Kjellstrand, and Thompson (2014) used their knowledge of a variety of factors related to school completion and dropout prevention to implement a program for middle and high school students at risk for dropping out of school. Their work found that monitoring school attendance, disciplinary referrals, and academic performance and building relationships with students to problem-solve these issues led to greater academic achievement and attendance and a decrease in disciplinary referrals. Hence, the intervention allowed students to control their academic performance by controlling the factors related to their previous poor academic performance. Control, then, is a powerful goal because it means that researchers achieved control over the behaviors that they study.

> The fourth goal of science is to control the conditions necessary to make a behavior occur and not occur.

LEARNING CHECK 5 ✓

1. State the four goals of science.

2. If researchers can make a behavior occur and not occur, then which goal of science have they met?

Answers: 1. Describe, explain, predict, control; 2. Control.

1.5 Approaches in Acquiring Knowledge

Many approaches lead to different levels of understanding of the behaviors and events we study using the scientific method. In this section, we introduce research that is basic or applied and research that is qualitative or quantitative.

Basic and Applied Research

Basic research is an approach where researchers aim to understand the nature of behavior. Basic research is used to answer fundamental questions that address theoretical issues, typically regarding the mechanisms and processes of behavior. Whether there are practical applications for the outcomes in basic research is not as important as whether the research builds upon existing theory. Basic research is used to study many aspects of behavior such as the influence of biology, cognition, learning, memory, consciousness, and development on behavior.

Basic research uses the scientific method to answer questions that address theoretical issues about fundamental processes and underlying mechanisms related to the behaviors and events being studied.

Applied research uses the scientific method to answer questions concerning practical problems with potential practical solutions.

Applied research, on the other hand, is an approach in which researchers aim to answer questions concerning practical problems that require practical solutions. Topics of interest in applied research include issues related to obesity and health, traffic laws and safety, behavioral disorders, and drug addiction. In educational research, applied research seeks to answer questions about educational practice that can be generalized to different educational settings. Examples of educational applied research include implementing different instructional strategies, character development, parental involvement, and classroom management. Researchers who conduct applied research focus on problems with immediate practical implications to apply their findings to problems that have the potential for immediate action.

Basic research is used to address theoretical questions regarding the mechanisms and processes of behavior; applied research is used to address questions that can lead to immediate solutions to practical problems.

While basic and applied research are very different in terms of the focus of study, we can use what is learned in theory (basic research) and apply it to practical situations (applied research), or we can test how practical solutions to a problem (applied research) fit with the theories we use to explain that problem (basic research). As an example, basic research using rats to test learning theories in the 1970s showed that adding sugar to a flavored drink increased how much the rats would consume of the flavor subsequently given without the added sugar (Holman, 1975). A similar result was shown with preschool-aged children in an applied research study in which researchers showed that adding sugar to grapefruit juice a few times enhanced liking for the grapefruit juice, even when it was subsequently consumed without the added sugar (Capaldi & Privitera, 2008; Privitera, 2008a). The applied research study in 2008, which was developed from basic research studies over 30 years earlier, proposed immediate solutions that could be applied to strategies for enhancing how much children like consuming low-sugar drinks.

Qualitative and Quantitative Research

Quantitative research uses the scientific method to record observations as numeric data. Most scientific research in the social sciences is quantitative because the data are numeric, allowing for a more objective analysis of the observations made in a study. Researchers, for example, may define *mastery* as the time (in seconds) it takes to complete a presumably difficult task. By defining mastery in seconds (a numeric value), the analysis is more objective—other researchers can readily measure mastery in the same way. Numeric values can also be readily entered into statistical formulas, from which researchers can obtain measurable results. Statistical analysis is not possible without numeric data.

Quantitative research uses the scientific method to record observations as numeric data. Most research conducted in the behavioral sciences is quantitative.

Qualitative research uses the scientific method to make nonnumeric observations, from which conclusions are drawn without the use of statistical analysis.

Qualitative research is different from quantitative research in that qualitative research does not include the measurement of numeric data. Instead, observations are made, from which conclusions are drawn. The goal in qualitative research is to describe, interpret, and explain the behaviors or events being studied. As an example, a qualitative researcher studying attraction may interview a small group of participants about their experiences with attraction. Each participant is allowed to respond however he or she wants. From this, the researcher will look at how the participants described attraction to interpret and explain what attraction is. Whereas in quantitative research, the researcher defines the variable of interest (e.g., attraction) and then makes observations to measure that variable, in qualitative research, the participants describe the variable of interest, from which researchers interpret and explain that variable.

Quantitative and qualitative research can be effectively used to study the same behaviors, so both types of research have value. For example, quantitative research can be used to determine how often and for how long (in minutes, on average) students study for an exam, whereas qualitative research can be used to characterize their study habits in terms of what they study, why they study it, and how they study. Each observation gives the researcher a bigger picture of how to characterize studying among students. In this way, both types of research can be effectively used to gauge a better understanding of the behaviors and events we observe.

1.6 Distinguishing Science From Pseudoscience

Pseudoscience is a set of procedures that are not scientific, and it is part of a system or set of beliefs that try to deceptively create the impression that the knowledge gained represents the "final say" or most reliable knowledge on its subject matter.

Throughout this book, you will be introduced to the scientific process, the general steps for which were elaborated in this chapter. As is evident as you read further, science requires that a set of systematic techniques be followed to acquire knowledge. However, sometimes knowledge can be presented as if it is scientific, yet it is nonscience, often referred to as *pseudoscience*; that being said, all nonscience is not pseudoscience (Hansson, 2015; Mahner, 2007).

The term *pseudoscience* is not to be confused with other terms often inappropriately used as synonyms, which include *unscientific* and *nonscientific*. A key feature of pseudoscience is intent to deceive: It is nonscience posing as science (Gardner, 1957; Hansson, 2015). For example, there are ways of knowing that do not at all purport to be based in science, such as those described in Section 1.3 in this chapter. These are not pseudoscience. As another example, an individual may engage in science, but the science itself is incorrect or rather poorly conducted (e.g., the individual misinterprets an observation or runs a careless experiment). Even if the "bad" science is intentional or fraudulent, "bad" science is rarely called pseudoscience. Therefore, to clarify, we can adopt two criteria here to define pseudoscience that delineates it as a narrower concept, adapted from Gardner (1957) and Hansson (2015):

(1) it is not scientific, and

(2) it is part of a system or set of beliefs that try to deceptively create the impression that the knowledge gained represents the "final say" or most reliable knowledge on its subject matter.

As an example to illustrate, consider the following three scenarios:

Scenario 1: A psychologist performs a study and unknowingly analyzes the data incorrectly, then reports erroneous conclusions that are incorrect because of his or her mistake.

Scenario 2: A psychologist makes a series of impromptu observations, then constructs an explanation for the observations made as if his or her conclusions were scientific.

Scenario 3: A psychologist reports that he or she has a personal belief and faith in God and believes that such faith is important.

> Pseudoscience is often described as nonscience that looks like science, but it is not.

In the cases above, only Scenario 2 meets the criteria for pseudoscience in that it is not scientific, and the psychologist tries to deceivingly leave the impression that his or her conclusions have scientific legitimacy, when they do not. Scenario 1 is a basic case of "bad" science, and Scenario 3 is simply a nonscientific way of knowing—there was no intent to give the impression that such faith is rooted in science. Being able to delineate science from pseudoscience can be difficult, and the demarcation between science and pseudoscience is often a subject of debate among philosophers and scientists alike. The examples given in this section provide some context for thinking about science versus pseudoscience, which should prove helpful as you read about science in this book.

1. Distinguish between basic and applied research.

2. What is the difference between quantitative and qualitative research?

3. Identify if the following is an example of pseudoscience; explain: A psychologist makes a series of observations while in a waiting room, then constructs an explanation for his observations as if his conclusions were scientific.

Answers: 1. Basic research is used to address theoretical questions regarding the mechanisms and processes of behavior, whereas applied research is used to address questions that can lead to immediate solutions to practical problems; 2. In quantitative research, all variables are measured numerically, whereas qualitative research is purely descriptive (variables are not measured numerically); 3. It is an example of pseudoscience because it is not scientific (i.e., there are no systematic procedures followed), and he tries to deceivingly leave the impression that his conclusions are scientific, when they are not.

CHAPTER SUMMARY

LO 1 Define science and the scientific method.

- **Science** is the acquisition of knowledge through observation, evaluation, interpretation, and theoretical explanation.

- Science is specifically the acquisition of knowledge using the scientific method, which requires the use of systematic techniques, each of which comes with a specific set of assumptions and rules that make it *scientific*.

LO 2 Describe six steps for engaging in the scientific method.

- The scientific process consists of six steps:

  Step 1: Identify a problem: Determine an area of interest, review the literature, identify new ideas in your area of interest, and develop a research hypothesis.

  Step 2: Develop a research plan: Define the variables being tested, identify participants or subjects and determine how to sample them, select a research strategy and design, and evaluate ethics and obtain institutional approval to conduct research.

  Step 3: Conduct the study. Execute the research plan and measure or record the data.

  Step 4: Analyze and evaluate the data as they relate to the research hypothesis, and summarize data and research results.

  Step 5: Communicate the results. Results can be communicated orally, in written form, or as a poster. The styles of communication follow standards identified by the APA.

  Step 6: Generate more new ideas. Refine or expand the original hypothesis, reformulate a new hypothesis, or start over.

LO 3 Describe five nonscientific methods of acquiring knowledge.

- **Tenacity** is a method of knowing based largely on habit or superstition. A disadvantage of tenacity is that the knowledge acquired is often inaccurate.

- **Intuition** is a method of knowing based largely on an individual's hunch or feeling that something is correct. A disadvantage of intuition is that the only way to determine the accuracy of an intuition is to act on that belief.

- **Authority** is a method of knowing accepted as fact because it was stated by an expert or respected source in a particular subject area. A disadvantage of authority is that there is typically little effort to challenge an authority, leaving authoritative knowledge largely unchecked.

- **Rationalism** is a method of knowing that requires the use of reasoning and logic. A disadvantage of rationalism is that it often leads to erroneous conclusions.

- **Empiricism** is a method of knowing based on one's experiences or observations. Disadvantages of empiricism are that not everyone experiences or observes the world in the same way, perception is often illusory, and memory is inherently biased.

LO 4 Identify the four goals of science.

- The four goals of science are to describe or define the variables we observe and measure, explain the causes of a behavior or event, predict when a behavior or event will occur in the future, and control or manipulate conditions in such a way as to make a behavior occur and not occur.

LO 5–6 Distinguish between basic and applied research, as well as between quantitative and qualitative research.

- **Basic research** uses the scientific method to answer questions that address theoretical issues about fundamental processes and underlying mechanisms related to the behaviors and events being studied. Applied research uses the scientific method to answer questions concerning practical problems with potential practical solutions.

- **Quantitative research** is most commonly used in the behavioral sciences and uses the scientific method to record observations as numeric data. **Qualitative research** uses the scientific method to make nonnumeric observations, from which conclusions are drawn without the use of statistical analysis.

LO 7 Delineate science from pseudoscience.

- **Pseudoscience** is a set of procedures that are not scientific, and it is part of a system or set of beliefs that try to deceptively create the impression that the knowledge gained represents the "final say" or most reliable knowledge on its subject matter.

- Being able to delineate science from pseudoscience can be difficult, and the demarcation between science and pseudoscience is still a subject of debate among philosophers and scientists alike.

applied research 22

authority 17

basic research 22

data or datum 12

empiricism 18

intuition 16

operational definition 8

population 10

pseudoscience 23

qualitative research 23

quantitative research 23

rationalism 17

research hypothesis or
hypothesis 7

sample 10

science 4

scientific method or
research method 4

score or raw score 12

tenacity 16

variable 8

REVIEW QUESTIONS

1. Science can be any systematic method of acquiring knowledge apart from ignorance. What method makes science a unique approach to acquire knowledge? Define that method.

2. The scientific method includes a series of assumptions or rules that must be followed. Using the analogy of a game (given in this chapter), explain why this is important.

3. State the six steps for using the scientific method.

4. A researcher reviews the literature and finds that taller men earn greater incomes than shorter men. From this review, he hypothesizes that taller men are more intelligent than shorter men. What method of knowing did he use to develop this hypothesis? Which method of knowing is used to determine whether this hypothesis is likely correct or incorrect?

5. A social psychologist records the number of outbursts in a sample of different classrooms at a local school. In this example, what is the operational definition for classroom interruptions?

6. Identify the sample and the population in this statement: A research methods class has 25 students enrolled, but only 23 students attended class.

7. True or false: Samples can be larger than the population from which they were selected. Explain your answer.

8. A friend asks you what science is. After you answer her question, she asks how you knew that, and you reply that it was written in a textbook. What method of knowing did you use to describe science to your friend? Define it.

9. You go out to eat at a restaurant with friends and have the most delicious meal. From this experience, you decide to go to that restaurant again because the food is delicious. What method of knowing did you use to make this decision? Define it.

10. State the four goals of science.

11. Studying the nature of love has proven challenging because it is difficult to operationally define. In this example, which of the four goals of science are researchers having difficulty meeting?

12. State which of the following is an example of basic research and which is an example of applied research.

    A. A researcher is driven by her curiosity and interest to explore the theoretical relationship between culturally responsive instruction and academic achievement of Black males.

    B. A researcher is interested in exploring the extent to which Black males who receive culturally responsive instruction are more likely to score higher on a science exam than those who do not receive the culturally responsive instruction.

13. Which research, basic or applied, is used to study practical problems in order to have the potential for immediate action?

14. State whether each of the following is an example of quantitative or qualitative research.

    A. A researcher interviews a group of teachers and asks them to explain how they feel about the Common Core State Standards. Each teacher is allowed to respond in his or her own words.

    B. A school administrator examines student attendance records after implementing a later school start time.

    C. A school psychologist interested in attention records the number of out-of-seat behavior of students.

    D. A witness to a bullying incident describes the incident to the school principal.

15. Is the following an example of pseudoscience? Explain.

    A researcher enters a home and uses a device that shows that some areas of the house have higher electromagnetic fields (EMFs) than others. He concludes that these EMF readings show scientific proof that ghosts or spirits are present in the rooms where the EMFs were highest.

ACTIVITIES

1. Recall that only behaviors and events that can be observed and measured (operationally defined) are considered scientific. Assuming that all of the following variables are both observable and measurable, state at least two operational definitions for each:

    The character development of elementary school students

    A student's ability to remember some event

    A teacher's patience

    The effectiveness of a professor's teaching style

The quality of life among high school students with autism

The level of drug use among teens

The amount of student texting during class time

The costs of obtaining a college education

2. We developed the following three hypotheses using Step 1 of the scientific method. Choose one of the ideas given, or use one of your own, and complete Step 2 of the scientific method.

A. *Scientific outcome 1:* The typical student obtains a C+ in difficult courses.

Scientific outcome 2: The typical student obtains a C+ in relatively easy courses.

Research hypothesis: Students will do less work in an easy course than in a difficult course.

B. *Scientific outcome 1:* The more education a woman has obtained, the larger her salary tends to be.

Scientific outcome 2: Today, more women earn a PhD in psychology than men.

Research hypothesis: Women in fields of psychology today earn higher salaries than their male colleagues.

C. *Scientific outcome 1:* Distractions during class interfere with a student's ability to learn the material taught in class.

Scientific outcome 2: Many students sign on to social networking sites during class time.

Research hypothesis: Students who sign on to social networking sites during class time will learn less material than those who do not.

3. Historically there has been great debate concerning the authority of scientific knowledge versus religious knowledge. What methods of knowing are used in science and religion? What are the differences between these methods, if any? What are the similarities, if any?

$SAGE edge™

SAGE edge offers a robust online environment featuring an impressive array of free tools and resources for review, study, and further exploration, keeping both instructors and students on the cutting edge of teaching and learning.

Access practice quizzes, eFlashcards, video, and multimedia at **edge.sagepub.com/priviterarme**.

Identify a problem

- Determine an area of interest.
- Review the literature.
- Identify new ideas in your area of interest.
- Develop a research hypothesis.

Develop a research plan

- Define the variables being tested.
- Identify participants or subjects and determine how to sample them.
- Select a research strategy and design.
- Evaluate ethics and obtain institutional approval to conduct research.

Generate more new ideas

- Results support your hypothesis—refine or expand on your ideas.
- Results do not support your hypothesis—reformulate a new idea or start over.

After reading this chapter, you should be able to:

1. Explain what makes an idea interesting and novel.

2. Distinguish between a hypothesis and a theory.

3. Distinguish between induction and deduction.

4. Describe the process of conducting a literature review.

5. Identify four ethical concerns for giving proper credit.

6. Describe the "3 Cs" of conducting an effective literature review.

7. Distinguish between a confirmational and a disconfirmational strategy.

8. Explain the issue of publication bias.

Communicate the results

- Method of communication: oral, written, or in a poster.
- Style of communication: APA guidelines are provided to help prepare style and format.

Conduct the study

- Execute the research plan and measure or record the data.

Analyze and evaluate the data

- Analyze and evaluate the data as they relate to the research hypothesis.
- Summarize data and research results.

GENERATING TESTABLE IDEAS

Hearsay, gossip, scuttlebutts, and rumors are a common phenomenon. A friend tells you that someone else likes you, or a classmate tells you that she heard that class is canceled today. Yet how can you trust your friend or classmate? One way would be to confirm that your friend heard it from the person who likes you, or your classmate heard it directly from the professor who canceled the class. In other words, the best information "comes straight from the horse's mouth." This idiomatic expression made popular in horse racing in the early 1900s is synonymous with reliability and observation.

The phrase is synonymous with the reliability of one's sources. In horseracing, a person who was so close to a horse that he or she could see inside the horse's mouth must have been a trusted source. This phrase is also synonymous with observation. Throughout history, unscrupulous horse traders falsified equine health records and ages, in hopes of persuading potential buyers to overpay for horses. The only way to know the health and age of a horse for sure was to look inside the horse's mouth for the truth. A horse's health and age could be estimated quite accurately by looking at the number and condition of his or her teeth. Consequently, to appraise a horse's worth, one must make an observation "straight from the horse's mouth."

In the same way that horse traders relied on trustworthy sources and observations to make judgments of a horse's worth, scientists develop their ideas or hypotheses based on the reliability of their sources and on their observations of phenomena. In this chapter, we will introduce the types of sources from which researchers generate ideas and the ways in which researchers can identify these sources based on whether the information reported in them "came straight from the horse's mouth."

edge.sagepub.com/ priviterarme

- Take the chapter quiz
- Review key terms with eFlashcards
- Explore multimedia links and SAGE articles

$SAGE edge™

2.1 Generating Interesting and Novel Ideas

It was the German-born American physicist Albert Einstein who once said, "I am neither especially clever nor especially gifted. I am only very, very curious." While it is more likely that Einstein was clever, gifted, and curious, his insight marks an important feature in science: Knowledge is only possible through inquiry. One characteristic of all good scientists is that they ask good questions. Einstein, for example, asked, "Are time and space the same thing?" His research was to answer this question, which led to his theory of relativity—a mathematical proof that the answer to his question is yes. For all the complexities of the theory of relativity, imagine that this research was inspired by such a simple question.

The object of research is to extend human knowledge beyond what is already known. Once a research study is complete, researchers will try to publish the results in a scientific journal called a **peer-reviewed journal.** After all, the scientific community will not know about a research study that is not published. To publish your work, you should be considerate of the aims of peer-reviewed scientific journals as you develop your ideas. Two criteria of importance to publishing a work can be met by answering the following two important questions regarding your idea:

> A **peer-reviewed journal** is a type of publication that specifically publishes scientific articles, reviews, or commentaries only after the work has been reviewed by peers or scientific experts who determine its scientific value or worth regarding publication. Only after acceptance from peer reviewers will a work be published.

- *Is my idea interesting?* An interesting idea can potentially benefit society, test a prediction, or develop areas of research where little is known. Peer-reviewed journals have a readership, and your idea must appeal to those who read that journal if you are to publish your ideas. In other words, journals prefer to publish papers that are going to be widely read and useful to their readers. The webpage for most peer-reviewed journals has an *aims and scope* section that you should read before deciding to submit your work to a particular journal. Not meeting the aims and scope of a journal can be grounds alone for rejection of a work.

- *Is my idea novel?* A novel idea is one that is original or new. You must be able to show how your idea adds to or builds upon the scientific literature. If you can demonstrate what we learn from your idea, then it is novel. It is valuable to replicate or repeat the results of other works; however, replication alone, without appreciable advancement of a fundamental new understanding or knowledge in an area, is often not sufficient to publish a work. Instead, the editors at peer-reviewed journals will prefer scientific reports of "original and significant" findings that extend, not simply repeat, scientific understanding or knowledge.

For any idea you have, the answer to both of these questions should be yes. Ultimately, it is your peers (i.e., other researchers in a field related to your idea) who will review your work before it can be published in a scientific journal. By answering yes to both

Table 2.1 Three Articles Concerning the Use of iPads in Elementary School

Reference	Description	Is the Idea Interesting?	Is the Idea Novel?
Falloon (2015)	The researcher used observations, display-recorded data, focus groups, and a survey to learn how features of the iPad affected students' collaboration.	Recent "research attention has turned towards mobile and touch screen technologies as offering new possibilities for supporting school learner collaboration" (p. 63).	This study "is profoundly different, and significantly extends earlier research. It is based on data collected over a period of almost 3 years in three different primary (elementary) school classrooms, where class and group sets of iPads were present 'fulltime', and used for the complete array of curriculum learning activities" (p. 63).
Milman, Carlson-Bancroft, and Boogart (2014)	Researchers examined how teachers differentiated instruction with the use of iPads.	As schools invest in new technologies, "interest continues to grow regarding the use of iPads in P–12 educational settings as mechanisms to increase student learning and achievement" (p. 119).	"There is a paucity of research on iPads in P–12 classroom Settings" (p. 120).
Carr (2012)	Researchers investigated the effect of the use of the iPad as a computing device on mathematics achievement.	An "investigation of the effects of iPads on fifth-grade mathematics achievement could not only fill a gap in the existing literature but also be used to inform elementary mathematics teachers" (p. 270).	"Scholarly research on the effects of iPad use on education has been limited in general and nonexistent for mathematics achievement" (p. 210).

Note: The citation for where the authors of each article explicitly state what makes their research interesting and novel is given.

questions, you should be able to effectively communicate the value of your idea to a broad scientific audience. Table 2.1 gives three examples of how the authors of a peer-reviewed article studying the use of iPads in elementary school classrooms communicated what made their ideas interesting and novel.

In this chapter, we specifically describe how scientists develop interesting and novel ideas—ideas that are based upon the review of reliable sources and can be tested; that is, we can make observations to confirm or disconfirm if the new idea is correct using the scientific method.

2.2 Converting Ideas to Hypotheses and Theories

In many ways, science may appear to be the search for new information. However, the information itself is of little value without organization. Imagine, for example, trying to find a book in a library that places books on shelves in a random order. The information is in the library; however, it will be difficult to find the information you seek. Moreover, we must do more than just catalog the information we obtain; we must also understand it. In other words, we identify the relevance or usefulness of information. Specifically, we identify the relevance of information by identifying how information can broaden our understanding of the phenomena we study.

The process of organizing information in science is similar to working on a puzzle. You begin with scattered pieces and guessing which pieces fit where. Once you have enough puzzle pieces in place, you can begin to organize other puzzle pieces based on what you know about the pieces in place. Some regions of the puzzle have a similar color and some have a similar design, and this organization can help you ultimately organize the remaining pieces until they all fit the puzzle. The pieces of the puzzle are like the observations we make. And the strategies we use to complete the puzzle are like the hypotheses and theories that researchers state.

A hypothesis, also defined in Chapter 1, is a specific, testable claim or prediction about what you expect to observe given a set of circumstances. For example, in Chapter 1, we tested the hypothesis that images on food packaging will increase healthy food choices among grade school children. The hypothesis we stated was a prediction that specifically identified the outcome we expect to observe (increased healthy food choices) given a specified set of circumstances (the foods are wrapped in packaging with emoticons). Using the puzzle analogy, each attempt to place puzzle pieces together is like an attempt to test a hypothesis. As we start to "put the pieces together," a theory can then develop.

A theory, however, is a broad statement used to account for or explain an existing body of knowledge and provide unique predictions to advance that body of knowledge. A theory essentially organizes evidence that has been rigorously tested and supported by scientific observations. If the findings of research studies point to a collective explanation for the observations made, then a theory develops. Returning to the puzzle analogy, imagine that we put together a puzzle without knowing what the image is that we are constructing. As we group pieces by colors and patterns, we will start to see an image appear in a similar way as we gain evidence and begin to "see" the nature of the phenomena we study. From that information, we can theorize what the puzzle image is. As

An idea should be interesting (appeal to others) and novel (provide new information).

A hypothesis is a specific, testable claim or prediction about what you expect to observe given a set of circumstances.

A theory is a broad statement used to account for an existing body of knowledge and also provide unique predictions to extend that body of knowledge. A theory is not necessarily correct; instead, it is a generally accepted explanation for evidence, as it is understood.

we continue to fit pieces of the puzzle together, we can then modify and refine our theory for what is in the image, similar to how we modify and refine theories of natural or behavioral phenomena as we gather more evidence about these phenomena.

While not exhaustive, there are three key criteria to consider when developing a good hypothesis or theory that is regarded as scientific:

1. Testable/falsifiable. A good theory or hypothesis must be stated in a way that makes it possible to reject it (i.e., it must be falsifiable). For example, we can state the theory that a belief in God leads to better health outcomes (Frampton, 2014). This theory does lead to falsifiable predictions that researchers can readily test. However, we cannot state the theory that God exists because the existence of God cannot be falsified and therefore cannot be accepted as a good theory. That is not to say science says God does not exist; that is to say that such a claim cannot be tested using the scientific process.

2. Replicable/precise. The mechanisms (i.e., presumed causes) and outcomes in a hypothesis or theory should be clearly defined and precise. For example, consider the theory that feelings of attraction promote commitment to a long-term relationship (see Frank, 1988, 2001). This theory is scientific if feelings of attraction (the mechanism) and what constitutes a long-term relationship (the outcome) are specifically defined, such that other researchers could also readily observe, measure, and repeat the procedures used to test this theory. Feelings of attraction may be measured using rating scales or perhaps by recording time spent holding hands in public, for example. It should also be explicitly defined how long is long enough to constitute a long-term relationship (e.g., 3 months? 1 year?). This needs to be clearly defined and precise so that other researchers could readily set up similar measures and procedures to see if they get similar results.

3. Parsimonious. Parsimony is a canon of science that simpler explanations should be preferred to more complex ones. For example, one poor theory popularized by television is the ancient alien theory, which posits that aliens have visited Earth in the past and influenced human civilizations. The theory, among other flaws, is unnecessarily complex. A simpler explanation is simply that man influenced human civilization. Evidence such as pyramid building and cultural norms such as burial practices can be explained without the need to appeal to ancient aliens visiting Earth and interacting with humans. Thus, one reason it is a poor theory for science is that simpler explanations can just as readily explain the evidence purported to support the theory itself.

> Parsimony is a canon of science that states that, all else being equal, simpler explanations should be preferred to more complex ones.

An advantage of a theory is that it not only states unique predictions but can also explain an existing body of research. Figure 2.1 shows the general pattern of developing

Conduct a literature review.

State or modify hypotheses to explain some behavior or event.

Test the predictions made by the new or modified hypotheses.

After working through various predictions, convert the hypotheses to a new or modified theory that can explain some behavior or event.

Test new predictions made by the theory.

State or modify the theory to explain some behavior or event. Discard the theory if the central tenets of the theory fail to be supported.

hypotheses and theories. Notice in the figure that a theory is just as open to testing as a hypothesis. Specifically, a theory is often tested in one of two ways:

- **The predictions made by a theory can be tested.** For example, the familiarity theory states that the more familiar children are with a food, the more they will eat the food (Pliner, 1982; Privitera, 2008b). We can test a "healthy" prediction of the theory to see if increasing a child's familiarity with vegetables will increase how much he or she eats vegetables.

- **The limitations of a theory can be tested.** For example, the familiarity theory is stated largely for children, with the assumption that adults have had too much prior experience with foods. Thus, one limitation of the theory is age. We could test this limitation by testing if adults will eat more foods they have never previously consumed before with greater familiarity to those foods. Or we could test a possible limitation by food type, by testing if children will eat more of any food with greater familiarity and, if not, to identify the food types where familiarity does not influence eating.

Hypotheses and theories allow researchers to organize a large body of research in a way that explains an understanding for evidence, as it is understood, and also provides predictions to organize the expectations for what we should observe. From this platform, we can state hypotheses to test our ideas, and we can also revise and develop our theories to better explain our observations—all with the hope of one day completing the puzzle of understanding human behavior.

> Researchers state hypotheses that, after being rigorously tested, can develop into a theory.

LEARNING CHECK 1 ✓

1. Explain why it is important for an idea to be interesting and novel. *People need to care about it & the idea needs to be new*

2. Distinguish between a hypothesis and a theory.

3. State three key criteria to consider when developing a good hypothesis or theory that is regarded as scientific.

Answers: 1. An idea should be interesting because peer-reviewed journals have a readership and the idea must appeal to those who read that journal in order to be published. An idea should be novel because you must be able to show how your idea adds to or builds upon the scientific literature; 2. A hypothesis is a specific, testable claim or prediction about what you expect to observe given a set of circumstances, whereas a theory is a broad statement used to account for an existing body of knowledge and also provide unique predictions to extend that body of knowledge; 3. Testable/falsifiable, replicable/precise, parsimonious.

2.3 Developing Your Idea: Deduction and Induction

The reasoning that scientists often use to develop their ideas is to begin with a theory or to begin with an observation, referred to as deductive and inductive reasoning, respectively. To

Figure 2.2   A Comparison of Deductive and Inductive Reasoning

Theory

Deduction. A "top-down" or "theory-driven" approach in which researchers begin with a specific claim or theory that generates predictions from which observations can be made to refute or support the claim or theory.

Hypothesis

Induction. A "bottom-up" or "data-driven" approach in which researchers begin by making general observations that lead to patterns from which they formulate hypotheses that make testable predictions—leading to the development of a new theory.

Observations

some extent, many scientists use a combination of both types of reasoning to develop their ideas. Each type of reasoning is introduced here and illustrated in Figure 2.2.

Deductive Reasoning

Many scientific reports will explicitly state theories that have been developed to explain a body of knowledge. A useful theory is one that leads to logical predictions of what we should and should not observe if the theory is correct. The reasoning we use to develop ideas to test those predictions is called deductive reasoning. Using deductive reasoning, you begin with a hypothesis or theory, then use that claim to deduce what you believe should occur, or not occur, if the claim is correct. The prediction you deduce will be used to refute or support the claim. Hence, using deductive reasoning, you start with an idea (the hypothesis or theory) to generate your ideas (predictions made by the hypothesis or theory). Using deductive reasoning, the hypothesis or theory guides the ideas you generate and observations you make.

> **Deductive reasoning** is a "top-down" type of reasoning in which a claim (a hypothesis or theory) is used to generate ideas or predictions and make observations.

To illustrate deductive reasoning, imagine that, based on a literature review, you state the following theory, which you call the "front row theory": Students who sit in the front row are smarter than students who sit in the back row. From this starting point, you deduce predictions of what will be observed if your theory is correct. One prediction, for example, is that students who sit in the front row will score higher on an exam than students who sit in the back row. You can test this prediction by recording the grades of students and recording where they sat in class. In this way, your theory guides what you choose to observe. Figure 2.3 illustrates the "front row theory" example using deductive reasoning.

Figure 2.3 The Process of Deduction and Induction for the Same Problem

Theory: Students who sit in the front row are smarter than students who sit in the back row.

Deduction

Hypothesis/predicted observation: Students who sit in the front row will score higher on exams than students who sit in the back row.

Induction

Observation: You observe that three students sitting in the front row always score highest on exams.

Note: In this example, both types of reasoning led to the same hypothesis.

Inductive Reasoning

Sometimes, you may find that your initial ideas are developed by your own data or observations. The type of reasoning you use to generate ideas from observations is called **inductive reasoning.** Using inductive reasoning, you make a casual observation (e.g., you see that all the students in Mr. Adams's history class raise their hand to participate in a discussion) or collect and measure data (e.g., you record the number of times each student raises his or her hand for 1 week). You then generate an idea to explain what you observed or measured (e.g., students raise their hand because Mr. Adams passes out candy to the students who participate in the discussions). The idea you generate to explain the observation is your hypothesis. Hence, using inductive reasoning, you start with an observation to generate new ideas; you generalize beyond the limited observations you made. Using inductive reasoning, then, the data or observations guide the ideas you generate and observations you make.

> **Inductive reasoning** is a "bottom-up" type of reasoning in which a limited number of observations or measurements (i.e., data) are used to generate ideas and make observations.

To illustrate the distinction between deductive and inductive reasoning, we can revisit the "front row theory" example to show how inductive reasoning could lead to the same idea we developed using deductive reasoning. Suppose you observe that three students sitting in the front row always score highest on exams. From this starting point, you hypothesize that all students who sit in the front row will score higher on exams than those who sit in the back row. You record the grades of all students and record where they sat in class. Notice that we arrive at the same idea and the same study to test that idea using both types of reasoning. Figure 2.3 illustrates the "front row theory" example using inductive reasoning.

> Inductive and deductive reasoning represent two ways in which researchers develop ideas for scientific testing.

1. Which of the following situations is an example of deductive reasoning, inductive reasoning, or both?

    A. You observe two students arguing loudly in a hallway. About 2 minutes into the argument, a teacher walks down the same hallway. After that, they no longer argue. From this you conclude that the presence of a teacher can prevent disruptive behavior in the hallways.

    B. While reading a professional paper, you come across a theory called model-lead-test that improves reading skills. You resolve that if this is true, then if you teach using the model-lead-test theory, the reading scores of your students will increase.

    C. You notice that students do better on a test after participating in a collaborative group project. You conclude then that providing more collaborative group projects will increase learning.

Answers: 1. A. induction; B. deduction; C. inductive.

2.4 Performing a Literature Review

To develop an idea, you must perform a literature review. The *literature* is the general body of published scientific knowledge. The *review* is the search you perform of this general body of knowledge. The literature is most often published in peer-reviewed journals and academic books. Other sources, such as newspapers, popular magazines, and Internet websites, are not part of the scientific literature because the information provided in these sources is not typically subjected to a peer review.

A key objective of the literature review is to develop new ideas that can be converted into a hypothesis that is both interesting and novel. Research is not an isolated process; rather, it is one of collaboration and peer review. Therefore, reviewing the general body of knowledge in your topic area is important to determine what is known and to develop ideas for what is yet to be discovered. In this section, we will explain how to get started with your literature review to develop new ideas and select a research topic. We will then explain how to use searchable databases and organize your search results.

A **literature review** is a systematic search for and recording of information identified in the general body of published scientific knowledge.

Getting Started: Choosing a Research Topic

Inquiry begins with a question. What topics interest you? What questions do you want to ask about those topics? When choosing a research topic, be sure to select one that interests you. The research process can be tedious. Asking questions about topics that interest you can make this process fun. Certainly, topics involving food, sports, family involvement, video gaming, teacher morale, instructional methods, or classroom discipline interest you as an educator. A researcher is probably studying just about any topic or behavior you can think of. It will be difficult to stay committed to a research project if you are not interested in the topic you are studying.

Getting Organized: Choosing Appropriate Sources

After you find an interesting research topic, you will review the literature about that topic. Keeping track of the types of sources you come across as you perform your review is important. A *source* is any published or printed article, chapter, or book from which information can be obtained. There can be thousands of sources for even a single research topic, and reviewing them all can be challenging. To organize the sources, you come across and make a literature review more efficient:

Choose a research topic that interests you.

- Begin with a search of review articles.

- Search only from peer-reviewed or other scientific sources.

You can categorize sources as primary and secondary. A secondary source is any source in which an author describes research or ideas that are not necessarily his or her own. Secondary sources can include textbooks, newspaper and magazine articles, online sources, and review articles. *Review articles* provide a full summary of a research topic by an author who is regarded as an expert on that topic. It is good to begin with these types of articles for the following two reasons:

> A secondary source is any publication that refers to works, ideas, or observations that are not those of the author.

- Key sources pertaining to a topic of interest are described in a review article.

- Review articles are typically published in peer-reviewed journals.

Review articles include dozens of the most up-to-date findings in an area of research. To summarize the literature for a topic, an author will review many sources from other researchers in that topic area. Each source reviewed in the article that was not the actual work of the author is called a secondary source. In a review article, the author or authors provide a thorough review of sometimes hundreds of secondary sources. By reading review articles, you can quickly review a diverse number of sources that you can be confident are related to your topic of interest.

Each time you come across a secondary source that interests you, you can find the reference cited in that review article and read it for yourself. As you review secondary sources, be sure to record the full reference of each source that interests you. For most sources, you should write down the author, publication year, title, journal, issue, and page numbers. Or you can create an electronic file or spreadsheet with this information to keep your search organized. You can be more efficient by having this information ready when it comes time to find the secondary sources that interest you.

A **primary source** is any publication in which the works, ideas, or observations are those of the author.

The original source of an idea or research is called a **primary source.** In an *empirical article*, in which the authors conduct a firsthand study, the introduction for these articles is a great place to find secondary sources. Empirical articles can often be readily identified because these include a detailed method and results section, in addition to a concluding discussion section. These additional sections are a primary source (or the original ideas/design of the authors). In your review, keep track of secondary sources so that you can find the primary source later. It is important to find and read a primary source from the original author of a work.

You should not develop your ideas based upon secondary sources because a secondary source is someone (e.g., the author of the review article) telling you what someone else (e.g., the original author of the work) observed. You need to check your sources. Find the primary source and read what the original author of that work did. You do this to check that what was reported in the review article was accurate and to be more confident in the ideas you develop from your review.

It can be more efficient to review secondary sources, and then primary sources, in a literature review.

Most of the primary and secondary sources you find in your review can be found using online databases. Many databases for searching only peer-reviewed and scientific works are available at colleges throughout the world. If you have access to these library databases, then this will make your search far easier and more efficient.

MAKING SENSE—PRIMARY AND SECONDARY SOURCES

A common misconception is that a source is either primary or secondary. In fact, most journal articles, especially those published in peer-reviewed journals, are a mix of both. Review articles mostly consist of secondary sources. However, secondary sources can also be found in original research articles from primary sources. For any research, authors must explain how their research is novel, and to do so, authors must show how their research study (primary source) builds upon the known body of research typically published by various different authors (secondary sources). For this reason, most articles published in peer-reviewed journals begin with an introduction, which is where authors will explain what is known (typically by reviewing secondary sources) and what is yet to be explained and so tested in their study (primary source).

After you spend days or weeks reviewing a research topic, it is often all too easy to forget whether the information you have came from primary or secondary sources. One contributing factor to this problem is that you can find secondary sources in most articles you read, even in articles you list as being a primary source. Keeping track of primary and secondary sources as you review them can minimize this problem.

Getting Searching: Using Online Databases

Online databases allow researchers to search for, save, and print thousands of primary and secondary sources in all topic areas in the education sciences. Popular databases in the education sciences, the contents of which are described in Table 2.2, include ERIC (Education Resources Information Center), PsycINFO, and Education Research Complete. Many of these databases offer peer-reviewed articles in full text, meaning that the full article is provided and can be downloaded and saved on your computer, usually as a PDF.

A full-text article is any article or text that is available in its full or complete published version.

A full-text database is any online database that makes full-text articles available to be downloaded electronically as a PDF or in another electronic format.

When searching for peer-reviewed articles, it is important to recognize the types of articles you can find. Searching in the databases suggested here is the safest way to ensure that you are finding only peer-reviewed articles. However, if you are ever uncertain as to whether your source is peer reviewed—whether using the databases suggested here or other databases such as Google Scholar—it is often beneficial to check that your source is indeed peer reviewed. You can do this by visiting the website for the journal and viewing the *about this journal* or *aims and scope* sections. For inexperienced students, it can also be a good idea to check with your professor or other more experienced professional.

In the remainder of this section, we will describe the general process for navigating online databases using ERIC as an example. Note that the screenshots for this database can vary from those shown in Figures 2.4 and 2.5 depending on the type of computer system you use to search ERIC. This example used the EBSCOhost search engine to access the ERIC database.

Table 2.2 Descriptions for Three Widely Used Online Databases in the Behavioral Sciences

Database	Description
ERIC	A bibliographic and full-text database that contains more than 1.2 million records, updated twice weekly for journal articles, books, conference and policy papers, technical reports, and other education-related materials (Educational Resource Information Center, n.d.).
PsycINFO	An abstract database containing more than 2.7 million records updated weekly, from more than 49 countries and in 29 languages. Ninety-nine percent of journals covered are peer reviewed from areas in psychology and related disciplines such as education (American Psychological Association [APA], 2013b).
Education Research Complete	This full-text database, available via EBSCOhost, covers areas of curriculum instruction, administration, policy, funding, and related social issues found in journals, books, and education-related conferences (EBSCO Industries, 2015).

After logging on to a database, typically using access provided by a college or research institution, you will see several search options under the advanced search tab. To illustrate the use of ERIC, we will use this database to perform a literature review on information about studying and elementary school student grades. Figure 2.4 shows the screen for this search. To begin a search, you need to select keywords for the database to search. For this example, the keyword *study habits* was entered in the top left cell, and the keyword *grades* was entered in the cell below it, and *elementary* was entered into the bottom cell. Be thoughtful when choosing keywords. It is unlikely that there is "no research on your topic." It is more likely that you are not using appropriate terms to search for your topic. So before giving up your search, use a thesaurus or check if you are using the correct technical jargon for your topic. It is likely that articles for your topic will appear once you start using more appropriate terms.

In the search, you have the option to search grade point average (GPA) *or* study habits by changing "and" to "or" in the dropdown box. As they are entered now, the database will search for GPA *and* study habits, which will narrow the search a bit. Note that the *and/or* options may appear across rows in other database displays. You can also limit your search to find keywords anywhere in an article, title, or abstract; by publication year; by author; and according to many other search options. Notice in Figure 2.4 that you can limit your search by publication type, date, educational level, or audience. To perform the search using the keywords and criteria you selected, click the "Search" option to the left.

Figure 2.4   A Screenshot of the Upper Portion of an Initial Search View in ERIC

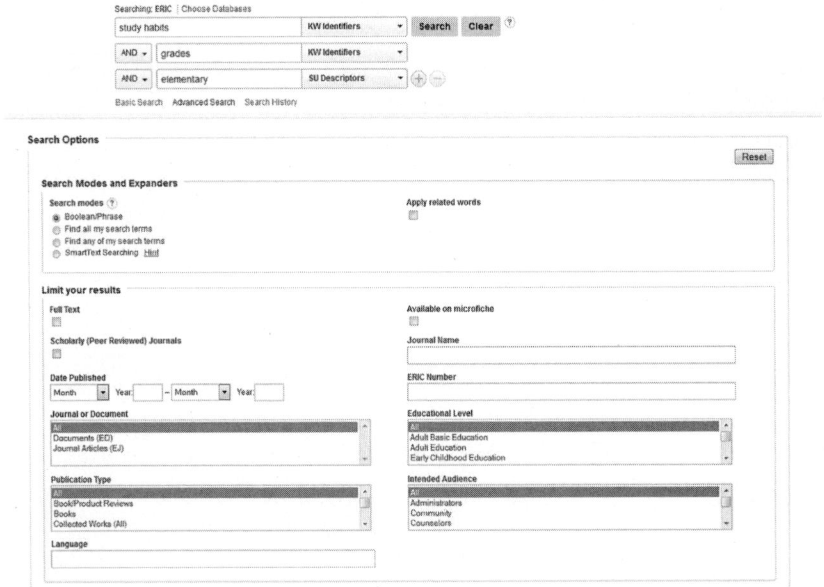

Note: In our search, we chose to search for the keywords *study habits, grades,* and *elementary* using the subject descriptors.

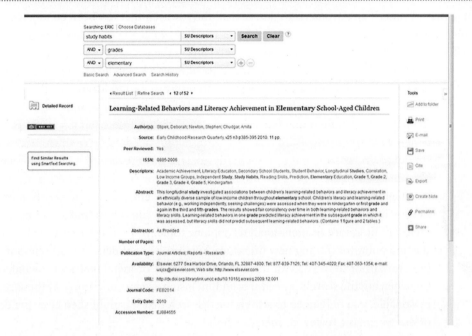

Note: These are the results of selecting the article authored by Stipek, Newton, and Chudgar (2010).

Clicking "Search" for the information entered in Figure 2.4 will display a list of sources related to the keywords you entered. Because the database is updated weekly, these results will change. Each article is listed with the title, year, author, journal, issue, and page information given. Many sources are full text, and all should include at least an **abstract** or brief overview of the article. If you selected the article authored by Stipek, Newton, and Chudgar (2010), for example, you would see the information shown in Figure 2.5. If the full-text article is available, then download and save it. If it is not, then saving the abstract and

> An **abstract** is a brief written summary of the purpose, methods, and results of an article, a chapter, a book, or another published document. The length of an abstract can vary; however, abstracts are usually 250 words or less.

reference information will make it easier for you to find the full-text article later. If a source is not available electronically, then it can likely be found using the interlibrary loan process at your college or university library.

Section 2.6 expands on this general description of working with a database by describing some common practices for conducting an effective literature review. We turn first to a discussion in Section 2.5 for how to properly cite research that is used in your research study.

SYSTEMATIC REVIEWS OF LITERATURE AND META-ANALYSES

During a search for literature in addition to articles of individual research studies, two other types of research articles that you might find are called a literature review (or systematic review of literature) and meta-analysis. A systematic review of literature is a synthesis of research studies conducted on a particular topic. The researcher will systematically conduct an extensive search for all the research conducted on the topic in a given period of time. The purpose is to describe all the research that has been conducted on the topic and to critically evaluate it. It establishes to what extent the topic has been studied and will identify consistencies, inconsistencies, and gaps in the research, which leads to directions for future research. In this type of research article, expect the researcher to clearly describe the search process, search terms used to locate the literature, criteria for articles to be included or excluded from the review, and the publication time frame for the articles. A meta-analysis takes a systematic review of literature one step further by combining the data derived from all of the studies to understand and to statistically analyze what the entire body of research says about the topic. There are different methods for conducting a meta-analysis, but the idea is to provide an overall estimate of the effect of an intervention or validity on a theoretical argument. If you are lucky enough to find a systematic review of literature or meta-analysis on your topic, you can use it as your starting point for finding new literature. You can be confident that all relevant literature prior to the date of the systematic review or meta-analysis is included by reviewing the search procedures and inclusion/exclusion criteria. If these seem reasonable, you only need to search for research that was published after the date of the systematic review or meta-analysis.

Online databases, such as ERIC, make research more accessible by allowing users to search thousands of articles in a single search.

LEARNING CHECK 3 ✓

1. What is a literature review?

2. Distinguish between primary and secondary sources.

3. List three online databases used by education scientists.

Answers: 1. A literature review is the systematic search for and recording of information discovered from the general body of published scientific knowledge; 2. A primary source is the works, ideas, or observations of the author, whereas a secondary source refers to works, ideas, or observations authored by other researchers; 3. PsycINFO, Education Research Complete, and ERIC.

CONNECTING TO THE CLASSROOM

Once you have identified a classroom- or school-based problem, performing a literature review is a very important first step to understanding the problem and identifying a potential solution. It is highly likely that you are not the only person to be experiencing a specific problem, and there is information about potential solutions available. A literature review can help you understand the whole picture of the issue. There may be aspects of the issue that you have not thought about that are important for you to know. It may also serve as a sense of relief to know that you are not alone in experiencing this issue.

We have an identified gap in education research called the research-to-practice gap. Research has identified evidence-based practices that are not being put to good use in everyday classrooms. Researchers publish their work in research journals and share it at education conferences that are not often read by educators. We need to do better in disseminating our work to a wider audience in ways that are usable. The U.S. Department of Education has established the What Works Clearinghouse (WWC, https://ies.ed.gov/ncee/wwc/) as a repository for identified evidence-based practices. The criteria for being included in the WWC are rigorous, so you can be confident in the practices that are identified as being effective. Once you identify a potential practice on the site, you can link onto a summary of the research studies that were used to identify it as an effective practice.

2.5 Ethics in Focus: Giving Proper Credit

One important reason for organizing your sources when conducting a literature review is to avoid confusion when giving credit for sources cited in your research study. Ethical problems arise if you cite these sources incorrectly or without reference to the primary source. Four ways to avoid such ethical problems are the following:

- **Always double-check your sources for accuracy.** When referring to a secondary source, be sure to cite it properly and accurately so that your readers can find the source should they wish to pursue the subject you are writing about. Readers may become frustrated if they try to locate the source and cannot find it. Accuracy in citations is a concern for you and even among researchers who publish in peer-reviewed scientific journals—Siebers and Holt (2000), for example, found many reference errors in leading medical journals, as shown in Table 2.3.

- **Obtain the primary source of an article you cite.** One way to find the primary source is to check the references of secondary sources, particularly review articles. In that way, you can find the original work that should be given proper credit. After all, "Citing the original article ensures that the person with priority for the discovery is provided proper credit. To cite a later source misallocates that credit" (Zigmond & Fischer, 2002, p. 231).

- **Avoid "abstracting."** Abstracting in this sense refers to instances in which an individual cites the full reference of some work after simply skimming through an abstract. This is poor practice because "citing references without scrutiny of the entire paper may lead to misrepresentation of the paper's actual findings" (Taylor, 2002, p. 167). When you cite a reference, be sure that you have read it in full to ensure that you properly represent the work.

Table 2.3 Error Rates in Articles Published by Five Leading Medical Journals in March 1999	
Total references checked	1,557
References with any error	300
Reference error rate (%)	19
Author errors	206
Title errors	101
Journal errors	20
Volume errors	15
Year errors	20
Page errors	49

Source: Data adapted from those presented by Siebers and Holt (2000).

- **Be aware of citation bias.** Citation bias occurs when an author or authors cite only evidence that supports their view and fail to cite conflicting evidence. For example, Ferguson (2010) identified such a problem in the video game violence literature. He noted that "a close look at the research on violence in video games reveals that findings are far less consistent than have been reported by some sources" (p. 72). What he revealed was that many articles in this area of research only cited one side for or against the dangers of video game violence. Make sure you cite sources for all findings in your area of interest, and be aware of possible citation biases when reviewing the work of others.

Citation bias is a misleading approach to citing sources that occurs when an author or authors cite only evidence that supports their view and fail to cite existing evidence that refutes their view.

In this section, we described four ethical concerns related to giving accurate and proper credit. The Office of Research Integrity offers a more exhaustive list of ethical considerations. To access the list, go to http://ori.dhhs.gov/education/products/ and select the "Misconduct" tab.

LEARNING CHECK 4 ✓

1. State the ethical pitfall that is described for each example given below:

   A. A student reads an interesting abstract of an article. He tries to find the full article but is unable to locate it. He still cites the full article in his research paper.

B. A professor reads an interesting review article stating that other researchers have shown a link between diet and addiction. She later writes about this link and gives credit to the review article but not the original researchers who showed this link.

C. An author makes a claim that watching television reduces the attention span of a child and cites only those sources that support his view even though some evidence exists that refutes his view.

D. A researcher reads an article that includes a study that piques his interest. When he goes to find the reference cited, he notices that the publication year is wrong.

Answers: 1. A. The student is guilty of abstracting; B. The professor has failed to obtain the primary source of an article cited; C. The work has a citation bias; D. The author of the article failed to double-check the sources for accuracy.

2.6 The "3 Cs" of an Effective Literature Review

This section presents some additional strategies for conducting an effective literature review. You can remember them as the "3 Cs," or being comprehensive, critical, and clever.

Be Comprehensive

Most of the sources available using online databases are peer-reviewed research journals, which are considered very reliable sources. These journals specialize; that is, they tend to publish articles only in a particular area of research. If you find an article relevant to your research topic in one journal, then it is likely that there are additional articles on that topic in other issues of that journal. To search the journal's archive, enter the journal title in an online database keyword search and search by journal.

Searching multiple databases can also enhance your search. Each database, such as PsycINFO or ERIC, includes a different list of journals to search from. It is very possible that an online search in one database will produce different results than an online search in another database. Hence, searching multiple databases can increase the total number of possible results to review for your topic of interest.

Keep in mind that each journal article follows a particular format. While many follow an APA (2009)–style format, not all journals will do so. Regardless of the formatting style used, each article will include a title, followed by an abstract, an introduction, method, results, discussion, and references. Table 2.4 lists and describes each of these sections. Usually, reading select portions of an article is sufficient to determine whether it is relevant to your research topic. Examining each article in the following order will help you search most efficiently.

Title. In many cases, if the title of an article does not pique your interest, then neither will the article.

Abstract. The abstract summarizes, typically in fewer than 250 words, the purpose and results of some work. Reading the title and abstract takes about 1 minute and allows you to discard many of the articles that are not relevant

Table 2.4 The Sections of Articles in Peer-Reviewed Journals

Section	Description
Title	A single sentence that captures the topic of a study
Abstract	A brief summary of the purpose and results of a study
Introduction	An overview of the research topic that explains how it is interesting and novel and identifies the hypotheses being tested
Method	A description of the materials, procedures, and participants or subjects in a study
Results	A summary of the statistical analyses that often includes figures and tables to summarize data
Discussion	The conclusion of the study that explains how the results of a study answered the hypotheses tested and sometimes offers ideas for future research
References	A listing for every source that was cited in the body of the article

to your research topic. Many online databases give you a minimum of the title and abstract of an article, making it easy to distinguish the articles you do need from those you do not.

Introduction and discussion. For the articles that you like, you can print and save the full text; if you are unable to access the article, see your librarian to learn how you can obtain a copy. Reading the introduction and discussion sections can allow you to determine if an article is truly relevant. If the article is relevant, then its list of secondary sources will identify other articles of possible interest.

Method and results. Once you have determined that an article is relevant to your research topic, carefully read through it. Be critical of the method and results published in an article and make sure that both are consistent with the conclusions drawn in the article.

References. Once you have fully reviewed articles of interest, you can search through the references listed at the end of each article to double-check that you have exhausted all articles related to your research topic of interest.

Also, keep in mind that one study rarely is sufficient to answer a research question or prove a claim, so you should not base your entire literature review on a single article or viewpoint. Scientists hold many opposing views and often present data that contradict scientific evidence published earlier. To be comprehensive, you should identify some of these opposing viewpoints and the contradictory evidence in those studies. Doing so can actually help you develop your own ideas to generate stronger hypotheses and theories.

Be Critical

To be critical means that you ask questions, know your sources, and are objective as you conduct your literature review. Each aspect of being critical is described here.

Ask questions. As you read an article, ask yourself questions about the participants that the researchers used, the methods or procedures employed, and the conclusions drawn. The article itself will provide most of the answers. Also, many researchers identify potential limitations or drawbacks to their study in the discussion section. As you read through this section, think of ways you could address them. Asking questions will help you generate your own ideas, and those ideas could eventually become part of your hypothesis.

Know your sources. Know where your information comes from. Know whether the information you find comes from a secondary or a primary source and whether it is peer reviewed. Most journals disclose their review policies in each issue. Also, be cautious when using online sources because they are often not subjected to a peer review. You must check the credibility of online sources closely, as a few may be peer reviewed, such as articles from open access publishers (e.g., AERA Open).

Remain objective. Be aware of your own biases. You may have some ideas before starting the literature review, which may affect what you decide to read and pay attention to during your search. If you keep an open mind, you may find sources that contradict your point of view. Knowing the opposing views may even help you generate some of your best ideas. After all, if you disagree with a point of view, then you should be able to explain why you disagree, which can often lead to new ideas or explanations.

Be Clever

Being clever means that you actively think of unique ways to advance the research you read about in your literature review; be innovative in your approach to advance scientific research. The following are five strategies you can use to be clever in your approach to generate new ideas for your research topic.

Identify flaws. There is some probability of an error in all published scientific data. In addition, scientists are not infallible—on some occasions

Being comprehensive means performing an effective literature review in a minimum amount of time.

Being critical means that you ask challenging questions rooted in the scientific literature.

they can, without intention, misinterpret, mislead, or misrepresent the data they publish. Consequently, some of the research you come across can be wrong or inaccurate. Identify these inaccuracies and conduct a study without them.

Identify contradictions. You may come across two or more studies with contradictory hypotheses or data. If you read these articles closely, you can develop hypotheses of your own that make predictions that can lend support to one or both studies. Your work will help clarify possible confusion in the published work.

Identify anomalies. Look for conclusions, interpretations, or data presented in articles that are inconsistent. For example, researchers often disregard scores called *outliers* that do not fit with most of the data as anomalies or errors. Often, anomalies are not errors, and they can lead to new ideas that result in new directions of research.

Consider subtleties. You may find that subtle changes to a study can make a big difference in a research result. An important issue, particularly in laboratory research, is whether research studies generalize to situations beyond those observed. Making subtle changes, such as observing participants with different demographic characteristics or measuring different variables, can have a significant impact on the results observed.

Think beyond the research. Princeton University psychologist Daniel Kahneman won the 2002 Nobel Prize in Economic Sciences for his landmark research applying psychology to economic theory. Well-known educator Maria Montessori was an Italian physician who developed her educational theory based on her observations of human development as a physician. Perhaps you can use a similar strategy to generate new ideas of your own by merging two different research topics to resolve the same problem.

> Being clever means that you are innovative in your approach to advance scientific research.

This brief list of strategies aims to help you see how knowing what to look for and how to generate new ideas can help you select a research topic. Your goal should be to generate your own new ideas, and the "3Cs" can help guide you in the right direction for achieving that goal.

LEARNING CHECK 5 ✓

1. List the order in which you should read sections of a research article as part of your literature review.

2. For each of the following examples, state the aspect of being critical that the student is ignoring.

A. A student reads through an article and just accepts every argument in the article without question.

B. A student cites an article as key evidence to justify her hypothesis but does not know whether the source is peer reviewed.

C. A student gets upset at a relevant article that contradicts his point of view, so he decides to put it aside and not include it in his paper.

3. State five clever strategies for generating new ideas that can help you select a research topic.

2.7 Testing Your Idea: Confirmation and Disconfirmation

Any idea you develop must be testable—it must make specific predictions that can be observed under specified conditions. In this section, we consider two ways to test a theory or hypothesis: a confirmational strategy in which a researcher tests *anticipated* outcomes and a disconfirmational strategy in which *unanticipated* outcomes are tested by a researcher.

Confirmational Strategy

A confirmational strategy is a method of testing a theory or hypothesis in which a positive result confirms the predictions made by that theory or hypothesis. A *positive result* confirms a hypothesis or theory and occurs when an effect or a difference is observed. A confirmational strategy is often used to test a new theory or hypothesis in terms of the predictions that it anticipates will occur if the theory or hypothesis is correct. Using an "if . . . then" logic statement, a confirmational strategy can be represented as follows:

> A confirmational strategy is a method of testing a theory or hypothesis in which a positive result confirms the predictions made by that theory or hypothesis.

If A is true, then B is true.

B is true.

Therefore, A is true.

The problem with using this type of logic, referred to as *affirming the consequent*, is that it can be fallacious or not true, as the following example demonstrates:

If you are a scientist (A), then you are educated (B).

You are educated (B).

Therefore, you are a scientist (A).

The conclusion that you are a scientist is not always true. While scientists are certainly educated, not all educated people are scientists. Thus, the logic is not valid. This problem of logical fallacy means that using the confirmational strategy alone to test theories and hypotheses is not good practice. To balance this major limitation, researchers also use a disconfirmational strategy.

Disconfirmational Strategy

A **disconfirmational strategy** is a method of testing a theory or hypothesis in which you test an outcome that is not predicted by the theory or hypothesis you are testing. A *positive result* in this case disconfirms a hypothesis or theory. Using this strategy, for example, suppose we hypothesize that students will increase the performance of a behavior if it is followed by a positive outcome, which is called a *theory of positive reinforcement*. To test this theory, we first we record the number of classroom disruptions in a day by disruptive students. Then some of the disruptive students receive pleasant verbal compliments from a teacher following appropriate behavior, such as following a teacher direction, and some do not. Finally, we record the number of classroom disruptions after 2 weeks of receiving the pleasant verbal compliments.

> A **disconfirmational strategy** is a method of testing a theory or hypothesis in which a positive result disconfirms the predictions made by that theory or hypothesis.

In this example, we applied both a confirmational and a disconfirmational strategy. Our hypothesis predicts that students who received the pleasant verbal compliments will perform the appropriate behaviors more often. As illustrated in Figure 2.6, this test is a confirmational strategy: If A, then B. For our hypothesis to be correct, we also must observe that students who did not receive the pleasant verbal compliments from the teachers will not perform appropriate behaviors more often. As illustrated in Figure 2.6, this test is a disconfirmational strategy: If A, then not C. If we do observe C, then the pleasant verbal compliments are not causing the increase in appropriate behavior.

A benefit of using the disconfirmational strategy is that we can refute a theory or hypothesis with a positive result. Alternatively, to refute a theory or hypothesis using a confirmational strategy, we would need to observe a *negative result*, meaning no effect or difference. As discussed in Section 2.8, because of problems related to statistical power (i.e., the likelihood of detecting an effect or a difference), negative results alone are rarely published in peer-reviewed journals. For this reason, a disconfirmational strategy is the best strategy for refuting a theory.

Theory of positive reinforcement operant conditioning: Students will increase performing a behavior that is followed by a pleasant outcome

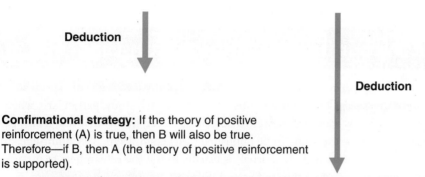

Deduction

Deduction

Confirmational strategy: If the theory of positive reinforcement (A) is true, then B will also be true. Therefore—if B, then A (the theory of positive reinforcement is supported).

Disconfirmational strategy: If the theory of positive reinforcement (A) is true, then C cannot be true (not C). Therefore—if C, then not A (the theory of positive reinforcement is refuted).

Key:
A = The theory of positive reinforcement.
B = Student increased performance of a behavior that was followed by a pleasant outcome.
C = Student increased performance of a behavior that was not followed by a pleasant outcome.
In this example, the theory of positive reinforcement anticipates B—a confirmational strategy is used to test this outcome. But the theory of positive reinforcement does not anticipate C—a disconfirmational strategy is used to test this outcome.

Note: In this example, the aversion theory anticipates B—a confirmational strategy is used to test this outcome. But the theory of positive reinforcement does not anticipate C—a disconfirmational strategy is used to test this outcome.

LEARNING CHECK 6 ✓

1. A researcher proposes the following theory: The more often students miss class, the worse their class grade will be. The following two studies, A and B, tested this claim. State the type of strategy, confirmational or disconfirmational, used in each study.

   A. You select a sample of high school students who have missed at least six classes during the semester. Half the students work full-time, and half do not work. You record the GPA of all students to see if there is a difference between groups. Because all students sampled in this study missed the same number of classes, the theory does not predict a difference between groups.

B. You obtain school records from a random sample of high school freshmen. You record the semester GPA and the number of classes missed during the semester for each student sampled. If the theory is true, then it should also be true that the more classes students miss during the semester, the lower their semester GPA will be.

2.8 Ethics in Focus: Publication Bias

Researchers conduct studies to observe an effect. An *effect* is any difference or significant outcome observed in a study. The failure to observe an effect in a study, particularly when the study is associated with low statistical power to detect the effect, means that few, if any, peer-reviewed journals will allow the study to be published (Dickersin, 1990; McCambridge, 2007). The response from reviewers for these journals is usually to tell the researchers to increase their statistical power and conduct the study again. For this reason, much of the peer-reviewed literature is biased in favor of studies showing positive results, a situation described as the publication bias. The **publication bias** is the tendency for editors of peer-reviewed journals to preferentially accept articles that show positive results and reject those that show only negative results.

negative results are usually not published

> **Publication bias** is the tendency for editors of peer-reviewed journals to preferentially accept articles that show positive results and reject those that show only negative results.
>
> The publication bias is also called the **file drawer problem** because researchers have a tendency to file away studies that show negative results, knowing that most journals will likely reject them.

Because editors of peer-reviewed journals and the peer reviewers themselves often reject a manuscript on the basis of a failure to show positive results (Liesegang, Albert, & Schachat, 2008), researchers are often deterred from even trying to submit negative results for publication (Calnan, Smith, & Sterne, 2006; Olson et al., 2002). As a result, many researchers do not even try to publish negative findings, instead choosing to file them away, a situation described as the **file drawer problem.**

The publication bias means that the size of an effect could be overstated for many behavioral phenomena reported in the peer-reviewed literature. For example, suppose you read a few studies showing that a new behavioral therapy for depression significantly reduces symptoms of depression in patients. If a researcher tests the effectiveness of this same behavioral therapy and finds no effect, it is likely that no peer-reviewed journal will accept it, so you will never find it or read about it. It is therefore possible that the effectiveness of this therapy is overstated because studies failing to show an effect are not included in the published peer-reviewed literature. Howard, Lau, et al. (2009) stated that "scientific progress is made by trusting the bulk of current knowledge" (p. 117), and the publication bias compromises this trust. Keep in mind that while positive results reported in the peer-reviewed literature can certainly be trusted, also take caution in knowing that many negative results may not be included in your search.

Positive results are more likely to be published in peer-reviewed journals than negative results.

LO 1 Explain what makes an idea interesting and novel.

- An interesting idea is any idea that appeals to the readership of peer-reviewed journals. A novel idea is one that is original or new.

LO 2 Distinguish between a hypothesis and a theory.

- A hypothesis is a specific, testable claim or prediction about what you expect to observe given a set of circumstances. A theory is a broader statement used to account for an existing body of knowledge and also provide unique predictions to extend that body of knowledge. A theory is not necessarily correct; instead, it is a generally accepted explanation for evidence, as it is understood.

- Three key criteria to consider when developing a good hypothesis or theory that is regarded as scientific are as follows: testable/falsifiable, replicable/precise, and parsimonious.

LO 3 Distinguish between induction and deduction.

- Deductive reasoning is a "top-down" type of reasoning in which a claim (hypothesis or theory) is used to generate ideas or predictions and make observations.

- Inductive reasoning is a "bottom-up" type of reasoning in which a limited number of observations or measurements (i.e., data) are used to generate ideas and make observations.

LO 4 Describe the process of conducting a literature review.

- Getting started: Find a research topic that interests you because it will make the scientific process more worthwhile.

- Getting organized: Review secondary sources to identify primary sources that are most relevant to your research topic. Then follow up and read the primary sources to check what is reported in those sources.

- Getting searching: Use online databases, such as PsycINFO, ERIC, and Education Research Complete. Each online database allows you to use keyword searches to review thousands of articles and books.

LO 5 Identify four ethical concerns for giving proper credit.

- These concerns are as follows: incorrectly citing reference articles, failing to obtain or give proper credit to a primary source, citing a source after only reading the abstract for that source, and citation bias.

- Citation bias occurs when citing only evidence that supports your view without also citing existing evidence that refutes your view.

LO 6 Describe the "3 Cs" of conducting an effective literature review.

- Be comprehensive. Journals specialize, so search a journal name if you know it contains articles that interest you. Read sections of research articles in the following order: title, abstract, introduction and discussion, method and results, and references. Also, be aware that one study rarely is sufficient to answer a research question or prove a hypothesis, so you should not base your entire literature review on a single article or viewpoint.

- Be critical. Ask questions as you read, know the types of sources you are using, and remain as objective as possible.

- Be clever. Some clever strategies are to identify flaws, identify contradictions, identify anomalies, consider subtleties, and think beyond the research.

LO 7 Distinguish between a confirmational and a disconfirmational strategy.

- A confirmational strategy is a method of testing a theory or hypothesis in which a positive result confirms the predictions made by that theory or hypothesis.

- A disconfirmational strategy is a method of testing a theory or hypothesis in which a positive result disconfirms the predictions made by that theory or hypothesis.

LO 8 Explain the issue of publication bias.

- Publication bias is the tendency for editors of peer-reviewed journals to preferentially accept articles that show positive results and reject those that show only negative results.

- The publication bias is also called the file drawer problem because researchers have a tendency to file away studies that show negative results, knowing that most journals will likely reject them. The publication bias means that the size of an effect could be overstated for many behavioral phenomena reported in the peer-reviewed literature.

KEY TERMS

abstract 45	file drawer problem 56	parsimony 35
citation bias 48	full-text article 43	peer-reviewed journal 32
confirmational strategy 53	full-text database 43	primary source 42
deductive reasoning 38	hypothesis 34	publication bias 56
disconfirmational strategy 54	inductive reasoning 39	secondary source 41
	literature review 40	theory 34

1. Why is it important for a research idea to be novel?

2. Researchers conducted a hypothetical study concerning self-image, parenting, and popular magazines. In their article, they stated the following:

   Popular magazines, such as *Cosmopolitan* (*Cosmo*), tend to portray women as the "fun, fearless female" (Machin & Thornborrow, 2003, p. 462). Considering that millions of girls in the United States read these popular magazines (Magazine Publishers of America, 2013), it is important to understand how this portrayal influences self-image among girls. In this study, the authors advance current knowledge by testing (1) the extent to which parents are aware of and approve of the content in these magazines and (2) the extent to which girls actively incorporate this portrayal into their own self-image.

   A. Identify the portion of this excerpt that describes what makes this research interesting.

   B. Identify the portion of this excerpt that describes what makes this research novel.

3. Is a theory or a hypothesis described as a statement that has been rigorously tested and supported by scientific observations?

4. Which type of source, primary or secondary, should you use to begin your literature review search? Why?

5. Name three educational databases used to perform a literature review. What article information is typically provided for available articles in these databases?

6. Which scenario listed below is ethical, and which is not? (Hint: Refer to Section 2.4.) Explain your answer.

   A. A student attends a conference and reads an abstract on a poster that she finds interesting as a source for her own paper. The presenter of the poster tells her that the research described in the abstract has been published in the journal of *Reading Research Quarterly*. The student finds the full-text article, reads it, and cites it in her paper.

   B. A student conducts a literature review by searching articles in ERIC. In his search, he finds three secondary sources that give many interesting primary sources. He is unable to find these primary sources; however, he still cites them in his own paper.

7. State the "3Cs" of an effective literature review.

8. What is the advantage of reading through the title and abstract of an article before reading further?

9. Which of the following terms best describes inductive or deductive reasoning?
    A. Top-down
    B. Bottom-up

10. The following explanation describes the reasoning you used to develop a theory. Identify the portion of the excerpt that (a) describes the use of inductive reasoning and (b) describes the use of deductive reasoning.

    You notice that among your students, those who are the most outgoing always have the most friends. You conclude that being outgoing is necessary to get friends. Using this conclusion as your theory, you predict that more outgoing students are more likely to have a lot of friends.

11. Distinguish between a confirmational and a disconfirmational strategy.

12. Explain why using a confirmational strategy alone to test a theory or hypothesis is poor practice.

13. What is the concern regarding publication bias?

ACTIVITIES

1. Choose a research topic that interests you and conduct a literature review as described in this chapter. In your search, find at least three articles that are relevant to your topic, and do the following:
    A. Without restating the abstract, briefly describe the study in each article you chose. Indicate whether the article is a primary or a secondary source.
    B. What information in the title and abstract of each source made it obvious to you that the source was a good reference for your topic?
    C. Include the following reference information for each source: author or authors, publication year, title, journal name, volume number, and page numbers.

2. The following three hypotheses have been tested in the published literature. You can use the citations to search for the full articles using ERIC. Choose one hypothesis and answer the questions that follow.

    Hypothesis 1: Parent literacy practices contribute to the literacy interests of their children (Hume, Lonigan, & McQueen, 2012).

    Hypothesis 2: Ability to generate and understand a number line is a critical precursor to mathematical competence (Rouder & Geary, 2014).

    Hypothesis 3: Teachers' sense of perceived threat and perceived efficacy are positively associated with the likelihood of intervening in a bullying incident (Duong & Bradshaw, 2013).

A. Deduce one prediction that is generated from the hypothesis you chose. Devise a study to test this prediction using a confirmational strategy.

B. Deduce one outcome that is not anticipated by the hypothesis you chose. Devise a study to test this unanticipated outcome using a disconfirmational strategy.

3. Over the course of the next week, observe the behavior and events you encounter. From your observations, use inductive reasoning to develop a research hypothesis and describe the behaviors or events that led to your hypothesis.

⑤SAGE edge™

SAGE edge offers a robust online environment featuring an impressive array of free tools and resources for review, study, and further exploration, keeping both instructors and students on the cutting edge of teaching and learning.

Access practice quizzes, eFlashcards, video, and multimedia at **edge.sagepub.com/priviterarme**.

Identify a problem

- Determine an area of interest.
- Review the literature.
- Identify new ideas in your area of interest.
- Develop a research hypothesis.

Develop a research plan

- Define the variables being tested.
- Identify participants or subjects and determine how to sample them.
- Select a research strategy and design.
- Evaluate ethics and obtain institutional approval to conduct research.

Generate more new ideas

- Results support your hypothesis—refine or expand on your ideas.
- Results do not support your hypothesis—reformulate a new idea or start over.

After reading this chapter, you should be able to:

1 Define research ethics.

2 Trace the history leading to the Nuremberg Code and state the 10 directives listed in the code.

3 Trace the history leading to the Belmont Report and state the three ethical principles listed in the report.

4 Identify the ethical concerns for two landmark studies in psychology: Milgram's obedience experiments and the Stanford prison study.

5 Describe the role of the IRB in regulating ethical research with human participants.

6 Describe the standards in the AERA code of conduct relating to human participant research.

7 Describe the standards in the AERA Code of Ethics relating to scientific integrity.

Conduct the study

- Execute the research plan and measure or record the data.

Communicate the results

- Method of communication: oral, written, or in a poster.
- Style of communication: APA guidelines are provided to help prepare style and format.

Analyze and evaluate the data

- Analyze and evaluate the data as they relate to the research hypothesis.
- Summarize data and research results.

chapter
three

....

RESEARCH ETHICS

....

Ethics is often thought of as the distinction between right and wrong, such as the Golden Rule: "Do unto others as you would have them do unto you." Sometimes ethics can even be confused with common sense; however, issues of ethics are far more difficult to resolve than common sense. The reason is that many concerns of ethics are universally recognized, but the interpretation or application for resolving these issues can vary based on the perspective of an individual.

One's perspective is shaped in different ways often depending on one's values and life experiences. The perspective an individual takes can have a substantial impact on the actions of an individual to address ethical concerns. Consider academic dishonesty, for example. Being a dishonest student is an ethical concern; however, the debate to address this concern can differ in perspective. A student may assess the consequences of cheating in the classroom with pressures for academic scholarships and college enrollment status; a teacher may assess the consequences of cheating on class grading; a school administrator may assess the fairness of awarding high school diplomas to students who cheat. In each case, the issue of academic honesty is addressed but from divergent perspectives.

Researchers also have divergent perspectives regarding ethical conduct in behavioral research. The information we obtain using the scientific method is typically important. For example, studying academic dishonesty is important. However, how we obtain information about academic dishonesty is also of ethical concern. For example, would it be ethical to tell a student to cheat in order to observe cheating? Is it ethical to video record a classroom to check for possible cheating during a test without making students aware that they are being recorded? The evaluation of these types of ethical questions and many more in scientific research is introduced in this chapter.

edge.sagepub.com/
priviterarme

- Take the chapter quiz
- Review key terms with eFlashcards
- Explore multimedia links and SAGE articles

$SAGE edge™

3.1 Ethics in Educational Research

The term *ethics* describes appropriate human action in areas such as business, medicine, health, religion, and research. In addition, most schools have ethical guidelines about cheating, academic dishonesty, and showing respect to classmates. In educational research, the term has special meaning. The term research ethics is used to identify the actions that a researcher must take to conduct responsible and moral research. Engaging in responsible research requires a researcher to anticipate what might happen, react to what is happening, and reflect on what did happen. Researchers must be aware of how a study will affect others in any positive or negative way.

> Research ethics identifies the actions that researchers must take to conduct responsible and moral research.

> Research ethics provide guidelines for responsible and moral research throughout the research process.

The research process begins with an idea or hypothesis from which researchers devise a research plan. In the plan, the researcher must make ethical considerations such as to anticipate what type of sample is needed and how to treat those in the sample. The difficulty of anticipating what will happen in a study is the biggest ethical challenge that researchers face. After all, the best-case scenario is to avoid ethical problems altogether, and the best way to do that is to fully anticipate concerns before the study is actually conducted.

We begin this chapter with an overview of the history of ethics in research that can also be found by taking the free certification Protecting Human Research Participants course at http://phrp.nihtraining.com. This course is offered by the National Institutes of Health specifically for researchers who receive federal funding to cover the costs of their research. We suggest that all individuals who plan to conduct human participant research complete this course prior to conducting research.

LEARNING CHECK 1 ✓

1. Define research ethics. What is the biggest ethical challenge that researchers face?

Answer: 1. Research ethics identifies the actions researchers must take to conduct responsible and moral research. The biggest ethical challenge that researchers face is to anticipate what will happen in a study.

3.2 The Need for Ethics Committees in Research: A Historical Synopsis

Guidelines for conducting ethical research are relatively new, particularly in the educational sciences. Ethical considerations in education research originate from the actions of researchers in other fields such as medicine and psychology. Researchers in the past were seldom required to consider the effects of their research on participants, and abuses often caused much pain and suffering. In this section, we describe two past events in which research caused harm to human subjects. These two events were instrumental in establishing ethical guidelines for all research and shaped our modern views of how to treat research participants.

The Nuremberg Code

The ethical conflict in research arises from researchers' desires to achieve *outcomes* regardless of the *means* required to achieve those outcomes. That is, before there were ethics committees, a few researchers valued what they learned from their study more than what they had to do to gain that knowledge. Hence, they favored the outcomes of their research over the means needed to achieve those results. Examples of harmful research on unwilling participants in which researchers sought outcomes above all else include the Nazi medical experiments in concentration camps during World War II. These experiments were unprecedented in the scope and degree of harm to unwilling participants.

These experiments, which took place between 1939 and 1945, included exposing prisoners to harmful gases, infecting them with diseases such as tuberculosis, immersing them in icy waters, placing them in compression chambers deprived of oxygen, and even cutting them with slivers of glass. These experiments, which often resulted in death, were conducted to learn something: the outcomes. The compression chamber experiments, for example, were conducted to determine the altitudes at which aircraft crews could survive without oxygen. However, these experiments were conducted with no concern for how prisoners were treated (the means) to gain that knowledge.

From 1945 to 1947, the individuals and physicians responsible for conducting the Nazi medical experiments were tried in international courts. Because of the enormous amount of evidence, shown in a file photo in Figure 3.1, and the number of defendants involved, many trials were required to investigate all the claims of misconduct. The first trial was held before the International Military Tribunal, which tried the most important and high-ranking criminals. Subsequent trials held under the Control Council Law No. 10 at the U.S. Nuremberg Military Tribunals prosecuted lesser war criminals. Among these trials included the Doctors' Trial between December 1946 and July 1947. In August 1947, the verdict from this trial included a section called Permissible Medical Experiments, which has come to be known as the Nuremberg Code—the first international code of research ethics. Table 3.1 lists the 10 directives of the Nuremberg Code.

> The Nuremberg Code (published in 1947) is the first international code for ethical conduct in research consisting of 10 directives aimed at the protection of human participants.

The Tuskegee Syphilis Study

A second event of unethical research behavior was the Tuskegee Syphilis Study. This study, which began in 1932, was performed on 600 Black men, 399 who had syphilis and 201 who did not. The health of the men was compared between the two groups for many decades. Most of those in the study were illiterate sharecroppers from one of the poorest counties in Alabama. Researchers told the men that they would be treated at no cost for "bad blood," a local term used

Source: Photo archive, U.S. Holocaust Memorial Museum, courtesy of National Archives and Records Administration, College Park, MD. Reprinted with permission. The views or opinions expressed in this book, and the context in which the images are used, do not necessarily reflect the views or policy of, nor imply approval or endorsement by, the United States Holocaust Memorial Museum.

Table 3.1	The Nuremberg Code

Ten Directives	
1	The voluntary consent of the human subject is absolutely essential.
2	The experiment should be such as to yield fruitful results for the good of society, unprocurable by other methods or means of study, and not random and unnecessary in nature.
3	The experiment should be so designed and based on the results of animal experimentation and a knowledge of the natural history of the disease or other problem under study that the anticipated results will justify the performance of the experiment.
4	The experiment should be so conducted as to avoid all unnecessary physical and mental suffering and injury.
5	No experiment should be conducted where there is an a priori reason to believe that death or disabling injury will occur; except, perhaps, in those experiments where the experimental physicians also serve as subjects.
6	The degree of risk to be taken should never exceed that determined by the humanitarian importance of the problem to be solved by the experiment.
7	Proper preparations should be made and adequate facilities provided to protect the experimental subject against even remote possibilities of injury, disability, or death.
8	The experiment should be conducted only by scientifically qualified persons. The highest degree of skill and care should be required through all stages of the experiment of those who conduct or engage in the experiment.
9	During the course of the experiment the human subject should be at liberty to bring the experiment to an end if he has reached the physical or mental state where continuation of the experiment seems to him to be impossible.
10	During the course of the experiment the scientist in charge must be prepared to terminate the experiment at any stage, if he has probable cause to believe, in the exercise of the good faith, superior skill, and careful judgment required of him, that a continuation of the experiment is likely to result in injury, disability, or death to the experimental subject.

Source: Reprinted from *Trials of War Criminals Before the Nuremberg Military Tribunals Under Control Council Law No. 10*, Vol. 2, pp. 181–182. Washington, DC: Government Printing Office, 1949.

to describe ailments ranging from fatigue to syphilis. In truth, the men did not receive proper treatment, and the researchers conducting the study never intended to treat the men. Their true purpose was to determine the course of the disease through death, the outcome.

In the 1940s, penicillin became widely available as an effective treatment for syphilis; one such common advertisement used to promote the use of penicillin is shown in Figure 3.2. Yet, with little apparent concern for the health and well-being of participants in this study, the researchers denied the men access to penicillin, and the study continued for another quarter-century. It was not until 1968 that a researcher would voice concerns about the study, ultimately leading to the termination of the study in 1972. Over the 40 years that this study continued, it was supported at one time or another by such government agencies as the U.S. Public Health Service (USPHS), the Centers for Disease Control and Prevention (CDC), and local chapters of the American Medical Association (AMA) and the National Medical Association (NMA). Table 3.2 shows a synopsis for this study and lists the changes that were made once the details of the study came to light.

LEARNING CHECK 2 ✓

1. Why were researchers prosecuted in the Nuremberg trials?

2. The _____ is the first international code of research ethics.

3. In the 1940s penicillin became widely available to treat syphilis. How did researchers of the Tuskegee Syphilis Study respond to this?

Answers: 1. Nazi physicians were prosecuted for conducting harmful experiments on concentration camp prisoners between 1939 and 1945; 2. Nuremberg Code; 3. The researchers denied treating the participants who had syphilis with penicillin, and they continued the study for another quarter-century.

Figure 3.2 A Poster Encouraging Early Syphilis Treatment for U.S. Citizens During the 1940s

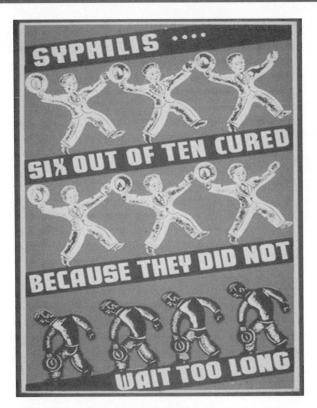

Source: Library of Congress; http://www.loc.gov/pictures/item/98514735. Public Domain.

Note: Although treatments were available, participants in the Tuskegee Syphilis Study were prevented from receiving treatment.

Table 3.2 Synopsis of the Tuskegee Syphilis Study

1932 Tuskegee Syphilis Study begins with a sample of 399 men with syphilis and 201 without. The men are told they are being treated for "bad blood," although none of the participants receive treatment.

1934 First papers are published suggesting health issues related to untreated syphilis.

1936 Local physicians insist that the men in the study not be treated. The decision is made to follow the men until death.

1940 Researchers hinder men from getting treatment ordered by the military draft effort.

1945 Penicillin accepted as an effective treatment for syphilis; USPHS researchers choose not to treat study participants with syphilis.

1947 USPHS establishes "Rapid Treatment Centers" to treat syphilis, although they continue to deny men in the study from being treated.

1968 Peter Buxtun, a venereal disease researcher with the USPHS, and others raise concerns about the ethics of the study.

1969 CDC reaffirms the need to continue the study and gains local support from the AMA and NMA chapters.

1972 The Associated Press publishes a newspaper report condemning the study, leading to public outrage; the Tuskegee Syphilis Study ends.

1973 Congress holds hearings, and a class-action lawsuit is filed by the National Association for the Advancement of Colored People on behalf of the study participants.

1974 A $10 million out-of-court settlement is reached, and the U.S. government promises to give lifetime medical benefits and burial services to all living participants; Congress establishes the National Commission for the Protection of Human Subjects of Biomedical and Behavioral Research to review the study and provide recommendations.

1979 The national commission drafts its recommendations in the Belmont Report.

1997 On May 16, President Bill Clinton formally apologizes on behalf of the nation.

Source: Adapted from McCallum, J. M., Arekere, D. M., Green, B. L., Katz, R. V., & Rivers, B. M. (2006). Awareness and knowledge of the U.S. Public Health Service syphilis study at Tuskegee: Implications for biomedical research. *Journal of Health Care for the Poor and Underserved, 17,* 716–733; and Centers for Disease Control and Prevention. (2011). *U.S. Public Health Service syphilis study at Tuskegee: The Tuskegee timeline.* Atlanta, GA: Author. Available at http://www.cdc.gov/tuskegee/timeline.htm.

The Belmont Report

Public outrage following the first published accounts of the Tuskegee Syphilis Study by the Associated Press in 1972 led Congress to establish a National Commission for the Protection of Human Subjects of Biomedical and Behavioral Research in 1974. This national commission was charged with identifying and developing ethical guidelines for all human participant research; in 1979, the commission drafted its recommendations in what is

The Belmont Report (published in 1979) is a published document that recommends three principles for the ethical conduct of research with human participants: respect for persons, beneficence, and justice.

Respect for persons is an ethical principle listed in the Belmont Report that states that participants in a research study must be autonomous agents capable of making informed decisions concerning whether to participate in research.

The Belmont Report provides three principles that all researchers must follow to engage in ethical research.

Beneficence is an ethical principle listed in the Belmont Report that states that it is the researcher's responsibility to minimize the potential risks and maximize the potential benefits associated with conducting a research study.

A type of analysis in which the researcher anticipates or weighs the risks and benefits in a study is called a risk-benefit analysis.

called the Belmont Report. The Belmont Report identifies three principles for the ethical conduct of research using human participants:

- Respect for persons
- Beneficence
- Justice

Respect for persons means that participants in a research study are treated as autonomous agents. That is, participants in a study must be capable of making informed decisions concerning whether to participate in a research study. A *capable* participant is one with the physical and mental capacity to participate. An *informed* participant is one with the ability to comprehend his or her potential role in a research study.

In addition to being capable and informed, all potential participants in research must be free of coercion or undue influence. To adhere to this recommendation, researchers must provide certain protections for special populations. For example, to protect children younger than 18 years, a parental waiver to participate in a research study is required; parents give consent for their underage children. This protection is especially important for protecting children who participate in sensitive areas of research such as those investigating possible pharmacological treatments for drug abuse (see Curry, Mermelstein, & Sporer, 2009) or children considered to be vulnerable such as those with a developmental disability.

Beneficence means that it is the researcher's responsibility to minimize the potential risks and maximize the potential benefits associated with a research study. Anticipating the risks and benefits in a study is also called a risk-benefit analysis. To apply a risk-benefit analysis, you must determine whether the benefits of a research study outweigh the risks. If not, then the study is potentially unethical.

The principle of beneficence can be subjective and difficult to assess. Researchers must anticipate potential risks, including the potential for physical and psychological harm, stress and health concerns, and loss of privacy or confidentiality. They must also anticipate potential benefits, including the potential for monetary gain, the acquisition of new skills or knowledge, and access to treatments for psychological or physical illnesses. To meet the challenges of anticipating potential risks and benefits in research, all research institutions appoint ethics committees that consist of many trained professionals from diverse educational backgrounds who provide additional review of the risks and benefits anticipated in a study before any research is conducted.

Justice refers to the fair and equitable treatment of all individuals and groups selected for participation in research studies in terms of the benefits they receive and the risks they bear from their participation in research. Justice is applied to ensure equality in the selection of potential participants in research. Educational researchers often select participants based on such criteria as age, gender, ethnicity, or educational need. The principle of justice ensures that any decision to include or exclude certain individuals or groups from participating in a research study is scientifically justified. For example, a study on the effects of response to intervention (RTI) on academic achievement can include only children who are at risk for or already underperforming in school. The scientifically justifiable reason to exclude children performing at grade level is that they are not in need of intensive educational intervention.

> **Justice** is an ethical principle listed in the Belmont Report that states that all participants should be treated fairly and equitably in terms of receiving the benefits and bearing the risks in research.

LEARNING CHECK 3 ✓

1. Name the study conducted from 1932 to 1972 that caused public outrage eventually leading to the Belmont Report.

2. State the principle of the Belmont Report that best describes each of the following:

   A. In a study on the effect of participating in school-sponsored sports on grades, researchers justify that nonschool athletes can be excluded from participating.

   B. Researchers decide not to conduct a study because the risks to participants outweigh the benefits.

   C. Researchers inform participants of the true purpose and intent of their study.

Answers: 1. The Tuskegee Syphilis Study; 2. A. justice; B. beneficence; C. respect for persons.

3.3 Ethics in Focus: Classic Examples From Psychology

There are classic examples of ethically problematic studies in psychology, many of which are landmark studies. Two such studies are described here: the Milgram obedience experiments and the Stanford prison study.

> Ethical concerns extend beyond medicine to examples in psychology and are as relevant today as they were in the past.

Milgram's Obedience Experiments

Beginning in the 1960s, Stanley Milgram conducted his obedience experiments that were staged to make the participant think that he or she was causing harm to another participant by administering electric shocks (Milgram,

1963). In his classic study conducted at Yale University, Stanley Milgram was the authority figure. He assigned one participant as a "teacher" and another person as the "learner," who, unbeknown to the participant, was paid to act as a participant. The general setup of the experiment is shown in Figure 3.4. The task of the learner (the actor) was to memorize word pairs. The task of the teacher was to state one word and wait for the learner to respond with the correct second word in the pair. For each incorrect response, the teacher was told by Milgram (the authority figure) to administer shocks to the learner in increments of 15 volts for each successive incorrect response. The experiment was set up to appear real to the participant. For example, the apparatus for administering shock was realistic and labeled with the different shock levels; the learner was prearranged to give incorrect answers and respond or act as if painful shocks were being administered. However, in truth, no shocks were ever administered. The results were astonishing: 100% of participants shocked the learner up to 300 volts, and 65% of participants shocked the learner to the maximum 450 volts—enough to kill a human being.

The key ethical concern of this study involved the significant stress placed on the participant. Although most participants followed the orders of the authority figure, most also complained and pleaded with the authority figure to stop the experiment very early on. For example, one participant complained, "He's [the learner] banging in there! I'd like to continue, but I can't do that to a man . . . I'll hurt his heart" (Milgram, 1963, p. 376). Clearly, participants experienced great stress in this experimental setting. To alleviate the stress caused

Figure 3.3 Milgram Obedience Experiment

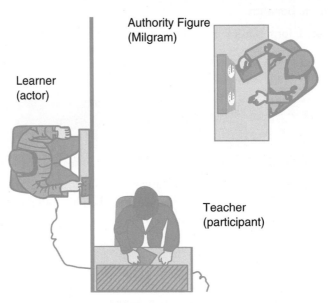

Authority Figure
(Milgram)

Learner
(actor)

Teacher
(participant)

Source: Milgram (1963). Reproduced with permission.

Note: The teacher (participant) administered "shocks" from another room to a learner (actor). The authority figure gave orders to the participant to continue as the experiment progressed.

by his manipulation, Milgram disclosed to participants the true intent of his experiment and that no shocks were ever administered, after the experiment was completed.

Stanford Prison Study

In the summer of 1971, Philip Zimbardo conducted the Stanford prison study (Haney & Zimbardo, 1977; Zimbardo, 1975). The aim of this study was to understand how social roles influence behavior. Participants were randomly assigned to be a prisoner or a guard. The prisoners were "arrested" and brought in by police, read their *Miranda* rights, and fingerprinted before being brought to the prison. The "prison" was constructed in the basement of the psychology building at Stanford University. The guards wore official uniforms and sunglasses and followed 8-hour shifts throughout the day. Once all "inmates" were in their cells, the study began, and the prison guards were left to run the prison. It did not take long for things to get out of hand. The guards became aggressive whenever a prisoner was disobedient in any way. At first, they took away prisoner privileges such as the opportunity to read or talk to other prisoners. It progressed later to taking away meals and bedding, tedious work such as cleaning toilets with bare hands, physical work such as doing push-ups while a guard stepped on the prisoner's back, and even "solitary confinement" in what was actually a utility closet. Keep in mind that these punishments were developed by the guards (not the researchers) during the study.

The prisoners faced increased psychological and physical harm as the guards' actions progressed. Some prisoners cried uncontrollably, became violent and rebellious, suffered from severe depression, and started referring to themselves by their "prison number," and one even developed a psychosomatic rash due to the stress. The ethical concern was for the welfare of the participants and the prisoners in particular. The study was planned to last 2 weeks. However, the punishments escalated in only a few days. Therefore, to resolve ethical concerns, the study was terminated after only 6 days because at that point, the risks to participant welfare far outweighed the benefits of continuing the study as planned.

Ethics in Educational Research

The goal of most educational research is to promote learning, prevent school failure, and understand the issues regarding the learning process. Education is a very socially sensitive topic and involves many key stakeholders such as students, parents, educational personnel, community members, and policy makers. There is often a delicate balance of quality research and the three principles for ethical conduct in research when the topic affects long-term quality of life and involves so many perspectives.

Let's go back and think about the three principles of ethical conduct—respect for persons, beneficence, and justice. What is the balance between quality research and the respect for persons when the participants are young children or children with a disability who may not have the capacity to understand their role in the research process? How about the element of being free from perceived coercion when the classroom teacher is conducting the research? What is the balance between quality research and beneficence when little is known about a potentially beneficial intervention? The risk could be in participating in an intervention that turns out to be not effective or the risk could be in not participating in an effective intervention. Justice involves the equity and fairness in the selection process. What is the balance between quality research and justice when there are more eligible students who could possibly benefit from an educational intervention than available resources in the study? The balance between quality research and the three principles of ethical conduct depend upon the perspective, whether they are the researcher, parent, teacher, or student. To help protect this balance between quality research and the three principles of ethical conduct, educational research is reviewed and approved by an institutional review board before it can begin.

CONNECTING TO THE CLASSROOM

One ethical dilemma that educators face when approached about conducting research about a new instructional strategy in the classroom is about the decision of who should receive the innovation and who will not. By conducting the literature review and identifying a potential solution to a problem, there is at least some notion that the new idea will be effective. The teacher or administrator will want all students to receive the new strategy. However, until we conduct the research study to determine if the strategy is effective and for whom, we really do not know if the strategy will be effective. Therefore, as you will learn as you read this text,

we must have some students who participate in the new strategy and others who do not participate. This is necessary so that we can compare the two strategies to decide if the new strategy is more effective. There are a lot of fads in education. You can probably think of a few that have come and gone already and some that may still be lingering (like learning styles). It is important to examine these new ideas before we implement them in schools. So, when thinking about the decision where some students may not get the new idea, remember that it can be more ethical to investigate it first before committing it to everyone.

An **institutional review board (IRB)** is a review board with at least five members, one of whom comes from outside the institution. These members review for approval research protocols submitted by researchers prior to the conduct of any human participant research. Every institution that receives federal funding must have an IRB.

A **research protocol** is a proposal, submitted by a researcher to an IRB, outlining the details of a study he or she wishes to complete and how he or she will address potential ethical concerns. Only upon approval by an IRB is a researcher allowed to conduct his or her study, and all researchers are bound to follow the protocol once it is approved.

3.4 Human Participant Research: IRBs and the AERA Code of Conduct

The ethical principles outlined in the Belmont Report are included in the Code of Federal Regulations issued by the U.S. Department of Health and Human Services (2007). Under these regulations, every institution receiving federal funding must have an **institutional review board (IRB)** for human participant research. IRBs have at least five members, one of whom comes from outside the institution. A primary function of the IRB is to review **research protocols** submitted by researchers at that institution. In a research protocol, the researchers provide details of a human participant study they wish to perform and describe how they will respond to any potential ethical conflicts. An IRB then categorizes the research as involving no risk, minimal risk, or greater-than-minimal risk and will make the final determination pertaining to the level of risk potentially involved in the research study. Only upon the IRB's approval are researchers permitted to conduct their research study.

The American Educational Research Association (AERA), the largest association of educational researchers worldwide, has adopted a method of assessing risk in its publication of the *Code of Ethics* (AERA, 2011). This code extends the ethical principles outlined in the Belmont Report to include five overarching principles (professional competence; integrity; professional, scientific, and scholarly responsibility; respect for people's rights, dignity, and diversity; and social responsibility) and 22 ethical standards.

First adopted in 1992 (AERA, 2011), this code identifies expected standards of ethical conduct in educational research and publication. The remainder of this chapter will discuss the important features of the 22 ethical standards, as they apply to ethical conduct in educational research.

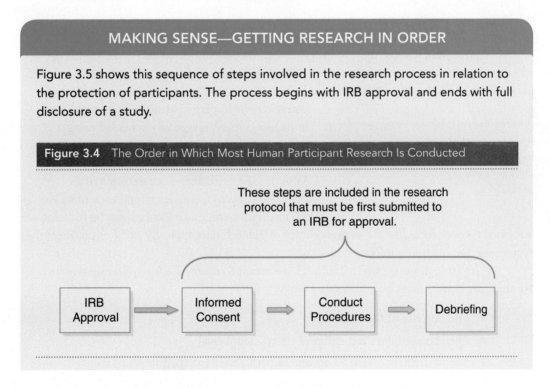

MAKING SENSE—GETTING RESEARCH IN ORDER

Figure 3.5 shows this sequence of steps involved in the research process in relation to the protection of participants. The process begins with IRB approval and ends with full disclosure of a study.

Figure 3.4   The Order in Which Most Human Participant Research Is Conducted

These steps are included in the research protocol that must be first submitted to an IRB for approval.

IRB Approval → Informed Consent → Conduct Procedures → Debriefing

Institutional Approval

Educational researchers are required to conform to the IRB requirements set forth by the educational agency such as those by public school systems and universities with whom they want to conduct research. An IRB application provides complete and accurate information regarding the purpose and process of the research being proposed. IRB approval is specifically required for research that involves the following:

- Waivers of informed consent
- Deception
- Audio, video, or photography

Once approved, the research protocol acts as a legal document to which the researcher(s) and the institution(s) must comply. Approval by an IRB ensures that any research that is conducted has been fully reviewed for ethical conduct beforehand.

1. What is an IRB, and what is the role of an IRB in human participant research?

Answer: An IRB is a review board with at least five members who review research protocols, which are used to categorize research as involving no risk, minimal risk, or greater-than-minimal risk. The IRB makes the final determination pertaining to the level of risk potentially involved in the research study.

Informed Consent to Research

In research, it is the right of every person to make informed decisions regarding whether to participate in a research study, as required in the Belmont principle of respect for persons. The AERA applies this principle by requiring that all participants give **informed consent** *prior* to participating in a research study. Informed consent is typically provided using a written informed consent form that is signed by participants and/or parents before a study begins. Table 3.3 shows an annotated example of an informed consent form, describing each of its key sections. Although more sections can be added to an informed consent form, the 10 sections shown in Table 3.3 are typically sufficient to meet the requirement of obtaining informed consent.

Informed consent is a signed or verbal agreement in which participants state they are willing to participate in a research study after being informed of all aspects of their role in the study.

The 10 sections shown in Table 3.3 are meant to meet AERA requirements, which are that participants must be informed of the following:

- The purpose of the research
- The expected duration and procedures being used
- The participant's right to decline or withdraw participation at any time
- Foreseeable consequences for declining or withdrawing
- Potential risks of participation
- Potential benefits of participation
- Limits of confidentiality
- Incentives of participation
- Information for whom to contact with regard to any questions a participant may have regarding the research and research participants' rights

A copy of the informed consent form must be submitted to an IRB as part of a research protocol. The AERA code of conduct also provides special provisions for persons who are legally incapable of giving informed consent, including minors. For example, researchers must attain **assent** when children are participants in research. In other words, for minors to participate in research, they must agree to participate only after receiving an appropriate explanation in reasonably understandable language. Obtaining consent from a child's parent or other legal guardian is also necessary.

> **Assent** is the consent of a minor or other legally incapable person to agree to participate in research only after receiving an appropriate explanation in reasonably understandable language.

The purpose of obtaining informed consent is to demonstrate the Belmont principle of respect for persons by providing all pertinent information in an informed consent form. Some additional guidelines for preparing and writing an informed consent form are as follows:

- Avoid exculpatory language. That is, participants should not be asked to waive or appear to waive any legal rights or to release the institution or its agents from liability for negligence.

- Use numeric values (such as <1%) to describe the probability of "rare" risks when possible. The more severe the potential risks, the less likely participants think they will occur, even when the same word is used to describe their probability (Fischer & Jungermann, 1996; Mazur & Merz, 1994; Rector, 2008).

- For participants requiring or requesting a translator, one must be provided to them, and the translator in addition to the participant should sign the form.

- Avoid technical jargon. Write in simple language at less than a high school level throughout the form.

- Write as if you are speaking to the participant. Use the second person using the pronoun *you* throughout the form.

- Use black, nonitalicized, 11-point font (or larger if appropriate) throughout the form.

An important, yet often overlooked, concern is what participants actually recall about a research study—particularly with regard to communicating risks (Lipkus, 2007; Parascandola, Hawkins, & Danis, 2002; Sieber, 2007). Evidence appears to indicate that participants actually recall very little (Flory & Emanuel, 2004). In one study intended to determine how researchers could improve participants' recall, the researchers paid participants $5 for each item correctly recalled in an informed consent form. As the data shown in Figure 3.6 indicate, this financial incentive increased recall of the items in the form (Festinger et al., 2009). Also, the finding that participants in this study recalled less than 20% of risks and benefits listed in an informed consent is somewhat concerning, particularly for research with the potential of severe risks to participants.

When possible, after parent consent is obtained, researchers should also obtain agreement from child participants, called an assent. Assents contain the basic information of the study and are written at a level that the child can understand. Assents should be read to young children and any other student who may have difficulty reading. It is possible to obtain agreement from young children or children with a disability using graphics such as a smiley/frown face or thumbs up/thumbs down images.

Table 3.3 Informed Consent Form

Introduction: State the purpose of requesting informed consent using this form.

> *Example for introduction:*
>
> The purpose of this form is to provide you with information to help you decide whether or not to allow your child to participate in this research.

Invitation/identification: Invite potential participants and identify the researchers who are involved in this study by name.

> *Example invitation line:*
>
> [Insert name of each researcher involved] at [insert university/institution name] invites you to participate in a research study.

Purpose: In two or three sentences, state what area of research you are investigating and why you are studying this area.

> *Example for a hypothetical educational intervention study:*
>
> The purpose of this study is to evaluate the effectiveness of this new iPad app to teach phonics. Your participation in this study can help us better understand if the iPad can teach phonics to struggling readers.

Description of research study: Describe exactly what you will do and what you require of participants in terms of their time and effort. In this section, you should also identify the approximate number of participants involved in the study.

> *Example for a parent consent form for a hypothetical educational intervention study:*
>
> If you decide to allow your child to participate, your child will join a study examining the effectiveness of the Early Reading Skills Builder (ERSB) curriculum to teach phonics involving at least 100 students. Your child will receive daily phonics instruction using the ERSB curriculum for 30 minutes as part of their typical reading instruction from their teacher. The study will begin September 1, 2018, and end December 15, 2018. The ERSB is an app that uses iPad technology to teach phonics skills with text-to-speech software. The ERSB is expected to improve your child's reading skills. We will also need to collect data on your child's reading skills. Once a week, we will ask your child to read a short passage for 5 minutes and record his or her reading errors.

Risks and benefits: This part of the consent form can be split into two sections, but all potential risks and benefits associated with participation in the research must be clearly stated.

Confidentiality: A statement should be made with regard to protecting each participant's privacy and confidentiality. This description should explicitly state how you will protect the participant's identity and for how long.

Example confidentiality paragraph:

All information obtained in this study is strictly confidential unless required by law. The results of this research may be used in reports, presentations, and publications, but the researchers will not identify your child. In order to protect your child's privacy and identity, all records of his or her participation will be given a unique number that does not allow anyone (including the project staff) to personally identify him or her. These records will be kept in a locked cabinet in a locked room where they will remain for at least 3 years following the completion of this research study or until the records can be safely destroyed.

Compensation: To recruit participants, it is often necessary to compensate them. The most common types of compensation are financial reimbursement and credit toward a college course. If the study does not involve compensation, then state it here.

Questions/contact information: The researcher must offer to answer any questions about the research and the participants' rights. When appropriate, it is advisable to include whom to contact in the event of a research-related injury or question. In all cases, the telephone number or address of a researcher must be provided. Some IRBs may also require you to include a contact number of the IRB.

Example questions/contact information paragraph:

If you have questions following your participation, they can be answered by [*insert name and contact information*]. If you have questions about your rights as a participant in this research, or if you feel you have been placed at risk, please contact [*insert name and contact information*].

Disclaimer: Explicitly state that participation is voluntary and that participants can quit or withdraw from the study at any time without penalty. When appropriate, also inform participants that they can refuse any portions of the study without withdrawing from the entire study.

Signature lines: A participant or parent must sign the informed consent form to be recognized as an individual voluntarily consenting to participate in a research study. For this reason, it is necessary to have each participant sign the form. The researcher should also sign the form. A statement similar to this should precede the signature and date lines.

Example signature line paragraph:

Parent statement: This form explains the nature, demands, benefits, and any risks associated with this research. I have read the informed consent form. I have had the chance to ask questions about this study, and those questions have been answered to my satisfaction. I am at least 18 years of age, and I agree for my child to participate in this research project. I understand that I will receive a copy of this form after it has been signed by me and the principal investigator of this research study.

_____	_____	_____
Parent signature	Printed name	Date
_____	_____	_____
Investigator signature	Printed name	Date

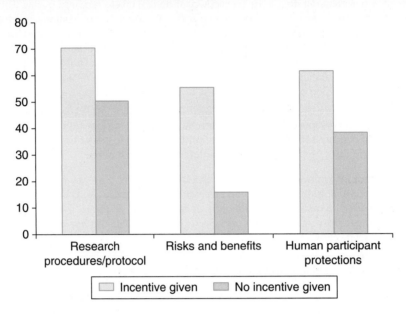

Source: Adapted from Festinger et al. (2009).

Note: Notice that participants who received an incentive of $5 for each item correctly recalled significantly increased their recall in each section of the form. Data are adapted from Festinger et al. (2009).

Informed Consent for Recording Voices and Images in Research

Informed consent appeals to the Belmont principle of respect for persons.

Some research uses video or voice recorders. Recording devices such as these are particularly useful in interviews and to observe instruction in classrooms. Before making recordings, however, researchers must obtain informed consent, with two exceptions. Researchers do not need to obtain informed consent when either of the following occurs:

- The research is conducted strictly in naturalistic settings and poses no anticipated risk of personal identification or harm.

- The research requires *deception*, and consent is obtained after the recordings have been made (the use of deception in research is described later in this section).

Client/Patient, Student, and Subordinate Research Participants

Researchers must also protect potential participants from adverse consequences associated with declining or withdrawing participation in a research study. For example, as an incentive for teachers to participate, researchers often offer a monetary stipend or gift such as books or classroom supplies. The informed consent must disclose the incentive and how the the incentive will be distributed if they withdraw from the study before it ends. All potential participants have the right to decline or withdraw participation at any time without undue influence or coercion.

Dispensing With Informed Consent for Research

To minimize bias and ensure the integrity of the data collected in a research study, it is sometimes permissible to initially exclude information in an informed consent form or dispense with or waive the need for an informed consent. An informed consent can sometimes "give away" what the study is about, which could bias participant responses during a study. To overcome this or a related concern, a researcher may wish to withhold specific information that is critical to a research hypothesis or seek a consent waiver. However, for an IRB to approve this action (i.e., not being fully forthcoming or waiving informed consent), the researcher must show that the potential of distress or harm to participants in a proposed study is minimal to none and that it is permitted by law and federal or institutional regulations.

Offering Inducements for Research Participation

Sometimes research participants will receive incentives to participate. Incentives can include monetary compensation, gift cards, or entry into a prize drawing. Whatever the incentive, researchers must ensure that it is not excessive or inappropriate. The idea here is that if a researcher made the incentive large enough, participants may participate in a study because the "payoff is too good to pass up," even when their actual intention would be to decline participation. Excessive incentives are viewed as a type of coercion or undue influence on the part of the researcher in order to gain participation. Therefore, excessive incentives should never be offered for participation in a study.

> While informed consent can be waived or information in an informed consent can be withheld or deceiving, such actions must never put a participant at greater-than-minimal risk and must be approved by an IRB.

Deception in Research

Deception in research occurs when participants are deliberately misled about the purpose or nature of a research study. Deception can be active (deliberately untruthful; e.g., telling a lie, often by using a cover story) or passive (omission of key information about a study; e.g., not telling participants what the true nature of the study is about). According to the AERA Code of Ethics, to use deception, the researcher must show the following:

> Deception is a strategy used by researchers in which participants are deliberately misled concerning the true purpose and nature of the research being conducted. Deception can be active (deliberately untruthful) or passive (omission of key information).
>
> A cover story is a false explanation or story intended to prevent research participants from discovering the true purpose of a research study.

- The deception is necessary, and the use of nondeceptive alternatives is not feasible.

- There is no more than minimal risk to the participants.

- The deception would not affect the participants' willingness to participate such as physical risks, discomfort, or unpleasant emotional experiences to participants as a result of the deception.

- Participants are informed of the deception as early as possible, meaning at the end of the study but no later than at the end of the data collection.

The use of deception is sometimes unavoidable. For example, in research investigating the effects of medication, when participants expect a drug treatment to cause some change, such as to relieve stress, they often report experiencing that change even if the drug treatment they received was actually fake. This response to the fake drug is called a *placebo effect*. To avoid a placebo effect, researchers use deception and do not let participants know whether they will actually receive a treatment (Kaptchuk, 1998; Miller, Wendler, & Swartzman, 2005). Deception may be used in educational research in sensitive areas such as academic dishonesty when full disclosure of what the study is about might lead to changes in participant behavior. For example, in a study by Evans and Lee (2011), children aged 8 to 10 years were placed in a room and asked to take a trivia quiz where the answer key was available to them but told not to look. When researchers left the room, they observed to see if the students looked at the answers and then later asked the children whether they had peeked at the answer key. The children were not told that their behavior in the room alone had been observed to see whether they would lie or tell the truth. The answer to one of the trivia quiz questions was also rigged such that the answer could only be answered correctly if they had peeked at the answer key. Determining if the use of deception is justified can still be subjective, which is why researchers must include any use of deception in their research protocol for an IRB to review.

Debriefing

Debriefing is required when deception is used in a research study. At the conclusion of a study, all participants and/or parents receive a **debriefing** in which the researcher discloses the true purpose of the study. A debriefing form can be read aloud to participants by the researcher. When no deception is used, participants can often be given a printed debriefing form to read on their own. Another option for debriefing in education research conducted across schools is to hold an information session for parents at the end of the study. The debriefing is included at the end of a study to meet the Belmont principle of respect for persons by being upfront with participants regarding their role in a research study. As part of a debriefing, the researcher should do the following:

- Take appropriate steps to answer participant questions and address any misconceptions or concerns the participants may have.

- Take reasonable steps to reduce risk or harm to participants if the researcher can justify delaying or withholding information in a debriefing.

> A **debriefing** is the full disclosure to participants of the true purpose of a study and is typically given at the end of a study.

- Take reasonable steps to protect participants if or when the researcher becomes aware that research procedures have harmed a participant.

The debriefing is especially important for studies that use deception because the debriefing informs the participant of the deception used. Consider, for example, the study conducted by Evans and Lee (2011) that used deception to study academic honesty. Both the participants and parents were debriefed after the research session where they also discussed issues of truth and lie telling.

> Whether or not deception is used, participants have a right to know the true purpose of a study prior to the conclusion of a study.

Suppose that the researchers let the children leave without disclosing what the study was about. This is an unethical situation that researchers want to avoid; the debriefing is a researcher's opportunity to "come clean," so to speak, when deception is used in a study. Interestingly, participants are rarely offended by being misled and instead often feel it is justified (Christensen, 1988; Resnick & Schwartz, 1973).

3.5 Ethics in Focus: Anonymity and Confidentiality

In the AERA (2011) *Code of Ethics*, researchers are required to protect the privacy of research participants. Consequently, researchers take steps to protect the anonymity and confidentiality of participants. **Anonymity** is the stricter standard in which the identity of a participant remains unknown to all people throughout a study. Hence, not even those involved in the study, including the researchers, can identify participants. This standard is often hard to meet, though, particularly for research that requires observing participants at multiple times, thereby requiring researchers to keep track of participants.

When anonymity is not possible, researchers instead take steps to protect the **confidentiality** of participants by ensuring that the identity of a participant is not made available to anyone who is not directly involved in a study. The researchers are able to identify participant information, and they promise not to share that information with anyone. Confidentiality allows researchers to track participants using personal identifiers and also protect participant information from being seen by anyone else, such as parents, friends, and other participants. Unfortunately, the terms *anonymity* and *confidentiality* are often used interchangeably, especially in ordinary speech. Be sure you are aware of the distinction between these terms when conducting research studies.

> **Anonymity** is a protection of individual identity in which the identity of a participant remains unknown throughout a study, even to those involved in a study.
>
> **Confidentiality** is a protection of individual identity in which the identity of a participant is not made available to anyone who is not directly involved in a study. Those involved in a study, however, are able to identify participant information.

1. State the principle in the Belmont Report that best describes the need for an informed consent and debriefing in human participant research.

2. A researcher informs participants of their rights as research participants prior to asking them to participate in a research study. By doing so, what AERA ethical standard does the researcher meet?

3. A researcher studying teacher judgments of student competency in a series of vignettes does not tell the teachers that the study is about how they rate the competency of similar students who differ only in ethnicity. What must the researcher do at the conclusion of the study?

4. Which protection of participant identity, anonymity or confidentiality, ensures that not even the researchers can identify participants?

Answers: 1. Respect for persons; 2. Informed consent to research; 3. They must give a debriefing in which they disclose the true intent or purpose of the study; 4. Anonymity.

3.6 Additional Ethical Considerations: Scientific Integrity

The remaining AERA (2011) *Code of Ethics* provides ethical guidelines for scientific integrity, which reflects the personal and professional conduct of the researcher. These additional considerations are discussed in this section.

> In ethics, scientific integrity is the extent to which a researcher is honest and truthful in his or her actions, values, methods, measures, and dissemination of research.
>
> In research, fabrication is to concoct methods or data that misrepresent aspects of a research study with the intent to deceive others.

Reporting Research Results

Researchers are expected to truthfully report data and never fabricate research results by making up data that were never observed or measured. If or when researchers make a mistake regarding the data they report, they must correct the mistake as soon as the mistake is discovered. While there aren't any recent examples of known fabrication of data in the education sciences, there are other recent examples in other fields of study. Recent examples of fabrication include a graduate student who, by her own admission, fabricated a series of articles in the field of personality and social psychology; a clinical researcher in the area of cancer prevention and treatment who fabricated patient data; and a researcher from an elite Ivy League medical school who fabricated up to 50% of reported data on sleep apnea in severely obese patients (Office of Research Integrity, 2011b). However infrequent, examples such as these occur each year.

Plagiarism

Researchers are expected to represent their own ideas in published work and, when they use ideas from other people, to appropriately give credit to others. If a researcher represents someone else's ideas as his or her own, then the researcher is guilty of **plagiarism.** Masters (2013) searched records of the National Science Foundation for cases of research plagiarism between 2007 and 2011. Her search located 61 cases of plagiarism. Plagiarism accounted for 88.4% of all cases of research misconduct. Keep in mind that you should feel free to use the work of others, so long as you acknowledge the source of those ideas. To avoid plagiarism, do not represent it as your own work. Indeed, you will read about the work of others throughout this book, but the sources and credits are given.

> **Plagiarism** is an individual's use of someone else's ideas or work that is represented as the individual's own ideas or work.

Publication Credit

When publishing or professionally presenting research data, all individuals who "have made a substantive contribution to an intellectual product" (AERA, 2011) to the work should be recognized as an author. Authors should be listed in order of their relative contribution to the work, with the first author listed being recognized as the individual having made the largest contribution. It is recommended that all potential authors discuss authorship prior to conducting a study to avoid possible concerns later.

> Researchers have an ethical responsibility to accurately and truthfully disclose the ideas and outcomes of a study.

Duplicate Publication of Data

The same work should never be published twice without recognition of what is being republished and why. It is unethical to duplicate or republish previously published data as original data unless it is "published with a citation to the first publication and undertaken consistent with any applicable laws and agreements" (AERA, 2011). Long, Errami, George, Sun, and Garner (2009) identified 212 pairs of duplicate articles in a review of those available on the search engine MEDLINE. Among the pairs of duplicate articles, on average the overlap between the original and the duplicate copy was 86.2% in the text and 73.1% among references cited. Also reported was that 71.4% of the duplicate pairs had a similar or identical table or figure. Avoiding **duplication** like this is an ethical concern.

Sharing Research Data for Verification

> **Duplication** is the republication of original data that were previously published.

Researchers are expected to share their data upon request from others for the purposes of verification or other analyses, which is one reason that researchers are expected to maintain their research data for years. One common way researchers share data today is by placing nonidentifiable data onto public archives such as the Odum Institute Dataverse Network (Howard W. Odom Institute for Research in Social Science, 2011). Researchers

Replication is the reproduction of research procedures under identical conditions for the purposes of observing the same phenomenon.

Peer review is a procedure used by editors of scientific journals in which a manuscript or work is sent to peers or experts in that area to review the work and determine its scientific value or worth regarding publication.

Researchers have a responsibility to protect data and confidentiality during and after the time in which a study is conducted.

can opt to make the data available upon permission or open to anyone without permission. At a minimum, the data upon which researchers base their conclusions should be made available to other scientists upon request in the following situations:

- The data do not compromise the confidentiality of participants.

- Sharing the data is expected if it does not violate any proprietary agreements already made.

Reviewers

To publish a scientific work, researchers can submit their work for publication in a scientific journal where their peers review their work. Once a **peer review** is complete, then an article can be rejected or accepted for publication in a scientific journal. As part of this process, peer reviewers can sometimes have access to information that should be protected. For this reason, the AERA (2011) *Code of Ethics* requires peer reviewers to respect the confidentiality and propriety rights of those who submit their work for review. Reviewers must also disclose any conflicts of interest when requested to review the work of others.

LEARNING CHECK 6 ✓

1. A researcher uses ideas described in another work and submits them as if they were his own ideas or work. What has the researcher done?

2. A researcher conducts a study and loses the data. She decides to make up the data instead and defends them as original data. What has the researcher done?

3. True or false: A peer reviewer is responsible for maintaining the confidentiality of those who submit their work for review.

Answers: 1. He plagiarized; 2. She fabricated data; 3. True.

CHAPTER SUMMARY

LO 1 Define research ethics.

- **Research ethics** identifies the actions that researchers must take to conduct responsible and moral research. In science, researchers must *anticipate* ethical considerations in a research plan, *react* to ethical concerns during a study, and *reflect* on what did happen in their study after the plan is executed.

LO 2 Trace the history leading to the Nuremberg Code and state the 10 directives listed in the code.

- The individuals and physicians responsible for the conduct of harmful experiments on concentration camp prisoners were put on trial between 1945 and 1947. Many trials were held during this time. The Doctors' Trial was prosecuted between December 1946 and July 1947. In August 1947, the verdict from this trial included a section that has come to be known as the Nuremberg Code, the first international code of research ethics.

LO 3 Trace the history leading to the Belmont Report and state the three ethical principles listed in the report.

- In 1932, the Tuskegee Syphilis Study began in which 600 Black men—399 with syphilis and 201 who did not have the disease—were studied to determine the course of the disease through death. The true purpose of the study was not revealed to the men. In the 1940s, penicillin became widely available as an effective treatment for syphilis; however, participants in the study were denied treatment, and the study continued for another quarter-century. In response to public outrage, the study ended in 1972; in 1974, Congress established the national commission that drafted the Belmont Report in 1979, which states three ethical principles: respect for persons, beneficence, and justice.

- **Respect for persons:** Participants in a research study must be autonomous agents capable of making informed decisions concerning whether to participate in research.

- **Beneficence:** It is the researcher's responsibility to minimize the potential risks and maximize the potential benefits associated with conducting a research study.

- **Justice:** All participants should be treated fairly and equitably in terms of receiving the benefits and bearing the risks in a research study.

LO 4 Identify the ethical concerns for two landmark studies in psychology: Milgram's obedience experiments and the Stanford prison study.

- Stanley Milgram at Yale University studied obedience using a manipulation in which participants thought they were administering significant levels of shock to another participant. One participant was told by Milgram (the authority figure) to administer shocks in increments of 15 volts to another participant (the confederate) for each incorrect response to a series of word pairs. The experiment was set up to appear real to the participant. However, in truth, no shocks were ever administered. The key ethical concern of this study involved the significant stress placed on the participant. To alleviate the stress caused by his manipulation, Milgram disclosed to participants that no shocks were ever administered, after the experiment was completed.

- Philip Zimbardo conducted the Stanford prison study in 1971. The aim of this study was to understand how social roles influence behavior. Participants were randomly assigned to be a prisoner or a guard. However, the guards began to use excessive force once the study began; the guards became aggressive whenever a prisoner was disobedient in any way, and the prisoners began to show signs of significant stress. The prisoners faced increased psychological and physical harm as the guards' actions progressed. The main ethical concern was for the welfare of the participants, and the prisoners in particular. Because the potential for serious harm to participants escalated in only a few days, the study was terminated after only 6 days.

LO 5 Describe the role of the IRB in regulating ethical research with human participants.

- An **institutional review board (IRB)** is a review board with at least five members, one of whom comes from outside the institution. These members review for approval research protocols submitted by researchers prior to the conduct of any research. Every institution that receives federal funding must have an IRB.

LO 6 Describe the standards in the AERA code of conduct relating to human participant research.

- All research requiring institutional approval is bound by the information in a research protocol, and the research can only be conducted after receiving approval.

- **Informed consent** is obtained prior to the conduct of research, and it must provide full information regarding all aspects of a research study.

- In most cases, informed consent must be obtained prior to the recording of voices or images obtained during research.

- Client/patient, student, and subordinate research participants must be protected from adverse consequences associated with declining or withdrawing from participation.

- In some situations, it is permissible to initially exclude information from an informed consent form so long as the potential harm to participants is minimal.

- Researchers should avoid offering excessive or inappropriate incentives that are likely to coerce participants.

- The use of **deception** is allowable in research in certain circumstances outlined by the AERA *Code of Ethics* aimed to protect human participants from harm.

- Researchers must disclose to participants the true purpose or intent of a study in a **debriefing**.

LO 7 Describe the standards in the AERA *Code of Ethics* relating to scientific integrity.

- Researchers must not **fabricate** research data and methods.

- Researchers must not **plagiarize.**

- All individuals making substantial contributions to a work must be recognized as authors.

- Researchers must not **duplicate** work published by them or another author.

- Researchers must store and maintain their data for the purposes of replication.

- Peer reviewers must respect the confidentiality and propriety rights of those who submit their work for peer review.

KEY TERMS

anonymity 83	duplication 85	plagiarism 85
assent 77	fabrication 84	replication 86
Belmont Report 70	informed consent 76	research ethics 64
beneficence 70	institutional review board (IRB) 74	research protocol 74
confidentiality 83	justice 71	respect for persons 70
cover story 81	Nuremberg Code 65	risk-benefit analysis 70
debriefing 83	peer review 86	scientific integrity 84
deception 81		

REVIEW QUESTIONS

1. Define research ethics and explain how researchers must anticipate, react, and reflect to conduct ethical research.

2. The conflict between ethics and research stems from the focus on *outcomes* versus *means*. Explain what this means.

3. Among the many trials held for harmful experiments on concentration camp prisoners was the Doctors' Trial, which led to what code? What is significant about this code?

4. In the 1940s, penicillin became widely available as an effective treatment for syphilis. Did the researchers in the Tuskegee Syphilis Study end the study and provide penicillin to the men with syphilis at this time?

5. Based on the timeline in Table 3.2, place the following events (A–E) in order of when they occurred.
    A. The Tuskegee Syphilis Study begins with a sample of 399 men with syphilis and 201 without.
    B. The Associated Press publishes a newspaper report condemning the study, leading to public outrage.
    C. The national commission drafts its recommendations in the Belmont Report.

D. Researchers hinder men from getting treatment ordered by the military draft effort.

E. President Bill Clinton formally apologizes on behalf of the nation.

6. State the principle of the Belmont Report that best describes each of the following:

   A. A researcher requests permission from teachers to record their instruction.

   B. Researchers studying the influence of play behavior in early development justify that only preschool-aged children can be included in the study.

   C. A study investigating the effects of a treatment to reduce bullying is approved by an IRB after the board determines that the benefits in the study outweigh the risks involved.

7. The AERA *Code of Ethics* requires that all research be approved prior to the conduct of the research.

   A. What is the name of the committee that is charged with reviewing research that uses human participants?

   B. What is the name of the document that researchers must submit to the review board committee?

8. State the five ethical principles incorporated in the AERA *Code of Ethics*.

9. Referring to Table 3.3, state 10 sections that should be included in an informed consent form.

10. Are researchers ever permitted to exclude information from an informed consent? Explain.

11. A researcher studying academic dishonesty uses a cover story in an informed consent form that tells participants that they are being asked to participate in a study concerning school pride.

    A. Is this type of deception allowed?

    B. What must researchers do at the end of the research study to disclose their deception?

12. State whether each of the following is an example of fabrication or plagiarism.

    A. A researcher submits a manuscript to a research journal that includes two figures summarizing data that were not actually recorded.

    B. A student uses the ideas from a book review to write a paper on the role of play in child development. She does not cite the book in her paper.

    C. A student notices a cool graphic that he decides to include in his research paper without giving credit to the original author of the graphic.

    D. A researcher notices that there are data missing, so she fills in the missing data with (made-up) scores that help show that her hypothesis is correct.

1. For each of the following research situations, state whether it is an ethical study. If you consider the study unethical, state how the hypothesis could potentially be studied in an ethical manner.

    A. Researchers hypothesize that a moderate level of music leads to greater mathematical test scores. To test this idea, they play music with low, moderate, or high volume during math instruction. They measure the number of items on a math test answered correctly, debrief the students, and dismiss them from the study.

    B. A psychologist hypothesizes that parental involvement in Head Start program activities improves end-of-year child academic achievement. To test this idea, she records the attendance of parents at the Head Start functions. This study was conducted in the natural setting of the Head Start functions.

    C. A researcher hypothesizes that corporal punishment, inconsistent discipline, and negative talk are related to attention-deficit/hyperactivity disorder symptoms. To test this idea, he contrives parent and child conflict-producing and non-conflict-producing activities in a lab setting then observes and records the parent and child behaviors.

    D. Researchers studying psychosexual development hypothesize that exposure to sexual content in television commercials will lead to lower self-image among teenage girls. To test this idea, they recruit teenage girls with positive self-image to participate. Half the girls are shown commercials with sexual content; the other half are shown commercials with neutral content. After the participants view the commercials, the researchers measure self-image in both groups, debrief the girls, and dismiss them from the study.

2. Suppose you are interested in testing the following hypothesis using the following research design:

    Hypothesis: Teachers will rate the same disruptive behavior of male students more severely than female students.

    Research design: You select a sample of 30 teachers. Each teacher reads six vignettes describing a mildly inappropriate behavior (chewing gum), moderately inappropriate behavior (swearing at a teacher), and highly inappropriate behavior (hitting a classmate) each with a male and female perpetrator. Teachers rate the severity of the disruptive behavior on a scale from 1 to 10.

    A. For this study, do you think a cover story is needed? Explain your answer and state a cover story you would use to distract from the true intent or purpose of the study.

    B. What precautions would you take to ensure minimal harm or psychological distress to participants? Include a justification of the use of deception.

    C. What information would you include in the debriefing? Explain each part of your answer.

3. Within the U.S. Department of Health and Human Services, the Office of Research Integrity is responsible for promoting integrity and monitoring research misconduct primarily in the behavioral and biomedical sciences. On the Office of Research Integrity website, there is a list of recent case summaries for research misconduct: http://ori.dhhs.gov/misconduct/cases/. Examine at least three cases of research misconduct posted on this website. Summarize the ethical misconduct for each case, and explain how you feel this type of misconduct could have been prevented or discovered sooner.

$SAGE edge™

SAGE edge offers a robust online environment featuring an impressive array of free tools and resources for review, study, and further exploration, keeping both instructors and students on the cutting edge of teaching and learning.

Access practice quizzes, eFlashcards, video, and multimedia at edge.sagepub.com/priviterarme.

DEFINING AND MEASURING VARIABLES, SELECTING SAMPLES, AND CHOOSING AN APPROPRIATE RESEARCH DESIGN

Identify a problem

- Determine an area of interest.
- Review the literature.
- Identify new ideas in your area of interest.
- Develop a research hypothesis.

Develop a research plan

- Define the variables being tested.
- Identify participants or subjects and determine how to sample them.
- Select a research strategy and design.
- Evaluate ethics and obtain institutional approval to conduct research.

Generate more new ideas

- Results support your hypothesis—refine or expand on your ideas.
- Results do not support your hypothesis— reformulate a new idea or start over.

After reading this chapter, you should be able to:

1   Describe two criteria that make variables suitable for scientific investigation.

2   Delineate the need for constructs and operational definitions in research.

3   Distinguish between continuous and discrete variables, as well as between quantitative and qualitative variables.

4   State the four scales of measurement, and provide an example for each.

5   Describe the following types of reliability: test-retest reliability, internal consistency, and interrater reliability.

6   Describe the following types of validity: face validity, construct validity, criterion-related validity, and content validity.

7   Define and give an example of intervention fidelity.

8   Identify the concerns of participant reactivity, experimenter bias, and sensitivity and range effects for selecting a measurement procedure.

9   Explain why the failure to replicate a result is not sufficient evidence for fraud.

Communicate the results

- Method of communication: oral, written, or in a poster.
- Style of communication: APA guidelines are provided to help prepare style and format.

Conduct the study

- Execute the research plan and measure or record the data.

Analyze and evaluate the data

- Analyze and evaluate the data as they relate to the research hypothesis.
- Summarize data and research results.

SCIENTIFIC VARIABLES, VALIDITY, AND RELIABILITY

While driving, you have probably asked, "How fast am I going?" While at work, maybe you have asked, "How much longer until I get out of work?" As a student, you may ask, "How much does college tuition cost?" In each case, the question you ask requires a definition and measurement of the variables (speed, time, tuition) about which you are asking a question.

To answer a question, you need a way to understand how that question can be answered. For example, to determine how "fast" you are going, you need to know how speed is measured— in miles or kilometers per hour. You can then use this measure of speed to find a measurable answer to the question "How fast am I going?" Similarly, you can measure time in seconds, minutes, or hours to answer the question "How much longer until I get out of work?" The expenses of tuition can likewise be measured in dollars to answer the question "How much does college tuition cost?" For each variable stated here, you define the variable in terms of how you will measure that variable—that is, speed is current miles per hour, time is minutes until work ends, and tuition is cost in dollars.

Defining how variables are measured is important because it ensures that others clearly understand how the questions of researchers are answered. In the example above, you know how to answer each question because you identified how you will measure or observe speed, time, and tuition. Similarly, researchers ask questions about behaviors, such as love, happiness, and stress. They then identify how they will measure or observe these variables so that others can clearly understand how their questions will be answered. We begin this chapter by further illustrating the importance and need for defining and measuring variables in science.

edge.sagepub.com/ priviterarme

- Take the chapter quiz
- Review key terms with eFlashcards
- Explore multimedia links and SAGE articles

4.1 Criteria for Defining and Measuring Variables

Using the scientific method, we typically need to first define the variables we will observe and measure to test a hypothesis. We can use an example to illustrate. Classroom textbooks will often highlight or color key terms to emphasize their importance in a text. Suppose you hypothesize that placing key terms in color increases the attention readers give to those words. To test this hypothesis using the scientific method, you must first ask the following questions:

- How will I observe or measure attention?

- Can other people observe attention in the same way I did?

To test this hypothesis, you must determine what you will observe, how you will observe it, and under what conditions it will be observed. In this example, you will measure or observe attention to the key terms. You could create two conditions: In Group Color, students read a text with key terms given in color; in Group No Color, students read the same text with key terms given in plain black font. You hypothesize that Group Color will spend more time attending to the key terms in the text than Group No Color. In this example, the measured variable, attention to the key terms, must meet two criteria to make it suitable for scientific investigation: The variable must be observable and be replicable.

> A **variable** (also defined in Chapter 1) is any value or characteristic that can change or vary from one person to another or from one situation to another.

A variable that is *observable* is one that can be directly or indirectly measured. A variable that is *replicable* is one that can be consistently measured. To meet both criteria, you must explain how the variable was measured (observable) and under what conditions the variable was measured so that other researchers can re-create the same conditions to measure the same variable you did (replicable). To measure attention to the key terms, for example, you can use a device that tracks eye movements and record the amount of time a student's eyes orient toward the key terms in the text. The longer a student's eyes orient toward a key term, the greater his or her attention to that word. As long as other researchers have a similar eye-tracking device, they can also measure attention in the same way that you did. Hence, as illustrated in Figure 4.1, attention is measured as time in milliseconds (observable) and could be observed again with an eye-tracking device (replicable), which makes the variable suitable for scientific study.

> For a variable to be suitable for scientific study, it must be observable and replicable.

In this chapter, we introduce the types of variables that researchers measure, how they measure them, and the extent to which a measure is informative. We then describe techniques researchers use to determine the reliability and validity of their measurements and some potential concerns or cautions for selecting a measurement procedure.

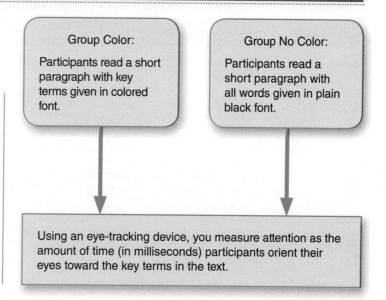

You measure *attention* in both groups to determine whether having key terms in color will result in greater attention paid to those words.

The variable, attention, is defined in milliseconds (observable) and could be observed again with an eye-tracking device (replicable), which makes the variable suitable for scientific study.

Group Color:

Participants read a short paragraph with key terms given in colored font.

Group No Color:

Participants read a short paragraph with all words given in plain black font.

Using an eye-tracking device, you measure attention as the amount of time (in milliseconds) participants orient their eyes toward the key terms in the text.

4.2 Constructs and Operational Definitions

An important challenge for researchers is to clearly explain how they will measure the variables they wish to study. To illustrate, consider the following three variables that researchers can measure: leadership, anxiety, and learning. Table 4.1 lists a description for each variable and three or four operational definitions that could be used to measure or define each variable. Recall from Chapter 1 that an operational definition describes a variable in terms of how it is measured.

The reason we use operational definitions is because it minimizes ambiguity caused by observing otherwise arbitrary phenomena. For example, we could describe *leadership* as the ability to lead school change. However, this description is ambiguous because one person may think about the ability to lead school change very differently from another person. After all, does "school change" refer to the increase in test scores, teacher morale, or a specific feature of the school such as inclusiveness or technology use? A general description of a variable is simply not good enough. Instead, researchers need to specifically define variables in terms of how those variables will be measured. As shown in Table 4.1, a single variable can have many operational definitions.

Keep in mind that many of the educational behaviors and events researchers observe are actually not observed at all—not directly anyway. For example, the first operational

Table 4.1 A Description and Operational Definitions for Three Constructs Studied in the Behavioral Sciences: Attraction, Anxiety, and Recall

Variable	Description	Operational Definitions
Leadership	The ability to lead school change.	1. The increase of school test scores in reading and mathematics 2. Teacher morale rating on a scale (from low morale to very high morale) 3. Percentage of time students with disabilities are included in grade-level instruction 4. Number of computers in the school
Anxiety	A state or feeling of worry and nervousness	1. Exam scores obtained in the presence of a teacher (the anxiety-provoking stimulus) 2. Anxiety rating (from low to very high) the day before end-of-year testing 3. Number of school absences in a semester due to school phobia
Learning	The ability to acquire new information	1. The number of correct answers made on a teacher-made exam 2. Number of times in which the new behavior is exhibited 3. Number of correct responses to a standardized achievement test 4. Number of items on homework assignments correct

definition listed for *learning* in Table 4.1 is the number of errors made on an exam. The more errors made on the exam, the worse the learning. Using this operational definition, we will observe the number of errors on an exam. *Learning*, then, is the word or **construct** we use to describe what we actually observed. In other words, we observe errors on an exam, and we infer that this observation reflects the ability for participants to *learn*.

Most of the educational behaviors and events researchers study are constructs. To identify or observe a construct, we identify the observable components or **external factors of the construct.** The operational definition of a construct is the external factor of that construct that we will observe. For example, the external factor of *learning* was the number of errors made on an exam, and two other ways we could observe *learning* are also given in Table 4.1. Many constructs are studied in the education sciences, including learning, anxiety, motivation, alertness, resilience, consciousness, cognition,

A **construct or hypothetical construct** is a conceptual variable that is known to exist but cannot be directly observed.

An **external factor of a construct** is an observable behavior or event that is presumed to reflect the construct itself.

intelligence, personality, and achievement. Each construct must be operationally defined to identify the external factor that will be observed for each construct.

Constructs are often a central component to an explanation provided by a theory. Constructs connect what is observed to a theoretical framework. For example, intelligence and learning are constructs to explain phenomena that we cannot directly observe. Intelligence and learning are inferred based on outcome of intelligence or learning such as a test score or performance of a new behavior. Being able to recognize the constructs that are central to a theory is important because constructs can be observed in many different ways—and each way you observe the construct should support the theory. If not, then the theory can be refuted.

> A construct is operationally defined to identify the external factor that will be observed or measured.

MAKING SENSE—OBSERVING CONSTRUCTS

How we define a construct depends on how we will observe it, and there are often many different ways to observe a construct. To illustrate, consider the following two studies used to measure the same construct, learning:

Study 1: In a study teaching new content to students, a researcher administers a test created for the study immediately after the new content is presented. We assume that the number of items correct on the test measures the amount of learning that took place.

Study 2: A researcher measures learning by administering a standardized achievement test such as the 10th edition of the Stanford Achievement Test (Harcourt Educational Measurement, 2002) 1 week after providing reading instruction.

These studies are the same in that both studies measure learning. The manner in which learning is measured is different in the two studies. In Study 1, the learning is a researcher-made test specific to the instruction provided. In Study 2, the researcher used a general measure of achievement provided by a test publisher. These hypothetical studies describe different experimental situations, each with a very different external factor that is presumed to measure the same construct, *learning*. Because the same construct can be measured in very different ways, it is important to know not only what was measured in a study but also how it was measured.

LEARNING CHECK 1 ✓

1. State two criteria that make a variable suitable for scientific investigation.

2. Which definition is an operational definition for school phobia? Explain.

    A. A fear of attending school

    B. The number of times a child refuses to go to school

3. For the following hypothetical research study, state (a) the construct and (b) the external factor for the construct.

   In a study on motivation to complete homework, a researcher provides laptops to one group of students and not to another to use for completing homework assignments. He counts the number of homework assignments completed by the students. He hypothesizes that the students who received the laptop to complete homework will be more motivated to complete the homework.

Answers: 1. A variable must be observable and replicable; 2. B is correct because it is defined in terms of how school phobia will be measured; 3. (a) motivation, (b) the number of homework assignments completed.

4.3 Types of Variables

Every variable or construct we study is defined in terms of how it is measured. The different types of variables we can measure fall into two categories:

- Continuous or discrete

- Quantitative or qualitative

Each category is discussed in this section. Many examples for how variables fit into each of these categories are given in Table 4.2.

> Constructs are often a central component to an explanation provided by a theory.

Continuous and Discrete Variables

Variables can be categorized as continuous or discrete. A **continuous variable** is measured along a continuum, meaning that continuous variables can be measured at any place beyond the decimal point. Consider, for example, that Olympic sprinters are timed to the nearest hundredths place (in seconds), but if the Olympic judges wanted to clock them to the nearest millionths place, they could. A **discrete variable,** on the other hand, is measured in whole units or categories, meaning that discrete variables are not measured along a continuum. For example, the number of brothers and sisters you have and your family's socioeconomic class (working class, middle class, upper class) are examples of discrete variables. Refer to Table 4.2 for more examples of continuous and discrete variables.

> A **continuous variable** is measured along a continuum at any place beyond the decimal point, meaning that it can be measured in whole units or fractional units.
>
> A **discrete variable** is measured in whole units or categories that are not distributed along a continuum.

> Whereas quantitative variables can be continuous or discrete, qualitative variables can only be discrete.

Quantitative and Qualitative Variables

Variables can be categorized as quantitative or qualitative. A **quantitative variable** varies by amount. These variables are measured in numeric units, so both

Section II: Defining and Measuring Variables, Selecting Samples, and Choosing an Appropriate Research Design

Table 4.2 A List of 20 Variables and How They Fit Into the Three Categories Used to Describe Them

Variables	Continuous vs. Discrete	Qualitative vs. Quantitative	Scale of Measurement
Sex (male, female)	Discrete	Qualitative	Nominal
Ethnicity (African American, Caucasian, Hispanic, Asian)	Discrete	Qualitative	Nominal
Number of vocabulary words recalled	Discrete	Quantitative	Ratio
Number of errors	Discrete	Quantitative	Ratio
Duration of attention (in seconds)	Continuous	Quantitative	Ratio
Ranking of favorite books	Discrete	Quantitative	Ordinal
Ratings of satisfaction (1 to 7)	Discrete	Quantitative	Interval
Free and reduced-price lunch status (eligible, not eligible)	Discrete	Qualitative	Nominal
Score (0% to 100%) on an exam	Continuous	Quantitative	Ratio
Number of students in your class	Discrete	Quantitative	Ratio
Standardized test score	Continuous	Quantitative	Interval
Time (in seconds) to memorize a list	Continuous	Quantitative	Ratio
The size of a reward (in grams)	Continuous	Quantitative	Ratio
Grade	Discrete	Quantitative	Ordinal
Political affiliation (Republican, Democrat)	Discrete	Qualitative	Nominal
Type of distraction (auditory, visual)	Discrete	Qualitative	Nominal
A letter grade (A, B, C, D, F)	Discrete	Qualitative	Ordinal
Reading fluency	Continuous	Quantitative	Ratio
A college student's SAT score	Discrete	Quantitative	Interval
Number of teachers with a master's degree	Discrete	Quantitative	Ratio

continuous and discrete variables can be quantitative. For example, we can describe students by age (a continuous variable) or grade level (a discrete variable). In both cases, the variables are measured by amount (in numeric units).

A **quantitative variable** varies by amount. A quantitative variable is measured as a numeric value and is often collected by measuring or counting.

A qualitative variable varies by class. A qualitative variable is often a category or label for the behaviors and events researchers observe and so describes nonnumeric aspects of phenomena.

A qualitative variable, on the other hand, varies by class. These variables are often labels for the behaviors we observe, so only discrete variables can be categorized as qualitative. For example, socioeconomic class (working class, middle class, upper class) is discrete and qualitative; so are many categories of mental disorders, such as attention-deficit hyperactivity disorder (with or without hyperactivity). Refer to Table 4.2 for more examples of quantitative and qualitative variables.

LEARNING CHECK 2 ✓

1. State whether each of the following is continuous or discrete.

   A. The time (in seconds) it takes a student to raise his or her hand after the teacher asks a question.

   B. The number of questions that students ask during a class.

   C. Type of drug use (none, infrequent, moderate, or frequent).

   D. Educational level (high school diploma or GED, associate's degree or technical school, college graduate, postgraduate degree).

2. State whether the variables listed in Question 1 are quantitative or qualitative.

Answers: 1. A. continuous, B. discrete, C. discrete, D. discrete; 2. A. quantitative, B. quantitative, C. qualitative, D. qualitative.

4.4 Scales of Measurement

Researchers can measure data using one of four scales of measurement. In the early 1940s, Harvard psychologist S. S. Stevens coined the terms *nominal, ordinal, interval,* and *ratio* to classify the scales of measurement (Stevens, 1946). Scales of measurement are rules that describe the informativeness of measured data. In this section, we discuss the extent to which data are informative on each scale of measurement. In all, scales of measurement are characterized by three properties: order, differences, and ratios. Each property can be described by answering the following questions:

Scales of measurement are rules for how the properties of numbers can change with different uses.

1. *Order:* Does a larger number indicate a greater value than a smaller number?

2. *Differences:* Does subtracting one set of numbers represent some meaningful value?

3. *Ratio:* Does dividing, or taking the ratio of, one set of numbers represent some meaningful value?

Table 4.3 Different Scales of Measurement and the Information They Provide Concerning the Order, Difference, and Ratio of Numbers

		Scale of Measurement			
		Nominal	Ordinal	Interval	Ratio
Property	Order	NO	YES	YES	YES
	Difference	NO	NO	YES	YES
	Ratio	NO	NO	NO	YES

Table 4.3 gives the answers to the questions for each scale of measurement. In this section, we begin with the least informative scale (nominal) and finish with the most informative scale (ratio).

Nominal

Numbers on a **nominal scale** identify something or someone; they provide no additional information. Common examples of nominal numbers include ZIP codes, license plate numbers, credit card numbers, student identification numbers, telephone numbers, and Social Security numbers. These numbers identify locations, vehicles, or individuals and nothing more. One credit card number, for example, is not greater than another; it is simply different.

In science, numbers on a nominal scale are typically categorical variables that have been **coded**—converted to numeric values. Examples of nominal variables include a person's race, sex, nationality, sexual orientation, hair and eye color, season of birth, marital status, or other demographic or personal information. Researchers may code men as 1 and women as 2. They may code the ethnicity as 1, 2, 3, and 4 for African American, Caucasian, Hispanic, and Asian, respectively. These numbers are used to identify sex or ethnicity and nothing more. We often code words with numeric values when entering them into statistical programs such as SPSS. Coding is largely done because it is often easier to compute data using statistical programs, such as SPSS, when data are entered as numbers, not words.

> **Nominal scales** are measurements in which a number is assigned to represent something or someone. Numbers on a nominal scale are often coded values.
>
> **Coding** is the procedure of converting a categorical variable to numeric values.

> The four scales of measurement are nominal, ordinal, interval, and ratio.

Ordinal

An **ordinal scale** of measurement is one that conveys order alone. Examples of variables

> **Ordinal scales** are measurements that convey order or rank only.

on an ordinal scale include finishing order in a competition, education level, and ranking. Ordinal scales indicate only that one value is greater than or less than another, so differences between ranks do not have meaning. Consider, for example, a hypothetical list of state rankings for the top high schools in the United States. Table 4.4 shows the rank, state, and percentage of high schools possibly rated as distinguished in that state for the top 20 states. Based on ranks alone, can we say that the difference between the high schools ranked 2 and 4 is the same as the difference between those ranked 8 and 10? In both cases, two ranks separate the schools. Yet, if you look at the actual scores for determining rank, you find that the difference between ranks 2 and 4 is 3.4 points, whereas the difference between

Table 4.4   A List of the Possible Top 20 State High Schools in the United States

Rank	State	Percentage of Distinguished High Schools
1	California	30.1
2	Connecticut	29.2
3	Maryland	27.1
4	North Carolina	25.8
5	Ohio	22.9
6	Illinois	21.0
7	Maine	19.5
8	Florida	19.1
9	Indiana	18.8
10	Wisconsin	17.2
11	New York	17.1
12	Texas	16.5
13	Colorado	15.3
14	New Hampshire	14.9
15	Georgia	14.5
16	New Jersey	14.2
17	Virginia	13.6
18	Nevada	12.9
19	Hawaii	12.2
20	Vermont	11.9

ranks 8 and 10 is 1.9 points. So the difference in points is not the same. Ranks alone do not convey this difference. They simply indicate that one rank is greater or less than another rank.

Interval

An interval scale of measurement can be understood readily by two defining principles: equidistant scales and no true zero. A common example for this in education science is the rating scale. Rating scales are taught here as an interval scale because most researchers report these as interval data in published research. This type of scale is a numeric response scale used to indicate a participant's level of agreement or opinion with some statement. An example of a rating scale is given in Figure 4.2. Here we will look at each defining principle.

An equidistant scale is a scale distributed in units that are equal distance from one another. Many behavioral scientists assume that scores on a rating scale are distributed in equal intervals. For example, if you are asked to rate your satisfaction with a spouse or job on a 7-point scale from 1 (*completely unsatisfied*) to 7 (*completely satisfied*),

> **Interval scales** are measurements that have no true zero and are distributed in equal units.
>
> A **true zero** is when the value 0 truly indicates nothing on a scale of measurement. Interval scales do not have a true zero.

like in the scale shown in Figure 4.2, then you are using an interval scale. Because the distance between each point (1 to 7) is assumed to be the same or equal, it is appropriate to compute differences between scores on this scale. So a statement such as "The difference in job satisfaction among men and women was 2 points" is appropriate with interval scale measurements.

However, an interval scale does not have a true zero. A common example of a scale with no true zero is temperature. A temperature equal to zero for most measures of temperature does not mean that there is no temperature; it is just an arbitrary zero point. Values on a rating scale also have no true zero. In the example shown in Figure 4.2, a 1 was used to indicate no satisfaction, not 0. Each value, including 0, is arbitrary. That is, we could use any number to represent none of something. Measurements of intelligence and achievement tests are interval levels of measurement because they do not have a true or absolute zero. The score of zero on an intelligence or achievement test does not mean the complete absence of either intelligence or achievement. The implication is that without a true zero, there is no absolute value to indicate the absence of the phenomenon you are observing,

---

Figure 4.2 An Example of a 7-Point Rating Scale for Satisfaction Used for Scientific Investigation

Satisfaction Ratings

| 1 | 2 | 3 | 4 | 5 | 6 | 7 |

Completely Unsatisfied   Completely Satisfied

so a zero proportion is not meaningful. For this reason, stating a ratio such as "Satisfaction ratings were three times greater among men compared to women" is not appropriate with interval scale measurements.

Ratio

Ratio scales are similar to interval scales in that scores are distributed in equal units. Yet, unlike interval scales, a distribution of scores on a ratio scale has a true zero. That is, a ratio scale value includes a value equal to 0 that indicates the absence of the phenomenon being observed. This is an ideal scale in behavioral research because any mathematical operation can be performed on the values that are measured. Common examples of ratio scale measurements include length, height, weight, and time. For scores on a ratio scale, order is informative. For example, a person who is 30 years old is older than another who is 20. Differences are also informative. For example, the difference between 70 and 60 seconds is the same as the difference between 30 and 20 seconds (the difference is 10 seconds). Ratios are also informative on this scale because a true zero is defined—it truly means nothing. Hence, it is meaningful to state that 60 pounds is twice as heavy as 30 pounds.

Ratio scales are measurements that have a true zero and are equidistant. A ratio scale is the most informative scale of measurement.

When possible, researchers often go out of their way to measure variables on a ratio scale. For example, if they want to measure reading, they may choose to measure fluency (number of errors in words read per minute). If they measure memory, they may choose to measure the amount of time it takes to memorize some list, or the number of errors made. In these examples, fluency and memory were measured using ratio scales, thereby allowing researchers to draw conclusions in terms of the order, differences, and ratios of values on those scales—there are no restrictions for variables measured on a ratio scale.

LEARNING CHECK 3 ✓

1. Participants ranked their favorite books in order from least to most preferred. Book rankings are on what scale of measurement?

2. State the two defining principles of interval scales.

3. State the scale of measurement for each variable listed below.

   A. Sex (male, female)

   B. Speed (in seconds)

   C. The latitude and longitude coordinates of a person's place of birth

   D. Grade level (1 to 12)

4. Which scale of measurement is the most informative?

Answers: 1. Ordinal scale; 2. An interval scale is equidistant and does not have a true zero; 3. A. nominal, B. ratio, C. interval, D. ordinal; 4. Ratio scale.

4.5 Reliability of a Measurement

Recall that a variable must be observable and replicable for it to be suitable for scientific investigation. The second criterion, that a variable be replicable, is most closely related to **reliability**—a replicable variable is one that has a reliable measurement. A measure is reliable inasmuch as it is consistent, stable, or repeatable across measures or across observations. We will introduce three types of reliability in this section:

- Test-retest reliability
- Internal consistency
- Interrater reliability

> **Reliability** is the consistency, stability, or repeatability of one or more measures or observations.
>
> **Test-retest reliability** is the extent to which a measure or observation is consistent or stable at two points in time.

Test-Retest Reliability

One type of reliability is the extent to which measurements or observations are consistent across time, called **test-retest reliability.** This type of reliability is shown when a measure or observation demonstrated at "Time 1" is again demonstrated using the same measure or observation procedure at "Time 2." When a measure is consistent over time, it is called a *stable* measure. Hence, test-retest reliability is the stability of a measure over time, with more stable measures being more reliable.

To demonstrate test-retest reliability, we can give participants the same measure at two times. The more consistent each participant's score from Time 1 to Time 2, the higher the test-retest reliability. To illustrate, Reddy, Fabiano, Dudek, and Hsu (2013) measured the test-retest reliability of the Classroom Strategies Scale (CSS). The CSS is a 20-item scale used to measure "how often teachers utilize specific empirically supported practices in their classrooms," including both instructional and classroom management strategies. Reddy et al. observed classrooms once and then again 2 weeks later. The researchers used a correlation to identify the stability or test-retest reliability of the scale; correlations are discussed in Chapter 8. Table 4.5 shows the correlation of the two parts of the CSS indicating how stable or consistent the scores were at both times. The key advantage of test-retest reliability is that you can determine the extent to which items or measures are replicable or consistent over time.

Internal Consistency

A type of reliability used to determine the extent to which multiple items for the same variable are related is called **internal consistency.** This type of reliability is shown when participants respond similarly to each item used to measure the same variable. Hence, internal consistency reflects the extent to which multiple items for the variable give the same picture of the behavior or event being measured.

> **Internal consistency** is a measure of reliability used to determine the extent to which multiple items used to measure the same variable are related.

To demonstrate internal consistency, we must show that scores or items for a single test or measure are related using a statistic called *Cronbach's alpha*, which is introduced in

Table 4.5 The Stability of Two Subscales of the CSS From Time 1 to Time 2 in a Sample of 57 Classrooms

Subscales of the CSS	Correlation Between Time 1 and Time 2 Observation Scores
Instructional strategies	$r = .70$
Classroom management strategies	$r = .86$

Source: Adapted from Reddy et al. (2013).

Note: Total scores remained stable over time. Data based on those presented by Reddy, Fabiano, Dudek, and Hsu (2013).

Chapter 13. In short, this statistic "splits" all items for the same measure every possible way and computes a correlation value for them all. The larger the value of Cronbach's alpha, the higher the internal consistency will be.

To illustrate the interpretation of internal consistency, suppose we gave the instructional practices subscale of the CSS to five participants. The results for this hypothetical study are shown in Table 4.6. Because each item measures the same phenomenon—use of empirically supported classroom instructional practices—we expect the participants to show a consistent pattern in their responses to each item. Indeed, a consistent pattern does emerge from the responses in Table 4.6. For example, notice that Andrew consistently responded on the high end of each item on the scale (i.e., five 3s and one 2); Joseph consistently responded on the low end (i.e., all 0s). When scores for each participant are consistent across items for the same measure, then the items give a consistent picture of the behavior being measured— use of empirically supported classroom instructional practices—and the measure is associated with high internal consistency.

Table 4.6 An Example of High Internal Consistency

Participants	Subscale						
	5	6	7	8	9	10	15
Andrew	3	3	3	2	3	3	2
Gregory	3	3	2	2	3	3	2
Rachel	2	2	2	2	2	2	2
Stephen	2	1	1	2	1	2	2
Joseph	0	0	0	0	0	0	0

Note: The data are for five hypothetical participants who were observed on the use of the empirically supported classroom instructional practices subscale of the CSS.

Section II: Defining and Measuring Variables, Selecting Samples, and Choosing an Appropriate Research Design

Interrater Reliability

A type of reliability used to compare the consistency of ratings or judgments of a behavior or event is called **interrater reliability (IRR).** This type of reliability is shown when observers make similar judgments of the same behavior or event. Hence, IRR is the extent to which the raters or observers are in agreement with what they observed.

> **Interrater reliability (IRR)** or **interobserver reliability** is a measure for the extent to which two or more raters of the same behavior or event are in agreement with what they observed.

To demonstrate IRR, we must show that scores or ratings are similar across raters using a statistic called *Cohen's kappa*, which is introduced in Chapter 13. In short, this statistic gives an estimate of the consistency in ratings of two or more raters. The more consistent the ratings, the higher the IRR will be. In behavioral research, raters are used to observe a behavior in a contrived or natural social situation or evaluate written or oral summaries created by participants. Multiple raters are used anytime different people could interpret an observation differently. To make sure that the observations made are reliable, the researcher uses multiple raters who independently observe the same behavior or event to get a consensus about what was observed. High IRR shows that observations made in a study reflect those that other observers would agree with. Low IRR, on the other hand, indicates a misunderstanding or confusion concerning the behavior or event being observed inasmuch as a consensus was not reached.

> Reliability is important inasmuch as we make consistent measurements or observations of a construct of interest.

LEARNING CHECK 4 ✓

1. Which of the following describes the reliability of a measure?
   A. Consistency
   B. Stability
   C. Repeatability
   D. All of the above

2. State the type of reliability measured for each of the following examples.
   A. A researcher has participants complete a seven-item leadership style survey and measures the extent to which responses for those seven items are consistent or the same for each participant.
   B. A researcher asks a sample of students who are obese to rank their favorite foods before eating in the school cafeteria and measures the extent to which participant rankings are consistent at both times.
   C. A researcher has two observers rate the same classroom and measures the extent to which the two raters agree in their judgments.

Answers: 1. D; 2. A. internal consistency, B. test-retest reliability, C. interrater reliability.

4.6 Validity of a Measurement

Reliability is important; however, it does not indicate the accuracy of a measure. For example, a clock that is 10 minutes off will consistently be 10 minutes off. In this case, the clock is not accurate but gives a reliably wrong estimate of time. For this reason, it is important to determine the extent to which a variable measures what it is intended to measure, which leads us to consider the validity of a measurement.

The **validity** of a measurement is the extent to which a measurement for a variable or construct measures what it is purported or intended to measure.

Recall that a variable must be observable and replicable for it to be suitable for scientific investigation. The first criterion that a variable be observable is most closely related to **validity**—a valid variable is one that is correctly or accurately observed. A measure is valid inasmuch as we measure what we intended to measure. For example, if we claim to be measuring attraction, then the measure is valid if we are indeed measuring attraction. We will introduce the following three types of validity in this section:

- Construct validity
- Criterion-related validity
- Content validity

Construct Validity

Another type of validity is used to determine the extent to which an operational definition for a construct is valid, called **construct validity.** This type of validity is shown when we determine that the operational definition for a variable or construct is actually measuring that variable or construct. For example, to measure the construct *learning*, an instructor may distribute a one-dimensional exam, such as multiple choice only. In this case, the operational definition for learning is an exam score, with higher scores indicating greater learning. However, scores on one-dimensional exams often do not measure learning but instead measure other factors, such as exam anxiety or stress (Dunn & Dunn, 1978; Morgan, Umberson, & Hertzog, 2014). Hence, one-dimensional exams often have low construct validity—it is not always true that low exam scores (the measure) reflect poor learning (the construct the exam is intended to measure).

Construct validity of a measurement is the extent to which an operational definition for a variable or construct is actually measuring that variable or construct.

Criterion-related validity of a measurement is the extent to which scores obtained on some measure can be used to infer or predict a criterion or expected outcome.

Criterion-Related Validity

Another type of validity, called **criterion-related validity,** examines the relationship between scores obtained on a measure for a construct and some criterion, outcome, or indicator of the construct. Criterion-related validity is the extent to which scores obtained on a measure for a variable or construct can be used to infer or predict a criterion or expected outcome of that variable or construct. This type of validity has many different subtypes, including *predictive validity*, *concurrent validity*, *convergent validity*, and *discriminant validity*. Table 4.7 defines and gives an example for each subtype of criterion-related validity.

Criterion-related validity is demonstrated when scores for a measure are related to, or predictive of, a certain outcome or criterion that is expected if, in fact, that measure is valid. Demonstrating any one of the subtypes of criterion-related validity is sufficient to demonstrate criterion-related validity. Although a detailed discussion of each subtype of criterion-related validity goes beyond the scope of this book, it is important to be familiar with the subtypes of criterion-related validity listed in Table 4.7. Examples demonstrating each subtype are also given in Table 4.7.

> Different types of criterion-related validity include predictive validity, concurrent validity, convergent validity, and discriminant validity.

Content Validity

A fourth type of validity, called **content validity,** determines whether the contents of a measure are adequate to capture or represent that construct. Content validity is the extent to which

> **Content validity** of a measurement is the extent to which the items or contents of a measure adequately represent all of the features of the construct being measured.

Table 4.7	Four Subtypes of Criterion-Related Validity	
Subtype of Criterion-Related Validity	**Definition**	**Example**
Predictive	The extent to which a measure predicts the outcomes it should.	SAT scores (measure) predict later college grade point average (GPA) (criterion).
Concurrent	The extent to which a measure can distinguish between groups it should be able to distinguish between.	A high school state end-of-grade test is related to high school GPA at the same time.
Convergent	The extent to which two or more different measures for the same construct are related or "converge."	One test of reading skills is related to another test of reading skills.
Discriminant	The extent to which one measure can be "discriminated" from another measure that it should not be related to.	A test for school anxiety (measure) predicts long-term school attendance (criterion). A high score on the test indicating higher anxiety will not be related to high rates of school absences.

the items or contents of a measure adequately reflect all of the features of the construct being measured. Hence, the more thorough a measure for a construct, the higher the content validity of the measure will be.

To demonstrate content validity, we must show that the items we use to measure a construct are representative of the construct as a whole. For example, a final exam should test an adequate sample of all topics taught during the semester; an exam of basic math skills should include more than just addition problems; an assessment for personality should measure more than just one personality trait. In each example, the validity of the measure reflected the extent to which an appropriate number of items were included to measure the construct as a whole.

> Validity is important in that we want to confirm that our measurements are indeed measuring what we intended to measure.

LEARNING CHECK 5 ✓

1. Face validity is a basic assessment of validity. Explain what this type of validity shows.

2. A researcher operationally defines student engagement as the number of times that a student raises his or her hand to answer a question posed by a teacher. To demonstrate construct validity, what must the researcher show?

3. Name four subtypes of criterion-related validity.

4. A researcher measures reading using a multidimensional assessment that encompasses all aspects of reading. For this reason, the researcher likely has high _____ validity.

Answers: 1. Face validity shows the extent to which a measure "looks like" it will measure what it is intended to measure; 2. The researcher must show that the frequency of raising a hand during class (the operational definition) is actually measuring student engagement (the construct); 3. Four subtypes of criterion-related validity are predictive validity, concurrent validity, convergent validity, and discriminant validity; 4. Content.

CONNECTING TO THE CLASSROOM

The use of tests to measure student achievement or aptitude is a routine task that can come with consequences. A teacher may use a reading test to create reading groups. A school psychologist will use tests to diagnose learning difficulties. We need to make sure that the tests we use provide a reliable and valid measure of achievement to feel confident in the decisions we make based on the test results. If you have access to the test manual, evidence of the technical adequacy (i.e., validity and reliability) will be provided. If you do not have access to the test manual or if you are looking for a test to use, you can find information about the technical adequacy in the Mental Measurement Yearbook with Tests in Print (MMYB) through a university library. Search in the MMYB database just like you would when conducting a library search for literature. An independent reviewer provides a review of what the test measures, how it was developed, and the technical adequacy. Below is a modified excerpt of the review of the technical adequacy for the Early Reading Assessment (ERA; Hammill, Pearson, Hresko, & Hoover, 2012) by Stacy L. Bliss, highlighting the reliability and validity information.

Section II: Defining and Measuring Variables, Selecting Samples, and Choosing an Appropriate Research Design

Reliability coefficients for the ERA composite score, calculated using coefficient alpha, were very high; coefficients ranged from .93 to .95 across age groups. Test-retest reliability with a time lapse ranging between 1 and 2 weeks was calculated with a subgroup of the standardization population. Resulting coefficients were .86 for the Early Reading Index (ERI), .77 to .80 for the core subtests, and .80 (PA, phonological awareness) and .70 (RV, receptive vocabulary) for the supplemental subtests. This reviewer considers the results to be in the acceptable range of above .70. Content validity was evaluated by examination of the **face validity** of the test questions, a comparison of the rationale for test format and items to the findings of the National Research Council and National Reading Panel (manual, p. 23), and examination of differential item functioning. To determine criterion validity, the authors compared the ERA with five other measures of early reading ability (i.e., Test of Early Reading Ability, Test of Preschool Early Literacy, Woodcock-Johnson III Tests of Achievement, Test of Silent Word Reading Fluency, and Test of Silent Reading Efficiency and Comprehension). The ERI composite showed large to very large correlations (.69–.82) with all other measures. Construct validity was examined by correlating ERA scores with age of examinee, correlating subtest scores with each other, and comparing ERA scores to the known reading ability of examinees. The test authors concluded the ERA showed adequate validity.

4.7 Intervention Fidelity

Intervention fidelity is related to both validity and reliability. When evaluating the effectiveness of interventions, it is important the intervention be delivered consistently (reliability) and as it is intended to be delivered (validity). Intervention or treatment fidelity refers to "how much" of an intervention is delivered as it was intended. In education research, a teacher will often deliver the intervention as designed by a researcher. If the intervention was not delivered as it was designed, then any outcome of the study is flawed. For example, in a study by Ahlgrim-Delzell et al. (2016), teachers were trained to implement a scripted curriculum to teach phonics-based reading to students with developmental disabilities. The curriculum required teachers to intervene in a certain way using systematic instruction and based on how students responded (no answer, incorrect, correct). Skipping one of the curriculum objectives, not following the scripted systematic instructional procedures, or not reacting to the types of student responses as they had been trained may have led to an incorrect conclusion about the effectiveness of the curriculum. In this study, graduate students went into the classrooms to observe the teachers' instruction and recorded it on an intervention fidelity form. The form listed all of the crucial steps in the intervention that needed to be performed by the teacher. At the end of the observation, the graduate students tallied the number of correct steps to obtain a percentage of the total number of steps performed correctly. A higher percentage of treatment fidelity means that the intervention was delivered as it was intended. Table 4.8 illustrates part of a treatment fidelity form from the Ahlgrim-Delzell et al. study.

> **Face validity** is the extent to which a measure for a variable or construct appears to measure what it is purported to measure.

Table 4.8 Example of Treatment Fidelity Form

Critical Components	Observed					
I. IDENTIFY LETTER GIVEN ITS SOUND	Time delay = 4-second delay					
	/m/	/s/	/a/			
Appropriate directions for items						
Provided appropriate wait time						
Provided error correction (prompt)						
Uses model then physical if no response						
Appropriate praise (NA if incorrect)						
II. FIRST SOUND IN WORDS	Time delay = 4-second delay					
	sit	man	soap	ant	apple	mud
Produced phoneme sounds correctly						
Appropriate directions for items						
Provided appropriate wait time						
Provided error correction (prompt)						
Uses model then physical if no response						
Appropriate praise (NA if incorrect)						

Source: Adapted from Ahlgrim-Delzell et al. (2016).

Note: NA = Not applicable.

By recording each step completed correctly with a checkmark, researchers could determine the percentage of intervention fidelity.

4.8 Selecting a Measurement Procedure

There are many things a researcher can do to help ensure that a measure for a variable or construct is reliable (repeatedly observed) and valid (actually measures what it was intended to measure). Researchers can be aware of, and control for, problems that can arise in the measurement procedures used. We will introduce four potential concerns that researchers should be aware of and control:

- Participant reactivity
- Experimenter bias

- Sensitivity

- Range effects

Participant Reactivity

In many research studies, the participants know that they are being observed. For most studies, participants are given an informed consent form that directly tells them that they are volunteering to participate in a study. The behavior of a participant can change in response to knowing that he or she is being observed, which is a phenomenon referred to as participant reactivity.

Participants most often react to their environment in one of three ways, as described in Table 4.8. Participants can be overly cooperative by behaving as if they are trying to please the researcher by acting in ways that they think are consistent with how the researcher wants them to behave—called participant expectancy. Participants can be overly apprehensive and withhold information the researcher is trying to study—called evaluation apprehension. Participants can also be overly antagonistic by

> Participant reactivity is the reaction or response participants have when they know they are being observed or measured.
>
> Three types of participant reactivity are participant expectancy (a participant is overly cooperative), evaluation apprehension (a participant is overly apprehensive), and participant reluctance (a participant is overly antagonistic).

behaving in ways that they think contradict how the researcher wants them to behave—called participant reluctance. In each example, the participant's behavior is a reaction to the knowledge that he or she is being observed and not a reflection of the manipulation or construct the researcher is trying to measure.

To avoid participant reactivity, researchers can simply not let participants know that they are being observed. However, for many research studies, this is not possible because participants are given an informed consent form prior to the conduct of the research procedures. In situations in which participants know that they are being observed, the following strategies can be used to minimize participant reactivity:

- **Reassure confidentiality.** A statement of confidentiality or anonymity is included in an informed consent form. Most research situations will protect the confidentiality of participants, and this point should be emphasized to remind participants that their responses will not be revealed. Reassuring confidentiality is especially effective for minimizing evaluation apprehension.

- **Use deception when ethical.** Participant expectancy and participant reluctance occur because the participant thinks that he or she has figured out the research hypothesis. To conceal the research hypothesis and therefore the true intent or purpose of the research study, it is often justified to use deception, especially when the true intent of the research study is transparent or obvious.

- **Minimize demand characteristics.** The research setting itself can sometimes give participants clues (usually unintentionally) about how to behave or react,

Table 4.9 Three Types of Participant Reactivity in Behavioral Research

Type of Participant Reactivity	Synopsis	Full Description
Participant expectancy	"The overly cooperative participant"	Plays the role of the "good participant" and behaves in ways he or she feels are consistent with the intent of the research study.
Evaluation apprehension	"The overly apprehensive participant"	Plays the role of the "shy participant" and conceals or withholds information he or she considers private or personal.
Participant reluctance	"The overly antagonistic participant"	Plays the role of the "bad participant" and behaves in ways he or she feels will disconfirm or contradict the intent of the research study.

A **demand characteristic** is any feature or characteristic of a research setting that may reveal the hypothesis being tested or give the participant a clue regarding how he or she is expected to behave.

Participant reactivity is problematic inasmuch as it can interfere with efforts to measure or observe a construct of interest.

typically in ways that promote the research hypothesis—such biases should be minimized or assessed to ensure that responding is due to the manipulation or construct being measured and not due to these "clues" (Robinson-Cimpian, 2014). Clues in the research setting that participants may use to decide how to behave are called **demand characteristics.** For example, suppose that a researcher studies sleep habits of high school students. In asking the students about their sleep habits, the researcher may inadvertently give them a clue as to which choice is consistent with the research hypothesis, such as in the wording of the question ("Students who perform poorly in school may not get enough sleep. How many hours of sleep per night do you typically get?"). To eliminate demand characteristics, participants should experience a similar research setting across conditions or groups.

Experimenter Bias

Experimenter bias is the extent to which the behavior of a researcher or experimenter intentionally or unintentionally influences the results of a study.

Expectancy effects are preconceived ideas or expectations regarding how participants should behave or what participants are capable of doing. Expectancy effects can often lead to experimenter bias.

In many research studies, the researcher knows the predicted outcome of interest. The extent to which a researcher uses his or her knowledge of the predicted outcome to influence the results of a study is called **experimenter bias.** This type of bias, which is most often unintentional, often results from **expectancy effects,** which are preconceived ideas or expectations that researchers have regarding how participants should behave or what participants are capable of doing.

To illustrate an experimenter bias, suppose a researcher developed an intervention in teaching a math or reading skill for at-risk students. A high school teacher was recruited and was asked by the researcher to provide the intervention to his or her first-period class of the day and not to the last class period of the day. Providing the new intervention during the first period may be biased in that the students are more alert and attentive than the last period of the day. During the study, the researcher observed classroom instruction and collected data on the teacher and students. It is possible that the researcher would view the classroom observations differently than someone else by rating the behaviors of students who received the intervention more positively.

Experimenter bias occurs anytime the researcher behaves or sets up a study in a way that facilitates results in the direction that is predicted. The following strategies can help minimize the problem of experimenter bias:

- **Get a second opinion.** It is often difficult to criticize yourself or your research plan. It could be that your plan is somehow biased and you do not notice it. A simple solution is to ask another colleague or friend for feedback first, before conducting the research study.

- **Standardize the research procedures.** To standardize the research procedures, you must ensure that all participants are treated the same. For example, you can read from a script verbatim, prerecord instructions for a study, or thoroughly train confederates prior to their participation in a study when appropriate to ensure that you treat participants similarly in a study.

> A **double-blind study** is a type of research study in which the researcher collecting the data and the participants in the study are unaware of the conditions in which participants are assigned.

- **Conduct a double-blind study.** A *blind* study is one in which the researcher or participants are unaware of the condition that participants are assigned. In a **double-blind study,** both the researcher and the participants are unaware of the conditions in which participants are assigned. When the researcher is blind to the predicted outcome or results of a study, the potential for experimenter bias is minimal.

> Experimenter bias can be problematic inasmuch as the researcher conducting the study is aware of the predicted outcomes of interest.

Sensitivity and Range Effects

The measure you choose for a construct or variable can sometimes limit your ability to observe that variable or construct. One limitation is the **sensitivity of a measure,** which is the extent to which a measure can change in the presence of a manipulation. For example, suppose we measure attention (the construct) in participants who are diagnosed with attention-deficit hyperactivity disorder as the amount of time spent attending to teacher instruction during one class session in 5-minute increments. Any increase of attention of less than 5 minutes would not be captured. This

> The **sensitivity of a measure** is the extent to which a measure can change or be different in the presence of a manipulation.

measure would then not be "sensitive" to smaller increments of attention span between 1 and 4 minutes.

Another possible limitation is range effect, which typically occurs when scores for a measure are clustered at one extreme. Scores can be clustered very high, called a ceiling effect, which can occur when a measure is too easy or obvious. This may occur, for example, if you give students 5 minutes to memorize only five items. Most people will likely be able to memorize the five items. Scores can also be clustered very low, called a floor effect, which typically occurs when a measure is too difficult or confusing. This may occur, for example, if you measure how much participants like stale popcorn at home or at a movie. If the stale popcorn tastes bad, then most participants will likely rate it very low no matter where they eat it.

A range effect can limit the sensitivity of a measure because scores will cluster very low or high for all groups, making it difficult to detect differences between groups. The following strategies can help maximize the sensitivity of a measure and minimize range effects:

> A range effect is a limitation in the range of data measured in which scores are clustered to one extreme. Scores can be clustered very low (floor effect) or very high (ceiling effect) on a given measure.
>
> A pilot study is a small preliminary study used to determine the extent to which a manipulation or measure will show an effect of interest.
>
> A manipulation check is a procedure used to check or confirm that a manipulation in a study had the effect that was intended.

- Perform a thorough literature review. There is a very good possibility that other researchers have already used a measure for the construct you wish to study. Review the literature to find what measures for the construct have been used and whether or not they were sensitive to detecting differences between groups. Then you can use the same measure in your study with the confidence of knowing that it will be a sensitive measure.

- Conduct a pilot study. If you are using a new measure, then start small. Begin with a pilot study, which is a small preliminary study. In the pilot study, you can evaluate whether the measure is sensitive to detecting changes in the presence of a manipulation before spending the time and money on a full-scale study.

- Include manipulation checks. You should consider that maybe the manipulation, and not the measure, is the reason that you are not detecting differences between groups. To check that a manipulation has the effect you intend, you can include a manipulation check. If, for example, you measure the speed of decision making when participants are hungry or full, you can check that participants are hungry or full (the manipulation) by asking participants to rate their hunger.

- Use multiple measures. Many constructs have more than one measure. Using two or more measures for the same variable can be more informative and make it more likely that at least one measure will detect differences between groups. For example, you could measure memory recall as the number of items correctly identified and the speed at which participants correctly identify items. The more measures you use, the more likely it is that at least one of them will be sensitive to detecting changes or group differences in your study.

1. Parents are asked to rate the quality of education at their child's school. One parent thinks the hypothesis is that the quality of education is higher in charter schools. Because their child attends a charter school, to appease the researcher, this parent intentionally overrates the quality of the education he or she thinks the child receives, which is an example of what type of participant reactivity?

2. State four strategies used to minimize participant reactivity.

3. State three strategies used to minimize experimenter bias.

4. A researcher uses a measure that participants in all groups scored very high on. What type of range effect should the researcher be concerned with?

5. State four strategies used to maximize the sensitivity of a measure and minimize range effects.

Answers: 1. Participant expectancy; 2. Reassure anonymity, use deception when ethical, measure less obvious variables, and minimize demand characteristics; 3. Get a second opinion, standardize the research procedures, and conduct a double-blind study; 4. Ceiling effect; 5. Perform a thorough literature review, conduct a pilot study, include manipulation checks, and use multiple measures.

4.9 Ethics in Focus: Replication as a Gauge for Fraud?

Many researchers assume that a replicable measure should be observed each time a researcher conducts a study. Researchers, who are ethically obligated to share their data for verification (see Chapter 2), can be subjected to criticism and even accused of fraud if other researchers reconduct their research procedures from an original study and do not obtain the same results as they did. However, a failure to replicate a result could likely be due to statistical error and not fraud. Any measure consists of a true score and a possible error that causes variability in that measure:

$$\text{Observed Score} = \text{True Score} + \text{Error}$$

An *error* is any influence in the response of a participant that can cause variability in his or her response. For example, a measure of life satisfaction can vary depending on a variety of factors, including a participant's current mood, relationship status, mental state, health, and even the time of day that the participant responds. Each factor can potentially contribute to an error in measurement inasmuch as each factor can cause responses on the life satisfaction measure to vary. Unfortunately, the potential errors of a measure are often not well understood and therefore are difficult to anticipate. For this reason, when a result is not replicated, always first consider potential sources of error in measurement that can likely explain why a result was not replicated.

A measure consists of a true score and error.

LO 1 Describe two criteria that make variables suitable for scientific investigation.

- A variable that is observable is one that can be directly or indirectly measured. A variable that is replicable is one that can be consistently measured. To meet both criteria, you must explain how the variable was measured (observable) and under what conditions the variable was measured so that other researchers can re-create the same conditions to measure the same variable you did (replicable).

LO 2 Delineate the need for constructs and operational definitions in research.

- Constructs are conceptual variables that are known to exist but cannot be directly observed. To observe a construct, we identify the observable components or external factors of the construct. The operational definition of a construct is the external factor or how we will observe the construct.

LO 3 Distinguish between continuous and discrete variables, as well as between quantitative and qualitative variables.

- A continuous variable is measured along a continuum, whereas a discrete variable is measured in whole units or categories. Continuous but not discrete variables are measured at any place beyond the decimal point.

- A quantitative variable varies by amount, whereas a qualitative variable varies by class. Continuous and discrete variables can be quantitative, whereas qualitative variables can only be discrete.

LO 4 State the four scales of measurement, and provide an example for each.

- The scales of measurement refer to how the properties of numbers can change with different uses. They are characterized by three properties: order, differences, and ratios. There are four scales of measurement: nominal, ordinal, interval, and ratio. Nominal values are typically coded (e.g., seasons, sex), ordinal values indicate order alone (e.g., rankings, grade level), interval values have equidistant scales and no true zero (e.g., rating scale values, temperature), and ratio values are equidistant and have a true zero (e.g., weight, height).

LO 5 Describe the following types of reliability: test-retest reliability, internal consistency, and interrater reliability.

- Reliability is the consistency, stability, or repeatability of one or more measures or observations. Three types of reliability are test-retest reliability, internal consistency, and interrater reliability.

- Test-retest reliability is the extent to which a measure or observation is consistent or stable at two points in time. Internal consistency is a measure of reliability used to determine the extent to which multiple items used to measure the same variable are related. **Interrater reliability** is a measure for the extent to which two or more raters of the same behavior or event are in agreement with what they observed.

LO 6 Describe the following types of validity: face validity, construct validity, criterion-related validity, and content validity.

- The **validity** of a measurement is the extent to which a measurement for a variable or construct measures what it is purported or intended to measure. Four types of validity are face validity, construct validity, criterion-related validity, and content validity.

- **Construct validity** is the extent to which an operational definition for a variable or construct is actually measuring that variable or construct. **Criterion-related validity** is the extent to which scores obtained on some measure can be used to infer or predict a criterion or expected outcome. Four types of criterion-related validity, described in Table 4.8, are predictive validity, concurrent validity, convergent validity, and discriminant validity. **Content validity** is the extent to which the items or contents of a measure adequately represent all the features of the construct being measured.

LO 7 Define and give an example of intervention fidelity.

- Intervention fidelity is the recording of the steps in an intervention delivered as it is intended to be delivered. It is presented as a percentage of steps performed correctly, with a higher percentage meaning greater fidelity.

LO 8 Identify the concerns of participant reactivity, experimenter bias, and sensitivity and range effects for selecting a measurement procedure.

- **Participant reactivity** is the reaction participants have when they know they are being observed or measured. To minimize participant reactivity, you can reassure confidentiality, use deception when ethical, measure less obvious variables, and minimize **demand characteristics.**

- **Experimenter bias** is the extent to which the behavior of a researcher influences the results of a study. To minimize experimenter bias, you can get a second opinion, standardize the research procedures, and conduct a **double-blind study.**

- The **sensitivity** of a measure is the extent to which it changes in the presence of a manipulation. A **range effect** is when scores on a measure all fall extremely high (**ceiling effect**) or low (**floor effect**) on the scale. To maximize the sensitivity of a measure and minimize possible range effects, you can perform a thorough literature review, conduct a **pilot study,** include **manipulation checks,** and use multiple measures.

LO 9 Explain why the failure to replicate a result is not sufficient evidence for fraud.

- Researchers can be subjected to criticism and even accused of fraud if other researchers reconduct their research procedures from an original study and do not obtain the same results as they did. However, a failure to replicate a result could be due to statistical error and not fraud. Any measure consists of a true score and a possible error that causes variability in that measure. An *error* is any influence in the response of a participant that can cause variability in his or her response. The error that causes variability, and not fraud, therefore could explain why a result was not replicated.

KEY TERMS

ceiling effect 118

coding 103

construct 98

construct validity 110

content validity 111

continuous variable 100

criterion-related
  validity 110

demand characteristics 116

discrete variable 100

double-blind study 117

evaluation
  apprehension 115

expectancy effects 116

experimenter bias 116

external factor of a
  construct 98

floor effect 118

hypothetical construct 98

internal consistency 107

interobserver reliability 109

interrater reliability
  (IRR) 109

interval scale 105

manipulation check 118

nominal scale 103

ordinal scale 103

participant expectancy 115

participant reactivity 115

participant reluctance 115

pilot study 118

qualitative variable 102

quantitative variable 101

range effect 118

ratio scale 106

reliability 107

scales of
  measurement 102

sensitivity of a
  measure 117

test-retest reliability 107

true zero 105

validity 110

variable 96

REVIEW QUESTIONS

1. State two criteria that make variables suitable for scientific investigation, and explain how to meet each criterion.

2. Which of the following choices is not an operational definition for a funny joke?
   A. Duration of time (in seconds) spent laughing during a 1-minute comedy skit
   B. Ratings on a scale from 0 (*not funny*) to 5 (*very funny*)
   C. The extent to which a joke or comment causes laughter

3. Below is a brief description of a hypothetical on teacher dress:
   A study tested the hypothesis that wearing different clothing can influence how people describe their teachers. Researchers first gained consensus on a list of

Section II: Defining and Measuring Variables, Selecting Samples, and Choosing an Appropriate Research Design

teachers who dressed in formal wear such as dresses and heals or suit coats and ties (e.g., cultivated, accurate) and casual wear such as jeans or khaki pants and T-shirts (e.g., easygoing, tolerant). They then asked some students to rate their teachers' personality traits. As predicted, they found that teachers in formal wear were rated with more "formal-appropriate traits," whereas teachers in casual wear were rated with more "casual-appropriate traits."

   A. What is the construct being measured in this study?

   B. What is the operational definition for the construct?

   C. Was the hypothesis confirmed? Explain.

4. For each of the following examples, (1) name the variable being measured, (2) state whether the variable is continuous or discrete, and (3) state whether the variable is quantitative or qualitative.

   A. A researcher records the month of birth for pre-K students.

   B. A teacher records the number of students who were absent for a final exam.

   C. A researcher asks children to choose which type of book they prefer (mystery, biography, science fiction, nonfiction, comedy). He records the choice of cereal for each child.

   D. A researcher measures the time (in seconds) that a teacher ignores a child with their hand raised before giving the child attention.

5. Rank the scales of measurement in order from least informative to most informative.

6. State the scale of measurement for each of the following variables:

   A. Number of parents who attend a parent-teacher conference

   B. The type of instruction (direct instruction or constructivist)

   C. Rating of school inclusiveness on a scale from 1 (*not inclusive*) to 10 (*very inclusive*)

   D. The ranking of a student's top five favorite music artists

7. A researcher measures leadership behavior using a new assessment she constructed with two subscales. Describe two ways the researcher could show that her new measure is reliable.

8. A researcher tests the hypothesis that female teachers are better at multitasking than male teachers. During an experimental session, female and male teachers completed as many classroom tasks as they could in 5 minutes. Three raters made judgments concerning the number of completed tasks for each participant. What type of reliability should the researcher demonstrate?

9. State four types of validity for research design.

10. A researcher operationally defines helping to tutor a peer. To demonstrate construct validity, what must the researcher show?

11. A researcher shows that students' self-efficacy, or belief in their abilities, can predict future college academic performance. Which type of criterion-related validity does this illustrate?

12. State whether each of the following examples is likely to have high or low content validity.

   A. A friend completely and honestly fills in the required fields concerning his personal information of a college application form.

   B. You find a job posting that does not explain key information concerning salary, benefits, and school location.

   C. A researcher measures the construct of teacher competence by having participants rate a group of characteristics known to be associated with it (e.g., caring, trustworthiness, commitment, content knowledge).

13. Explain three strategies that can minimize participant reactivity.

14. To avoid experimenter bias, a researcher conducts a double-blind study. Why is this is a good strategy to minimize experimenter bias?

15. Explain four strategies that can maximize the sensitivity of a measure and minimize range effects.

ACTIVITIES

1. Choose three of the following constructs and answer the questions below for each.

(1) Attractiveness	(2) Satisfaction	(3) Obsession
(4) Engagement	(5) Intelligence	(6) Spirituality
(7) Resilience	(8) Creativity	(9) Persuasiveness
(10) Success	(11) Popularity	(12) Learning
(13) Athleticism	(14) Leadership	(15) Social justice

   A. State two operational definitions for each construct. The operational definition for each construct must be on a different scale of measurement.

   B. State whether each external factor or operational definition is continuous or discrete and quantitative or qualitative.

   C. State the scale of measurement for each external factor or operational definition.

2. Write down the five most important characteristics you look for in a great teacher. For example, these characteristics may include compassion, leadership, sense of humor, intelligence, and attractiveness. For each characteristic you list, state whether it is a construct, and describe at least one way you would operationally define it.

3. The following three hypotheses have been tested in the published literature. You can use the citations to search for the full articles using ERIC. Choose one hypothesis, and answer the questions that follow.

Hypothesis 1: Parent involvement contributes to child adjustment in school (Hoglund, Jones, Brown, & Aber, 2015).

Hypothesis 2: Children who are deaf display lower levels of social competence (Hoffman, Quittner, & Cejas, 2015).

Hypothesis 3: Classrooms with a higher percentage of girls reduce the academic consequences associated with exposure to children with emotional and behavioral disorders (Gottfried & Harven, 2014).

A. Devise a research study to test one hypothesis and explain whether your study has face validity. How might you assess the reliability of your measure?

B. Explain two strategies you will use to minimize participant reactivity and to minimize experimenter bias.

C. Explain one strategy you will use to maximize the sensitivity of your measure.

$SAGE edge™

SAGE edge offers a robust online environment featuring an impressive array of free tools and resources for review, study, and further exploration, keeping both instructors and students on the cutting edge of teaching and learning.

Access practice quizzes, eFlashcards, video, and multimedia at **edge.sagepub.com/ priviterarme**.

Identify a problem

- Determine an area of interest.
- Review the literature.
- Identify new ideas in your area of interest.
- Develop a research hypothesis.

Develop a research plan

- Define the variables being tested.
- Identify participants or subjects and determine how to sample them.
- Select a research strategy and design.
- Evaluate ethics and obtain institutional approval to conduct research.

Generate more new ideas

- Results support your hypothesis—refine or expand on your ideas.
- Results do not support your hypothesis— reformulate a new idea or start over.

Communicate the results

- Method of communication: oral, written, or in a poster.
- Style of communication: APA guidelines are provided to help prepare style and format.

Conduct the study

- Execute the research plan and measure or record the data.

Analyze and evaluate the data

- Analyze and evaluate the data as they relate to the research hypothesis.
- Summarize data and research results.

After reading this chapter, you should be able to:

1 Identify the different types of data collection instruments that researchers use.

2 Distinguish between the different types of tests that researchers use.

3 Identify and construct open-ended, partially open-ended, and restricted questionnaire items.

4 Identify nine rules for writing valid and reliable questionnaire items.

5 Describe the different methods of administering questionnaires.

6 Distinguish between the different levels of structure in an interview.

7 Describe the types of documents used in research.

chapter
five

....

INSTRUMENTATION

....

In Chapter 4, we described how researchers define and measure variables involved in research. Sometimes we can measure variables directly such as speed, "How many words per minute does a student read correctly?" or how often a behavior occurs, "How many times does a student raise his or her hand to answer a question during math class?" Other variables such as achievement, personality, or stress have to be inferred through the administration of tests or surveys. In this chapter, we will review the various ways that researchers use to collect data on the variables of interest in their study. Researchers can use instruments such as tests or questionnaires, observations, interviews/focus groups, or existing data collected by others.

Understanding how researchers collect their data is important because the strength and quality of the study depend on the appropriateness and quality of the measure used to collect the data. Have you ever heard the phrase "Garbage in, garbage out?" This applies to research. If the data collected in a study are flawed, the results and interpretations are then also flawed. For example, let's say a researcher is studying the effects of a student collaboration technique on achievement of social studies knowledge. Instead of administering a test of social studies knowledge, the researcher administers a survey to teachers to estimate the students' knowledge. A survey of teachers is the best way to measure student knowledge so the conclusions drawn from this study are very limited. This chapter will describe and illustrate the various ways that researchers collect data.

> edge.sagepub.com/
> priviterarme
>
> - Take the chapter quiz
> - Review key terms with
>   eFlashcards
> - Explore multimedia links
>   and SAGE articles
>
>

5.1 Classifying Data Collection Instruments

We can classify data collection instruments by the process in which the data are collected and the type of data that are collected. Some forms of data collection involve instruments that administer a predetermined, standard set of items designed to measure a characteristic or skill of the participant. These are called **tests.** Tests can measure many different things in the areas of aptitude, achievement, or personality, but the outcome of a test is a numerical value that describes the performance of the individual taking the test. Some forms of data collection involve instruments to administer a predetermined, standard set of items designed to measure an attitude or perception of the participant. These are called questionnaires. The outcome of a questionnaire is often also numerical to describe the extent to which a participant subscribes to a certain attitude or perception, but some questionnaires include open-ended written responses, too. Other forms of data collection involve observing behavior in a naturalistic setting to describe the behavior. These are called observations. Observations can be numeric or narrative but are a more direct way to measure behavior since it is a firsthand way to measure behavior and not a self-report like tests or questionnaires. Sometimes researchers will ask questions directly to the participants and record their answers. These are called **interviews.** Interviews can be used to collect information about the attitudes and perceptions of individuals where the data are in a narrative form. Finally, researchers can use existing documents as a source of data. **Documents** are narrative data and might include such things as newspapers, TV news reports, or minutes of school meetings. In this chapter, we will review each of these types of data collection instruments in more detail. Table 5.1 summarizes the different data collection instruments.

> Using data collection instruments allows us to gather data across many behaviors of interest.

A **test** is a predetermined, standard set of items designed to measure a characteristic or skill.

Interviews are used to collect information about the attitude and perceptions of individuals one-on-one or in groups. They can be structured, semi-structured, or unstructured.

Documents are narrative data and might include such things as like newspapers, TV news reports, or minutes of school meetings.

An **unobtrusive observation** is a technique used by an observer to record or observe behavior in a way that does not interfere with or change a participant's behavior in a research setting.

Researchers use many techniques to make naturalistic observations. We use naturalistic observation to observe a behavior as it would naturally occur, so we typically do not want participants to know that they are being observed. In other words, we want to make **unobtrusive observations,** which are observations that do not interfere with or change a participant's behavior. If participants knew that they were being observed or were influenced by the observations made, then their behavior would not be a natural response in a natural setting—instead, their behavior would be a reaction to being observed. Making unobtrusive observations, then, can minimize or eliminate participant reactivity because participants do not know they are being observed using unobtrusive observation strategies. Four strategies used to make unobtrusive observations are introduced here.

- *Remain hidden.* To remain hidden, we can never be seen by participants. We could hide behind a curtain or one-way mirror, or we could place hidden cameras in

Table 5.1 Types of Data Collection Instruments

Type of Instrument	Type of Data	Description
Test	Numerical	A standard set of items in a prescribed way to all individuals taking the test to describe an individual's performance on the test.
Questionnaire	Numerical or narrative	A set of predetermined questions designed to measure an attitude or perception of the participant. They can have closed-ended or open-ended written responses.
Observation	Numerical or narrative	A direct way to measure behavior by observing behavior in a naturalistic setting to describe the behavior.
Interview	Narrative	Interviewers ask questions directly to the participants and record their answers. To describe their attitude and perceptions of individuals where the data are in a narrative form.
Documents	Narrative	Existing narrative materials such as school policies, videos, or Individual Education Plans (IEPs).

a research setting so that observations can be recorded surreptitiously. In both cases, we remain hidden and out of view of the participants.

- *Habituate participants to the researcher.* In some situations, we may need to be physically in the research setting. One strategy is to allow participants to habituate to, or get used to, our presence. For example, to observe students or a professor in the classroom, we can sit quietly in a classroom for a few class days before actually recording data. This allows for unobtrusive observations inasmuch as those in the classroom habituated to our presence.

- *Use a confederate.* To be present in a research setting, we can also employ a confederate or coresearcher. The confederate would play a role in the study, such as pretending to be a participant. If the confederate is convincing in that role, then he or she can make unobtrusive observations while being present in the research setting. The observations would be unobtrusive so long as participants viewed the confederate as "one of them."

- *Use indirect measures.* A clever strategy is to indirectly measure some behavior in a way that does not make obvious what it is that we are measuring. For example, we could measure recycling behavior by rummaging through trash or recycling bins, which is probably not fun but effective nonetheless. In this way, we can make unobtrusive observations in that our research does not "tip off" participants that they are being observed.

> Making unobtrusive observations minimizes participant reactivity in a setting; we can remain hidden, habituate participants to our presence, use a confederate, or use indirect measures.

5.2 Tests and Measures

There are many kinds of tests, but most administer a standard set of items in a prescribed way to all individuals taking the test. Tests will have a specific set of administration procedures so everyone takes the same test under the same set of circumstances. Having a uniform set of procedures for administering a test is an important element of a test. This way, an individual's performance on the test can be compared to other individuals' performance. We can classify tests according to (a) what they are measuring (aptitude, achievement, or personality), (b) the type of comparison and interpretation that is made by the test (norm referenced or criterion referenced), and (c) how it is intended to be used (whether they are large-scale, commercially available standardized tests, smaller locally developed tests, or researcher developed).

Standardized Aptitude, Achievement, and Personality Tests

A standardized test is a test that is commercially available with standardized test administration procedures, a set of calibrated items, and a uniform measure of the outcome of the test. Most educational standardized tests are typically scored correct or incorrect where there is one correct answer. You have likely taken a standardized test sometime during your lifetime. Examples include the Weschler Individual Achievement Test, GRE or SAT school admission tests, MMPI (Minnesota Multiphasic Personality Inventory), and the Stanford-Binet Intelligence Test.

A **standardized achievement test** is designed to measure current learned skills and knowledge associated with different age or grade levels. Some tests measure one content area such as reading comprehension or mathematical skills while others assess multiple content areas and are often called achievement batteries. General achievement tests determine whether an individual has learned the content expected at that age or grade level. Diagnostic achievement tests evaluate specific strengths and weaknesses in the content area. The test will sample the relevant content from the discipline with the assumption that the content has been delivered through effective instruction. Screening tests are quick assessments developed to primarily assess the readiness of a child to begin school by meeting developmental milestones. They can be used to identify children who may be "at risk" and in need of further evaluation for specialized assistance or services. Screening tests typically involve a variety of skills such as gross and fine motor skills, listening, and basic academic skills. These tests rely heavily on predictive validity and should be interpreted with caution because many factors influence a young child's readiness such as health and family environment.

In contrast, a **standardized aptitude test** is designed to measure the potential of an individual to learn and is used to predict future performance. You have likely heard of one type of aptitude test called an IQ test, a measure of intelligence or ability. The items on an aptitude test are not the type of skills directly taught in school. An aptitude test will include things like

> A **standardized achievement test** measures current learned skills associated with different age or grade levels.
>
> A **standardized aptitude test** measures the potential of an individual to learn and is used to predict future performance.

arranging blocks to match a design, complete a maze, or answer general knowledge questions such as "What should you do if a stranger asks you for money?" Aptitude tests assume that individuals have inherently different strengths and weaknesses, and they seek to measure this inherent ability. There are many different types of aptitudes such as verbal, mathematical, abstract, or verbal reasoning. Different careers require different types of skills so aptitude tests are often used to determine an individual's strengths in relation to the specific skills needed for a specific job. In education, we use aptitude tests to determine a student's ability to acquire the information being taught in school. In research, aptitude tests are rarely used to measure the effect of the independent variable since aptitude is inherent, not learned. Researchers may use aptitude tests instead as one way to describe the participants or in participant selection. Saleh, Lazonder, and Tong (2007) used ability testing to classify students as high, average, or low ability to examine the differential effects of structured collaborative learning of students with the different ability levels. One finding was that structured collaborative learning increased the verbal collaborative episodes for students with low and high ability but decreased the verbal collaborative episodes for students with average ability.

Selecting and evaluating the appropriateness of one of these standardized tests for use in a research study is based on several factors. First, commercially available, standardized achievement tests are not associated with any specific school or school system curriculum. So it is important to inspect the items to determine if they align with the curriculum and instruction actually provided to the participants. It is also important to evaluate the evidence of reliability and validity of the test. Recall our discussion of validity and reliability in Chapter 4, where reliability estimates the stability of the score derived from the test—stable across multiple times taking the test, across scorers, across multiple forms, or across items within the test. Validity evaluates the test's connection to theorized construct—if it is measuring what it says it is measuring through expert review of the content, its relationship to other tests measuring the same content, and the relationship of items to each other. An instrument used in research should have adequate reliability and validity in the measure of the content area. The selection of a standardized test should also consider the ability of the individual to access the items of the test adequately. For example, visual or hearing impairments or processing difficulties can interfere with an individual taking the test and may measure something other than the content

> A standardized test can be readily tested for reliability and validity of the instrument.

area. A researcher measuring mathematical ability of students with a reading disability would want to select a test that is not reliant on reading word problems.

> A **standardized personality test** measures an individual's affective traits or psychological makeup.

Standardized personality tests are tests that are designed to measure an individual's affective traits or psychological makeup. While some are used to identify psychopathology, in education, they are used to measure traits related to learning such as motivation, self-concept, cognitive style, and career interests. Most personality tests are self-report, whereby individuals respond to items on a questionnaire. The items are typically statements with which the individuals indicate whether the statement is true/not true of them. With children, some of these tests can be administered as in interviews to a parent/guardian or caregiver.

Norm-Referenced and Criterion-Referenced Tests

Instruments used in research can also be classified by the type of comparison or interpretations of the score obtained by taking the test. Have you ever taken a test where the instructor said they graded on a curve? This is a norm-referenced test, where your performance and grade were determined by the performance of others in the class who took that test. A test that compares one individual's performance on the test to other individuals' performance on the same test is called a norm-referenced test. The score obtained by an individual is compared to the performance of other individuals taking the same test. The comparison is made to a defined referent or norm group, typically of individuals of the same age. Norms are established when the test is developed by having many individuals take the test and statistically evaluating and classifying their performance. These tests will include items that are easy (correctly answered by most of the individuals taking the test), moderately difficult (correctly answered by some of the individuals taking the test), and difficult items (correctly answered by few of the individuals taking the test) so that test scores can be differentiated.

A **norm-referenced test** compares an individual's performance to the performance of others who took that test.

A **criterion-referenced test** compares an individual's performance on the test to a predetermined standard or criterion.

A test that compares one individual's performance on the test to a predetermined level of performance is called a criterion-referenced test. Instead of being compared to how others performed on the test, the comparison here is with a standard or criterion. The criterion is usually a percentage of items answered correctly and is usually paired with a description of the level of performance. Examples of common criterion-referenced tests are the test you took to get your driver's license and a college exam with an established grading scale where 90% = an A, 80% = a B, and so on. Many school systems and state boards of education use criterion-referenced scales such as "meet," "do not meet," or "exceed expectations" to classify the performance of schools and students. The criteria are established in advance and usually are developed through professional judgment to determine cut points for each level of the scale. This is also called standard setting. One form of criterion-based test often used in educational research is a curriculum-based measure (CBM). These tests are distinguished from other standardized tests in that they are very quick, often 1 to 2 minutes (e.g., how many words the student can read correctly in 1 minute), and are designed to be administered frequently for progress monitoring. DIBELS (Good & Kaminski, 2011) and AIMSweb (2014) are two popular CBMs.

Locally Developed Tests and Researcher-Developed Tests

All of the standardized tests that we have reviewed so far are large-scale, commercially available tests. But other smaller scale tests can be useful in research. *Locally developed tests* are designed to be used by a specific community. An example of a locally developed test is the annual state student performance test. Most states administer annual standardized achievement tests of student performance based on grade-level state education standards to measure the progress of students through the state-mandated curriculum. This type of testing was required by the No Child Left Behind Act of 2001. While many state curricula are based on standards aligned to national organizations such as the International Reading Association or the National Council of Teachers of Mathematics, the specific curricula upon which the tests are based vary from state to state. The types of scores and interpretations made of the scores on the tests are also very idiosyncratic. A passing score in one state may not be a passing score in another state. Although these tests are to be connected to the instruction being delivered in the classroom, more so than the large-scale standardized tests we described earlier in this section, states often revise or recalibrate their tests so they are not always comparable from year to year.

In addition to using large-scale, standardized tests, researchers and teachers often develop specific tests to assess the specific knowledge being taught. This is called a curriculum-based assessment (CBA) or curriculum-based measure (CBM). Both CBM and CBA are curriculum based, but the CBM is commercially available and not tied to a specific curriculum. When a teacher or researcher creates a test to use in his or her classroom, this is a CBA. When a teacher or researcher uses a test that accompanies a published curriculum, this is a CBM. CBAs are not commercially available while CBMs are; both are directly tied to the curriculum being taught.

Tests used in research come in many different forms to be used with specific purposes—as a general measure of achievement or personality or a measure of specific skills taught, to screen for or diagnose strengths and weaknesses. Researchers will often combine different subtests of these assessments to measure the skills involved in the research in different ways. A combination of standardized assessments and CBA (or CBM) is common. The CBA and CBM are *proximal measures* because they are closely tied to the curriculum being taught. The use of a published standardized assessment is a *distal measure* since it is not so closely tied to the curriculum being taught and can serve to illustrate that the learning is generalized to other assessments.

> A locally developed test is designed to be used by a specific community.

> A curriculum-based assessment is created by a teacher or researcher to directly measure what is taught.

> A curriculum based measure is created by a curriculum publisher to accompany the published curriculum.

> A proximal measure is closely tied to the intervention.

LEARNING CHECK 1 ✓

1. What are the five types of data collection instruments?

2. What do achievement tests, aptitude tests, and a personality test measure?

3. What is the difference between norm-referenced and criterion-referenced tests?

4. Is each of the following a locally developed test or researcher-developed test?

   A. A school system develops a test to measure character traits of students.

   B. A researcher develops a curriculum-based test of biology knowledge.

> A distal measure is not tied to the intervention to illustrate that learning is generalized.

Answers: 1. Test, questionnaire, interview, observation, document; 2. Achievement tests measure learned skills, aptitude tests measure potential to learn, and personality tests measure psychological traits. 3. Norm-referenced tests compare an individual's performance to other individuals' performance, and criterion-referenced tests compare an individual's performance to a set criterion. 4. A. Locally developed, B. researcher developed.

5.3 Types of Questionnaire Items

A **questionnaire** is a common measurement tool in the education sciences consisting of a series of questions or statements to which participants indicate responses. A survey can also be called a *self-report* questionnaire because many surveys specifically include questions in which participants report about themselves—their attitudes, opinions, beliefs, activities, emotions, and so on.

> A **questionnaire** is a series of questions or statements, called items, in print form or an interview to measure the self-reports or responses of respondents.

A **questionnaire** can be administered in printed form, or it can be distributed orally in an interview. While a questionnaire can be used as a measurement tool in many research designs, the survey research design specifically refers to the use of questionnaires in a systematic survey method to quantify, describe, or characterize an individual or a group. In this chapter, we will introduce the types and writing of questions included in questionnaires, how to administer surveys (i.e., survey method), and some limitations associated with using surveys in the education sciences. In Chapter 9, we will examine how to use questionnaires in a survey research design.

> A **respondent** is a person who has completed and returned a questionnaire.

A questionnaire consists of many questions or statements to which participants respond. A questionnaire is sometimes called a *scale*, and the questions or statements in the questionnaire are often called *items*. Three types of questions or statements can be included in a survey: open-ended items, partially open-ended items, and restricted items. Each type of item is described here.

Open-Ended Items

When researchers want participants to respond in their own words to a survey item, they include an **open-ended item** in the survey. An open-ended item is a question or statement that is left completely "open" for response. It allows participants to give any response they feel is appropriate with no limitations. For example, the following three items are open-ended questions that Holfeld and Leadbeater (2015) could also have asked:

> An **open-ended item** is a question or statement in a survey that allows the respondent to give any response in his or her own words, without restriction.

- What are your views on cyberbullying by girls (or boys)?

- How do you think the victims of cyberbullying feel?

- In what ways do you feel that you have been cyberbullied?

Open-ended items can also be given as a statement and not a question. For example, the researchers could have asked participants in the focus group to respond to the following survey item:

"Describe an experience you had as a victim of cyberbullying." In this example, the open-ended item is phrased as a statement and not a question; however, the response will still be open-ended.

Open-ended items are most often used with the qualitative research design because the responses in the survey are purely descriptive. For all other research designs—those that are quantitative—the challenge is in coding the open-ended responses of participants. It is difficult to anticipate how participants will respond to an open-ended item, so the researcher must develop methods to code patterns or similarities in participant responses. Coding the responses to open-ended items, however, requires researchers to do both of the following:

- Tediously anticipate and list all possible examples of potential responses in terms of how participants might write or express their responses.

- Use multiple raters and additional statistical analyses to make sure the coding is accurate.

For the reasons listed here, open-ended survey items are not often used in quantitative research, with partially open-ended or restricted items being favored among quantitative researchers.

Partially Open-Ended Items

Researchers can include items, called **partially open-ended items,** which give participants a few restricted answer options and then a last one that allows participants to respond in their own words in case the few restricted options do not fit with the answer they want to give. The open-ended option is typically stated as "other" with a blank space provided for the participant's open-ended response. For example, the Holfeld and Leadbeater (2015) study also included the following partially open-ended item:

> A **partially open-ended item** is a question or statement in a survey that includes a few restricted answer options and then a last one that allows participants to respond in their own words in case the few restricted options do not fit with the answer they want to give.

Which form of cyberbullying do you think is most harmful?
- A. Text message sent directly to the person
- B. Online post to social media
- C. Sharing a private picture with others
- D. Other ____

In this item, participants either chose an option provided (text message sent directly to the person, online post to social media, or sharing a private picture with others) or provided their own open-ended response (other ___). Using an online game could be another response not listed by the researchers that could have been recorded as "other." For the researchers, it is easier to manage the participant responses, or data, when an open-ended item includes a few restricted options. To enter participant responses, researchers can code each answer option as a number. The last open-ended option could be coded further or just analyzed without further coding. For example, we could report only the percentage of participants choosing the last open-ended option, without analyzing the specific open-ended responses given. In this way, coding and analyzing partially open-ended items can be less tedious than for open-ended items.

Restricted Items

The most commonly used survey item in quantitative research, called a *restricted* item (or interval scale), includes a restricted number of answer options. A restricted item does not give participants an option to respond in their own words; instead, the item is restricted to the finite number of options provided by the researcher. A **Likert scale** is the most common form of a restricted interval scale item. A Likert scale is named after Rensis Likert (Likert, 1932), who was the first to use a scale with a finite number of *points* to measure the level of agreement. Likert (pronounced lick-ert) scales use scale points of agreement, as illustrated below:

A **Likert scale** is a numeric response scale specifically to rate the level of agreement with a question or statement.

1	2	3	4
Strongly agree	Somewhat agree	Somewhat disagree	Strongly disagree

Another common application of a restricted interval scale is to have participants use the scale to describe themselves. For example, the responses to the item "I have been the victim of a cyberbully" could be set up this way:

I have been the victim of a cyberbully: (Circle one)

1	2	3
Never	A few times	Often

A response scale does not necessarily have to be numeric. For example, young children cannot count, let alone use numeric scales to describe themselves. The use of pictorial scales is common in special education research. In these cases, pictorial scales, such as the one shown in Figure 5.1, can be used. Reynolds-Keefer, Johnson, Dickenson, and McFadden (2009) used this pictorial scale to measure reading attitudes. The researchers coded each picture using a numeric scale; however, the children used the facial expressions to describe how much they liked reading.

The main advantage of using restricted interval scale items is that survey responses can be easily entered or coded for the purposes of statistical analysis. The main limitation of using restricted items is that the analysis is restricted to the finite number of options provided to participants. However, when the options available to participants are exhaustive of all options they could choose, this limitation is minimal.

1. State the type of survey item for each of the following items:

   A. How do you feel about the effectiveness of your professor's teaching style?

   B. On a scale from 1 (*very ineffective*) to 7 (*very effective*), how would you rate your professor?

   C. Is your professor's greatest strength his or her (a) teaching style, (b) knowledge of the material, (c) concern for students, or (d) other ___ (please explain)?

2. A _____ is a numeric response scale used to indicate a participant's rating or level of agreement with a question or statement.

Answers: 1. A. open-ended item, B. restricted item, C. partially open-ended item; 2. Rating or Likert scale.

5.4 Rules for Writing Survey Items

Writing survey items is a thoughtful endeavor. The items that you write must be valid and reliable. In other words, the items must actually measure what you are trying to measure (valid), and the responses in the survey should be consistently observed across participants and over time (reliable). When an item or a measure is not valid and reliable, it is often due to a *measurement error*, or variability in responding due to poorly written survey items. In this section, we describe the following nine rules used to write valid and reliable survey items that can minimize the likelihood of measurement error:

1. Keep it simple.

2. Avoid double-barreled items.

3. Use neutral or unbiased language.

4. Minimize the use of negative wording.

5. Avoid the response set pitfall.

6. Use rating scales consistently.

7. Limit the points on a rating scale.

8. Label or anchor the rating scale points.

9. Minimize item and survey length.

Keep It Simple

Everyone who takes a questionnaire should be able to understand it. The best strategy is to use less than a high school–level vocabulary in writing the survey items. We use this strategy to make sure that participants' responses reflect their actual responses and are not given because they are confused about what the question is asking. For example, we could have participants rate how full they feel by asking, "To what extent do you support *inclusion?*" However, some participants may not know that *inclusion* means to integrate a student with a disability to be educated in the general education all day, so it would be better to plainly ask, "To what extent do you support educating a student with a disability in the general education all day?" In sum, keep the language simple.

> Use simple words or language in a survey.

Avoid Double-Barreled Items

Ask only one question or give only one statement for each item. Double-barreled items are questionnaire items that ask participants for one response to two different questions or statements embedded in the same item. For example, to study

> Double-barreled items are survey items that ask participants for one response to two different questions or statements.

teacher's job satisfaction, we could ask participants to indicate their level of agreement with the following statement:

I love being a teacher and everything about it.

1	2	3	4	5	6
Strongly disagree	Moderately disagree	Slightly disagree	Slightly agree	Moderately agree	Strongly agree

This item for teacher's job satisfaction is double barreled. It is not necessarily true that people who love being a teacher also love everything about being a teacher. Any time a sentence uses a conjunction, such as *and*, it is likely that the item is double barreled. The solution is to split the question into separate items. For example, we can change the double-barreled item into two separate items, each with a separate rating scale. We could write the first item as "I love being a teacher" and the second item as "I love everything about teaching" to allow participants to give a separate response to each individual item.

> Do not use double-barreled items in a survey.

Use Neutral or Unbiased Language

Do not use *loaded terms*, or words that produce an emotional reaction, such as language that is or could potentially be considered offensive by a respondent. Potentially offensive language is inappropriate, and it can also lead people to respond in reaction to the language used rather than in reaction to the question itself. In other words, responses may be caused by the choice of wording in a survey item and may not reflect the honest response of the participant. Some suggestions include identifying persons 18 years and older as *women* and *men* and capitalizing *Black* and *White* to identify racial and ethnic groups. Person-first language is also required in many publications specializing in populations with a disability. Person-first language means that we refer (and think) about people as being a person first and the disability second. For example, we say "student with autism" not "the autistic student." The best way to avoid potentially offensive language is to know your audience. More guidelines are provided in the publication manual (APA, 2009).

Likewise, do not use *leading terms* or *leading questions*, or words or questions that indicate how people should respond to an item. For example, a leading question would be, "How bad are your problems with your boss?" In this example, it is implied that you have a problem, which may or may not be true. So the use of the word *bad* is a leading term in this sentence, and it should be removed. A better way to phrase this question would be, "What is the nature of your relationship with your boss?" In this case, you are not implying what the nature of that relationship is, and the respondent is not being led toward one response or another. Thus, the solution for fixing survey items with loaded terms or leading questions is often to simply rephrase or rewrite the item to avoid this pitfall.

> Use appropriate and unbiased language in surveys.

Minimize the Use of Negative Wording

The use of negative wording can trick participants into misunderstanding a survey item. *Negative wording* is the use of words in a sentence or an item that negates or indicates the opposite of what was otherwise described. The rule is to avoid asking participants in a survey item what they would *not* do, which can require rephrasing a sentence or survey item. For example, the survey item "How much do you *not* like working?" can be rephrased to "How much do you *dislike* working?" It may seem like a small change, but it can effectively reduce confusion.

Avoid the Response Set Pitfall

Avoid using negative wording in a survey item.

When respondents notice an obvious pattern in the responses they provide, they will often use that same pattern to respond to future items in that survey. For example, suppose we ask participants to indicate their level of agreement with the following items on a 5-point scale to measure student commitment to academic success:

I have the study skills needed for academic success.

I have the time management skills needed for academic success.

I monitor my progress toward academic success.

On the 5-point scale, suppose 1 indicates *strongly disagree* and 5 indicates *strongly agree*. For each item, *strongly agree* would be a rating of 5. If there were 20 questions like this, then participants would start to see a pattern, such as high ratings always indicate greater agreement. If participants are in general agreement, they may begin marking 5 for each item without reading many of the items because they know what the scale represents. However, the ratings participants give

A **response set** is the tendency for participants to respond the same way to all items in a survey when the direction of ratings is the same for all items in the survey.

would reflect the fact that they saw a pattern and may not necessarily reflect their true ratings for each item. To avoid this problem, called a **response set,** mix up the items in a survey so that ratings are not all on the same end of the scale for a given measure.

To illustrate how to avoid the response set pitfall, let's take the items from the student academic success items and 5-point Likert scale from above and add a fourth item.

Do not include predictable response patterns in a survey.

I have the study skills needed for academic success.

I have the time management skills needed for academic success.

I monitor my progress toward academic success.

I lack confidence in my academic success.

Notice that the last item is flipped—if participants agree, then they would rate on the low end of the scale for this last listed item only. If a questionnaire has a few items flipped like this, responses on this scale are unlikely to result from a response set. However, for the scale to make sense, higher overall ratings must indicate greater agreement. The first three items are stated such that higher scores do indicate greater agreement. Suppose, for example, a participant rates the first three items a 5. The participant's total score so far, then, is 5 × 3 items = 15.

The fourth item is a **reverse-coded item,** meaning that we need to code responses for the item in reverse order. The participant rates his or her response on the 1 to 5 scale, but when we score it, we will reverse it to a 5 to 1 scale. Hence, a 1 is scored as a 5, a 2 is a 4, a 3 remains a 3, a 4 is a 2, a 5 is scored as a 1. By doing so, a 5 for the reverse-coded item again indicates the highest agreement, and a 1 indicates the lowest agreement—consistent with the scale for the other items in the survey. Returning to our example, suppose that our participant rates the fourth item a 2. We reverse code this item and score it as a 4, then calculate the total score, which is 15 (first three items) + 4 (fourth item) = 19 (total score).

> A **reverse-coded item** is an item that is phrased in the semantically opposite direction of most other items in a survey and is scored by coding or entering responses for the item in reverse order from how they are listed.

Because the fourth item was reverse coded, the survey can now be scored such that higher scores indicate greater daily intake of sugar, and the survey can also be written so as to avoid a response set pitfall.

Use Rating Scales Consistently

Another rule is to use only one rating scale at a time. In the simplest scenario, use only one scale if possible. The B & C: PVWS Cyberbullying scale, for example, uses the same frequency scale for the eight items in the questionnaire from 0 (*never*) to 4 (*every day*). Having only one response scale makes it clear how respondents must respond to all items in a survey. If a survey must use two or more different scales, then the items in the survey should be grouped from one type of scale to the next. Begin with all items for one scale (e.g., items with a scale rated from *very dissatisfied* to *very satisfied*) and then give directions to clearly indicate a change in the scale for the next group of items (e.g., items with a scale rated from *not at all* to *all the time*). Consistent use of rating scales in a survey ensures that participants' responses reflect their true ratings for each item and not some confusion about the meaning of the scale used.

> Be clear about the rating scale(s) used in surveys.

Limit the Points on a Rating Scale

To construct a response scale, keep the scale between 5 and 8 points (Dillman, Smyth, & Christian, 2014). Experts in *psychometrics*, a field involved in the construction of measurement scales, suggest that response scales should have a midpoint or intermediate response level. Having fewer than 3 points on a response scale violates this suggestion, and response scales with more than 10 points can be too confusing.

There are two exceptions to the rule of limiting a rating scale to 3 to 10 points. One exception is that a 2-point scale is appropriate for dichotomous scales in which only two responses are possible. For example, dichotomous scales with true/false, yes/no, or agree/disagree as the response options are acceptable. A second exception is that **bipolar**

> **Bipolar scales** are response scales that have points above (positive values) and below (negative values) a zero point.

scales,those that have points above and below a zero point, can be 3 to 10 points above and below the zero point. Hence, a bipolar scale, such as the one shown below with 11 points, can have up to 21 points, or 10 points above and 10 points below zero.

How do you feel about your ability to find a teaching job that will make you happy?

| −5 | −4 | −3 | −2 | −1 | 0 | 1 | 2 | 3 | 4 | 5 |

Extremely pessimistic   No opinion   Extremely optimistic

> As a general rule, use 3 to 10 points on the rating scale for each item in a survey.

Label or Anchor the Rating Scale Points

> Anchor or label the end points of a rating scale.

Notice that in the examples of Likert and Likert-type scales that we have sometimes labeled all of the response points or only labeled some of them. To clearly indicate what a rating scale means, we use adjectives to describe the points of a rating scale. When we only label the end points of the scale, the labels are called **anchors.**Anchors are often listed below the end points on a rating scale, such as those given for the bipolar scale for the previous rule. An item that only labels the two end or anchor points is called a semantic differential scale. Notice also in the bipolar scale that the midpoint is labeled. Indeed, we can include anchors for the end points and label every other point on a scale if we choose.

> **Anchors**are adjectives that are given to describe the end points of a rating scale to give the scale greater meaning.

Minimize Item and Survey Length

> A semantic differential scale is one where only the two end anchor points are labeled.

As a general rule, you want to make sure that each item in a survey is as brief as possible. Being concise is important to ensure that respondents read the full item before responding. Likewise, a survey itself can be too long, although it is difficult to determine or define what constitutes "too long." The best advice is to write the survey to be as short and concise as possible, yet still able to convey or measure what it is intended to measure. Keep in mind that participants will fatigue or simply get tired of answering survey items. If this occurs, then a participant may start to "browse" survey items or even make up responses just to "get the survey over with." It is not to say that all participants will do this, but some will do this, and we want to avoid this problem of fatigue. The obvious solution is to make the survey and the items in the survey as brief or concise as possible. A survey that is no longer than 10 to 15 minutes is typically preferred to one that takes an hour to complete.

The time to complete a survey tends to be more important than the number of items in the survey. For example, a survey with a few open-ended items may take 15 to 20 minutes to complete, whereas a survey that has 30 restricted items may take only a minute or two to complete. To minimize survey length, then, the key goal is to minimize how long (over time) it takes a person to complete all items in a survey and not necessarily to minimize the number of items in the survey per se.

Other Types of Questionnaire Items

A restricted interval scaled item is only one way to create a questionnaire item. Other types of questionnaire items include checklist and **rank order scales.** A **checklist** is a list of items from which the respondent selects one or more options.

Which one of the following is the favorite part of your job?

- Collaborating with colleagues
- Professional development to improve my teaching skills
- Interacting with the children
- Mentoring preservice teachers
- Monitoring student academic progress
- Instructional time in class
- Interacting with parents

> A **rank order scale** is a scale to order the options in a sequence such as preference, priority, or desire.
>
> A **checklist** is a list of items from which the respondent selects one or more options.

The item could be stated in this way using the same list of options, but now the respondent selects all that apply instead of one. "Which of the following contribute to your satisfaction with your job: (Check all that apply)."

A rank order item asks the respondent to order the options in a sequence. Rank ordering an item can provide additional information about the importance or preference of a respondent. Perhaps a respondent selected all four items when asked which ones contribute to job satisfaction above or responded strongly agree to all the items in a Likert scale. We can get more information if we ask the respondent to rank order the items. Using the same options, we could state the item this way: "With 1 being the biggest contributor and 7 being the least contributor, rank order the following items from 1 to 7 in their contribution to your satisfaction with your job."

Minimize item and survey length.

LEARNING CHECK 3 ✓

1. Which rule or rules for writing survey items does each of the following items violate? Note: Assume that each item is rated on a 5-point scale from 1 (*completely untrue*) to 5 (*completely true*):

   A. I am a likable person and my students like me.

   B. On a scale from 1 (*very unlikely*) to 13 (*very likely*), what are the chances you will still be working in the education field 5 years from now?

   C. There is a problem with white flight from inner-city public schools.

   D. Misogynistic men do not make good high school teachers.

2. True or false: How an item is worded can affect the reliability and validity of responses given for that item.

Answers: 1. A. avoid double-barreled items, B. limit the points on a rating scale, C. use neutral or unbiased language, D. keep it simple and minimize the use of negative wording; 2. True.

5.5 Administering Questionnaires

Once a questionnaire is constructed, it is administered to participants in a systematic fashion using a survey method. A questionnaire can be written (in print or electronically) or spoken (such as in an interview). A written questionnaire can be administered in person, by mail, or using the Internet. An interview questionnaire can be administered face to face, by telephone, or in focus groups. Each method of administering a questionnaire is described in this section.

Written Surveys

In-person surveys. A method that can effectively get participants to respond to a survey is to be physically present while participants complete the survey. The reason that more participants are willing to complete a survey administered in person is that you, the researcher, can be there to explain the survey, observe participants taking the survey, and answer any questions they may have while they complete the survey. This method is more time-consuming, however, because it requires the researcher to be present while each and every participant completes the survey.

Mail surveys. An alternative that can require less of the researcher's time is to send the questionnaire in the mail. However, mail questionnaires pose the potential risk of respondents choosing not to complete and return them to the researcher (i.e., nonresponse). Mail questionnaires can also be costly in terms of both the time it takes to prepare the surveys (e.g., printing and addressing surveys) and the money spent to send them out to potential respondents (e.g., postage stamps and envelopes) but not as costly as in-person questionnaires. The following are four strategies that can increase how many people complete and return a mail questionnaire:

- Include a return envelope with the return postage already paid.

- Let potential respondents know in advance that the survey is being sent.

- Include a cover letter detailing the importance of completing the survey.

- Include a gift for the potential respondent to keep, such as a pen or gift card.

Internet surveys. A popular and cost-effective survey option is to administer surveys online. This option is inexpensive in that a questionnaire can be administered to a large group of potential respondents with little more than a click of a button. Online surveys can be administered via links provided in an e-mail or using online questionnaire construction sites, such as SurveyMonkey.com. The main concern for using online surveys is that the results of these surveys may be limited to individuals who have access to computers with online capabilities and to individuals who know enough about using computers that they can complete and submit the questionnaire correctly. When comparing the rates of response to Internet and mail surveys, despite being in the "digital age," more people will respond to a mail survey than an Internet-based survey (Dillman et al., 2014).

> A written survey can be administered in person, by mail, or using the Internet.

Teachers can administer a questionnaire to obtain opinions or information from students. The use of a questionnaire is almost endless. Here are some ideas where a questionnaire can be useful to a teacher.

1. What students think of a certain classroom activity
2. How much time they spend studying or doing homework
3. How they study
4. Outside class interests that may be incorporated into class
5. How they feel about their teacher
6. School climate
7. Experiences with bullying
8. Getting to know students such as favorite song or TV show
9. Access to technology
10. Fundraising ideas

Interview Surveys

Face-to-face interviews. A researcher could administer a survey orally to one participant at a time or to a small group. The advantage of a face-to-face interview is that the researcher can control how long it takes to complete the survey inasmuch as it is the researcher asking the questions. The drawback of face-to-face interviews is that they require the interviewer to be present for each survey and can be prone to interviewer bias, meaning that the interviewer's demeanor, words, or expressions in an interview may influence the responses of a participant. For this reason, face-to-face interviews, while used in quantitative research, tend to be more commonly applied in qualitative research for which interviewing is a primary method used to describe an individual or a group.

> **Interviewer bias** is the tendency for the demeanor, words, or expressions of a researcher to influence the responses of a participant when the researcher and the participant are in direct contact.

Telephone questionnaires. A questionnaire can also be administered via the telephone. Phone interviews can be interpersonal (e.g., the researcher asks the questions) or automated (e.g., computer-assisted technology asks the questions). One advantage of automated telephone questionnaires is that they can save time and reduce the likelihood of interviewer bias. Another advantage is that telephone questionnaires can be administered at random by generating telephone numbers at random from within the area or region using random digit dialing from phone numbers listed in the phone directory. The key disadvantage of telephone questionnaires is that they often result in few people willingly agreeing to complete the questionnaire. Also, the passage of new laws restricting telephone surveying and the increased reliance on cellphones with unlisted phone numbers has made this method of administering questionnaires less common in the education sciences.

Each questionnaire administration method described here can vary substantially on how effectively researchers obtain representative samples. Obtaining representative samples is important because survey methods are often used for the purpose of learning about characteristics in a population of interest. For example, we sample a few potential voters to identify the candidate who is likely to obtain the most votes in the population, not just among those sampled. Therefore, it is important that the sample we select to complete a questionnaire is representative of the population. It is important to understand the population that is being studied to understand what type of survey administration may result in the most responses.

Administering a questionnaire in person or face to face can make it more likely that we can obtain a representative sample in some populations like older adults. Administering the questionnaire by mail, telephone, or Internet, on the other hand, may limit the representativeness of our sample because a smaller proportion of those who receive the survey will respond and actually complete the questionnaire but may be the preferred method for a younger population. Issues related to this problem of response rate are discussed in Section 9.5 in Chapter 9.

Random digit dialing is a strategy for selecting participants in telephone interviews by generating telephone numbers to dial or call at random.

5.6 Interviewing

Our fourth form of data collection instrument is an interview. An interview is a series of questions that are presented to a participant and the responses are verbal. The responses are typically recorded verbatim using a recording device and transcribed later. Interviews require establishing **rapport** with the person being interviewed so that the individual(s) are motivated to respond honestly. A properly conducted interview can obtain more in-depth information than a questionnaire because the interviewer can ask follow-up questions based on the responses of the interviewee. The interviewer can also observe the behavior of the person being interviewed, which may also lead to further questioning. Interviews are also helpful when a written questionnaire is not possible such as with young children or individuals with disabilities who are unable to read or write or those who need extra support to respond.

The term **rapport** is used to describe a relationship in which people understand the feelings and ideas of others and communicate them well.

A **structured interview** is an interview with a specific set of questions and response options.

A **semi-structured interview** is an interview with a set of questions that are presented to all the individuals being interviewed but the responses are open-ended.

Interviews can be structured, semi-structured, or unstructured. A **structured interview** is an interview with a specific set of questions and response options. A face-to-face questionnaire is an example of a structured interview. The interviewer reads closed-ended questions and response options like a questionnaire item verbatim and records the answer by marking the option selected by the interviewee. Structured interviews are presented to the person being interviewed in the same way—same questions, same order, and same response options. They are quantitative, where each of the response options is assigned a numerical value just like a written questionnaire. A **semi-structured interview** is an interview with a set of questions that are presented to all the individuals being interviewed but the responses are open-ended. "What are the characteristics of an effective teacher?" is an example of a semi-structured interview question. The interviewee is allowed to answer orally without the use of specific choices. This type of interview also allows for follow-up questions to clarify and expand upon a response. Unstructured interviews are interviews where there is no predetermined set of questions. The interviewer has a general idea of the types of questions to be asked, but the questions can differ from interviewee to interviewee. Pillay, Dunbar-Krige, and Mostert (2013) used an unstructured interview with students with socioemotional behavioral disorder about reintegrating back into the classroom after a period of time in a specialized learning environment. The students completed a series of incomplete sentences and wrote a life essay. By using an unstructured interview, the researchers could ask specific questions based on the information contained in the incomplete sentence and life essay task of each student.

> Unstructured interviews are interviews where there is no predetermined set of questions.

Earlier when discussing face-to-face questionnaires, we defined interviewer bias as the tendency for the demeanor, words, or expressions of a researcher to influence the responses of a participant when the researcher and the participant are in direct contact. This is also called interviewer effect. Bias sounds more insidious, involving preexisting views that influence what the interviewer sees and hears, but the effect that an interviewer can have on the interviewee is broader than that. It is very important that an interviewer be trained in interviewing practices to avoid unintentional interviewer effect. Gaining rapport with the person being interviewed is an essential element to interviewing. The interviewer should be pleasant and engaging in order to develop a relationship with the interviewee so the interviewee feels comfortable in sharing personal information. Sometimes the characteristics of the interviewer, such as ethnicity or age, can influence an interviewee under certain circumstances. In such cases, matching an interviewee with an interviewer of similar personal characteristics may be necessary.

Interviews can also be conducted in groups called focus groups. *Focus group interviews* are interviews where participants interact in response to the question posed by the interviewer. Focus groups are usually a small group of about three to eight people. Questionnaire items in a focus group are mostly open-ended, and the researcher plays more of a moderator role than an interviewer role. The goal of a focus group is to get participants talking to each other so that they share their ideas and experiences on a predetermined topic. The conversations are typically recorded and then analyzed. While focus groups can reveal new directions and ideas for a given research topic, they are associated with the same problems mentioned for face-to-face interviews.

> An interview questionnaire can be administered face to face, individually or in groups, by telephone, or in focus groups.

5.7 Ethics in Focus: Maintaining Confidentiality of Collected Data

Existing documents can also be a source of information for researchers conducting qualitative research. They can serve as the primary source of information or in addition to other types of data collection instruments. The term *document* is used broadly to include such things as published records like newspapers or meeting minutes, photographs, social media posts, and media files like videos or audio recordings. Ahlgrim-Delzell and Rivera (2015) used existing video recordings of teachers' classroom literacy lessons from 2004 and 2010 to illustrate the changes in the teachers' understanding of literacy. Grove (2014) reviewed school policies, school curriculum, and teacher lesson plans to explore student learning experiences with narratives (oral retelling) as they progress through the curriculum. Document reviews involve a process of analyzing the content of the document called content analysis, which we discuss further in Chapter 20.

Regardless of how data are collected, it is a responsibility of the researcher to keep the information collected in confidence. One way that researchers can maintain confidentiality is to not use the participant's real name during the data collection process. During an interview, the researcher can ask the participant to select a pseudonym or fake name to use during the interview to avoid using his or her real name. In focus group interviews, the researcher may even have nametags or card tents to place in front of the individual and ask the participants to write down their preferred pseudonyms. A second way researchers can maintain confidentiality is to provide participants with a numerical identification number. A list of the participant names and the assigned identification numbers are kept separately from the data that are collected. These numbers are then used on the data that are collected and in the databases that store the information. If real names are collected on forms and included in the database during the time that data are being collected, a third way that researchers can maintain confidentiality is to delete the names from the electronic records once all the data are collected. Whenever names are paired with collected data, these files must be stored in such a way as to prevent access by unauthorized personnel. The researcher can keep the files in a locked filing cabinet if the data are collected on paper, use a password on the computer where the electronic data are stored, or in the case of very sensitive information, encryption of the file may be needed. It is the researchers' responsibility to ensure that confidentiality of the information they collect is maintained in a manner to prevent breach of confidentiality.

LEARNING CHECK 4 ✓

1. Why is it important that an interviewer receive training before conducting interviews?

2. Which of the following type of interview is most likely being used: unstructured, semi-structured, or structured?

   A. A principal interviews students involved in an altercation in the cafeteria. She is trying to find out what happened.

   B. A researcher conducts an interview with a set of specific questions but asks follow-up questions to get more in-depth information.

   C. You receive a phone call to participate in a questionnaire. The interviewer reads the question and the four response options that you choose from.

3. A researcher is studying cyberbullying. What type of documents might the researcher want to review?

Answers: 1. To learn how to avoid unintentional interviewer effect and how to gain rapport; 2. A. unstructured, B. semi-structured, structured; 3. Emails, tweets, Facebook posts, Instagram photos.

LO 1 Identity the different types of data collection instruments that researchers use.

- *Tests* are instruments that administer a predetermined, standard set of items designed to measure a characteristic or skill of the participant. Educational tests measure achievement, aptitude, or personality.

- *Questionnaires* are self-report instruments where individuals describe their attitude or perception. Questionnaires can be open-ended or closed-ended.

- *Observations* involve observing behavior in a naturalistic setting to describe the behavior firsthand. They can be numeric or narrative.

- *Interviews* are used to collect information about the attitude and perceptions of individuals one-on-one or in groups. They can be structured, semi-structured, or unstructured.

- *Documents* are narrative data that seek to obtain information from written works such as newspapers, TV news reports, or minutes of meetings.

LO 2 Distinguish between the different types of tests that researchers use.

- A **standardized achievement test** measures current learned skills associated with different age or grade levels.

- A **standardized aptitude test** measures the potential of an individual to learn and is used to predict future performance.

- A **standardized personality test** measures an individual's affective traits or psychological makeup.

- A **norm-referenced test** compares an individual's performance to the performance of others who took that test.

- A **criterion-referenced test** compares an individual's performance on the test to a predetermined standard or criterion.

- A locally developed test is designed to be used by a specific community.

- A researcher-developed test is one made by the researchers specifically for the study.

LO 3 Identify and construct open-ended, partially open-ended, and restricted questionnaire items.

An **open-ended item** is a question or statement in a survey that allows the respondent to give any response in his or her own words, without restriction. This type of question is most often used in qualitative research.

A **partially open-ended item** is a question or statement in a survey that includes a few restricted answer options and then a last option that allows participants to respond in their own words in case the few restricted options do not fit with the answer they want to give.

A restricted item is a question or statement in a survey that includes a restricted number of answer options to which participants must respond. This type of question is most often used in quantitative research.

LO 4 Identify nine rules for writing valid and reliable questionnaire items.

Nine rules for writing valid and reliable survey items are as follows:

- Keep it simple.
- Avoid double-barreled items.
- Use neutral or unbiased language.
- Minimize the use of negative wording.
- Avoid the response set pitfall.
- Use rating scales consistently.
- Limit the points on a rating scale.
- Label or anchor the rating scale points.
- Minimize survey length.

LO 5 Describe the different methods of administering questionnaires.

A survey can be written (in print or electronically) or spoken (such as in an interview). A written survey can be administered in person, by mail, or using the Internet. An interview survey can be administered face to face, by telephone, or in focus groups. In-person and face-to-face surveys have the best response rates. Also, written surveys are preferred to interview surveys in quantitative research partly because interviews are prone to a possible interviewer bias.

LO 6 Distinguish between the different levels of structure in an interview.

- A structured interview is an interview with a specific set of questions and response options.
- A semi-structured interview is an interview with a set of questions that are presented to all the individuals being interviewed but the responses are open-ended.
- Unstructured interviews are interviews where there is no predetermined set of questions.

LO 7 Describe the types of documents used in research.

- Documents are existing materials such as published written works, photographs, video or audio recordings, or social media.

anchors 142

bipolar scales 141

checklist 143

criterion-referenced
    test 132

documents 128

double-barreled
    item 138

focus group 147

interviewer bias 145

interviewer effect 147

interviews 128

Likert scale 136

norm-referenced
    test 132

open-ended item 134

partially open-ended
    item 135

questionnaire 134

rank order scale 143

rapport 146

response set 140

reverse-coded item 141

semi-structured
    interview 146

standardized achievement
    test 130

standardized aptitude
    test 130

standardized personality
    test 131

structured interview 146

test 128

unobtrusive observation 128

unstructured interview 147

REVIEW QUESTIONS

1. Which form of data collection is best used to study the following topics?
   A. Mathematics knowledge
   B. Disposition to be a teacher
   C. Readiness to begin kindergarten
   D. The opinion of parent satisfaction with their child's education
   E. Why an 11th grader is truant from school

2. Distinguish between an open-ended and a partially open-ended question.

3. Identify the problem or flaw with each of the following survey items. Assume that each item is rated on a 5-point scale from 1 (*strongly disagree*) to 5 (*strongly agree*).
   A. I hate driving behind old people.
   B. I am happy when I am teaching, and I do not like the other responsibilities.
   C. I have difficulty engaging in convoluted situations.

4. State two problems with the following scale for a survey item:

1	2	3	4	5	6	7	8	9	10	11

   Neither agree or disagree

5. State four strategies that researchers use to make unobtrusive observations.

6. A researcher in a gym setting makes observations without anyone being seen from an observation room. What type of strategy did the research use to make unobtrusive observations?

7. What does it mean for a researcher to habituate participants to his or her presence?

8. Measuring recycling behavior by rummaging through trash or recycling bins is an example of what type of measure?

9. Develop one semi-structured and one structured interview question that you might ask at a parent-teacher conference.

10. What types of interviews consist of no predetermined set of questions?

ACTIVITIES

1. Think about all the ways that your school system measures student, teacher, and school outcomes. What kinds of measures do they use?

2. Follow the eight rules for writing valid and reliable items to construct a short 6- to 10-item questionnaire to measure a behavior that you are interested in. Then give the questionnaire to at least five people, and summarize the responses given for each item in your survey.

3. Choose a quantifiable behavior and someone to observe. Decide what observation strategy you will use (interval, frequency, duration, or latency). Develop a way to record the behavior. Observe and record the behavior.

4. Select a topic of interest to you. Write some semi-structured and structured interview questions and select a few people to interview. What things did you do to gain rapport?

$SAGE edge™

SAGE edge offers a robust online environment featuring an impressive array of free tools and resources for review, study, and further exploration, keeping both instructors and students on the cutting edge of teaching and learning.

Access practice quizzes, eFlashcards, video, and multimedia at edge.sagepub.com/priviterarme.

Identify a problem

- Determine an area of interest.
- Review the literature.
- Identify new ideas in your area of interest.
- Develop a research hypothesis.

Generate more new ideas

- Results support your hypothesis—refine or expand on your ideas.
- Results do not support your hypothesis—reformulate a new idea or start over.

After reading this chapter, you should be able to:

1. Explain why researchers select samples that are representative of a population of interest.

2. Distinguish between subjects and participants as terms used to describe those who are subjected to procedures in a research study.

3. Distinguish between probability sampling methods and nonprobability sampling methods.

4. Delineate two nonprobability sampling methods: convenience sampling and quota sampling.

5. Delineate four probability sampling methods: simple random sampling, stratified random sampling, systematic sampling, and cluster sampling.

6. Define and explain sampling error and the standard error of the mean.

7. Define and explain sampling bias and nonresponse bias.

8. Identify potential ethical concerns related to sampling at schools.

Develop a research plan

- Define the variables being tested.
- Identify participants or subjects and determine how to sample them.
- Select a research strategy and design.
- Evaluate ethics and obtain institutional approval to conduct research.

Conduct the study

- Execute the research plan and measure or record the data.

Communicate the results

- Method of communication: oral, written, or in a poster.
- Style of communication: APA guidelines are provided to help prepare style and format.

Analyze and evaluate the data

- Analyze and evaluate the data as they relate to the research hypothesis.
- Summarize data and research results.

chapter
six

SAMPLING FROM POPULATIONS

As a student, you have surely had a teacher hand out grades for an exam you took earlier. Given the strong tendency for students to compare themselves to other students, you have likely on occasion asked students sitting near you to tell you their grade on the same exam—to get a better sense of how you performed on the exam. If the few people you ask all did worse than you on the exam, then you will probably feel much better; if they all did better than you, then you will probably feel worse.

The reason you did not ask all students in the class how they did on the exam is because of the constraints of the class. When you received your grade, your class was in session. You certainly could not walk to the front of the class and take a poll. Instead, the only students who could be quickly polled without disrupting the class were the students near where you were sitting. In this example, the population was all students in class who took the exam, and the sample was the few students who told you their grade. In science, we likewise have constraints that require us to select samples to understand behavior in a population. For example, human behaviors, such as love or depression, are expressed in all people. We certainly cannot ask all people how they experience these behaviors, so we ask only a few of them who are accessible or close by.

Now of course we still need to consider that only a few people were asked. Why, for example, did asking only a few students make you feel so much more confident in how well or poorly you performed on the exam? An answer requires an understanding of how samples are selected from populations, as is explored in this chapter. Specifically, in this chapter, we explore approaches that educational researchers take to select samples from populations so that we can be confident that the observations made in a sample will also be observed in the larger population.

6.1 Why Do Researchers Select Samples?

A population can be identified as any group of interest. A population is specifically a group that a researcher is interested in answering a question about. For example, suppose you ask why high school students join school clubs. In this case, students who join school clubs make up the group, called the population, that you are interested in. You identified a population of interest just as researchers identify populations they are interested in.

Remember that researchers select samples mostly because they do not have access to all individuals in a population. Imagine having to identify every student who has been absent from school, experienced test anxiety, been bullied, suffered with depression, or did not eat breakfast before coming to school. It is not possible for us to identify all individuals in such populations. So researchers use data gathered from samples (a portion of individuals from the population) to make inferences concerning a population.

To make sense of this, suppose you want to get an idea of how teachers in general feel about a new state testing policy. To find out, you ask 20 teachers at random throughout the day whether or not they like the new testing policy. Now, do you really care about the opinion of only those 20 teachers you asked? Not really—you actually care more about the opinion of teachers in general. In other words, you only asked the 20 teachers (your sample) to get an idea of the opinions of teachers in general (the population of interest). Sampling from populations follows a similar logic, and in this chapter, we introduce strategies that researchers use to select samples from populations. We then describe many of the errors, biases, and ethical concerns related to sampling, particularly when we select human participants.

> Researchers select samples to learn more about populations of interest to them.

6.2 Subjects, Participants, and Sampling Methods

Sampling from populations is unique in that researchers thoughtfully determine what groups to study and how to select them for a study. To begin, we distinguish between *participants* and *subjects* based on ethics guidelines provided by the American Psychological Association (APA, 2009). We also introduce the categories of sampling that are described in this chapter.

Subjects and Participants

Using the APA (2009) guidelines provided in the code of conduct, we refer to humans as **participants** and nonhuman groups as **subjects.** The reason for this distinction is in the semantics of how we use language. A "subject of research" implies that an individual is subjected to the study, regardless of his or her consent. This is not the case with

> The term **participant** is used to describe a human who volunteers to be subjected to the procedures in a research study.
>
> The term **subject** is used to describe a nonhuman that is subjected to procedures in a research study and to identify the names of research designs.

human groups because humans provide informed consent prior to participation, and only upon signing the consent form will they participate in a study. Therefore, humans are participants in a study inasmuch as they voluntarily choose to participate. Nonhuman groups, however, do not volunteer. Instead, the researchers and ethics review boards (i.e., an institutional animal care and use committee; see Chapter 3) decide for these groups whether or not they will be subjected to the procedures in a study. In this way, then, nonhuman groups are subjects in research, and humans are participants. This distinction is made throughout the book.

The term *subject* is also used to identify the names of research designs. For example, as will be described in Chapters 10 and 11, when different participants or subjects are observed in each group, the research design is called a *between-subjects design;* when the same participants or subjects are observed in each group, the research design is called a *within-subjects design. Subjects* is used to identify each research design, regardless of whether human or nonhuman groups are studied.

Selecting Samples From Populations

When researchers identify a population of interest, the population they identify is typically very large. For this reason, researchers often categorize populations as being a target population or an accessible population.

The target population is all members of a group of interest to a researcher. The target population of interest to a researcher is typically very large—so large that we can rarely select samples directly from it. For example, suppose we want to study school choice and what is most important to parents in choosing a school for their child or children. In this example, the target population of interest is prospective U.S. students. The size of that population is very large and spread out across the country. We could not possibly give all members of this group an opportunity to participate in our study.

> A target population is all members of a group of interest to a researcher.
>
> The accessible population, also called the sampling frame, is the portion of the target population that can be clearly identified and directly sampled from.

By contrast, an accessible population, also called the sampling frame, is a portion of the target population that can be clearly identified and directly sampled from. The sampling frame is a smaller group of the target population. It is a specific list of potential participants that is representative of the target population. This group is generally in close proximity to the researcher, such that all members of the accessible population could potentially have an opportunity to participate in a study. For example, we could identify parents at one or more local elementary schools (the sampling frame) and select a sample of parents from that accessible population to represent larger target population of parents.

While most samples are selected from accessible populations as represented in the sampling frame, the goal is still to describe characteristics in the target population. In other words, researchers select samples to learn more about the characteristics of individuals in a target population. However, as illustrated in Figure 6.1, most samples are selected from an accessible population, and characteristics in an accessible population are not always the same as those in the larger target population. For this reason,

Researchers typically select samples from an accessible population and generalize observations made with samples to the target population of interest.

Figure 6.1   The Process of Nonprobability Sampling

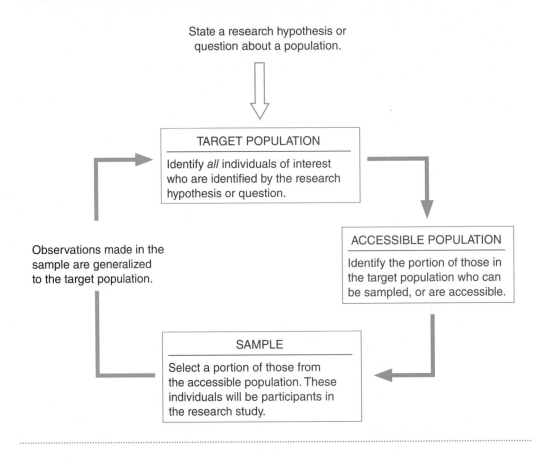

State a research hypothesis or
question about a population.

TARGET POPULATION

Identify *all* individuals of interest
who are identified by the research
hypothesis or question.

ACCESSIBLE POPULATION

Identify the portion of those in
the target population who can
be sampled, or are accessible.

Observations made in the
sample are generalized
to the target population.

SAMPLE

Select a portion of those from
the accessible population. These
individuals will be participants in
the research study.

researchers must use careful procedures that allow them to select samples from accessible
populations that mimic or have similar characteristics as those in the target population.

If researchers want to generalize the results they observe in a sample to those in
the target population, then they need to make certain that the sample is representative of
the target population. A **representative sample**
is a sample that has characteristics that resemble
those in the target population. This can be difficult
when we know little about the characteristics of
individuals in a target population. However, when
we do know about characteristics in the target population, then we can use a sampling
procedure that ensures that those characteristics will also be represented or included in the
sample that is selected from that population.

A **representative sample** is one in which the
characteristics of individuals or items in the sample
resemble those in a target population of interest.

The methods that researchers use to select samples from one or more populations
can be categorized as probability and nonprobability sampling. **Probability sampling** is
a category of sampling in which a sample is selected directly from the target population;

nonprobability sampling is a category of sampling in which a sample is selected from the accessible population. Sampling directly from the target population using probability sampling is possible in situations in which the exact probability of selecting each individual in a target population is known.

However, it is rare that researchers know the exact probability of selecting each individual in a target population because it is difficult to identify all individuals in very large populations, let alone know the exact probability of selecting each individual. For this reason, nonprobability sampling methods, which are discussed in the next section, are most commonly used to select samples in educational research.

Probability sampling is a category of sampling in which a sample is selected directly from the target population. Probability sampling methods are used when the probability of selecting each individual in a population is known and every member of the population has an equal chance of being selected.

Nonprobability sampling is a category of sampling in which a sample is selected from the accessible population. Nonprobability sampling methods are used when it is not possible to select individuals directly from the target population.

LEARNING CHECK 1 ✓

1. Distinguish between subjects and participants based on guidelines provided by the APA.

2. Distinguish between a target population and an accessible population.

3. Why is it important to select a representative sample?

4. Which type of sampling, probability or nonprobability sampling, involves selecting participants from the accessible population?

Answers: 1. Subjects are nonhumans that are subjected to procedures in a research study, and this term is also used to identify the names of research designs. Participants are humans who are subjected to procedures in a research study; 2. The target population is all members in a group or population of interest to a researcher. The accessible population is a portion of the target population that can be clearly identified and directly sampled from; 3. Because researchers want to generalize the results they observe in a sample to those in the target population; 4. Nonprobability sampling.

6.3 Methods Of Sampling: Nonprobability Sampling

Researchers can rarely identify all members of a target population, which is why they often select samples from an accessible population that can be identified and listed in the sampling frame. For example, suppose a study investigates neural response patterns in the brain of participants as the participants study. In this example, the target population is all people who study. It would be difficult to identify this entire group, so an accessible population—of a group of schools, for example—would be identified and sampled from. Hence, researchers use nonprobability sampling, as illustrated in Figure 6.1, when it is not possible to identify all members of a target population. Two types of nonprobability sampling methods discussed in this section are convenience sampling and quota sampling.

Convenience Sampling

Convenience sampling is a method of sampling in which subjects or participants are selected for a research study based on how easy or convenient it is to reach or access them and based on their availability to participate.

A **convenience sample,** as indicated in the name, is selected out of convenience or ease, meaning that participants are selected based on their availability to participate. A commonly used sampling method in experimentation is to select college students, who are the most convenient sample available to many behavioral researchers. The reason that college students are the most convenient group to sample from is because many college behavioral science professors conduct their research at the university or college by which they are employed.

Many educational researchers are also university professors. Other educational researchers are employed by not-for-profit organizations or for-profit businesses. Instead of college students, they create a subject pool of school-aged children, school employees, or parents from school districts located near them. The educational researchers form relationships with local school system administrators to be able to conduct research with teachers, students, and/or parents. School systems often have specific policies related to what kind of research can be conducted in schools and under what conditions school employees and students can participate in research. The reason these subject pools are created is so that researchers can have access to a group that is available to participate in educational research. Selecting a sample from a local school district is an example of convenience sampling. The ethical implications of creating subject pools for the purposes of research are described in Section 6.8.

A subject pool is a group of accessible and available participants for a research study. In educational settings, a subject pool is created using school system policies that allow students, parents, and school employees to participate in educational research under certain conditions.

A drawback of convenience sampling is that it does not ensure that a sample will be representative of the target population because the sample was selected out of convenience—a "first come, first serve" kind of approach. In a convenience sample, more convenient individuals have a better chance of being selected than those who are less convenient. Because we cannot know how "convenient" and "inconvenient" individuals are different, we cannot know whether the sample we selected is representative of the target population. To make a convenience sample representative of a larger target population of interest, researchers can use the following two strategies:

1. Researchers can use *quota sampling*, in which they select subgroups of the population that resemble or represent characteristics in a target population of interest.

2. Researchers can use a *combined sampling method*, in which they combine convenience sampling with a probability sampling method.

We begin by describing quota sampling, which is a common sampling method using nonhuman subjects. In Section 6.4, we describe four probability sampling methods that can be combined with convenience sampling to ensure that a sample is representative of the target population of interest to a researcher.

Quota Sampling

A **quota sample** is selected based on known or unknown criteria or characteristics in the target population. Researchers use quota sampling to ensure that the characteristics upon which subjects or participants are selected are represented in a sample.

For situations in which little is known about the characteristics of a target population, researchers use **simple quota sampling.** For example, Bleakley, Hennessy, Fishbein, and Jordan (2009) used a type of simple quota sampling to select a group of high school students to participate in a survey about sexual behavior. A simple quota sampling method can be useful to select participants to ensure that the sample is representative of the target population of high school students.

Using simple quota sampling, an equal number of subjects or participants are selected based on a characteristic or demographic that they share. For example, as illustrated in Figure 6.2 (left side), in a brain imaging study, we may be concerned that men and women process information differently and we will thus select an equal number of men and women to participate in the research study. Other characteristics of interest can include age, education level, marital status, and any other demographic characteristic believed to be representative of the target population. In the study of sexual behavior of high school students, the researchers wanted to ensure representation of the survey respondents based on age, gender, and ethnicity. Simple quota sampling is often used when the target population is not well understood, such as sampling students who cheat on exams—this group would be unlikely to admit cheating and therefore would be difficult to identify.

For situations in which certain characteristics are known in the population, researchers use **proportionate quota sampling.** Using proportionate quota sampling, subjects or participants are selected such that known characteristics or demographics are proportionately represented in the sample. For example, we know that approximately 25% of the American population is obese and 75% is not obese. Based on these known proportions, we could select a sample in which 25% of participants were obese, and 75% were not, as illustrated in Figure 6.2. Assuming the target population of interest was the American population, we have now proportionately represented health categories (obese, not obese) in our sample.

Quota sampling is one method of sampling used to ensure that a sample is representative of the target population of interest to a researcher. Another strategy used to ensure that a sample is representative of the target population is to combine convenience

> Convenience sampling is the most common method of sampling in behavioral research.

> **Quota sampling** is a method of sampling in which subjects or participants are selected based on known or unknown criteria or characteristics in the target population.

> **Simple quota sampling** is a type of quota sampling used when little is known about the characteristics of a target population. Using this type of quota sampling, an equal number of subjects or participants are selected for a given characteristic or demographic.

> **Proportionate quota sampling** is a type of quota sampling used when the proportions of certain characteristics in a target population are known. Using this type of quota sampling, subjects or participants are selected such that the known characteristics or demographics are proportionately represented in the sample.

Figure 6.2 Simple and Proportionate Quota Sampling

Simple Quota Sampling	Proportionate Quota Sampling
POPULATION	POPULATION
Unknown	25% Obese 75% Nonobese

An equal number of men and women are selected from the accessible population for a brain imaging study.

Obese and nonobese participants are selected from the accessible population such that the proportions of those selected resemble proportions in the target population.

When demographics in a population are unknown or the same, simple quota sampling is used; proportionate quota sampling is used when specific demographic information is known in a target population.

---

sampling with probability sampling methods—four probability sampling methods are introduced in the next section.

Purposeful Sampling

> Purposeful sampling requires selecting participants with certain required characteristics or experiences.

Purposeful sampling (also called purposive sampling) is used when the researcher needs specific characteristics to be represented in the sample. The study requires that the participants have certain characteristics or experiences so the researcher purposefully seeks to find participants with these characteristics or experiences. An example of purposeful sampling is if the researcher was interested in studying algebraic instruction of experienced middle school teachers. The researcher would intentionally seek out a sample of these teachers by defining each element of the sample. Middle school could be defined as Grades 6 through 8. Algebra teachers could be defined as math teachers who taught at least one algebra course in the past school year. An experienced teacher could be defined as a teacher with at least 5 years of teaching experience. The researcher will then recruit sixth-, seventh-, or eighth-grade teachers with at least 5 years of teaching experience who have taught at least one algebra course in the past year.

1. Name three types of nonprobability sampling methods.

2. Name two strategies that researchers use to ensure that characteristics in a convenience sample are representative of characteristics in a target population.

3. Which type of quota sampling is used when characteristics in a target population are unknown?

4. When would a researcher use purposeful sampling?

Answers: 1. Convenience sampling and quota sampling; 2. Researchers can use *quota sampling*, in which they select subgroups of the population with characteristics that resemble or represent characteristics in a target population. Researchers can also use a combined sampling method, in which they combine convenience sampling with a probability sampling method; 3. Simple quota sampling; 4. When he or she needs participants with specific characteristics or experiences.

6.4 Methods of Sampling: Probability Sampling

> Probability sampling and nonprobability sampling methods are ways in which samples are selected to inform us about a target population.

Probability sampling methods, as illustrated in Figure 6.3, are used when the probability of selecting each individual in a target population is known. Four probability sampling methods introduced in this section are simple random sampling, simple and proportionate stratified random sampling, systematic sampling, and cluster sampling.

Simple Random Sampling

For small populations of interest, a simple random sample can be selected because each individual can be identified and the likelihood of selecting each individual is known. Using simple random sampling, the likelihood of selecting each individual in the population is known, so we can use a random procedure to select individuals from the population, such as using the random number table, which is given in Appendix B.1 with instructions for how to use it.

To ensure that the probability of selecting each individual is always the same, researchers use sampling with replacement. To use sampling with replacement, each individual selected is replaced before the next selection. To illustrate how this works, suppose we have a population of a college class of 10 students. The probability of selecting

> **Simple random sampling** is a method of sampling subjects and participants such that all individuals in a population have an equal chance of being selected and are selected using sampling with replacement.
>
> **Sampling with replacement** is a strategy used with simple random sampling in which each individual selected is replaced before the next selection to ensure that the probability of selecting each individual is always the same.

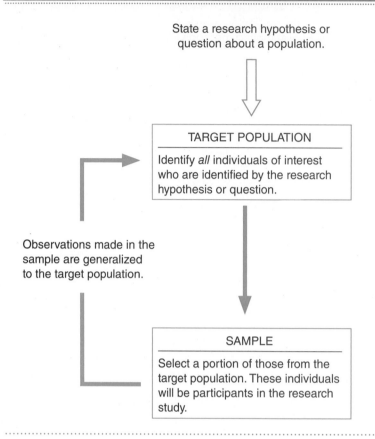

State a research hypothesis or
question about a population.

TARGET POPULATION

Identify *all* individuals of interest
who are identified by the research
hypothesis or question.

Observations made in the
sample are generalized
to the target population.

SAMPLE

Select a portion of those from the
target population. These individuals
will be participants in the research
study.

the first student is 1 in 10 or 10%. If we return the student we selected back into the class before selecting again, then 10 students will remain in the class when we select again, and the probability of the next selection will again be 1 in 10 or 10%.

However, most researchers use **sampling without replacement,** which means that each individual selected is not replaced before the next selection. For example, if we did not replace the student we selected before selecting another student, then there would only be 9 students left in the population, so the probability of the next selection would be 1 in 9 or 11%. Hence, in this example, the probability of selecting each student changed when we sampled without replacement.

Sampling without replacement is a nonrandom sampling strategy most often used by behavioral researchers in which each individual selected is not replaced before the next selection.

For very large populations, however, sampling without replacement is associated with negligible changes in probabilities from one selection to the next. For example, with a population of 100 individuals, the probability (p) of the first selection is 1 in 100 or $p = .01$, and the probability of the second selection using sampling without replacement is 1 in 99 or $p = .01$—when rounding to the hundredths place, there is no difference in probability. As the

Section II: Defining and Measuring Variables, Selecting Samples, and Choosing an Appropriate Research Design

population size increases, these probabilities become more and more negligible, and most populations of interest to educational researchers have thousands or millions of individuals. For this reason, sampling without replacement can still be used to select a simple random sample so long as the population size is large.

Unfortunately, when the selection of participants is left completely to chance, this can lead to the selection of a sample that is not representative of the population. For example, if we selected a simple random sample of elementary schoolteachers, then we could end up with a sample of 20 male schoolteachers. However, female schoolteachers are estimated to constitute about 80% of the population, so a sample of 20 male schoolteachers would not be representative of the larger population. In other words, the sample would misrepresent the demographic characteristic of gender. To avoid the problem of selecting samples that are not representative of the population, we can use one of three alternative sampling methods that are described in this section.

Stratified Random Sampling

One sampling method used to obtain a representative sample, called stratified random sampling, involves dividing the population into subgroups or "strata," then randomly selecting participants from each subgroup using a simple random sampling procedure. Participants selected from each subgroup are then combined into one sample that is representative of each stratum from which participants have been selected. Populations should be divided into strata based on characteristics that are relevant to the research hypothesis. For example, Klar and Brewer (2013) stratified middle schools in one southeastern state by their geographic region and then selected school principals to participate in each stratum in a study examining the role of the school principal.

> **Stratified random sampling** is a method of sampling in which a population is divided into subgroups or strata; participants are then selected from each subgroup using simple random sampling and are combined into one overall sample.
>
> Stratified random sampling can involve selecting an equal number of participants in each subgroup, called **simple stratified random sampling,** or selecting a different proportion of participants in each subgroup, called **proportionate stratified random sampling.**

To represent a certain characteristic of a population in a sample, researchers could use simple stratified random sampling by selecting an equal number of participants in each subgroup or stratum. For example, to stratify middle schools by geographic regions, researchers can split the population of middle schools into three strata (urban, rural, suburban) and then randomly select the same number of principals from each stratum. Participants selected in each stratum can then be combined into one large sample that has an equal number of principals from each geographic region.

As another strategy to represent a certain characteristic of a population in a sample, researchers could use proportionate stratified random sampling. Using this strategy, researchers select participants in each subgroup or stratum, such that the numbers in each stratum are proportionately represented similar to proportions in the population. For example, suppose that 50% of middle schools in the state are urban, 30% suburban, and 20% rural. In this case, illustrated in Figure 6.4, the researcher can split the population into three strata (urban, suburban, rural) and then randomly select participants such that 50% of those selected are urban, 30% are suburban, and 20% are rural. When the three strata are combined, the proportion of those from each geographic region in the sample will be identical to the proportions that exist in the population of middle schools in that state.

Notice that stratified random sampling is similar to quota sampling in that an equal or proportionate number of subjects or participants can be selected based on known characteristics in a population. Notice also the similarity in Figures 6.2 and 6.4. The difference is that quota sampling uses convenience sampling and not random sampling to select participants; however, both strategies ensure that certain characteristics in a sample are representative of the population.

> With stratified random sampling, the strata are subgroups in a target population of interest.

Systematic Sampling

> **Systematic sampling** is a method of sampling in which the first participant is selected using simple random sampling, and then every *n*th person is systematically selected until all participants have been selected.

A probability sampling method that begins with random sampling and then switches to a systematic procedure is called **systematic sampling.** Using this sampling method, a researcher randomly selects the first participant and then selects every *n*th person until all participants have been selected. Hence, the researcher uses simple random sampling to select the first participant and then uses a systematic sampling procedure to select all remaining participants (i.e., by selecting every *n*th person). For example, the 2011

Figure 6.4   Simple and Proportionate Stratified Random Sampling

Simple Stratified
Random Sampling

POPULATION
_____
freshmen = sophomores =
juniors = seniors

An equal number
of participants is
selected from each
subgroup.

Proportionate Stratified
Random Sampling

POPULATION
_____
30% freshmen
30% sophomores
20% juniors
20% seniors

A proportion of
participants is
selected from each
subgroup to resemble the
proportion of those in the
population.

Note: When subgroups contain similar numbers of persons in the population, then simple stratified random sampling is used; proportionate stratified random sampling is used when subgroups are not equal.

Trends in International Mathematics and Science Study (TIMSS) used a systematic sampling procedure to select specific schools from a list by selecting one school at random, then selecting every *n*th school until all eligible schools were selected to participate. The sampling interval *n* was determined by the number of schools in the country divided by the number of schools needed for the sample (Martin & Mullis, 2011).

To further illustrate systematic sampling, suppose that a professor has a class of 90 students. The professor wants to select a sample of 30 students from this class. To achieve this sample size, the professor will need to select every third student ($90 \div 30 = 3$). The first participant is selected using simple random sampling, such as by using the random number table given in Appendix B.1 to select the first participant. The next 29 participants in the sample are chosen systematically, meaning that every third person is selected until 30 participants are in the sample. One way to use the systematic procedure would be to have students count off by threes, starting with the randomly selected first participant saying "Three" and the next student beginning back at "One." The students who say "Three" will then be the remaining 29 participants in the sample.

Cluster Sampling

For situations in which the population of interest is spread out across a wide region or the participants are situated in naturally occurring groups, researchers can use cluster sampling. When a population is spread out across a wide region, this can make random and systematic sampling very difficult because the population is hard to access and efforts to select a sample would be too time-consuming and costly. A solution to this problem is to sample from smaller segments or clusters within the population using a probability sampling method called **cluster sampling**. When conducting research in schools, potential participants are organized in naturally occurring clusters (i.e., classrooms). It would be very difficult to conduct research where only some students in a classroom participate. Therefore, large-scale educational research such as the TIMSS study often use cluster sampling. Using cluster sampling, we divide the population into clusters and then select all individuals in some of those clusters who we think are representative of the population as a whole. Hence, some clusters will be completely omitted from the sample.

> **Cluster sampling** is a method of sampling in which subgroups or clusters of individuals are identified in a population, and then a portion of clusters that are representative of the population is selected such that all individuals in the selected clusters are included in the sample. All clusters that are not selected are omitted from the sample.

Cluster sampling is different from stratified random sampling in that some subgroups are omitted from a sample using cluster sampling, whereas a random sample of individuals in each subgroup is included in a sample using stratified random sampling, as illustrated in Figure 6.5. The advantage of using cluster sampling is that it breaks down a population into clusters when it is difficult to reach all clusters or if the potential participants are located in natural clusters. Clusters selected are representative of all clusters in the population.

As an example to illustrate cluster sampling, suppose we want to study concerns of bullying behavior in New York State (NYS) public high schools. The population of public high school students in NYS is spread out over a wide region and can occur in naturally occurring intact groups. To use cluster sampling, we first break up the population into clusters, such as by district. Then we choose a sample of districts by selecting three or four districts (we could choose any number of districts) that we think are representative of the characteristics of students in the larger population of NYS public schools. Once those districts have been selected, all students in those districts will be selected for the sample. All districts that were not selected will be omitted from the sample.

A limitation of cluster sampling is that it limits a sample to individuals in the chosen clusters, and there can be substantial variation between clusters within one population. For instance, bullying behavior in Queens, New York, will likely be different from bullying behavior in Buffalo, New York; bullying behavior

Figure 6.5 The Distinction Between Stratified Random Sampling and Cluster Sampling

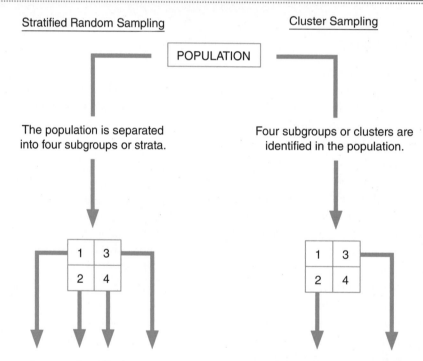

Stratified Random Sampling

Cluster Sampling

POPULATION

The population is separated into four subgroups or strata.

Four subgroups or clusters are identified in the population.

A sample or portion of individuals in each subgroup (1, 2, 3, 4) is included in the sample.

The population is likely contained within a localized and accessible region, so including all subgroups in the sample is practical.

All individuals in the selected subgroups (2, 3) are included in the sample. The remaining subgroups (1, 4) are left out of the sample.

The population is likely spread out and largely inaccessible, making it more practical to include select clusters that are accessible.

Using stratified random sampling, a portion of individuals in each subgroup is selected in a sample. Using cluster sampling, all individuals in a sample or portion of subgroups are included in a sample.

Section II: Defining and Measuring Variables, Selecting Samples, and Choosing an Appropriate Research Design

will likely be different for schools in wealthier neighborhoods as well. Other important factors include, race, gender, and school size. To select a representative sample, each of these characteristics should be represented in the selected clusters because only individuals in those clusters will be included in the sample.

In all, the six sampling methods described in this chapter are some of the most common methods used in educational research to select participants for research studies. Table 6.1 summarizes each of the probability and nonprobability sampling methods described in Sections 6.3 and 6.4.

Table 6.1 The Probability and Nonprobability Sampling Methods Described in Sections 6.3 and 6.4

Type of Sampling	Description	Population Sampled From	Expected Quality of the Sample
Nonprobability Sampling Methods			
Convenience sampling	A sampling method in which participants are selected based on availability or convenience	Accessible population	The sample is not random and not representative.
Quota sampling	A sampling method in which available or convenient subgroups of participants are selected, typically in a way that resembles the target population	Accessible population	The sample is not random but can be representative.
Probability sampling methods			
Simple random sampling	A sampling method in which all individuals in a population have an equal chance of being selected	Target population	The sample is random but not always representative.
Stratified random sampling	A sampling method in which a population is divided into subgroups or strata, and then a random sample of participants is selected from each subgroup and combined into one overall sample	Target population	The sample is random and representative, particularly for proportionate stratified sampling.
Systematic sampling	A sampling method in which the first participant is randomly selected, then every nth person is systematically selected from there until all persons have been selected	Target population	The sample is systematic (not random) and not always representative.
Cluster sampling	A sampling method in which subgroups or clusters of individuals are identified in a population. A sample of clusters is then selected, and all individuals in those clusters are included in the sample	Target population	The sample is not random but can be representative with the careful selection of clusters.

1. To use simple random sampling, should a researcher use sampling with replacement or sampling without replacement?

2. What sampling method involves selecting all individuals from a portion of subgroups in a population?

3. A researcher investigates how political attitudes (Republican, Democrat) are related to attitudes toward teaching evolution in a school classroom. To select the sample, she is given access to a database identifying the political affiliations and mailing addresses for all local residents in her area. She splits the list into two subgroups (Republican, Democrat) and then selects a sample or portion of individuals from each subgroup. To select participants from each subgroup, she uses a random procedure to select the first address and then selects every sixth address after that until 300 participants from each subgroup are selected. What three sampling methods has she combined to select this sample?

Answers: 1. Sampling with replacement; 2. Cluster sampling; 3. Convenience sampling (only local residents have a chance of being selected), simple stratified random sampling (the list is separated into subgroups, and an equal number of participants are selected from each subgroup), and systematic sampling (she chooses every sixth address on the list after a random start).

MAKING SENSE—REPRESENTATIVE VERSUS RANDOM SAMPLES

Using random sampling does not always mean that the sample selected is representative of characteristics in a population. For researchers, the larger concern is for a sample to be representative because they want to be able to describe characteristics in a population based on observations they make with samples. The more the characteristics in the sample resemble those in the population, the more representative of the population the sample will be.

The convenience sampling method is often used in the education sciences but does not use a random sampling procedure. However, if we know characteristics in the target population, then we can represent them in our sample by combining convenience sampling with a probability sampling method. For example, to study class behavior among middle school students, we can select a convenience sample of local middle school students and use stratified sampling to split the pool of potential participants by grade level (sixth, seventh, eighth), as illustrated in Figure 6.6. We can then randomly select participants from each class year among those available in the convenience sample. In this example, grade level is now represented in the convenience sample.

In a published study, Christon, Arnold, and Myers (2015) used a similar strategy in a study on the psychosocial interventions provided to students with autism. The researchers selected a convenience sample of professionals recruited through newspaper ads and professional organization membership lists, which produced an eligible pool of 17,423 potential participants in the sampling frame list. Then they used a simple stratified random sampling method by separating the eligible pool of 17,423 people on the list into different disciplines (i.e., education, psychology, medical, social work, occupational and physical therapy, and speech/language/hearing) and then randomly selecting 200 professionals from each discipline to participate in their study. Hence, the researchers combined a convenience sampling method (a convenient pool of qualified individuals through ads and organizational membership lists) with a probability sampling method (simple stratified random sampling) to ensure that the characteristic of discipline was represented in their sample.

Figure 6.6 Probability Sampling Used With Convenience Sampling to Make the Sample More Representative of the Population

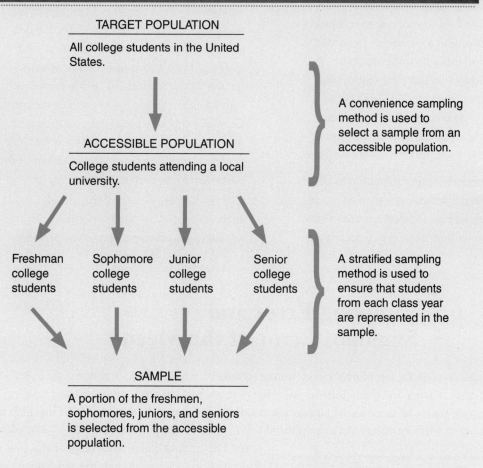

Note: In this example, the accessible population (a convenience sample) is split into grade levels, and then participants are randomly selected from each group (a stratified sample) to ensure that the grade levels are represented in the sample.

A teacher who is interested in examining his or her own practice and uses his or her students in the study begins with a convenience sample, but a random sampling technique can be used to select some of the students instead of using all of them. Selecting some of the students can make the investigation more manageable. Here are some ways to use the random sampling techniques:

- Simple random—print a class roster and cut the names into slips of paper and place student names into a container. Draw out names of students who will participate or number students on the class roster. Use the random number function in Excel to generate the desired number of random numbers. Match to the student numbers. These are the students who will participate.

- Stratified random—separate students based on the desired characteristic such as grade level or gender into different groups. Then select students from each group separately

using a simple random technique described above.

- Systematic random—decide how many students are needed to participate in the study. Take the number of students on the class roster and divide it by the number needed for the study. This provides the sampling interval (or nth). Put the class roster in alphabetic order (this is considered to be a random order). Take the alphabetized class roster, close your eyes, and point to a place on the roster. Do not start at the top of the list! The name where the finger pointed is the first participant for the study. Now count to the sampling interval (nth). This is the second participant. Continue this way until all the participants are selected. When the end of the roster is reached, continue counting at the top of the roster until you end up where you started.

- Cluster random—each of the above techniques can be used for groups of students like classrooms or class periods.

6.5 Sampling Error and Standard Error of the Mean

Regardless of the sampling strategy we use to select a sample, there is always a probability of error. Hence, the characteristics we observe in a sample are not always the same or representative of those in the population from which the sample was selected. This difference between what we observe in a sample and what is true in the population is called **sampling error.** The implication of sampling error is that two random samples selected from the same population can produce very different scores or outcomes.

To illustrate sampling error, suppose that a small hypothetical population of three people (A, B, C) scored an 8, 5, and 2, respectively, on some

Sampling error is the extent to which sample means selected from the same population differ from one another. This difference, which occurs by chance, is measured by the standard error of the mean.

assessment. The mean or average score on the assessment in this population, then, is the sum of each score divided by the total number of scores summed:

$$\text{Population Mean} = \frac{8+5+2}{3} = 5.0.$$

If there is no sampling error, then each sample we select should show that the average score on this assessment is 5.0. Any other outcome indicates a sampling error in our estimate of the assessment score in the population. To illustrate, suppose we select all possible samples of two people from this population of three people. Table 6.2 shows all nine possible samples that we could select and the sample mean score on the assessment that we would obtain in each sample. Notice that the possible sample means we could select vary from 2.0 to 8.0. The distance that sample mean values can deviate from the value of the population mean, called the **standard error of the mean,** is used as a measure of sampling error. Hence, if we do select one sample from this population, there is a possibility, due to chance, that the sample mean will not equal the mean assessment score in the population.

> The **standard error of the mean** is the standard deviation of a sampling distribution of sample means. It is the standard error or distance that sample mean values can deviate from the value of the population mean.

> The standard error of the mean is a measure of sampling error.

One way to reduce standard error is to increase the size of the sample. If we select a sample from a population of 100 people, then a sample of 90 people will give us more accurate information about that population than a sample of just 10 people. In terms of sampling error, the sample of 90 people will be associated with a smaller standard error. To put it another way, the larger the sample, the more information you have and therefore the less variation or error there will be between mean scores in a population and those in a randomly selected sample.

LEARNING CHECK 4 ✓

1. How is standard error related to sampling error?

2. Name one way to reduce sampling error.

Answers: 1. Sampling error, which occurs by chance, is measured numerically by the standard error of the mean; 2. Increase the sample size.

6.6 Potential Biases in Sampling

Selecting a sample can be prone to bias either due to the fault of the researcher, *sampling bias,* or due to the fault of the participants, *nonresponse bias.* Both biases, which are introduced in this section, can limit the extent to which researchers can use observations in a sample to describe characteristics in a population.

Table 6.2 The Participants, Individual Scores, and Sample Mean for Each Possible Sample of Size 2 From This Population of Size 3

Although the population mean is 5.0, average scores in each sample can vary from 2.0 to 8.0.

Participants Sampled (*n* = 2)	Scores for Each Participant	Sample Mean for Each Sample
A,A	8,8	8.0
A,B	8,5	6.5
A,C	8,2	5.0
B,A	5,8	6.5
B,B	5,5	5.0
B,C	5,2	3.5
C,A	2,8	5.0
C,B	2,5	3.5
C,C	2,2	2.0

Sampling Bias

One source of bias can result from the research procedures developed by the researcher. This type of bias, called **sampling bias,** occurs when sampling procedures employed in a study favor certain individuals or groups over others. Sampling bias can lead to the selection of a sample that is not representative of the target population but is instead representative of only the overrepresented groups in the sample. Suppose, for example, that we study attitudes toward inclusion of students with disabilities in general education classrooms by sampling individuals from a list of Council for Exceptional Children (CEC) members. Whatever the result, it is likely to be biased in favor of those who favor inclusion.

> **Sampling bias,** or **selection bias,** is a bias in sampling in which the sampling procedures employed in a study favor certain individuals or groups over others.

Sampling bias can be particularly problematic for research that uses online surveys or computer-based surveys, which have increased significantly in use among researchers over the past decade. Using online surveys is easier and more cost-effective; however, problems with the sampling procedures include the technology aptitude of participants, system incompatibilities (e.g., potential respondents cannot open the survey), and institutional gatekeeping policies that recognize the survey as spam (see Hartford, Carey, & Mendonca, 2007). Each problem with the sampling procedures leads to sampling bias in that these problems limit the potential portion of the population that is sampled in favor of participants with greater aptitude and experience with computers and those with access to more compatible computer systems.

Nonresponse Bias

Another source of bias can result from the nonresponsiveness of participants. This type of bias, called **nonresponse bias,** occurs when participants choose not to respond to a survey or request to participate in a study. The reason that nonresponse bias can be a problem is that individuals in a population who respond to surveys or postings asking for participants, such as in a school newspaper or poster, are likely to be systematically different from those who do not.

> **Nonresponse bias** is a bias in sampling in which a number of participants in one or more groups choose not to respond to a survey or request to participate in a research study.

Hence, nonresponse bias could limit a sample to be representative of only the portion of the population that is willing to respond to a survey or request to participate in a study.

To illustrate nonresponse bias, suppose we select a sample of children who are obese. One problem we will face is that the parents of these children are less likely to give their written or verbal authorization, called *active consent*, to allow their children to participate (see Mellor, Rapoport, & Maliniak, 2008) largely due to the perceived negative stereotype associated with being obese. If many parents choose not to give active consent, then any results we observe in a sample may be limited to only that portion of the population of children who are obese who also have parents who are willing to give consent. It is not possible to know for sure if the results we observe in our sample would also be observed with children who are obese who have parents not willing to give consent.

6.7 Ethics in Focus: Research in Schools

In schools across the country, parents, teachers, and students are recruited to participate in educational research. Most school systems have policies regarding research activities that can take place in schools and a formal system to approve such research. This system typically includes obtaining permission from the school district before contacting individual school administrators and/or teachers. Ethical research in schools contributes to the mission and goals of the school system. Some common goals of schools are to improve (a) student outcomes, (b) staff effectiveness, (c) program effectiveness, or (d) conditions for learning. So educational researchers need to be able to illustrate how a given study may influence one or more of these goals.

Educational researchers need to also consider ethical issues that relate to the practicality of conducting research in schools. Some of these considerations include use of staff time, school and teacher resources, affordability or cost to teachers and schools, number of students to be affected by the study, and ease of implementation. Take, for example, a study investigating a computer-based problem-solving strategy to improve math achievement. This study requires a sufficient number of computers in the classroom for the students, use of a specific computer program, redirection of teacher instructional time, and the selection of some students to participate while others do not. It also requires interruptions of class time for the researchers to collect data for the study. While the implications of the study are important (i.e., improving math achievement), there are ethical concerns. Do the researchers only recruit from schools that already have enough classroom computers or should they supply some? Who purchases and installs the computer programs? What instructional time will be replaced by the new problem-solving intervention? What might happen to students receiving the problem-solving instruction if it is found not to be effective? How would students and/or parents of those students who did not receive the instruction feel if it were found to be effective? These questions represent the type of ethical considerations educational researchers face when planning and implementing research in schools. Researchers need to consider the risks and benefits of these ethical considerations when designing studies.

LEARNING CHECK 5 ✓

1. Distinguish between sampling bias and nonresponse bias.

2. State two rules that make the creation of subject pools an ethical practice.

Answers: 1. Sampling bias is a bias in sampling in which the sampling procedures employed in a study favor certain individuals or groups over others, whereas nonresponse bias is a bias in sampling in which a number of participants in one or more groups choose not to respond to a survey or request to participate in a study; 2. Class grades are never contingent on actual participation in a research study, and students are given alternative options to receive a grade.

CHAPTER SUMMARY

LO 1 Explain why researchers select samples that are representative of a population of interest.

- Researchers select samples from a population to learn more about the population from which the samples were selected. If researchers want to generalize the results they observe in a sample to those in the target population, then they need to make certain that the sample is representative of the target population. A representative sample is a sample that has characteristics that resemble those in the target population.

LO 2 Distinguish between subjects and participants as terms used to describe those who are subjected to procedures in a research study.

- The term participant is used to describe a human who volunteers to be subjected to the procedures in a research study. The term subject is used to describe a nonhuman that is subjected to procedures in a research study and is used to identify the names of research designs.

LO 3 Distinguish between probability sampling methods and nonprobability sampling methods.

- Probability sampling is a category of sampling in which a sample is selected directly from the target population; nonprobability sampling is a category of sampling in

Section II: Defining and Measuring Variables, Selecting Samples, and Choosing an Appropriate Research Design

which a sample is selected from the accessible population. Sampling directly from the target population using probability sampling is possible in situations in which the exact probability of selecting each individual in a target population is known. However, it is rare that researchers know the exact probability of selecting each individual in a target population, so nonprobability sampling methods are most commonly used to select samples in behavioral research.

LO 4 Delineate two nonprobability sampling methods: convenience sampling and quota sampling.

- A **convenience sample,** as indicated in the name, is selected out of convenience or ease, meaning that participants are selected based on their availability to participate. A drawback of convenience sampling is that it does not ensure that a sample will be representative of the target population. To make a convenience sample representative of a target population of interest, researchers can use quota sampling or a combined sampling method.

- **Quota sampling** is a method of sampling in which subjects or participants are selected based on the characteristics they share to ensure that these characteristics are represented in a sample. For situations in which little is known about the characteristics of a target population, researchers use **simple quota sampling.** For situations in which certain characteristics are known in the population, researchers use **proportionate quota sampling.**

  For situations in which little is known about the characteristics of a target population, researchers use simple quota sampling.

  For situations in which certain characteristics are known in the population, researchers use proportionate quota sampling.

LO 5 Delineate four probability sampling methods: simple random sampling, stratified random sampling, systematic sampling, and cluster sampling.

- **Simple random sampling** is a method of sampling subjects and participants such that all individuals in a population have an equal chance of being selected and are selected using sampling with replacement.

- **Stratified random sampling** is a method of sampling in which a population is divided into subgroups or strata; participants are selected from each subgroup using simple random sampling and are combined into one overall sample. We can select an equal number of participants from each subgroup (**simple stratified random sampling**) or a number of participants from each subgroup that is proportionate with those in the population (**proportionate stratified random sampling**).

- **Systematic sampling** is a method of sampling in which the first participant is randomly selected, and then every nth person is systematically selected until all participants have been selected.

- **Cluster sampling** is a method of sampling in which subgroups or clusters of individuals are identified in a population, and then a portion of clusters that are representative of the population is selected such that all individuals in the selected clusters are included in the sample. All clusters that are not selected are omitted from the sample.

LO 6 Define and explain sampling error and the standard error of the mean.

- The extent to which sample means selected from the same population differ from one another is called **sampling error.** This difference, which occurs by chance, is measured by the **standard error of the mean,** which is the standard error or distance that sample mean values can deviate from the value of the population mean.

LO 7 Define and explain sampling bias and nonresponse bias.

- **Sampling bias** is a bias in sampling in which the sampling procedures employed in a study favor certain individuals or groups over others, whereas **nonresponse bias** is a bias in sampling in which a number of participants in one or more groups choose not to respond to a survey or request to participate in a study. Both biases can result in the selection of samples that are not representative of the population.

LO 8 Identify potential ethical concerns related to sampling at schools.

- Sampling participants at schools could place the burden of participation too heavily on the population of students. Most school systems have policies regarding research activities that can take place in schools and a formal system to approve such research. This system typically includes obtaining permission from the school district before contacting individual school administrators and/or teachers. Ethical research in schools contributes to the mission and goals of the school system. Some common goals of schools are to improve (a) student outcomes, (b) staff effectiveness, (c) program effectiveness, and (d) conditions for learning.

KEY TERMS

accessible population 157

cluster sampling 167

convenience sampling 160

nonprobability
   sampling 159

nonresponse bias 175

participant 156

probability sampling 158

proportionate quota
   sampling 161

proportionate stratified
   random sampling 165

quota sampling 161

representative sample 158

sampling bias 174

sampling error 172

sampling frame 157

sampling with
   replacement 163

sampling without
   replacement 164

selection bias 174

simple quota sampling 161

simple random
   sampling 163

simple stratified random
   sampling 165

standard error of the
   mean 173

stratified random
   sampling 165

subject 156

systematic sampling 166

target population 157

1. Which of the following best describes the reason why researchers select samples from populations of interest?

    A. Researchers make observations with samples to learn about, or generalize to, populations.

    B. Researchers select samples to avoid having to describe the characteristics of an entire population.

    C. Researchers make observations in populations to learn about the samples they will select.

2. Distinguish between a target population and an accessible population.

3. Which method of sampling requires that the probability of selecting each individual in a population is known?

4. Identify the target population, the accessible population (sampling frame), and the sample for the following hypothetical study.

    A consultant is hired by a school district to test the hypothesis that "school spirit days" (any days where teachers and students wear clothing with school colors or logo) improve school attendance or morale. To test this hypothesis, the consultant obtains a list of all the schools in the district and randomly selects 10 schools to participate in the study.

5. Identify the target population, the accessible population (sampling frame), and the sample for the following hypothetical study.

    A professor who teaches three sections of a research methods class tests the hypothesis that his research methods class prepares students for a career in research. To test this hypothesis, the professor obtains a list of all students in each of his three sections and randomly selects 25 students from each section to participate in a study.

6. A researcher selects a sample from an accessible portion of a target population. What sampling method, probability sampling or nonprobability sampling, is described in this example?

7. What is the most common nonprobability sampling method used to select human participants for a research study? Which nonprobability sampling method is typically used to obtain animal subjects in behavioral research?

8. State the nonprobability sampling method described in each example.

    A. A researcher studies student perceptions of global warming by selecting high school participants from a subject pool at the local high school and has each student complete a global warming attitudes survey.

    B. A researcher conducts a study on eating in a school cafeteria by asking students as they enter the cafeteria if they are willing to participate in a study while they eat lunch. The researcher selects the first 50 girls and the first 50 boys who volunteer to participate in the study.

9. State the probability sampling method described in each example.

   A. To determine why many students at a local school are not eating the fruits and vegetables provided in the school cafeteria, a researcher obtains a list of all students at the school and separates the list into two subgroups: students who eat the fruits and vegetables provided in the school cafeteria and students who do not. The researcher randomly selects 12 students from each subgroup to be in her sample.

   B. A professor obtains a list of all registered students in his class and randomly selects 40 students from the list to participate in a course evaluation.

   C. An administrator at a local elementary school identifies that 24 classes are taught throughout the day at her school. From this list, she selects 12 classes and measures preparedness among all students in those 12 classrooms.

   D. A psychologist randomly selects one athlete to participate in a study from a list of all athletes at the school. Then, beginning with the randomly selected athlete, he selects every fourth athlete on the list to also participate in the study.

10. What is sampling error, and how is it measured?

11. Distinguish between sampling bias and nonresponse bias.

12. Which ethical principle was a concern for the creation of subject pools? Explain.

ACTIVITIES

1. Researchers select samples from populations to learn more about the populations from which they selected the samples. Give an analogy from an everyday experience you have had to illustrate why researchers select samples from populations.

2. Choose any research topic that interests you and develop a research hypothesis. Answer the following items, which should be part of your research plan:

   A. Identify the target population and accessible population addressed by your research hypothesis.

   B. Describe the sampling method you will use. If you plan to use a combined sampling method, then identify each method you plan to combine. Make sure you identify your exact procedure for selecting participants.

   C. Explain how the sample you select is, or is not, representative of the target population.

$SAGE edge™

SAGE edge offers a robust online environment featuring an impressive array of free tools and resources for review, study, and further exploration, keeping both instructors and students on the cutting edge of teaching and learning.

Access practice quizzes, eFlashcards, video, and multimedia at edge.sagepub.com/priviterarme.

Identify a problem

- Determine an area of interest.
- Review the literature.
- Identify new ideas in your area of interest.
- Develop a research hypothesis.

Develop a research plan

- Define the variables being tested.
- Identify participants or subjects and determine how to sample them.
- Select a research strategy and design.
- Evaluate ethics and obtain institutional approval to conduct research.

Generate more new ideas

- Results support your hypothesis—refine or expand on your ideas.
- Results do not support your hypothesis—reformulate a new idea or start over.

After reading this chapter, you should be able to:

1. Identify three categories of research design: experimental, quasi-experimental, and nonexperimental.

2. Explain how a gradient of control can be used to understand research design.

3. Define and explain internal and external validity.

4. Describe three elements of control required in an experiment.

5. Describe factors that threaten the internal validity of a research study.

6. Describe factors that threaten the external validity of a research study.

7. Define and explain mundane and experimental realism.

Conduct the study

- Execute the research plan and measure or record the data.

Communicate the results

- Method of communication: oral, written, or in a poster.
- Style of communication: APA guidelines are provided to help prepare style and format.

Analyze and evaluate the data

- Analyze and evaluate the data as they relate to the research hypothesis.
- Summarize data and research results.

chapter
seven

CHOOSING A RESEARCH DESIGN

Education is about understanding the process of learning. You are in many ways an educational researcher when you ask questions about student learning and seek to answer those questions. For example, if you have students who are struggling in your class, you may ask, "How can I improve my teaching to increase my students' grades?" While you may not have considered the formal scientific process to answer your question, it can nonetheless be used to answer your question.

One way to think of research design is as a set of rules for how to make observations to answer questions. Each research design has a unique set of rules to help you control, manage, and organize what will be observed and how it will be observed. In this way, research design is similar to a board game, which has many rules to control, manage, and organize how you are allowed to move game pieces on a game board. Most board games, for example, have rules that tell you how many spaces you can move on the game board at most at a time and what to do if you pick up a certain card or land on a certain spot on the game board. The rules, in essence, define the game. Each board game only makes sense if players follow the rules.

Likewise, in science, the rules stated in a research design allow us to make sense of the conclusions we draw from the observations we make. In a board game, we follow rules to establish a winner; in science, we follow rules to establish conclusions from the observations we make. There are many ways in which you could observe your teaching—for example, videotape, observation reports by a teacher colleague or mentor, while using a specific teaching strategy, in a specific content area, or in a less controlled setting such as a library or study hall. In this chapter, we will explore the basic nature of the major categories of research design introduced in this book and organize how these research designs differ based on the types of conclusions they allow you to draw from the observations you make.

edge.sagepub.com/
priviterarme

- Take the chapter quiz
- Review key terms with eFlashcards
- Explore multimedia links and SAGE articles

7.1 Designing a Study to Answer a Question

Conducting a study is important because it allows you to make observations using the scientific process to answer your research question. The type of study you conduct depends largely on the type of question you are asking. To conduct a research study, you need to be thoughtful of the extent to which you are actually answering your question. To illustrate, suppose you are a teacher and want to know if student collaboration promotes greater student learning. To answer this question, you organize one group of students into collaborative learning groups and a second group of students work as individuals. If you find that the students in the collaborative learning groups perform better, then can we conclude that the collaborative groups caused the difference between student learning outcomes?

The answer to your question depends on how thoughtful your research design was. For example, ability influences learning, so the student ability level in each group should be the same. Otherwise, if the ability level of one group of students was greater than the other, then maybe the ability level caused the differences between the two groups and not the collaboration. Other factors that could also influence learning as a result of collaboration include the content area, task being performed by the students, or gender. These additional factors should also be controlled to clearly show that the collaboration itself caused the differences between groups. In other words, designing a study is a careful, thoughtful, and often clever endeavor.

A **research design** is the specific methods and procedures used to answer a research question.

A research study applies specific methods and procedures, called the **research design**, to answer a research question. The types of research questions that you can ask are generally categorized as *exploratory*, *descriptive*, or *relational* questions. Each type of question is described with examples given in Table 7.1. In this chapter, we introduce many types of research designs used in the education sciences. In this book, Chapters 7 to 12 will describe in greater detail each type of research design introduced in this chapter.

LEARNING CHECK 1 ✓

1. State the type of question being asked for each example.

   A. How often do students complete homework assignments?

   B. What if the way that animals learn is similar to the way that humans learn?

   C. Is family income related to enrollment in charter schools?

Answers: 1. A. descriptive, B. exploratory, C. relational.

Table 7.1 The Three Types of Questions That Researchers Ask

Type of Question	Question Stated	Description/Goal	Examples
Exploratory	"What if"	To "get an idea of" or "explore" an area of research that is not well understood. Rarely do these questions provide definitive answers; rather, they lead to a stronger focus for subsequent research.	1. What if a high-fat, high-sugar diet leads to attention-deficit hyperactivity disorder? 2. What if human memory has an infinite capacity for storage?
Descriptive	"What is" "How"	To characterize, explain, or "describe" variables that are related to a specific group of individuals. These questions are not concerned with relationships between variables; rather, they are concerned with simply describing variables.	1. What is the average number of articulation errors in 4- to 5-year-old children? 2. How many minutes do elementary school-aged students spend watching TV per day?
Relational	"Does" "Is"	To determine the extent to which specified relationships exist between variables. These questions provide (1) causal explanations or (2) descriptions of the relationship between two or more variables.	1. Do low levels of serotonin in the brain cause depression? 2. Is free or reduced-price lunch status related to achievement?

7.2 Categories of Research Design

To answer a research question, you can choose a research design that falls into one of the following three categories, summarized in Figure 7.1:

- Experimental research design
- Quasi-experimental research design
- Nonexperimental research design

Each type of research design is distinguished by the level of control that is established in the design. The term **control** is used in research design to describe (a) the manipulation of a variable and (b) holding all other variables

Control in research design is (a) the manipulation of a variable and (b) holding all other variables constant. When control is low, neither criterion is met; when control is high, both criteria are met.

Figure 7.1 The Three Categories of Research Design

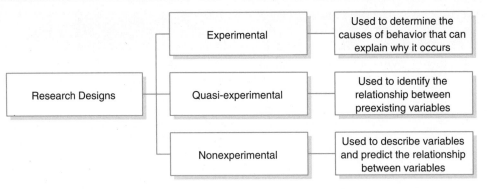

constant. When control is low, neither criterion (a) nor (b) is met. For example, suppose we observe play behavior among children at a park. The variable is play behavior; some children play quietly, and others play loudly. The children determine how loudly they play—the play behavior, then, is not manipulated or controlled by the researcher. Also, many other factors (e.g., the types of toys available to play with or the behavior of other children) can influence a child's play behavior at a park. Because the researcher does not manipulate the variable or hold these other variables constant, the study has low control.

Alternatively, when control is high, both criteria (a) and (b) are met. For example, to study play behavior, a researcher can have the children play one at a time on a playground. In one group, the children are told to play quietly; in another group, the children are told to play loudly. By manipulating the play behavior of the children (quiet play, loud play), the researcher establishes greater control. In addition, because all of the children play alone on the same playground, factors such as the types of toys available to play with or the behavior of other children are now held constant—all children, whether they play quietly or loudly, play alone with the same playground of toys. In this example, the researcher has established greater control by meeting both criteria (a) and (b) needed to establish control in a research design.

In this section, we introduce each research category, and we briefly describe the types of research designs that fall into each category. We will specifically distinguish between the levels of control established with each design because *control* is the key feature that can distinguish between categories of research design.

An **experimental research design** is the use of methods and procedures to make observations in which the researcher fully controls the conditions and experiences of participants by applying three required elements of control: randomization, manipulation, and comparison/control.

Experimental Research Designs

The staple of all designs is the experimental research design. The **experimental research design** is the use of methods and procedures to make observations in which the researcher fully controls the conditions and

Figure 7.2   Experimental Research Designs

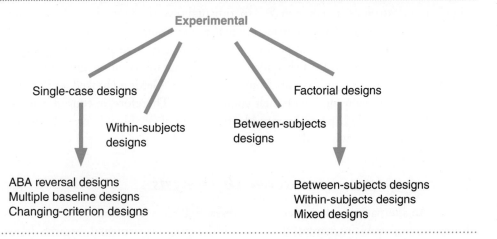

experiences of participants by applying three required elements of control: randomization, manipulation, and comparison/control. Each element of control is discussed in greater detail in Section 7.4. Figure 7.2 identifies many experimental research designs introduced in this book.

A key strength of the experimental research design is that it is the only research design capable of demonstrating cause and effect. To demonstrate that one factor causes changes in a dependent variable, the conditions and experiences of participants must be under the full control of the researcher. In the social sciences, such as psychology and sociology, this often means that an experiment is conducted in a laboratory and not in the environment where a behavior naturally operates. Suppose, for example, we study the effects of winning and losing on the desire to gamble. In a natural environment, it would be difficult to know if winning or losing causes changes in a person's desire to gamble because many other factors can vary in that setting. Some factors include the person's reasons for gambling that day, the amount of money available to gamble, the number of gamblers in a group, the types of games being played, and even the bright lights and sounds in the casino. We may be able to observe differences related to one's desire to gamble, but identifying the specific causes in that natural environment would be very difficult. To identify if winning or losing causes changes in a person's desire to gamble, Young, Wohl, Matheson, Baumann, and Anisman (2008) conducted an experiment by bringing students into a laboratory and having them experience a "virtual reality" casino in which the events, including winning and losing, were specifically controlled by the researchers. In this controlled setting of a virtual casino, the researchers specifically identified that high-risk gamblers have a much greater desire to gamble following a large win than following a series of small wins in a virtual casino setting. A key limitation of the experimental research design is that behavior that occurs under controlled conditions may not be the same as behavior that occurs in a natural environment.

Control is a key feature of research designs. Experimental designs have the greatest control over the conditions and experiences of participants.

In the education sciences, researchers rarely examine educational-related behaviors in a controlled lab setting. Our work primarily occurs in the natural educational setting—schools and classrooms. This can make experimental research more difficult in attempt to control and/or document those outside influences. For example, let's say you are a researcher exploring the difference between phonics-based and whole language–based reading instruction. You can control which student received what intervention and for how long at school, but you can't control parents from purchasing a "Getting Hooked on Phonics" CD from the Internet and using it with their child at home. Therefore, in educational research, researchers often include procedures to identify potential outside influences such as treatment diffusion or implementation fidelity.

Quasi-Experimental Research Designs

An alternative to the experimental research design for situations in which it is difficult or impossible to manipulate a factor is the quasi-experimental research design. The quasi-experimental research design is the use of methods and procedures to make observations in a study that is structured similar to an experiment, but the conditions and experiences of participants are not under the full control of the researcher. The conditions and experiences of participants are not under the full control of the researcher when the factor is not manipulated (i.e., it is "quasi-independent") or when the research design lacks a comparison/control group. This is probably the most common form of research in education because of the inability to randomly assign individual participants to treatment/comparison or control groups. Educational researchers instead assign intact classrooms or schools to treatment/comparison or control groups. Because of this lack of full control over the individual participants, this research is considered quasi-experimental. A quasi-independent variable is any factor in which the levels of that factor are preexisting. Quasi-independent variables of interest to researchers include characteristics of student participants, such as their gender (male, female), ability level (low, average, high), ethnicity, or free and reduced-price lunch status. When a factor is preexisting, participants cannot be randomly assigned to each level of that factor, but it allows researchers to study factors related to the unique characteristics of participants.

A quasi-experimental research design is the use of methods and procedures to make observations in a study that is structured similar to an experiment, but the conditions and experiences of participants lack some control because the study lacks random assignment, includes a preexisting factor (i.e., a variable that is not manipulated), or does not include a comparison/control group.

A quasi-independent variable is a variable with levels to which participants are not randomly assigned and that differentiates the groups or conditions being compared in a research study.

An example of an educational quasi-experiment is a study by Mann, Smith, and Kristjansson (2015), who investigated the effectiveness of the REAL Girls program on girls with preexisting problem behaviors that affected their school performance. Middle school girls from two public schools were recruited. The students from one middle school were assigned to participate in the REAL Girls program (treatment group) and students from the second middle school served as the control/comparison group and received delayed treatment. This study is considered quasi-experimental because the individual students were

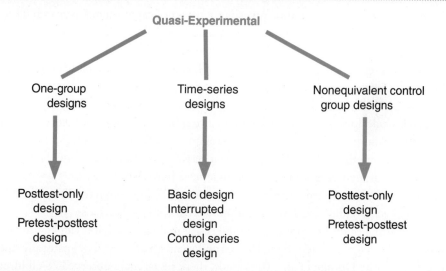

Figure 7.3 Quasi-Experimental Research Designs

Quasi-Experimental

One-group designs
- Posttest-only design
- Pretest-posttest design

Time-series designs
- Basic design
- Interrupted design
- Control series design

Nonequivalent control group designs
- Posttest-only design
- Pretest-posttest design

not randomly assigned to the groups. Assignment to the treatment group was by school, not by student. The researchers found that the REAL Girls program improved the academic self-efficacy, school connectedness, and identity of the girls.

A key limitation of the quasi-experimental research design is that researchers do not have full control to manipulate the independent variable (i.e., quasi-independent variable) and thus cannot demonstrate cause and effect. Referring back to the Mann et al. (2015) quasi-experiment, it is not possible to know if the REAL Girls program *caused* changes in academic self-efficacy, school connectedness, or identity because other factors, such as peer influences or home situations, could also be related to these factors and therefore could also be causing the changed attitude about school. Any time a factor is preexisting (i.e., quasi-independent), then any other factors related to it could also be causing changes in a dependent variable. Figure 7.3 identifies the many quasi-experimental research designs introduced in this book. Each research design is listed in Figure 7.3.

> A quasi-experimental research design is structured similar to an experiment, but the conditions and experiences of participants are not under the full control of the researcher.
>
> A nonexperimental research design is the use of methods and procedures to make observations in which the behavior or event is observed "as is" or without an intervention from the researcher.

Nonexperimental Research Designs

A common research design used in the education sciences is the nonexperimental research design. The nonexperimental research design is the use of methods and procedures to make observations in which the conditions or experiences of participants are not manipulated. A *manipulation* occurs when the researcher creates the conditions in which participants are observed; however, this is not always possible to study behavior. For example, we cannot manipulate the content of existing documents at different times in history, such as an analysis of Individualized Educational Plans (IEPs) under different special education laws.

Another example is that we often cannot manipulate interactions in natural settings, such as those between a student and a teacher or between an athlete and a coach. Situations such as these are certainly worthy of scientific investigation, so nonexperimental research designs have been adapted to study these types of situations.

In many situations, we want to study behavior in settings where the behavior or variables being observed cannot be manipulated. Figure 7.4 identifies many nonexperimental research designs introduced in this book—each design will be introduced in greater detail in Chapters 8 and 9. A key characteristic that differentiates nonexperimental designs from all other research designs is that the behavior or event being observed is observed "as is" or without intervention from the researcher. For example, Durden, Escalante, and Blitch (2014) observed teachers in ethnically diverse preschool classrooms to examine how the teachers implemented culturally relevant pedagogical practices. In this study, teachers were observed as they went about their typical day for 1 year as the researchers observed the physical environment, teacher-child interactions, and nonverbal communications.

A key strength of the nonexperimental research design is that it can be used to make observations in settings in which the behaviors and events being observed naturally operate. Referring back to the Durden et al. (2014) study, these researchers observed 28 children and 51 teachers (graduate students and preservice teachers) in two preschool classrooms. Likewise, we can observe other situations in natural settings—that is, a prisoner and a guard in a prison or an athlete and a coach during a game. In each example, we make observations in a setting where the subjects or participants being observed would naturally interact.

A key limitation of the nonexperimental research design is that it lacks the control needed to demonstrate cause and effect. For example, if the classroom environment lacked

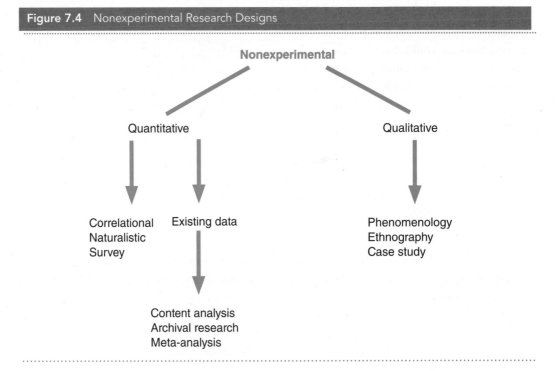

Figure 7.4 Nonexperimental Research Designs

Section II: Defining and Measuring Variables, Selecting Samples, and Choosing an Appropriate Research Design

an ethnically and gender diverse library of books, toys, and games, we cannot know for sure that non–culturally relevant pedagogical practices caused that lack of diversity because other factors (e.g., monetary resources, classroom space, administrative decisions) could also explain the type of classroom supplies present. It is often difficult to anticipate all alternative explanations for what is observed in a natural setting. Using a nonexperimental research design, then, we can speculate about potential causes for the observations we make, but we cannot know for sure without greater control.

MAKING SENSE—"CAUSE" AS THE STANDARD OF RESEARCH DESIGN?

As shown in Figure 7.5, we could characterize a research design as either having demonstrated cause and effect (i.e., experimental research design) or having failed to establish the control needed to do so (i.e., nonexperimental and quasi-experimental designs). This characterization can lead to the erroneous conclusion that the best or superior research designs are those that demonstrate cause—this conclusion is not true.

Certainly, one of the goals in science discussed in Chapter 1 is to *explain* the causes of the behaviors and events we observe. An experimental research design is the only design capable of meeting this goal. However, it is also a goal in science to *describe* the behaviors and events we observe and to determine the extent to which we can *predict* their occurrence in different situations. Nonexperimental and quasi-experimental research designs are well adapted to meet these goals. Studying behavior is complex, and we must understand that not all behaviors and events can be brought under the full control of a researcher. Therefore, nonexperimental and quasi-experimental research designs are an essential and valuable tool that allows researchers to meet the goals of science and add to an understanding of the behaviors and events they observe.

Figure 7.5 Classifying Research Designs by Whether They Can Demonstrate Cause and Effect

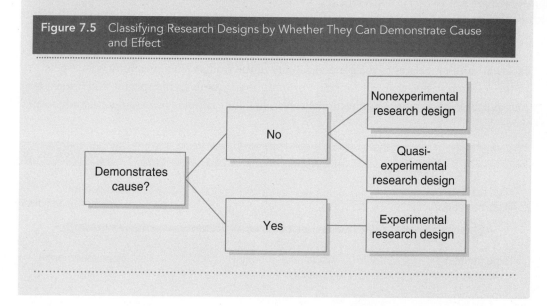

7.3 Internal and External Validity

Categorizing research design is rather difficult. Indeed, there is not even full agreement among scientists about what types of research designs fit into each category. In other research methods textbooks, for example, many of the quasi-experimental designs listed in Figure 7.3 are instead taught as being nonexperimental designs. However, try not to get bogged down in the categorization of research design. Instead, use the three main categories of research design—experimental, quasi-experimental, and nonexperimental—as a way to organize the general types of designs used.

Categorization can oversimplify the complexity of research design. For example, you will find in Chapter 9 that the single-case design is taught as a type of experiment; however, not all researchers agree on this categorization. In Chapter 12, you will find that sometimes we can combine research designs that belong to different categories. The idea here is that thinking of research design only in terms of categories takes away from the true complexity of research design. A better approach is to think of research design along a gradient of control, as illustrated in Figure 7.6. Experimental research designs have the greatest control in that the conditions and experiences of participants are under the full control of the researcher. This control is less in a quasi-experimental research design and can be absent in a nonexperimental research design.

> Internal validity is higher with greater control; external validity is higher with fewer constraints.

The level of control in a research design directly relates to internal validity or the extent to which the research design can demonstrate cause and effect. The more control in a research design, the higher the internal validity. Experimental research designs have the greatest control and therefore the highest internal validity; nonexperimental research designs typically have the least control and therefore the lowest internal validity.

A second validity for research design, called external validity, relates to the generalizability of the study. Generalizability is an aspect of the research design that can constrain or limit observations to the specific conditions or manipulations in a study. An educational researcher, for example, may conduct a study in an

Internal validity is the extent to which a research design includes enough control of the conditions and experiences of participants that it can demonstrate a single unambiguous explanation for a manipulation—that is, cause and effect.

External validity is the extent to which observations made in a study generalize beyond the specific manipulations or constraints in the study.

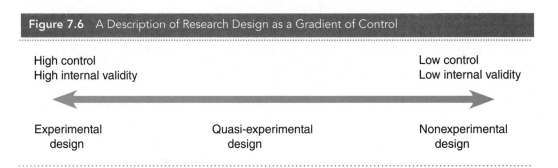

Figure 7.6 A Description of Research Design as a Gradient of Control

High control
High internal validity

Low control
Low internal validity

Experimental
design

Quasi-experimental
design

Nonexperimental
design

urban school setting with only males. The constraints in this study are the school setting and use of only male participants. Would the findings of this study in this situation be the same in other situations, such as in a rural setting or with females? The more an observation generalizes beyond the specific conditions or constraints in a study, the higher the external validity. The fewer the constraints or the more natural the settings within which observations are made, the higher the external validity of a research study tends to be.

7.4 Demonstrating Cause in an Experiment

Any study that demonstrates cause is called an **experiment.** To demonstrate cause, an experiment must follow strict procedures to ensure that all other possible causes have been minimized or eliminated. Therefore, researchers must control the conditions under which observations are made to isolate cause-and-effect relationships between variables. Figure 7.7 uses an example to show the steps of a typical experiment. We will work through this example to describe the basic structure of an experiment.

An **experiment** is the methods and procedures used in an experimental research design to specifically control the conditions under which observations are made to isolate cause-and-effect relationships between variables.

General Elements and Structure of Experiments

An experiment includes three key elements of control that allow researchers to draw cause-and-effect conclusions:

1. Randomization (random sampling and random assignment)

2. Manipulation (of variables that operate in an experiment)

3. Comparison/control (a control group)

The hypothetical experiment illustrated in Figure 7.7 illustrates a hypothetical experiment to determine the effect of distraction on student test scores. To employ **randomization,** we use

Three required elements of control in an experiment are randomization, manipulation, and comparison/control. Each element of control is described further in this section.

Randomization is the use of methods for selecting individuals to participate in a study and assigning them to groups such that each individual has an equal chance of being selected to participate and assigned to a group.

Researchers use randomization to ensure that individuals are selected to participate at random (random sampling or random selection) and are assigned to groups at random (**random assignment**).

An **independent variable** or **factor** is the variable that is manipulated in an experiment. The levels of the variable remain unchanged (or "independent") between groups in an experiment. It is the "presumed cause."

The **levels of a factor** are the specific conditions or groups created by manipulating that factor.

In an experiment, random assignment is used to control for individual differences.

Individual differences are the unique characteristics of participants in a sample that can differ from one participant to another.

A **confound** or confounding variable is a variable not accounted for in a research study that could be causing or associated with observed changes in the independent variable(s).

The **dependent variable** is the variable that is believed to change in the presence of the independent variable. It is the "presumed effect."

random sampling by selecting a sample at random from a population of students, and we then use **random assignment** to assign students to one of two groups at random. In one group, the teacher sits quietly while students take an exam (low-distraction condition); in the other group, the teacher rattles papers, taps her foot, and makes other sounds during an exam (high-distraction condition).

Random sampling is a method of selecting participants such that all individuals have an equal chance of being selected to participate. Random assignment is a method of assigning participants to groups such that each participant has an equal chance of being assigned to each group. To use random assignment, we identify the **independent variable** or **factor** that will be manipulated in an experiment (note that *manipulation* is the second element of control in an experiment). We then assign participants to each **level** of that factor using a random procedure, such as using a random numbers table to assign participants to groups. (Note that a random numbers table is given in Appendix B.1 with instructions for how to use it.) As shown in Figure 7.7, in our experiment, we manipulated "distraction" (the factor), which has two levels (low, high). We then randomly assigned participants to one level or the other. Each level of the independent variable is a group in our design.

Random assignment was first introduced in research with plant seeds (Fisher, 1925, 1935) and has since been applied to research with humans. What was learned in studies with plants is that random assignment controls for the **individual differences** in the characteristics of plants, and the same principle can be applied to human participants. An individual difference is any characteristic that can differentiate people, including their ethnicity, gender, ability level, free and reduced-price lunch status, age or grade, school attendance, or any other characteristic that may differ between people in a specific study.

We use random assignment with humans to control for individual differences in participant characteristics by ensuring that the characteristics of participants in each group of an experiment vary entirely by chance. If we do not control for individual differences, then any number of participant characteristics could differ between groups and explain an observed difference between groups. The individual differences would be a **confound,** or an alternative explanation for an observation in an experiment by affecting the independent variable. In our hypothetical experiment regarding distraction during an exam, a possible confounding variable may be hearing acuity. If students from one group had lower hearing acuity than the other, it may serve as an alternate explanation of the independent variable.

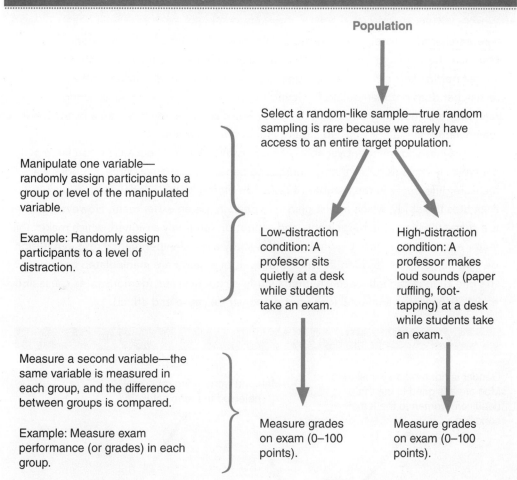

We create at least two groups in an experiment so that a presumed cause (high distraction) can be compared to a group where it is absent or minimal (low distraction). We can then compare grades in each group to determine the difference or effect that distraction had on exam grades. The measured variable in an experiment is called the **dependent variable.** If a difference is observed between the low- and high-distraction groups, then we conclude that distraction levels caused the difference because we used randomization, manipulation, and comparison/control to design the experiment.

Uncontrolled variables that directly affect the dependent variable are called extraneous variables. Like confounding variables, they add error to the experiment by affecting the results of the study. Possible extraneous variables in our hypothetical study of distraction on test scores may be tiredness, time of day, or student interest in the content area. Additional factors to be considered to draw cause-and-effect conclusions are described in Section 7.6.

An extraneous variable is one that is not controlled for in the study that affects the dependent variable.

In an experiment, the independent variable is manipulated to create groups; the dependent variable is measured in each group.

A researcher must manipulate the independent variable or factor in an experiment. Manipulating the factor means that the researcher creates the levels of that factor so that participants can then be assigned to a level or group at random. If the researcher does not manipulate the levels of the factor, then participants cannot be randomly assigned to groups, and the study is not an experiment. When a factor is not manipulated, the factor is called a quasi-independent variable.

Quasi-independent variables can be readily identified because these factors are typically characteristics that are unique to participants. For example, suppose we measure differences in the number of tasks completed by men and women. Figure 7.8 illustrates this study, which at first glance appears to be an experiment. However, gender is a characteristic of the participants and cannot be randomly assigned, which makes this factor a quasi-independent variable and this study a quasi-experimental research design. Be careful, therefore, to identify when the levels of a factor are manipulated because this one change can influence whether a study is experimental (demonstrates cause and effect) or quasi-experimental (does not demonstrate cause and effect).

Figure 7.8 A Quasi-Experimental Research Design

Gender is not randomly assigned. Men are assigned to the male condition; women to the female condition.

Men and women are randomly selected to participate.

Male condition:
Men are asked to complete as many tasks as possible in 5 minutes.

Female condition:
Women are asked to complete as many tasks as possible in 5 minutes.

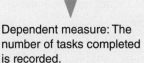

Dependent measure: The number of tasks completed is recorded.

Dependent measure: The number of tasks completed is recorded.

Note: Although experimental procedures are used, the factor (gender) was preexisting, which makes this a quasi-experimental research design.

7.5 Ethics in Focus: Beneficence and Random Assignment

In an experiment, researchers manipulate the levels of an independent variable and randomly assign participants to groups to establish control. Researchers also include a control or comparison group. In the example illustrated in Figure 7.7, a high-distraction condition was compared to a low-distraction condition. This example is likely associated with little ethical concern because manipulating the levels of distraction did not necessarily result in significant benefits or risks to participants. However, some situations may produce big differences in how participants are treated in each group. In these situations, there can be an ethical concern that relates to *beneficence*, which is the equal distribution of potential costs and benefits of participation (see Chapter 3).

Random assignment ensures that all participants in the research study have an equal chance of being assigned to a group and, therefore, an equal chance of receiving whatever benefits and costs are associated with participation in that group. Random assignment, however, may not be sufficient when one group has obviously greater benefits than another group. For example, studies that examine effectiveness of different instructional methods can have significant benefits for those participants receiving a superior type of instruction; thus, the control group (no instruction condition) or a comparison group (alternate or typical instruction) can be viewed as relatively disadvantaged. In these situations, researchers will often compensate the disadvantaged group, such as giving the control or comparison group access to the superior instruction at some time after the study, referred to as *compensatory equalization of treatments* (see Kline, 2008) or delayed treatment. Such compensation is provided to participants to meet the ethical standard of beneficence, as required in the American Educational Research Association (2011) code of conduct.

> Random assignment ensures that participants have an equal chance of receiving the benefits or taking the risks associated with participation in a group.

LEARNING CHECK 3 ✓

1. State three elements of control in an experiment that allow researchers to draw cause-and-effect conclusions.

2. An educational researcher tests whether attitudes toward full inclusion of students with disabilities in general education classes differ based on grade band (elementary, middle, or high school). Identify the independent variable and the dependent variable in this example.

3. A researcher examining the effects of a new math intervention fails to control for the reading ability of the students taking the math test. Is the reading ability of the students an extraneous or confounding variable?

Answers: 1. Randomization, manipulation, and comparison/control; 2. Independent variable: grade band. Dependent variable: Attitudes toward full inclusion; 3. Extraneous variable.

Conducting an experiment in an educational context is difficult because of the natural grouping of students into classrooms. In the context of a classroom setting, it is a challenge to assign individual students to receive different experiences. Here are some things to think about when thinking about undergoing a study within a classroom.

- Can the students be randomly assigned individually to a treatment or comparison group? The answer to this question is not always no, even within a classroom. For example, if you are interested in examining different ways to manage small group work, you could randomly assign individual students to a small group and then randomly assign the small groups different ways to operate (such as some groups with certain roles and rules and other groups without the roles and rules).

- Consider how much control you can have over the intervention—who gets it and how much they get. An experiment about different types of homework would be more difficult to control than an experiment of different ways to manage small groups during a class activity. Homework is conducted outside of the teacher purview and therefore will have less control than a small group activity that occurs under the direction of the teacher.

- Recruit your students to be a part of your investigation. Prior to beginning the study, inform the students what you plan to do and why. Avoid statements that predict that one form of intervention may be better than another; instead, simply say you want to know which intervention is better. Let them know that you will be seeking their input after the study. You can pass out a short survey or hold a focus group discussion to see what your students think.

- If conducting an experiment with treatment and comparison groups, make sure to treat each group equitably. Each group should receive an equal amount of your attention and feel important to the study. Both groups should get "something" (i.e., comparable treatment) rather than one group get something and the other group get nothing.

- If it is not possible to manage two different interventions in one classroom, then randomly assign different classrooms to the different interventions. Make sure the classrooms are "equal." You can do this if you teach the same course during two different class periods and students are essentially equal in the sense that they have the same type of students. For example, you will not be able to compare a class designated as AP (Advanced Placement) to a non-AP-designated class.

7.6 Threats to the Internal Validity of a Research Study

Validity was first introduced in Chapter 4 to describe measurement, or the extent to which a variable measures what it is intended to measure. In this chapter, we introduce validity to describe research design, or the extent to which the claim of a researcher fits with what was actually observed in a research study. Factors that threaten (i.e., decrease) the internal validity of a research study are those factors that vary systematically with an independent variable. (Internal validity was introduced in Section 6.3 in this chapter.) Therefore, any threat to the internal validity of a study is a potential confound that must be controlled.

The following is a list of common threats to the internal validity of a research study, which are introduced in this section:

- History and maturation

- Regression and testing effects

- Instrumentation and measurement

- Heterogeneous attrition

- Environmental factors

- Treatment factors

History and Maturation

One threat to internal validity, called a **history effect,** refers to an unanticipated event that co-occurs with a treatment or manipulation in a study. History effects threaten internal validity when the event itself can also explain a research finding. For example, suppose researchers in New York City wanted to study the benefits of reading and so measured well-being on September 7, 2001, and again on September 14, 2001, among a group of participants who read each day for 1 hour during that time. A history effect, or unanticipated event, may have been the 9/11 terrorist attacks, which occurred during the study. If benefits of reading scores decreased, it was just as likely due to the 9/11 attacks (history effect) as it was to the reading manipulation. Other more subtle examples include holidays (e.g., measuring achievement after the winter break), school-related events (e.g., measuring instructional amount of instructional time after the Special Olympics or school pep rally), and public policy (e.g., measuring teacher stress levels before and after a change in education policy). In each case, 9/11, a holiday, school-related events, or public policy (history effects) can also explain any changes in benefits or reading, achievement, instructional time, or stress, respectively.

Another concern relates to **maturation**, which is a threat to internal validity in which a participant's physiological or psychological state changes over time during a study. Maturation refers to internal changes that exist within an individual and are not related to external events. Maturation includes factors such as age, learning, hunger, physical development, and boredom. As an example, suppose that a speech therapist shows that 3- to 4-year-old children improve their speech following her therapy, as illustrated in Figure 7.9. However, 3- to 4-year-old children develop speech naturally during that age period. Some

> Factors that threaten internal validity vary systematically with the levels of an independent variable.

> A **history effect** is a possible threat to internal validity in which an unanticipated event co-occurs with a treatment or manipulation in a study.
>
> **Maturation** is a possible threat to internal validity in which a participant's physiological or psychological state changes over time during a study.

Figure 7.9 Maturation

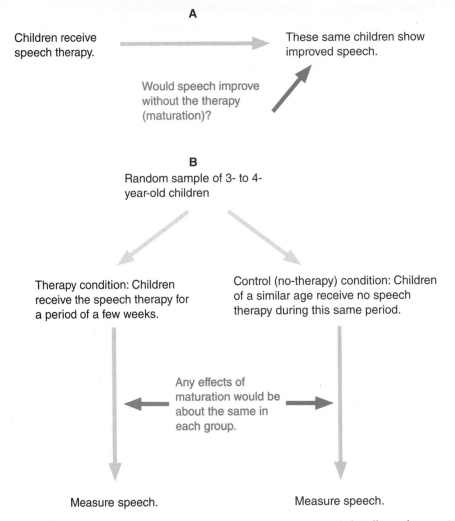

A

Children receive speech therapy. → These same children show improved speech.

Would speech improve without the therapy (maturation)?

B

Random sample of 3- to 4-year-old children

Therapy condition: Children receive the speech therapy for a period of a few weeks.

Control (no-therapy) condition: Children of a similar age receive no speech therapy during this same period.

Any effects of maturation would be about the same in each group.

Measure speech.

Measure speech.

(A) A child's speech could be due to maturation. (B) An experiment that controls for effects of maturation by including an appropriate control condition.

changes during the therapy, then, could simply be due to natural development and not to her specific therapy. One way to eliminate this problem would be to conduct an experiment that includes a no-therapy control condition, also illustrated in Figure 7.9.

Regression and Testing Effects

Regression toward the mean is a change or shift in a participant's performance toward a level or score that is closer to or more typical of his or her true potential or mean ability on some measure, after previously scoring unusually high or low on the same measure.

Some possible threats to internal validity are related to performance. Two examples of this are regression toward the mean and testing effects. **Regression toward the mean** occurs when unusually high or low performance at one time shifts toward a level or score that is more typical or closer to the mean of an individual's true ability at a second time. You see this firsthand any time you obtain a better score on a makeup exam after "bombing" the first exam. One very possible explanation for the change in performance is regression toward the mean or toward one's true abilities.

Regression toward the mean usually occurs when participants are selected from the bottom or top percentile (extreme groups) in a population because initial scores will be unusually high or low for that group. For example, suppose you select a low-performing high school to examine changes in test scores of students after changing the start time to 1 hour later. You then give them a test before and after changing the school start time. As illustrated in Figure 7.10, without a control group that does not have the earlier start time, any improvement in scores on this test could be due to regression toward the mean.

A **testing effect** may be another explanation for the results. Testing effects occur when performance on a test or measure improves the second time it is taken. In the start time study,

> A **testing effect** is the improved performance on a test or measure the second time it is taken due to the experience of taking the test.

the improvement in test scores could be due to a testing effect inasmuch as participants may have learned something about the test the first time they took it. To distinguish between regression toward the mean and testing effects, keep in mind that regression toward the mean can be attributed to an increase or a decrease in performance from one time to another, whereas testing effects are attributed primarily to an increase in performance from one time to another. As illustrated in Figure 7.10, including an appropriate control group (i.e., a no–later start time group) can eliminate both threats to internal validity.

Instrumentation and Measurement

Sometimes an error in the measurement of a variable can threaten the internal validity of a research study. The possible threat of **instrumentation** refers to instances in which the measurement of the dependent variable changes due to low reliability of the instrument. Recall in Chapter 4 we discussed the reliability of measurements in terms of stability (test-retest), internal consistency (how items relate to each other), equivalence (having multiple forms of the same test), and interrater reliability (multiple raters). If the test does not measure the dependent variable consistently, whether it is over time such as a pre- and posttest or across different forms or raters, then

> **Instrumentation** is a possible threat to internal validity in which the measurement of the dependent variable changes due to an error during the course of a research study.

the change in scores during a study may be due to the inadequate ability (i.e., low reliability) of the instrument and not due to a change in participants as a result of the independent variable.

Instrumentation can be problematic when it is inherently prone to error, such as low reliability, but instrumentation may also be a problem due to inadequate training to use the measure. This can be a problem when the dependent measure requires some expertise to administer. For example, suppose three raters rate the time a participant held eye contact with a teacher during instruction. Learning to measure duration of eye contact should be a part

Figure 7.10   Regression Toward the Mean and Testing Effects

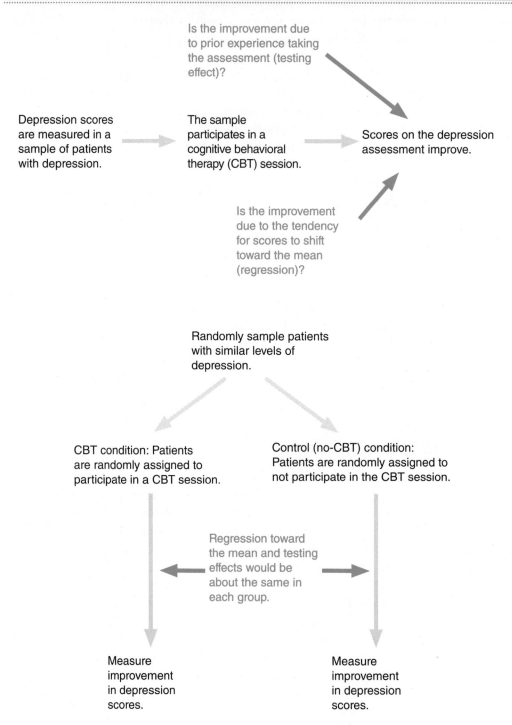

Is the improvement due to prior experience taking the assessment (testing effect)?

Depression scores are measured in a sample of patients with depression.

The sample participates in a cognitive behavioral therapy (CBT) session.

Scores on the depression assessment improve.

Is the improvement due to the tendency for scores to shift toward the mean (regression)?

Randomly sample patients with similar levels of depression.

CBT condition: Patients are randomly assigned to participate in a CBT session.

Control (no-CBT) condition: Patients are randomly assigned to not participate in the CBT session.

Regression toward the mean and testing effects would be about the same in each group.

Measure improvement in depression scores.

Measure improvement in depression scores.

(A) Improved depression scores could be due to regression or testing effects. (B) An experiment that controls for the effects of both factors by including an appropriate control condition.

of the study protocol. If not properly trained, the raters will get better at rating the dependent variable (duration of eye contact) over time. One way to deal with getting better at administering the dependent variable is to intermix the order of the observations such that all of one condition is not run before another. If all female participants, for example, were observed prior to those in the male participants, then it is possible that ratings were better for the group that was observed last (the male group). In this case, instrumentation can threaten the internal validity of the study because the experience of the raters varies systematically with the levels of the factor, as illustrated in Figure 7.11.

> **Attrition**, or **experimental mortality**, is a possible threat to validity in which a participant does not show up for a study at a scheduled time or fails to complete the study.
>
> **Heterogeneous attrition** is a possible threat to internal validity in which rates of attrition are different between groups in a study.

Attrition or Experimental Mortality

A common threat to internal validity can arise when a study is conducted across time such as multiple trials, days, or weeks. The problem of **attrition**, or **experimental mortality**, occurs when a participant does not show up for a study at a scheduled time

Figure 7.11	Instrumentation

A random sample of recent college graduates is selected to participate.

Male condition:
Participants have a mock interview with a male interviewer.
Dependent variable: The time a participant held eye contact (judged by three raters).

Female condition:
Participants have a mock interview with a female interviewer.
Dependent variable: The time a participant held eye contact (judged by three raters).

Instrumentation

Raters estimated the dependent measure for this group last.
So they were more experienced— possibly resulting in more consistent measures.

Raters estimated the dependent measure for this group first.
So they were less experienced— possibly resulting in less consistent measures.

The experience of the raters (instrumentation) varies systematically with the independent variable (gender of interviewer), which threatens the internal validity of the study.

or fails to complete the study. A type of attrition that specifically threatens internal validity is called **heterogeneous attrition** , which occurs when attrition rates in one group are more or less than attrition rates in another group. Heterogeneous attrition is a threat to internal validity because attrition rates are different in each group. To illustrate, suppose you randomly assign children with a behavioral disorder to receive or not receive an intervention. In this case, the intervention group is likely to be a more tedious or demanding group for the children. If more children in the intervention than the no-intervention group drop out of the study, then attrition rates are now different between groups, and thus attrition rates vary systematically with the levels of the independent variable, as shown in Figure 7.12. Hence, the different rates of attrition can also potentially explain differences between groups in this example.

Another type of attrition, called **homogeneous attrition** , occurs when rates of attrition are the same in each group. Because attrition rates are the same in each group, homogeneous attrition does not threaten internal validity. It can, however, threaten the external validity of the study as defined and described further in Section 7.7.

Environmental Factors

Often, it is characteristics or dynamics of the study itself and the actions of the researcher that can a pose threats to internal validity. These types of threats are collectively referred to as *environmental factors*. Environmental factors include the time of day when a study is conducted, how researchers treat participants, and the location of the study.

Figure 7.12 Heterogeneous Attrition

Randomly sample children with a
behavioral disorder.

Intervention condition:
Children receive an intervention
aimed to alleviate the disorder.

Control condition:
Children do not receive the intervention and
instead receive some neutral treatment to
fill in the time.

**Heterogeneous
attrition**

High attrition rate: A high
percentage of participants drop
out of the study from this group.

Low attrition rate: A low percentage
of participants drop out of the
study from this group.

Note: In this example, attrition rates vary systematically with the independent variable, which threatens the internal validity of the study.

Environmental factors can vary from one research design to another, so these factors should be carefully considered before conducting a study.

An environmental factor can only threaten the internal validity of a study when it varies systemically with the levels of an independent variable. Suppose, for example, you conduct a study to determine how participants judge the time they spend studying. In one group, participants rate their studying time each evening for a week; in a second group, participants rate their studying at the end of the week. In this case, if participants in one group had a test scheduled that week and those in a second group did not have a test scheduled that week, then this new factor (scheduled test) could threaten the internal validity of the study because it varies systematically with the levels of the independent variable (the rating format daily or weekly). Each environmental factor should be held constant so that only the rating format varies between groups.

Another way that the actions of the researcher can pose a threat to the internal validity of a study is when the researcher plays a role in the study itself. This is called experimenter effects. A researcher has a conflict of interest when it comes to the outcomes of the study. A researcher has spent time and effort in preparing for a study, and even if a hypothesis is not explicitly stated, there is an idea of what the outcome of the study may be. When the researcher then plays a role in the study such as conducting the educational intervention or collecting data on the dependent variable, this bias may alter the findings. For example, the researcher may alter effects of the intervention by being overly enthusiastic with the treatment group and not the control group or unconsciously help the students in the treatment group during the posttest. To combat this possibility, educational researchers should train others, called interventionists, to deliver the treatment and collect data. Many times, this could be the regular school teacher or a trained graduate student or other member of the research team.

Treatment Factors

Treatment factors can also affect the internal validity of a study when conducting an experimental study. These factors include threats called treatment replications, diffusion of treatment, and participant effects. The treatment replication threat to internal validity involves delivering the treatment for a long enough period of time after which the effect is expected to occur. If the treatment is not delivered long enough, the effect of the treatment may not be seen, even if the treatment is a successful one. For example, a researcher designs an intervention to use graphic organizers, understand social studies content, and deliver the graphic organizer treatment for only one social studies session. It is unlikely that the effect of the graphic organizer will be seen. The time it takes to see the desired effect varies with the intervention and the participants. Prior research conducted by other researchers and personal experience of the researcher can provide information on the length of time a specific treatment should be delivered.

A second treatment factor that can affect the interval validity of a study is called diffusion of treatment. This is when the treatment inadvertently gets delivered to the control group. Treatment diffusion may occur in two ways when participants are within close proximity to each other. One way that treatment diffusion can occur is when the person delivers the treatment in the view of all participants, both treatment and control. For example, a researcher is delivering two different types of reading instruction to separate reading groups that occur within the classroom. While one group is receiving one type of reading instruction, the other group could be listening in or watching. A second way that treatment diffusion occurs is when the participants of different conditions (i.e., treatment and control groups) talk to each other about the study. Participants in the treatment group may share vital information about the treatment that changes the behavior of the participant in the control group. Another way that treatment diffusion can occur in research that is conducted in educational settings is when some form of the treatment is delivered to participants in the control group outside of the educational setting. Take the parent who purchased that "Getting Hooked on Phonics" CD for his or her child who happened to be in the whole language condition of a study. This would be treatment diffusion. Researchers should monitor for treatment diffusion whenever this possibility exists through observation and communication with the interventionists.

It is also possible for participants to alter their behavior as a result of simply being selected to participate in a research study. These effects are called participant effects or reactivity effects. Participant effects can be a potential threat to internal validity because the change in participant behavior is not due to the effect of the treatment but is related to just being a part of a research study. The most common of these effects are known as social desirability, the Hawthorne effect, John Henry (or compensatory rivalry) effect, and resentful demoralization. **Social desirability** is when participants change their behavior to put themselves in the best light. They respond in ways that are not true to themselves but in a way that they think would be more socially desirable. This is more likely to occur when the research involves less socially desirable topics such as bullying or academic cheating. The participants may respond in a more socially desirable way by not reporting that they were a perpetrator or victim of a bully or by minimizing the extent of cheating. The other forms of participant effects are related to which condition the participant is assigned. The **Hawthorne effect** occurs when the participants are selected as part of the treatment group and change their behavior because they believe they are getting special treatment. On the other hand, participants who are assigned to the control group may try harder because they were not selected to receive the special treatment. This is called the **John Henry effect** or compensatory rivalry. This is like the old Avis rental car commercial, where they say, "We are number two, so we try harder." Participants assigned to the control group may instead feel demoralized or resentful because they were not selected for the treatment group. This is called **resentful demoralization.** In this case, the participant's behavior changes because he or she is less motivated.

There are several ways to reduce the possibility of participant effects. One way is to less than fully disclose the object of the study so the participant does not know the exact behavior that is under study. We discussed this back in Chapter 3. The researcher will need to share enough about the study so the participant can weigh the risks and benefits of participating but may not know the exact behavior the researcher is interested in studying. Another way to reduce the possibility of participant effects is to offer an alternate or

Social desirability is when the participants change their behavior to put themselves in the best light. They respond in ways that are not true to themselves but in a way that they think would be more socially desirable.

Hawthorne effect occurs when the participants are selected as part of the treatment group and changes their behavior because they believe they are getting special treatment.

John Henry effect (compensatory rivalry effect) is when a participant who is assigned to the control group may try harder because he or she was not selected to receive the special treatment.

Resentful demoralization is when a participant assigned to the control group may instead feel demoralized or resentful because he or she was not selected for the treatment group.

Table 7.2 Internal and External Validity

Type of Validity	What Is Common Among Threats to This Validity?	What Are the Common Threats to This Validity?
Internal validity	All threats vary systematically with the levels of the factor or independent variable.	History, maturation, regression toward the mean, testing effects, instrumentation, heterogeneous attrition, environmental factors, and treatment factors that vary or are different between groups
External validity	All threats are held constant across groups in a study.	Sampling and participant characteristics, homogeneous attrition, research settings, timing of measurements, and the operationalization of constructs

unrelated intervention so both groups get something. Table 7.2 summarizes the threats to internal validity that were described in this section and also describes the threats to external validity that will be introduced in Section 7.7.

LEARNING CHECK 4 ✓

1. What is characteristic of a factor that threatens the internal validity of a research study?

2. A teacher records scores for 10 students who took a midterm and a makeup midterm exam. She finds that scores improved on the makeup exam. Which two factors can likely threaten the internal validity of this result?

3. Explain why heterogeneous attrition, and not homogeneous attrition, is a threat to internal validity.

4. Name the different treatment factors that can affect internal validity.

Answers: 1. Factors that threaten the internal validity of a research study vary systematically with the levels of the independent variable. 2. Regression toward the mean and testing effects; 3. Heterogeneous attrition, but not homogeneous attrition, occurs when attrition rates differ between groups and, therefore, only heterogeneous attrition is a threat to internal validity because it varies systematically with the levels of an independent variable. 4. Treatment replications, diffusion of treatment, social desirability, Hawthorne effect, John Henry effect (compensatory rivalry), and resentful demoralization.

7.7 Threats to the External Validity of a Research Study

Threats to internal validity vary systematically with the levels of an independent variable. However, it can also be problematic when factors that are held constant between groups threaten the external validity of a study. Factors that threaten the external validity of a study limit the extent to which observations made by a researcher generalize beyond the constraints of the study. (External validity was introduced in Section 6.3 in this chapter.) Hence, the factor that is held constant becomes the constraint to which observations are limited.

External validity is a broad term and can be subcategorized into at least four validities, each of which is described in Table 7.3. The following common threats to the external validity of a research study are described in this section:

- Population validity
- Ecological validity
- Temporal validity
- Outcome validity
- Treatment validity

Factors that threaten external validity are held constant across groups in a study.

Population Validity: Sampling and Participant Characteristics

Results observed in a study can sometimes be constrained to the sample. The extent to which results generalize to the population from which a sample was selected is called **population validity**. Researchers select samples to learn more about the populations from which the samples were selected. Sampling directly from the target population will result in the highest

Population validity is the extent to which results observed in a study will generalize to the population from which a sample was selected.

Table 7.3 Five Subcategories for External Validity

Subcategory of External Validity	Description	Threats to This Subcategory of External Validity
Population validity	The extent to which results observed in a study will generalize to the target population	Sampling methods and participant characteristics
Ecological validity	The extent to which results observed in a study will generalize across settings or environments	Research settings
Temporal validity	The extent to which results observed in a study will generalize across time and at different points in time	Timing of measurements, changes in our understanding of constructs over time
Outcome validity	The extent to which results observed in a study will generalize across different but related dependent variables	Operationalization of constructs
Treatment validity	The extent to which results observed in a study will generalize across different ways the intervention or treatment is conceptualized and administered	Implementing the treatment in different ways and varying amounts of time

population validity. However, this sampling method is often too difficult, so researchers more often select a sample of participants from a portion of the target population that is accessible, as described in Chapter 6, and illustrated here in Figure 7.13. When researchers select samples from an accessible population, they use strategies to ensure that characteristics in the sample are similar to those in the larger population, which will increase the population validity of a study.

One threat to population validity is **homogeneous attrition,** which occurs when the same number of participants from different conditions of a study does not show up at a scheduled time or fails to complete a study. In these cases, it is possible that participants who drop out or do not show up for a study are systematically different from those who do participate in the full study. Hence, the observations we make in the study will have low population validity in that results may be limited to only those participants who show up to participate and may not generalize to those

> **Homogeneous attrition** is a threat to population validity in which rates of attrition are about the same in each group.

Figure 7.13

Population

Select a random-like sample—true random sampling is rare because we rarely have access to an entire target population.

Manipulate one variable—randomly assign participants to a group or level of the manipulated variable.

Example: Randomly assign participants to a level of distraction.

Low-distraction condition: A professor sits quietly at a desk while students take an exam.

High-distraction condition: A professor makes loud sounds (paper ruffling, foot-tapping) at a desk while students take an exam.

Measure a second variable—the same variable is measured in each group, and the difference between groups is compared.

Example: Measure exam performance (or grades) in each group.

Measure grades on exam (0–100 points).

Measure grades on exam (0–100 points).

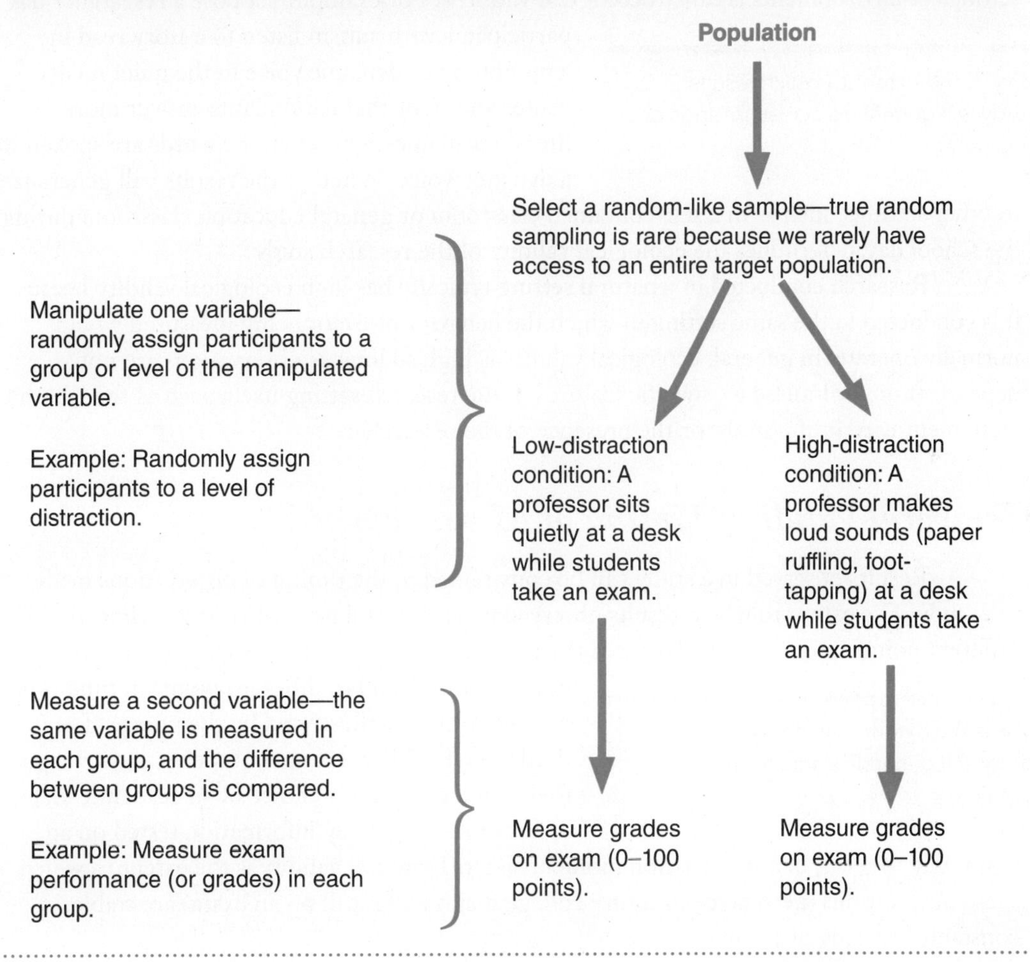

who do not. If differences between participants who complete and do not complete a study are related to changes in the dependent variable, this can lead to bias in the study (Goldkamp, 2008; Scott, Sonis, Creamer, & Dennis, 2006).

The key concern for population validity is that an effect that is observed in a study will only occur in that study. However, keep in mind that even when researchers use appropriate sampling methods, many results in a study can be constrained to a variety of factors even within a given population. For example, characteristics of teachers vary by grade band, and definitions of disabilities vary by state. If we study teacher characteristics or students with disabilities in the United States, then we must recognize that differences exist for these factors within the U.S. population. Issues of population validity, then, extend far beyond the methods used to select samples from populations. For this reason, it is important to be cautious in the extent to which we generalize observations to a larger population.

Ecological Validity: Research Settings

Results observed in a study can be constrained to the research setting in which observations were made. The extent to which results observed in a study will generalize across settings or environments is called ecological validity. For example, suppose a researcher has participants with autism listen to a story read in a monotone or dynamic voice in the quiet media center and finds that participants answer more literal recall questions when the words are spoken in a dynamic voice. Whether the results will generalize to other settings, such as in a self-contained classroom or general education classroom during the school day, determines the ecological validity of the research study.

> Ecological validity is the extent to which results observed in a study will generalize across settings or environments.

Research conducted in a natural setting typically has high ecological validity because it is conducted in the same setting in which the behavior or event being measured would normally operate. In general, ecological validity is high so long as observations are not dependent on, or limited to, specific features of the research setting itself, such as the lab, the equipment used in the study, or the presence of the researcher.

Temporal Validity: Timing of Measurements

Results observed in a study can be constrained to the timing of observations made in a study. The extent to which results observed in a study will generalize across time and at different points in time is called temporal validity. The timing of measurements refers to the passage of time and to different points in time. The passage of time is illustrated by the phrase "Let me think about it." For example, students may change their mind about their choice of an academic major, or they may forget key information tested on an exam only to recall that information moments later. Temporal validity is the extent to which these observations (i.e., choice of future college major and recall on an exam) are stable, constant, or steady over time.

> Temporal validity is the extent to which results observed in a study will generalize across time and at different points in time.

Temporal validity may also be related to how our explanations of behaviors change over time. As a result of research or changing attitudes, we may come to view or understand behaviors differently. We have many examples of this in education. One example of how ideas change over time is attention-deficit hyperactivity disorder (ADHD; Lange, Reichl, Lange, Tucha, & Tucha, 2010). In the 1960s, ADHD was called minimal brain dysfunction and referred to a class of learning problems presumed to be neurologically based and also included learning disability. This term was replaced in the 1970s with *hyperkinetic reaction in childhood* and recognized the hyperactivity aspect. In the late 1970s and early 1980s, the term *attention-deficit disorder* was introduced and distinguished with and without hyperactivity but was quickly replaced in the late 1980s with ADHD. This is the term we currently use to describe a persistent pattern of inattention and/or hyperactivity, but now there are three distinct subtypes: predominantly inattention, predominantly hyperactive, and combined. Autism and learning disability follow a similar pattern or change in understanding and diagnosis. We must consider these changes when evaluating the impact of temporal validity of research.

Outcome Validity: Operationalization of Constructs

Results observed in a study can be constrained to how the researcher defines the dependent variables. The extent to which results observed in a study generalize across related dependent measures for a variable or construct is called outcome validity. For example, if a study showed that a new behavioral intervention helped children stay on task, then it would have high outcome validity if it also showed that it reduced the number of times children disrupted the class. Disrupting class (outcome) is a different but related dependent variable to staying on task (outcome).

> **Outcome validity** is the extent to which the results or outcomes observed in a study will generalize across different but related dependent variables.

As another example, if a study showed an effect of increased hunger, then it would have high outcome validity if it also showed an effect of increased calories consumed in a meal, for example. In this example, calories consumed in a meal (outcome) are a different but related dependent variable to hunger (outcome). Outcome validity, then, is the extent to which the outcomes or results of a research study can be generalized across different but related dependent variables. Hence, high outcome validity allows researchers to generalize a result or outcome beyond the specific measures used in a study.

Treatment Validity: Operationalization of Treatments

Results of a study can be constrained by the extent to which a treatment is conceptualized and implemented. The extent to which the treatment can be generalized is called treatment validity. The question is whether the treatment can be implemented as it is conceptualized to other individuals. The key to treatment validity is the thorough description of the different components of the treatment, who

> **Treatment validity** is the extent to which the treatment can be generalized, whether the treatment can be implemented as it is conceptualized to other individuals.

delivered the treatment (such as teacher, paraeducator, or certified therapist), and dosage of the treatment (number and duration of treatments). Interventions that are difficult to implement or extend over a long period of time may be more difficult to generalize.

LEARNING CHECK 5 ✓

1. What is characteristic of a factor that threatens the external validity of a research study?

2. State five subcategories of external validity.

3. A researcher found that targeted professional development increased the job satisfaction of middle school teachers. Teachers' increased job satisfaction persisted for 6 months after the training. This study has high _____, which is a subcategory of external validity.

Answers: 1. Factors that threaten external validity are held constant across conditions in a study; 2. Population validity, ecological validity, temporal validity, outcome validity, and treatment validity; 3. Temporal validity.

7.8 External Validity, Experimentation, and Realism

Researchers who conduct laboratory studies are aware that studies conducted in laboratories generally have low external validity, so they make efforts to increase the external validity of their studies. Because researchers can control all aspects of the study in the laboratory, laboratory studies tend to have high internal validity. To increase the external validity of laboratory studies, researchers can take additional steps to make the experimental situation *look* and *feel* as "real" as possible.

The extent to which an experimental situation *looks* real is called **mundane realism.** Suppose, for example, that you want to study gambling behavior. To establish mundane realism, you could create a casino-like setting in a laboratory with flashing lights, coin slots, and other games of risk. If the appearance of the setting looks real to participants, then the study has high mundane realism. Although field experiments, like one in an actual casino, will have higher mundane realism than laboratory experiments, efforts to mimic a "real" setting, such as a casino setting, can substantially increase the external validity of laboratory experiments.

Mundane realism is the extent to which a research setting physically resembles or looks like the natural or real-world environment being simulated.

Experimental realism is the extent to which the psychological aspects of a research setting are meaningful or feel real to participants.

The extent to which an experimental situation *feels* real is called **experimental realism.** In the casino gambling study, the more that participants feel as if they are in a casino during the study, the higher the experimental realism will be. If you set up a "real" casino-like setting in the laboratory, then it would likely have high mundane realism in that it *looks* like a real casino. However, if the study was conducted in a laboratory or academic building, then participants may not entirely *feel* like they are at a real casino—because they realize where they are. In this way, it is important to reflect on both types of realism, as each type is distinct.

To enhance the experimental realism in a study, it is important that the manipulations in a study are meaningful to participants. For example, inherent physical abilities are meaningful to athletes, so we could manipulate high and low self-esteem by manipulating whether an athlete receives positive or negative feedback concerning his or her physical abilities. This manipulation would increase the experimental realism of the study because the manipulation is personally meaningful to participants. In all, making such considerations to increase the mundane realism, the experimental realism, or both in a study will increase the external validity of a research result.

> Increasing the mundane and experimental realism of a study will increase the external validity of the study.

7.9 A Final Thought on Validity and Choosing a Research Design

Selecting a research design requires careful thoughtful planning and some creativity. Be aware that few, if any, research designs will demonstrate high internal and high external validity in the same design. Indeed, some research designs have low internal validity, such as nonexperimental research designs, whereas others have low external validity, such as laboratory experiments. However, the goal in educational research is not to solve the world's educational problems in one study; this goal may not even be possible or realistic. Instead, the goal in educational research is to move forward and advance our knowledge of education and the behaviors and events that operate within it. Researchers are responsible for stating a question and choosing a research design that can answer their question. Researchers must choose an appropriate research design that can answer their question, and they must recognize the limitations of the research designs they choose.

Each research design used in behavioral research has strengths and limitations. Whether a study has high or low internal or external validity will vary from one study to another. For this reason, the greatest advancement of knowledge is found when many different types of research designs, with a complement of strengths and weaknesses, are employed to address the same problem. To advance knowledge, then, you do not have to design the perfect experiment; instead, you must choose an appropriate research design and be cautious to understand its strengths and weaknesses when drawing conclusions from the observations you make. In this way, to advance scientific knowledge, it is as important to be aware of the limitations and strengths of the research designs used to answer a research question.

> High internal and external validity is not a prerequisite for "good" research designs. All research designs have limitations, and it is important that researchers recognize them.

Section III (Chapters 8 to 12) and Section IV (Chapters 13 to 15) will describe the research designs listed for each category of research design in Figures 7.2 to 7.4 in this chapter. You can revisit these figures as you read to help you organize how to think about research design in the chapters ahead.

LO 1 Identify three categories of research design: experimental, quasi-experimental, and nonexperimental.

- A research design is the specific methods and procedures used to answer research questions. The types of research questions that researchers ask are generally categorized as exploratory, descriptive, or relational questions.

- A nonexperimental research design is the use of methods and procedures to make observations in which the behavior or event being observed is observed "as is" or without any intervention from the researcher.

- An experimental research design is the use of methods and procedures to make observations in which the researcher fully controls the conditions and experiences of participants by applying three required elements of control: randomization, manipulation, and comparison/control.

- A quasi-experimental research design is the use of methods and procedures to make observations in a study that is structured similar to an experiment, but the conditions and experiences of participants are not under the full control of the researcher. Specifically, the study includes a preexisting factor (i.e., a variable that is not manipulated: a quasi-independent variable) or lacks a comparison/control group.

LO 2 Explain how a gradient of control can be used to understand research design.

- Categorizing research can oversimplify the complexity of research design. Another way to approach research design is to think of it along a gradient of control. The more control present in a study, the more suited the design will be to demonstrate that one variable causes a change in a dependent variable. Studies with high control will be experimental; the less control in a study, the more quasi-experimental or nonexperimental the research design.

LO 3 Define and explain internal and external validity.

- Internal validity is the extent to which a research design includes enough control of the conditions and experiences of participants that it can demonstrate cause and effect.

- External validity is the extent to which observations made in a study generalize beyond the specific manipulations or constraints in the study.

LO 4 Describe three elements of control required in an experiment.

- An experiment has the following three elements of control that allow researchers to draw cause-and-effect conclusions:

  Randomization (random sampling and random assignment)

  Manipulation (of variables that operate in an experiment)

  Comparison/control (a control group)

- Randomization is used to ensure that individuals are selected to participate and assigned to groups in a study using a random procedure. Manipulation means that a researcher created the levels of the independent variable, thereby allowing the researcher to randomly assign participants to groups in the study. A comparison or control group is used to allow researchers to compare changes in a dependent variable in the presence and in the absence of a manipulation.

LO 5 Describe factors that threaten the internal validity of a research study.

- Factors that threaten the internal validity of a research study will vary systematically with the levels of an independent variable. These factors include history effects, maturation, regression toward the mean, testing effects, instrumentation, heterogeneous attrition, and environmental factors that can vary between groups in a study.

LO 6 Describe factors that threaten the external validity of a research study.

- Factors that threaten the external validity of a research study are those that are held constant across groups in a study. These factors include four subcategories of external validity:
  - Population validity, or the extent to which observations generalize beyond a sample to the population
  - Ecological validity, or the extent to which observations generalize across settings
  - Temporal validity, or the extent to which observations generalize across time or at different points in time
  - Outcome validity, or the extent to which observations generalize across different but related dependent variables

LO 7 Define and explain mundane and experimental realism.

- Mundane realism is the extent to which a research setting physically resembles or *looks* like the natural environment being simulated. Experimental realism is the extent to which the psychological aspects of a research setting are meaningful or *feel* real to participants. A study with high mundane and experimental realism will have high external validity.

KEY TERMS

attrition 203	ecological validity 210	external validity 192
confound 194	experiment 193	Hawthorne effect 206
control 185	experimental mortality 203	heterogeneous attrition 203
dependent variable 195	experimental research design 186	history effect 199

homogeneous attrition 209

independent variable 194

individual differences 194

instrumentation 201

internal validity 192

John Henry effect (compensatory rivalry effect) 206

levels of a factor 194

maturation 199

nonexperimental research design 189

outcome validity 211

population validity 208

quasi-experimental research design 188

quasi-independent variable 188

random assignment 194

randomization 193

regression toward the mean 200

research design 184

resentful demoralization 206

social desirability 206

temporal validity 210

testing effect 201

treatment validity 211

REVIEW QUESTIONS

1. Choose the category of research design that best fits with the description given.

   A. Generally associated with high external validity

   B. Associated with the highest internal validity

   C. Structured as an experiment but lacks the control needed to demonstrate cause and effect

2. State the only category of research design that can demonstrate a cause-and-effect relationship between two factors.

3. In terms of controlling the conditions and experiences of participants:

   A. Which category of research design has the least control?

   B. Which has the most control?

   C. What is the relationship between control and internal validity?

4. State three elements of control that allow researchers to draw cause-and-effect conclusions.

5. Based on the following description of a hypothetical study, identify (a) the independent variable and (b) the dependent variable.

   A researcher believes that students will recall words that appear first and last on a list of vocabulary words more than the words that appear in the middle of the list. She presents each student with a list of 20 words to memorize in 3 minutes, and the words correctly recalled are recorded.

6. State whether each factor listed below is an example of an independent variable or a quasi-independent variable. Only state "quasi-independent variable" for participant variables that cannot be manipulated.

   A. Marital status

   B. Political affiliation

   C. Amount of delay prior to recall

   D. Type of school setting (urban, rural, suburban)

   E. Time spent in reading instruction

   F. Type of feedback (negative, positive)

7. What is characteristic of threats to internal validity? What is characteristic of threats to external validity?

8. A researcher measures the effectiveness of a drug intervention program by measuring the number of arrests of teenagers for drug possession before and after the program. One problem is that police initiate a crackdown on drugs in schools during this same time. What is the history effect in this example?

9. A researcher measures responsiveness to a drug treatment in high school students who volunteered or were mandated to participate. One problem that arises is that many students drop out of the program before the study is completed.

   A. What type of threat to validity does this example illustrate if dropout rates are the same among volunteer and mandated students? Is this a threat to internal or external validity?

   B. What type of threat to validity does this example illustrate if dropout rates differ between volunteer and mandated students? Is this a threat to internal or external validity?

10. Distinguish between regression toward the mean and testing effects as threats to internal validity.

11. Which subcategory of external validity is most likely threatened by homogeneous attrition? Explain.

12. A researcher uses an intervention program at a local youth center to help children with behavioral disorders. The researcher finds that the program was effective in an urban community but not in a rural community. What subcategory of external validity is low in this example? Explain.

13. A researcher measures a student's motivation to succeed as the amount of time spent studying. In a second study, the researcher conducts the same study but instead measures a student's motivation to succeed as the percentage of classes attended during a semester. Different results were observed in each study. What subcategory of external validity is low in this example? Explain.

14. State whether the following study has high mundane realism, high experimental realism, or both. Explain.

A researcher measures gambling behavior among addicted gamblers. The study is conducted at a local casino (the researcher reserved a portion of the casino for the duration of the study). She manipulated whether participants won or lost a predetermined game and recorded the amount of money participants gambled for 1 hour after this manipulation.

ACTIVITIES

1. A researcher hypothesizes that teachers will be more patient if they are also a parent. (a) Describe a research design to test this hypothesis. (b) Explain why you cannot choose an experimental research design for this example. Hint: Consider characteristics of quasi-independent variables.

2. Suppose you choose to conduct a study on fighting at school, eating behavior in school cafeterias, or safety concerns in high poverty area schools. Choose one topic and select and describe a research design.

3. Choose any research topic that interests you and state a research hypothesis. Identify the following information:

   A. Identify whether or not you will use an experimental research design to test your hypothesis. Explain.

   B. Identify factors that may threaten the internal validity of your study. Explain how your research design controls, or fails to control, for these threats to internal validity.

   C. Identify factors that may threaten the external validity of your study. Explain how your research design controls, or fails to control, for these threats to external validity.

NONEXPERIMENTAL RESEARCH DESIGNS

Identify a problem

- Determine an area of interest.
- Review the literature.
- Identify new ideas in your area of interest.
- Develop a research hypothesis.

Develop a research plan

- Define the variables being tested.
- Identify participants or subjects and determine how to sample them.
- Select a research strategy and design.
- Evaluate ethics and obtain institutional approval to conduct research.

Generate more new ideas

- Results support your hypothesis—refine or expand on your ideas.
- Results do not support your hypothesis—reformulate a new idea or start over.

After reading this chapter, you should be able to:

1. Identify and define the naturalistic research design.

2. Distinguish between natural and contrived research settings.

3. Identify and describe how researchers make unobtrusive observations.

4. Describe how researchers operationalize observation periods in a naturalistic or contrived setting.

5. Describe how researchers quantify and manage observation periods in a naturalistic or contrived setting.

6. Identify and describe three existing data research designs: archival research, content analysis, and meta-analysis.

Conduct the study

- Execute the research plan and measure or record the data.

Communicate the results

- Method of communication: oral, written, or in a poster.
- Style of communication: APA guidelines are provided to help prepare style and format.

Analyze and evaluate the data

- Analyze and evaluate the data as they relate to the research hypothesis.
- Summarize data and research results.

chapter eight

NATURALISTIC AND EXISTING DATA RESEARCH DESIGNS

Often, we may be interested in making observations in settings where a behavior nature operates (e.g., where it naturally occurs), or you may be interested in collected data that already exists for a given behavior or events (e.g., academic records). To illustrate, consider the classroom as a naturalistic setting of interest. Suppose you are a researcher and are interested in classroom management variables, such as how teachers manage disruptive behavior in a classroom, how students verbally interact during group collaborative assignments, or how students interact with a peer with a disability.

In a *naturalistic design*, we make our observations in settings where the behaviors of interest naturally occur. For such a study, we could have an administrator, other teacher, or a researcher make observation during a regular class period. Methodologically, the observer needs to be prepared to record observations as it occurs. Keep in mind that the participants in that setting control what happens, not the researcher. If a teacher interacts with a student, that encounter needs to be systematically recorded. The methods using a naturalistic design allow that to happen in such a dynamic setting.

In an *existing data design*, our observations are of data that is retrieved from exiting sources. For such a study, we could instead review previous evaluations of the teacher and even student records for anything from academic grades to recorded incidents of misbehavior or misconduct. Keep in mind that the researcher needs a plan for not only what data will be retrieved but also how it will be retrieved, and even for what time periods. The methods using an existing data allow this to happen to ensure the data can be used to draw valid conclusions.

In this chapter, we introduce research designs that allow us to make these types of observations. We further explore ways of adding information about the observations we make and how to appropriately interpret them.

edge.sagepub.com/priviterarme

- Take the chapter quiz
- Review key terms with eFlashcards
- Explore multimedia links and SAGE articles

$SAGE edge™

NATURALISTIC DESIGNS

Many research designs can be used to test the same hypotheses. This chapter is separated into two major sections; each section describes a nonexperimental research design: the naturalistic and existing data designs. To introduce how each research design can be used to test the same hypothesis, we will begin each major section by developing a new research design to test the same hypothesis.

Suppose we hypothesize that fruits will be eaten more if they are made more convenient. We could use a naturalistic observation to test this hypothesis by observing student selections in the school cafeteria. Before we make observations in this setting, we categorize the fruits as being in a convenient or an inconvenient location in the cafeteria line and then record the number of fruits chosen by the students. This is a naturalistic design because we will make observations in a natural setting (i.e., a school cafeteria) and observe the behavior of students as they would naturally behave in that setting. If we set up the study correctly, we can use the observations we make at the school cafeteria to test the hypothesis that fruits will be eaten more if they are made more convenient.

8.1 An Overview of Naturalistic Design

A naturalistic design is a nonexperimental research design that can be used to make observations in natural settings or in places where the behaviors being observed naturally operate. For example, we could observe buying behavior in the school store, parenting behavior during parent-teacher conferences, relations between coach and student athlete during practice, or the interactions of children at a preschool. In each example, we make a **naturalistic observation,** meaning that we make an observation in the natural setting where we would expect to observe those behaviors.

> A naturalistic design is a nonexperimental research design used to make observations in natural settings or places where the behaviors being observed naturally operate.

The naturalistic research design is associated with high external validity. Recall that external validity is the extent to which observations made in a study generalize beyond the specific manipulations or constraints in the study. Because we do not attempt to overtly manipulate the conditions of the environment using a naturalistic observation, we do not limit or constrain the observations we make. Hence, observations made in natural settings will generalize beyond the limited constraints of the study because we do not limit or constrain the environment using a naturalistic observation. However, also keep in mind that in certain cases, the external validity of observations in a natural setting can still be limited. For example, the reasons why young people join gangs in Los Angeles may be very different from why they join gangs in a rural area of South Carolina. In this example, external validity is limited to the region in which the observations are made.

> The naturalistic research design is generally associated with high external validity but low internal validity.

While external validity is generally high using the naturalistic research design, this design is also associated with low internal validity. Recall that internal validity is the extent to which a research design has enough control of the conditions and experiences of participants that it can demonstrate a single unambiguous explanation for an observed effect—that is, cause and effect. Because we do not overtly manipulate the conditions in a natural environment, we typically have limited control over other possible factors that could be causing the observations we make. Therefore, we cannot necessarily determine what is causing the behaviors that we observe using a naturalistic observation.

8.2 The Research Setting: Natural and Contrived Settings

A **natural setting** is a location that is, or appears to be, the environment where the behavior or event being observed typically occurs. When the natural setting is the location where the behavior typically occurs, the researcher does not have to arrange or manipulate the setting in any way. However, making observations in this setting can be difficult. It can be expensive in that the researcher has to travel to locations where the behaviors naturally occur. It can be time-consuming in that the researcher has to wait for the behaviors to occur, which can also be frustrating because the researcher can spend days or weeks waiting to observe a behavior, such as waiting to observe mating displays among animal species.

An alternative to making observations in natural settings is to instead observe behavior in an arranged or **contrived setting**. A contrived setting is one that is arranged or manipulated to appear the same as the natural environment within which a behavior of interest naturally occurs. A contrived setting should *look* and *feel* natural to increase the external validity of the observations made in that setting—the more a contrived setting looks and feels real, the more likely we are to observe that behavior as it would naturally occur in a natural setting.

> A **natural setting** is a location or site where a behavior of interest normally occurs.
>
> A **contrived setting,** or **structured setting,** is a location or site arranged to mimic the natural setting within which a behavior of interest normally occurs to facilitate the occurrence of that behavior.

To illustrate a research situation in which a contrived setting could be used, we can use the naturalistic observation design to study English language use of young English language learners (ELLs) (see Appelt, 2015; Rader-Brown & Howley, 2014). Suppose we measure English language use among ELL children as they play with peers in a pre-K classroom. An example of a contrived pre-K classroom is illustrated in Figure 8.1. We could create this pre-K classroom in a laboratory or any other location within a school or clinic. To make observations in this setting, we could ask parents to tell their children that they are going to visit a new classroom, then observe the children as they play in the contrived pre-K classroom. Creating a contrived setting, such as the one illustrated in Figure 8.1, has two important advantages.

Researchers make naturalistic observations in a natural or contrived setting.

- We can control many factors that are otherwise impossible to control in a natural setting. In a typical pre-K classroom, for example, we cannot control how many children are in the classroom at a time, where the toys are located, the appearance of the classroom, or the characteristics of the other children. However, in a contrived setting, we can control all of these factors, as described in Figure 8.1. This greater level of control allows us to increase the internal validity of the observations we make in a contrived setting.

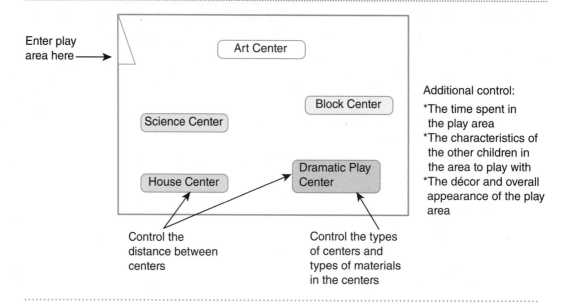

Enter play area here →

Art Center

Block Center

Science Center

Dramatic Play Center

House Center

Additional control:
*The time spent in the play area
*The characteristics of the other children in the area to play with
*The décor and overall appearance of the play area

Control the distance between centers

Control the types of centers and types of materials in the centers

- Second, we can structure the setting to facilitate the occurrence of a behavior. In the pre-K classroom, for example, we can provide only materials that promote interactive play, as illustrated in Figure 8.1, to facilitate the chance of observing play behavior among the children in the classroom. We could also place more popular toys in that area to further enhance our chance of observing play behavior.

LEARNING CHECK 1 ✓

1. Define the naturalistic design.

2. State whether each of the following describes a natural or a contrived setting:

   A. A study on athletic ability in a room arranged to look like a gym

   B. A study on the quality of child care conducted at three local preschools

   C. A study on teacher performance conducted at the school

Answers: 1. Naturalistic design is the observation of behavior in the natural setting where it is expected to occur, with limited or no attempt to overtly manipulate the conditions of the environment where the observations are made; 2. A. contrived, B. natural, C. natural.

8.3 Techniques for Making Unobtrusive Observations

Researchers use many techniques to make naturalistic observations. These techniques are used to ensure that observations are unobtrusive and measurable and that the time period of observations is managed. Each technique is described in this section.

We use a naturalistic observation to observe a behavior as it would naturally occur, so we typically do not want participants to know that they are being observed. In other words, we want to make unobtrusive observations, which are observations that do not interfere with or change a participant's behavior. If participants knew that they were being observed or were influenced by the observations made, then their behavior would not be a natural response in a natural setting—instead, their behavior would be a reaction to being observed. Making unobtrusive observations, then, can minimize or eliminate participant reactivity because participants do not know they are being observed using unobtrusive observation strategies. Four strategies used to make unobtrusive observations are introduced here.

> An **unobtrusive observation** is a technique used by an observer to record or observe behavior in a way that does not interfere with or change a participant's behavior in a research setting.

- *Remain hidden.* To remain hidden, we can never be seen by participants. We could hide behind a curtain or one-way mirror, or we could place hidden cameras in a research setting so that observations can be recorded surreptitiously. In both cases, we remain hidden and out of view of the participants.

- *Habituate participants to the researcher.* In some situations, we may need to be physically in the research setting. One strategy is to allow participants to habituate to, or get used to, our presence. For example, to observe students or a professor in the classroom, we can sit quietly in a classroom for a few class days before actually recording data. This allows for unobtrusive observations inasmuch as those in the classroom habituated to our presence.

- *Use a confederate.* To be present in a research setting, we can also employ a confederate or coresearcher. The confederate would play a role in the study, such as pretending to be a participant. If the confederate is convincing in that role, then he or she can make unobtrusive observations while being present in the research setting. The observations would be unobtrusive so long as participants viewed the confederate as "one of them."

- *Use indirect measures.* A clever strategy is to indirectly measure some behavior in a way that does not make obvious what it is that we are measuring. For example, we could measure recycling behavior by rummaging through trash or recycling bins, which is probably not fun but effective nonetheless. In this way, we can make unobtrusive observations in that our research does not "tip off" participants that they are being observed.

> Making unobtrusive observations minimizes participant reactivity in a setting; we can remain hidden, habituate participants to our presence, use a confederate, or use indirect measures.

8.4 Making Observations

Imagine you are sitting on a bench "people watching" at a mall as you wait for a friend. What might you observe? A couple passing by you holding hands? A mother sharing a conversation with her daughter? A teenager reading a book alone on another bench? These are not uncommon observations one could make at a mall, yet rarely do we consider *how* we make such observations—that is, how do we decide what we are observing?

In the natural setting of a mall, we could begin considering these rules. For example, how do you decide that the couple strolling by you holding hands is in love? How might you observe the nature of the relationship between the mother and the daughter? Or how might you evaluate the content of the book that the student reads on the other bench? In other words, how do you define the constructs you observe each day—constructs such as love, interactions, and content? Specifically, how do we define our observations so that others will see and interpret our observations the same way?

In our examples here, you may identify love by recording how long the couple holds hands; the nature of the relationship between the mother and daughter could be determined by evaluating the content of the conversations they have; content of a book could be evaluated by genre or subject matter. "People watching" can be a great exercise in applying the rules that scientists use to make observations. The rules for observing behavior in quantitative studies in natural settings, such as school settings, are introduced in this chapter. We will discuss qualitative observations in Chapter 10.

In each example, we make a **naturalistic observation**, meaning that we make an observation in the natural setting where we would expect to observe those behaviors.

Naturalistic observation is the observation of behavior in the natural setting where it is expected to occur, with limited or no attempt to overtly manipulate the conditions of the environment where the observations are made.

Operationalizing Observations

The challenge of observing behaviors in a natural setting is being able to know when you actually observed the behavior. Let's suppose that we were interested in studying English language use among ELL children in a pre-K classroom. To know when we are observing English language use, we need to define exactly what "counts" as English language use, which means that we need to anticipate all the different ways that the children communicate. To do this, we define **behavior categories** to identify the specific types of behaviors we intend to measure in the research setting like we did in Figure 8.2.

To list behavior categories, we first identify all the categories of the construct we are measuring, then list examples of what "counts" in each category. In the English language use study, we could anticipate the following categories of language use: questioning, direct request, question answering, praise, admonishment, event description, and no English language use. To define each category of language use, we then need to list examples of how we think the children will communicate in the pre-K classroom so that an observer can recognize that behavior when he or she sees it. For example, we could list "A child says 'I will bake some cookies'" as an example of event description. We would need as exhaustive of a list as possible for all the behavior categories we created.

Behavior categories are the specific types of behaviors that researchers want to measure in the research setting and are typically organized as a list of examples that "count" in each category or for each type of behavior.

Once the researcher has identified the behavior categories and the examples of behaviors that "count" in each category, he or she can make observations. In many cases, what "counts" in each category can be a subjective interpretation, even with the most careful preparation. For example, suppose a child starts to speak in English but then switches to

Spanish within the same sentence—does that still "count" as English language use? To ensure that observations made in a naturalistic observation are reliable, multiple observers are often used to observe the same research setting. Then the level of agreement of each rater, called *interrater reliability*, can be measured. To improve interrater reliability, each rater or observer should be formally trained and have time to prepare and learn the behavior categories that he or she is being asked to observe. One way to accomplish this is to make sure all raters have a list of the examples in front of them with a checklist for coding or recording each occasion that they observed the behavior, similar to the checklist shown in Figure 8.2.

> Researchers define behavior categories using examples that operationalize, or make measurable, each category.

Quantifying Observations

When researchers make an observation, they need to record or quantify that observation in terms of how it was measured. Researchers can use many methods to quantify observations. The following are four such methods.

- An **interval method** is used by dividing an observational period into intervals of time, then recording whether or not certain behaviors occur in each interval. Observations are split into equal time intervals. We use this method to break down long observation intervals of time into smaller units of time.

> An **interval method** is a method used to quantify observations made in a study by dividing an observational period into equal intervals of time and then recording whether or not certain behaviors occur in each interval.
>
> A **frequency method** is a method used to quantify observations made in a study by counting the number of times a behavior occurs during a fixed or predetermined period of time.

- A **frequency method** is used by counting the number of times a behavior occurs during a fixed period of time. The interval method is illustrated in the checklist in Figure 8.2. We use this method when the behavior we observe occurs

---

Figure 8.2   A Checklist for a 10-Minute Observation Period of English Language Use

Type of English Language Use	Frequency
Questioning	
Direct requests	
Question answering	
Praise	
Admonishment	
Event description	
No English language use	

Note: Observers rate or place a checkmark in the appropriate box as they observe the behaviors over time.

often because, if it did not, then we would not have enough observations of the behavior. For example, the frequency method could be used to count the number of times a teenager uses cusswords around other friends; however, this behavior may occur much less around the teen's parents, so a frequency method may not be the best method to quantify observations in this case.

- A **duration method** is used by recording the amount of time or duration that a participant engages in a certain behavior during a fixed period of time. We use this method to record behaviors that participants engage in over a period of time. For example, we can use the duration method to record the length of time the child engaged in tantrum behavior or the amount of time it took a participant to solve a math problem. For this method, the behavior being observed must have a clearly defined start and end before we make observations. For example, we define "completing a math problem" as starting when the problem is given to the participant and finishing when the problem is solved.

A **duration method** is a method used to quantify observations made in a study by recording the amount of time or duration that participants engage in a certain behavior during a fixed period of time.

A **latency method** is a method used to quantify observations made in a study by recording the time or duration between the occurrences of behaviors during a fixed period of time.

- A **latency method** is used by recording the time or duration between behaviors during a fixed period of time. We use this method to record behaviors that are repeated. For example, we may record the time (i.e., latency) in seconds between when a teacher asks a question and the student raises his or her hand to answer or the latency between each time a student looks at his or her phone during a class. Like the duration method, the behavior being observed using the latency method must have a clearly defined start and end before we make observations.

The four methods of quantifying behaviors described here are among the most common methods applied in the behavioral sciences but are not the only methods used. Other methods for quantifying behaviors include the *topography method* (the shape or style of behavior is recorded), the *force method* (the intensity of a behavior is recorded), and the *locus method* (the location of a behavior is recorded). Ultimately, each method is used to quantify or make measurable the behaviors observed in a natural setting.

Managing the Observational Period

A naturalistic observation requires strong time management on the part of the researcher because behaviors can occur at any time and at different rates. Having strong time management becomes even more important when the researcher needs to observe multiple behaviors during a single observation period. To minimize any possible stress on the part of the observer or researcher, he or she must plan for how observations will be made. The most effective strategy is often to use a recording device, such as a video or audio device, when possible. This allows researchers to view the observation setting as often as they need, thereby giving them more time to make their judgments because recordings can be replayed repeatedly.

However, the use of recording devices may not always be possible due to ethical concerns, such as putting cameras in a person's home or maybe a lack of funding to afford expensive video equipment. Whatever the reason, many naturalistic observations do not use recording devices, and in those cases, we can use one of the following three strategies to manage the observation period:

- **Time sampling** is used by splitting a fixed period of time into smaller intervals of time, then making observations during alternating intervals. For example, suppose we record behaviors that occur during a 5-minute period. Using a time sampling strategy, we could first divide the 5-minute observation period into intervals of 30 seconds. We then record observations for the first 30-second interval; take a break for the next 30-second interval, maybe using that time to check that all behaviors were accurately recorded; and again record observations for a 30-second interval, repeating this pattern until the 5-minute observational period has ended.

- **Event sampling** is used by splitting a fixed period of time into smaller intervals of time, then recording a different behavior in each time interval. In the dentist's office waiting room study, for example, we could split a 5-minute observation period into ten 30-second intervals, then record each of the five types of play behavior twice over the full 5-minute observation period: once in the first half and again in the second half of the observation period. Using event sampling, we want to make sure that each event is recorded for the same duration (each type of play behavior will be observed for 1 minute total) and spread out at different points in time (each type of play behavior will be observed in the first and second half of the 5-minute observation period).

> **Time sampling** is a strategy used to manage an observation period by splitting a fixed period of time into smaller intervals of time and then making observations during alternating intervals until the full observation period has ended.
>
> **Event sampling** is a strategy used to manage an observation period by splitting a fixed period of time into smaller intervals of time and then recording a different behavior in each time interval.
>
> **Individual sampling** is a strategy used to manage an observation period by splitting a fixed period of time into smaller intervals of time and then recording the behaviors of a different participant in each time interval.

- **Individual sampling** is used by splitting a fixed period of time into smaller intervals of time, then recording the behavior of a different participant in each time interval. This strategy is similar to event sampling, except that we switch from one participant to another instead of from one event to another. For example, to observe two participants during a 4-minute interval, we could split the observation period into four intervals of 1 minute each and then alternate recording the behavior of each participant in each interval until the 4-minute period is complete. Similar to event sampling, it is important that all participants be recorded for the same duration and spread out at different points in time. This strategy can be most useful when we want to preserve the order in which participants behave over time (e.g., she did this first, then she did this).

Minimizing Bias in Observation

Interpreting what we observe can be difficult because each person is inherently biased inasmuch as each person has a unique perspective. This is one reason why we compare the reliability of ratings made by multiple observers in a study—to check that each rater had similar ratings or interpretations of the behaviors or events observed in a study. One particular concern is observer or experimenter bias, which was introduced in Chapter 4. Observer bias occurs any time the observer knows the intent or purpose of a research study because this knowledge of the purpose of the study could influence how he or she observes or interprets a research situation, often unknowingly. A solution, when possible, is for a primary investigator to train observers and not reveal the purpose of the study to the observers. So long as the observers are *blind* to the purpose of the study, then the influence of observer bias is unlikely.

Another caution is to only record behaviors as they were quantified and not to make interpretations during an observation. It is a human tendency to interpret or find a cause of what was observed. As an example of this tendency, paranormal investigators will often infer changes in polarity and unexplained noises in a dark room as evidence of activity from spirits. In truth, the polarity of the Earth naturally fluctuates, and unexplained noises are just that—unexplained. An interpretation of these observations as being caused by the presence of spirits is unnecessary; however, this typically will not stop many from trying to infer meaning from these observations.

> Observer bias can lead to misinterpretation of what is observed.

In a research situation, an observer is rarely needed to interpret behavior. Instead, the job of an observer is typically to record the occurrence or absence of a behavior, and that is all. For an observer, interpretations should be considered at a later time and not during an observational period.

LEARNING CHECK 2 ✓

1. State four ways that a researcher can make unobtrusive observations.

2. How are behavior categories typically defined in naturalistic research?

3. To measure nervousness, a researcher counts the number of times that a student says the word *um* during a class presentation. Which method was used to quantify nervousness?

4. A researcher records the attentiveness of students in a classroom setting for 10 minutes, then takes a break for 10 minutes. This pattern is repeated for a 60-minute observation period. Which method of sampling was used to manage the observation period?

5. What are two sources of bias during an observation period?

Answers: 1. Remain hidden, habituate participants to the researcher, use a confederate, and use indirect measures; 2. As a list of examples that "count" in each behavior category; 3. Frequency method; 4. Time sampling; 5. Observer or experimenter bias, and the tendency of observers to infer meaning from what was observed.

8.5 Ethics in Focus: Influencing Participant Behavior

In many situations, a researcher may find that making naturalistic observations can be an ethical alternative to conducting an experiment. For example, if a researcher wanted to conduct a study on reactions to bullying behavior of adolescent girls, in a contrived setting, the researcher would need to manipulate the environment with a confederate to simulate bullying behavior. Such a study would be largely unethical in an experiment because we would need to randomly assign adolescent girls to various types of bullying behavior. Randomly assigning participants to be a victim of bullying would be a serious ethical concern.

The ethical concern pertains to what is being asked of participants due to the direct influence of the researcher. If potentially dangerous behavior, such as bullying, is observed, then the researcher should have no influence over the behavior of participants, if at all possible. In our example, if the researcher observed bullying behavior in the hallway of a middle school with no influence over the bullying incident, how it began or how it played out, this would be an unobtrusive observation. The adolescent girls were not influenced in any way by the actions of the researcher. Randomly assigning adolescent girls to various bullying conditions could have been dangerous, so observing in the school hallway was an ethical alternative that allowed the researcher to study bullying behavior in this setting.

EXISTING DATA DESIGNS

In the chapter opening, we stated the following hypothesis: Fruits will be eaten more if they are made more convenient. To answer the hypothesis, we could also use an existing data design. For example, suppose we reviewed online testimonials provided by students who successfully lost weight. We could analyze the content of those testimonials to find if there are themes or recurring phrases in the content. If we find, for example, that a high percentage of testimonials indicate that students ate more fruits when they were in more convenient locations in the cafeteria, then this would lend support to the hypothesis that fruits will be eaten more if they are made more convenient. If we set up the study correctly, we can use this existing data analysis to show support for the hypothesis that fruits will be eaten more if they are made more convenient.

In this final section, we introduce the research design that was illustrated here: the existing data design.

8.6 An Overview of Existing Data Designs

In many cases, researchers can analyze data that have already been recorded in some form. **Existing data designs** are research designs for handling and analyzing data that already exist, such as a written document, data collected as part of an earlier study,

> An **existing data design** is the collection, review, and analysis of any type of existing documents or records, including those that are written or recorded as video, as audio, or in other electronic form.

school records, or as an electronic or audio recording. Existing data can be qualitative, such as written records of the words in an Individualized Education Plan (IEP), and existing data can be quantitative, such as school records that reveal student test scores, student demographics, and school characteristics.

As noted earlier in this chapter for naturalistic observations, obtaining data that already exist is one strategy used to make unobtrusive observations. For example, to study student performance across schools that participate in the national Communities in Schools (CIS) initiative, a researcher could obtain data already collected by school districts that have schools participating in the CIS initiative. In this example, the researcher obtained data from the school districts. The researcher did not obtain the data directly from a participant. Obtaining existing data can also be more economical than selecting samples used to measure data in that it can save time and money. When the data already exist, researchers do not need to spend their time and money selecting a sample and observing participants in the sample because the data that will be analyzed already exist.

Existing data designs are used to analyze data that already exist.

8.7 Archival Research, Content Analysis, and Meta-Analysis

Existing data designs are used to describe behavior based on an analysis of data that already exist in some form. Two particular cautions should be made any time you select data from existing records:

1. Existing records can provide a selective record of behaviors observed, called **selective deposit.** For example, a detective may screen a host of records to admit into evidence, including some (e.g., phone records) but excluding others (e.g., letters written by a defendant).

2. Only certain types of records may survive over time, called **selective survival.** For example, some government documents of previously classified events may have been shredded, so the surviving records are biased in favor of only those records that were kept.

Selective deposit is the process by which existing records are selectively recorded or deposited into document files that can be accessed for analysis.

Selective survival is the process by which existing records survive or are excluded/decay over time.

Each caution can limit the generalizability of your results inasmuch as the selective records of behavior and the selective survival of existing records represent only those data that remain over time; it is not possible to draw conclusions about data that are not available for analysis. Three existing data designs described in this section are archival research, content analysis, and meta-analysis.

Archival Research

One type of existing data design, called archival research, is used to characterize or describe existing archives or historical documents. The documents are then described or summarized

in terms of how they address a research hypothesis. For example, Porowski and Passa (2011) used public school data from seven states to study differences in high school dropout rates among Communities in Schools (CIS) and non-CIS high schools over a 4-year period. The results of their study showed that CIS high schools made stronger gains in on-time graduation rates than the comparison non-CIS high schools.

Existing data can be obtained from any recorded document, including newspapers, books, magazines, medical reports, school records, websites, criminal records, and historical or government documents. These records can be used to study anything from high school sporting events to the teacher attitudes or education policy. The biggest challenge often is obtaining a copy of the existing data you need. The U.S. Department of Education (DOE) collects a vast amount of data from nationally representative samples of public schools on a wide variety of topics such as education funding, teacher shortages, school safety, and student outcomes after high school graduation, just to name a few. These data are stored in the National Center for Education Statistics (NCES). Most of these data are available for free public use at http://catalog.data.gov/dataset?groups=education2168#topic=educat ion_navigation. NCES encourages educational researchers to investigate new questions using the data they have collected. A quick literature search identifies over 500 journal articles and technical reports that used NCES data between 2012 and 2016. Some NCES databases require special permission to protect the data from certain disclosures. NCES offers training to educational researchers of the types of data that are collected, variables in the databases and how they are measured, and the requirements for obtaining permission to access the data. Accessing the restricted data requires a signed agreement between the researcher and the DOE regarding measures to protect confidentiality of the participants. Even though the data do not include direct identifying information such as names, it may be possible for researchers to combine several variables in a database to figure out who the participant might be. The agreement prevents the researchers from doing so. Access to some NCES data may also require specific computer configuration such as accessing the data from a computer that is kept in a separate, secure room and not connected to the Internet. In addition to national databases, individual school systems at all levels—pre-K to 12, community colleges, and 4-year universities—collect and maintain school data for long periods of time.

Some education-related data have been collected by the DOE longitudinally—over an extended period of time. This allows researchers to analyze trends over time. For example, the National Education Longitudinal Study (NELS) is a survey of a range of educational topics administered to students, teachers, parents, and school administrators. It was first conducted in 1988 with follow-up surveys in 1990, 1992, 1994,

Archival research measures potential relationships (often statistical in nature) based on existing data.

and 2000. Another example is the School Survey on Crime and Safety (SSOCS) conducted between 1999 and 2010. This survey collected data from a national sample of schools (as reported by the school principal) on topics related to school safety such as school security, staff training, and frequency of crime and violence in the school. A study by Han (2014) examined the SSOCS data of 2,500 public schools and found school mobility (changing schools) is negatively associated with students' levels of aspiration and school achievement, as well as positively associated with students' insubordination. These findings can lead to school policy changes to address the needs of students who frequently change schools. It is highly unlikely that Han (or the other researchers who use nationally collected databases) could have collected these data on their own considering the time, expense, and other resources necessary to gather this amount of data. This makes the NCES data an extremely valuable resource for education researchers.

Content Analysis

Another type of existing data design, called **content analysis,** uses archival records to analyze the content of specific events or behaviors, such as depth of knowledge in end-of-chapter questions in school textbooks or content of school wellness policies. Unlike archival research, which is used mostly to describe existing data as summary statistics, content analysis is used to analyze or interpret the detailed content in the records. For example, to analyze school wellness policies, we could review the school policies or qualitative interviews of school nurses or athletic coaches. Using a content analysis, we can analyze the content of the wellness policies or interviews by recording the types of wellness activities included in the policy or perceptions of the policy. To describe these data, we must analyze the actual content of the materials. To use a content analysis, the following must be identified:

> A **content analysis** is a type of existing data design in which the content of written or spoken records of the occurrence of specific events or behaviors is described and interpreted.

- The unit of analysis in the document or existing record. What information or content in the document will you specifically analyze, code, or interpret?

- The operational definition for the content analyzed. What words or features in the content are of interest? How will you be able to identify that content?

As an example, Ahlgrim-Delzell and Rivera (2015) analyzed the content of video recordings of literacy lessons in 2004 and 2010 to compare the types of literacy skills taught to students with developmental disability. In this study, the existing data were video recordings of instruction taken during the two time periods. To use a content analysis, the researchers needed to identify the unit of analysis in the recordings. In their study, the unit of analysis was a literacy skill. They also needed to give an operational definition for what content they would analyze in the instructional recordings. In their study, they defined a literacy skill as a skill listed in the National Reading Panel (2000) or the National Early Literacy Panel (2009) reports. Using this definition, the researchers analyzed the content of video to record the frequencies of each type of literacy skill present.

Similar to archival research, a content analysis is typically used to test some hypothesis. In the Ahlgrim-Delzell and Rivera (2015) study, the hypothesis was that literacy instruction in 2010 would include more components of literacy related to learning to read and comprehension than in 2004 as a result of increased research in this area for this population. To test this hypothesis, the researchers watched each video and coded the type of literacy skills taught in the lesson. As shown in Table 8.1, their findings show support for their hypothesis that the 2014 videos of literacy lessons included more components of literacy related to reading and comprehension.

> A content analysis is used to analyze or interpret the content of specific events or behaviors that have already been recorded or archived.

Meta-Analysis

An existing data design used to review findings from many research studies is called a **meta-analysis.** This type of analysis is often used when there are results across a series of studies that are not in agreement. Some studies may show evidence that an intervention is effective, whereas others may not show this effect. A meta-analysis can help sort out these inconsistencies by summarizing the results across a large group of studies or research papers. Specifically, a meta-analysis is used to combine, analyze, and summarize data across a group of related studies to make statistically guided decisions about the strength or reliability of the reported findings in those studies.

> A **meta-analysis** is a type of existing data design in which data are combined, analyzed, and summarized across a group of related studies to make statistically guided decisions about the strength or reliability of the reported findings in those studies.

Table 8.1 Percentage of Teachers Including the Component of Literacy in a Literacy Lesson in 2004 and 2010

Types of Literacy Skill	2004 (%)	2010 (%)
Vocabulary	100.0	83.3
Alphabet knowledge	33.37	0
Concept of print	66.7	83.3
Comprehension	66.7	100
Phonological memory	50.0	83.3
Phonological awareness	0	50
Phonics	0	66.7

Source: Adapted from data presented by Ahlgrim-Delzell and Rivera (2015).

As a general outline for how to conduct a meta-analysis, the following three steps can provide a useful framework for conducting a meta-analysis:

1. Select the relevant variable(s) or topic(s). To operationalize a relevant variable or topic, we need to know what question we are asking. For example, suppose we ask if a new behavioral therapy is effective. We could identify the relevant topic in this example as all studies testing the utility of this new therapy.

2. Select a set of studies related to the relevant variable(s) or topic(s). Here we now need to refine our criteria for what "counts" as a study on this topic. The design and analysis used and even the participants observed may vary substantially from one study to another. What type of participants should be included? Should we exclude certain designs—such as qualitative designs that report nonnumeric data? What type of data do we need, and do the studies report sufficient data to include them in a meta-analysis? Also important is quality—both of the journal and the methodology. These should be evaluated, and data reported in higher-quality journals and data from studies with stronger methodology should be given greater weight or "count" more in the meta-analysis. These evaluations can be checked by an interrater reliability check.

3. Perform the meta-analysis. Once you have identified your topic and refined your criteria to collect data from the sample of studies that fit your topic, you can now apply meta-analytic techniques. In general, a meta-analysis is used to either compare studies or combine studies (Rosenthal, 1984). For example, we can compare if this new behavioral therapy produces significantly different effects for men compared to women. Or we could combine the data reported in the studies and report the overall utility or effect of this new behavioral therapy. While there are many statistical alternatives when evaluating data, a meta-analysis is most often reported as **effect size.**

> **Effect size** is a statistical measure of the size or magnitude of an observed effect in a population, which allows researchers to describe how far scores shifted in a population or the percentage of variance in a dependent variable that can be explained by the levels of a factor.

> Effect size can be interpreted in terms of differences, proportions, and degree of association.

Effect size, which is an estimate of the size of an observed effect or change in a population, is introduced in greater detail in Chapter 14 of this book. In a meta-analysis, effect size is used to describe the size of an effect for data reported across a series of related research studies. Researchers can compute effect size in many different ways, depending on the type of data available. Estimates of effect size, which differ in terms of how each is reported, can be interpreted in terms of the following:

- Differences. An effect size measure for this interpretation is Cohen's *d*. The interpretation is typically in terms of how far scores shift in a population (e.g., how much greater benefit a student gains from a new instructional strategy) or how scores differ between two populations (e.g., the difference in benefits gained in boys compared to girls from a new instructional strategy). This effect size measure, which is reported in standard deviation units, can be represented as follows:

$$\text{Effect size} = \frac{\text{Sample mean difference}}{\text{Sample standard deviation}}.$$

- Proportions. The effect size measure for this interpretation is typically eta squared (η^2). The interpretation is in terms of the proportion of variance in a dependent variable that can be explained or accounted for by a manipulation or event (e.g., the proportion of variance in reduced disruptive behavior that can be explained by a new engagement strategy). Proportion of variance ranges between 0 and 1, with larger values indicating greater effect size, and can be represented as follows:

$$\text{Effect size} = \frac{\text{Variability explained}}{\text{Total variability}}.$$

- Degree of association. The effect size measure for this interpretation is typically the correlation coefficient (r). The interpretation is in terms of the degree of association or relationship between two factors, X and Y (e.g., the degree of association between different leadership styles and teacher satisfaction). A correlation coefficient ranges between -1.0 and $+1.0$, with values further from 0 indicating a stronger relationship between two factors, and can be represented as follows:

$$\text{Effect size} = \frac{\text{Variance of } X \text{ and } Y \text{ together}}{\text{Variance of } X \text{ and } Y \text{ separately}}.$$

A meta-analysis uses these statistical measures to summarize findings across many studies. For example, Jeynes (2015) conducted a meta-analysis to test the relationship between father involvement and student academic achievement using Cohen's d as a measure of effect size. The researchers reviewed the literature and selected 66 studies related to this topic. In their study, they computed the effect size of findings for all studies to measure how father involvement and student academic achievement were related. Their results, a portion of which are shown in Table 8.2, indicate that father involvement was associated with academic achievement for children overall. The effect size is lightly greater for children of color and children aged 1 to 10 years.

MAKING SENSE—CONTENT ANALYSIS VERSUS META-ANALYSIS

In content analysis, the researcher will collect information found in documents or records such as school crime reports in newspapers, videos of teacher instruction, or types of goals identified in Individualized Education Plans (IEPs). The information is compiled, typically in the form of frequency counts, to describe the content of the documents (or records).

In meta-analysis, the researcher will collect research studies on a specific independent or quasi-independent variable such as play therapy, self-monitoring, or leadership style. The results are compiled, typically in the form of means, standard deviations, and correlation coefficients, to describe the observed effect of the independent variable.

Table 8.2 Estimates of Effect Size for Father Involvement With Student Academic Achievement

Type of Father Involvement	Effect Size
Father involvement overall	.16
Father involvement for children of color	.22
Father involvement for youth ages 1 to 10	.20
Father involvement for youth ages 11 to 20	.15

Source: Adapted from data presented by Jeynes (2015). Reproduced with permission.

A key advantage of a meta-analysis is that it increases **statistical power,** or the likelihood of detecting an effect or mean difference in one or more populations. A meta-analysis increases statistical power because it combines the sample sizes across many research studies, then computes effect size. Increasing sample size is one way to increase power. By combining many studies, a meta-analysis also combines the samples in those studies—thereby increasing, more than any individual study included in the analysis, the likelihood of detecting an effect (see Cooper & Rosenthal, 1980).

Statistical power, or **power,** is the likelihood that data in a sample can detect or discover an effect in a population, assuming that the effect does exist in the population of interest.

A key disadvantage of a meta-analysis is that it is prone to *publication bias,* which was defined in Chapter 2. Howard, Lau, et al. (2009) drew an analogy of this problem to calculating a baseball player's batting average, which is the proportion of times at bat that a player hits the ball into fair play and gets on base. To illustrate this analogy, suppose you compute a player's batting average only on his "good hitting days" and do not count the days that he did not get a hit. In this case, you would overestimate a player's true batting average because you only counted days that the player got a hit. The same is true for a meta-analysis in that the editors of peer-reviewed journals have a tendency to publish positive results or results that show an effect, while omitting those studies that fail to show an effect. Hence, many studies that do not show an effect are possibly not included in calculations of effect size in a meta-analysis because such studies are not often published in peer-reviewed journals. In this way, a meta-analysis can be prone to overestimating the true size of an effect in a population.

A meta-analysis increases statistical power but is prone to publication bias.

CONNECTING TO THE CLASSROOM

The What Works Clearinghouse (WWC) sponsored by the U.S. Department of Education (https://ies.ed.gov/ncee/wwc/) compiles research studies on various interventions and uses meta-analysis to evaluate the observed effect of the interventions. To be included in the meta-analysis, each study is first evaluated for its quality based on a series of quality indicators. If the study is deemed to be of sufficient quality, the results are combined with other studies of sufficient quality for analysis. The analysis provides an Effectiveness Rating, which is a summary of the quality of the research, magnitude of the findings, and the consistency of the findings across the studies included in the summary. It ranges from negative effect to mixed results to positive effect. The analysis also provides an Improvement Index, which is the expected change in percentile rank if the student receives the intervention. It ranges from –50 to 50.

Looking for some information on an intervention or new ideas? This is a good place to start. The results of the meta-analyses are presented in an easy-to-read table format. The criteria for interventions to be included in the WWC are rigorous. If the intervention you are looking for is not included in the WWC, it does not automatically mean that it is not effective; ineffective interventions also are listed. It may be that there are not yet enough studies that have investigated the intervention or the studies are not of sufficient quality to be included. In this case, you need to rely on the individual studies of that intervention to form your own opinion.

8.8 Ethics in Focus: Existing Data and Experimenter Bias

A concern any time you review existing data is to consider all data that are relevant to your research topic. Experimenter bias, intentionally or not, can occur when you selectively review only those records with data that fit with the conclusions you want to draw, so you disregard all other existing data. This can be a problem because, unlike sampling participants, researchers must often probe or sift through existing data records prior to including them in an analysis to make sure each record is relevant to the topic being studied. To avoid experimenter bias, you should have multiple researchers search existing data records during the initial review process. By doing so, you can reduce bias in that a consensus can be reached by many researchers prior to selecting which existing data records are included in or omitted from a research study.

LEARNING CHECK 3 ✓

1. State the type of existing data research design described in each example.
   A. A researcher selects 77 related studies that are published in peer-reviewed journals to analyze the extent to which student evaluations are related to student learning.
   B. A researcher analyzes the appropriateness of content in advertising themes during television programming aimed at children.
   C. A researcher reviews IEP records to determine the types of academic and social skills being taught.
2. How does a meta-analysis increase statistical power?

Answers: 1. A. meta-analysis, B. content analysis, C. archival research, 2. A meta-analysis increases statistical power because it combines the sample size from many studies.

LO 1 Identify and define the naturalistic research design.

- The naturalistic research design applies a naturalistic observation strategy to make observations in natural settings. Naturalistic observation is the observation of behavior in the natural setting where it is expected to occur, with limited or no attempt to overtly manipulate the conditions of the environment where the observations are made.

LO 2 Distinguish between natural and contrived research settings.

- A natural setting is a location or site where a behavior of interest normally occurs. A contrived setting is a location or site arranged to mimic the natural setting within which a behavior of interest normally occurs, to facilitate the occurrence of that behavior.

LO 3 Identify and describe how researchers make unobtrusive observations.

An unobtrusive observation is a technique used by an observer to record or observe behavior in a way that does not interfere with or change a participant's behavior in that observed research setting.

To make unobtrusive observations, researchers can remain hidden, habituate participants to their presence, use a confederate, or use indirect measures.

LO 4 Describe how researchers operationalize observation periods in a naturalistic or contrived setting.

Researchers operationalize observations by identifying behavior categories of interest. Behavior categories are the specific types of behaviors that researchers want to measure in the research setting and are typically organized as a list of examples that "count" in each category or for each type of behavior.

LO 5 Describe how researchers quantify and manage observation periods in a naturalistic or contrived setting.

To quantify observations, researchers can use the following methods:

- Interval method (record whether or not certain behaviors occur in a given interval)
- Frequency method (record the number of times a behavior occurs during a fixed period of time)
- Duration method (record the amount of time that a participant engages in a certain behavior during a fixed period of time)
- Latency method (record the time or duration between the occurrences of behaviors during a fixed period of time)

To manage observation periods, researchers can use the following methods:

- Time sampling (making observations in alternating intervals of an observation period)

- **Event sampling** (recording different events or behaviors in each interval of an observation period)
- **Individual sampling** (recording the behavior of different individuals in each interval of an observation period)

LO 6 Identify and describe three existing data research designs: archival research, content analysis, and meta-analysis.

- **Archival research** is a type of existing data design in which events or behaviors are described based on a review and analysis of relevant historical or archival records.

- **Content analysis** is a type of existing data design in which the content of written or spoken records of the occurrence of specific events or behaviors is described and interpreted.

- A **meta-analysis** is a type of existing data design in which data are combined, analyzed, and summarized across a group of related studies to make statistically guided decisions about the strength or reliability of the reported findings in those studies.

  - Data are often reported as **effect size** in a meta-analysis. A meta-analysis increases **statistical power** by combining the sample sizes from many studies but is also prone to a publication bias because negative results, or those that do not show an effect, tend to be omitted from the peer-reviewed literature.

KEY TERMS

archival research 233	frequency method 227	power 238
content analysis 234	individual sampling 229	selective deposit 232
contrived setting 223	interval method 227	selective survival 232
duration method 228	latency method 228	statistical power 238
effect size 236	meta-analysis 235	structured setting 223
event sampling 229	natural setting 222	time sampling 229
existing data design 231	naturalistic observation 226	unobtrusive observation 225

REVIEW QUESTIONS

1. Identify which statement, A or B, is false, and explain what makes the statement false.
   A. Naturalistic observation often involves the use of unobtrusive observations.
   B. Naturalistic observation is an experimental research design.

2. A researcher reviews academic transcripts to determine the percentage of high school students who enter college with at least some college credits. Which existing data research design did the researcher use?

3. To study whether a media bias exists, a researcher analyzes the content of the recordings of prime-time coverage for three major news networks (CNN, MSNBC, and FOX) during a 1-week period. Which existing data research design did the researcher use?

4. Name one advantage and one disadvantage of conducting a meta-analysis.

5. Name the type of effect size and the statistic used in the following hypothetical studies.

   A. A study of the relationship between ethnicity of the student and amount of praise/criticism by the teacher

   B. A study of the difference in reading comprehension achieved by graphic organizers and metacognition strategies

   C. A study of the amount of variance in school attendance explained by parental involvement

6. A researcher in a gym setting counts the number of times that individuals look at themselves in a mirror while they exercise during a 30-minute observation period. What method did the researcher use to quantify her observations?

7. State three sampling methods that researchers use to manage an observational period.

8. A researcher plays a video of an interview and records the behavior of the interviewer, then replays the video and records the behavior of the interviewee. What sampling method did the researcher use to manage the observational period?

9. A key disadvantage of a meta-analysis is that it is prone to: [fill in the blank].

10. True or false: Experimenter bias is always intentional.

ACTIVITIES

1. For any three of the following factors, identify a naturalistic and a contrived research setting that could be used to study the factor.

   A. Computer skills

   B. Student engagement

   C. Peer tutoring

   D. Teaching style in the classroom

   E. Expressions of happiness

2. Choose any behavioral research topic of interest, and state three different types of existing data you could obtain to study your topic.

⑤SAGE edge™

SAGE edge offers a robust online environment featuring an impressive array of free tools and resources for review, study, and further exploration, keeping both instructors and students on the cutting edge of teaching and learning.

Access practice quizzes, eFlashcards, video, and multimedia at edge.sagepub.com/priviterarme.

Identify a problem

- Determine an area of interest.
- Review the literature.
- Identify new ideas in your area of interest.
- Develop a research hypothesis.

Develop a research plan

- Define the variables being tested.
- Identify participants or subjects and determine how to sample them.
- Select a research strategy and design.
- Evaluate ethics and obtain institutional approval to conduct research.

Conduct the study

- Execute the research plan and measure or record the data.

Analyze and evaluate the data

- Analyze and evaluate the data as they relate to the research hypothesis.
- Summarize data and research results.

Communicate the results

- Method of communication: oral, written, or in a poster.
- Style of communication: APA guidelines are provided to help prepare style and format.

Generate more new ideas

- Results support your hypothesis—refine or expand on your ideas.
- Results do not support your hypothesis—reformulate a new idea or start over.

After reading this chapter, you should be able to:

1 Describe the difference between the four different types of surveys.

2 Explain how response rates to survey research can limit the interpretation of survey results.

3 Identify how to appropriately handle and administer surveys.

4 Describe the steps involved in survey research.

5 Describe the five common types of correlational designs.

6 Identify and describe the direction and strength of a correlation.

7 Explain how causality, outliers, and restriction of range can limit the interpretation of a correlation coefficient.

8 Explain how linear regression can be used to predict outcomes.

SURVEY AND CORRELATIONAL RESEARCH DESIGNS

You have probably made or heard the popular comment "Is it just me, or [fill in the blank here]?" This question is really a survey that asks others to indicate their level of agreement with some viewpoint—for example, "Is it just me, or is it hot in here?" or "Is it just me, or was this exam difficult?" We largely ask such questions to gauge the opinions of others. Many examples likely occur every day, from completing a customer satisfaction survey to asking your friends what they plan to order at a restaurant to get a better idea of what you might want to order. Really, we could survey people to measure all sorts of constructs, including love, attachment, personality, motivation, cognition, and many other constructs studied by behavioral scientists.

We can also identify how constructs such as love, attachment, personality, motivation, and cognition are related to other factors or behaviors such as the likelihood of depression, emotional well-being, and physical health. In everyday situations, you may notice relationships between temperature and aggression (e.g., the hotter it is outside, the more often you see people fighting at a sports stadium) or between class participation and grades (e.g., students with higher grades tend to also participate more in class). Hence, there is a natural tendency for us to engage the world under the assumption that behavior does not occur in isolation. Instead, behavior is related to or influenced by other factors in the environment.

It is therefore not uncommon at all for humans to observe the world by asking people to answer questions about themselves or by observing how human behavior is related to other factors such as health and well-being. The same is true in science. In this chapter, we describe how we can use the scientific method to evaluate or survey participant responses and identify relationships between factors.

> **edge.sagepub.com/priviterarme**
>
> - Take the chapter quiz
> - Review key terms with eFlashcards
> - Explore multimedia links and SAGE articles
>
> **⑤SAGE edge™**

SURVEY DESIGNS

Many research designs can be used to test the same hypotheses. This chapter is separated into two major sections; each section describes a nonexperimental research design: the survey designs and correlational designs. To introduce how each design can be used to test the same hypothesis, we will begin each major section by developing a new research design to test the same hypothesis.

Suppose we hypothesize that cyberbullying victimization is more prevalent with older children and among girls (DePaolis & Williford, 2015; Holfeld & Leadbeater, 2015). We could use a survey research design by asking a sample of schoolchildren to indicate in a questionnaire how often they have been cyberbullied. If the hypothesis is correct and we set up this study correctly, we should find support for our hypothesis. We will return to this hypothesis with a new way to answer it when we introduce correlational designs. We begin this chapter with an introduction to the research design that was illustrated here: the survey research design.

9.1 An Overview of Survey Designs

Have you ever received a phone call or been approached in a public area to stop and answer a few questions about your opinion? You may be asked about what TV or radio station you listen to most or asked what you think about your school. A nonexperimental research design used to describe an individual or a group by having participants complete a questionnaire using a survey method is called the **survey research design.** A survey research design administers a questionnaire in a systematic fashion to quantify, describe, or characterize the opinions or experiences of individuals. Recall from Chapter 5 that a questionnaire can be administered in written form or orally as an interview. Surveys have a wide variety of uses and topics covering health, employment, political affiliation, household purchasing habits, and education, just to name a few. They are widely used in education designed to learn about your opinions and attitudes. Surveys can be large, covering a national sample like those distributed by the U.S. Department of Education covering many topics such as early childhood, school staffing, private schools, and libraries. Surveys can also cover a smaller section of the population. Feuerborn, Tyre, and King (2015) used a survey of school staff from 36 schools to assess staff perceptions of schoolwide expectations of student behavior and discipline. Chen, McCray, Adams, and Leow (2014) surveyed 346 preschool teachers on their beliefs and confidence in teaching and assessing math. You can see how versatile a survey can be across topics and participants.

> The **survey research design** is the use of a questionnaire, administered either in written form or orally using a systematic survey method, to quantify, describe, or characterize a group of individuals.

Surveys can be classified as either longitudinal or cross-sectional. *Longitudinal surveys* administer a questionnaire to the same participants repeatedly over a period of time to understand the changes that occur in attitudes and opinions over that time.

These surveys are usually administered once a year. The U.S. Department of Education early childhood study is longitudinal. Beginning in 1998, they followed children from kindergarten to eighth grade regarding development and school experiences. A new cohort from kindergarten to fifth grade beginning in 2010 is currently being followed. In 2007, the U.S. Department of Education began a longitudinal study of beginning teachers that will last 10 years until 2017. Longitudinal surveys can provide valuable information about how attitudes and perceptions change over time but are costly and time-consuming. We have to wait 10 years to understand the changes of beginning teachers.

> A trend longitudinal survey follows different samples of individuals from the same population over time.

There are three types of longitudinal surveys—trend, cohort, and panel studies. Trend studies focus on the same population but use different samples of the population for each time the questionnaire is administered. An example of this type of longitudinal survey study would be if a researcher was interested in learning how teachers felt about the implementation of the *Common Core State Standards in English Language Arts* (National Governors Association and Council of Chief State School Officers, 2010). Each year, the researchers would sample a new group of teachers to obtain their opinions. They can see how opinions change over time by comparing teacher responses each year. Because the sample of specific teachers changes each year, it is important that the sampling frame from which the teachers were selected be representative of teachers. Cohort studies examine changes over time of a specific group of people with a common characteristic. An example of this type of longitudinal survey study would be if a researcher was interested in learning how specific types of teachers, such as high school English teachers within their first 5 years of teaching, felt about the implementation of the *Common Core State Standards in English Language Arts*. Each year, the researchers would sample a new group of teachers with the same common characteristic to obtain their opinions. A panel longitudinal study is one where the same sample is surveyed over time. Using the same example of teacher opinions about the *Common Core State Standards in English Language Arts*, each year the survey would be administered to the same people over time to examine how their opinions change.

> A cohort longitudinal survey follows different samples of individuals with a common characteristic over time.

> A panel longitudinal survey follows the same sample of individuals over time.

> **Longitudinal survey** is the same questionnaire administered repeatedly over a period of time to the same participants repeatedly to understand the changes that occur in attitudes and opinions.

CONNECTING TO THE CLASSROOM

The type of survey design selected for a study depends on the purpose of the study. Here are some examples of how the different survey designs could be used.

Purpose: gather current opinions of parents on school uniforms
Design: cross-sectional

(Continued)

(Continued)

Purpose: examine current differences of opinions of teachers, parents, and students on school uniforms
Design: cross-sectional

Purpose: examine changes of opinions of parents in your school on school uniforms over time
Design: trend longitudinal

Purpose: examine changes of opinions of low-income parents in your school on school uniforms over time
Design: cohort longitudinal

Purpose: examine changes of opinions of the same parents in your school on school uniforms over time
Design: panel longitudinal

Cross-sectional surveys administer a questionnaire once to a sample of people to examine attitudes and perceptions as a "snapshot" in time. Upon completion of the study, researchers can compare differences of opinion among groups of people with different characteristics within the sample. In our example of the opinions of the *Common Core State Standards*, researchers could compare opinions of early career teachers to experienced teachers of those from rural school systems or urban school systems from surveys that were all collected at the same time.

A **cross-sectional survey** administers the survey just once but can examine differences of opinion of distinct groups of individuals who completed the survey.

MAKING SENSE—LONGITUDINAL VERSUS CROSS-SECTIONAL SURVEY DESIGNS

Longitudinal surveys, whether they are trend, cohort, or panel studies, gather information from individuals over time where the individuals respond to the same questions more than once. Cross-sectional surveys are administered at one point in time so that individuals respond to the questions only once.

LEARNING CHECK 1 ✓

1. What is the purpose of a survey research design?

2. Decide what type of survey research is used in each of the following hypothetical studies.

   A. The study examined the changes of opinions of the same group of students over time on their preference for school club offerings.

   B. The study examined the changes of opinions of students over time on their preference for school club offerings.

C. The study examined the current opinions of students on their preference for school club offerings.

D. The study examined the changes of opinions of freshman students over time on their preference for school club offerings.

9.2 Surveys, Sampling, and Nonresponse Bias

When administering a questionnaire, it is important to obtain a high survey **response rate.** A response rate is the portion of participants who agree to complete a questionnaire among all those who were asked to complete the questionnaire. When the response rate is low, the concern is that any results from the survey study will be limited to only those people who were actually willing to complete the questionnaire. When the response rate is high, we can be more confident that the sample of those who completed the survey is representative of the larger population of interest.

> **Response rate** is the portion of participants who agree to complete a survey among all individuals who were asked to complete the survey.

Issues related to response rates center on the possibility of a *nonresponse bias*, which occurs when participants who choose not to complete a questionnaire or choose not to respond to specific items in a questionnaire are different from those who do respond to the survey. Although at least a 75% response rate should be obtained to minimize bias, the typical response rate to survey research in published peer-reviewed research is often less than 50% (Baruch, 1999; Baruch & Holtom, 2008; Shih & Fan, 2008). The problem of low response rates is that people who respond to the questionnaire may be different from those who do not respond. Because we cannot know how people who fail to respond would have responded if they had completed the questionnaire, it is difficult to know the exact characteristics of this group of nonresponders. For this reason, we cannot know for sure whether survey results of those who do respond are representative of the larger population of interest, which includes those who do not respond to surveys.

While the low response rates in published research can be problematic, there is good reason to publish the results from these journals. Although low response rates can limit the population validity (a subtype of external validity; see Chapter 7) of results from a survey, researchers are not always interested in generalizing results to a population. To establish some external validity, researchers often use survey results to instead generalize to a theory, called *theoretical generalization*, or generalize to

> **Theoretical generalization** is the extent to which results in a survey or another research study are consistent with predictions made by an existing theory.
>
> **Empirical generalization** is the extent to which results in a survey or another research study are consistent with data obtained in previous research studies.

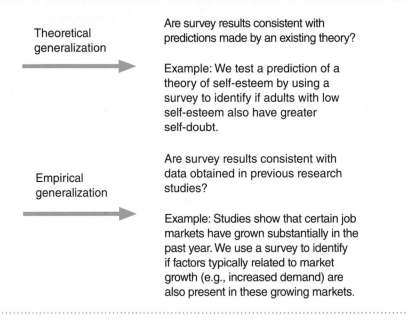

Theoretical generalization

Are survey results consistent with predictions made by an existing theory?

Example: We test a prediction of a theory of self-esteem by using a survey to identify if adults with low self-esteem also have greater self-doubt.

Empirical generalization

Are survey results consistent with data obtained in previous research studies?

Example: Studies show that certain job markets have grown substantially in the past year. We use a survey to identify if factors typically related to market growth (e.g., increased demand) are also present in these growing markets.

other observations, called *empirical generalization*. Each type of generalization is illustrated in Figure 9.1 with an example given for each type. As long as survey results are rooted in existing theories and data, researchers "can afford to be lenient [to some extent] about sample quality in academic research" (Blair & Zinkhan, 2006, p. 6).

MAKING SENSE—RESPONSE RATES

A response rate is typically calculated by dividing the number of completed surveys by the number of individuals in the sampling frame who were asked to complete the survey. A survey request was sent to 300 individuals, and 126 individuals completed the survey. To calculate the response rate, divide 126 by 300 (which equals .42) and then multiply by 100 to get the percentage (42%).

9.3 Survey Methods

The survey method is the systematic process of administering the questionnaire. The process used by the researcher in administering the questionnaire begins with developing the questionnaire and determining the mode in which it is delivered (such as phone, Internet, face to face). Table 9.1 lists some additional steps in the survey method that researchers should take when using a survey method to administer a questionnaire.

Once developed, the questionnaire should be piloted with a group of participants who are as much like the potential respondents but will not be participating in the study. For

Table 9.1 Additional Steps in the Survey Process

Develop the questionnaire
Determine the mode in which the questionnaire will be administered
Pilot the questionnaire with "like" participants who will not be part of the survey study
Determine the number and type of contacts sent to potential respondents
Monitor receipt of questionnaires (response rate, missing data)
Send reminders to nonrespondents
Investigate potential response bias

example, researchers studying teacher job satisfaction can use a few teachers from a different school or school system that will not be in the research study to pilot the questionnaire. *Pilot* means to test the questionnaire before using it in the research study. The questionnaire can be tested for ease of use, time it takes to complete, and clarity of the items. To pilot the questionnaire, have the pilot participants take the questionnaire in the mode in which it will be delivered during the research study. Once complete, ask the participants about how easy it was to complete or if there were items that were confusing. A pilot can also test the flow or links in an Internet questionnaire that may not work or be incorrect. Pilot testing typically only requires a few participants but can save a lot of time and energy later on if a flawed questionnaire is sent out to participants before being piloted.

It is possible to use more than one mode to administer a questionnaire within a single survey research study. One way to improve response rates to surveys is to employ a multimodal process to announce, administer, and follow up on the questionnaire. Researchers of the teacher job satisfaction survey may decide to announce the upcoming survey and send a link to the questionnaire via an email. In the email, they can offer to send a paper copy of the questionnaire instead. They then can remind nonresponders to complete the questionnaire by sending a postcard in the mail. Using more than one mode to administer the questionnaire can improve the response rates by capturing the preferred method of taking the questionnaire of different participants but also reminds them to complete it.

It is important to monitor the questionnaires as they are completed to determine if the survey process is proceeding as planned. By looking over the responses to the surveys, the researchers can be aware of possible glitches in the survey method or the questionnaire. Perhaps the researchers for the teacher job satisfaction notice that no surveys have been returned from a specific school or that many of the respondents skipped a certain item. The researchers could investigate the problem and fix it so that it doesn't affect the findings.

The final step in a survey research study is to investigate possible **response bias.** Recall response bias occurs whenever the individuals who respond to a survey respond differently from those who do not. The potential for response bias exists

> **Response bias** occurs whenever the individuals who respond to a survey respond differently than those who do not.

whenever we have less than a 100% response rate, yet just because we have a low response rate does not mean that we have response bias. To examine potential response bias, a researcher can do two things. One way to examine potential response bias is to contact those who did not respond to the survey in an attempt to get them to respond using a different contact mode. Researchers who initially sent out the email link to the Internet teacher job satisfaction survey may call some of the people who did not take the Internet survey and ask them to take it over the phone. A comparison of the answers by the initial nonresponders who completed the survey using the alternate contact to the answers of the responders may reveal a difference in response patterns indicative of response bias. The second way to examine potential response bias requires the researcher to have some information about the individuals on the sampling frame. In addition to contact information, the sampling frame may contain demographic information such as gender, ethnicity, or other variables pertinent to the study. If available, the researcher could compare the differences between the individuals who responded to those who did not using these variables to identify potential response bias.

9.4 Ethics in Focus: Handling and Administering Surveys

To show respect for persons, which is a key principle in the Belmont Report, the researcher has certain ethical responsibilities regarding how to handle and administer surveys in a research study. The following are four responsible and appropriate ways to handle and administer surveys:

- The survey itself should not be offensive or stressful to the respondents. The respondents should, under reasonable circumstances, be satisfied or comfortable with their survey experience such that they would not feel distress if asked to complete the survey again. If they would feel distress, then the survey may pose potential psychological risks to the respondents.

- Do not coerce respondents into answering questions or completing a survey. All respondents should be informed prior to completing the survey, typically in an informed consent form, that they can skip or choose not to answer any survey items, or the entire survey, without penalty or negative consequence.

- Do not harass respondents in any way for recruitment purposes. Because of high nonresponse rates, researchers often actively recruit potential respondents through e-mail or phone call reminders. The potential respondents must not view these recruitment efforts as harassing or intrusive.

- Protect the confidentiality or anonymity of respondents. Personally identifiable information of respondents should be protected at all times. If the researcher requires respondents to provide personally identifiable information, then such information should be safeguarded while in the possession of the researcher.

1. What is the response rate for a survey that sent out 1,500 surveys and received 850 completed surveys?

2. What is a potential problem when a survey has less than a 75% response rate?

3. What step in the survey method is missing from the following survey description?

A researcher developed a survey to be administered by Internet-based survey software. The researcher decided to invite 150 participants through an e-mail message with a link to the survey. As the surveys were completed, the researcher monitored the responses using the survey software and sent a reminder to those who had not yet replied after 2 weeks. At the end of the survey, the researcher compared the respondents to the nonrespondents on several key characteristics.

Answers: 1. 56.7%; 2. Nonresponse bias; 3. A pilot is missing.

CORRELATIONAL DESIGNS

In the chapter opening, we stated the following hypothesis: Cyberbullying victimization is more prevalent with older children and among girls. To answer the hypothesis, we used a survey design to begin this chapter. However, we could use a correlational research design to test this hypothesis as well. To use the correlational design, for example, we could ask a sample of participants who drive to indicate in a questionnaire their age (in years) and how often they have been the victim of cyberbullying (per month). If the hypothesis is correct and we set up this study correctly, then we should expect to find that increased victimization from cyberbullying is associated with older students and girls.

Notice that we used survey data (based on responses in a questionnaire) to record the data. Surveys are often used with a correlational research design. However, keep in mind that any time we use data to determine whether two or more factors are related/correlated, we are using the correlational design, even if we used a survey or questionnaire to record the data. In this final section, we introduce the research design that was illustrated here: the correlational research design.

9.5 The Structure of Correlational Designs

It is often difficult to determine that one factor causes changes in another factor. For example, in the cyberbullying study used to introduce each major section in this chapter, we cannot reasonably determine that being older or female causes cyberbullying victimization because we cannot control for other possible factors that can cause a change in cyberbullying behavior. Other possible factors include how often students use social media, types of social media they use, experiences with face-to-face bullying, social status in school, or how they define cyberbullying. In these situations, when it is difficult to control for other possible factors that could be causing changes in behavior, we use the **correlational research design** to determine the

A **correlational research design** is the measurement of two or more factors to determine or estimate the extent to which the values for the factors are related or change in an identifiable pattern.

extent to which two factors are related, not the extent to which one factor causes changes in another factor.

To set up a correlational research design, we make two or more measurements for each individual observed. For the purposes of introducing the correlational research design, we will introduce situations in which only two measurements are made. Each measurement is for a different variable that we believe is related. For example, colleges record the relationship between SAT scores and college grade point average (GPA) to determine admittance criteria. Higher SAT scores in high school are related to a higher freshman college GPA, which is why many colleges use SAT scores as part of their criteria for accepting students to enroll. The correlation establishes the extent to which two factors are related, such that values for one variable may predict changes in the values of a second variable.

A correlation can be established in any setting. In a naturalistic setting, for example, we could measure the correlation between customer satisfaction in a restaurant and timeliness to serve patrons. In a classroom setting, we could expose students to a unique teaching style and record how much they like that teaching style. Using existing data school records, we could identify the correlation between school ranking and any number of student demographic characteristics. In each example, we make two measurements for each individual (or document when using existing records), and one measurement for each of the two variables being examined.

The different types of correlational designs can be characterized by the number of independent variables, the timing of the independent and dependent variables, and how the dependent variable is measured. Table 9.2 defines some of the most common forms of correlational designs by their distinguishing characteristic and provides an example. The independent variable might be collected at the same time as the dependent variable (e.g., simple correlation) or at different times (e.g., predictive). There might be just one independent variable (e.g., comparative) or more than one (e.g., multiple regression). Each design is described below.

Simple correlation. **Simple correlation** examines the relationship between one independent and one dependent variable at one point in time. The information for both variables is gathered at the same time. For example, the researcher could gather information on job satisfaction among teachers and also ask them how long they have been teaching to see if job satisfaction increases or decreases with time spent teaching.

Comparative. A **comparative design** investigates the relationship between one independent and one dependent variable. In this specific case, the independent variable consists of at least two groups such as male and female teachers or freshman, sophomore, junior, and senior high school students. This type of correlational study looks at the difference in the relationships between the groups of the independent variable on the dependent variable. Does the relationship between job satisfaction differ for male and female teachers?

Prediction. In a **prediction design,** the independent variable occurs before the dependent variable. The researcher might use information from the past as the independent variable to predict the presence or amount of a current dependent variable

Simple correlation design examines the relationship between one independent and one dependent variable at one point in time. The information for both variables is gathered at the same time.

Comparative design investigates the relationship between one independent and one dependent variable where the independent variable consists of at least two groups.

Prediction design uses one independent variable to predict the later occurrence of the dependent variable.

or might collect information now on the independent variable and wait for the passage of time to collect information on the dependent variable. For example, a researcher might ask you to eat Cheerios and record the amount you eat each day and then measure your cholesterol a year after you began eating the Cheerios. The researcher wants to predict the relationship between eating Cheerios and cholesterol level.

> **Multiple regression** is a prediction design with more than one independent variable to predict one dependent variable.
>
> **Logistic regression** is a prediction design where the dependent variable(s) is/are dichotomous—pass/fail, case/not case.

Multiple regression. **Multiple regression** is similar to a prediction study except there is more than one independent variable used to predict one dependent variable. A prediction is usually more accurate if more than one variable is included. For example, when predicting cholesterol level, adding amount of exercise and other eating habits will likely be a better predictor of cholesterol level than just eating Cheerios each day.

Logistic regression. **Logistic regression** is another prediction design, but in this design, the dependent variable is dichotomous—pass/fail, case/not case. There can be one or more independent variables used to predict the dependent variable. Sometimes the research question is whether something will or will not occur such as passing a course (pass or not), winning an election (win or not), or report a bullying incident (report or not). If the outcome variable is one of two options, then logistic regression is the design used.

Table 9.2 Distinguishing Characteristics of Common Correlational Designs

Correlational Design	Characteristic	Example
Simple correlation	One independent variable and dependent variable, both collected at same point in time	What is the relationship between longevity and job satisfaction among teachers? Both length of time teaching and job satisfaction are collected at the same time.
Comparative	One independent variable and one dependent variable where the independent variable is two or more groups	What is the relationship between gender and job satisfaction? Gender has at least two groups: male and female.
Prediction	One independent variable and dependent variable; the independent variable occurs before the dependent variable	This study investigated if attending a Head Start program or not predicted third-grade academic performance. Head Start occurred years before third grade.
Multiple regression	More than one independent variable to predict one dependent variable (also prediction)	Attitudes toward technology, barriers to technology implementation, ease of use of the technology, and technological self-efficacy predicted whether teachers adopted technology in their classrooms. Four independent variables were used to predict one dependent variable.
Logistic regression	The dependent variable is dichotomous (yes/no, case/not case, also prediction)	How well does course format (online or face to face) predict passing the course? Passing the course is dichotomous (pass or not pass).

The correlation coefficient is a statistic used to measure the strength and direction of the linear relationship, or correlation, between two factors. The value of r can range from −1.0 to +1.0.

Once we measure two variables, we then compute a statistical measure called the **correlation coefficient** to identify the extent to which the values of the two variables or factors are related or change in an identifiable pattern. The correlation coefficient ranges from −1.0 (the values for two factors change in opposite directions) to +1.0 (the values for two factors change in the same direction) and is used to identify a pattern in terms of the *direction* and *strength* of a relationship between two factors—each way of describing the relationship between two factors is introduced in this section.

In behavioral research, we mostly describe the linear (or straight-line) relationship between two factors. For this reason, we will limit this introduction to the direction and strength of a linear relationship between two factors.

A **scatterplot**, also called a **scatter diagram** or **scattergram**, is a graphical display of discrete data points (x, y) used to summarize the relationship between two factors.

Data points are the x- and y-coordinates for each plot in a scatterplot.

The **regression line** is the best-fitting straight line to a set of data points. A best-fitting line is the line that minimizes the distance that all data points fall from it.

9.6 Describing the Relationship Between Variables

The *direction* of a relationship between two factors is described as being positive or negative. The *strength* of a relationship between two factors is described by the value of the correlation coefficient, *r*, with values closer to $r = \pm 1.0$ indicating a stronger relationship between two factors. The direction and strength of correlation can be readily identified in a graph called a **scatterplot**. To construct a scatterplot (also called a **scatter diagram** or **scattergram**), we plot each pair of values, called **data points,** along the *x*-axis and *y*-axis of a graph to see whether a pattern emerges.

The extent to which two factors are related is determined by how far data points fall from a **regression line** when the data points are plotted in a graph. The regression line is the best-fitting or closest-fitting straight line to a set of data points. The best-fitting straight line is the one that minimizes the distance of all data points that fall from it. We will use the regression line to illustrate the direction and strength of the relationship between two factors using the correlational research design.

The pattern of a set of data points can indicate the extent to which two factors are related.

A **positive correlation** is a positive value of r that indicates that the values of two factors change in the same direction: As the values of one factor increase, values of the second factor also increase; as the values of one factor decrease, values of the second factor also decrease.

The Direction of a Relationship

In a scatterplot, a **positive correlation** means that as values of one factor increase, values of a second factor also increase; as values of one factor decrease, values of a second factor also decrease. If two factors have values that change in the same direction, we can graph the correlation using a straight line. In Figure 9.2, values on the *y*-axis increase as values on the *x*-axis increase.

Figure 9.2a shows a *perfect* positive correlation, which occurs when each data point falls exactly on a straight line, although this is rare. More commonly, as shown in Figure 9.2b, a positive correlation is greater than 0 but less than 1.0, where the values of two factors change in the same direction but not all data points fall exactly on the regression line.

A **negative correlation** means that as values of one factor increase, values of the second factor decrease. If two factors have values that change in the opposite direction, we can graph the correlation using a straight line. In Figure 9.3, values on the *y*-axis decrease as values on the *x*-axis increase.

> A **negative correlation** is a negative value of *r* that indicates that the values of two factors change in different directions, meaning that as the values of one factor increase, values of the second factor decrease.

Figure 9.3a shows a *perfect* negative correlation, which occurs when each data point falls exactly on a straight line, although this is also rare. More commonly, as shown in

---

Figure 9.2 A Perfect Positive (a) and a Positive (b) Linear Correlation

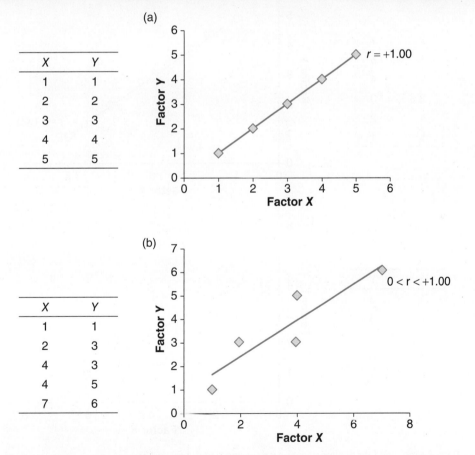

Note: Both the table and the scattergram show the same data for (a) and (b).

Figure 9.3b, a negative correlation is greater than –1.0 but less than 0, where the values of two factors change in the opposite direction, but not all data points fall exactly on the regression line.

The Strength of a Relationship

A zero correlation ($r = 0$) means that there is no linear pattern or relationship between two factors. This outcome is rare because usually by mere chance at least some values of one factor, X, will show some pattern or relationship with values of a second factor, Y. The closer a correlation coefficient is to $r = 0$, the weaker the correlation and the less likely that two factors are related; the closer a correlation coefficient is to $r = \pm1.0$, the stronger the correlation and the more likely that two factors are related.

Figure 9.3   A Perfect Negative (a) and a Negative (b) Linear Correlation

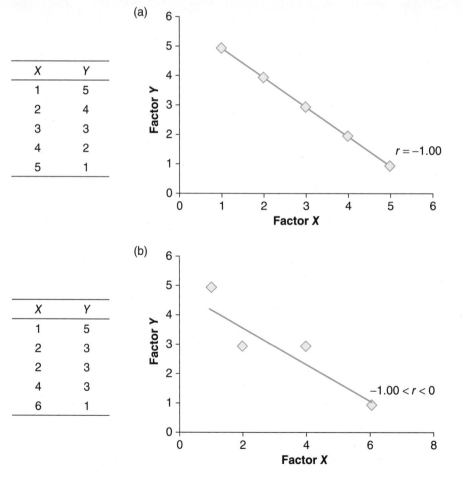

X	Y
1	5
2	4
3	3
4	2
5	1

X	Y
1	5
2	3
2	3
4	3
6	1

Note: Both the table and the scattergram show the same data for (a) and (b).

The strength of a correlation reflects how consistently values for each factor change. When plotted in a graph, a stronger correlation means that the values for each factor change in a related pattern—the data points fall closer to a regression line, or the straight line that best fits a set of data points. Figure 9.5 shows two positive correlations between exercise (Factor *X*) and body image satisfaction (Factor *Y*), and Figure 9.6 shows two negative correlations between absences in class (Factor *X*) and quiz grades (Factor *Y*). In both figures, the closer a set of data points falls to the regression line, the stronger the correlation—hence, the closer a correlation coefficient is to $r = \pm 1.0$.

> The closer a set of data points falls to a regression line, the stronger the correlation.

Figure 9.4 The Consistency of Scores for a Positive Correlation

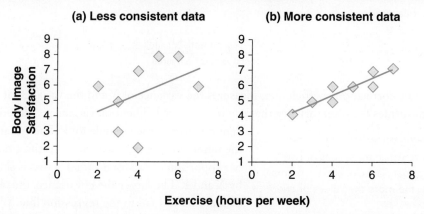

Note: Both figures show approximately the same regression line, but the data points in (b) are more consistent because they fall closer to the regression line than in (a).

Figure 9.5 The Consistency of Scores for a Negative Correlation

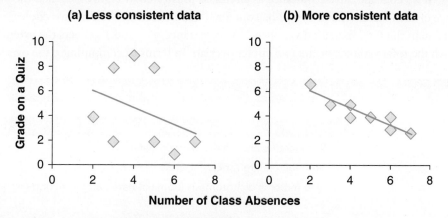

Note: Both figures show approximately the same regression line, but the data points in (b) are more consistent because they fall closer to the regression line than in (a).

The Correlation Coefficient

The most commonly used formula for computing r is the **Pearson correlation coefficient,** which is used to determine the strength and direction of the relationship between two factors on an interval or a ratio scale of measurement. Alternative formulas for computing a correlation with many scales of measurement exist, as identified in Table 9.2; however, each of these alternative formulas was derived from the formula for the Pearson correlation coefficient, so only the Pearson formula will be described in this section. The formula for the Pearson correlation coefficient is a measure of the variance of data points from a regression line that is shared by the values of two factors (X and Y), divided by the total variance measured:

> The **Pearson correlation coefficient** is used to measure the direction and strength of the linear relationship of two factors in which the data for both factors are on an interval or a ratio scale of measurement.

$$r = \frac{\text{Variance shared by } X \text{ and } Y}{\text{Total variance measured}}.$$

The correlation coefficient, r, measures the variance of X and the variance of Y, which constitutes the total variance that can be measured. The total variance is placed in the denominator of the formula for r. The variance in the numerator, called **covariance,** is the amount or proportion of the total variance that is shared by X and Y. The larger the covariance, the closer data points will fall to the regression line. When all data points for X and Y fall exactly on a regression line, the covariance equals the total variance, making the formula for r equal to +1.0 or −1.0, depending on the direction of the relationship between two factors. The farther that data points fall from the regression line, the smaller the covariance will be compared with the total variance in the denominator, resulting in a value of r closer to 0.

> **Covariance** is the extent to which the values of two factors (X and Y) vary together. The closer data points fall to the regression line, the more the values of two factors vary together.

If we conceptualize covariance as circles, as illustrated in Figure 9.7, then the variance of each factor (X and Y) will be contained within each circle. The two circles, then, contain the total measured variance. The covariance of X and Y reflects the extent to which the total variance or the two circles overlap. In terms of computing r, the overlap

Table 9.3 The Scales of Measurement for Factors Tested Using Correlation Coefficients

Correlation Coefficient	Scale of Measurement for Correlated Variables
Pearson	Both factors are interval or ratio data.
Spearman	Both factors are ranked or ordinal data.
Point-biserial	One factor is dichotomous (nominal data), and a second factor is continuous (interval or ratio data).
Phi	Both factors are dichotomous (nominal data).

Figure 9.6 Covariance Between X and Y

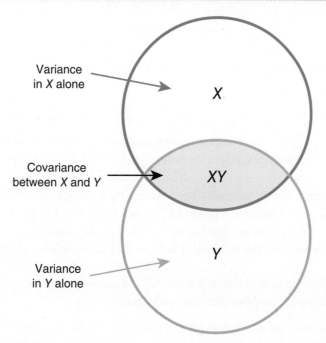

Variance in X alone

Covariance between X and Y

Variance in Y alone

Note: Each circle represents the variance of a factor. The variances of two factors covary inasmuch as the two circles overlap. The more overlap or shared variance of two factors, the more the two factors are related.

or covariance is placed in the numerator; the total variance contained within each circle is placed in the denominator. The more the two circles overlap, the more the covariance (in the numerator) will equal the independent variances contained within each circle (in the denominator)—and the closer *r* will be to ±1.0.

LEARNING CHECK 3 ✓

1. The value of the _____ provides an estimate of the strength and direction of the relationship between two factors.

2. A professor measures a negative correlation between time spent partying and grades. Interpret this result.

3. A researcher records a correlation of $r = +.02$.

   A. Identify the direction of this correlation.

   B. Identify the strength of this correlation.

4. How will the data points appear in a graph for two factors with values that change consistently?

Answers: 1. correlation coefficient (*r*); 2. As time spent partying increases, grades decrease; 3. A. the direction of the correlation is positive, B. the strength of the correlation is weak because .02 is close to 0; 4. The data points will fall close to the regression line.

9.7 Limitations in Interpretation

Fundamental limitations using the correlational method require that a significant correlation be interpreted with caution. Among the many considerations for interpreting a significant correlation, in this section, we consider causality, outliers, and restriction of range.

Causality

Correlation does not demonstrate cause.

Using a correlational design, we do not manipulate an independent variable, and we certainly make little effort to control for other possible factors that may also vary with the two variables we measured. For this reason, a significant correlation does not show that one factor causes changes in a second factor (i.e., causality). To illustrate, suppose we measure a significant negative correlation between the self-rated mood of students and the amount of food they eat daily (in calories per day). We will look at four possible interpretations for this correlation.

1. Decreases in how children feel (mood) can cause an increase in the amount they eat (eating). This possibility cannot be ruled out.

2. Increases in the amount children eat (eating) can cause a decrease in how they feel (mood). So the direction of causality can be in the opposite direction. Hence, instead of changes in mood causing changes in eating, maybe changes in eating cause changes in mood. This possibility, called reverse causality, cannot be ruled out either.

3. The two factors could be systematic, meaning that they work together to cause a change. If two factors are systematic, then Conclusions 1 and 2 could both be correct. The worse children feel, the more they eat, and the more children eat, the worse they feel. This possibility, that each factor causes the other, cannot be ruled out either.

Reverse causality is a problem that arises when the direction of causality between two factors can be in either direction.

Reverse causality occurs when the direction of causality for two factors, A and B, cannot be determined. Hence, changes in Factor A could cause changes in Factor B, or changes in Factor B could cause changes in Factor A.

A confound or confound variable is an unanticipated variable not accounted for in a research study that could be causing or associated with observed changes in one or more measured variables.

4. Changes in both factors may be caused by a third unanticipated confound or confound variable. Perhaps biological factors, such as increased parasympathetic activity, make children feel worse and increase how much they want to eat. So, it is increased parasympathetic activity that could be causing changes in both mood and eating. This confound variable and any number of additional confound variables could be causing changes in mood and eating and cannot be ruled out either.

Figure 9.7 summarizes each possible explanation for an observed correlation between mood and eating. The correlational design cannot distinguish between these four possible explanations. Instead, a significant correlation shows that two factors are related. It does not provide an explanation for how or why they are related.

Outliers

Another limitation that can obscure the correlation or relationship between two factors is when an outlier is in the data. An **outlier** is a score that falls substantially above or below most other scores in a data set and can alter the direction and the strength of an observed correlation. Figure 9.9a shows data for the relationship between income and education without an outlier in the data. Figure 9.9b shows how an outlier, such as the income earned by a child movie

> An **outlier** is a score that falls substantially above or below most other scores in a data set.

Figure 9.7 Four Potential Explanations for a Significant Correlation

1. Changes in mood cause changes in eating:

Mood ⟶ Eating

2. Changes in eating cause changes in mood (reverse causality):

Mood ⟵ Eating

3. The two variables work together (systematically) to cause an effect:

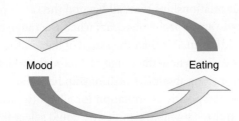

Mood   Eating

4. Changes in both factors are caused by a third confound variable:

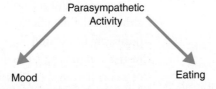

Parasympathetic Activity

Mood   Eating

Note: Because factors are measured but not manipulated using the correlational method, any one of these possibilities could explain a significant correlation.

Figure 9.8   The Effects of an Outlier

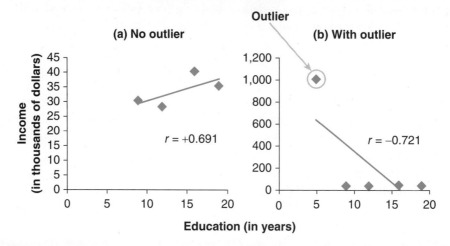

Note: (a) The graph displays a typical correlation between income and education, with more education being associated with higher income. (b) The graph shows the same data with an additional outlier of a child movie star who earns $1 million. The inclusion of this outlier changed the direction and the strength of the correlation.

star, changes the relationship between two factors. Notice in Figure 9.9 that the outlier changed both the direction and the strength of the correlation.

Restriction of Range

When interpreting a correlation, it is also important to avoid making conclusions about relationships that fall beyond the range of data measured. The **restriction of range** problem occurs when the range of data measured in a sample is restricted or smaller than the range of data in the general population.

Figure 9.9 shows how the range of data measured in a sample can lead to erroneous conclusions about the relationship between two factors in a given population. This figure shows the positive correlation for a hypothetical population (top graph) and the correlations in three possible samples we could select from this population (smaller graphs below). Notice that, depending on the range of data measured, we could identify a positive correlation, a negative correlation, or zero correlation from the same population, although the data in the population are actually positively correlated. To avoid the problem of restriction of range, the direction and the strength of a correlation should only be generalized to a population within the limited range of measurements observed in the sample.

> Outliers can change the strength and the direction of a correlation or relationship between two factors.

Restriction of range is a problem that arises when the range of data for one or both correlated factors in a sample is limited or restricted, compared with the range of data in the population from which the sample was selected.

Figure 9.9 The Effects of Restriction of Range

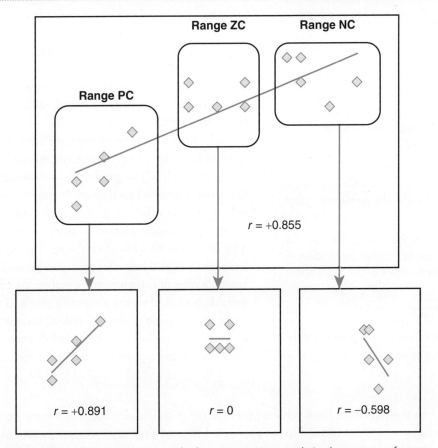

Note: In this population, shown in the top graph, there is a positive correlation between two factors ($r = +.855$). Also depicted are three possible samples we could select from this population. Range PC shows a positive correlation ($r = +.891$), Range ZC shows a zero correlation ($r = 0$), and Range NC shows a negative correlation ($r = -.598$)—all within the same population. Because different ranges of data within the same population can show very different patterns, correlations should never be interpreted beyond the range of data measured in a sample.

9.8 Correlation, Regression, and Prediction

The correlation coefficient, r, is used to measure the extent to which two factors (X and Y) are related. The value of r indicates the direction and strength of a correlation. When r is negative, the values of two factors change in opposite directions; when r is positive, the values of two factors change in the same direction. The closer r is to ± 1.0, the stronger the correlation, and the more closely two factors are related.

A correlation cannot describe data beyond the range of data observed in a sample.

We can use the information provided by r to predict values of one factor, given known values of a second factor. Recall that the strength of a correlation reflects how closely a set of data points fits to a regression line (the straight line that most closely fits a set of data points). We can use the value of r to compute the equation of a regression line and then use this equation to predict values of one factor, given known values of a second factor in a population. This procedure is called **linear regression** (also called **regression**).

> **Linear regression,** also called **regression,** is a statistical procedure used to determine the equation of a regression line to a set of data points and to determine the extent to which the regression equation can be used to predict values of one factor, given known values of a second factor in a population.
>
> The **predictor variable** (X) is the variable with values that are known and can be used to predict values of another variable.
>
> The **criterion variable** (Y) is the to-be-predicted variable with unknown values that can be predicted or estimated, given known values of the predictor variable.

To use linear regression, we identity two types of variables: the predictor variable and the criterion variable. The **predictor variable** (X) is the variable with values that are known and can be used to predict values of the criterion variable; the predictor variable is plotted on the x-axis of a graph. The **criterion variable** (Y) is the variable with unknown values that we are trying to predict, given known values of the predictor variable; the criterion variable is plotted on the y-axis of a graph. If we know the equation of the regression line, we can predict values of the criterion variable, Y, so long as we know values of the predictor variable, X. To make use of this equation, we identify the following equation of a straight line:

$$Y = bX + a.$$

In this equation, Y is a value we plot for the criterion variable, X is a value we plot for the predictor variable, b is the slope of a straight line, and a is the y-intercept (where the line crosses the y-axis). Given a set of data, researchers can find the values of a and b, then use the equation they found to predict outcomes of Y.

To illustrate the use of the regression line to predict outcomes, consider a study conducted by Chen, Dai, and Dong (2008). In this study, participants completed a revised version of the Aitken Procrastination Inventory (API), and their level of procrastination was recorded. The researchers found that the following regression equation could be used to predict procrastination (Y) based on known scores on the API (X):

$$\hat{Y} = 0.146X - 2.922.$$

In this equation, $\hat{Y}$ is the predicted value of Y given known scores on the API, $a = 2.922$, and $b = 0.146$. Using this information, we could have a student complete the API, plug his or her API score into the equation for X, and solve for $\hat{Y}$ to find the procrastination level we predict for that student.

The equation of the regression line can be used to predict outcomes of a criterion variable.

The advantage of using linear regression is that we can use the equation of the regression line to predict how people will behave or perform. A caution of using this procedure, however, is that smaller correlations, or those closer to $r = 0$, will produce inaccurate predictions using the equation of the regression line because the data points will fall far from it. Likewise, the stronger the correlation, or the closer to $r = \pm 1.0$, the more accurate the predictions made using the equation of the regression line because the data points will fall closer to it.

LEARNING CHECK 4 ✓

1. A correlational design does not demonstrate cause. Why?

2. True or false: An outlier can influence both the *direction* and the *strength* of an observed correlation.

3. _____ occurs when the range of data for one or both correlated factors in a sample is limited or restricted, compared to the range of data in the population from which the sample was selected.

4. What procedure is used to predict outcomes of one factor given known values of a second factor?

Answers: 1. Because we do not manipulate an independent variable, and we make little effort to control for other possible factors that may also vary with the two variables we measured; 2. True; 3. Restriction of range; 4. Linear regression.

CHAPTER SUMMARY

LO 1 Describe the difference between the four different types of surveys.

- A trend longitudinal survey follows different samples of individuals from the same population over time.

- A cohort longitudinal survey follows different samples of individuals with a common characteristic over time.

- A panel longitudinal survey follows the same sample of individuals over time.

- A cross-sectional survey administers the survey just once but can examine differences of opinion of distinct groups of individuals who completed the survey.

LO 2 Explain how response rates to survey research can limit the interpretation of survey results.

- The problem of low response rates is that people who respond to surveys are probably different from those who do not respond. Because we cannot collect data from people who fail to respond, it is difficult to know the exact characteristics of this group of nonresponders. For this reason, we cannot know for sure whether survey results of those who do respond are representative of the larger population of interest, which includes those who do not respond to surveys.

LO 3 Identify how to appropriately handle and administer surveys.

- To appropriately handle and administer surveys, the survey itself should not be offensive or stressful to the respondent; do not coerce respondents into answering questions or completing a survey; do not harass respondents in any way for recruitment purposes; protect the confidentiality or anonymity of respondents.

LO 4 Describe the steps involved in survey research.

- The survey process includes creating and piloting the questionnaire, administering and monitoring the administration of the questionnaire, sending reminders, and investigating possible response bias.

LO 5 Describe the five common types of correlational designs.

- **Simple correlation** examines the relationship between one independent and one dependent variable at one point in time. Data for both variables are gathered at the same time.

- **Comparative designs** examine the relationship between one independent and one dependent variable, when the independent variable is at least two groups to be compared.

- In **prediction designs,** the independent variable has occurred before the dependent variable. The independent variable will be used to predict the dependent variable.

- **Multiple regression** is a prediction, but more than one independent variable is used to predict the dependent variable.

- **Logistic regression** is another design aimed at making a prediction. There may be more than one independent variable. The dependent variable is dichotomous (yes/no, case/not case).

LO 6 Identify and describe the direction and strength of a correlation.

- The **correlation coefficient,** r, is used to measure the extent to which two factors (X and Y) are related. The value of r indicates the direction and strength of a correlation. When r is negative, the values for two factors change in opposite directions; when r is positive, the values for two factors change in the same direction. The closer r is to ± 1.0, the stronger the correlation and the more closely two factors are related.

- When plotted in a graph, the strength of a correlation is reflected by the distance that data points fall from the **regression line.** The closer that data points fall to a regression line, or the straight line that best fits a set of data points, the stronger the correlation or relationship between two factors.

LO 7 Explain how causality, outliers, and restriction of range can limit the interpretation of a correlation coefficient.

- Three considerations that must be made to accurately interpret a correlation coefficient are as follows: (1) correlations do not demonstrate causality, (2) outliers can change the direction and the strength of a correlation, and (3) never generalize the direction and the strength of a correlation beyond the range of data measured in a sample (restriction of range).

LO 8 Explain how linear regression can be used to predict outcomes.

- We can use the information provided by r to predict values of one factor, given known values of a second factor using a procedure called **linear regression.** Specifically, we can use the value of r to compute the equation of a regression line and then use this equation to predict values of one factor, given known values of a second factor in a population. Using the following equation of the regression line, $Y = bX + a$, we can predict values of the criterion variable, Y, so long as we know values of the predictor variable, X.

KEY TERMS

comparative design 254

confound variable 262

correlation coefficient 256

correlational research
  design 253

covariance 260

criterion variable 266

cross-sectional survey 248

data points 256

linear regression 266

logistic regression 255

longitudinal survey 247

multiple regression 255

negative correlation 257

outlier 263

Pearson correlation
  coefficient 260

positive correlation 256

prediction design 254

predictor variable 266

regression 266

regression line 256

response bias 251

response rate 249

restriction of range 264

reverse causality 262

scatterplot 256

simple correlation
  design 254

survey research design 246

REVIEW QUESTIONS

1. What are three reasons that more participants are willing to complete a questionnaire administered in person?

2. Which type of bias can occur when a questionnaire is administered in an interview?

3. State four responsible and appropriate ways to handle and administer questionnaires.

4. A community decides that ethnic diversity in each of their schools is important. They make changes to the school boundaries so that no school has greater than 80% nonwhite student membership. What is the best way to track parent and teacher satisfaction of a school's minority status over time? Why?

5. A hypothetical study found that students (a) from lower socioeconomic status, (b) who had parents and friends who had not completed high school, (c) had been suspended or expelled at least once, and (d) previously were held back and not promoted to the next grade at least once were more likely to drop out of high school. What type of correlation design is described here? Why?

6. Are the following scenarios a positive or negative correlation?

   A. A researcher reports that the farther college students are from their parents, the more often they communicate with their parents (either by phone or by e-mail). Is this an example of a positive or a negative correlation?

   B. An instructor reports that as the number of student interruptions during class decreases, student scores on in-class quizzes increase. Is this an example of a positive or a negative correlation?

7. The following graphs display the data points for a linear correlation. Based on the information provided in these graphs, answer the following questions.

   A. Which graph displays the negative correlation? Explain.

   B. Which graph displays the stronger correlation? Explain.

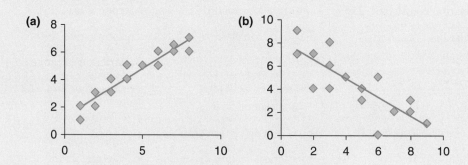

8. True or false: Outliers can change the direction and strength of a correlation.

9. When does restriction of range limit the interpretation of a significant correlation?

10. What is the relationship between the predictor variable and the criterion variable?

ACTIVITIES

1. Think of a topic of interest to you. Outline the steps you would take to administer a questionnaire using the different types of survey designs: longitudinal (trend, cohort, and panel) and cross-sectional.

2. Think of two factors that you predict will be related. Measure each factor in a sample of at least 10 people. Create your own scatterplot on a piece of graph paper. Summarize the result in terms of the direction and the strength of the correlation between the two factors you measured.

$SAGE edge™

SAGE edge offers a robust online environment featuring an impressive array of free tools and resources for review, study, and further exploration, keeping both instructors and students on the cutting edge of teaching and learning.

Access practice quizzes, eFlashcards, video, and multimedia at edge.sagepub.com/priviterarme.

Identify a problem

- Determine an area of interest.
- Review the literature.
- Identify new ideas in your area of interest.
- Develop a research hypothesis.

Develop a research plan

- Define the variables being tested.
- Identify participants or subjects and determine how to sample them.
- Select a research strategy and design.
- Evaluate ethics and obtain institutional approval to conduct research.

Generate more new ideas

- Results support your hypothesis—refine or expand on your ideas.
- Results do not support your hypothesis—reformulate a new idea or start over.

After reading this chapter, you should be able to:

1 Define qualitative research.

2 Distinguish between the holistic perspectives of qualitative and quantitative research.

3 Understand the three prominent theoretical perspectives of qualitative researchers.

4 Identify the steps involved in qualitative research.

5 Describe the four possible roles of the qualitative researcher.

6 Distinguish between the different types of sampling procedures for qualitative research.

7 List the three main types of data collection in qualitative research.

8 Describe how qualitative observations are different from quantitative observations.

9 Identify three key questions of concern for the use of the Internet as a method for selecting samples in qualitative research.

Communicate the results

- Method of communication: oral, written, or in a poster.
- Style of communication: APA guidelines are provided to help prepare style and format.

Conduct the study

- Execute the research plan and measure or record the data.

Analyze and evaluate the data

- Analyze and evaluate the data as they relate to the research hypothesis.
- Summarize data and research results.

chapter

ten

....

INTRODUCTION TO QUALITATIVE RESEARCH

....

In the Chapter 8 opening, we stated the following hypothesis: Fruits will be eaten more if they are made more convenient. To answer the hypothesis, we used a naturalistic observation. We placed fruits in a convenient location in the school cafeteria and recorded the number of fruits selected by students as they went through the cafeteria line. However, a qualitative analysis could provide insight into the validity of this hypothesis as well. For example, suppose we spend time in the school cafeteria for a few weeks and observe the food selection process of students. We could write down a narrative description of the students' behavior of what they selected and where the food items were located. We could record other information as well, such as whether students talked with other students about their selections or record the comments they made about the selections offered. We could also interview some of the students about their food choices. If many of the students describe that they eat foods that are easier to reach, then we can describe their experiences in this way.

In qualitative research, we are really interested in the process of food selection and the perspective of the student making the food choice, not just the outcome of the number of fruits selected depending on where they were located. If we set up the study correctly, we can use this qualitative analysis to show support for the hypothesis that fruits will be eaten more if they are made more convenient.

> **edge.sagepub.com/ priviterarme**
>
> - Take the chapter quiz
> - Review key terms with eFlashcards
> - Explore multimedia links and SAGE articles
>
> **⑤SAGE edge™**

10.1   What Is Qualitative Research?

In Chapter 1, we introduced the **qualitative research design** as a method used to collect nonnumeric, **narrative data** from which conclusions are drawn without the use of statistical analysis. Denzin and Lincoln (2011) define qualitative research as an empirical, scientific approach to examine phenomena in a natural setting and interpret the phenomena in light of the meanings that people have about the phenomena. As described above in the food selection example, qualitative research could be used to collect naturalistic information in the school cafeteria with the purpose to provide deep, rich descriptions of food selection behavior, thoughts, or emotions from the students' perspectives. As with quantitative research, specific qualitative designs are used to answer different types of research questions. We will describe the more common qualitative designs in Chapters 11 and 12. In this section, we introduce the philosophy of conducting qualitative research, which is very different from other research designs taught in this book.

> The **qualitative research design** is the use of the scientific method to collect nonnumeric, narrative data from which interpretations are drawn from participant perspectives.
>
> **Narratives** (or narrative data) are words collected via interviews or documents that are used for analysis.

A Holistic Perspective

A core assumption in science is that of **determinism,** which is an assumption that all actions in the universe have a cause. In quantitative research—that is, all research described in this book, except that described in this chapter and Chapters 11 and 12—we observe the behavior of many individuals and measure that behavior exactly the same way for all individuals. By doing so, we must assume that there is a single reality or truth in nature that can be measured the same way for all people. Behavior, then, is a measurable phenomenon that can be understood independent of the context in which any one individual experiences it. That is, behavior is a universal phenomenon.

> **Determinism** is an assumption in science that all actions in the universe have a cause.

Qualitative research also adopts the assumption of determinism; however, it does not assume that behavior itself is universal. Instead, qualitative research identifies behavior as something experienced differently by each individual, so behavior cannot be measured independent of how the individual experiences it. In all, the perspective of qualitative research is based on a holistic, or "complete picture," view that emphasizes the following two principles:

1. There is no single reality in nature; hence, *reality changes.* Reality, or the truth about behavior that science is used to discover, is in the eye of the beholder. In other words, each person experiences a slightly different reality. From this view, the participant is no longer an object of study used to measure behavior, as is the case in quantitative research. Instead, the participant is an expert in his or her own life because we aim to understand the participant's unique experiences to study the causes of his or her behavior. The focus, then, is not on behavior itself but specifically on people's perceptions and interpretations of their experiences.

2. Behavior does not occur independent of context; hence, *behavior is dynamic.* Context is the individual, psychological, social, political, historical, and cultural setting within which an individual behaves at any given time. From a qualitative perspective, people's perceptions and interpretations of their experiences, which we call behavior, can only be understood in the specific context within which the behavior occurs. Hence, behavior operates differently in different contexts; an analysis of behavior outside of the particular context in which it occurs, then, will be incomplete.

> Qualitative research is based on the holistic view that reality changes and behavior is dynamic.

10.2 Foundations of Qualitative Research

While both quantitative and qualitative research designs use rigorous, scientific methods to plan, gather, and analyze data, the foundations of these two methods are distinctly different, as shown in Table 10.1. The *focus of qualitative research is process oriented* rather than outcome oriented, examining why and how a behavior, thought, or emotion occurs. In the case of the food selection study, qualitative researchers can observe or interview participants to describe the process of food selection. We already mentioned that *qualitative data are narrative* rather than numeric; words instead of numbers are used to describe the observation or gathered through interviews. The *participants of qualitative research are considered coresearchers,* as the experts in their own life and perspectives rather than an object of study. The qualitative researcher's role is to adequately describe the participant's behavior, thought, or emotion. The researcher will often consult with the participant to ensure that the description is accurate. This *relationship between the researcher and participant is interactive,* whereby the researcher develops rapport with the participant, often over a period of time, to obtain information and verify its accuracy. Recall in quantitative research that the researcher directs the progression of the study and what the participant will do. The role of the researcher can vary along a continuum of **observer** and participant, a balance that we will describe shortly. The *process of data collection and analyzing the data is emergent* rather than structured in that data are collected and then analyzed (as described later in this chapter) repeatedly in an

> **Observer** is a research role where the observer is neither seen nor heard. The researcher is as unobtrusive as possible in the situation being observed and the participants may not even know that they are being observed.

iterative process. Data are collected and then analyzed to determine if more data are needed and what kind of data may be needed. This process continues until the data are saturated. Data saturation occurs when no new information is derived from the data collection process and all the needed information is obtained. The information derived from the participant(s) is then used to describe a pattern that emerges from the data using *thematic analysis* rather than statistical analysis. This analysis can be used to formulate a theory or hypothesis. Using data to formulate a theory or hypothesis is a form of **inductive reasoning** rather than the **deductive reasoning** used in quantitative studies. The *results of qualitative research are descriptive* summaries of the responses of the participants rather than statistical summaries, often using quotes to illustrate a point. Table 10.1 distinguishes the foundational differences between qualitative and quantitative research.

Inductive reasoning is a "bottom-up" type of reasoning in which a limited number of observations or measurements (i.e., data) are used to generate ideas and make observations.

Deductive reasoning is a "top-down" type of reasoning in which a claim (a hypothesis or theory) is used to generate ideas or predictions and make observations.

....

10.3   Theoretical Perspectives in Qualitative Research

The theoretical perspective of qualitative researchers guides their view of the world and how they interpret it; therefore, it is very important for qualitative researchers to understand their own theoretical perspective and to share this with the consumers of their research.

Positivism/postpositivism is a philosophical view that there is one reality that can be studied using a structured scientific method, verified, and understood.

Constructivism is a philosophical view that maintains there are multiple realities, in which that people construct their own meaning of the world.

Critical theory is a group of philosophical views that contend that reality is defined by social entities such as culture, race, class, politics, and gender.

There are three broad prominent qualitative theoretical perspectives that include **positivism/postpositivism**, **constructivism**, and **critical theory**. Positivism/postpositivism is a philosophical view shared by both quantitative and qualitative researchers where the belief is that there is one reality that can be studied using a structured scientific method, verified, understood, and tested as theories. Postpositivism varies slightly from positivism in that it contends that reality cannot be fully understood. Positivist/postpositivist qualitative researchers may use frequency counts or other descriptive statistics to describe their findings. Similar to the constructivist learning theory, the constructivist paradigm maintains there are multiple realities and that people construct their own meaning of the world based on their own experiences. Using this theoretical approach, the researcher and participants co-create an understanding of reality through their interaction with the final aim to construct a consensual understanding and description of reality. The critical theoretical perspective is actually a group of paradigms that believe that reality is defined by social entities such as culture, race, class, politics, and gender. Some specific qualitative critical theories include feminism, ethnic, Marxist, cultural studies, and

	Quantitative Research	Qualitative Research
Orientation	Focus is on the outcome of the study, impacts or effects of an independent variable.	Focus is on the process of a behavior, how or why a behavior, thought, or emotion occurs.
Data	Numeric. Behavior is operationalized in terms of how it is measured.	Words. Participant perceptions and experiences are described in words as the participant describes them.
Participants	An object of study whose identity is to be protected.	A coresearcher; an expert in his or her own life.
Relationship between the researcher and the participant	Directional. The researcher directs the progression of a study. Researcher → Participant	Interactive. The participant is regarded as a "coresearcher" in a study. The researcher may also become a participant. Researcher ← → Participant
Process	Structured. Step-by-step procedures for data collection and analysis are planned in advance.	Emergent. Iterative process with data collection and analysis informing each other and determining the study is complete when data are saturated.
Data analysis	Statistical analysis occurs after data collection where there is one interpretation.	Thematic analysis occurs concurrently with data collection where there can be multiple interpretations.
The role of theory and reasoning in measurement	Deductive reasoning. A theory or hypothesis is used to justify what will be observed or measured in a study.	Inductive reasoning. Any participant response is recorded in a study. A theory or hypothesis emerges as data are collected.
Results	Statistical. Summarizes only those scores that were measured.	Descriptive. Summarizes all responses provided by participants.

queer theory. Each has a unique perspective with the commonality of looking at reality through the specific social perspective.

LEARNING CHECK 2 ✓

1. What are the eight ways in which the foundations of qualitative and quantitative research differ?

2. Are the following descriptions qualitative or quantitative research?

   A. A research study investigates the effectiveness of an intervention by counting the number of correct answers on a test.

B. A research study reviews the data collected to determine if more information is needed to answer the research question.

C. A researcher designs a study to formulate a hypothesis on how singing affects social development of preschoolers.

3. What theoretical perspective is reflected in the following statements?

A. Understanding how the world works depends on the social and economic factors in which the individual operates.

B. Scientific evidence reveals how the world works.

C. Humans generate their own knowledge of how the world works.

10.4 Steps in Qualitative Research

Recall we mentioned above that qualitative research is an iterative process to gather narrative information to describe behavior, thought, or emotion. Figure 10.1 illustrates the iterative process of qualitative research. The first two steps to generate the research questions and design the study are the same as with quantitative research. Chapters 11 and 12 describe six of the more common qualitative designs. The iterative process includes Steps 3 through 6 to collect, analyze, generate findings, and validate findings until the data have reached the saturation point. Data are gathered and then analyzed to determine what additional data are needed. As additional data are gathered, findings are generated and validated. We will discuss how qualitative researchers collect data in this chapter. We will discuss the process for analyzing, generating findings, and validating the findings in Chapter 20. The saturation point is the point at which no new information is being gathered. At this point, the study is considered complete and a report can be generated.

Data saturation occurs when data collection provides no new information.

10.5 Role of the Researcher and Entry Into the Field

As we mentioned above, the role of the researcher in qualitative research is interactive with the participant. This interaction falls on a continuum from observer to participant. In some research, qualitative researchers will remain hidden, unknown to the participants as being a researcher as in the observer role. In other cases, the researcher may use a confederate. A confederate is an individual who acts as a participant in the presence of the participants but is really a member of the research team and operates under the direction of the researchers. The qualitative researcher may use a confederate when he or she cannot directly participate in the

Section III: Nonexperimental Research Designs

Figure 10.1   Steps in the Iterative Process of Qualitative Research

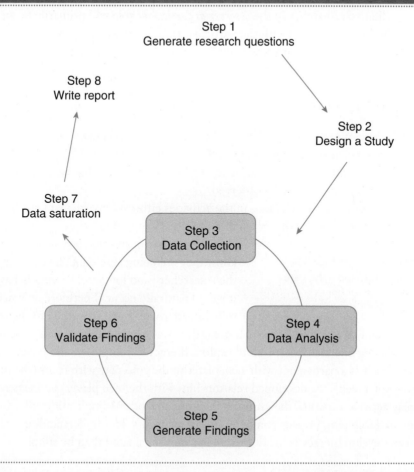

Step 1
Generate research questions

Step 8
Write report

Step 2
Design a Study

Step 7
Data saturation

Step 3
Data Collection

Step 6
Validate Findings

Step 4
Data Analysis

Step 5
Generate Findings

study. For example, in a study on teen behavior, the presence of an adult will likely change the behavior of the teens so a teen confederate may be necessary. Table 10.2 illustrates the four different roles that a qualitative researcher can play in their research. By adding a level of participation to the observation, the researcher can access different types of information that may be missed by simple observation. By participating in the activities being investigated, researchers can develop a rapport with the participants that affords them the opportunity to observe behavior as it would naturally occur. The information gained from participating can add to the understanding of the topic being investigated.

Observer

A qualitative researcher who serves only as an observer is the proverbial fly on the wall, neither seen nor heard. The researcher is as unobtrusive as possible in the situation being observed and the participants may not even know that they are being observed. She or he will be in the background and only watch what is happening. She or he will not interact with the participants or be a part of the activity being observed.

Observer as Participant

A qualitative researcher in the *observer as participant* role will primarily be an observer but will have limited interaction with the participants. In this case, the participants know they are being observed and may even know why they are being observed, but the researcher is a neutral third party.

Participant as Observer

In the case of *participant as observer*, the researcher is engaged with the participants of the study and may be viewed as a friend or colleague. The participants know that this person is the researcher and thus the researcher is an outsider in the sense that he or she is not a member of the group or event being observed.

The downside of participating in the activities either as a participant as observer or an observer as participant is the threat of reactivity. **Reactivity** is when the participants alter their behavior in some way because they know they are being studied. When this happens, the researcher is no longer observing behavior as it would naturally occur. Therefore, it is necessary to habituate participants in a study to the presence of the researcher. For example, Hayes-Moore (2015) was interested in studying the use of digital role-playing in a teen book club to explore literacy development and imagination. By immersing herself as a participant with a character in the role-play with teens (she disclosed that she was not a teen), she developed relationships with the teen players and experienced the role-play activity as part of the group to then understand the implications of using this technology in developing literacy competencies of teenagers. Her understanding of how role-play can develop literacy is likely greater having participated than by simply observing it.

> **Reactivity** is when the participants alter their behavior in some way because they know they are being studied.

Complete Participant

A complete participant role is when the researcher is fully embedded in the event or activity being observed. They are fully engaged as a member of the group. In this case, the participants do not know this person is a researcher. While this is a great way to get an in-depth understanding of the topic of the investigation without the threat of reactivity, by being a member of the group, the researcher has the potential to interfere with the activity or event being observed. The question is whether the actions would have been the same if the researcher was not present and engaging with the participants.

CONNECTING TO THE CLASSROOM

Conducting a qualitative research study in your own classroom is likely be more difficult than with a quantitative study given the hierarchical teacher-student relationship already established. With this relationship established, students may not be as open to sharing their true thoughts or feelings. One solution is the use of a confederate such as an older student (with parent permission), guidance counselor, or faculty member from a local university to assist in conducting the interviews or observations. Another way to gather information from your own students is indirectly through documents such as in a writing assignment or other project. Want to know students' opinions about bullying, their favorite subject at school, or how they use the Internet at home? Ask them to write about it, paint/draw/collage an art project, or prepare a class presentation.

Table 10.2 Roles of a Qualitative Researcher

Role	Description	Example
Observer	The researcher is only an observer and does not engage in the activities under investigation.	A researcher observes a literacy lesson from the back of the room and does not interact with the teacher or students (Jordan, 2015).
Observer as participant	The researcher has minimal involvement in the activities under investigation.	A researcher sings along with preschool children during observations but only interacts when approached by a child (Niland, 2015).
Participant as observer	The researcher takes an active role in the activities under investigation, typically by assuming the role being studied.	The researcher participates in an online role-play club for teens, disclosing that she is a researcher. She documents her observations and collects artifacts from her role-play activities with the teens (Hayes-Moore, 2015). Also called overt observations.
Complete participant	The researcher is a full participant of the activities under investigation, typically observing covertly.	A researcher poses as a student, completing assignments and interacting with the instructor, to learn about the experiences of students in a Massive Online Open Course (MOOC). Also called covert observations.

The role of a qualitative researcher as observer and/or participant requires skill in gaining entry into the field. Entry to the field simple means gaining access to the participants and developing the relationship necessary to obtain the information needed for the study. For educational researchers, this means gaining access to schools, classrooms, teachers, students, parents, or administrators who have the information that the researcher is seeking. Skill is needed to identify a site, select the participants, and guide the relationship with the participants to facilitate the research process. This requires consent of the members of the group not only in the form of informed consent but also in the ability of the researcher to become immersed in the group being studied. For example, in the Hayes-Moore (2015) study, she gained access to participants by posing as a player in a teen role-play game. She disclosed that she was not a teen, and the group allowed her to participate in the role-play game. If some of the teens had objected to her participation, her experience would have been different. She also could have not been allowed to play at all. Becoming a full participant in the research avoids the possibility of being denied entry because there is

> **Overt observation** is when the researcher takes an active role in the activities under investigation, typically by assuming the role being studied.

typically not a disclosure of the research, but this type of access may have ethical implications that we will address later in the chapter.

One common way to gain entry into the field is to use personal contacts that can ease entry. One example is having a key contact within the group who can "vouch" for the researcher with other members of the group. For example, McCormick, Schmidt, and Clifton (2015) were interested in studying gay-straight alliances on the academic experiences of lesbian, gay, bisexual, transgender, and questioning (LGBTQ) youth. They recruited school counselors who worked with LGBTQ youth as their key contact to identify and recruit participants. Educational qualitative researchers also access participants with whom they already have some type of relationship. Unrau, Ragusa, and Bowers (2015) were interested in studying how teachers motivate students to read. They recruited teachers who were earning their master's degree at their universities. Villa and Baptiste (2014) recruited preservice teachers at their university who had taken class where the researcher had been the instructor. It is also possible to obtain participants with whom the researcher does not have a previous relationship. In a study by Scarbrough and Allen (2015), one of the researchers heard about the partnership of an English teacher and a teaching artist/performance poet to co-teach poetry to high school students. The researcher simply asked to observe their co-taught poetry lessons.

10.6   Sampling in Qualitative Research

Because qualitative researchers need access to specific participants who have knowledge of the topic under investigation, they use purposeful (or purposive) nonprobability sampling techniques. Recall in probability sampling techniques, the researcher knows the probability of an individual being selected as a participant of the study. In nonprobability sampling techniques, we do not know the probability of a person being selected as a participant and therefore will not be able to know how well the participants represent some target population. Take, for example, a study of bullying where the researcher is interested in the perspective of teen victims of bullying. Casting a wide net to randomly sample teens at local high schools will likely obtain teens who have not been victims of bullying. Sampling in this way would be a waste of time, effort, and money, so qualitative researchers have to employ other techniques to obtain the specific participants who have the specific information they need. Qualitative researchers then study these participants in depth to provide deep, rich descriptions of the topic.

Qualitative research swaps the large sample sizes of quantitative research for smaller samples that are studied in greater detail. The smaller sample size is another reason that it is imperative that the participants possess the knowledge the researcher needs. There is no set number of participants who are needed for a qualitative study as there is in quantitative studies. It is possible to have a sample size of 1 in qualitative research, as in the case study design described in Chapter 12. Scarbrough and Allen (2015) studied one co-teaching pair and Niland (2015) observed one preschool classroom to investigate the role of singing in social development. A study by Peck, Maude, and Brotherson (2015) is considered a large sample for qualitative research. They interviewed 18 teachers regarding their expression of empathy in their relationships with young children with disabilities and their families.

There are many different ways that qualitative researchers select their participants depending on the aim of the research study. Some types of qualitative sampling seek participants with similar experiences or views while other types of sampling seek participants with different experiences or views. Table 10.3 describes the more common types of qualitative sampling and provides an example.

- **Criterion sampling** is when the researcher develops a set of predetermined criteria by which to select participants. The criteria define the specific characteristics of the participants that the researcher thinks is important. Once the criteria are established, the researcher seeks to find the individuals who meet the criteria.

- The **critical case sampling** strategy selects a few essential cases for understanding the issue. The researcher will need to define what characteristics or knowledge the critical case possesses. It is similar to criterion, but it selects just a few individuals who are crucial to gaining understanding.

- **Typical case sampling** selects individuals who are average or representative of the issue being investigated. Using this technique, the researcher is interested in understanding the issue under ordinary circumstances.

- **Opportunistic (or emergent) sampling** takes advantage of the knowledge gained as a result of conducting a study. During the study, the researcher becomes aware of new information and takes advantage of this by adding individuals who can contribute to the understanding of the new information being learned. This is useful when conducting an exploratory study of a relatively new phenomenon.

- In **snowball sampling,** the researcher typically begins with one or two participants who he or she knows can provide information about the topic under investigation. The researcher will ask these participants if they know someone else who can provide additional information and may be willing to talk to him or her. These new participants are also asked if they know someone else. The sample becomes larger as the study continues, like making a snowball by rolling it through the snow. This is a good technique when the researcher knows few potential participants at the onset of a study or if the targeted participants are difficult to find or small in number.

- **Extreme case sampling** identifies highly unusual cases for the issue being investigated. These cases would be considered "the exception to the rule." This allows the researcher to develop a deeper understanding of the issue by examining the outliers and not just the typical.

Criterion sampling is when the researcher develops a set of predetermined criteria by which to select participants.

Critical case sampling selects a few essential cases for understanding the issue. The researcher will need to define what characteristics or knowledge the critical case possesses.

Typical case sampling selects individuals who are average or representative of the issue being investigated.

Opportunistic sampling obtains participants serendipitously to take advantage of circumstances or new events as they arise.

Snowball sampling begins with one or two participants who can provide information about the topic under investigation. The researcher will ask these participants if they know someone else who can provide additional information. These new participants are also asked if they know someone else.

Extreme case sampling identifies highly unusual cases (the exception to the rule) as the sample.

Maximum variation sampling maximizes the diversity of the sample by including typical and extreme cases. The individuals selected represent the entire spectrum of possible cases rather than a homogeneous group.

Negative (disconfirming) case sampling seeks to find individuals who do not fit into the emerging patterns identified in the analysis.

- Maximum variation sampling maximizes the diversity of the sample by including typical and extreme cases. The individuals selected represent the entire spectrum of possible cases rather than a homogeneous group like criterion sampling.

- Negative (disconfirming) case sampling seeks to find individuals who do not fit into the emerging patterns identified in the analysis.

Table 10.3 Qualitative Sampling Techniques

Technique	Description	Example
Criterion	Participant(s) meet predetermined criteria (such as similar experience or view).	Peck, Maude, and Brotherson (2015) selected early childhood professionals employed in inclusive preschool settings with children aged 3 to 5 years.
Critical case	Participant(s) possess critical or important elements needed to understand the topic.	Jordan (2015) selected one teacher with 20 students to study scaffolding of student engagement during literacy instruction based on qualifications of the teacher (34 years of experience, teacher of the year, curriculum specialist) and school/class demographics (92% economically disadvantaged, 63% limited English proficiency).
Typical case	Participants are considered typical or average.	Tarman and Kuran (2015) used typical case sampling to select social studies texts for their investigation of the depth of knowledge (using Bloom's Taxonomy) of the assessment questions provided by the texts.
Opportunistic	Participants are selected to take advantage of circumstances or new events as they arise.	Gurley, Anast-May, and Lee (2015) studied a 2-year-long school leadership academy created by a school district-university partnership to meet the school district need for school leaders. One of the researchers was a part of the development of and instructor for the academy.
Snowball	Participants nominate others who can add information on the topic.	To investigate why Black males drop out of school, Bell (2014) asked participants to recommend other participants who could contribute additional information.
Extreme case	Participants are considered unusual.	Tubin (2015) used a three-step process to select the most successful schools (based on high graduation rate, low dropout rate, and reputation/nomination) in Israel to investigate what makes these schools so successful.
Maximum variation	Participants are selected based on diverse variations of the topic and opposite ends of a continuum such as high/low, success/failure.	To study democratic citizenship instruction, Ersoy (2014) selected two schools—one public school with a high percentage of low socioeconomic families and one private school with more affluent families—to illustrate the differences.
Negative case	Participants are selected who are opposite of what the initial findings suggest, an outlier.	Sutherland, Stuhr, and Ayvazo (2014) used negative case sampling of teachers learning to teach using the adventure-based learning (ABL) model of physical education. Negative cases were identified as those teachers who did not fit into the ABL model and identified themes.

By seeking individuals who do not fit into the identified pattern, the researcher can develop a deeper understanding of the issue being investigated and identify limitations of the study.

LEARNING CHECK 3 ✓

1. Name the steps in qualitative research.

2. Which role is the qualitative researcher taking in the following scenarios?

   A. A researcher observes a series of aspiring principal professional development sessions and talks to some of the participants during breaks about the observations.

   B. A researcher joins a teacher book club disclosing that she is using her participation for a research study.

   C. A researcher assumes an undercover role of a substitute teacher in a low-performing school.

   D. A researcher observes and narratively records the behavior of a disruptive student.

3. What form of sampling is being used to study why teachers leave the field of teaching in the following scenarios.

   A. The researcher locates a couple of teachers who have left the field and asks them to name a few more they know who might be willing to participate.

   B. The researcher lists the following specific criteria in order for participants to be eligible to participate in her study: licensed teacher from an accredited teaching program, taught in public school for less than 5 years, and currently employed in a noneducation job.

   C. After administering a survey, a researcher selected teachers with less than 5 years of teaching experience and those with more than 20 years of teaching experience who indicate they are contemplating leaving teaching to interview.

Answers: 1. Generate research question(s), design a study, then in an iterative fashion collect and analyze, generate and validate findings until data are saturated, write a report; 2. A. observer as participant, B. participant as observer, C. participant; 3. A. snowball, B. criterion, C. maximum variation.

MAKING SENSE—SELECTING A SAMPLING STRATEGY

A researcher will select a sampling strategy that best fits the research question. He or she will select the strategy that offers the best way to get the information needed to answer the research question given the availability of such individuals. When beginning a new line of inquiry, it might be best to start with typical case or criterion sampling to identify the most common characteristics. As knowledge of the line of inquiry and the individuals involved develops, negative, extreme, or critical case sampling can add depth of understanding to what is already known. In some cases, it might be difficult to find the participants needed. In this case, snowball sampling can be useful in identifying additional participants.

10.7 Types of Qualitative Data

There are three main types of qualitative data that include narrative descriptions of naturalistic observations, interviews or focus groups, and document reviews that gather information indirectly from the participants. Other types of qualitative data include visual images such as pictures, videos or film, sounds, and virtual data. Observations, interviews, focus groups, and documents were described in Chapter 5. The descriptions of interviews, focus groups, and document reviews in that chapter are applicable here, too. The description of naturalistic observations, though, was from a quantitative perspective to define and count the behaviors involved in the study. In this section, we will look at conducting observations from a qualitative perspective and the other types of qualitative data.

Qualitative Observations

Qualitative observations are deep, rich descriptions of what is being observed in naturalistic settings. These observations typically occur over a period of time and require rapport with all participants. Notes are taken during the observation to help the observer recall what was observed. These notes are usually short phrases because the observer is still observing while taking the notes. These observation notes are transferred to field notes as soon as possible after the observation. **Field notes** typically include two parts. The first part of field notes is to expand and detail the observation using the original notes, including "who," "what," "where," and "when" of the observation to describe what was seen and/or heard. These notes are the raw data the researcher will later analyze, so the more detailed the better. For example, instead of simply saying that a "student was disruptive," the field notes should describe what the student did, such as "When the teacher passed back the graded assignments, the student looked at the paper, stood up, and spoke in a loud and deep tone to the teacher that she was unfair, then he threw the papers she had just passed out on the ground. He sat back in his desk with some force to make the desk move a few inches and pounded his fist on top of the desk once." The second part of field notes is a reflection of the observation. Reflections can include "how" or "why" thoughts or other interpretations of the observation, including emotional reactions to the observation. One interpretation could be that he was upset about the grade that he received on the assignment. The researcher reflects upon not only the participants under observation but also himself or herself. Reflections can also include how this observation compared with other observations. These reflections seek to describe and interpret the observation. In the case of the disruptive student, field note reflections might include notes about how the student, teacher, and researcher felt about the interaction described; why the student and teacher reacted in this way; or how and why the researcher reacted to this observation. Thompson (2014) described her experience in writing field notes as such:

> While a little notepad in my pocket helped for quick jottings to later jog my memory, I mainly wrote fieldnotes on my laptop, alone in my room.

Field notes are notes taken during and after the observation period to document what was seen and heard. They can also include an interpretation of the observation.

In that sense, the notes constitute memory work, where I remembered to document and reflect on the research. My fieldnotes describe interactions and conversations, senses and spaces, my ongoing decision-making and interpretations. I elaborated both on the everyday and more dramatic "crisis events." . . . Adopting reflexivity to situate the knowledges produced . . . I questioned my reactions and assumptions, desperately wanting to recognize and deconstruct essentialist constructions. I also wrote about how others reacted, such that my notes also consider participant concerns. (p. 248)

Types of Qualitative Data and Technology

With the growth and ease of technology, other types of visual data are emerging in qualitative work such as the use of graphics, photographs, film, and social media. Visual data can be useful as they record behavior as it naturally occurs but also retains it for scrutiny by others. Consider the recent use of video recording of police and civilian interactions being shared on the Internet. Not only do we see the actions in the actual encounter (sometimes with audio), but such recordings can be easily shared with others and repeatedly viewed so that the actions can be verified. We might see something on the second or third viewing that we didn't see the first time.

Qualitative researchers may create visual data by video-recording observations or interviews themselves or they can use visual data created by others. Ahlgrim-Delzell and Rivera (2015) used videos of teachers during reading lessons taken in 2010 and 2014 to explore the changes made by teachers in their reading instruction as a result of professional development and participating in research on reading instruction. Videos of teachers reading

Figure 10.2 Illustration of the Qualitative Data Analysis Process in a Hypothetical Qualitative Study

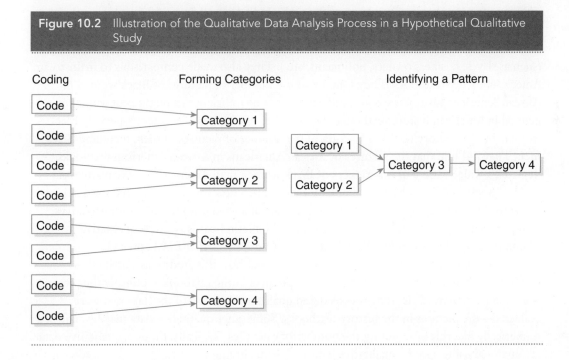

lessons taken before the professional development and research studies were compared to videos taken a year after the final study was completed. By using videos, the researchers did not have to depend on teacher perception of their teaching. The videos could be replayed as often as needed to make sure something was not missed. Different coders could watch the videos, giving an increased sense of reliability of the coding. Muthersbaugh, Kern, and Charvoz (2014) used images created by the participants as part of their qualitative data. They asked students to create watercolor paintings depicting their views of the environment during the Lewis and Clark expedition and now. They asked the students to describe the two different paintings to capture students' views on how the environmental landscape has changed. The paintings were used during interviews where the students described what they drew. Researchers could ask why certain elements of the painting were included or not included. In this case, students were able to verbally describe their paintings, but this may also be a good technique with students who are not able to verbally describe their perceptions. This type of use of visual images is called elicitation. The images are used to elicit information from the participants. Use of photos to elicit information from participants is called photo elicitation, and use of videos to elicit information from participants is called video elicitation.

Visual data can also include publicly available visuals such as photographs or movies. Such photos can be found in archives of newspapers and magazines or on display at places like museums. These images can be used to capture a historical or current perspective of the object under investigation. Burton Blatt and Fred Kaplan (1974) used pictures taken of individuals in residential institutions for people with disabilities in the United States during the 1960s to tell the story about the conditions under which these people lived. The book is predominately the pictures with limited little text other than to label the pictures as the pictures themselves tell the story. Schocker and Woyshner (2013) analyzed images of women in U.S. history textbooks to explore gender and ethnic diversity in an African American history textbook used by their local school system. First, they counted the number of images of Black women in the textbook, and then they looked at how the women were portrayed (such as slaves, business owners, politicians, etc.). They also made comparisons to mainstream American history textbooks. They found that the number of pictures of Black women in African American history textbooks reflected the same imbalance of pictures of women in general in American history textbooks. The number of pictures of women, especially Black women, in U.S. history texts is a fraction of the number of pictures of men, including Black men. They did find that the pictures of African Americans in African American textbooks depicted a wider variety of experiences of Black women than American history textbooks.

Social media such as Facebook or Twitter are a new source of material for qualitative research. The postings and tweets can be saved and analyzed just like any other narratives. Using Internet sources such as these or blogs and bulletin boards is a new qualitative orientation called netography. We will discuss netography further in Chapter 11.

You might be asking yourself right now about how this study was classified as qualitative when they counted the number of pictures in the textbook. Counting the pictures is a numeric activity. This study is considered qualitative because of the data that were collected—the pictures in the history textbooks. Sometimes qualitative data may be analyzed numerically like this by counting the number of examples. Typically, though, qualitative data are analyzed using specific qualitative data analysis techniques.

10.8 Ethics in Focus: Using the Internet in Qualitative Research

One of the research studies used in this chapter used an online role-play game (Hayes-Moore, 2015). In this article, she expresses some difficulty in navigating some of the ethical guidelines in obtaining institutional review approval for her human subject research. A major issue she encountered was being able to verify the demographic makeup of the participants. Although each player created a role-play profile that included age and gender, because the profiles were self-generated, she could not verify their accuracy. She could not exactly outline who her participants were. This illustrates one of the ethical considerations needed when conducting Internet-based research.

The Internet can be a tool in which to collect qualitative data but also a field site, such as with the Hayes-Moore (2015) study. Special considerations in using the Internet as a tool or field site include the concept of human subjects research that directly interacts with "human subjects," whether avatars or digital information should be considered human subject research, and the expectations of privacy in public forums such as tweets and public Facebook posts (Association of Internet Researchers, 2012). Conception of human subjects research as described in the Belmont Report or guidelines of professional organizations such as the American Educational Research Association or American Psychological Association envision human subject research as having direct interaction with the participants and that the researcher has some control over these interactions. This is not the case with Internet-based research. Consider the difference between collecting information via e-mail or an interview and obtaining information from an avatar. Information obtained through e-mail or an interview is directly connected to an individual, but is an avatar a person or human subject? How about collecting data from tweets? Should research using avatars and social media be considered human subjects research at all? Finally, what is the expectation of privacy when individuals post in public forums? If an individual posts in a public forum, is there an expectation about how that information can be used by others, including researchers? There are now tools that can be used to extract posts such as tweets in aggregated form, called data mining, which researchers can use. Should an individual have an expectation that his or her post or tweet may be later mined by others for research? If so, how does the notion of informed consent apply in this situation? These are questions that need to be answered as Internet-based research becomes more common. The concepts of protection from harm, vulnerability, and personal identifying information still apply, but the concept of what constitutes a human subject and how these notions can be maintained is likely different.

CHAPTER SUMMARY

LO 1 Define qualitative research.

- An empirical, scientific approach to examine phenomena in a natural setting and interpret the phenomena in light of the meanings that people have about the phenomena.

LO 2 Distinguish between the holistic perspectives of qualitative and quantitative research.

- Both perspectives believe that all actions have a cause.

- Quantitative research assumes that there is a single reality for all people.

- Qualitative research operates under the assumption that behavior is not universal. Behavior is understood within how the individual experiences it. Each individual experiences reality differently, and behavior occurs in the context of the individual's perceptions of reality.

LO 3 Understand the three prominent theoretical perspectives of qualitative researchers.

- Positivism/postpositivism is a philosophical view that there is one reality that can be studied using a structured scientific method, verified, and understood.

- Constructivism is a philosophical view that maintains there are multiple realities and that people construct their own meaning of the world.

- Critical theory is a group of philosophical views that contend that reality is defined by social entities such as culture, race, class, politics, and gender.

LO 4 Identify the steps involved in qualitative research.

- The first two steps are to generate the research questions and design the study. Collecting, analyzing, generating, and validating findings are iterative and continue until the data are saturated. Once no new information is needed to answer the research question, a report is written.

LO 5 Describe the four possible roles of the qualitative researcher.

- An observer simply observes and does not engage in the activities under investigation.

- An observer as participant observes and has minimal involvement in the activities under investigation.

- A participant as observer takes an active role in the activities under investigation, typically by assuming the role being studied.

- A participant actively participates in the activities under investigation, typically observing covertly.

LO 6 Distinguish between the different types of sampling procedures for qualitative research.

- Criterion sampling involves selecting participant(s) who meet predetermined criteria (such as similar experience or view).

- Critical case sampling selects participant(s) who possess critical or important elements needed to understand the topic.

- **Typical case sampling** selects participants because they are considered typical or average.

- **Opportunistic sampling** obtains participants serendipitously to take advantage of circumstances or new events as they arise.

- Participants of **snowball sampling** are nominated by other participants who can add information on the topic.

- **Extreme case sampling** selects participants who are considered unusual.

- Participants in **maximum variation sampling** are selected based on diverse variations of the topic or because they represent opposite ends of a continuum.

- **Negative case sampling** involves selecting cases that are opposite of the initial findings of the study.

LO 7 List the three main types of data collection in qualitative research.

- Qualitative data include observations, interviews or focus groups, and document reviews.

LO 8 Describe how qualitative observations are different from quantitative observations.

- Qualitative observations are deep, rich descriptions (not numeric counts) of what is being observed in naturalistic settings. Notes are taken during the observation to help the observer recall what was observed. These original notes can be expanded to add details about the observations made and to add reflections the researcher may have of the observation. These are called field notes.

LO 9 Identify three key questions of concern for the use of the Internet as a method for selecting samples in qualitative research.

- Can we verify the demographic makeup of the participants?

- Is conducting research with digital information considered human participant research?

- Are data posted in public forums considered private information?

KEY TERMS

constructivism 276

criterion sampling 283

critical case sampling 283

critical theory 276

data saturation 278

deductive reasoning 276

determinism 274

extreme case sampling 283

field notes 286

inductive reasoning 276

maximum variation sampling 284

narrative data 274

negative case sampling 284

observer 275

observer as participant 280

positivism/postpositivism 276

reactivity 280

opportunistic sampling 283

qualitative research
design 274

snowball sampling 283

overt observation 281

typical case sampling 283

REVIEW QUESTIONS

1. How does the idea of determinism differ in quantitative and qualitative research?

2. Which of the eight ways in which qualitative and quantitative research differ is represented in the following scenarios:

   A. The researcher develops rapport with the participant to gain information from him or her.

   B. Numeric data are collected.

   C. The researcher allows the theory to emerge from the data as they are collected.

3. Distinguish the similarities and differences in the three broad prominent qualitative theoretical perspectives.

4. Describe the general process of qualitative research.

5. Why is entry into the field so important in qualitative research?

6. Compare and contrast the four different roles that a researcher can take in qualitative research.

7. Why do qualitative studies use smaller samples and nonprobability sampling?

8. Which of the qualitative sampling techniques is used in the following scenarios?

   A. The researcher locates an individual who is opposite of what the initial findings suggest.

   B. The researcher is studying the effects of implementing the Common Core curriculum and is asked to join a school advisory board. She decides to include fellow board members in her study.

   C. The school system is studying a later start time for high school. They implement the study in the lowest performing high school in the school system.

9. How are quantitative observations from Chapter 5 different from qualitative ones?

10. What are other types of qualitative data besides observations that qualitative researchers can use? Provide some examples.

1. Let's plan a study about how learning styles affect learning outcomes. Decide
   A. what role you will play
   B. what kind of data you will collect
   C. how you will gain access to students
   D. what sampling procedure to use

2. Select a topic that interests you. Choose three different forms of sampling and describe how you can use them to study your topic.

3. Observe a classroom for 15 minutes. Decide what you will observe and then take notes during the observation. Later expand these notes to include a deeper description of what you observed and reflect upon what you observed and formulate some ideas about what you think was happening.

4. Ask 10 people to give you three wishes. Code their wishes and develop categories or themes to include all of the wishes.

$SAGE edge™

SAGE edge offers a robust online environment featuring an impressive array of free tools and resources for review, study, and further exploration, keeping both instructors and students on the cutting edge of teaching and learning.

Access practice quizzes, eFlashcards, video, and multimedia at edge.sagepub.com/priviterarme.

Identify a problem

- Determine an area of interest.
- Review the literature.
- Identify new ideas in your area of interest.
- Develop a research hypothesis.

Develop a research plan

- Define the variables being tested.
- Identify participants or subjects and determine how to sample them.
- Select a research strategy and design.
- Evaluate ethics and obtain institutional approval to conduct research.

Generate more new ideas

- Results support your hypothesis—refine or expand on your ideas.
- Results do not support your hypothesis— reformulate a new idea or start over.

After reading this chapter, you should be able to:

1. Identify and describe three qualitative research designs: phenomenology, ethnography, and grounded theory.

2. Describe netnography and autoethnography.

3. Distinguish between the different contexts in which participants self-describe.

4. Distinguish between the three forms of bias that may occur when using the participant as observer role.

5. Describe grounded theory.

Conduct the study

- Execute the research plan and measure or record the data.

Communicate the results

- Method of communication: oral, written, or in a poster.
- Style of communication: APA guidelines are provided to help prepare style and format.

Analyze and evaluate the data

- Analyze and evaluate the data as they relate to the research hypothesis.
- Summarize data and research results.

chapter eleven

PHENOMENOLOGY, ETHNOGRAPHY, AND GROUND THEORY DESIGNS

Qualitative research has become increasingly important for understanding educational issues. Recall that qualitative designs are descriptive and process oriented with a key aim of seeking to describe, explore, and explain phenomena. Qualitative research designs can use techniques from the naturalistic observation design described in Chapter 8 and the observation, interviewing, and document review techniques described in Chapters 5 and 10. In this chapter, we describe three qualitative designs: phenomenology, ethnography (as well as netnography and autoethnography), and grounded theory. Three additional designs (narrative, case study, and critical theory) are described in Chapter 12. The selection of a qualitative design depends on the research question. Just as in quantitative research, a particular design is aligned to specific goals of the research and how the findings are interpreted.

Let us continue to use the hypothesis from Chapter 8: Fruits will be eaten more if they are made more convenient. To answer the hypothesis, we used a naturalistic observation. We placed fruits in a convenient location in the school cafeteria and recorded the number of fruits selected by students as they went through the cafeteria line. In Chapter 10, we discussed how we could also conduct this study using qualitative tools: interviews, focus groups, or observations. Now we can look at this study from specific qualitative perspectives or designs. We could look at food selection as a phenomenon or event and examine how students experience making a food selection (phenomenology).

> **edge.sagepub.com/priviterarme**
>
> - Take the chapter quiz
> - Review key terms with eFlashcards
> - Explore multimedia links and SAGE articles
>
> **⑤SAGE edge™**

We might want to look at food selection as an aspect of culture (ethnography). We could use a well-known app used by students to scour for comments about food selection (netnography). Or if we wanted to generate a theory about convenience of food and child food selection, we could use a grounded theory perspective.

11.1 An Overview of Phenomenology Designs

One qualitative research design, called **phenomenology,** is the study of the conscious experiences of phenomena from the first-person point of view. A **conscious experience** is any experience that a person has lived through or performed and can bring to memory in such a way as to recall that experience. A conscious experience can be an experience such as divorce, natural disaster, or living with a disability or health issue. When applied to education, we can examine how these experiences affect various aspects of education such as access to educational systems and educational attainment. The phenomenological approach assumes that there is some essence of the lived experience that is shared by those who have experienced it. The goal is to understand the essence of the lived experience that is shared. To understand this shared essence, the researcher interviews participants about their first-person account (e.g., "I did/see/think . . .") of the experience. The researcher then constructs a narrative to describe or summarize the experiences described in the interviews. Other methods used to collect data are observation and videotape, although in-depth interviews are the primary method for the phenomenology research design.

Phenomenology is the qualitative analysis of the conscious experiences of phenomena from the first-person point of view of the participant.

Conscious experience is any experience that a person has lived through or performed and can bring to memory in a such a way as to recall that experience.

Objects of awareness are those things that bring an experience to memory or consciousness.

The narrative a researcher constructs is used to describe any type of conscious experience such as teachers interacting with parents, participating in professional development, or surviving in an era of high accountability. To write a qualitative narrative, the researcher must be considerate of the *intentionality* or meaning of a participant's conscious experiences. It is often easiest to identify the intentionality of a participant's conscious experiences by first identifying **objects of awareness,** which are those things that bring an experience to memory or consciousness. Objects of awareness tend to direct conscious experiences and also illuminate the intentionality of a participant's conscious experiences.

11.2 An Example of Phenomenology Research

To illustrate the phenomenological design, let's consider the following study published by Bleiler (2015). Bleiler became interested in a pair of university faculty (one from the mathematics department and one from a mathematics education department) who she met at a conference (opportunistic sampling). They were team teaching mathematics courses for preservice teachers. She employed a phenomenological design because she was interested in investigating the lived experiences of and reflections upon this collaborative teaching phenomenon. Bleiler describes this experience as extraordinary because of the cross-department collaboration of the practices of teaching. She used six sources of data (triangulation) that included individual interviews, paired interviews, field notes from observations of planning sessions, video recordings of class sessions, audio recordings of planning sessions, and student questionnaires. She describes her role as an observer as participant, mostly observing but occasionally participating as the co-teacher of the class. She describes her analytic process in four stages to read and reread the interviews and listening to the audiotapes, then coding the data using Atlas.ti software, developing themes using the codes, then searching for patterns and connections across the themes. She employed member checking at each stage of the analysis to ensure that she accurately represented their perspectives. Her analysis found two themes, one in which the instructor from the teacher education department reflects upon her justifications for instructional decision making and one in which the instructor from the mathematics department reflects on increased understanding of student needs. Both themes were combined into one overarching theme called "increasing awareness of our practice through interaction across communities." All participants reflected on their own practice as a result of their collaboration across different departments (i.e., communities) and teaching perspectives. Here is an example of how Bleiler reports her findings.

> Angela perceived her role as one in which she would provide insight into the recommendations and practices of the mathematics education community to a newcomer in that community (her co-instructor, Dejan). She felt a constant pressure to be able to provide a well-articulated and explicit rationale for those recommendations. In attempting to provide a strong rationale, she found it challenging to articulate to an outsider what seemed to be tacit disciplinary knowledge of the mathematics education community. She struggled with the notion that much of her professional decision making seemed to come from her "gut," and in dichotomizing the dimensions of her pedagogy as art versus science, strived toward the scientific dimension in order to communicate with and convince Dejan of the community's goals. Through attempts at articulation of the philosophy guiding her and her community's practice, Angela found herself reflecting more deeply about some of the major issues involved in the professional preparation of PSMTs, making greater sense of her own practice through contrast with the practices of her co-instructor. (p. 239)

In this paragraph, Bleiler employed an etic perspective using her researcher perspective to describe the participant experience. She followed this paragraph with a quote from the participant as an example of this description. Her results section continued to describe the reflections on collaboration from the two participants, with each description followed by quotes to illustrate how she arrived at her description.

11.3 Considerations for Participant Self-Descriptions

In writing narratives, the author should make additional considerations that increase the trustworthiness of the research. These additional considerations should account for the context within which participants self-describe their experiences. Table 11.1 describes seven key considerations that should be made to account for the context of the experiences described by a participant. Being able to consistently make each consideration in your writing is very important and requires a great deal of practice and training. In all, constructing narratives that identify the intentionality of conscious experiences and the context of those experiences will strengthen the trustworthiness of the research. In this way, phenomenology allows for the detailed analysis of individual conscious experience in a way that conforms to criteria of trustworthiness.

Phenomenology is used to describe first-person accounts of conscious experiences.

Table 11.1 Key Considerations of the Context of Self-Description That Can Influence How Participants Self-Describe Their Conscious Experiences

Context of Self-Description	Description (Example)
Historical	Relevant political, societal, geographic, temporal, and personal histories (e.g., pre– vs. post–Common Core implementation)
Political/governmental	Current political and legal issues that affect an individual (e.g., passage of No Child Left Behind [2001] or Student Success [2015] Acts)
Societal/cultural/religious	Social, cultural, or religious idiosyncrasies (e.g., separation of church and state, neighborhood schools and desegregation)
Geographic	Different social settings or localities (e.g., urban vs. rural schools)
Temporal	Individuals adapt or change over time, even during a research study (e.g., an interviewee changes his or her demeanor during the course of an interview)
Gender	This applies to both the researcher and the participant (e.g., a male interviewer asks questions of a sexual nature to female participants)
Familiarity	We often can only describe experiences when we reflect on them (e.g., a state of fear or anger clouds intention at the time of an experience)

A key distinction between quantitative and qualitative research is in the data collection process. Unlike quantitative research, which tends to measure only those variables that are relevant to a hypothesis, qualitative research describes characteristics of phenomena without numeric measurement. For example, a quantitative researcher may hypothesize that the longer a student studies, the better the student will perform on an exam. Based on this hypothesis, the researcher will measure minutes spent studying and the score on an exam. However, a qualitative researcher using a phenomenological approach would observe studying and record anything that is observed or self-described by a participant as his or her experiences of doing well on an exam. In other words, the participant's responses, and not always some hypothesis, guide the direction of qualitative research. There is little effort to fully structure, control, or predetermine the data collection process using qualitative research. Instead, the participant is regarded as a coresearcher or expert in his or her own life. Hence, as illustrated in Figure 11.1 for qualitative research, participants have greater control in the data collection process.

A qualitative researcher does not predetermine measures or theories within which the data must fit. Instead, the researcher plays the role of a learner in that the researcher aims to learn about the participant who is an expert in his or her own life and experiences. From this view, then, the participant is allowed greater control during the research study, such as being allowed to ask questions himself or herself in an interview, because the participant's expert descriptions are valued as part of the data collection process.

Figure 11.1 The Extent to Which Researchers Control Data Collection in Qualitative and Quantitative Research From a Phenomenological Perspective

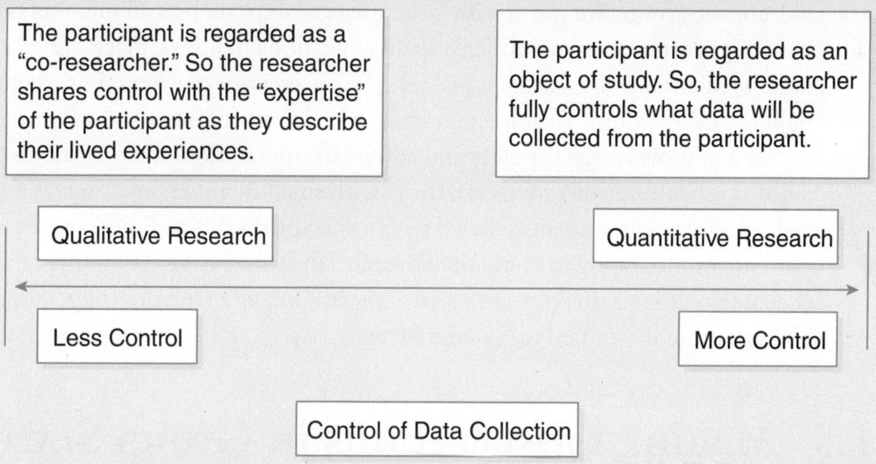

The participant is regarded as a "co-researcher." So the researcher shares control with the "expertise" of the participant as they describe their lived experiences.

The participant is regarded as an object of study. So, the researcher fully controls what data will be collected from the participant.

Qualitative Research

Quantitative Research

Less Control

More Control

Control of Data Collection

1. What is the primary purpose of the phenomenology design?

2. What are the seven contextual considerations in which participants can self-describe their experiences?

Answers: 1. To capture the conscious, lived experiences of the participants; 2. Historical, political/governmental, societal/cultural/religious, geographical, temporal, gender, familiarity.

11.4 An Overview of Ethnography Designs

A qualitative research design used to describe and characterize the behavior and identity of a group or culture is called **ethnography.** The perspective for this research is that groups of people will eventually evolve a culture over time, meaning that they will form an identity that will guide some worldview or way of life for the members of that culture. Ethnography is used to understand the intricacies of culture as it is defined and described by members of that culture. A culture is a "shared way of life" that includes patterns of interaction (e.g., cultural norms), shared beliefs and understandings (e.g., beliefs about the goal of education), adaptations to the environment (e.g., teacher classroom assignments, implementing new teaching standards), and many more factors that can lead to a group or cultural identity. Ethnography is used to describe the culture (e.g., the shared beliefs, values, and worldview), and members of that group or culture are regarded as experts in their lives, and researchers conduct the study, in part, to learn from and about them.

> **Ethnography** is the qualitative analysis of the behavior and identity of a group or culture as it is described and characterized by the members of that group or culture.

Ethnography is used to study macro-level and micro-level groups and cultures. Macro-level cultures or groups are those with large membership, such as all members of a country, government, or continent. In an educational context, macro-level groups could be members of a state school system or preservice teachers. For example, we could use ethnography to study culture and beliefs of teachers and administrators in Title I schools versus teachers and administrators in non–Title I schools. Micro-level cultures or groups are those with small membership, such as a first-grade classroom or students labeled with a specific disability. For example, we could use ethnography to study the dynamics in an inclusive classroom versus a self-contained special education classroom. In sum, any type of group, culture, or subculture can be studied using ethnography.

> Ethnography is used to describe the identity of groups or cultures as defined by their members.

11.5 Making Observations in Group Settings

To observe a group or culture, it is often necessary to get close up to or participate in that group or culture. To do this, ethnographic researchers often use the participant as observer or observer as participant role discussed in Chapter 10, which means that the researcher becomes a participant in or member of the group or culture for the length of the study. Researchers use the participant as observer role to study a group or culture similar to the way that an investigative reporter joins a group or culture to investigate its members' actions. When researchers use participant observation to make observations, they need to remain neutral in how they interact with members of the group. If they show a bias, then any observations may be specific to the bias and may not be characteristic of the group or culture as a whole. Three types of bias in how researchers can interact with members of a group or culture are described in Table 11.2.

An added challenge of using participant observation to study a group or culture is that many of the members can be aware of the researcher's presence, which can then lead to participant *reactivity* (see Chapter 10). Researchers typically use one of two strategies to gain entry into a group or culture without causing participants to react or change their behavior in reaction to the researchers' presence:

- Researchers can covertly or secretly enter a group. This strategy can work for larger groups; however, the physical presence of a "new" member, covert or not, in a small group can result in participant reactions that are not always obvious or predictable (often categorized as the participant role).

- Researchers can announce or request entry into a group. This strategy is used when it is not possible to enter a group covertly. By being upfront and honest with members of a group, the researcher can try to get the group to habituate to his or

> The participant as observer role is a method of observation in which researchers participate in or join the group or culture that they are observing.

Table 11.2   Three Common Pitfalls Associated With the Participant as Observer Role

Type of Bias	Description
The "eager speaker" bias	The researcher tends to focus on or speak mostly with those who are eager to speak to them while largely ignoring those who do not. This is poor practice inasmuch as those who do not speak with the researcher do make important contributions to the overall identity of a given group or culture.
The "good citizen" bias	The researcher assumes that he or she knows how members should contribute to the group or culture. As a result, members who actively participate with the researcher tend to be held in higher regard, or as "good citizens," than those who do not. This is poor practice inasmuch as the researcher shows bias against members who do not actively participate.
The "stereotype" bias	The tendency is for a researcher to positively or negatively regard a group or culture in a way that influences how the researcher treats members of the group. Researchers can be overly positive toward members if they hold the group in high regard (e.g., teachers) or overly negative to members if they hold the group in low regard (e.g., students who have been expelled or suspended).

Source: Adapted in part from suggestions made by Parker (2005).

her presence or accept him or her as a member of the group (often categorized as the participant as observer role).

11.6 An Example of Ethnography Research

To illustrate the ethnographic design, let's consider the following published study by Singh, Sylvia, and Ridzi (2015). Singh et al. were interested in studying how Burmese refugee families in New York interacted with books and a book distribution program. This specific program was typical of the eight programs in New York (typical case sampling). They employed an ethnographic design because the participants were refugees from Burma, and differences in culture and religion were important elements to consider. They observed 32 literacy sessions (prolonged engagement) with an observer role taking field notes, reviewed instructional plans (document review), and conducted individual interviews with the program participants and instructors (triangulation). Data collection and analysis were conducted in a recursive process using the analysis to guide further data collection. In the first stage of analysis, codes were assigned to field notes, interview transcripts, and documents. The codes were then reviewed to develop themes (thematic analysis). They employed peer debriefing by having each researcher code independently them comparing the assigned codes. The analysis identified four themes: (a) the contrast of literacy practices in the United States and Burma, (b) the use of modeling as a means of communication (since not all of the participants were proficient English speakers), (c) using parents to support teachers, and (d) changes in parent literacy activities at home. Here is an example of how Singh et al. reported their findings when describing the theme of the different literacy practices in the United States and Burma:

> In ethnography, researchers use participant as observer or observer as participant roles to observe groups and cultures, and they use field notes and interviews to record observations.

The focus on the oral tradition was not exclusively due to culture; it also reflected their lives in the camps, and the subsequent lack of available educational resources for the families to use at home for themselves and their children. While the families explicitly pointed out to the lack of resources available to them in the refugee camps, they were able to articulate similarities in the concepts taught by the program. The following is an excerpt from an interview with Enu that exemplifies this notion:

> They are teaching the same in Thailand. Like read a book, sing a song, play . . . to the kids right. There is one difference—we don't have much instrument or material in Thailand. Because in Thailand, we need money to buy, but sometime there is money but no material to buy. We sing a song, we play, and we have a snack. One difference, in Thailand, they teach in Karen, but here, they learn English. (p. 41)

In this paragraph, Singh et al. employed an etic perspective using a researcher perspective to describe the participant experience. Paragraphs that describe the themes are followed with a quote from the participant as an example of this description (etic).

11.7 An Overview of Netnography and Autoethnography Research

Netnography (Kozinets, 2010) is a branch of ethnography that uses social media, taking "net" from the word *Internet* and "graphy" from *ethnography*. This branch of ethnography examines the culture of the online world by examining computer-mediated social interaction. The field site is a group of individuals with a common interest engaged in a virtual community such as discussion boards, gaming sites, and blogs. A key to netnography is the context in which the study takes place. In this case, the selection of the appropriate online community is very important. The researcher needs to be familiar with the various online communities in the area being investigated. Netnography research may also be conducted along the observer-participant continuum. Recall that we looked at a study by Hayes-Moore (2015) in Chapter 10, who conducted a study as a participant as observer on literacy in a role-playing game. In this study, Hayes-Moore was a participant in the observer-participant continuum as she pretended to be a player of the role-playing game. A strict observer could simply copy the discussions of others and not participate in the group being observed. Lynch (2015) used netnography by collecting data from teacher message boards regarding gender-based play to understand teacher perspectives on gender and play. She copied discussions by searching for key words like *play based* and *centers*. Recall that this type of data collection is also called data mining. **Data mining** is when social media posts are perused for key words or phrases particular for the field under study and copied into files for later use. A key advantage to netnography is that it uses naturally occurring text; is less obtrusive than ethnography or ways to collect data such as interviews, focus groups, or surveys; and is an efficient and cost-effective way to collect data. Netnography is an unobtrusive way to collect conversational

> **Netnography** is a branch of ethnography that uses social media to examine the culture of the online world by examining computer-mediated social interaction.
>
> **Data mining** is when social media posts are perused for keywords or phrases particular for the field under study and copied into files for later use.

> Data mining is a form of data collection where social media posts are perused for key words and phrases and copied into files for later use.

CONNECTING TO THE CLASSROOM

Interested in conducting a netnographic study of your own? Here are some places to look for education-related data.

You can use education-related blogs as a source of data. Here is a link to TEACH100, a maintained list of the top 100 blog sites for education: https://teach.com/teach100.

Google Groups has groups for educators called GEGs (Google Educator Groups) that you can join. Google does not run the groups; it only provides the Internet space. The groups are organized by a volunteer leader. Here is a link to the GEG main page: https://www.google.com/landing/geg/. You can join an existing group or volunteer to organize a new one.

Yahoo! also sponsors groups for educators. You can see the list of groups

(Continued)

(Continued)

here: https://groups.yahoo.com/neo/dir/1600077623.

Using social media for a study of child experiences requires keeping up with the kids! Where do kids go on the Internet? Gaggle, a company that creates online digital learning products for schools, keeps an updated list of the social networks that kids use. Here is a link to the list: https://www.gaggle.net/top-social-networking-sites-and-apps-kids-use/.

If considering using social media, keep in mind that much of the communication will also include images such as logos, pictures, videos, and emojis. Plan ahead how you will code that kind of data.

Remember that research ethics described throughout this text applies to data gathered from the Internet, too. Although communication on the Internet in general is not considered private, unless stated on the site, you should consider the use of informed consent, maintain confidentiality by using pseudonyms, and submit an application for approval by an appropriate institutional review board (IRB).

Autoethnography is a branch of ethnography where the researcher studies the culture of oneself and how the self is a part of the culture.

data because there is no "seen" observer; as such, reactivity is not an issue.

Autoethnography is an emerging branch of ethnography where instead of studying the culture of others, the researcher studies the culture of oneself and how the self is a part of the culture. The researchers use their own experiences to understand the culture in which they are a part. This approach requires introspection, acute self-awareness, and the ability to self-question. An autoethnographer will provide deep, rich descriptions of personal experiences that tell a story and how culture and the cultural experience shaped the story. Autoethnography may use interviews with others, field notes, document reviews, or other media sources of information as a form of triangulation. The distinction between a biography and an authoethnography is the inclusion of qualitative methods. They will identify codes, themes, and patterns that are shared as they tell the story. This sounds easy, but the ability to self-examine and question how culture affects the self is actually very difficult. Many autoethnographers describe how a single study may take years to develop. Autoethnography is quite controversial because of its subjectivity, but those engaged in autoethnography assert that it combines both the art of storytelling and science.

Hains-Wesson and Young (2017) conducted an autoethnographic study of the development of reflective practice in STEM (science, technology, engineering, and math) teachers. The researchers and nine STEM teachers generated or conducted (a) self-reflections, (b) collaborative reflections, (c) a review of current literature on the development of self-reflection, and (d) a focus group interview with nine STEM teachers. Self-reflections were the "personal perceptions of experience, knowledge, and observations" of reflective practice. Collaborative reflections focused on the perceptions of collaborative episodes such as friendly discussions, meetings, and e-mails. These reflections were systematically recorded as journal entries. The journal entries were supplemented with the review of literature and the focus group. They first conducted a thematic analysis of the journal entries and focus group and then added a second analysis of the literature review. They derived three essential themes: (a) distinguishing between generic and STEM-specific reflective practice, (b) using the scientific method to guide reflective practice, and (c) identifying examples and exemplars of reflective STEM practice.

1. What is the primary purpose of the ethnography design?

2. Which form of bias is present in the following scenarios?

   A. A researcher is conducting a study in an English as a second language (ESL) classroom. He speaks in a normal tone and pace with most of the students but speaks louder, slower, and simpler to a student in a wheelchair.

   B. A researcher is conducting a study in an English as a second language (ESL) classroom. She interacts with a small group of students who appear enthusiastic to talk to her while other more shy students are overlooked.

3. Identify two branches of ethnography and describe how they study culture.

Answers: 1. To understand cultural behavior and identity; 2. A. stereotype bias, B. eager speaker bias; 3. Netnography studies the culture of online communities and autoethnography studies the culture of the self rather than the culture of others.

11.8 An Overview of Grounded Theory Designs

Grounded theory is an empirical, inductive approach for developing a theory from data that are systematically gathered and analyzed (Strauss & Corbin, 1994). Although it is commonly thought of and employed as a qualitative method, it could be also used with quantitative data. The distinction is the incorporation of inductive logic rather than strict use of deductive logic. It is an alternative to the quantitative view to formulate a theory and then collect data to confirm the theory (deductive logic) by instead collecting the data first and formulating a theory from the data (inductive logic). Once a theoretical position is identified through inductive logic, use of the grounded theory takes an additional step to use deductive logic to gather additional information by asking more focused questions about the theory. This last step requires theoretical sensitivity. Coined by Glaser (1978), **theoretical sensitivity** is the use of personal experience and professional immersion into the field of study to be able to give meaning to the data collected. The emphasis is on the systematic process in which data are collected and analyzed using the iterative process outlined in Chapter 10. The data are collected and in the same fashion as described in Chapters 5 (interviews, observations, and documents/artifacts) and 10, but with the idea to generate a theory and use of theoretical sampling.

Within the iterative process of data collection and analysis, the researcher interviews or observes a small sample of participants and then decides with whom he or she needs to speak/observe next to obtain additional information. This is called **theoretical sampling.** The process of continually gathering, analyzing data, and determining what

> **Grounded theory** is an empirical, inductive approach for developing a theory from data that are systematically gathered and analyzed.
>
> **Theoretical sensitivity** is the use of personal experience and professional immersion into the field of study to be able to give meaning to the data collected.
>
> **Theoretical sampling** is selecting participants based on whether they possess the information needed to develop the theory.

Constant comparative method is a process of continually gathering data, analyzing data, and determining what additional data are needed.

Data saturation occurs when the information gathered is redundant and no new information is obtained.

Selective coding involves organizing the categories or themes that articulate a theory.

additional data are needed is called the **constant comparative method.** This process continues until the data are saturated. **Data saturation** occurs when the information gathered is redundant and no new information is obtained. The general process of analyzing the data described in Chapter 10 of coding and categorizing the codes applies here, too. The difference lies in the final step of the data analysis that organizes the categories or themes to articulate a theory. This last step is called **selective coding.**

11.9 An Example of Grounded Theory Designs

To illustrate the grounded theory design, let's consider the following published study by Ruppar, Gaffney, and Dymond (2015). Ruppar et al. were interested in examining teachers' decision making about literacy instruction for students with severe disability. They selected four special education teachers who had previously responded to a survey about literacy instruction who taught at different grade levels and different program arrangements (i.e., self-contained classrooms or self-contained school) with unique approaches to literacy instruction (maximum variation). They employed a grounded theory design because of the complex social nature of the literacy phenomenon. They conducted interviews with follow-up questionnaires and emails, conducted 8 hours of observations that were videotaped and photographed, and reviewed Individualized Education Plans (triangulation) over 6 months (prolonged engagement). Data were gathered in a specific sequence where information from the previous step was analyzed and used to guide the information gathered at the next step (iterative process). Data collection and analysis were conducted in a recursive process using the analysis to guide further data collection. Teachers confirmed that the observations and interviews were representative of their literacy instruction (member checking). In the first stage of analysis, the researchers used NVivo QSR software to assign codes for each teacher individually in an open coding process. The codes were then reviewed across teachers to combine or reassign codes to develop categories in an axial coding process. To draft their theory regarding literacy decision making, the researchers narrowed their focus to four categories and searched for confirming and disconfirming evidence in the materials (negative case analysis). A second author reviewed the draft theory and suggested alternative explanations (peer debriefing). The analysis identified four themes regarding teachers' decision making about literacy: (a) context; (b) beliefs about students, teaching, and learning; (c) expectations; and (d) self-efficacy. They provide a graphic depiction of the relationship of the four themes and the elements coded within each theme (see Figure 11.2). Each element of the theory is thoroughly described with supporting evidence from the data collected, including descriptions of observations and quotes from the interviews.

Figure 11.2 Preliminary Theoretical Framework of Teacher Decision Making About Literacy for Students With Severe Disabilities (Ruppar, Gaffney, & Dymond 2015)

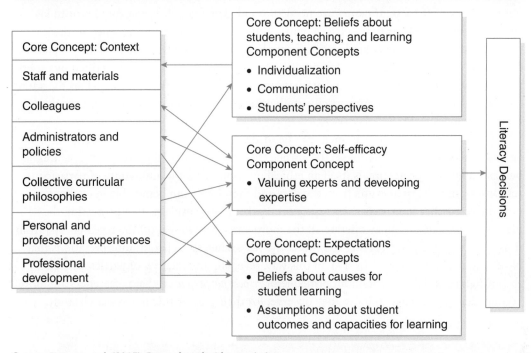

Source: Ruppar et al. (2015). Reproduced with permission.

11.10 Ethics in Focus: Anonymity in Qualitative Research

A unique characteristic of qualitative research is that the identity of participants is not entirely concealed because the researcher is engaged in some form of interaction such as interviews and observations. Instead, the real name or pseudo name (pseudonym) for a participant is often published and directly linked to the data collected. Of the qualitative studies described in this chapter, for example, Ruppar et al. (2015) and Singh et al. (2015) used pseudonyms for the names of the participants and the settings where the study took place. Hayes-Moore (2015) did not need pseudonyms since the names used in the role-play were already pseudonyms created for characters in the role-play game. Lynch (2015) copied Internet-based discussion board posts without names and did not mention any names in her results. Blieler (2015) did use the names of the two faculty members involved in the collaboration (Angela and Dejan) and did not mention if they are pseudonyms or not. The setting is described as a large public university located in the southeast United States, so even if Angela and Dejan are the real names, we would be hard-pressed to really know who they are.

Sometimes researchers ask the participants what pseudonym they would like to use. In contrast to qualitative research, participant identities are concealed and rarely, if ever, linked to the data measured in quantitative research. Instead, participants are assigned a unique number to identify them. If names are needed to link data from different sources or to keep track of participants over time, a list of names and the unique numbers assigned to them is created and stored in a separate location from the data collected from them. The reason for concealing participant identities is to protect the participants from being identified by others, particularly when the data measured are potentially harmful to participants, such as the study of LGTBQ youth. Concealing participant identities therefore shows high regard for the Belmont principle of *respect for persons*.

However, the same argument can be made that revealing participant identities is an ethical position. McLaughlin (2003) argued that the view that all participants are "fragile beings" in need of protection is itself an ethical position. Also, the anonymity of participant responses conceals participants from the data and therefore from being able to challenge how the researcher interprets their responses. Parker (2005) explains that protecting the identity of participants "may operate all the more efficiently to seal off the researcher[s] from those they study, actually serving to protect the researcher[s] . . . [from] interpretations that have been made in a report" (p. 17). In this way, revealing the identity of participants also shows high regard for the Belmont principle of *respect for persons* in that researchers are more accountable, particularly to those they observe, for their part or role in a research study.

LEARNING CHECK 3 ✓

1. What is the purpose of the grounded theory design?

2. How do qualitative researchers protect participant identity?

3. Which qualitative research design is used to study the conscious experiences of phenomena from the first-person point of view?

4. State the type of qualitative research design described in each of the following examples.

   A. A researcher joins a parent-teacher association for 6 months to study how these groups operate.

   B. A researcher conducts an in-depth interview of a principal and asks him to reflect on his experiences in providing professional development. She reports his first-person accounts in a narrative.

   C. A researcher data mines for information on drug abuse from Twitter posts.

   D. A researcher conducts interviews and observations in a self-contained classroom for students with emotional and behavioral disorders to formulate a theory regarding the stigma associated with being labeled with this disorder.

Answers: 1. To formulate a theory from the data; 2. Use pseudonyms or do not mention names at all; 3. Phenomenology; 4. A. ethnography, B. phenomenology, C. netnography, D. grounded theory.

LO 1 Identify and describe three qualitative research designs: phenomenology, ethnography, and grounded theory.

- **Phenomenology** is the qualitative analysis of the conscious experiences of phenomena from the first-person point of view.

- **Ethnography** is the qualitative analysis of the behavior and identity of a group or culture as it is described and characterized by the members of that group or culture.

- **Grounded theory** is the qualitative analysis of data to formulate a theory from the data.

LO 2 Describe netnography and autoethnography.

- **Netnography** is a branch of ethnography. It uses Internet-based narrative data instead of directly interviewing or observing participants to understand the culture of online communities.

- **Autoethnography** is a second branch of ethnography where a researcher examines the culture of himself or herself and how culture shaped the self.

LO 3 Distinguish between the different contexts in which participants self-describe.

- Historical self-description includes relevant political, societal, geographic, temporal, and personal histories.

- Political/governmental self-description includes current political and legal issues that affect an individual.

- Societal/cultural/religious self-description includes social, cultural, or religious idiosyncrasies.

- Geographic self-description includes different social settings or localities.

- Temporal self-description includes how individuals adapt or change over time.

- Gender self-description includes how gender influences thinking and interactions.

- Familiarity self-description includes how we describe experiences when we reflect on them.

LO 4 Distinguish between the three forms of bias that may occur when using the participant as observer role.

- "Eager speaker" bias is when the researchers tend to focus on or speak mostly with those who are eager to speak to them, while largely ignoring those who do not.

- "Good citizen" bias is when the researcher assumes that he or she knows how members should contribute to the group or culture. As a result, members who actively participate with the researcher tend to be held in higher regard, or as "good citizens," than those who do not.

- "Stereotype" is when the researcher regards some members of the groups more positively or negatively and that influences how the researcher treats different members of the group.

LO 5 Describe grounded theory.

- Grounded theory is an empirical, inductive approach for developing a theory from data that are systematically gathered and analyzed using inductive reasoning and theoretical sampling.

KEY TERMS

autoethnography 304

conscious experiences 296

constant comparative method 306

data mining 303

data saturation 306

ethnography 300

grounded theory 305

netnography 303

objects of awareness 296

phenomenology 296

reactivity 301

selective coding 306

theoretical sampling 305

theoretical sensitivity 305

REVIEW QUESTIONS

1. A researcher states that he views each participant as a coresearcher and not as an object of study. Which perspective, qualitative or quantitative, does this statement describe? Explain.

2. State the type of qualitative research design that is most closely associated with the following terms:

    A. Conscious experience

    B. Cultural identity

    C. First-person narrative

    D. Data mining

    E. Theoretical sampling

    F. Constant comparative method

3. A young researcher joins a parent-teacher association posing as a parent and becomes immersed into the association activities to study members of the association.

    A. What method of observation did the researcher use?

    B. What type of qualitative research design often requires the use of this method of observation?

4. A researcher is interested in studying the experiences of a first-year teacher in a Title I school using a phenomenology perspective.

   A. What is the phenomenon being studied?

   B. What type of data will the researcher collect?

5. In the study above about first-year teachers, they make the following statements. What context of self-description is best applied to these statements?

   A. I think the high school boys test me more than they seem to test the male teachers.

   B. This used to be an area of our city with high poverty, but because it is close to the downtown area, there are some younger people who work in the corporate offices downtown who want to live closer to work so the student body is changing.

   C. We recently lost all of our teacher assistants due to a state budget cut.

6. A researcher is interested in examining the culture of a student-led Internet support group.

   A. What type of qualitative design would be most appropriate?

   B. What type of data can the researcher collect?

7. What makes autoethnographic qualitative research difficult?

8. A researcher is interested in generating some ideas about how high school students form social cliques to exclude others.

   A. What type of qualitative design would be most appropriate?

   B. What type of data can the researcher collect?

9. What makes grounded theory different from the other qualitative designs?

10. Why do qualitative researchers need theoretical sensitivity?

ACTIVITIES

1. For any of the three following topics, identify a qualitative design that could be used to study the topic. Describe why you selected this design.

   A. Classroom teaching style

   B. Student learning style preference

   C. Gender differences in learning algebra

   D. Teacher perceptions of the Common Core Standards

   E. Inquiry-based teaching

   F. Teacher reflection on preservice preparation

   G. Parent-teacher relationships

   H. Effect of media on student engagement

2. Choose one of the topics above and design an ethnographic study.

   A. Write the research question.

   B. Determine how you will select your participants.

   C. Determine what type of data you will collect.

   D. Describe how you will analyze the data.

3. Choose one of the topics above and design a phenomenology study.

   A. Write the research question.

   B. Determine how you will select your participants.

   C. Determine what type of data you will collect.

   D. Describe how you will analyze the data.

4. Choose one of the topics above and design a netnographic study.

   A. Write the research question.

   B. Determine how you will select your participants.

   C. Determine what type of data you will collect.

   D. Describe how you will analyze the data.

5. Choose one of the topics above and design a grounded theory study.

   A. Write the research question.

   B. Determine how you will select your participants.

   C. Determine what type of data you will collect.

   D. Describe how you will analyze the data.

$SAGE edge™

SAGE edge offers a robust online environment featuring an impressive array of free tools and resources for review, study, and further exploration, keeping both instructors and students on the cutting edge of teaching and learning.

Access practice quizzes, eFlashcards, video, and multimedia at edge.sagepub.com/priviterarme.

Identify a problem

- Determine an area of interest.
- Review the literature.
- Identify new ideas in your area of interest.
- Develop a research hypothesis.

Develop a research plan

- Define the variables being tested.
- Identify participants or subjects and determine how to sample them.
- Select a research strategy and design.
- Evaluate ethics and obtain institutional approval to conduct research.

Generate more new ideas

- Results support your hypothesis—refine or expand on your ideas.
- Results do not support your hypothesis—reformulate a new idea or start over.

Communicate the results

- Method of communication: oral, written, or in a poster.
- Style of communication: APA guidelines are provided to help prepare style and format.

Conduct the study

- Execute the research plan and measure or record the data.

Analyze and evaluate the data

- Analyze and evaluate the data as they relate to the research hypothesis.
- Summarize data and research results.

After reading this chapter, you should be able to:

1   Identify and describe three qualitative research designs: narrative inquiry, case study, and critical theory.

2   Identify and describe the three dimensions of narrative inquiry.

3   Define the eight considerations for narrative inquiry.

4   Distinguish between the three types of case studies.

5   Distinguish between case studies that are general inquiry and designed for theory development.

6   Describe the tenets of the three types of critical theories described in this chapter.

NARRATIVE INQUIRY, CASE STUDY, AND CRITICAL THEORY DESIGNS

Throughout this book, we have been using our food selection example to illustrate how this research question could be answered using different research designs. Recall our hypothesis from Chapter 8: Fruits will be eaten more if they are made more convenient. We can explore this idea using three different qualitative designs presented in this chapter. Let's say we were interested in capturing the essence of food selection through the process of in-depth human stories. We could collect rich and deep descriptions of food selection as described by the participants. This is called narrative inquiry. We could also delve into how individuals make food selections by examining one "case." We would use the "case" to illustrate how food selections are made. This is the case study qualitative design. If we were interested in how our social structures (such as culture, gender, and politics) shape our food selections, we can use the critical theory qualitative design. In each design, our exploration of the notion of food selection is sculpted by the philosophical underpinnings of the design. Each design looks at the research question from a different perspective.

In this chapter, we describe three more qualitative designs: narrative inquiry, case study, and critical theory. Narrative inquiry and critical theory are relative newcomers to the field of education. Recall that the selection of a qualitative design depends on the research question whereby a particular design is aligned to specific goals of the research and how the findings are interpreted. Narrative inquiry is designed to supply human stories that capture the essence of the human experience; case study uses a "case" to illustrate, explore, or compare ideas present in the cases; and critical theory is used to explore and challenge ideas and generate theories defined by social entities such as culture, race, class, politics, and gender.

edge.sagepub.com/
priviterarme

- Take the chapter quiz
- Review key terms with eFlashcards
- Explore multimedia links and SAGE articles

$SAGE edge™

NARRATIVE RESEARCH DESIGNS

12.1   An Overview of Narrative Research

Narrative inquiry evolved from a movement to better understand social and cultural differences in life experiences. It is the use of human stories to understand phenomena and experiences. It is based on the premise that we come to understand and give meaning to our lives through the use of stories. **Human stories** are in-depth descriptions of actual lived experiences. In gathering human stories, attention is placed not only on the facts in the story but also how the individual constructed the story and what purpose the story serves. The use of human stories is not exclusive to narrative inquiry; other qualitative designs such as ethnography and phenomenology also use the art of storytelling. The distinction of narrative inquiry is how the stories are constructed by the researcher. Clandinin, Pushor, and Orr (2007) describe narrative stories as having three dimensions that they call "commonplaces" that include temporality, sociality, and place. Looking at the human story narrative through these three commonplaces simultaneously is what distinguishes narrative inquiry from the other qualitative designs. Table 12.1 describes each of these dimensions. Our experiences are constructed within these three dimensions. **Temporality** is based on the belief that our experiences of places, things, and events in the story have a past, present, and future that are in a constant state of revision as the story is formed. Narrative inquiry attempts to capture how the story is formed and revised. **Sociality** is the social conditions under which the story is formed. Personal stories are shaped by the social conditions under which they are formed. The relationship between the researcher and participant is part of the social condition in which the story is formed. **Place** recognizes that human stories take place somewhere, in some concrete space. Narrative inquiry acknowledges that these stories are linked to the place where they are formed. The collection of human stories can provide a deep and rich description of a **phenomenon** or experience. Narrative inquiry studies these meaningful stories and retells them to help us understand the phenomenon or experience.

Narrative inquiry is the use of human stories to understand phenomena and experiences.

A **human story** is an in-depth description of actual lived experiences.

Temporality is dimension of narrative inquiry to understand that events have a past, present, and future.

Sociality is a dimension of narrative inquiry that includes the personal, social, and relationship with the researcher.

Place recognizes that human stories take place somewhere, in some concrete space.

Phenomenon is a situation or a person's perception of the experience; it refers to what the inquiry is about.

12.2   Considerations for Narrative Inquiry

The basic process of narrative inquiry is the same as with other forms of qualitative research as described in Chapter 10 with differences specific to this design. The participants are those who have stories to tell about the topic. The data are the stories collected as interviews

Table 12.1 Three Dimensions of Narrative Inquiry

Dimension	Description
Temporality	Events have a temporal transition in the past, present, and future. Narrative inquiry attempts to understand people in transition.
Sociality	Sociality includes three conditions: personal, social, and the relationship with the researcher. Personal conditions are the "feelings, hopes, desires, aesthetic reactions, and moral dispositions" of the participant and researcher (Connelly & Clandinin, 2006, p. 480). Social conditions are the environment and other people that form each individual's context.
Place	The physical boundaries where the inquiry and events take place.

Source: Adapted from Clandinin, Pushor, and Orr (2007).

or focus groups with supporting observations and documents that help tell the story. The interviews or focus groups can vary from semi-structured to unstructured conversations. The interviews or focus groups can use artifacts such as photographs or items that invoke memories to initiate the storytelling. Data are coded and categorized into themes to retell the life story. The major difference in this design comes from the perspective of retelling the life story attending to the three commonplaces (temporality, sociality, and place). Clandinin et al. (2007) describe eight elements to consider when designing and interpreting a narrative inquiry. Table 12.2 lists and defines these eight elements.

The first element to consider is justification. **Justification** is the reasons why the study is important along three dimensions: personal, practical, and social. Personal justification refers to the researcher's interest in the inquiry. Why is the researcher interested in this topic? What is the researcher's relationship to this topic? Practical justification examines how the inquiry will change practices or thinking of the researcher and others. Social justification is about the importance of topic. Is the topic or issue important? So what? Who cares? The second consideration is identification of the phenomenon. What is the phenomenon being investigated through the narrative point of view? The research method is the third consideration. The researcher needs to plan recruitment of participants and study procedures in such a way to be able to tell the story. The researcher needs to think about how the story might unfold. This includes making decisions about what type of data need to be collected. Data analysis and interpretation is the fourth consideration. Data analysis and interpretation incorporates the three commonplaces. It is centered on how to examine them within the study and how to describe the characteristics of three commonplace features. The fifth element, **positioning,** is the comparison of the narrative inquiry with other research conducted on the topic. This is similar to a literature review, comparing and contrasting (i.e., positioning) the results and interpretations to the findings of other studies. **Uniqueness,** the sixth element, refers to the ability of the narrative inquiry to provide additional information about the phenomenon that is not known or cannot be known

Justification is the reason why the study is important along three dimensions: personal, practical, and social (12).

Positioning is the comparison of the narrative inquiry with other research conducted on the topic (12).

Uniqueness is a consideration of narrative inquiry that refers to what new information is provided by the study (12).

by using other designs or methods. Narrative inquiry provides a unique lens through which we can study the issue; this element requires the researchers to identify what new information can be gained by conducting the study using this perspective. Ethical consideration is the seventh element. Ethical considerations for the participant permeate through the research process because of the personal relationship between the researcher and the participant. The researcher considers the participant and how the participant might react as he or she creates the narrative and shares it with others. The final written description is a negotiation between the researcher and participant. The final element is representation. Representation refers to the form of the story, how to structure the story and reflect the three commonplaces for the specific audience.

12.3   An Example of Narrative Research

In education, narrative inquiry can serve as a way that educators, students, and other stakeholders can share personal experiences or stories with each other so we can learn from them. Let's look at an example by Kennedy-Lewis, Murphy, and Grosland (2016). In this study, they seek to tell the stories of three persistently disciplined middle school students to better understand them and their experiences. They selected the three students based on their discipline history of office referrals and number of in-school and out-of-school suspensions (critical case sampling). They conducted interviews and collected drawings to supplement the verbal accounts. Each interview transcript was coded and then organized into themes for each individual separately to

Table 12.2   Eight Considerations for Narrative Inquiry

Element	Description
Justification	Justification refers to the reasons why the study is important. This includes the interest in the inquiry (personal), how the inquiry will change thinking or practices (practical), and what larger educational issue may be involved (social).
Phenomenon	Phenomenon refers to what the inquiry is about.
Research method	Research method refers to planning the inquiry within the changing life space in which it occurs and deciding what types of data need to be collected and composed.
Analysis and interpretation	Analysis and interpretation refers to thinking about the data within the three dimensions of temporality, sociality, and place.
Positioning	Positioning refers to how this study relates to other studies.
Uniqueness	Uniqueness refers to what new information is provided by this study.
Ethical	Ethical refers to the additional considerations of the relationship between the researcher and participant that is formed by sharing personal stories and how these stories are shared with others.
Representation	Representation refers to how the narrative is presented as a story.

Source: Adapted from Clandinin, Pushor, and Orr (2007).

tell separate stories with selected student quotes to illustrate the theme. They then shaped the themes in a story for each participant. Below in an excerpt of the story of Haley:

"It's like I have to force myself to get up when I got to go to school."

Haley, an introverted 14-year-old eighth grade student of mixed racial descent, speaks softly and reluctantly about her experiences. During our interviews, we read a combination of sadness and disgust in her countenance when she described how she feels about school, which her words affirmed. This general malaise remained throughout our interviews as she described having a lack of rapport with educators at her school. Despite Haley's depressed and lethargic demeanor, she expresses much anger at the school system for being unresponsive to her needs. She states that teachers do not really care, as evidenced by their ignoring her or helping other students when she has asked them something. She believes that the reason some teachers don't care is "because they're just getting their paycheck at the end of the day." Regarding the apathy she perceives from educators at school whenever she makes a request, Haley states:

"It's like if I would have told somebody, I feel nothing would have got done because that's just how this school system is . . . you tell somebody and they'll say they'll do something about it, it never gets resolved and then when a fight happens that you told, that you're trying to prevent and you just can't take it no more, you get in trouble and you're wondering, I told you all. I told you about this but you guys never did nothing about it. . . . I just really can't wait to get out of this school." (p. 11)

Notice how the results are presented as a life story with a description from the researcher point of view (etic) and a supporting quote from the student.

CASE STUDY DESIGNS

12.4 An Overview of Case Study Designs

Another qualitative research design, the **case study,** can be used to examine in depth one entity such as one individual (e.g., a teacher or student), group (e.g., preservice teachers or students with a learning disability), organization (school or school district), or event (e.g., implementation of new curriculum or Special Olympics competition). The name *case study* is used because the focus of study (e.g., the individual, group, organization, or event) is called a "case."

A case is any identified, bounded unit. It could an individual such as one teacher, a specific group of individuals such as all the teachers at one school, an organization such as all employees of a school system, or community such as by including all stakeholders of a school system (parents, interested citizens, school board members, etc.). Figure 12.1 illustrates how a case may be bounded. A case study may include more than one case if the researcher is interested in comparing different cases. Other examples of how a case may be defined include an event (all attendees at an event such as at a parent-teacher night at school) or role (superintendents across school systems). Once the case is defined, the researcher will collect information from only those that are defined as being a case.

12.5 Types of Case Study Designs

The following are three types of case studies; each type is further described in Table 12.3:

An **illustrative case study** (or intrinsic case study) investigates rare or unknown cases, such as the academic effects of concussions by looking at individuals who happened to suffer from a concussion. Hence, we use this case study to understand a particular case or person (e.g., a person who suffered a concussion). A case can be selected because it is particularly interesting or because it is typical. An example of an illustrative case study is a study by Achinstein, Curry, and Ogawa (2015). Their "critical case study" examined an urban high school as it attempted to challenge traditional low expectations for Latina/o students by "relabeling" them to see themselves as college-bound students. They described this case as "one that holds strategic importance" because of its extensive efforts to challenge the traditional low expectations for this population.

> A **case study** is the qualitative analysis of an individual, group, organization, or event used to illustrate a phenomenon, explore new hypotheses, or compare the observations of many cases.
>
> Three types of case studies are the **illustrative case study** (used to investigate rare or unknown phenomena), the **exploratory case study** (used to explore or generate hypotheses for later investigation), and the **collective case study** (used to compare observations of many cases).

An **exploratory case study** (or instrumental case study) is a preliminary analysis that explores potentially important hypotheses, such as possible concerns regarding the methods used to study adult education programs in a local community. Hence, we use a case or person to better understand a more general phenomenon (e.g., methods to study adult education) rather than to understand the complexities of the specific case. A study by Liou, Martinez, and Rotheram-Fuller (2015) can be classified as an exploratory case study as it explored a mentoring framework between teachers and students to improve school experiences for students of color.

A **collective case study** compares the individual analysis of related cases, such as comparing behavioral symptoms expressed by three children with autism in a classroom. A collective case study approach was used by Rutledge, Cohen-Vogel, Osborne-Lampkin, and Roberts (2015) compared two low-performing and two high-performing high schools in the manner in which they attended to both the academic and social learning needs of students.

Table 12.3 Three Types of Case Studies in Behavioral Research

Type of Case Study	Description
Illustrative (or intrinsic case study)	Pertains to rather unique cases where little is known about an individual, a group, or an organization. This can provide new insights and a better understanding of rare or largely unknown phenomena and often leads to the introduction of a common language for describing the phenomena being studied.
Exploratory (or instrumental case study)	Explores potentially important hypotheses that may include a preliminary or pilot study conducted prior to the conduct of a large-scale research study. This type of study explores or provides important information pertaining to the selection of research questions, measurements, and potential limitations that may arise when the large-scale study is conducted.
Collective	Compares the individual analysis of related cases. For example, researchers may conduct a case study on behavior problems associated with three children with autism in the classroom. The collective description for each case (or child) can provide insights into the extent to which observations will generalize to other cases but not to the general population.

In each example, the level of analysis is to make observations with one individual or group at a time. For each type of case study, researchers can use field notes, interviewing, naturalistic and participant observation, and the retrieval of records or documents related to the case. Most case studies use a combination of these methods to understand the complexities of the case, be able to provide a rich description of the case, and increase the trustworthiness of the research.

> A case study is an in-depth qualitative analysis of a single individual, group, or organization.

As part of an analysis, a case study typically includes a **case history** of the individuals, groups, or organizations being observed. Case histories provide a historical background of the individual, group, or organization observed. This can include demographic characteristics; family, school, or medical history; and what makes the case interesting to the researcher. A case history can often be the only information provided in a case study. In other case studies, the researcher may include a manipulation, such as administering a learning assessment to a child with a learning disorder or a treatment and describing the outcome. Combining a case history and a treatment to describe the outcome of the treatment is a common case study technique in the medical community.

> A **case history** is an in-depth description of the history and background of the individual, group, or organization observed. A case history can be the only information provided in a case study for situations in which the researcher does not include a manipulation, a treatment, or an intervention.
>
> **General inquiry** is an application of a case study where the purpose is to learn about certain cases of interest used to advance general knowledge (12).

In all, case studies have the following two common applications in education:

> The case study can be used to make qualitative and quantitative analyses.

1. **General inquiry.** In this sense, researchers tend to ask a lot of questions instead of stating hypotheses. The purpose or intent of the case study, then, is to learn about certain cases of interest. For example, the study by Rutledge et al. (2015) mentioned above can also be classified as a general inquiry type of case study. Their research was not theory driven in that

Theory development is an application of case study where the researchers state hypotheses to develop new theories or to test existing theories (12).

they did not set up the study to test an idea they had. Rather, the researchers made observations and conducted interviews and collected school documents to record and learn about practices in high-performing high schools that were not present in low-performing high schools. Case studies are often used to advance knowledge regarding naturally occurring social groups, such as schools, and rare or unknown cases, such as individuals with a disability or mental disease.

2. **Theory development.** In this sense, researchers state hypotheses to develop new theories or to test existing theories. For example, Liou et al. (2015) observed and interviewed high school students to test a theory of critical mentorship between students and teachers to improve student outcomes. Case studies are particularly effective for testing the effectiveness of a new treatment or therapy because it is often more ethical to conduct these tests on a case-by-case basis.

12.6 Combining Case Study Design With Quantitative Data

A case study, while considered a qualitative design, can also incorporate quantitative data. This means that a case study, in addition to providing a narrative description of the case, can also include quantitative data analysis. An example of this is a study by Asef-Vaziri (2015). Asef-Vaziri conducted a comparative case study of flipped classroom versus a traditional classroom. A flipped classroom refers to a process whereby students access prepared content outside of the classroom using a Leaning Management System and participating in activities and discussions in class with the teacher thereby flipping the traditional model. In the traditional classroom model, the teachers deliver content in the classroom and students do activities or homework outside of the classroom. The researchers narratively described the case through the use of classroom observations and also reported test scores, final grades, and class attendance.

MAKING SENSE—INTERPRETATION OF CASE STUDY RESEARCH

You likely have heard about the recent controversy regarding the connection between the childhood MMR (measles, mumps, rubella) vaccine and subsequent diagnosis of autism. The study that sparked this controversy was conducted by Wakefield et al. (1998). It used a case study design to temporally describe the medical history (including vaccinations) and behavioral history of a child who was subsequently diagnosed with autism. Although the article clearly stated that a case study historical account could not be interpreted as a cause-and-effect relationship between the MMR vaccination history and onset of autism, the authors continued to publicly interpret this study in just that way. Case study research, as a type of qualitative research, seeks to describe and interpret experiences and processes. The authors correctly stated that they could not make cause-and-effect interpretations.

Over the years, Wakefield continued to publicly make this claim of cause and effect between the MMR vaccination and diagnosis of autism. Most of his coauthors of the study retracted his claims, and the study was officially retracted from the journal *The Lancet* in 2010. Subsequently, many quasi-experimental studies (Chapter 13) have been conducted and have found no relationship between the MMR vaccination (or other chemicals associated with vaccinations such as mercury and thimerosal) and diagnosis of autism. A list of these studies can be found on the Autism Science Foundation website (http://autismsciencefoundation.org/what-is-autism/autism-and-vaccines/). Despite the retractions and subsequent research using designs that specifically examine the relationship between variables, there continues to be some parents who now refuse to vaccinate their children. Places with lower vaccination rates have seen a resurgence of these childhood diseases.

This is a cautionary tale of how misinterpreting research findings can have drastic consequences.

LEARNING CHECK 2 ✓

1. What is the primary purpose of case study?

2. Which type of case study is represented in the following scenarios?

   A. A researcher is interested in developing a framework for how teachers form their professional identity and sense of self-efficacy.

   B. A researcher is interesting in comparing the parent-teacher associations of low- and high-performing high elementary schools.

   C. A researcher is interested in describing how teachers adapted to a newly adopted state curriculum.

Answers: 1. To analyze one case (individual, group, or organization); 2. A. exploratory, B. collective, C. illustrative.

CRITICAL THEORY DESIGNS

12.7 An Overview of Critical Theory Designs

Critical theory is a group of qualitative designs that operate under the assumption that "reality"

Critical theory is a group of qualitative designs that operate under the assumption that "reality" is shaped by our social, political, cultural, economic, ethnic, and gender-related experiences. It seeks to empower individuals to change the social structures.

is shaped by our social, political, cultural, economic, ethnic, and gender-related experiences (Denzin & Lincoln, 2011). Critical theory has three essential elements: (1) inquiry is situated in a social justice perspective, (2) interpretations are based on critiquing the social structures, and (3) the findings are used to motivate change. Critical theory research attempts to reconstruct individual (micro-level) and collective (macro-level) knowledge as it relates to personal experiences with the social structures of the society. It focuses these experiences as struggles with power, equity, and justice and seek to empower, resocialize, and liberate individuals and groups by focusing on these experiences. Once exposed, the goal is to change the social structures that contribute to these inequities. The critical theory method involves a dialogue between the researcher and participant(s) to uncover the knowledge shaped by these experiences as a social critique. As a method, critical theory studies seek participants who are "marginalized" by their social, political, cultural, economic, ethnic, or gender-related experiences with power. Information is gathered through observations and interviews with analysis to reflect and describe the experiences. Analysis and interpretation mostly use dialogical and discourse techniques that we will discuss in Chapter 20.

12.8   Types of Critical Theory Designs

Some of the critical theories included in this group of qualitative designs are queer theory, critical race theory, and feminism. Each type of critical theory concentrates on one or more aspects of the experiences with power. For example, feminism focuses on experiences of gender, and critical race theory focuses on experiences of ethnicity. These theories can be used as informative descriptions of experiences of teachers, administrators, and students as they interact with these sources of power in educational contexts. Table 12.4 briefly describes these critical theories and provides an example of how these theories can be used in education. Queer theory is based on the idea that identities are not fixed or binary (such as homosexual/heterosexual). Identities and experiences are constructed by many elements and not just gender or sexual orientations. It examines how social construction of knowledge, organization of society, and societal practices privilege some and discriminate against others. Although often used to study issues of homosexuality, queer theory refers to any behavior that is considered odd or out of the ordinary. Critical race theory (CRT) examines how society and culture intersect with race and power. CRT views race as a socially constructed idea, a hierarchical system that places Whites above other races. The differential values assigned to different races depend on the function White people want different races to take in society. CRT seeks to describe how race frames life experiences. Feminist theory is the study of how gender bias, oppression, and inequity shape the experiences of women. It is particularly concerned with how the differential power and status of women in society marginalize and disadvantage them and define how they are treated in social settings. While all of these theories deal with a different aspect of power (sexuality, race, and gender) in developing societal norms

Queer theory examines how social construction of knowledge, organization of society, and societal practices privilege some and discriminate against others based on sexual orientation or other odd behavior (12).

Critical race theory is a qualitative design that examines how society and culture intersect with race and power (12).

Feminist theory examines how differential power marginalizes and disadvantages women and defines how they are treated in social settings (12).

Table 12.4 Descriptions and Examples of Critical Theories

Critical Theory	Basic Tenets	Example
Queer theory	• Identities and experiences are constructed by many elements • Examines how some individuals are privileged and others are not • Refers to any behavior that is considered odd or out of the ordinary	Lapointe (2015) used queer theory to understand motivation for becoming a member of a gay-straight alliance among high school students.
Critical race theory	• Race is a socially constructed hierarchical system that places privileges on Whites • Seeks to describe how race frames life experiences	Aviles de Bradley (2015) used critical race theory to understand the role that race plays in the educational experiences of homeless youth.
Feminism theory	• Gender bias, oppression, and inequity shape the feminine identity • Examines how differential power marginalizes and disadvantages women and defines how they are treated in social settings	Beard (2012) used Black feminist theory to describe the values and decision making of an African American female school superintendent.

and expectations, they each examine how society defines who has power and privilege and marginalizes others. The purpose of the study is to elucidate how the differential power struggle shapes life experiences and emancipates the individuals in order to change society.

LEARNING CHECK 3 ✓

1. What is the primary purpose of critical theory research?

2. Which type of critical theory is represented in the following scenarios?

   A. A researcher is interested in developing a framework for how female teachers form their professional identity and sense of self-efficacy.

   B. A researcher is interested in understanding the experiences of minority students in predominately nonminority schools.

   C. A researcher conducts a study to describe the social experiences of LGBTQ students.

Answers: 1. To study how "marginalized" people are shaped by their social, political, cultural, economic, ethnic, or gender-related experiences with power; 2. A. feminism, B. critical race theory, C. queer theory.

CONNECTING TO THE CLASSROOM

In this era of accountability where teachers and schools are rated based on student academic performance, there is an emphasis on creating programs that address issues related to the needs

(Continued)

(Continued)

of students. Here are some of the topics we hear a lot about in education today:

- We have a disparity in academic achievement among students from low-income families. Students from lower-income families often have lower achievement levels.

- There is a documented underrepresentation of women in STEM (science, technology, engineering, and mathematics) fields.

- LGBTQ (lesbian, gay, bisexual, transgender, and questioning/queer) youth are victims of bullying and discrimination that place them in physical and psychological risk that limits their education.

Consider how the use of critical theory might be useful in identifying the social structures in education that create disparities in which some youth succeed and some don't. Critical race theory could examine how the educational system itself affects differential academic achievement among different races. Queer theory could examine how the educational system supports the culture of intolerance of behavior considered out of the ordinary that leads to bullying and discrimination. Feminist theory could examine why girls are not attracted to careers in STEM. With an emphasis on empowerment and change of the status quo, application of critical theory appears to be well suited for addressing some of the current issues in education today.

12.9 Ethics in Focus: Retelling Human Stories

One of the eight considerations for narrative research is ethics. The notion of ethics here is deeper than simply receiving institutional review board approval to conduct human subjects research. Recall that narrative research is the retelling of a human story. Think about what it would take for a researcher to get such a story. It takes a lot of time and a close relationship in order for the participant to be comfortable with telling the story and the researcher to get the story just right. There may be some differences between how the researcher and participant see the story, so there is an element of negotiation. The researcher and participant will often negotiate in how to tell the story and interpret the experiences. There needs to be a strong relationship and trust in how the researcher will share the story with others and subsequently how others will think about the story. There is also the consideration of what happens to this relationship when the research is complete. These issues are particularly important when retelling the story of children. In narrative research, because of the long-term, close relationship and connection needed to gather the human story, narrative research must also think about an "ethic of caring" to protect their participants from harm. Narrative researchers need to consider such protection from harm when planning, considering the vulnerability of the participants at each step of the process, including an exit strategy.

LO 1 Identify and describe three qualitative research designs: narrative inquiry, case study, and critical theory.

- **Narrative inquiry** is the use of human stories to understand phenomena and experiences.
- **Case study** is the qualitative analysis of an individual, a group, an organization, or an event used to illustrate a phenomenon, explore new hypotheses, or compare the observations of many cases.
- **Critical theory** is a group of qualitative designs that operate under the assumption that "reality" is shaped by our social, political, cultural, economic, ethnic, and gender-related experiences.

LO 2 Identify and describe the three dimensions of narrative inquiry.

- **Temporality**—events have a temporal transition in the past, present, and future. Narrative inquiry attempts to understand people in transition.
- **Sociality** includes three conditions; personal, social, and relationship with the researcher. Personal conditions are the "feelings, hopes, desires, aesthetic reactions, and moral dispositions" of the participant and researcher. Social conditions are the environment and other people who form each individual's context.
- **Place** includes the physical boundaries where the inquiry and events take place.

LO 3 Define the eight considerations for narrative inquiry.

- **Justification** refers to the reasons why the study is important. This includes the interest in the inquiry, how the inquiry will change thinking or practices, and what larger educational issue may be involved.
- **Phenomenon** refers to what the inquiry is about.
- **Research method** refers to planning the inquiry within the changing life space in which it occurs and deciding what types of data need to be collected and composed.
- **Analysis and interpretation** refer to thinking about the data within the three dimensions of temporality, sociality, and place.
- **Positioning** refers to how this study relates to other studies.
- **Uniqueness** refers to what new information is provided by this study.
- **Ethical** refers to the additional considerations of the relationship between the researcher and participant that is formed by sharing personal stories and how these stories are shared with others.
- **Representation** refers to how the narrative is presented as a story.

LO 4 Distinguish between the three types of case studies.

- Illustrative case study pertains to unique cases where little is known about an individual, a group, or an organization. This can provide new insights and a better understanding of the phenomenon.

- Exploratory case study explores potentially important hypotheses to better understand a more general phenomenon.

- Collective case study will review and compare several cases.

LO 5 Distinguish between case studies that are general inquiry and designed for theory development.

- In general inquiry, researchers tend to ask a lot of questions instead of stating hypotheses. The purpose or intent of the case study, then, is to learn about certain cases of interest.

- Theory development case studies state hypotheses to develop new theories or to test existing theories.

LO 6 Describe the tenets of the three types of critical theories described in this chapter.

- Queer theory is based on the idea that identity is constructed by many elements and not just gender or sexual orientations. It refers to any behavior that is considered odd or out of the ordinary.

- Critical race theory is based on the belief that race is a socially constructed, hierarchical system that places Whites above other races, and the different values placed on different races depend on the function White people want them to take in society. Critical race theory seeks to describe how race frames life experiences.

- Feminist theory is the study of how gender bias, oppression, and inequity shape the feminine identity. It is particularly concerned about how women are treated in social settings and how this treatment shapes our knowledge of the world.

KEY TERMS

1. State the type of qualitative research design that is most closely associated with the following terms:

    A. Marginalized

    B. Case history

    C. Temporal transition

    D. Gender bias

    E. Human story

2. Which dimension of narrative inquiry is represented by the following descriptions?

    A. Within the story, the researcher describes the location where the events occurred.

    B. Within the story, the researcher describes the emotional context under which the inquiry takes place.

3. Which consideration for narrative inquiry is represented in the following statements?

    A. The researcher describes the transformative relationship between himself or herself and the participant.

    B. The researcher describes that the inquiry is about how an African American male decides to become a high school science teacher.

    C. The researcher tells the reader that this study will add to what we know about who decides to become a teacher by examining how the combination of gender and race affects this decision.

4. A researcher is interested in retelling the life story of a Latina preservice teacher.

    A. What type of qualitative research design can be used? Why?

5. A researcher is interested in studying the experiences of girls in an algebra class.

    A. What type of qualitative design can be used? Why?

6. A researcher is interested in studying teacher self-efficacy by conducting the study with teachers at one low-performing elementary school and one high-performing elementary school. What type of qualitative design can be used? Why?

7. A researcher is interested in studying the use of technology in schools. What perspective would the researcher take in the following designs?

    A. Narrative

    B. Critical race theory

    C. Illustrative case study

8. What is the unique feature of the three critical theories among the other qualitative designs?

9. What are the two common applications of case study in education?

10. Why is an ethic of caring so important to narrative research?

1. For any of the three following topics, identify a qualitative design that could be used to study the topic. Describe why you selected this design.

   A. Classroom teaching style

   B. Student learning style preference

   C. Gender differences in learning algebra

   D. Teacher perceptions of the Common Core Standards

   E. Inquiry-based teaching

   F. Teacher reflection on preservice preparation

   G. Parent-teacher relationships

   H. Effect of media on student engagement

2. Choose one of the topics above and design a narrative inquiry study.

   A. Write the research question.

   B. Determine how you will select your participants.

   C. Determine what type of data you will collect.

   D. Describe how you will analyze the data.

3. Choose one of the topics above and design a case study.

   A. Write the research question.

   B. Determine how you will select your participants.

   C. Determine what type of data you will collect.

   D. Describe how you will analyze the data.

4. Choose one of the topics above and design a critical theory study.

   A. Write the research question.

   B. Determine how you will select your participants.

   C. Determine what type of data you will collect.

   D. Describe how you will analyze the data.

QUASI-EXPERIMENTAL, EXPERIMENTAL, AND MIXED-METHODS RESEARCH DESIGNS

Identify a problem

- Determine an area of interest.
- Review the literature.
- Identify new ideas in your area of interest.
- Develop a research hypothesis.

Develop a research plan

- Define the variables being tested.
- Identify participants or subjects and determine how to sample them.
- Select a research strategy and design.
- Evaluate ethics and obtain institutional approval to conduct research.

Conduct the study

- Execute the research plan and measure or record the data.

Analyze and evaluate the data

- Analyze and evaluate the data as they relate to the research hypothesis.
- Summarize data and research results.

Communicate the results

- Method of communication: oral, written, or in a poster.
- Style of communication: APA guidelines are provided to help prepare style and format.

Generate more new ideas

- Results support your hypothesis—refine or expand on your ideas.
- Results do not support your hypothesis—reformulate a new idea or start over.

After reading this chapter, you should be able to:

1 Define and identify a quasi-experiment and a quasi-independent variable.

2 Identify and describe two one-group quasi-experimental research designs: the posttest-only and pretest-posttest designs.

3 Identify and describe two nonequivalent control group quasi-experimental research designs: the posttest-only and pretest-posttest designs.

4 Identify and describe three time-series quasi-experimental research designs: basic, interrupted, and control designs.

5 Define the single-case experimental design.

6 Identify and describe three types of single-case research designs: the reversal, multiple-baseline, and changing-criterion designs.

7 Identify in a graph the stability and magnitude of a dependent measure, and explain how each is related to the internal validity of a single-case design.

8 Identify three ways that researchers can strengthen the external validity of a result using a single-case design.

QUASI-EXPERIMENTAL AND SINGLE-CASE EXPERIMENTAL DESIGNS

In the educational world, the environment or situation you find yourself in can be dynamic. You need look no further than within a school classroom. Suppose, for example, that a teacher gives an exam in which the average student scored a 50%. Why were the exam grades so low? Was the teacher ineffective in his or her teaching? Did the students study for the exam? Was the exam itself not fair? Was the material being studied too difficult or at too high a level? In this example, the answer can be difficult to identify because the classroom environment is constrained by preexisting factors—the time, date, and content area of the exam; the teacher and students in the class were not assigned by a researcher but instead were determined by the parents and school administrators. Accounting for these preexisting factors is important to determine why the exam grades were low.

The above example involves a classwide issue. In other situations, the issue may involve only one or a few students. What if in the above example most students did well on the exam and only a few students were failing the course? There may also be a classroom situation when there is one child with disruptive behavior within a classroom of students. Other educational questions may involve a low-incidence population of students such as those with severe intellectual disability, autism, or speech language impairment. In these cases, we wouldn't need to observe the entire classroom to determine why the grades of the students were low or why the one student is disruptive, so it would be advantageous to observe the behavior of only the target individuals. For example, we could observe the few students who are failing the course as the teacher implements a different instructional strategy or the student with disruptive behavior as a new positive reinforcement strategy is implemented to see if the behavior changes over time as a result of the new strategies.

In this chapter, we introduce quasi-experimental designs used in science to make observations in group settings that are constrained by preexisting factors. We also introduce methods used to assess the behavior of a single participant using single-case experimental designs, typically used when a large sample is not needed or cannot be obtained.

edge.sagepub.com/
priviterarme

- Take the chapter quiz
- Review key terms with eFlashcards
- Explore multimedia links and SAGE articles

⑤SAGE edge™

QUASI-EXPERIMENTAL DESIGNS

Suppose we hypothesize that high school graduates who attend college will value an education more than those who do not attend college. To test this hypothesis, we could select a sample of high school graduates from the same graduating class and divide them into two groups: those who attended college (Group College) and those who did not attend college (Group No College). We could then have all participants complete a survey in which higher scores on the survey indicate a higher value placed on obtaining an education. If the hypothesis is correct and we set up this study correctly, then participants in Group College should show higher scores on the survey than participants in Group No College.

A **quasi-experimental research design** is the use of methods and procedures to make observations in a study that is structured similar to an experiment, but the conditions and experiences of participants lack some control because the study lacks random assignment, includes a preexisting factor (i.e., a variable that is not manipulated), or does not include a comparison/control group.

Notice in this example that participants controlled which group they were assigned to—they either attended college or did not. Hence, in this example, the factor of interest (whether or not students attended college) was a quasi-independent variable. When a researcher does not manipulate a factor in a study (i.e., quasi-independent), this typically means that the study is a type of quasi-experimental research design. In this chapter, we separate the content into two major sections: quasi-experimental designs and single-case experimental designs. We begin this chapter with an introduction to the type of research design illustrated here: the quasi-experimental research design.

13.1 An Overview of Quasi-Experimental Designs

In this major section, we introduce a common type of research design called the quasi-experimental research design. The **quasi-experimental research design,** also defined in Chapter 6, is structured similar to an experiment, except that this design does one or both of the following:

1. It includes a **quasi-independent variable** (also defined in Chapter 6).

2. It lacks an appropriate or equivalent comparison/control group.

In the example used to introduce this section, the preexisting factor was college attendance (yes, no). The researchers did not manipulate or randomly assign participants to groups. Instead, participants were assigned to Group College or No College based on whether they attended college prior to the study. In other words, the participants, not the researcher, controlled which group they were assigned to. In this way, the study described to introduce this section was a quasi-experiment—the study was structured like an experiment in that differences in how students value college were compared between groups, but it lacked a manipulation (of the groups: whether students attended or did not attend college) and randomization (of assigning participants to each group).

> A **quasi-independent variable** is a preexisting variable that is often a characteristic inherent to an individual, which differentiates the groups or conditions being compared in a research study. Because the levels of the variable are preexisting, it is not possible to randomly assign participants to groups.

Hence, a quasi-experiment is not an experiment because, as illustrated in Figure 13.1, the design does not meet all three requirements for demonstrating cause. In the college attendance study, for example, additional unique characteristics of participants, other than whether or not they attended college, could also be different between groups and therefore could also be causing differences between groups. For example, levels of motivation and academic ability may also be different between people who attend and do not attend college. When other possible causes cannot be ruled out, the design does not demonstrate cause.

In this major section, we introduce three categories of quasi-experimental research designs used in the behavioral sciences:

- One-group designs (posttest only and pretest-posttest)

- Nonequivalent control group designs (posttest only and pretest-posttest)

- Time-series designs (basic, interrupted, and control)

13.2 One-Group Designs

In some situations, researchers ask questions that require the observation of a single group. When only one group is observed, the study lacks a comparison group and so does not demonstrate cause. These designs may also be referred to as "preexperimental" designs. Two types of one-group experiments are the following:

> A quasi-experiment resembles an experiment but includes a quasi-independent variable and/or lacks a control group.

- One-group posttest-only design
- One-group pretest-posttest design

One-Group Posttest-Only Design

The type of quasi-experiment most susceptible to threats to internal validity is the **one-group posttest-only design,** which is also

> A **one-group posttest-only design** is a quasi-experimental research design in which a dependent variable is measured for one group of participants following a treatment.

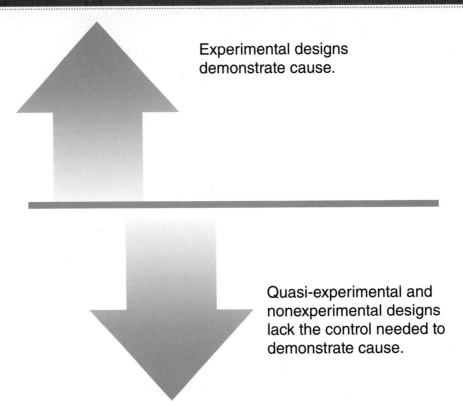

Experimental designs demonstrate cause.

Quasi-experimental and nonexperimental designs lack the control needed to demonstrate cause.

Note: The line represents the requirements for demonstrating cause: randomization, manipulation, and comparison/control. A quasi-experiment lacks at least one of these requirements and so fails to demonstrate cause.

One-group research designs lack a comparison/control group.

called the *one-shot case study* (Campbell & Stanley, 1966). Using the one-group posttest-only design, a researcher measures a dependent variable for one group of participants following a treatment. For example, as illustrated in Figure 13.2, after a teacher provides instruction on the steps of long division (the treatment), she or he may record the number of division problems solved correctly on a practice worksheet (the dependent variable) to test their learning.

The major limitation of this design is that it lacks a comparison or control group. Consider, for example, the number of division problems solved correctly on the practice worksheet. If the number of problems solved correctly is high following the instruction, can we conclude that the instruction is effective? How can we know for sure if the number of correct answers would have been high even without the instruction? We cannot know this because we have nothing to compare this outcome to; we have no

Figure 13.2   The One-Group Posttest-Only Quasi-Experimental Design

TREATMENT: Quasi-Independent Variable		MEASUREMENT: Dependent Variable
Students receive a lecture on a topic.	→	Measure an exam score.

comparison/control group. Hence, the design is susceptible to many threats to internal validity, such as history effects (unanticipated events that can co-occur with the exam) and maturation effects (natural changes in learning). In all, these limitations make the one-group posttest-only design a poor research design.

One-Group Pretest-Posttest Design

One way to minimize problems related to having no control or comparison group is to measure the same dependent variable in one group of participants before (pretest) and after (posttest) a treatment. Using this type of research design, called a **one-group pretest-posttest design,** we measure scores before and again following a treatment, then compare the difference between pretest and posttest scores. The advantage is that we can compare scores after a treatment to scores on the same measure in the same participants prior to the treatment. The disadvantage is that the one-group design does not include a no-treatment control group or a business-as-usual comparison group and therefore is still prone to many threats to internal validity, including those associated with observing the same participants over time (e.g., testing effects and regression toward the mean).

> A **one-group pretest-posttest design** is a quasi-experimental research design in which the same dependent variable is measured in one group of participants before (pretest) and after (posttest) a treatment is administered.

To illustrate the one-group pretest-posttest design, we will look at the research example illustrated in Figure 13.3. McCaleb, Anderson, and Hueston (2008) measured teacher perceptions of school violence before and after a three-part workshop on school violence. Their results showed a change in perception of school violence from before to after the treatment. A limitation of this design is that participants were not randomly assigned to groups. This means that any other factors related to perception of school violence, such as previous experiences in school violence, teaching experience, or being a victim of a crime outside of school, were beyond the control of the researchers and could have also influenced the results. Also, because the study lacked a control or comparison group with teachers who did not attend the workshop, the design was susceptible to many threats to internal validity, as stated previously.

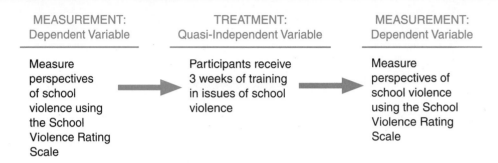

Figure 13.3   The One-Group Pretest-Posttest Quasi-Experimental Design

MEASUREMENT: Dependent Variable	TREATMENT: Quasi-Independent Variable	MEASUREMENT: Dependent Variable
Measure perspectives of school violence using the School Violence Rating Scale	Participants receive 3 weeks of training in issues of school violence	Measure perspectives of school violence using the School Violence Rating Scale

Note: Based on a design used by McCaleb, Anderson, and Hueston (2008).

13.3 Quasi-Experimental Design: Nonequivalent Control Group Designs

A **nonequivalent control group** is a control group that is matched upon certain preexisting characteristics similar to those observed in a treatment group but to which participants are not randomly assigned. In a quasi-experiment, a dependent variable measured in a treatment group is compared to that in the nonequivalent control group.

Selection differences are any differences, which are not controlled by the researcher, between individuals who are selected from preexisting groups or groups to which the researcher does not randomly assign participants.

Nonequivalent control group quasi-experimental research designs include a comparison/control group that is nonequivalent.

In some cases, researchers can use nonequivalent control/comparison groups when it is not possible to randomly assign participants to groups. A **nonequivalent control group** is a type of control/comparison group that is matched upon certain preexisting characteristics similar to those observed in a treatment group but to which participants are not randomly assigned. For example, suppose a teacher provides instruction using cooperative learning groups for one U.S. history class and provides traditional whole-group instruction in another U.S. history class, then compares grades on the U.S. history topic. The classes are matched on certain characteristics: Both classes are on the same topic (U.S. history), offered at the same school, and taught by the same teacher. However, the class taught using the traditional method is a nonequivalent comparison group because students in that class were not randomly assigned to that class. Any preexisting differences between students in the two classes, called **selection differences,** could therefore explain any differences observed between the two classes. Two types of nonequivalent control group quasi-experiments are the following:

- Nonequivalent control group posttest-only design

- Nonequivalent control group pretest-posttest design

Nonequivalent Control Group Posttest-Only Design

Using the **nonequivalent control group posttest-only design,** a researcher measures a dependent variable following a treatment in one group and compares that measure to a nonequivalent control/comparison group that does not receive the treatment. The nonequivalent control/comparison group will have characteristics similar to the treatment group, but participants will not be randomly assigned to this group, typically because it is not possible to do so. For example, as illustrated in Figure 13.4, suppose a teacher provides a new teaching method in a high school biology class and gives a traditional method in another biology class, then tests all students on the material taught. In this example, the nonequivalent control group was selected because it matched characteristics in the treatment group (e.g., all students were taking a biology class). Students, however, were not randomly assigned to the classes, so the comparison is a nonequivalent control group.

> A **nonequivalent control group posttest-only design** is a quasi-experimental research design in which a dependent variable is measured following a treatment in one group and also in a nonequivalent control group that does not receive the treatment.

A key limitation of this research design is that it is particularly susceptible to the threat of selection differences. In the example illustrated in Figure 13.4, because the high school students registered for the biology class were assigned to a specific class by a school administrator, the researcher did not control which class they enrolled in. Therefore, any preexisting differences between students in the two classes, such as how busy the students' daily schedules are or how much they study, are actually causing differences in grades between classes. For this reason, the nonequivalent control group posttest-only design demonstrates only that a treatment is associated with differences between groups and not that a treatment caused differences between groups, if any were observed.

Figure 13.4 The Nonequivalent Control Group Posttest-Only Quasi-Experimental Design

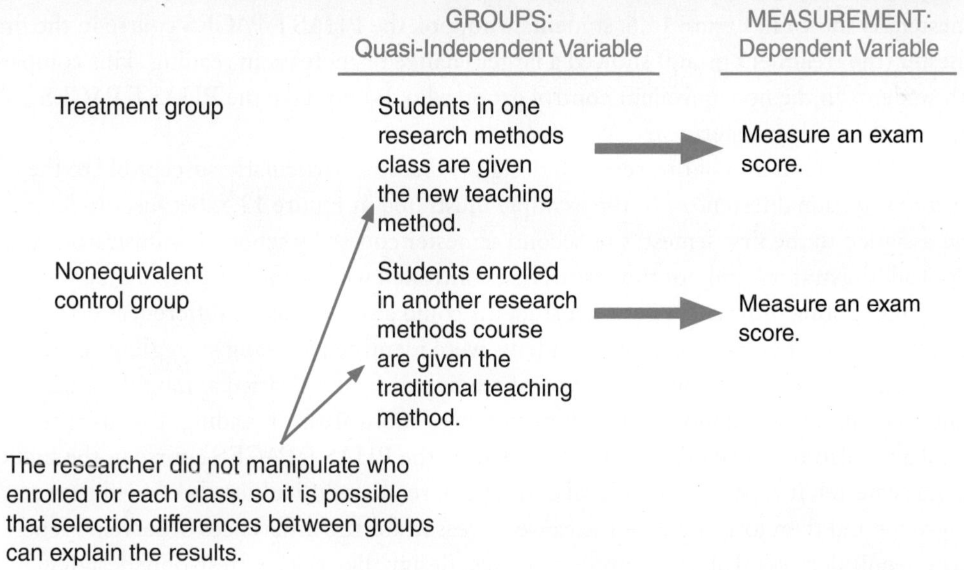

	GROUPS: Quasi-Independent Variable	MEASUREMENT: Dependent Variable
Treatment group	Students in one research methods class are given the new teaching method.	Measure an exam score.
Nonequivalent control group	Students enrolled in another research methods course are given the traditional teaching method.	Measure an exam score.

The researcher did not manipulate who enrolled for each class, so it is possible that selection differences between groups can explain the results.

Nonequivalent Control Group Pretest-Posttest Design

One way to minimize problems related to not having a comparison group is to measure a dependent variable in one group of participants observed before (pretest) and after (posttest) a treatment and also measure that same dependent variable at pretest and posttest in another nonequivalent control group that does not receive the treatment. This type of design is called the **nonequivalent control group pretest-posttest design.** The advantage of this design is that we can compare scores before and after a treatment in a group that receives the treatment and also in a nonequivalent control group that does not receive the treatment. While the nonequivalent control group will have characteristics similar to the treatment group, participants are not randomly assigned to this group, typically because it is not possible to do so. Hence, selection differences still can possibly explain observations made using this research design.

> A **nonequivalent control group pretest-posttest design** is a quasi-experimental research design in which a dependent variable is measured in one group of participants before (pretest) and after (posttest) a treatment and that same dependent variable is also measured at pretest and posttest in another nonequivalent control group that does not receive the treatment.

To illustrate the nonequivalent control group pretest-posttest design, we will look at the research example in Figure 13.5. Lovett, Lacerenza, DePalma, and Frijters (2012) used several measures of reading (i.e., word attack, word reading, and passage comprehension) to measure the reading skills of high school students who were identified as struggling readers. These researchers hypothesized that a reading intervention called PHAST PACES that teaches word identification strategies, knowledge of text structures, and reading comprehension strategies would increase reading skills among the struggling readers. To test this hypothesis, struggling readers were assigned by school administrators to the PHAST PACES course in the first semester (the treatment group) or second semester (the nonequivalent control group) of high school. All of the struggling readers were given the battery of reading tests before and after the implementation of PHAST PACES in the first semester. As shown in Figure 13.6, students who took the PHAST PACES course in the first semester (the treatment group) showed a larger change or increase in reading skills compared with students in the nonequivalent control group who did not take the PHAST PACES course in the first semester.

A key limitation of this research design is that it is particularly susceptible to the threat of selection differences. In the example illustrated in Figure 13.5, because students were assigned to the first semester or second semester course by school administrators, the school administrators, and not the researcher, controlled what semester course they were in. Any preexisting differences between students could also be causing differences classes in the reading skills. For example, while students were identified as being struggling readers on a battery of pretests, the level and type of reading difficulties varied among the students. Some students struggled more than others in one or more areas of reading. Because the school administrators decided which students took the PHAST PACES course in the first or second semester, it is possible that level and type of reading difficulties also varied between the groups and therefore could be the cause or reason for the differences observed. Hence, the nonequivalent control group pretest-posttest design, like the posttest-only design,

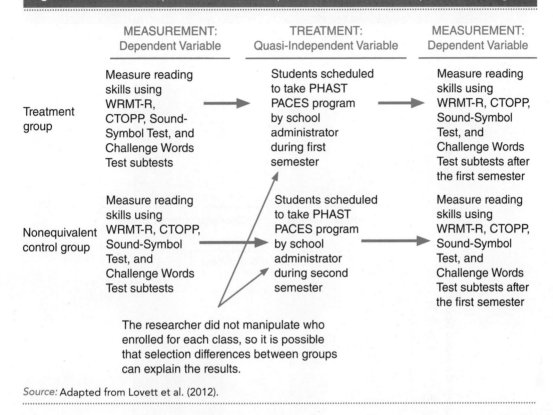

	MEASUREMENT: Dependent Variable	TREATMENT: Quasi-Independent Variable	MEASUREMENT: Dependent Variable
Treatment group	Measure reading skills using WRMT-R, CTOPP, Sound-Symbol Test, and Challenge Words Test subtests	Students scheduled to take PHAST PACES program by school administrator during first semester	Measure reading skills using WRMT-R, CTOPP, Sound-Symbol Test, and Challenge Words Test subtests after the first semester
Nonequivalent control group	Measure reading skills using WRMT-R, CTOPP, Sound-Symbol Test, and Challenge Words Test subtests	Students scheduled to take PHAST PACES program by school administrator during second semester	Measure reading skills using WRMT-R, CTOPP, Sound-Symbol Test, and Challenge Words Test subtests after the first semester

The researcher did not manipulate who enrolled for each class, so it is possible that selection differences between groups can explain the results.

Source: Adapted from Lovett et al. (2012).

demonstrates only that a treatment is associated with differences between groups and not that a treatment caused differences between groups, if any were observed.

13.4 Quasi-Experimental Design: Time-Series Designs

In some situations, researchers observe one or two preexisting groups at many points in time before and after a treatment, and not just at one time, using designs called the time-series quasi-experimental designs. Using these types of designs, we compare the pattern of change over time from before to following a treatment. Three types of time-series quasi-experimental designs are as follows:

> Time-series quasi-experimental research designs involve many observations made before and after a treatment.

- Basic time-series design

- Interrupted time-series design

- Control time-series design

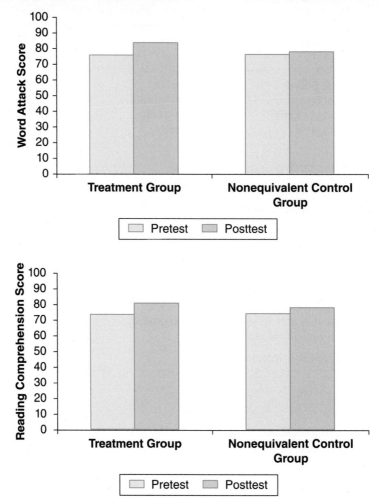

Source: Lovett et al. (2012). Reproduced with permission.

Basic Time-Series Design

When researchers manipulate the treatment, they use a basic time-series design to make a series of observations over time before and after a treatment. The advantage of measuring a dependent variable at multiple times before and after a treatment is that it eliminates the problem associated with only having a snapshot of behavior. To illustrate, suppose we test a treatment for improving alertness during the day. To use the basic time-series design, we record alertness at

> A basic time-series design is a quasi-experimental research design in which a dependent variable is measured at many different points in time in one group before and after a treatment that is manipulated by the researcher is administered.

multiple times before and after we give participants the treatment, as illustrated in Figure 13.7. Notice in the figure that a pretest (at 12 p.m.) and posttest (at 4 p.m.) measure can be misleading because the pattern observed before and after the treatment recurred without the treatment at the same time the day before and the day after the treatment was given. The basic time-series design allows us to uniquely see this pattern by making a series of observations over time.

Using the basic time-series design, the researcher manipulates or controls when the treatment will occur. The advantage of this design is that we can identify if the pattern of change in a dependent variable before and after the treatment occurs only during that period of time and not during other periods of time when the treatment is not administered. The disadvantage of this design is that only one group is observed, so we cannot compare the results in the treatment group to a group that never received the treatment.

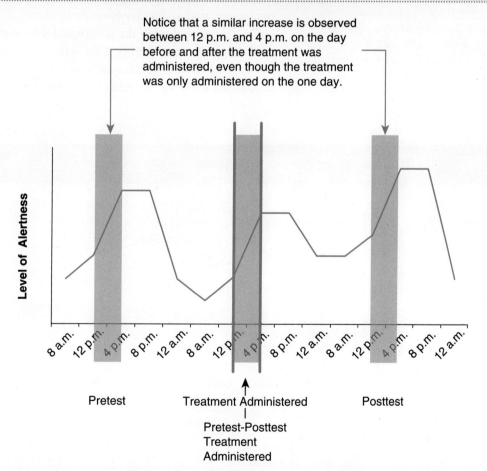

Figure 13.7 The Time-Series Quasi-Experimental Design

Notice that a similar increase is observed between 12 p.m. and 4 p.m. on the day before and after the treatment was administered, even though the treatment was only administered on the one day.

Level of Alertness

8 a.m.　12 p.m.　4 p.m.　8 p.m.　12 a.m.　8 a.m.　12 p.m.　4 p.m.　8 p.m.　12 a.m.　8 a.m.　12 p.m.　4 p.m.　8 p.m.　12 a.m.

Pretest

Treatment Administered
|
Pretest-Posttest
Treatment
Administered

Posttest

Note: A time-series design is used to compare the pattern of behavior before and after the treatment. In this example, the pattern that occurs before and after the treatment recurs at the same time of day, even without the treatment.

Interrupted and Control Time-Series Designs

In some situations, educational researchers will measure a dependent variable multiple times before and after a naturally occurring treatment or event. Examples of a naturally occurring treatment or event in education include changes in educational policy such as class size and curriculum adoptions. These events occur beyond the control of the researcher, so the researcher loses control over the timing of the manipulation. In these situations, when multiple measurements are taken before and after a naturally occurring treatment, researchers use the **interrupted time-series design.**

As an example of the interrupted time-series design, Madsen, Hicks, and Thompson (2011) measured physical activity reports from the California Healthy Kids Survey 1 year before and 6 years after implementing a Playworks. For this study, the line in Figure 13.8 shows that the days per week of physical activity (exercise, dance, or play sports) increased in the San Francisco Bay Area, 6 years following the implementation of the Playworks curriculum.

An advantage of the interrupted time-series design is that we can identify if the pattern of change in a dependent variable changes from before to following a naturally occurring treatment or event.

An **interrupted time-series design** is a quasi-experimental research design in which a dependent variable is measured at many different points in time in one group before and after a treatment that naturally occurred.

Figure 13.8 Interrupted Time-Series Design: Physical Activity Reports 1 Year Before and 6 Years After Implementing Playworks

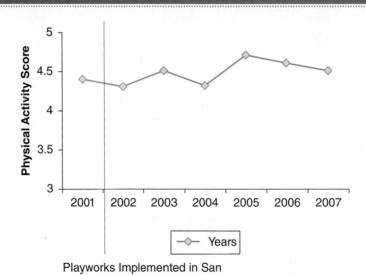

Playworks Implemented in San Francisco Bay Area in 2002

Note: Data are adapted from those reported by Madsen, Hicks, and Thompson (2011). Reproduced with permission by Wiley.

The disadvantage of this design, like that for the basic time-series design, is that only one group is observed, so we cannot compare the results in the treatment group to a group that never received a treatment. To address this disadvantage, we can include a matched or nonequivalent control group.

A basic or interrupted time-series design that includes a matched or nonequivalent control group is called a **control time-series design.** Byrnes (2009) examined the achievement scores of middle grade schools in Pennsylvania that were privatized to an education management organization 6 years before and 5 years after the privatization. He included a control group of schools from Pennsylvania that were not privatized by also recording achievement scores during the same period of time. As shown in Figure 13.9, achievement scores in the nonprivatized schools were greater than those of the privatized schools. The addition of this control group can increase how confident we are in the effect of privatizing schools with education management organizations.

> A **control time-series design** is a basic or interrupted time-series quasi-experimental research design that also includes a nonequivalent control group that is observed during the same period of time as a treatment group but does not receive the treatment.

As a caution, keep in mind that the students in each of the schools are preexisting groups in that the researcher did not assign students to the schools or which schools would be privatized. It is therefore possible, like for all other designs that use a nonequivalent control group, that selection differences, such as differences in attendance rates or student demographics (e.g., free and reduced-price lunch eligibility or percentage of minority students) between students in each of the schools, could have caused the different observed pattern of achievement scores and not the privatization of

Figure 13.9 Control Time-Series Design: Pennsylvania Achievement Scores 6 Years Before and 5 Years After Privatizing Schools to an Education Management Organization

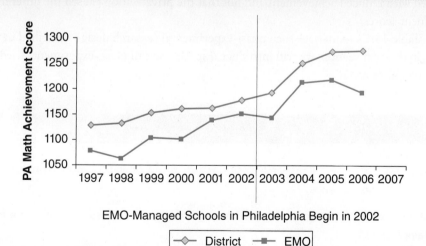

Note: Data are adapted from Byrnes, V. (2009). Getting a feel for the market: The use of privatized school management in Philadelphia. *American Journal of Education, 115,* 437–455. Reproduced with permission by the University of Chicago Press.

Table 13.1 The Quasi-Experimental Research Designs

Type of Quasi-Experimental Design	Description	Key Limitation
One-group posttest only	Observe one group after (posttest) a treatment	No control group for comparison
One-group pretest-posttest	Observe one group before (pretest) and after (posttest) a treatment	No control group for comparison
Nonequivalent control group posttest only	Observe treatment and nonequivalent control groups after (posttest) a treatment	No random assignment between groups
Nonequivalent control group pretest-posttest	Observe treatment and nonequivalent control groups before (pretest) and after (posttest) a treatment	No random assignment between groups
Basic time-series design	Make many observations over a period of time before and after a treatment manipulated by the researcher	No control group for comparison
Interrupted time-series design	Make many observations over a period of time before and after a naturally occurring treatment	No control group for comparison
Control series design	A time-series design with a matched or nonequivalent control group	No random assignment between groups

school management (the treatment). For this reason, we conclude that the privatization was associated with reduced achievement and not that the privatization caused the difference in achievement scores.

Table 13.1 summarizes each quasi-experimental research design described in this chapter. In the next section, we will introduce a special case of quasi-experiments used in developmental research.

LEARNING CHECK 1 ✓

1. The quasi-experimental research design is structured similar to an experiment, except [complete the sentence].

2. State the type of quasi-experimental research design described in each of the following examples:

   A. A researcher records the time (in seconds) it takes a group of students to complete a computer-based task following an online "how-to" course.

B. A researcher records the rate of school attendance at a school for 2 years before and 2 years after a reduced school attendance reward program was implemented.

C. A researcher records teacher satisfaction for 3 months before and 3 months after a training seminar. He compares satisfaction scores for teachers at one school compared to the satisfaction scores for teachers at another school who did not receive the seminar.

MAKING SENSE—IDENTIFYING QUASI-EXPERIMENTAL DESIGNS

While reading a journal article, you might find a thorough description of the steps of the study, but the specific type of design is not named. Diagramming the steps of the study can help identify the design. We use a notation system to diagram studies. The system uses these notations:

X = exposure to the independent variable

O = observation (or data collection) of the dependent variable(s)

A, B, C, etc. = groups of participants

Diagrams for the quasi-experimental designs are as follows:

One-group posttest only	A	X	O					
One-group pretest-posttest	A	O	X	O				
Nonequivalent control group posttest only	A	X	O					
	B	X	O					
Nonequivalent control group pretest posttest	A	O	X	O				
	B	O	X	O				
Basic and interrupted time series	A	O	O	O	X	O	O	O
Control time series	A	O	O	X	O	O		
	B	O	O	X	O	O		

Diagramming the number of groups, as well as timing the measurement of the independent and dependent variable(s), can help you identify the type of design if it is not specifically named in the description of the study.

Much of the research in education involves the identification of effective educational programs, policies, and practices. An effective educational program, policy, or practice either improves student outcomes such as achievement, engagement, or motivation or decreases behaviors that interfere with educational attainment such as disruptive behavior at school or truancy. This research, which involves testing a potentially effective program, policy, or practice and evaluating its effect on students, must follow rigorous research methods. A panel of educational research experts convened by the U.S. Department of Education, Institute for Education Sciences, created the *What Works Clearinghouse Procedures and Standards Handbook* (U.S. Department of Education, 2010) that outlines the rigorous methods that must be followed to be considered a high-quality study.

Most of the research designed to identify effective educational programs, policies, and practices are group designs. The nonequivalent group quasi-experimental designs discussed in this chapter lack one of the most important elements of a high-quality study that can be used to identify effective

practices—random assignment to groups. Nonequivalent group designs rely on intact groups such as a group of students within classrooms where random assignment to the treatment and control/comparison groups may not be possible. One way educational researchers can overcome this problem of lack of random assignment to groups is to provide some evidence of baseline (preintervention) equivalence of the groups. To provide this evidence, researchers examine the differences in important characteristics of the groups that may affect the outcomes, such as gender, ethnicity, or performance on the dependent measure using statistics. A second way to provide equivalent groups is to make statistical adjustments to account for any preexisting group differences when conducting the statistical analysis of the results of the study.

When reading research in consideration for implementation as an effective practice to improve student educational outcomes, if the study uses a quasi-experimental design, look for information that either (a) demonstrates that the groups are equivalent before the study is conducted or (b) accounts for group differences during analysis once the study is completed.

SINGLE-CASE EXPERIMENTAL DESIGNS

In this section, we begin by identifying a new research design to test the following research hypothesis: Giving positive reinforcement to a student who is disruptive in class only while he or she stays on task will increase on-task behavior in the classroom. To answer this hypothesis, we could measure the time (in minutes) that the disruptive student stays on task. We could observe the student for a few days with no positive reinforcement. Then we could observe the student for a few days with positive reinforcement given as he or she works on the task. Then we could again observe the student for a few more days with no positive reinforcement. If the hypothesis is correct and we set up this study correctly, then we should expect to find that the time (in minutes) spent on task was high when the positive reinforcement was given but low during the observation periods before and after when no positive reinforcement was given. The unique feature of this design is that only one participant was observed.

In this final section, we introduce the research design that was illustrated here: the single-case experimental design.

13.5 An Overview of Single-Case Designs

In some cases, educational researchers want to observe and analyze the behavior of an individual case. An individual case can be a single participant or a single cluster of participants such as a classroom. We can study individual cases using a research design called the **single-case experimental design.** A single-case design is unique in that the individual case serves as

its own control compared to at least two conditions or phases, without and with an intervention (Kazdin, 2011). In addition, the dependent variable is repeatedly measured in a single-case design across conditions for each individual case and is not averaged to compare groups. Single-case designs are useful in education to evaluate the effectiveness

> A **single-case experimental design** is an experimental research design in which an individual case serves as his, her, or its own control, and the dependent variable measured is analyzed for each individual case.

of interventions when applied to individual cases, as illustrated above, rather than groups. Although it can be applied to individual clusters, single case is most often applied with individual students in educational settings. In contrast, all other experimental research designs, introduced in Chapters 10 to 12, are grouped designs.

Single-case designs have three main characteristics. These characteristics include an individual case, manipulation, and repeated measurements.

1. As described above, the single-case design involves the analysis of an individual case whereby the individual case is compared to itself. However, to establish experimental control, the control must be repeated at least three times (Horner, Swaminathan, Sugai, & Smolkowski, 2012). These demonstrations of control can be across three cases (such as across individual people or classrooms), settings (such as across different times of day or different places), or materials (such as reading from different books or academic content areas).

2. *Manipulation* involves control over the absence and delivery of the independent variable across the phases or treatments that are experienced by each case. The researcher must control when the independent variable or treatment is delivered. If there is more than one independent variable or treatment, then the researcher is in control over when each is delivered across the different phases of the study.

> The single-case design, which is also called the *single-subject, single-participant,* or *small n design,* is most often used in applied areas of special education.

> The single-case design is characterized by an individual case that serves as its own control with repeated measurements across phases of the study.

3. Repeated measurement involves the frequent measurement of the dependent variable across all phases of the study. The dependent variable is measured at least three times in each phase of the study.

An advantage of analyzing the data one participant at a time is that it allows for the critical analysis of each individual measure, whereas averaging scores across groups can give a spurious appearance of orderly change. To illustrate this advantage, suppose that a researcher measures the effect of an academic intervention for incarcerated adolescents. The hypothetical data, shown in Table 13.2, show that the adolescents as a group gained on average 25 points on the assessment. However, Student C scored the same. An analysis of each individual student could be used to explain this outlier; a grouped design would often disregard this outlier as "error" so long as weight loss was large enough on average.

The single-case designs described in this chapter include reversal design (AB design), multiple-baseline design, changing-criterion design, and alternating treatment design (ABC design).

Table 13.2 The Value of an Individual Analysis

Participant	Baseline Assessment Score	Assessment Score following Academic Intervention	Assessment Increase
Adolescent A	70	85	15
Adolescent B	50	80	30
Adolescent C	66	66	0
Adolescent D	58	83	25

Average assessment gain: 17.5 points

Adolescent C was the only participant to not gain points on the assessment. An individual analysis would investigate why, whereas a group analysis would mostly disregard this anomaly as long as average assessment increase was large enough.

Note: In this example, an individual analysis could be used to explain why Student C was the only student not to improve his or her test score.

13.6 Single-Case Baseline-Phase Designs

Single-case designs are typically structured by alternating baseline and treatment phases over many trials or observations. In this major section, we will introduce three types of single-case experimental research designs:

- Reversal design
- Multiple-baseline design
- Changing-criterion design

Reversal Design

One type of single-case design, called the **reversal design,** involves observing a single case prior to (A), during (B), and following (A) a treatment or manipulation. The reversal design is structured into **phases,** represented alphabetically with an A or a B. Each phase consists of many observations or trials. The researcher begins with a **baseline phase (A),** in which no treatment is given, then applies a treatment in a second phase (B), and again returns to a baseline phase (A) in which the treatment is removed. This type of research design can be represented as follows:

A **reversal design,** or **ABA design,** is a single-case experimental design in which a single participant is observed before (A), during (B), and after (A) a treatment or manipulation.

A **phase** is a series of trials or observations made in one condition.

The **baseline phase (A)** is a phase in which a treatment or manipulation is absent.

A (baseline phase) → B (treatment phase) → A (baseline phase)

If the treatment in Phase B causes a change in the dependent variable, then the dependent variable should change from baseline to treatment, then return to baseline levels when the treatment is removed. For example, we opened this section with the hypothesis that giving positive reinforcement to a disruptive student while he or she is on task will increase the amount of on-task behavior in the classroom. To test this hypothesis, we measured the time in minutes that the disruptive student spent on task in a class with no positive reinforcement (baseline, A) for a few trials, then with positive reinforcement (treatment, B) for a few trials, and again with no positive reinforcement (baseline, B) for a few more trials. If the positive reinforcement (the treatment) was successful, then the time (in minutes) spent on task would be higher when the positive reinforcement was given but lower during the observation periods before and after when no positive reinforcement was given. The second baseline phase minimizes the possibility of threats to internal validity. Adding another B and A phase would further minimize the possibility of threats to internal validity because the pattern of change would be repeated using multiple treatment phases.

A visual inspection of the data, and not inferential statistics, is used to analyze the data when only a single participant is observed. When visually inspecting data in single-case studies, we are looking to identify a functional relationship between the independent and dependent variables. To analyze the data in this way, we look for three types of patterns that indicate that a treatment caused an observed change within a phase and three types of patterns across phases (*What Works Clearinghouse Procedures and Standards Handbook*; U.S. Department of Education, 2010). Figure 13.10 illustrates the three types of patterns to look for within a phase:

- A *change in level* is displayed graphically, as shown in Figure 13.10 (Graph A), when the level of the dependent variable within the baseline phases is obviously less than or greater than the level of the dependent variable within the treatment phase.

- A *change in trend* is displayed graphically, as shown in Figure 13.10 (Graph B), when the direction or pattern of change within the baseline phases is different from the pattern of change within the treatment phase. In the typical case, a dependent variable gradually increases or decreases in the treatment phase but is stable or does not change in the baseline phases.

- A change in *variability* is displayed graphically, as shown in Figure 13.10 (Graph C), when the pattern of data points within the baseline phases is different from the pattern of data points within the treatment phase. Typically, the pattern of data points in the treatment phase will be less variable than the pattern of the data points in the baseline phase.

Overlap (Graph D), immediacy of the effect (Graph E), and the consistency of data in similar phases (Graph F) make it possible to infer that some treatment is causing an effect or a change in behavior.

Visual inspection of single-case data also includes looking at the pattern of data across phases. We look for three additional patterns of the data across phases, as illustrated in Figure 13.11.

- *Overlap* is displayed in Figure 13.11 (Graph D) when the pattern of change in one phase overlaps the data in the other phase. The smaller the amount of overlap across baseline and treatment phases is also indicative of a functional relationship between the independent and dependent variables.

Figure 13.10 Three Ways to Identify if a Treatment Caused Changes in a Dependent Variable Within the Phase

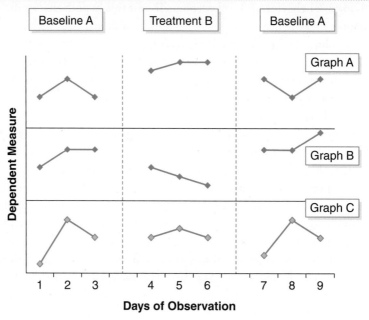

Source: Adapted from Wu & Chiang (2014).

Note: A change in level within a phase (Graph A), a change in trend (Graph B), and the variability (Graph C) make it possible to infer that some treatment is causing an effect or a change in behavior.

Section IV: Quasi-Experimental, Experimental, and Mixed-Methods Research Designs

- *Immediacy of the effect* is displayed in Figure 13.11 (Graph E) when the direction or pattern of change in the phases occurs immediately following the implementation or withdrawal of the treatment in the different phases. The more immediate the change is from one phase to another, the more compelling the argument is for a functional relationship between the independent and dependent variables.

- *Consistency of data in similar phases* is displayed in Figure 13.11 (Graph F) when the pattern of change in similar phases (all baseline A or all treatment phases B) is consistent with each other. The greater the consistency of the pattern of data across similar phases, the greater the likelihood of a functional relationship.

The reversal design is typically conducted in educational research to investigate the effectiveness of interventions that may benefit the individual participant. Often this means that researchers will be asked by ethics committees to end their study with a treatment phase (B), which was the phase that was beneficial to the participant. For this reason, many reversal designs are at least four phases, or ABAB, so as not to return to baseline to end an experiment.

A limitation of the reversal design is that the change in a dependent variable in a treatment phase must return to baseline levels when the treatment is removed. However,

Figure 13.11 Three Additional Ways to Identify if a Treatment Caused Changes in a Dependent Variable Across Phases

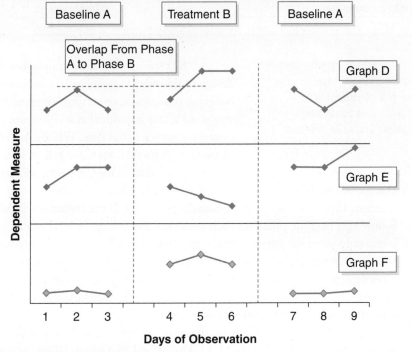

Source: Adapted from Ridgers et al. (2014).

The overlap across levels (graph D), immediacy of the effect across levels (graph E), and consistency across levels (graph F) also make it possible to infer that some treatment is causing an effect or a change in behavior.

when applied to interventions that affect learning, a return to baseline is not possible. When a participant is taught a new skill, for example, it is often not possible to undo what the participant learned—as fully expected, the behavior will not return to baseline. There may also be times when returning to baseline would be detrimental to the participant such as reducing harmful behavior like self-injury. In these situations, when it is not possible for changes in a dependent variable to return to baseline, a reversal design cannot be used.

Multiple-Baseline Designs

For situations in which it is not possible for changes in a dependent variable to return to baseline levels following a treatment phase, researchers can use the multiple-baseline design. The multiple-baseline design is a single-case design in which the treatment is successively administered over time to different participants, for different educational materials, or in different settings. This design allows researchers to systematically observe changes caused by a treatment without the need of a second baseline phase and can be represented as follows:

Case #1	Baseline _____	Treatment _____
Case #2	Baseline _____	Treatment _____
Case #3	Baseline _____	Treatment _____

A visual inspection of the data, and not inferential statistics, is used to analyze the data when only a single participant is observed.

A multiple-baseline design is a single-case experimental design in which a treatment is successively administered over time to different participants, for different behaviors, or in different settings.

By representing the multiple-baseline design in this way, a *case* refers to a unique time, behavior, participant, or setting. Treatment phases staggered to the individual cases illustrate control over the changes in the data. While the treatment phase is implemented for Case 1, Cases 2 and 3 remain in baseline. Once Case 1 demonstrates a change in level of pattern, then Case 2 will enter treatment while Case 3 remains in baseline. Case 3 will enter the treatment phase last. If the treatment causes an effect following a baseline phase for each case, then the change in level or pattern should begin only when the baseline phase ends, which is different for each case. If this occurs, then we can be confident that the treatment is causing the observed change. This design minimizes the likelihood that something other than the treatment is causing the observed changes if the changes in a dependent variable begin only after the baseline phase ends for each case.

The start of a treatment phase varies using the multiple-baseline design to determine if the changes in a dependent variable begin only after each baseline phase ends.

To illustrate the multiple-baseline design, we will look at the research example illustrated in Figure 13.12. Dukes and McGuire (2009) used a multiple-baseline design to measure the effectiveness of a sex education intervention, which they administered to multiple participants with a moderate intellectual disability. The researchers recorded participant knowledge of sexual functioning using the Sexual Consent and Education Assessment

(SCEA K-Scale; Kennedy, 1993), on which higher scores indicate greater ability to make decisions about sex. Each participant was given a baseline phase for a different number of weeks. Scores on the SCEA K-Scale were low in this baseline phase. As shown in Figure 13.12 for three participants, only after the baseline period ended and the intervention was administered did scores on the scale increase. Scores also remained high for 4 weeks after the program ended. Hence, the results showed a change in level from baseline to intervention for each participant.

Each participant in the sex education study received the intervention (or the treatment) in successive weeks: Tina (Week 11), Josh (Week 12), and Debbie (Week 13). Because the treatment was administered at different times, and changes in the dependent variable only occurred once the treatment was administered, the pattern showed that the treatment, and not other factors related to observing participants over time, caused the observed changes in SCEA K-Scale scores.

Figure 13.12 Results From a Multiple-Baseline Design for Three Participants Receiving a Sex Education Intervention

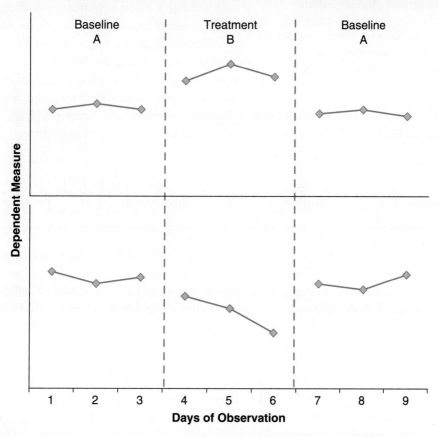

A change in level (graph A), a change in trend (graph B), and a change in variability (graph C) make it possible to infer that some treatment is causing an effect or a change in behavior.

Source: Adapted from Dukes & McGuire (2009). Reproduced with permission by Wiley.

The advantage of a multiple-baseline design is that it can be used when we expect a treatment will not return to baseline, such as when we study learning on some measure, as illustrated in Figure 13.12 for our example. One limitation to the multiple-baseline design in an educational context is the collection of data at each instructional session. For some studies that have multiple tiers of the intervention, such as across participants and settings, this can result in a lot of data collection. To make this design more efficient, the multiple-probe design is often used. Instead of collecting data at each session, data are collected at prescribed times (called probes) and in sufficient number to still provide visual evidence of the pattern of data in each of the phases. A second limitation of a multiple-baseline design is that the design is used when only a single type of treatment is administered. This same limitation applies to the reversal design. For situations when we want to administer successive treatments, then, we require a different type of single-case experimental design.

Changing-Criterion Designs

A **changing-criterion design** is a single-case experimental design in which a baseline phase is followed by successive treatment phases in which some criterion or target level of behavior is changed from one treatment phase to the next. The participant must meet the criterion of one treatment phase before the next treatment phase is administered.

For research situations in which we want to change a criterion or treatment after the participant meets an initial criterion or responds to one particular treatment, we can use a **changing-criterion design.** Using the changing-criterion design, we begin with a baseline phase, which is followed by many successive treatment phases to determine if participants can reach different levels or criteria in each treatment phase. The criterion can be changed as often as necessary or until some final criterion is met.

To illustrate the changing-criterion design, we will look at the research example illustrated in Figure 13.13. Plavnick (2012) used the changing-criterion design to increase the number of seconds that a student with autism attended to a video displayed on a cellphone of same-age peers modeling how to communicate using words and picture cue cards. In a baseline phase, the student looked at the video once for 1 second out of six trials. Then a series of manipulations followed. Each time the student attended to the screen of the cellphone while the video was played, he was rewarded with a preferred edible. The initial criterion was 2 seconds. This criterion was increased over time between 2 and 4 seconds after three consecutive sessions of meeting the previous criterion. As shown in Figure 13.13, each time the criterion, or the number of seconds required to gain a reward, was increased, the student's attending behavior increased.

Two advantages of the changing-criterion design are that it does not require a reversal to baseline of an otherwise effective treatment and that it enables experimental analysis of a gradually improving behavior. A limitation of the design is that the target

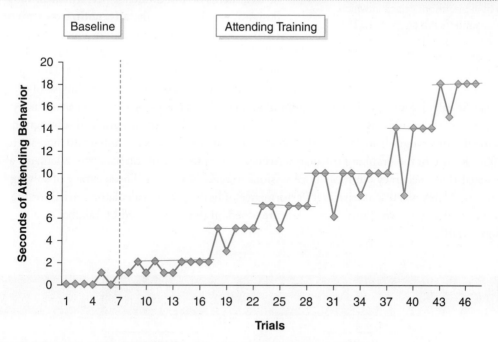

Figure 13.13 A Changing-Criterion Design to Increase the Number of Seconds a Single Student With Autism Attended to a Video

Source: Adapted from Plavnick (2012). Reproduced with permission.

Note: At baseline, Sam attended to the video once for 1 second. He began with 2 seconds, then 5 seconds, 7 seconds, 10 seconds, 14 seconds, and finally 18 seconds in order to receive the reward. The changing criterion is highlighted in the treatment phase by the dotted lines. Notice that as the criterion was increased, the student increased the number of seconds he looked at the video displayed.

behavior must already be in the participant's repertoire. For example, the student with autism needed to look at the video on the cellphone at least once to be able to increase the amount of time spent attending to the video. Also, researchers should be cautious to not increase or decrease the criterion too soon or by too much, which may impede the natural learning rate of the participant being observed.

With the reversal, multiple-baseline, and changing-criterion designs, notice that only one treatment is being evaluated. In some cases, researchers want to compare treatments to compare the effectiveness of each. For this type of research, we use the alternating treatment or ABC design.

Alternating Treatment Design

For situations where we want to compare different treatments or treatment conditions, we can use the alternating treatment design. The premise here is to alternate the treatment conditions during the treatment phase and compare how the individual performs under different conditions or treatments. If the performance of the participant does not

An **alternating treatment (ABC) design** is a single-case experimental design in which a baseline phase is followed by a treatment phase in which the conditions or treatments are alternated. The performance of the participant is compared under the different conditions or treatments.

change under the different conditions or treatments, then we can conclude that the different conditions or treatments do not influence performance. This design is also known as the **alternating treatment (ABC) design** and is illustrated in Figure 13.14.

Baseline data illustrate the accuracy of the participant prior to using the calculator. During the treatment (intervention) phase, the use of a scientific calculator (triangles) and a graphing calculator (squares) is alternated so accuracy of solving math problems can be compared. Notice at baseline, the accuracy in subtraction computations ranges from 0% to 20%. During treatment, there is an immediate increase to 100% for use of the graphing calculator. Accuracy with the use of the scientific calculator also reached 100% accuracy but took more sessions to reach that level. The accuracy of solving word problems was 0% at baseline. Performance of both types of calculators varied for the accuracy of solving word problems. Data are based on those presented by Yakubova and Bouck (2014).

Figure 13.14 An Alternating Treatment Design to Compare Two Types of Calculators on the Subtraction and Word Problem Accuracy of a Student With Mild Intellectual Disability

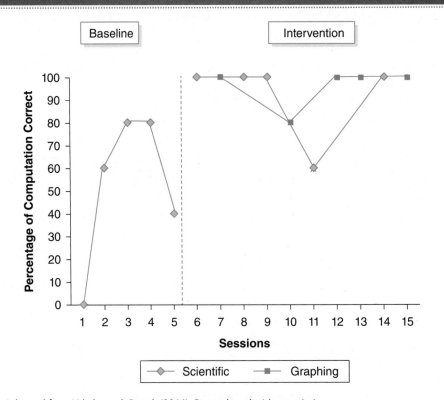

Source: Adapted from Yakubova & Bouck (2014). Reproduced with permission.

The advantage of the alternating treatment design is the ability to directly compare different conditions or treatments in the same study. One disadvantage is a possible carryover effect in comparing the treatment or conditions. The learning from one condition or treatment may carry over to the other condition or treatment. Therefore, the conditions or treatments must be distinctly different. Yakubova and Bouck (2014) compared two different types of calculators that operate differently to solve novel math problems. A second disadvantage to the alternating treatment design is that the alternated treatments must be able to alternate rapidly from treatment session to the next and the dependent variable must be able to change rapidly. For example, studies to compare effects of medications for attention-deficit hyperactivity disorder (ADHA) cannot be used in an alternating treatment design as many medications cannot be alternated or combined safely, and a medication may take time to take effect.

13.7 Application of Single-Case Designs in an Applied School Setting

Experimental designs have three main characteristics that enable these designs to infer cause-and-effect conclusions. These characteristics include manipulation, comparison, and randomization. Single-case designs do include manipulation of the independent variable and a comparison across individuals or conditions. *Randomization* typically implies random selection in nonexpermiental designs or random assignment to treatment/comparison groups in experimental designs. Randomization is important to the generalizability of the study to a larger population and in the application of inferential statistics. In single-case designs, randomization can include different forms of randomization depending on the type of single-case study. For example, conditions can also be randomized by randomly determining the presentation of the conditions. In single-case designs with more than one participant, participants can be randomly assigned to the order in which they will enter the treatment. In an applied educational setting where much of the educational research is conducted, such randomization is not always possible. Educational research is conducted in the confines of the schedule of school activities during the day, which may interfere with randomizing treatment conditions that need to occur rapidly. Single-case researchers also often purposefully select the order of entry of the participants based on who they believe will respond quicker to the intervention since the subsequent participants cannot enter until the preceding participant has demonstrated change. Randomly selecting a slower responding participant to enter treatment first will delay the entry of the other participants and extend the length of the study. Single-case researchers also underemphasize the need for randomization since inferential statistics cannot be used to analyze single-case data. To counteract the potential lack of generalizability, single-case research will include a more in-depth description of the participants, often providing a detailed description of each of the participants individually.

13.8 Single-Case Designs in the Identification of Effective Educational Programs, Policies, and Practices

The use of statistics is an important element in measuring student outcomes and defining effective educational programs, policies, and practices. We mentioned earlier in this chapter that analysis of single-case research is primarily through visual analysis. The data provided in single-case research do not lend themselves easily to quantitative analysis because they violate many of the assumptions needed to apply to statistics. One example of this violation is the assumption of independent data. This means that the data being analyzed need to be independent of each other. In the case of group-designed research, all participants in the group are considered independent since they represent different participants. In the case of single-case research, the data collected come from the same participant over time; hence, the data are not independent. Therefore, single-case research is not currently used to identify effective educational practices by the What Works Clearinghouse (http://ies.ed.gov/ncee/wwc/). Statisticians are currently working on this issue to develop a statistical procedure so that single-case studies can be used to identify effective educational practice that can be included in the What Works Clearinghouse.

Even though single-case research is not used to identify effective educational programs, policies, and practices in the What Works Clearinghouse, it is still a very useful research tool that can be used to evaluate the effectiveness of educational work with individual participants. The *What Works Clearinghouse Procedures and Standards Handbook* (U.S. Department of Education, 2010) does supply guidelines that can be used to judge the quality of single-case research. A high-quality single-case research study will include (a) more than one assessor of the dependent variable and information regarding interrater agreement of the multiple assessors; (b) at least three demonstrations of the effect of the treatment across participants, materials, or settings; (c) at least three data points in the baseline phase; and (d) at least 20 to 30 data points across phases depending on the specific design.

LEARNING CHECK 2 ✓

1. When would a single-case design be used instead of a group design?

2. Identify whether each of the following is an example of a reversal design, a multiple-baseline design, a changing-criterion design, or an alternating treatment design:

   A. A researcher gives a child successively greater levels of positive reinforcement after an initial baseline phase to reduce how often the student shouts out during class. The successive treatments are administered until the child has reached a level where she is no longer shouting out in class.

B. A researcher records the duration of time a participant stays on task in math class 4 days before, 4 days during, and 4 days after a behavioral intervention strategy is implemented.

C. A researcher records the number of times a child raises her hand in class for 5 days before and 10 days while implementing two different types of reinforcement that are provided on alternate days.

D. A researcher records the level of engagement made by three participants. Each participant was given a treatment phase after 3, 4, or 5 days of a baseline phase; no baseline phase was given after the treatment was administered.

3. For a single-case experimental study, why would a researcher use a multiple-baseline design instead of a reversal design?

13.9 Validity, Stability, Magnitude, and Generality

The analysis of single-case experimental research designs is based largely on a visual inspection of the data in a graph and not based on statistical analyses that require data to be grouped across multiple participants or groups. The specific visual features in a graph that indicate the validity of an observation are described in this section.

> The stability and magnitude of change across phases in a single-case design determine the extent to which a researcher has established control. The greater the control, the higher the internal validity.

Internal Validity, Stability, and Magnitude

Recall from Chapter 6 that internal validity is the extent to which we can demonstrate that a manipulation or treatment causes a change in a dependent measure. Importantly, the extent to which we establish experimental control of all other possible causes is directly related to the internal validity of a research study. The greater the control we establish, the higher the internal validity.

A single-case design requires a visual analysis of the graphical data of a single participant. The level of control and therefore the internal validity of a single-case design can be determined when the following two features are observed in a graph using this type of analysis:

- The stability in the pattern of change across phases

- The magnitude or size of the change across phases

In a visual inspection of a graph, the **stability** of a measure is indicated by the consistency in the pattern of change in each phase. The stability

> **Stability** is the consistency in the pattern of change in a dependent measure in each phase of a design. The more stable or consistent changes in a dependent measure are in each phase, the higher the internal validity of a research design.

of a dependent measure is illustrated in Figure 13.15. Data in a given phase can show a stable level, as in Figure 13.15a; show a stable trend, as in Figure 13.15b; or be unstable, as in Figure 13.15c. The stability of a measure in each phase is important because when a measure is unstable, changes are occurring in a dependent variable even when the researcher is not manipulating the behavior. When a dependent measure is stable, we can be confident that any changes in level or trend were caused by the manipulation because changes only occurred between each phase and were otherwise stable or consistent within each phase. Therefore, the more stable a measure, the greater the control and the higher the internal validity in an experiment.

Another level of control can be demonstrated by the magnitude of change, which is the size of the change in a dependent measure observed between phases. When a measure is stable *within* each phase, we look at the magnitude of changes *between* phases. For a treatment to be causing changes in a dependent measure, we should observe immediate changes as soon as the treatment phase is administered. We can observe an immediate change in level, as shown in Figure 13.16a, or we can observe an immediate change in trend, as shown in Figure 13.16b. The greater the magnitude of changes between phases, the greater the control and the higher the internal validity in a single-case experiment.

> Magnitude is the size of the change in a dependent measure observed between phases of a design. The larger the magnitude of changes in a dependent measure between phases, the higher the internal validity of a research design.

Figure 13.15 A Stable Level (a), a Stable Trend (b), and an Unstable Response (c)

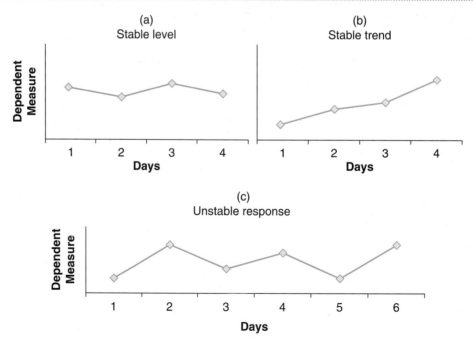

Note: Graphs (a) and (b) show a response that indicates high internal validity, whereas graph (c) indicates low internal validity.

Figure 13.16 Internal Validity and Control

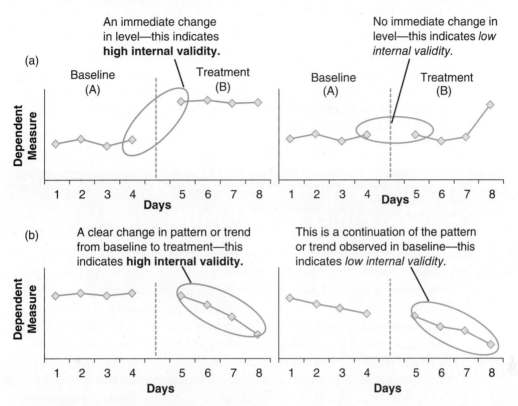

Note: Identifying an immediate change in level (top row, a) or a change in trend (bottom row, b) that would indicate a high level of control and high internal validity.

External Validity and Generality

Recall from Chapter 6 that external validity is the extent to which observations generalize beyond the constraints of a study. A single-case design is typically associated with low population validity, which is a subcategory of external validity. In other words, it is not possible to know whether the results in the sample would also be observed in the population from which the sample was selected because single-case experimental designs are associated with very small sample sizes. However, the results in a single-case design can have high external validity in terms of generalizing across behaviors, across subjects or participants, and across settings. The following is an example of each way to generalize results to establish the external validity of a single-case experiment:

- As an example of generalizing across behaviors, a researcher may examine the extent to which an intervention for reducing aggression toward others generalizes to or reduces self-injury. In this example, the therapist generalizes across behaviors, from aggression toward others (Behavior 1) to self-injury (Behavior 2).

- As an example of generalizing across subjects or participants, a researcher may examine the effectiveness of an intervention to improve reading skills across multiple participants.

- As an example of generalizing across settings, a teacher may want to determine the extent to which an intervention to increase social exchanges with peers during recess generalizes to increases in social exchanges with peers during group activities during science. In this example, the researcher generalizes across settings, from social exchanges during recess (Setting 1) to social exchanges during science (Setting 2).

13.10 Ethics in Focus: The Ethics of Innovation

Many single-case experiments look at early treatments for behaviors needed for learning (such as attending to task or engagement) or improving academic skills. When these types of behaviors are studied using a single-case design, the treatment is typically hypothesized to have benefits, such as increasing the frequency of behaviors needed for learning, reducing the frequency of behaviors that interfere with learning, or teaching new skills. Researchers will end an experiment with the treatment phase that was most beneficial, so as to maximize the benefits that participants receive. In a reversal design, this means that researchers end the study in a B phase (e.g., ABAB). A multiple-baseline design, an alternating treatment, and a changing-criterion design already end in a treatment phase. Adding a treatment phase or otherwise adapting a single-case design is quite manageable for researchers because they observe only one or a few subjects or participants in a single-case experiment. Observing such a small sample size allows researchers the flexibility to make changes, such as when they add or omit treatments to maximize benefits to participants. Teachers can use this design to make data-based decisions regarding the efficacy of the instruction they provide in producing the desired change in the students.

> Researchers often generalize observations in single-case experiments across behaviors, across subjects or participants, and across settings.

The flexibility of a single-case design also allows for greater "investigative play" (Hayes, 1981, p. 193) or greater freedom to ask innovative or new questions about treatments with unknown causes or with unknown costs or benefits. Single-case designs allow for the conduct of such innovative research to rigorously evaluate potential, yet untested, treatments with small samples, thereby testing the treatment without exposing such a treatment to large groups of participants, particularly when the potential costs of implementing such a treatment are largely unknown or untested. In this way, single-case designs can be used as an initial research design for testing some of the most innovative research in the behavioral sciences, which can then be tested in larger group studies.

1. Perform a visual inspection of the following data. Does the graph illustrate a study with high internal validity? Explain.

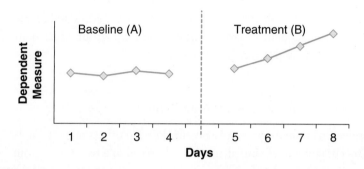

2. A researcher uses a single-case design to record the number of minutes spent studying in a baseline phase and a calming music treatment phase with a student who studied in a school media center and the same student who studied in a study hall room. Based on this description, can the researcher generalize across behaviors, across participants, or across settings?

3. Single-case designs allow for greater freedom to ask innovative or new questions about educational interventions with unknown costs or benefits. Why can a single-case design be an ethically appropriate research design to test the effectiveness of such treatments?

Answers: 1. Yes, because the data in baseline are stable, and a change in trend from baseline to treatment; 2. Generalize across settings; 3. Because single-case designs are used with small samples, thereby testing the treatment without exposing such a treatment to large groups of participants.

CHAPTER SUMMARY

LO 1 Define and identify a quasi-experiment and a quasi-independent variable.

- A quasi-experimental research design is structured similar to an experiment, except that this design lacks random assignment, includes a preexisting factor (i.e., a variable that is not manipulated), or does not include a comparison/control group.

- A quasi-independent variable is a preexisting variable that is often a characteristic inherent to an individual, which differentiates the groups or conditions being compared in a research study. Because the levels of the variable are preexisting, it is not possible to randomly assign participants to groups.

LO 2 Identify and describe two one-group quasi-experimental research designs: the posttest-only and pretest-posttest designs.

- The one-group posttest-only design is a quasi-experimental research design in which a dependent variable is measured for one group of participants following a treatment.

- The one-group pretest-posttest design is a quasi-experimental research design in which the same dependent variable is measured in one group of participants before and after a treatment is administered.

LO 3 Identify and describe two nonequivalent control group quasi-experimental research designs: the posttest-only and pretest-posttest designs.

- A nonequivalent control group is a control group that is matched upon certain preexisting characteristics similar to those observed in a treatment group but to which participants are not randomly assigned. When a nonequivalent control group is used, selection differences can potentially explain an observed difference between an experimental and a nonequivalent control group.

- The nonequivalent control group posttest-only design is a quasi-experimental research design in which a dependent variable is measured following a treatment in one group and is compared to a nonequivalent control group that does not receive the treatment.

- The nonequivalent control group pretest-posttest design is a quasi-experimental research design in which a dependent variable is measured in one group of participants before (pretest) and after (posttest) a treatment and that same dependent variable is also measured at pretest and posttest in a nonequivalent control group that does not receive the treatment.

LO 4 Identify and describe three time-series quasi-experimental research designs: basic, interrupted, and control designs.

- The basic time-series design is a quasi-experimental research design in which a dependent variable is measured at many different points in time in one group before and after a treatment that is manipulated by the researcher.

- The interrupted time-series design is a quasi-experimental research design in which a dependent variable is measured at many different points in time in one group before and after a treatment that naturally occurs.

- A control time-series design is a basic or interrupted time-series quasi-experimental research design that also includes a nonequivalent control group that is observed during the same period of time as a treatment group but does not receive the treatment.

LO 5 Define the single-case experimental design.

- The single-case experimental design is an experimental research design in which an individual case serves as its own control and the dependent variable measured is analyzed for each individual case and is not averaged across groups or across participants. This design has specific requirements of the number of data points within and across phases to be considered high quality.

LO 6 Identify and describe three types of single-case research designs: the reversal, multiple-baseline, and changing-criterion designs.

- The reversal design is a single-case experimental design in which a single case is observed before (A), during (B), and after (A) a treatment or manipulation.

- The multiple-baseline design is a single-case experimental design in which a treatment is successively administered over time to different participants, for different behaviors, or in different settings.

- The changing-criterion design is a single-case experimental design in which a baseline phase is followed by successive treatment phases in which some criterion or target level of behavior is changed from one treatment phase to the next. The participant must meet the criterion of one treatment phase, before the next treatment phase is administered.

- The alternating treatment design is a single-case experimental design in which the baseline phase is followed by a treatment phase where at least two treatments are delivered on alternating sessions. The treatments are then compared to determine which one was more effective.

LO 7 Identify in a graph the stability and magnitude of a dependent measure, and explain how each is related to the internal validity of a single-case design.

- The stability of a measure is the consistency in the pattern of change in a dependent measure in each phase of a design. The more stable or consistent changes in a dependent measure are in each phase, the higher the internal validity of a research design.

- The magnitude of change in a measure is the size of the change in a dependent measure observed between phases of a design. A measure can have a change in level or a change in trend. The larger the magnitude of change, the greater the internal validity of a research design.

LO 8 Identify three ways that researchers can strengthen the external validity of a result using a single-case design.

- A single-case design is typically associated with low population validity (a subcategory of external validity). However, researchers can strengthen the external validity of a result using a single-case design by generalizing across behaviors, across subjects or participants, and across settings.

KEY TERMS

ABA design 351

alternating treatment design (ABC) 358

baseline phase (A) 351

basic time-series design 342

changing-criterion design 356

control time-series design 345

interrupted time-series design 344

magnitude 362

multiple-baseline design 354

nonequivalent control group 338

nonequivalent control group posttest-only design 339

nonequivalent control group pretest-posttest design 340

one-group posttest-only design 335

one-group pretest-posttest design 337

phase 351

quasi-experimental research design 334

quasi-independent variable 335

reversal design 351

selection differences 338

single-case experimental design 349

stability 361

REVIEW QUESTIONS

1. A quasi-experimental research design is structured similar to an experiment, with what two exceptions?

2. State whether each of the following factors is an example of an independent variable or a quasi-independent variable. Only state "quasi-independent variable" for participant variables that cannot be manipulated.

   A. The age of participants

   B. Time allotted for taking an exam

   C. A teacher's prior teaching experience

   D. Time of day a study is conducted

   E. A participant's state of residence

   F. Amount of time spent studying

3. How does a one-group pretest-posttest design improve on the posttest-only quasi-experimental design? What is the major limitation of all one-group designs?

4. What is a nonequivalent control group, and why does this type of group make it difficult to determine cause and effect using a nonequivalent control group quasi-experimental design?

5. What is the key difference between the basic and interrupted time-series quasi-experimental research designs?

Section IV: Quasi-Experimental, Experimental, and Mixed-Methods Research Designs

6. A reversal design is used to test the hypothesis that low lighting in a room reduces how quickly students read. As shown in the figure for one student, a student reads passages of similar length in a room with normal lighting (baseline), then in the same room with dim lighting (treatment), and then again with normal lighting. Do the results shown in the figure support the hypothesis? Explain.

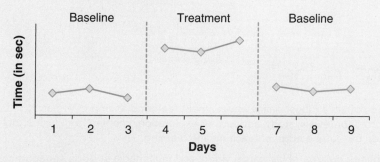

7. What is the most likely reason that a researcher uses a multiple-baseline design instead of a reversal design?

8. Define the changing-criterion design and explain when the design is used.

9. Describe how an alternating treatment design differs from the other single-case designs.

10. In the following scenarios, is the researcher generalizing across behaviors, participants, or settings?

   A. A researcher examines the generalizability of an educational intervention for increasing vocabulary acquisition by testing the same treatment to increase reading comprehension.

   B. A researcher examines if the effectiveness of a new learning system used in a classroom is also effective when used in a home (for homeschooled children).

ACTIVITIES

1. Use an online database, such as PsycINFO, to search scientific research articles for any topic you are interested in. Perform two searches. In the first search, enter a search term related to your topic of interest, and enter the term *longitudinal* to find research that used this design in your area of interest. Select and print one article. In the second search, again enter a search term related to your topic of interest, and this time enter the term *cross-sectional* to find research that used this design in your area of interest. Again, select and print one article. Once your searches are complete, complete the following assignment:

   A. Write a summary of each article, and explain how each research design differed.

   B. Describe at least two potential threats to internal validity in each study.

   C. Include the full reference information for both articles at the end of the assignment.

2. A researcher proposes that parental involvement will improve school attendance of the child. (a) Write a research plan to test this hypothesis using a single-case experimental design. (b) What is the predicted outcome or pattern if the hypothesis that parental involvement will improve attendance is correct? (c) Graph the expected results. (d) Identify the extent to which your results demonstrate high or low internal validity.

$SAGE edge™

SAGE edge offers a robust online environment featuring an impressive array of free tools and resources for review, study, and further exploration, keeping both instructors and students on the cutting edge of teaching and learning.

Access practice quizzes, eFlashcards, video, and multimedia at edge.sagepub.com/priviterarme.

Identify a problem

- Determine an area of interest.
- Review the literature.
- Identify new ideas in your area of interest.
- Develop a research hypothesis.

Develop a research plan

- Define the variables being tested.
- Identify participants or subjects and determine how to sample them.
- Select a research strategy and design.
- Evaluate ethics and obtain institutional approval to conduct research.

Generate more new ideas

- Results support your hypothesis—refine or expand on your ideas.
- Results do not support your hypothesis— reformulate a new idea or start over.

After reading this chapter, you should be able to:

1. Delineate the between-subjects design and the between-subjects experimental design.
2. Distinguish between an experimental group and a control group.
3. Explain how random assignment, control by matching, and control by holding constant can make individual differences about the same between groups.
4. Identify the appropriate sampling method and test statistic for independent samples to compare differences between two group means, and among two or more groups.
5. Delineate the within-subjects design and the within-subjects experimental design.
6. Demonstrate the use of counterbalancing and control for timing using a within-subjects experimental design.
7. Identify the appropriate sampling method and test statistic for related samples to compare differences between two or more group means.
8. Contrast the use of a between-subjects versus a within-subjects design for an experiment.
9. Identify the appropriate sampling method for a factorial design used in an experiment.
10. Identify and describe three types of factorial designs.
11. Identify the implications of using a quasi-independent factor in a factorial design.
12. Describe the higher-order factorial design.

Conduct the study

- Execute the research plan and measure or record the data.

Communicate the results

- Method of communication: oral, written, or in a poster.
- Style of communication: APA guidelines are provided to help prepare style and format.

Analyze and evaluate the data

- Analyze and evaluate the data as they relate to the research hypothesis.
- Summarize data and research results.

EXPERIMENTAL DESIGNS: BETWEEN SUBJECTS, WITHIN SUBJECTS, AND FACTORIAL

Often, we may be interested in making comparisons between groups created by one or more independent variables. To illustrate, consider the school cafeteria where integrating healthy food choices is critical. Suppose we integrate a new lunch program into the school. Let us identify three ways to evaluate the effectiveness of this new lunch program.

In a *between-subjects design*, we compare between two or more groups in which different participants are observed in each group. For such a study, we could implement the new lunch program for half the school, and leave the regular lunch program in place for the other half of students, then compare the number of healthy food choices in each group of children. The independent variable would be the new lunch program (implemented, not implemented) and the dependent variable would be the number of healthy food choices by children in each group.

In a *within-subjects design*, we compare between two or more groups in which the same participants are observed in each group. For such a study, we could implement the new lunch program for the entire school, then compare the number of healthy food choices among children for a period of time before, then after the program is implemented. The independent variable would be time (before, after lunch program is implemented) and the dependent variable would again be the number of healthy food choices by children.

In a *factorial design*, we compare between groups created by two or more independent variables in which the same or different participants are observed in each group. For such a study, we could implement the new lunch program for the entire school, then compare the number of healthy food choices by gender from before, then after the program is implemented. The independent variables would be gender (boys, girls) and time (before, after lunch program is implemented) and the dependent variable would again be the number of healthy food choices by children.

In this chapter, we introduce the structure of all three of these types of designs. We further explore other ways of adding information about the nature of observed effects and how to appropriately interpret them.

14.1 Conducting Experiments: Between-Subjects Design

A **between-subjects design** is a research design in which different participants are observed one time in each group or at each level of a factor.

A **between-subjects experimental design** is an experimental research design in which the levels of a between-subjects factor are manipulated, and then different participants are randomly assigned to each group or to each level of that factor and observed one time.

A **between-subjects factor** is a type of factor in which different participants are observed in each group or at each level of the factor.

The most common reason for conducting an experiment is to identify factors that cause changes in behavior in a population. The term *experiment* is used almost synonymously with *science*. It is the staple for how researchers conduct research; however, keep in mind that other than the single-case design, to this point we have only introduced nonexperiments and quasi-experiments. In this chapter, we introduce the **between-subjects experimental design** in which we manipulate the levels of a **between-subjects factor** and then randomly assign different participants to each group or to each level of that factor. The between-subjects experimental design, described in Figure 14.1, is a **between-subjects design** that meets the three requirements for demonstrating cause and effect (first introduced in Chapter 7):

1. Randomization (random sampling and/or random assignment)

2. Manipulation (of variables that operate in an experiment)

3. Comparison/control (or a control group)

In Figure 14.1, Step 3 meets the requirement for randomization. Step 1 may also be a random selection of participants, but in some educational research, the group of participants selected to participate may be convenient (i.e., using students and teachers from the nearby school system) or purposeful (i.e., selecting a school that has the lowest achievement rating or has high levels of behavioral incidents). Step 2 meets the requirements for manipulation (of the levels of an independent variable) and comparison/control (by creating two or more groups). Steps 4 and 5 allow researchers to compare differences in a dependent variable between two or more groups and use statistical analyses to determine if the differences observed in the sample are also likely to exist in the population from which the sample was selected. A decision in Step 6 is then made regarding the research hypothesis tested. In this section, we will introduce the procedures used in each step of the between-subjects experimental design, as described in Figure 14.1.

Figure 14.1 The Steps Used for a Between-Subjects Experimental Design

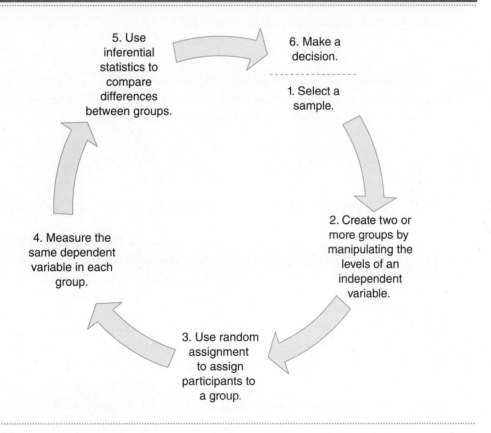

5. Use inferential statistics to compare differences between groups.

6. Make a decision.

1. Select a sample.

2. Create two or more groups by manipulating the levels of an independent variable.

3. Use random assignment to assign participants to a group.

4. Measure the same dependent variable in each group.

14.2 Experimental Versus Control Group

Each type of research design introduced in this book can be distinguished by the level of control that is established by a researcher. The term control, also defined in Chapter 7, is used in research design to describe (a) the manipulation of a variable and (b) holding all other variables constant. In an experiment, control is high, and therefore both criteria (a) and (b) must be met in a between-subjects experiment.

A staple of the between-subjects experiment is that results in an experimental group can be compared to those in a control/comparison group. For this reason, we begin here by clarifying the distinction

Control in research design is (a) the manipulation of a variable and (b) holding all other variables constant. When control is low, neither criterion is met; when control is high, both criteria are met.

between a control group, a comparison group, and an experimental group. The **experimental group,** or **treatment group,** is a group that receives a treatment (the independent variable) or is exposed to a manipulation believed to cause changes in a dependent variable. The **control group** is a group that is treated the same as an experimental group, except that participants are not treated; that is, the manipulation is omitted. The **comparison group** is a group that received a different treatment from the experimental or treatment group. Although many educational researchers use the term *control group* (a group that receives nothing), it is rare when such a group actually receives nothing. In educational research, we often ask questions about a new idea or intervention in comparison to the traditional or business-as-usual intervention. When comparing two interventions, the traditional or business-as-usual group is called a comparison group. You may also see the term *placebo control group.*

Participants in a control group must be treated exactly the same as those in the experimental group, minus the manipulation. For example, suppose we hypothesize that an after-school peer tutoring will increase high school grade point average (GPA). In an experiment, we implement the after-school peer tutoring to one group but not to a control group. The groups are the same except for the receipt of the after-school tutoring. A comparison group could receive a different form of after-school tutoring that the school had been using, perhaps from teachers. If we observe differences between groups, then it is likely due to the administration of the new peer tutoring because both groups were otherwise treated the same.

> The **experimental group** or **treatment group** is a condition in an experiment in which participants are treated or exposed to a manipulation or level of the independent variable that is believed to cause a change in the dependent variable.
>
> The **control group** is a condition in an experiment in which participants are treated the same as participants in an experimental group, except that the manipulation believed to cause a change in the dependent variable is omitted.
>
> The **comparison group** is a condition in an experiment in which participants are treated with a different treatment from the experimental or treatment group.

> Participants in a control group are treated identical to those in a treatment group, minus the manipulation.

MAKING SENSE—CREATING APPROPRIATE CONTROL GROUPS

The control group must be treated exactly the same as an experimental group, except that the members of this group do not actually receive the treatment believed to cause changes in the dependent variable. As an example, let's take a study by Scheiter, Schubert, Gerjets, and Stalbovs (2015), who were interested in testing the effectiveness of learning strategies relevant to multimedia instruction (Smartboard).

(Continued)

(Continued)

To test these learning strategies, the students in the experimental group received training in the specific strategies relevant to learning through the use of a multimedia Smartboard. The students in the placebo-control group were treated the same by receiving the same amount of training on general learning strategies not related to the use of multimedia (Smartboard). Both groups then received instruction on the same novel academic content with the Smartboard. Knowledge of the academic content, the dependent variable, was measured through a 20-item test of the after instruction.

Note that simply omitting the multimedia relevancy of the training is not sufficient. The control group in our example still receives some training in non-multimedia content and use of the Smartboard. Other important factors for experiments like these include some control of other variables that might affect the outcome. In this study, the researchers also gathered information on reading skills and prior knowledge of the participants to ensure that these factors are the same for all participants. These added levels of control ensure that both groups are truly identical, except that one group received multimedia strategy training and a second group did not. In this way, researchers can isolate all factors in an experiment, such that only the manipulation that is believed to cause an effect is different between groups.

LEARNING CHECK 1 ✓

1. What are the three requirements for demonstrating cause and effect in an experiment?

2. Identify the experimental group and the control/comparison group in the following description of an experiment:

   To test whether adding spoken text to a computer-based Venn diagram was more effective than the traditional text-only computer-based Venn diagram in increasing student learning, students were randomly assigned to interact with an interactive computer-based Venn diagram using either spoken text or text only. A knowledge test of the Venn diagram was administered after interacting with the Venn diagram.

3. What type of group is the control group in this example: control group, comparison group, or business-as-usual comparison group?

14.3 Manipulation, Variability, and the Independent Variable

An important characteristic of an experiment is that participants are assigned to groups using a random procedure. To use random assignment, defined in Chapter 6, the researcher must manipulate the levels of an independent variable to create two or more groups. In this section, we introduce the types of manipulations used in an experiment, how researchers employ random assignment, and some additional strategies researchers use to control the assignment of participants to groups in an experiment.

Experimental Manipulations

To make an **experimental manipulation,** the researcher must identify an independent variable, then create the groups that constitute the levels of that independent variable. For example, suppose that we study the effects of class size on student learning. In this example, class size is our independent variable only if we manipulate the levels of that variable. As shown in Figure 14.2 for an experiment, we could create two classes and randomly assign participants to one of the two classes. In this case, we created the instruction provided in these classes and controlled the assignment of participants to each class. As shown in Figure 14.2 for the

> An **experimental manipulation** is the identification of an independent variable and the creation of two or more groups that constitute the levels of that variable.

quasi-experiment, however, if we observed students who were already assigned to a class with a small or large class size, then the study would no longer be an experiment because we did not control which students attended each class; someone else controlled to which class they were assigned.

Random Assignment and Control

An experimental manipulation allows researchers to create groups to which participants can be randomly assigned. Random assignment, defined in Chapter 6, is a procedure used to ensure that each participant has the same likelihood of being selected to a given group. One way to do this would be to refer to Appendix B.1 and follow the directions given for using random assignment.

Figure 14.2 Identifying an Experimental Manipulation

This is a *quasi-experiment* because students were chosen from classes they were already attending. So class size was a preexisting variable or a quasi-independent variable.

Variables:
Independent variable:
Class size (small, large)
Dependent variable:
Learning (exam score)

EXPERIMENT

An equal number of students are randomly assigned to attend one of two classes.

QUASI-EXPERIMENT

Two groups, each with an equal number of students, are chosen from a class to which they are already assigned.

This is an *experimental manipulation* because the researcher creates the small- and large-class-size classes to which participants will be randomly assigned.

For half the students the class size is small.

For half the students the class size is large.

Half the students are attending a class with a small class size.

Half the students are attending a class with a large class size.

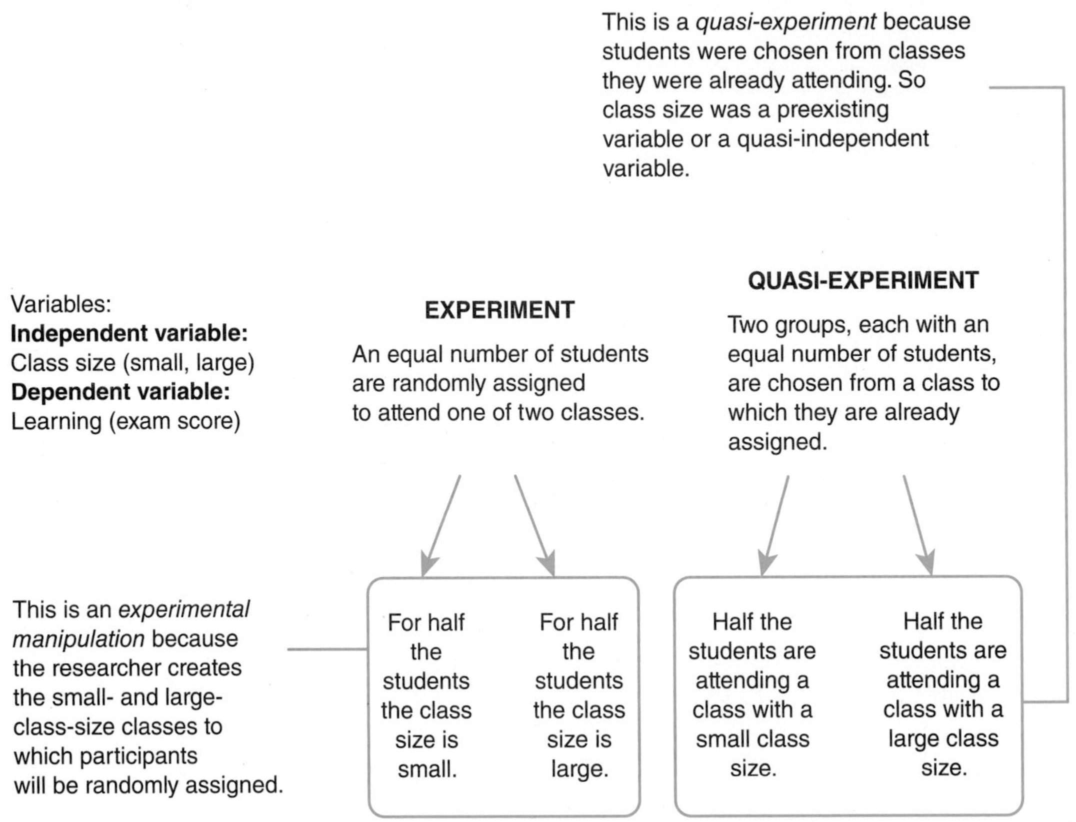

Note: A distinction between manipulating the independent variable (class size) in an experiment and observing preexisting groups of students in classes of different size in a quasi-experiment.

Random assignment allows researchers to assume that the individual differences of participants are about the same between groups.

The primary advantage of random assignment is that it makes the individual differences of participants about the same in each group. Individual differences, defined in Chapter 7, are the unique characteristics of participants that make them unique or different from other participants. Individual differences can include intelligence, marital status, income, education level, self-esteem, mood, age, political views, race, citizenship, genetic predispositions, and gender. If any of these characteristics is not directly controlled by the researcher, then these characteristics, or individual differences, and not the levels of the independent variable, may be causing an effect or a difference between groups.

Random assignment ensures that participants, and therefore the individual differences of participants, are assigned to groups entirely by chance. When we do this, we can assume that the individual differences of participants in each group are about the same (Fisher, 1925, 1935). Hence, if we use random assignment, then we can be confident that any differences observed between groups can be attributed to the different levels of the independent variable that were manipulated by the researcher and not to individual differences between participants.

Restricted Measures of Control

Keep in mind that when we use random assignment, we can *assume* that individual differences are about the same in each group. However, this is not always the case; sometimes researchers do not want to leave it to chance that individual differences are about the same between groups. In these cases, researchers can take steps to control the assignment of participant characteristics to each group by using **restricted random assignment.** Two strategies of restricted random assignment are as follows:

- Control by matching
- Control by holding constant

Researchers can match certain participant characteristics they wish to control in each group by using **control by matching.** Using this strategy, we assess or measure the characteristic we want to control, group or categorize participants based on scores on that measure, and then use a random procedure to assign participants from each category to a group in the study. For example, Berenhaus, Oakhill, and Rusted (2015) studied how sensorimotor activities influenced memory of a story among children aged 7 to 11. To conduct their study, the researchers first matched participants in each group by age and comprehension ability such that these two specific factors were the same in each group; therefore, the researchers established control of both factors. Any group differences in memory of a story, then, could not be attributed to age and comprehension ability because these factors were the same in each group.

To illustrate how to employ control by matching, we can use the example of controlling intelligence. To use control by matching, we first measure intelligence in a sample of children—we can measure intelligence using the Peabody Picture Vocabulary Test (PPVT; Dunn, 1979). We then categorize participants based on their intelligence scores and randomly assign the children in each intelligence category to each group, as described in Figure 14.3. In this way, we restrict random assignment to each category of intelligence.

Researchers can also establish control by limiting the types of participants who are included in a study using **control by holding constant.**

Restricted random assignment is a method of controlling differences in participant characteristics between groups in a study by first restricting a sample based on known participant characteristics, then using a random procedure to assign participants to each group. Two strategies of restricted random assignment are control by matching and control by holding constant.

Control by matching is a type of restricted random assignment in which we assess or measure the characteristic we want to control, group, or categorize participants based on scores on that measure and then use a random procedure to assign participants from each category to a group in the study.

Control by holding constant is a type of restricted random assignment in which we limit which participants are included in a sample based on characteristics they exhibit that may otherwise differ between groups in a study.

Figure 14.3 The Procedures for Using Control by Matching

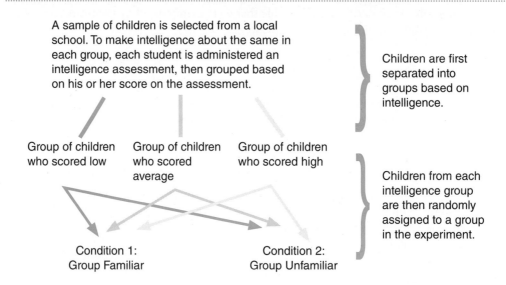

A sample of children is selected from a local school. To make intelligence about the same in each group, each student is administered an intelligence assessment, then grouped based on his or her score on the assessment.

Children are first separated into groups based on intelligence.

Group of children who scored low

Group of children who scored average

Group of children who scored high

Children from each intelligence group are then randomly assigned to a group in the experiment.

Condition 1: Group Familiar

Condition 2: Group Unfamiliar

Note: Children in this example are grouped by intelligence; then children in each intelligence group are randomly assigned to a group in the experiment.

Using this strategy, we exclude participants who exhibit characteristics that may otherwise differ between groups in a study. For example, Ahlgrim-Delzell et al. (2016) studied how an app-based phonics curriculum with systematic instruction influenced word-reading ability of students with developmental disability. Because using an app requires a physical skill and learning phonics requires foundational literacy skills, the sample was restricted to only those participants who had the physical capacity to touch responses on an iPad and had acquired the foundational literacy skills needed to be ready to learn phonics—hence, physical capacity and literacy skills were held constant between groups. In this example, the researchers also could have controlled other characteristics by holding them constant such as school attendance, level of disability, or type of disability and then randomly assign participants to the different groups. In this way, we hold constant (or make the same) certain participant characteristics between groups.

Variability and the Independent Variable

From a methodological view, the manipulation of the levels of an independent variable and the random assignment of participants to each level or group is the way we control for the possibility that individual differences differ between groups. As an added measure of control, we can also measure individual differences numerically in terms of error variance. We can measure the

Error variance or **error** is a numeric measure of the variability in scores that can be attributed to or is caused by the individual differences of participants in each group.

variance or differences between groups and then measure how much of that variance or difference between groups can be attributed to individual differences due to *error* or random variation.

Random variation is measured by determining the extent to which scores in each group overlap. The more that scores in each group overlap, the larger the error variance; the less that scores overlap between groups, the smaller the error variance. To illustrate error variance, Figure 14.4 shows data for two hypothetical experiments in which there is a 3-point treatment effect between two groups in both experiments; that is, the mean difference between the two groups is 3.0. When scores do not overlap, shown in Figure 14.4a, all scores for the group receiving Treatment A are smaller than scores for the group receiving Treatment B. This result indicates that the manipulation or the different levels of the independent variable likely caused the 3-point treatment effect because individuals at each level, or in each group, are behaving differently.

When scores do overlap, shown in Figure 14.4b, individual differences become a likely explanation for an observed difference between two or more groups in an experiment. Although the same 3-point treatment effect was observed in Figure 14.4b, some participants receiving Treatment B behaved as if they received Treatment A; that is, their scores overlap

Two types of restricted random assignment are control by matching and control by holding constant.

Figure 14.4 A Hypothetical Example of Two Experiments in Which There Is No Overlap (a) in One Experiment and There Is Overlap (b) in Scores Between Groups in the Second Experiment

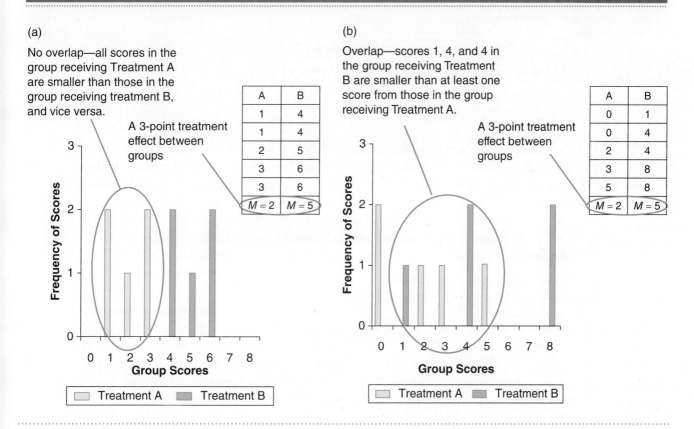

(a)

No overlap—all scores in the group receiving Treatment A are smaller than those in the group receiving treatment B, and vice versa.

A 3-point treatment effect between groups

A	B
1	4
1	4
2	5
3	6
3	6
M = 2	M = 5

(b)

Overlap—scores 1, 4, and 4 in the group receiving Treatment B are smaller than at least one score from those in the group receiving Treatment A.

A 3-point treatment effect between groups

A	B
0	1
0	4
2	4
3	8
5	8
M = 2	M = 5

Groups are different. Notice that no persons in Treatment B are behaving as if they are in Treatment A—no scores from Treatment B fall within the shaded region or range of scores for Treatment A. Hence, there is no overlap, and the data can be clearly divided by group.

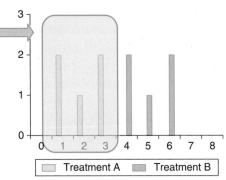

People are different. Notice that three persons in Treatment B are behaving as if they are in Treatment A—three scores from Treatment B fall within the shaded region or range of scores for Treatment A. Hence, people are different because there is a lot of overlap and the data cannot be clearly divided by group.

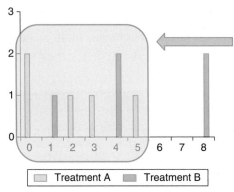

The data given here are the same as those given in Figure 10.4.

with the scores of those receiving Treatment A. When scores overlap with those for other groups, it indicates that individual differences may be causing the 3-point treatment effect between groups. Hence, the manipulation that created the two groups is not likely causing the differences between groups when participants responding substantially overlap from one group to the next.

To measure error variance and differences between groups, we identify a test statistic that is used to make a decision regarding whether an effect observed in a sample is also likely to be observed in a population from which the sample was selected. For this reason, you will find that the categorization of experiments, beginning in Section 14.7, is based upon the type of test statistic used for that experimental situation. Table 14.1 shows each between-subjects experimental design and the parametric test statistic used with each design, to be introduced in this chapter.

A test statistic is a mathematical formula that allows researchers to determine the extent to which differences observed between groups can be attributed to the manipulation used to create the different groups.

Table 14.1 The Type of Between-Subjects Experimental Design and the Corresponding Test Statistic Used With That Design

Experimental Research Design (between subjects)	Test Statistic
Two independent samples	Two-independent-sample t test
Multiple independent samples	One-way between-subjects analysis of variance

The smaller the error variance, the more likely we are to conclude that a manipulation of an independent variable caused an observed difference between two or more groups.

14.4 Ethics in Focus: The Accountability of Manipulation

Because the researcher creates or manipulates the levels of an independent variable in an experiment, he or she bears greater responsibility for how participants are treated in each group. For example, in the study by Ahlgrim-Delzell et al. (2016) on the effectiveness of the iPad phonics curriculum for students with development disability, only one group of students received the phonics instruction. The placebo control group received nonphonics-based literacy instruction to interact with books using the iPad. This comparison treatment was created not only to control for instructional time and use of the iPad but also served as an ethical responsibility to provide the comparison group with an alternate, yet evidence-based literacy instruction. Once the study was completed, the teachers were allowed to keep the iPads and curriculum materials to use with all of the students. A true control group that receives no treatment is rarely possible in an educational context where the treatment is an educational intervention. Therefore, educational researchers often use business-as-usual, placebo control, or some other comparison group. In this way, all participants have an opportunity to benefit from instruction, albeit different from the instruction under investigation.

LEARNING CHECK 2 ✓

1. True or false: When we use random assignment, we can assume that the individual differences of participants are about the same in each group.

2. A researcher studying the effects of media on self-esteem limits his sample to high school females. Is the researcher using control by matching or control by holding constant in this example?

3. When the manipulation of the levels of an independent variable is likely to be causing an effect, should we expect to observe small or large error variance?

Answers: 1. True; 2. Control by holding constant; 3. Small error variance.

14.5 Comparing Two or More Independent Samples

To conduct the between-subjects design, participants are selected in a certain way, and a particular test statistic for two groups is used. The goal in experimentation is to minimize the possibility that individual differences, or something other than a manipulation, caused differences between groups. Methodologically, we ensure that participants are selected in such a way that random assignment can be used, which will make individual differences about the same in each group. Statistically, we add another level of control by using a test statistic to determine the likelihood that something other than the manipulation caused differences in a dependent measure between groups. Each level of control is described in Table 14.2.

Note that the test statistics introduced in this chapter can also be used in quasi-experiments. However, because the quasi-experiment does not methodologically control for individual differences (i.e., random assignment is not used in a quasi-experiment because the levels of the factor already exist), the design cannot demonstrate cause and effect. Both levels of control (methodological and statistical) are present in the between-subjects experimental design. Therefore, the between-subjects experimental design can demonstrate cause and effect. How participants are selected to two groups and how the test statistic is used to analyze measured data are introduced in this section.

Selecting Two Independent Samples

Using the between-subjects design, different participants are observed in each group. When participants are observed in this way, the sample is called an independent sample. Figure 14.5 shows two ways to select two independent samples, and each way is described in this section.

> In an independent sample, different participants are independently observed one time in each group.

The first way, shown in Figure 14.5a, is to select a sample from two populations. This type of sampling is commonly used to conduct quasi-experiments for situations in which the levels of a factor are preexisting. For example, suppose we hypothesize that high school students who have a part-time job will use their study time more efficiently. We record the time spent studying and how they used their study time in a sample of students who, prior to the study, had a part-time job or did not have a

Table 14.2 Two Levels of Control in Experimentation

Between-Subjects Experimental Design		Checklist	
Level of Control	How?	Quasi-Experiment	Experiment
Methodological	Use random assignment		√
Statistical	Compute test statistic	√	√

Note: Only when both levels of control are established can we demonstrate cause and effect.

part-time job. Referring to Figure 14.5a, Population 1 consists of students who had a part-time job; Population 2 consists of students who did not have a part-time job. Each sample is selected from a different population, so each sample constitutes a different group.

The second way to select independent samples, shown in Figure 14.5b, is to select one sample from the same population and randomly assign participants in the sample to two groups. This type of sampling is commonly used in experiments that include randomization, manipulation, and a comparison/control group. The only way to achieve an experiment is to randomly assign participants selected from a single population to different groups. For example, suppose we hypothesize that paying high school students for earning higher grades will improve their performance on an exam. To test this, we could select a group of high school students and have them study a word list and test their recall. In one group, participants are paid for better scores, and in a second group, participants are not paid. Referring to Figure 14.5b, the population would be high school students, from which each sample was selected and randomly assigned to be paid (Group 1) or not paid (Group 2) for earning grades.

To select participants for an experiment, it is most appropriate to sample from one population and then randomly assign participants to different groups.

The Use of the Test Statistic

Once participants have been assigned to groups, we conduct the experiment and measure the same dependent variable in each group. For example, suppose we test the hypothesis that personalizing instruction can affect learning outcomes. To test this hypothesis, we can select a sample of participants from a single population and randomly assign them to one of two groups. In Group Personalization, participants receive algebra story problems using their interest such as music, sports, and movies; in Group No Personalization, different participants receive algebra story problems that are not created using their personal interests. Personalization versus no personalization is the manipulation. After the manipulation, participants in both groups are given 15 minutes to solve as many story problems as they can. If the hypothesis is correct, then Group Personalization should complete more story problems than Group No Personalization. The number of completed story problems, then, is the dependent variable measured in both groups.

To compare differences between groups, we compute a *test statistic*, which is a mathematical formula that allows us to determine whether the manipulation (personalization vs. no personalization) or error variance (other factors attributed to individual differences) is likely to explain differences between the groups. In most cases, researchers measure data on an interval or a ratio scale of measurement. In our example, the number of story problems completed is a ratio scale measure. In these situations, when data are interval or ratio scale, the appropriate test statistic for comparing differences between two independent samples is the two-independent-sample *t* test. This test statistic follows a common form:

A two-independent-sample *t* test, also called an independent-sample *t* test, is a statistical procedure used to test hypotheses concerning the difference in interval or ratio scale data between two group means, in which the variance in the population is unknown.

$$t = \frac{\text{Mean differences between groups}}{\text{Mean differences attributed to error}}.$$

Figure 14.6 Two Methods of Selecting Two Independent Samples

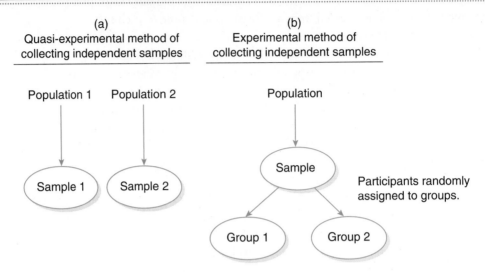

(a)
Quasi-experimental method of
collecting independent samples

(b)
Experimental method of
collecting independent samples

Population 1   Population 2

Population

Sample 1   Sample 2

Sample

Participants randomly
assigned to groups.

Group 1   Group 2

Note: Selecting participants from a single population is appropriate for experiments because participants can then be randomly assigned to different groups.

The numerator of the test statistic is the actual difference between the two groups. For example, suppose that participants in Group Music came up with five practical uses for a paper clip on average, and Group No Music came up with two practical uses on average. The mean difference, then, between the two groups is 3 (5 − 2 = 3). We divide the mean difference between two groups by the value for error variance in the denominator. The smaller the error variance, the larger the value of the test statistic will be. In this way, the smaller the error variance or the less overlap in scores between groups, the more likely we are to conclude that the manipulation, and not factors attributed to individual differences, is causing differences between groups.

> The two-independent-sample *t* test is used to compare differences in interval and ratio data between two groups in an experiment.

Selecting Multiple Independent Samples

Using the between-subjects design, we can also observe more than two groups. How different participants can be selected to more than two groups and how to use the test statistic to analyze measured data are introduced in this section.

Researchers use similar sampling methods to select different participants to two groups and to multiple groups. The two ways to select different participants to multiple groups are described in Figure 14.6. The first way, shown in Figure 14.6a, is to select a sample from two or more populations. For example, suppose we hypothesize that leadership style of a school principal affects teacher retention. To test this hypothesis, select school principals who we observe to be transformational, transactional, and laissez-faire. Referring to Figure 14.6a, Population 1 consists of principals who are transformational; Population 2 consists of principals who are transactional; Population *k* consists of principals who are laissez-faire. Each sample is selected from a different population, so each sample constitutes a different group. We would then look at teacher retention in each of the three leadership styles. Because participants determine the group to which they are assigned, this sampling method is commonly used for quasi-experiments.

The second way to select independent samples, shown in Figure 14.6b, is to select one sample from the same population and randomly assign participants in the sample to two or more groups. Using this sampling method, we could select a random sample of teachers and then randomly assign them to transformational, transactional, or laissez-faire manner principals. Referring to Figure 14.6b, the population would be teachers in a school system, from which one sample was selected and randomly assigned to transformative (Group 1), transactional (Group 2), or laissez-faire (Group *k*) principals. Then compare teacher retention rates. This sampling method is commonly used for experiments because it makes the random assignment of participants to groups possible.

> To select participants for an experiment, it is most appropriate to sample from one population and then randomly assign participants to different groups.

The Use of the Test Statistic

Once participants have been assigned to groups, we conduct the experiment and measure the same dependent variable in each group. For example, suppose we want to test the hypothesis that principals with a laissez-faire leadership style will retain fewer teachers from year to year, compared to a transformational or transactional leader. To test this hypothesis, we could create the three leadership groups (transformational, transactional, laissez-faire) and randomly assign teachers to each group.

Figure 14.7 An Example for How Adding Groups Can Be More Informative

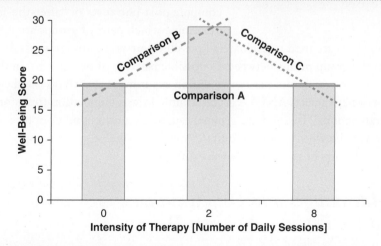

The results for three groups, in which any one comparison of two groups could have led to a conclusion that there is no effect (Comparison A: between 0 and 8), a positive effect (Comparison B: between 0 and 2), or a negative effect (Comparison C: between 2 and 8) of increasing the intensity of the therapy. Only when we observe all three groups do we see a full pattern of the results emerge.

The one-way between-subjects ANOVA is a statistical procedure used to test hypotheses for one factor with two or more levels concerning the variance among group means. This test is used when different participants are observed at each level of a factor and the variance in a given population is unknown.

To compare differences between groups, we will compute a *test statistic*, which allows us to determine if the manipulation (transformational, transactional, laissez-faire) or error variance (other factors attributed to individual differences) is likely to explain differences between the groups. In most cases, researchers measure data on an interval or a ratio scale of measurement. In our example, the number of teachers retained is a ratio scale measure. In these situations, when data are interval or ratio scale, the appropriate test statistic for comparing differences among two or more independent samples is the one-way between-subjects analysis of variance (ANOVA). The term *one-way* indicates the number of factors in a design. In this example, we have one factor or independent variable (type of leadership style).

An ANOVA is computed by dividing the variability in a dependent measure attributed to the manipulation or groups by the variability attributed to error or individual differences. When the variance attributed to error is the same as the variance attributed to differences between groups, the value of F is 1.0, and we conclude that the manipulation did not cause differences between groups. The larger the variance between groups relative to the variance attributed to error, the larger the value of the test statistic and the more likely we are to conclude that the manipulation, and not individual differences, is causing an effect or a mean difference between groups.

A post hoc test is a statistical procedure computed following a significant ANOVA to determine which pair or pairs of group means significantly differ. These tests are needed with more than two groups because multiple comparisons must be made.

A pairwise comparison is a statistical comparison for the difference between two group means. A post hoc test evaluates all possible pairwise comparisons for an ANOVA with any number of groups.

The one-way between-subjects ANOVA informs us only that the means for at least one pair of groups are different—it does not tell us which pairs of groups differ. For situations in which we have more than two groups in an experiment, we compute post hoc tests or "after-the-fact" tests to determine which pairs of groups are different. Post hoc tests are used to evaluate all possible pairwise comparisons, or differences in the group means between all possible pairings of two groups. In the leadership style and teacher retention experiment, we would use the one-way between-subjects ANOVA to determine if the manipulation (transformational, transactional, laissez-faire groups) caused the mean number of teacher retention to vary between groups. We then would compute post hoc tests to determine which pairs of group means were different.

Advantages and Disadvantages of the Between-Subjects Design

The key advantage of using a between-subjects design is that it is the only design that can meet all three requirements of an experiment (randomization, manipulation, and the inclusion of a comparison/control group)

The smaller the error variance, the more likely we are to conclude that a difference between two groups was caused by a manipulation and not individual differences in an experiment.

to demonstrate cause and effect. In a between-subjects design, we use random assignment to assign different participants to one and only one group. In this way, we can use random assignment, which would otherwise not be possible if the same participants were observed in each group. A second advantage is that the between-subjects design places less of a burden on the participant and the researcher. Observing participants on only one occasion eliminates the problem of attrition or dropout rates and can ease the burden on researchers because they do not have to track each participant beyond that one observation.

The key disadvantage, however, is that the sample size required to conduct a between-subjects design can be large, particularly with many groups. For example, if we observed 30 participants in each group, then we would need 60 participants in a two-group design ($30 \times 2 = 60$), 90 participants in a three-group design ($30 \times 3 = 90$), and 120 participants in a four-group design ($30 \times 4 = 120$). It can be difficult to recruit the large number of participants needed to conduct a between-subjects design, particularly in small research settings with limited participant pools (such as students with developmental disability, speech/language or vision and hearing impairments) and funding. In this way, a between-subjects design can sometimes be too impractical, so a researcher will use an alternative design that requires the selection of fewer participants—this alternative research design is described in the next section.

A one-way between-subjects ANOVA determines if two or more group means significantly differ; post hoc tests determine which pairs of group means significantly differ.

A between-subjects design allows for participants to be randomly assigned to one group but can require large sample sizes, particularly with many groups.

LEARNING CHECK 3 ✓

1. State whether each of the following between-subjects designs is an example of a quasi-experiment or an experiment:

   A. A researcher compares differences in resilience among students in urban, rural, and suburban school systems.

   B. A researcher measures job satisfaction among teachers randomly assigned to receive a small, moderate, or large bonus during the summer.

2. What test statistic is used to compare differences in interval or ratio data between two or more groups to which different participants were assigned?

3. Why do researchers compute post hoc tests?

4. Name three types of measurements for a dependent variable.

5. What is the key advantage and disadvantage of using a between-subjects design?

Answers: 1. A. quasi-experimental; B. experimental; 2. The one-way between-subjects ANOVA; 3. To determine which pairs of group means significantly differ following a significant ANOVA; 4. Self-report measures, behavioral measures, and physiological measures; 5. The key advantage is that participants are observed only once, which allows for the use of random assignment. The key disadvantage is that the sample size required to conduct a between-subjects design can be large, particularly with many groups.

14.6 Conducting Experiments: Within-Subjects Design

A **within-subjects design,** also called a **repeated measures design,** is a research design in which the same participants are observed one time in each group of a research study.

A **within-subjects experimental design** is an experimental research design in which the levels of a within-subjects factor are manipulated, and then the same participants are observed in each group or at each level of the factor. To qualify as an experiment, the researcher must (1) manipulate the levels of the factor and include a comparison/control group and (2) make added efforts to control for order and time-related factors.

A **within-subjects factor** is a type of factor in which the same participants are observed in each group or at each level of the factor.

For a between-subjects design, a different set of participants is observed in each group. However, it is not always possible or practical to conduct such a study. In this chapter, we introduce an alternative research design called the **within-subjects design,** which is a research design in which the same participants are observed in each group. Specifically, we will introduce the **within-subjects experimental design** in which we manipulate the levels of a **within-subjects factor,** then observe the same participants in each group or at each level of the factor. The steps for conducting a within-subjects experimental design are described in Figure 14.8.

Two common reasons that researchers observe the same participants in each group are as follows:

1. To manage sample size. When many groups are observed or when many participants are observed in each group, it is often more practical to observe the same participants in each group. For example, if we observe 30 participants in three groups, then a between-subjects design would require 90 participants ($30 \times 3 = 90$), whereas a within-subjects design would require only 30 participants observed three times.

2. To observe changes in behavior over time. This is often the case for studies on learning or within-participant changes over time. As an example, if a researcher was interested in studying student engagement as the result of teacher-directed opportunities to respond, the researcher would need to measure student engagement over time to get an accurate picture of student engagement before and after the teacher implemented the teacher-directed opportunities to respond to the intervention.

> In a within-subjects design, the same participants are observed in each group.

The within-subjects experimental design, described in Figure 14.8, does not meet the randomization requirement for demonstrating cause and effect. We do manipulate the levels of an independent variable and include at least two conditions (at least one of which is a comparison or control condition such as with and without the teacher-directed opportunities to respond) in Steps 2 and 3. However, because the same participants are observed in each condition, we cannot use random assignment; we therefore do not use randomization, which is a requirement in an experiment. Step 4 is therefore included as an added measure to control for possible order and time-related factors associated with observing the same participants over time.

14.7 Controlling Time-Related Factors

Step 4 in Figure 14.8, the step where we control for order and time-related factors, is required for a within-subjects design to qualify as an experiment. The reason Step 4 is required is that when we observe the same participants over time, factors related to observing participants over time can also vary between conditions. This is not a problem in a between-subjects design because different participants are observed one time in a group and not over time. When time-related factors covary with the levels of an independent variable (i.e., the manipulation), these factors can then threaten the internal validity of an experiment.

Time-related factors include those introduced in Chapter 7, such as maturation, testing effects, regression toward the mean, attrition, and **participant fatigue,** which occurs when a participant becomes tired of participating further in an experiment. These time-related factors must be controlled or made the same between groups, such

> **Participant fatigue** is a state of physical or psychological exhaustion resulting from intense research demands typically due to observing participants too often or requiring participants to engage in research activities that are too demanding.

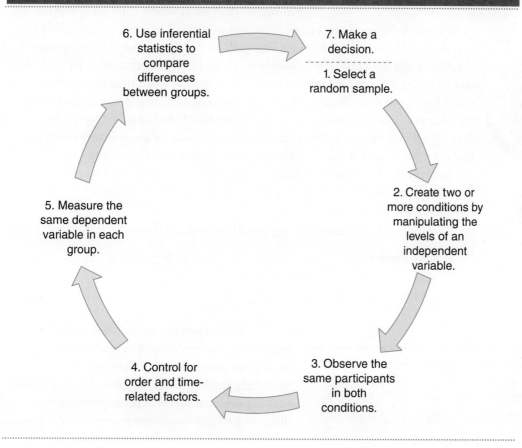

Figure 14.8   The Steps Used for a Within-Subjects Experimental Design

6. Use inferential statistics to compare differences between groups.

7. Make a decision.

1. Select a random sample.

2. Create two or more conditions by manipulating the levels of an independent variable.

3. Observe the same participants in both conditions.

4. Control for order and time-related factors.

5. Measure the same dependent variable in each group.

that only the levels of the independent variable are different between groups. Again, the goal here is to conclude that the manipulation is causing differences between groups. Therefore, we need to control for factors that may covary with the manipulation—that is, factors related to observing the same participants over time.

To control for time-related factors, researchers make efforts to control for order effects. Order effects occur when the order in which a participant receives different treatments or participates in different groups in the study causes the value of a dependent variable to change. Order effects are observed throughout the literature. For example, consideration must be made for the order of questions and the response options in a survey, which can influence participant responses to items in that survey (Garbarski, Schaeffer, & Dykema, 2015; Rasinski, Lee, & Krishnamurty, 2012); the order in which different hypothetical situations, such as educational scenarios, are presented can influence the judgments made about the scenario (Bublitz, Philipich, & Blatz, 2015); and, when presented with two different interventions, our response to the intervention can be influenced by the order in which the interventions are presented (Varghese & Nilsen, 2013).

Order effects are a threat to internal validity in which the order in which participants receive different treatments or participate in different groups causes changes in a dependent variable.

Carryover effects are a threat to internal validity in which participation in one group "carries over" or causes changes in performance in a second group.

To illustrate further, suppose a researcher measures the rate at which children complete each of two behavioral tasks to increase engagement. The goal is to conclude that the two behavioral tasks cause changes in a dependent variable. However, children could use knowledge about one task to help them complete the second task (testing or carryover effect); if the tasks were difficult, then the children could have been more fatigued for the second task (fatigue); if there was a lot of time between the two tasks, then the children could have matured by the time they completed the second task (maturation). Any one of these factors could also explain differences between groups unless we control for time-related factors to eliminate these threats to the internal validity of an experiment. To control for these threats to internal validity, researchers can use two strategies:

Two strategies to control for order effects are to control order and control timing.

1. Control order (counterbalancing, partial counterbalancing)

2. Control timing

Controlling Order: Counterbalancing

Researchers can control the order in which participants receive different treatments or participate in different groups using a procedure called counterbalancing. Using this procedure, we balance or offset the order in which participants receive different treatments or participate in different groups.

Counterbalancing is a procedure in which all possible order sequences in which participants receive different treatments or participate in different groups are balanced or offset in an experiment.

Counterbalancing is used to balance or offset the different orders in which participants could receive different treatments or participate in different groups. This type of counterbalancing is used when the number of treatments or different groups is small—usually two groups but not more than three. As an example, Reid, Barody, and Purpura (2015) used complete counterbalancing with two groups (conventional number line task, modified number line task). One group was asked to complete a traditional number line task by drawing a line to indicate the place of the numbers 1 to 9 on a number line with 0 and 10 provided first, then asked to complete a modified number line task by drawing a line where a bunny will land after 2 to 9 jumps on a number line, where 1 and 10 are provided with a picture of a bunny at 0 and a carrot at 10; that order was reversed for a second group. In this way, the researchers could control for the possibility that the order of group assignment somehow influenced responses in each group.

To calculate the number of possible orders, make the following calculation in which k is the number of treatments or groups:

Number of possible order sequences = $k!$

As k increases, so do the number of possible order sequences. There are 2 possible order sequences when $k = 2$ ($2 \times 1 = 2$), 6 possible order sequences when $k = 3$ ($3 \times 2 \times 1 = 6$), and 24 possible order sequences when $k = 4$ ($4 \times 3 \times 2 \times 1 = 24$). With only 2 or 6 order sequences, researchers could counterbalance every possible order. However, counterbalancing 24 order sequences would be difficult. For example, Figure 14.8 shows how counterbalancing would be used with two groups. Notice that counterbalancing, shown in Figure 14.8b, offsets or balances the possible order sequences in each group. By comparison, counterbalancing 24 possible order sequences would be very difficult. With a larger number of groups, then, researchers use a different type of counterbalancing: partial counterbalancing.

With four treatments (A, B, C, and D), we can ensure that a limited number of order sequences are representative of all order sequences, as shown in Figure 14.9. Of the 4 (out of 24 possible) order sequences chosen in Figure 14.9, each treatment occurs one time in each column or position, and each treatment precedes and follows each treatment one time (e.g., AB in row 1, BA in row 3). To use partial counterbalancing, order sequences can be chosen systematically or at random, but the two criteria for selecting representative order sequences must be met. As a special case of partial

Using a counterbalancing procedure, the order in which participants receive different treatments or participate in different groups is balanced or offset in an experiment. Two types of counterbalancing are complete and partial counterbalancing.

Complete counterbalancing is a procedure in which all possible order sequences in which participants receive different treatments or participate in different groups are balanced or offset in an experiment.

Partial counterbalancing is a procedure in which some, but not all, possible order sequences in which participants receive different treatments or participate in different groups are balanced or offset in an experiment.

A Latin square is a matrix design in which a limited number of order sequences are constructed such that (1) the number of order sequences equals the number of treatments, (2) each treatment appears equally often in each position, and (3) each treatment precedes and follows each treatment one time.

Counterbalancing does not eliminate order effects; rather, it balances these effects, such that they are equal or the same in each treatment or group.

Figure 14.9 Counterbalancing With Two Groups or Treatments

(a)
**WITHOUT
COUNTERBALANCING**

PARTICIPANT	TREATMENT	
	A	B
A	1 ⟶	2
B	1 ⟶	2
C	1 ⟶	2
D	1 ⟶	2
E	1 ⟶	2
F	1 ⟶	2
G	1 ⟶	2
H	1 ⟶	2

Notice that all participants experienced Treatment A first, then B. In this case, the order of presenting treatments (order effects) varies with the levels of the independent variable.

(b)
**WITH
COUNTERBALANCING**

PARTICIPANT	TREATMENT	
	A	B
A	1 ⟶	2
B	2 ⟵	1
C	1 ⟶	2
D	2 ⟵	1
E	1 ⟶	2
F	2 ⟵	1
G	1 ⟶	2
H	2 ⟵	1

Notice that half the participants in each group experienced Treatment A first, then B; and half experienced Treatment B first, then A. Counterbalancing, then, makes order effects the same in each treatment.

Note: The numbers and arrows in the figures indicate which treatment participants experienced first and which they experienced second.

counterbalancing, we can use a procedure called a Latin square to select representative order sequences. This procedure is widely used in the behavioral sciences (for a critical review, see Reese, 1997) and was the procedure used to select the four representative order sequences shown in Figure 14.9 (right side). The steps to construct a Latin square are given in Appendix B.2.

Controlling Timing: Intervals and Duration

Another way to control for threats to internal validity associated with observing the same participants over time is to control timing. Researchers can control timing by controlling the following:

- Interval between treatments or groups

- Total duration of an experiment

Figure 14.10 An Unbiased Subset or Selection of 4 Order Sequences From 24 Possible Sequences for Treatments A, B, C, and D

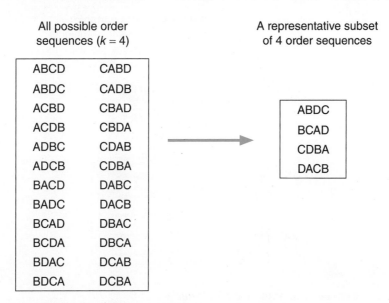

All possible order sequences (k = 4)

ABCD	CABD
ABDC	CADB
ACBD	CBAD
ACDB	CBDA
ADBC	CDAB
ADCB	CDBA
BACD	DABC
BADC	DACB
BCAD	DBAC
BCDA	DBCA
BDAC	DCAB
BDCA	DCBA

A representative subset of 4 order sequences

ABDC
BCAD
CDBA
DACB

Note: Notice on the right side that A, B, C, and D occur once in each column or position, and each treatment precedes and follows each treatment one time (e.g., AB in row 1 and BA in row 3).

MAKING SENSE—COUNTERBALANCING AS A BETWEEN-SUBJECTS FACTOR

Using counterbalancing ensures that the number of possible order sequences is the same in each group. For example, with two groups (A and B), half participate first in Group A and then in Group B, and half participate first in Group B and then in Group A, as shown in Figure 14.10. The order of participation is not a threat to internal validity in this case because the same number of participants in each group has each possible order sequence.

In some cases, however, there may be reason to believe that one order sequence is associated with larger changes than the other. For example, in the Reid et al. (2015) study described above, the researchers were concerned about the possibility that first completing a traditional number line task could affect completion of the modified number line task. As illustrated in Figure 14.10, researchers can include *order* as a between-subjects factor and the groups (traditional or modified number line) as a within-subjects factor. In this way, researchers can test whether the order of presenting the number line tasks causes changes in a dependent variable (e.g., improved accuracy using the modified number line task). The experimental design described here is introduced later in this chapter on factorial designs.

Within-subjects variable:
Groups are the within-subjects
variable. The same participants
were observed in each group.

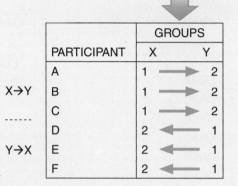

PARTICIPANT	GROUPS	
	X	Y
A	1 →	2
B	1 →	2
C	1 →	2
D	2 ←	1
E	2 ←	1
F	2 ←	1

ORDER

X→Y

Y→X

Between-subjects variable: Order
is the between-subjects variable.
Half the participants (A, B, C)
experienced Group X, then Y, and
half (D, E, F) experienced the reverse
order: Group Y, then X.

Note: Notice that participants can be grouped based on which order sequence they received (the between-subjects variable).

We control the interval between treatments or groups to minimize possible testing and carryover effects. For example, the Reid et al. (2015) study also used time to minimize the carryover effect by waiting 2 to 7 days between sessions to make sure, in part, that performance in one number line task session did not carry over to the next number line task session.

As another way to control timing, we can control the total duration of an experiment to minimize the total demands placed on participants, which, when great, can lead to participant attrition or fatigue. For example, in educational research, studies on attention-sustaining tasks like learning a list of vocabulary words or completing mathematical word problems can control the duration of the experiment by limiting the number of words or word problems used or by controlling the length of the intervention sessions and thereby eliminating the concern of participant attrition or participant fatigue.

For a given experiment, we may require very different ways to control timing. However, as a general rule, increasing the interval between treatments or groups, while also minimizing the total duration of an experiment, is often the most effective strategy for

Two ways to control timing are to control the interval between treatments or groups and to control the total duration of an experiment.

minimizing common threats to internal validity that are associated with observing the same participants over time.

Controlling for order effects by using counterbalancing or controlling timing can minimize the threats to internal validity associated with observing the same participants over time. In addition, as described in this section, a within-subjects design can minimize individual differences between groups and reduce variability in an experiment.

When the same participants are observed in each group, the individual differences of participants are also the same in each group. For example, as shown in Figure 14.11, if we observe five participants in each of two groups, then the individuals who make up those groups are the same. Referring to Figure 14.11, the individual differences that make Eman, Diego, Aiden, Sam, and Grace unique are the same in each group because these same five individuals are observed in both groups. Hence, when we observe the same participants in each group, we can assume that the individual differences of participants are also the same in each group.

Figure 14.12 A Within-Subjects Design With Five Participants

The same five participants are observed in each group. Hence, the individual differences of participants are also the same in each group.

	Groups	
	1	2
	Hannah	Hannah
	Adam	Adam
	Aiden	Aiden
	Sam	Sam
	Grace	Grace

Note: The same five participants (Eman, Diego, Aiden, Sam, and Grace) are observed in each group.

LEARNING CHECK 4 ✓

1. For a within-subjects experimental design, the same participants are observed in each group or at each level of an independent variable. Which requirement of an experiment (manipulation, randomization, or comparison/control) is not met using this design?

2. State two ways that researchers control for order effects.

3. How can researchers ensure that order sequences are representative using partial counterbalancing?

4. State two strategies used to minimize the possible ethical concern of participant fatigue in experiments that use a within-subjects design.

> The within-subjects design minimizes individual differences between groups because the same participants are observed in each group.

Answers: 1. Randomization (random assignment); 2. Researchers control order and control timing; 3. By ensuring that each treatment or group appears equally often in each position, and each treatment or group precedes and follows each treatment or group one time; 4. Minimize the duration needed to complete an experiment, and allow for a reasonable time interval or rest period between treatment presentations.

14.8 Comparing Two or More Related Samples

To conduct the within-subjects design, participants are selected in a certain way, and a particular test statistic for two groups is used. The goal in experimentation is to minimize

Figure 14.13 Between-Groups Variability for a Hypothetical Sample of Four Participants With Data Given

	Treatments	
Participant	Q	Z
A	3	4
B	0	3
C	2	3
D	3	6
	M = 2	M = 4

Between-groups variability.
The variability caused by the manipulation of the levels of the independent variable.

the possibility that individual differences, or something other than a manipulation, caused differences between groups. Methodologically, we control for order and timing to control for time-related factors associated with observing the same participants in each group. Statistically, we add another level of control by using a test statistic to determine the likelihood that something other than the manipulation caused differences in a dependent measure between groups. Each level of control is described in Table 14.3.

Note that the test statistics introduced in this chapter can also be used in quasi-experiments. However, because the quasi-experiment does not methodologically control for individual differences (i.e., a quasi-experiment lacks a manipulation or control for order effects and timing), the design cannot demonstrate cause and effect. Both levels of control (methodological and statistical) are present in the within-subjects experimental design. Therefore, the within-subjects experimental design can demonstrate cause and effect. Table 14.4 shows each within-subjects experimental design and the test statistic used with each design, to be introduced in this chapter. How participants are selected

Figure 14.14 Two Sources of Error for a Sample of Four Participants With Data Given

Error Variance = Within-Groups Variability + Between-Persons Variability

	Treatments	
Participant	Q	Z
A	3	4
B	0	3
C	2	3
D	3	6
	M = 2	M = 4

	Treatments	
Participant	Q	Z
A	3	4
B	0	3
C	2	3
D	3	6
	M = 2	M = 4

Within-groups variability:
Differences occur within each column for each group, even though all participants in each column experienced the same manipulation.

Between-persons variability:
Differences occur between participants. For example, Person A increased 1 point from Group Q to Group Z, and Person B increased 3 points. These differences, attributed to individual differences, are assumed to be equal to 0 in a within-subjects design.

The sum of within-groups and between-persons variability is the total value of error. In a within-subjects design, however, we assume that the value of the between-persons variability is equal to 0. Hence, the within-groups variability is the only measure of error in a within-subjects design.

Table 14.3 Two Levels of Control in Experimentation

Within-Subjects Experimental Design		Checklist	
Level of Control	How?	Quasi-Experiment	Experiment
Methodological	Control order and timing		√
Statistical	Compute test statistic	√	√

Note: Only when both levels of control are established can we demonstrate cause and effect.

Table 14.4 The Type of Within-Subjects Experimental Design and the Corresponding Test Statistic Used With That Design

Experimental Research Design (Within Subjects)	Test Statistic
Two related samples	Related-samples *t* test
Multiple related samples	One-way within-subjects analysis of variance

to two groups and how the test statistic is used to analyze measured data are introduced in this section.

Selecting Two Related Samples

Using the within-subjects design, the same participants are observed in each group. When participants are observed in this way, the sample is called a related sample. The following are two ways to select two related samples, and each way is described in this section:

- The same participants are observed in each group.

- Participants are matched, experimentally or naturally, based on the common characteristics or traits that they share.

As shown in Figure 14.15, we can select one sample from one population and observe that one sample of participants in each group. This type of sampling, used with a *repeated measures design*, can be used in an experiment only if we manipulate the levels of the independent variable and control for order effects. For example, we can investigate whether music-integrated math instruction improves math achievement among elementary-aged children (by using an experiment). We could select a sample of

> In a related sample, also called a dependent sample, the same or matched participants are observed in each group.

The **matched-samples design** is a within-subjects research design in which participants are matched, experimentally or naturally, based on preexisting characteristics or traits that they share.

In a repeated measures research design, the same participants are observed in each group. This way of selecting samples can be used in an experiment.

elementary-aged children and manipulate whether music is played during math instruction (music, no music). To counterbalance the order in which participants are assigned to groups, we could play music in one session of math instruction and no music in a second session of math instruction for half the children; the other half of children would have the reverse order: no music in the first session, then music in the second session. By doing so, we would satisfy Steps 2 to 4 of the within-subjects experimental design, as described in Figure 14.15.

Another way to select related samples is to match participants based on preexisting characteristics or traits that they share. This type of sampling, called a **matched-samples design,** cannot be used in an experiment because groups are created based on preexisting characteristics of the participants and not on a manipulation made by the researcher. Hence, a matched-samples design is more often used to select samples for quasi-experiments or nonexperiments.

Using the matched-samples design, participants can be matched as naturally occurring pairs or can be matched experimentally based on a common characteristic of interest, as described in Table 14.5. Naturally occurring pairs are matched based on characteristics inherent to each individual. For example, we could match participants by age or grade level, ethnicity, or primary language spoken, then test if these matched pairs differ in their attitudes regarding use of technology in the classroom.

Experimentally matched pairs are matched based on an experimental matching procedure in which a researcher matches participants based on their scores or responses on a dependent measure. For example, a researcher can measure intelligence, personality type, or education level, then match participants based on their responses or scores on those measures. Once participants are matched, researchers can test if these

Figure 14.15 Selecting Participants to Two Groups in a Within-Subjects Design

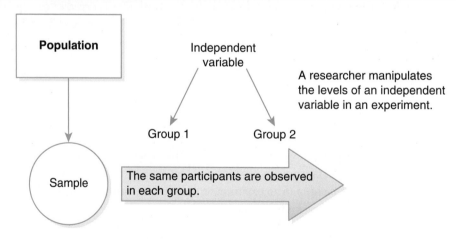

Note: In a within-subjects design, one sample of participants is selected from a population and is observed in each group or at each level of the independent variable.

Table 14.5 Two Types of Matching in a Matched-Samples Design

Type of Matching	Description	Example
Naturally occurring matched pairs	Participants are matched based on preexisting characteristics inherent to each individual.	Researchers match participants on age, ethnicity, and gender. The participants then participate in a study in which the differences in scores for each matched pair of are compared.
Experimentally matched pairs	Participants are matched based on their scores on a dependent measure for some characteristic of interest.	Researchers measure reading comprehension in a sample of children, then match them based on their scores. Participants with the two highest scores are paired, then the next two highest scores are paired, and so on. Children then participate in a study in which the differences in scores for each matched pair are compared.

matched pairs differ in their attitudes regarding use of technology in the classroom, for example. Using a matched-samples design, one member of each pair constitutes a group, and the differences in scores for each matched pair are compared.

> A matched-samples research design uses a quasi-experimental sampling method because participants are matched or assigned to groups based on preexisting characteristics or traits that they share.

The Use of the Test Statistic

Once participants have been selected, we observe the same participants in each group and also measure the same dependent variable in each group. To illustrate the use of a test statistic, suppose we test the hypothesis that personalized reading selections will increase engagement in reading. To test this hypothesis, we select a sample of participants and present them with two types of reading materials (personalized to the interests and not personalized to their interests). The personalized reading material is the manipulation. To be an experiment, we must also counterbalance the order that participants in each group are presented with the reading materials, then record the amount of time (in minutes) that participants read the materials. If the hypothesis is correct, we should expect participants to read longer when provided with reading materials that are personalized for their interests.

To compare differences between the personalized reading materials, we compute a *test statistic*, which is a mathematical formula that allows us to determine whether the manipulation (personalized vs. not personalized) or error variance (other factors attributed to individual differences) is likely to explain differences between the groups. In most cases, researchers measure data on an interval or a ratio scale of measurement. In our example, time spent reading is a ratio scale measure. In these situations, when data are interval or ratio scale, the appropriate test statistic for comparing differences between two related samples is the **related-samples *t* test.**

> A **related-samples *t* test,** also called a **paired-samples *t* test,** is a statistical procedure used to test hypotheses concerning the difference in interval or ratio scale data for two related samples in which the variance in one population is unknown.

The numerator of the test statistic is the actual difference between the two groups. For example, suppose that participants spent 10 minutes reading nonpersonalized material and 60 minutes reading personalized material, on average. The mean difference, then, between the two types of reading materials is 50 minutes (60 − 10 = 50). We divide the mean difference between two groups by the difference attributed to error in the denominator. In the denominator, we make the value of the between-persons error equal to zero by reducing two columns of data (one column for each group) to one column of difference scores—by subtracting across the rows for each participant. As illustrated in Figure 14.16, when we reduce a hypothetical data set to one column of difference scores, the between-persons variability is eliminated; that is, it is equal to zero. The result is that the value of error in the denominator of the test statistic will be smaller, thereby making the value of the test statistic larger than if we did not perform this subtraction procedure.

> A related-samples *t* test reduces the data to one column of difference scores, thereby eliminating the between-persons variation.

Between-persons variability is a source of variance in a dependent measure that is caused by or associated with individual differences or differences in participant responses across all groups.

Selecting Multiple Related Samples

Using the within-subjects design, we can also observe more than two groups. How different participants can be selected to more than two groups and how the test statistic can be used to analyze measured data are introduced in this section.

Only the repeated measures design can be used to observe participants in more than two groups. A matched-samples design cannot be used because it is limited to situations in which participants are paired into two groups. As shown in Figure 14.17 using a repeated measures design, participants are selected from a single population and observed in multiple groups in an experiment.

Figure 14.16 Eliminating Between-Persons Variability by Computing Difference Scores

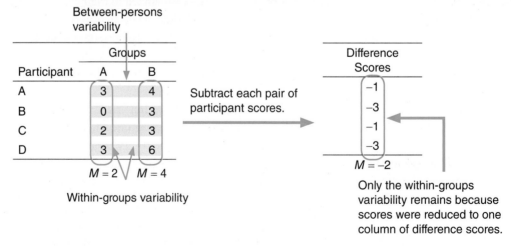

Note: Computing difference scores eliminates variability between persons by reducing the data to a single column of difference scores.

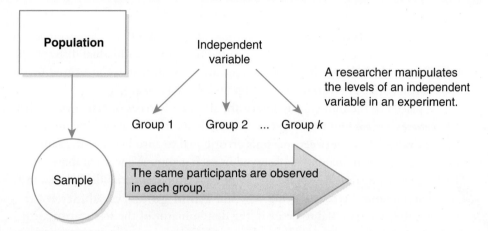

Population

Independent variable

Group 1   Group 2   ...   Group k

A researcher manipulates the levels of an independent variable in an experiment.

Sample

The same participants are observed in each group.

Note: In a within-subjects design, one sample of participants is selected from a population and is observed in each group or at each level of the independent variable.

To illustrate the repeated measures design with more than two groups, suppose we test the hypothesis that White teachers will make judgments of student behavior differently based on the ethnicity of the student (based on a study by Chan, Lam, & Covault, 2009). To test this hypothesis, we ask teachers to read and rate student behaviors in three scenarios to see if what they are told about the ethnicity of the students in the scenarios will affect their ratings of praise or criticism of the behaviors in the scenarios. Teachers read the same scenarios three times but are given different information about the ethnicity of the student in each scenario—they are told that the ethnicity is African American, Hispanic, or White. To be an experiment, we must control for order effects, or the order of presenting the manipulation (whether the ethnicity is described as African American, Hispanic, or White). We hypothesize that ratings of praise will be higher for African American and Hispanic scenarios than White scenarios even though they read the same scenarios each time.

> Only the repeated measures design can be used when the same participants are observed in more than two groups.

The Use of the Test Statistic

To compare differences between groups, we will compute a *test statistic*, which allows us to determine whether the manipulation (describing the wine as inexpensive, moderately expensive, or expensive) or error attributed to individual differences is likely to explain group differences in ratings of liking. In most cases, researchers measure data on an interval or a ratio scale of measurement. In our example, ratings of liking are an interval scale measure. In these situations, when data are interval or ratio scale, the appropriate test statistic for comparing differences among two or more related samples is the **one-way within-subjects analysis of variance (ANOVA).** This test statistic follows a common form:

> The **one-way within-subjects ANOVA** is a statistical procedure used to test hypotheses for one factor with two or more levels concerning the variance among group means. This test is used when the same participants are observed at each level of a factor and the variance in a given population is unknown.

$$F = \frac{\text{Variability between groups}}{\text{Variability attributed to error}}.$$

In the one-way within-subjects ANOVA, we compute the between-persons variability and remove it, thereby leaving only within-groups variability as a measure of error in the denominator of the test statistic.

ANOVA measures the variance of differences between groups divided by the variance of differences attributed to error or individual differences. Figure 14.18 shows the three sources of variation that are measured by the test statistic. The variance of group means, or **between-groups variability,** is placed in the numerator. There are also two sources of error: variability *between persons* and *within groups*. In the denominator, we will again make the value of the between-persons error equal to zero because the same, not different, participants are observed in each group. We will compute the between-persons variability and remove it from the variability placed in the denominator, thereby leaving only the **within-groups variability** as the variability attributed to error in the denominator of the test statistic.

The one-way within-subjects ANOVA informs us only that at least one group is different from another group—it does not tell us which pairs of groups differ. For situations in which we have more than two groups in an experiment, we compute post hoc tests in the same way that we did for the

Figure 14.18 Three Sources of Variability in a Within-Subjects Design With More Than Two Groups

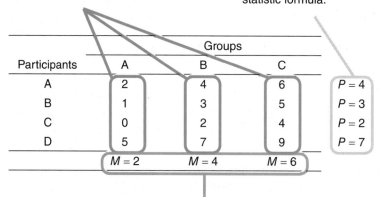

Within-groups variability is the variability of scores within each group. This variability is placed in the denominator of the test statistic formula.

Between-persons variability is calculated by computing the average score of each person (P) in each row. This variability is not included in the test statistic formula.

Between-groups variability is the variance of group means. This variability is placed in the numerator of the test statistic formula.

between subjects earlier in this chapter. Post hoc tests are used to evaluate all possible pairwise comparisons, or differences between all possible pairings of two group means. In the ratings-of-wine experiment, we would use the one-way within-subjects ANOVA to determine if the manipulation (describing the wine as inexpensive, moderately expensive, or expensive) caused mean ratings of liking to vary between groups. We would then use post hoc tests to determine which pairs of group means were different.

> **Between-groups variability** is a source of variance in a dependent measure that is caused by or associated with the manipulation of the levels (or groups) of an independent variable.
>
> **Within-groups variability** is a source of variance in a dependent measure that is caused by or associated with observing different participants within each group.

14.9 Comparing Between-Subjects and Within-Subjects Designs

The between-subjects design is an experimental research design in which we use randomization and manipulation, as well as include a comparison or control group. The within-subjects design is an experimental research design in which we use manipulation and include a comparison or control group, then control for timing and order effects because randomization is not used. The key advantage of using each type of research design is described in this section.

Between-Subjects Design: Randomization

The between-subjects design allows researchers to randomly assign participants to groups or to the levels of an independent variable; the within-subjects design does not. The advantage of using random assignment is that it makes individual differences about the same in each group. Participants are observed one time in one group that they were assigned to entirely by chance. We can then measure a dependent variable in each group and compare differences between groups.

Interestingly, the advantage of using random assignment is that participants are observed one time in one group. Yes, random assignment makes individual differences about the same in each group; however, observing the same participants in each group, using a within-subjects design, means that the individual differences of participants are also the same in each group. The problem when we observe the same participants in each group and do not randomly assign participants to one group is that we must control for effects resulting from the order that participants are observed, which can threaten internal validity; this concern is not a problem using a between-subjects design.

Within-Subjects Design: Economizing and Power

The advantage of using a within-subjects design is that fewer participants are required overall (economizing) because the same participants are observed in each group. This is a particular advantage for studying small populations, such as Olympic athletes or children with autism. These groups can be difficult to sample in large numbers, so observing a smaller sample of the same participants in each group can be more practical. Also, researchers may have limited funding or other limited resources that prevent them from recruiting large samples. In these types of situations, a within-subjects design can be a practical alternative to a between-subjects design to conduct an experiment.

A second advantage of using the within-subjects design is that the test statistic has greater power to detect significant differences between groups using a within-subjects design (Hampton, 1998). Recall from Chapter 8 that *power* is the likelihood that we can detect an effect, if one exists in a population. In other words, using a within-subjects design, if an effect exists in the population, then we are more likely to detect it (i.e., conclude that a manipulation caused two or more groups to be different) than if we ran a between-subjects analysis on the same data. The reason we have greater power is because of how we compute the test statistics for a within-subjects versus a between-subjects design.

1. Which type of design, the between-subjects or the within-subjects design, allows for the random assignment of participants to groups?

2. True or false: The between-subjects design has greater power to detect an effect than the within-subjects design.

3. Which type of design, the between-subjects or the within-subjects design, is associated with a smaller value of error variance, assuming the data are the same?

Answers: 1. Between-subjects design; 2. False. The within-subjects design has greater power; 3. Within-subjects design.

14.10 Conducting Experiments: Factorial Experimental Designs

In between-subjects and within-subjects designs sections of this chapter, the complexity of the experimental research designs has varied in two ways:

1. We changed the levels of one factor. We described tests for differences between two groups and tests for the variance among more than two groups or levels of one factor.

2. We changed how participants were observed. In the between-subjects section, we described research designs in which different participants were observed in each group or at each level of one factor. In the within-subjects section, we described research designs in which the same participants were observed in each group or across the levels of one factor.

For each experimental research design, we manipulated the levels of a single factor. In this section, we will describe research situations in which we manipulate the levels of two factors observed in the same experiment. For example, in the scenarios where teachers rated behaviors of students, we manipulated the ethnicity of the student. Suppose we also manipulated the behavior described in the scenario as positive or negative. Now we have two factors: ethnicity of the student in the scenario and the behavior in the scenario. To make it simpler, let's just look at Hispanic and White students and positive and negative behavior. As shown in Table 14.6, in this case we have one factor (ethnicity) with two levels (Hispanic and White) and a second factor, behavior (positive, negative). By crossing the levels of both factors, we create four unique groups.

The design shown in Table 14.6 is called a **factorial design,** which is used to compare

> A **factorial design** is a research design in which participants are observed across the combination of levels of two or more factors.

A factorial design is a research design in which participants are observed across the combination of levels of two or more factors.

A factorial experimental design is a research design in which groups are created by manipulating the levels of two or more factors, then the same or different participants are observed in each group using experimental procedures of randomization (for a between-subjects factor) and using control for timing and order effects (for a within-subjects factor).

A complete factorial design, or completely crossed design, is a factorial design in which each level of one factor is combined or crossed with each level of the other factor, with participants observed in each cell or combination of levels.

differences between groups created by combining the levels of two or more factors. Specifically, we will introduce the factorial experimental design in which we create groups by manipulating the levels of two or more factors, then observe the same or different participants in each group using experimental procedures of randomization (for a between-subjects factor) and using control for timing and order effects (for a within-subjects factor). In this section, we will only discuss situations in which participants are observed at each level of both factors, which is called a complete factorial design. For the example shown in Table 14.6, this means that we describe situations in which we observe participants in each cell in the table (or in each group).

14.11 Types of Factorial Designs

The factorial design can include between-subjects factors, within-subjects factors, or both. In this section, we will introduce three types of factorial designs for situations in which the levels of two factors are manipulated, using an example to illustrate each type. The three types of factorial designs introduced in this section are the following:

- Between-subjects design (a design in which all factors are between-subjects factors)

- Within-subjects design (a design in which all factors are within-subjects factors)

Table 14.6 A Factorial Research Design With Two Factors (Ethnicity, Behavior)

		Behavior	
		Positive	Negative
Ethnicity	Hispanic	Scenario of Hispanic student displaying positive behavior	Scenario of Hispanic student displaying negative behavior
	White	Scenario of White student displaying positive behavior	Scenario of White student displaying negative behavior

Note: In this example, combining the levels of each factor creates four unique groups, which are described in the cells of the table.

- Mixed factorial design (a design with at least one between-subjects factor and at least one within-subjects factor)

Between-Subjects Factorial Designs

We use a **between-subjects factorial design** when we observe different participants in each group created by combining the levels of at least two factors (i.e., independent variables). Hence, once we select the sample, we assign different participants to each group. To illustrate the between-subjects factorial design, consider an experiment conducted by Al-Dujaily, Kim, and Ryu (2013), which is illustrated in Table 14.7. In this study, researchers recorded learning outcomes as a result of personality type (introvert, extravert) and type of online learning (intelligent learning system that tracked student work and tailored individual feedback, nonintelligent learning system). For the between-subjects factorial design to be an experiment, the researchers must have done each of the following:

> A **between-subjects factorial design** is a research design in which the levels of two or more between-subjects factors are combined to create groups, meaning that different participants are observed in each group.

1. Manipulate the levels of each factor. In this example, the researchers had to manipulate the type of personality and the type of online learning system.

2. Cross the levels of the two factors to create the groups. In this example, we have two factors each with two levels (introvert/extravert and intelligent learning system/not intelligent learning system). If we cross the levels of each factor, then we have $2 \times 2 = 4$ groups.

3. Randomly assign different participants to each group. Then compare group differences in the dependent variable (learning outcomes).

Table 14.7 An Experiment in Which the Type Personality (Introvert, Extravert) and the Type of Online Learning (Intelligent, Not Intelligent) Were Manipulated

		Type Online Learning System		
		Intelligent	Not Intelligent	
Type of Personality	Introvert	Intelligent online learning system and introverts	Not intelligent online learning system and introverts	
	Extravert	Intelligent online learning system and extraverts	Not intelligent online learning system and extraverts	

Source: Data and design are adapted from those reported by Al-Dujaily, Kim, & Ryu (2013).

Note: The cells in the table represent the groups created by combining the levels of each factor. Using the within-subjects factorial design, the same subjects are observed in each cell or group.

Using the between-subjects factorial design, the total number of participants (*N*) is equal to the number of participants in each group (*n*) multiplied by the number of levels for each factor. In this experiment, we had two factors, each with two levels. Suppose that 10 participants were observed in each group (*n*); the total number of participants would be as follows:

$$N = 10 \times 2 \times 2 = 40 \text{ participants.}$$

Within-Subjects Factorial Designs

In a between-subjects factorial design, we combine the levels of two or more between-subjects factors.

We use a within-subjects factorial design when we observe the same participants in each group created by combining the levels of at least two factors (i.e., independent variables). To illustrate a within-subjects factorial design, consider the experiment illustrated in Table 14.8. In this study, researchers measured the number of times students were off-task in each of six environments that varied by the frequency of reinforcement for staying on task (throughout the day, at the end of the day, at the end of the week) and type of reinforcement (social praise such as "Good job!," stickers placed on a display board). For the within-subjects factorial design to be an experiment, the researchers must have done each of the following:

A within-subjects factorial design is a research design in which the levels of two or more within-subjects factors are combined to create groups, meaning that the same participants are observed in each group.

1. Manipulate the levels of each factor. In this example, the researchers manipulated the frequency and type of reinforcement.

2. Cross the levels of the two factors to create the groups. In this example, we have two factors, one with two levels and one with three levels. If we cross the levels of each factor, then we have $2 \times 3 = 6$ groups.

3. Control for order effects due to observing the same subjects in each group or in each environment in this example. Then compare group differences in the dependent variable (activity levels).

In a within-subjects factorial design, we combine the levels of two or more within-subjects factors.

As shown in Table 14.8 using hypothetical data, we see that rewards scattered throughout the day are better to keep students on task and that social praise is slightly better than stickers.

Using the within-subjects factorial design, the total number of participants (*N*) is equal to the number of participants in one of the groups because the same participants are observed in each group. In this experiment, 25 students were observed in each group, so the total number of subjects was 25.

A mixed factorial design is a research design in which different participants are observed at each level of a between-subjects factor and also repeatedly observed across the levels of the within-subjects factor.

Mixed Factorial Designs

We use a mixed factorial design when we create groups by crossing the levels of at least

Table 14.8 A Within-Subjects Factorial Design in Which the Frequency of Reinforcement (throughout the day, at the end of the day, at the end of the week) and Type of Reinforcement (social praise, sticker board) in an Environment Were Manipulated

		Frequency of Reinforcement		
		Throughout Day	Once a Day	Once a Week
Type of Reinforcement	Social praise	3	6	10
	Sticker board	4	8	12

Note: The cells in the table represent the groups created by combining the levels of each factor. Using the between-subjects factorial design, different participants are observed in each cell or group. The numbers in the cells are the hypothetical mean numbers of times per day the students were off task.

one between-subjects factor and one within-subjects factor. To illustrate a mixed factorial design, consider an experiment conducted by Dickens and Meisinger (2016), which is illustrated in Table 14.9. In this study, researchers tested how two factors affected the reading comprehension using a 2 × 2 mixed factorial design, with reading skill (normal, at risk) varied between subjects and reading modality (oral, silent) varied within subjects. For the mixed factorial design to be a true experiment, the researchers must have done each of the following:

1. Manipulate the levels of each factor. In this example, the researchers manipulated how participants read the passage and reading ability.

2. Cross the levels of the two factors to create the groups. In this example, we have two factors each with two levels. If we cross the levels of each factor, then we have 2 × 2 = 4 groups.

3. Randomly assign different participants to each level of the between-subjects factor. In educational research, such as in our example, the between-subjects factor is often not manipulated by random assignment but is a characteristic of the individual such as reading ability. Although the researchers may label their study as mixed factorial, they are violating this assumption regarding mixed factorial designs.

4. Control for order effects due to observing the same participants at each level of the within-subjects factor (reading modality). Then compare group differences in the dependent variable (reading comprehension).

> In a mixed factorial design, we combine the levels of at least one between-subjects factor and one within-subjects factor.

Using the mixed factorial design, the total number of participants (*N*) in an experiment is equal to the number of participants in the within-subjects groups times the number of levels of the between-subjects factor. Suppose that 30 participants were randomly assigned to each level of the between-subjects factor (normal reading ability to at-risk reading ability). In this case, the total number of participants would be as follows:

$$N = 30 \times 2 = 60 \text{ participants each observed two times.}$$

LEARNING CHECK 7 ✓

1. A researcher conducts a 4 × 2 factorial design with 10 participants observed in each group. How many participants are needed to conduct this experiment if he or she conducts each of the following designs?

   A. A between-subjects factorial design

   B. A within-subjects factorial design

   C. A mixed factorial design in which the first variable is a within-subjects factor

   D. A mixed factorial design in which the second variable is a within-subjects factor

2. Which type of factorial design includes the manipulation of a between-subjects factor and a within-subjects factor?

Answers: 1. A. 80 participants, B. 10 participants, C. 20 participants, D. 40 participants; 2. A mixed factorial design.

14.12 Including Quasi-Independent Factors in an Experiment

We have described the factorial design using examples for how the design is used in an experiment. In other words, in each example, both factors were manipulated, such that participants could be randomly assigned to groups, or the same participants could be

Table 14.9 A Mixed Factorial Design

		Reading Ability	
		Normal	At-Risk
Reading Modality	Oral	Group 1	Group 2
	Silent	↓	↓

Source: Design is adapted from that reported by Dickens & Meisinger (2016).

Note: With reading ability (normal, at risk) as the between-subjects factor and the reading modality (oral, silent) as the within-subjects factor. Using a mixed factorial design, the same subjects were observed in each level of the within-subjects factor.

observed in each group and the researcher could then control for order effects (e.g., use counterbalancing). Hence, in each example, we manipulated the levels of two independent variables. Because the manipulation of an independent variable is a requirement for demonstrating cause and effect, each example thus far is one that could be used in an experiment.

The factorial design, however, can also be used when we include preexisting or quasi-independent factors. When all factors in a factorial design are quasi-experimental, the design is not an experiment because no factor is manipulated. For example, if we measure reading comprehension scores among participants with different genders (male, female) and disability status (autism, no disability), then the study is a quasi-experiment because the participants determined their group assignment; both factors were preexisting. We would still use a factorial design to analyze the health scores, but we would not conclude that one or both factors caused changes in the dependent variable (health scores). Instead, we could only conclude that these factors were related to or associated with observed changes because the study conducted is a quasi-experiment.

When at least one factor in a factorial design is manipulated (an independent variable), the design is typically called an experiment, even if a quasi-independent variable is included in the design, such as the reading modality and reading skill study. Often, researchers will include a quasi-independent variable called a **participant variable** in an experiment when it relates to the hypothesis being tested. Participant variables are typically demographic characteristics—that is, characteristics of the participants in a study. Examples of participant variables include intelligence level, age, gender, race, ethnicity, education level, personality type, and body weight.

> A **participant variable** is a quasi-independent or preexisting variable that is related to or characteristic of the personal attributes of a participant.

When a quasi-independent variable is included in a factorial design, we do not show cause and effect for any effect that involves that quasi-independent factor. Instead, we conclude that the levels of a quasi-independent variable are related to or associated with changes in a dependent variable. To illustrate how to interpret the effects of a factorial design with a quasi-independent variable, consider a 2×2 mixed factorial design by Dickens and Meisinger (2016) described above to determine if reading skill and reading modality would influence reading comprehension. The researchers manipulated whether the children read silently or orally (modality). The quasi-independent participant variable was reading skill (normal, at risk). The design of this experiment is illustrated in Table 14.9. The advantage of including the preexisting factor (reading skill) is to test the generality of their findings across the levels of the quasi-independent variable.

> An effect of a quasi-independent variable shows that the factor is related to changes in a dependent variable. It does not demonstrate cause and effect because the factor is preexisting.

14.13 Higher-Order Factorial Designs

In this chapter, we used the two-way factorial design to illustrate how to conduct experiments using this design. However, factorial designs are not limited to testing only two

A **higher-order factorial design** is a research design in which the levels of more than two factors are combined or crossed to create groups.

A **higher-order interaction** is an interaction for the combination of levels of three or more factors in a factorial design.

factors. When a factorial design includes more than two factors, it is called a **higher-order factorial design.**

The "way" of a factorial design indicates the number of factors being combined or crossed to create groups. In the two-way factorial design, we cross two factors to create groups; in a three-way factorial design, we cross three factors. The number of factors we cross to create groups is the number of "ways" of a factorial design. One consequence of adding factors is that the number of possible effects we could observe also increases. For example, in a three-way factorial design, we could observe any combination of three main effects, two two-way interactions, and one three-way interaction. The three-way interaction is called a **higher-order interaction** because it shows that the combination of levels of more than two factors is associated with changes in a dependent variable. To show how the number of possible effects increases as we increase the number of factors in a factorial design, Table 14.10 lists the possible main effects and interactions for a three-way and a four-way factorial design.

Interpreting a higher-order interaction can be challenging, although a three-way interaction can be readily interpreted—to graph such a finding, we would need to plot the data on three axes, however. For example, we may observe a three-way interaction in which participant final exam scores vary by the gender (male, female), ethnicity, and content area (science, mathematics, English language arts) of the person being rated. To plot one data point, we would record, for example, that a male (one axis) who is Hispanic (a second axis) and has science as a content area (a third axis) scored 89 on the final exam. A four-way interaction or higher is very difficult to interpret because the number of axes needed to plot the data makes it difficult to understand exactly what the interaction is showing. For this reason, researchers will often limit the number of factors in a factorial design to two or three, if possible, to avoid the possibility of observing higher-order interactions with four or more factors.

Higher-order factorial designs allow us to observe the effects of three or more factors in the same design.

Table 14.10 The Possible Main Effects and Interactions in Three-Way and Four-Way Factorial Designs

	Three-Way Factorial Design	Four-Way Factorial Design
Main effects	A, B, C	A, B, C, D
Two-way interactions	A × B, B × C, A × C	A × B, B × C, C × D, A × C, A × D, B × D
Three-way interactions	A × B × C	A × B × C, B × C × D, A × B × D, A × C × D
Four-way interactions	—	A × B × C × D

1. How are our conclusions in a factorial design limited when the design includes at least one quasi-independent factor?

2. What is a higher-order interaction?

Answers: 1. When a quasi-independent factor is included in a factorial design, we do not show cause and effect for any effect that includes that quasi-independent factor; 2. A higher-order interaction is an interaction for the combination of levels of three or more factors in a factorial design.

CHAPTER SUMMARY

LO 1 Delineate the between-subjects design and the between-subjects experimental design.

- A between-subjects design is a research design in which different participants are observed one time in each group of a research study.

- A between-subjects experimental design is an experimental research design in which the levels of a between-subjects factor are manipulated, and then different participants are randomly assigned to each group or to each level of that factor and observed one time. We follow six steps to use the between-subjects design in an experiment:
  ○ Select a random sample.
  ○ Create two or more groups by manipulating the levels of an independent variable.
  ○ Use random assignment to select participants to a group.
  ○ Measure the same dependent variable in each group.
  ○ Use inferential statistics to compare differences between groups.
  ○ Make a decision.

LO 2 Distinguish between an experimental group and a control group.

- An experimental group is a condition in an experiment in which participants are treated or exposed to a manipulation, or level of the independent variable, that is believed to cause a change in a dependent variable.

- A control group is a condition in an experiment in which participants are treated the same as participants in a treatment group, except that the manipulation believed to cause a change in the dependent variable is omitted.

LO 3 Explain how random assignment, control by matching, and control by holding constant can make individual differences about the same between groups.

- The random assignment of participants to different groups ensures that participants, and therefore the individual differences of participants, are assigned to groups entirely by chance. When we do this, we can assume that the individual differences of participants in each group are about the same.

- **Restricted random assignment** is a method of controlling differences in participant characteristics between groups in a study by first restricting a sample based on known participant characteristics, then using a random procedure to assign participants to each group. Two strategies of restricted random assignment are the following:
  - In **control by matching,** we assess or measure the characteristic we want to control, group or categorize participants based on scores on that measure, and then use a random procedure to assign participants from each category to a group in the study.
  - In **control by holding constant,** we limit which participants are included in a sample based on characteristics they exhibit that may otherwise differ between groups in a study.

LO 4 Identify the appropriate sampling method and test statistic for independent samples to compare differences between two group means and among two or more groups.

- Using the between-subjects design, we select an **independent sample,** meaning that different participants are observed in each group. To select participants to an independent sample, we can select two groups from different populations (a quasi-experimental method), or we can sample from a single population and then randomly assign participants to two groups (an experimental method).

- The appropriate test statistic for comparing differences between two group means for the between-subjects design is the **two-independent-sample t test.** Using this test statistic establishes statistical control of error or differences attributed to individual differences. The larger the value of the test statistic, the more likely we are to conclude that a manipulation, and not error, caused a mean difference between two groups.

- To select participants to an independent sample with two or more groups, we can select groups from many different populations (a quasi-experimental method), or we can select groups from a single population and then randomly assign participants to two or more groups (an experimental method).

- The appropriate test statistic for comparing differences between two or more groups using the between-subjects design is the **one-way between-subjects ANOVA.** If significant, then at least one pair of group means is different, and we conduct **post hoc tests** to determine which pairs of group means are significantly different. The larger the value of the test statistic, the more likely we are to conclude that the manipulation, and not error, caused a mean difference between two groups. Using this statistical procedure establishes statistical control of error or differences attributed to individual differences.

LO 5 Delineate the within-subjects design and the within-subjects experimental design.

- A within-subjects design is a research design in which the same participants are observed one time in each group of a research study.

- A within-subjects experimental design is an experimental research design in which the levels of a within-subjects factor are manipulated, and then the same participants are observed in each group or at each level of the factor. To qualify as an experiment, the researcher must (1) manipulate the levels of the factor and include a comparison/control group and (2) make added efforts to control for order- and time-related factors.

LO 6 Demonstrate the use of counterbalancing and control for timing using a within-subjects experimental design.

- When we observe the same participants over time, factors related to observing participants over time can also vary between groups. When time-related factors covary with the levels of the independent variable (the manipulation), it can threaten the internal validity of an experiment.

- For the counterbalancing procedure, the order in which participants receive different treatments or participate in different groups is balanced or offset in an experiment. Two types of counterbalancing are as follows:
  - Complete counterbalancing in which all possible order sequences are included in an experiment.
  - Partial counterbalancing in which some, but not all, possible order sequences are included in an experiment. One example of partial counterbalancing is the Latin square.

- We can also control for order effects by controlling timing. We can control the interval between treatments or groups and the total duration of an experiment. As a general rule, increasing the interval between treatments and minimizing the total duration of an experiment is often the most effective strategy to minimize threats to internal validity that are associated with observing the same participants over time.

LO 7 Identify the appropriate sampling method and test statistic for related samples to compare differences between two or more group means.

- Using a within-subjects design, the same participants are observed in each group. When participants are observed in this way, the sample is called a related sample. There are two ways to select related samples for two groups:
  - The repeated measures design in which we select a sample from one population and observe that one sample of participants in each group. This type of sampling can be used in an experiment when researchers control for order effects and manipulate the levels of the independent variable.
  - The matched-samples design in which participants are matched, experimentally or naturally, based on characteristics or traits that they share. This type of sampling

cannot be used in an experiment because groups are created based on preexisting characteristics of the participants and not on a manipulation made by the researcher.

- The appropriate test statistic for comparing differences between two group means using the within-subjects design is the related-samples t test.

- For more than two groups, the repeated measures design is used to observe participants. Using a repeated measures design, participants are selected from a single population and observed in multiple groups in an experiment. The appropriate test statistic for comparing differences between two or more group means using a within-subjects design is the one-way within-subjects ANOVA.

LO 8 Contrast the use of a between-subjects versus a within-subjects design for an experiment.

- A between-subjects design allows for the use of random assignment; a within-subjects design does not. The advantage of using random assignment is that we do not need to control for order effects using a between-subjects design; however, we do need to control for order effects using a within-subjects design.

- An advantage of using a within-subjects design is that fewer participants are required overall (economizing) because the same participants are observed in each group. A second advantage of using the within-subjects design is that the test statistic for this design has greater power to detect an effect between groups.

LO 9 Identify the appropriate sampling method for a factorial design used in an experiment.

- The appropriate sampling method for a factorial design used in an experiment is to select one sample from the same population and then randomly assign the same or different participants to groups created by combining the levels of two or more factors. This type of sampling is used in experiments because we can include randomization, manipulation, and a comparison or control group.

LO 10 Identify and describe three types of factorial designs.

- Between-subjects design (a design in which all factors are between-subjects factors). Using this design, we manipulate the levels of both factors, cross the levels of each factor to create groups, and randomly assign different participants to each group.

- Within-subjects design (a design in which all factors are within-subjects factors). Using this design, we manipulate the levels of both factors, cross the levels of each factor to create groups, and control for order effects due to observing the same participants in each group.

- Mixed factorial design (a design with at least one between-subjects factor and one within-subjects factor). Using this design, we manipulate the levels of both factors, cross the levels of each factor to create groups, randomly assign different participants to each level of the between-subjects factor, and control for order effects due to observing the same participants at each level of the within-subjects factor.

- We identify any type of factorial design by the number of levels of each factor. We find the number of groups in a factorial design by multiplying the levels of each factor. For example, a 3 × 4 factorial design has two factors, one with three levels and one with four levels, and with 3 × 4 = 12 groups. How participants are assigned to each group depends on whether we manipulate the levels of a within-subjects factor or the levels of a between-subjects factor.

LO 11 Identify the implications of using a quasi-independent factor in a factorial design.

- The factorial design can be used when we include quasi-independent factors. When all factors in a factorial design are quasi-experimental, the design is not an experiment because no factor is manipulated; the design is a quasi-experiment. When at least one factor in a factorial design is manipulated (i.e., an independent variable), then the design is typically called an experiment; however, any effects involving the quasi-independent variable cannot demonstrate cause—only effects of the experimentally manipulated variable can demonstrate cause.

LO 12 Describe the higher-order factorial design.

- A higher-order factorial design is a research design in which the levels of more than two factors are combined or crossed to create groups.

- The higher-order factorial design allows researchers to analyze higher-order interactions for the combination of levels of three or more factors. Because a higher-order interaction is difficult to interpret, researchers will often try to limit the number of factors in a factorial design to two or three, if possible.

KEY TERMS

between-groups variability 407

between-persons variability 404

between-subjects design 374

between-subjects experimental design 374

between-subjects factor 374

between-subjects factorial design 411

carryover effects 394

comparison group 377

complete factorial design 410

control 376

control by holding constant 381

control by matching 381

control group 377

counterbalancing 394

dependent samples 401

error 382

error variance 382

experimental group 377

experimental manipulation 379

factorial design 409

factorial experimental design 410

higher-order factorial design 416

REVIEW QUESTIONS

1. State the six steps to conduct a between-subjects experimental design.

2. A researcher selects a sample of female teachers and assigns half the teachers to one professional development group and the other half of teachers to a different professional development, such that all teachers have an equal probability of being selected to one or the other group. What type of procedure was used to assign teachers to groups in this example?

3. A researcher studying resilience of elementary school teachers is concerned that gender differences could be problematic because there are so few male teachers. What type of restricted random assignment strategy can the researcher use to make sure that an equal number of male and female teachers are represented in the sample? Explain.

4. State the way of selecting independent samples that is used with experiments, and explain why it is appropriate for an experiment.

5. Name the test statistic for a between-subjects design (1) used to compare differences between two group means and (2) used to compare differences among two or more group means. Name the test statistic used to compare differences between two group means using a within-subjects design. Name the test statistic used to compare differences among two or more group means using a within-subjects design.

6. Three requirements of an experiment are randomization, manipulation, and the inclusion of a comparison or control group. Which of these requirements is not met when we use the within-subjects design? Explain.

7. What are the two ways that researchers compensate for not using random assignment in a within-subjects experimental design?

8. Explain why each of the following order effects is a threat to internal validity.

   A. Carryover effect

   B. Participant fatigue

9. State whether each of the following is an example of a between-subjects design or a within-subjects design.

   A. A sample of principals is asked to rate the effectiveness of six teachers.

   B. A sample of children is randomly assigned to counting skills with one of four types of manipulatives.

10. State whether each of the following is an example of a repeated measures design or a matched-samples design.

    A. Researchers measure reading fluency in a sample of high school students across four reading passages.

    B. Researchers record the amount of time (in minutes) that parent-child pairs spend on social networking sites to test for generational differences between the pairs.

    C. Researchers compare perceptions of safety in four different schools among pairs of participants matched based on whether they were a victim or perpetrator of bullying.

11. Using the within-subjects design, what strategy is used to eliminate between-persons variability from the denominator of the test statistic in the following situations?

    A. When comparing two group means

    B. When comparing two or more group means

12. Explain why the within-subjects design has greater power to detect an effect than the between-subjects design.

13. What type of factorial design is described in each of the following situations?

    A. The same participants are observed in each group.

    B. The same participants are observed at each level of one factor and repeatedly observed across the levels of a second factor.

    C. Different participants are observed in each group.

14. A researcher conducts a 3 × 2 factorial design with 15 participants observed in each group. How many participants are needed to conduct this experiment if he or she conducts each of the following designs?

    A. Between-subjects factorial design

    B. Within-subjects factorial design

    C. A mixed factorial design in which the first factor is a within-subjects factor

    D. A mixed factorial design in which the second factor is a within-subjects factor

15. A researcher has male and female middle school students read a vignette describing a peer performing an immoral act for reasons of preservation, protection, or self-gain. Participants rated the morality of the peer described in the vignette. Identify the quasi-independent variable in this design.

1. A school system noticed that its bus drivers are tardy or sick most often on Fridays compared to any other day of the week. Based on this observation:

   A. Design an experiment using a between-subjects design to test why most bus drivers are tardy or sick on Fridays.

   B. Specify how your design is experimental. In other words, explain how you will use manipulation, randomization, and comparison/control in your design.

2. A school superintendent is concerned that parent satisfaction is low in schools where teacher turnover is high. She hypothesizes that the greater the number of teacher turnover, the worse the parent satisfaction will be. To test this hypothesis:

   A. Design an experiment using a within-subjects experimental design to test her hypothesis regarding parent satisfaction and teacher turnover.

   B. Specify how your design is experimental. In other words, explain how you will use manipulation and comparison/control, and explain how you will control for possible order effects in your design.

3. A Latin square was introduced in this chapter as a type of partial counterbalancing strategy. Refer to the directions for constructing a Latin square given in Appendix B.2 to construct a Latin square to partially counterbalance each of the following:

   A. The order sequences for three treatments

   B. The order sequences for four treatments

4. Conduct a literature review by searching an online database (e.g., ERIC) and typing in keywords to search for factorial designs. From your search, choose any two factorial designs that interest you the most. For the purposes of this activity, you should choose designs with only two or three factors so that you can more readily understand the design. Complete the following assignment:

   A. Identify each factor and the number of levels of each factor. Also state whether each factor is an independent variable or a quasi-independent variable.

   B. Identify if the design is a between-subjects, within-subjects, or mixed factorial design. If you choose a mixed factorial design, then also identify the between-subjects factor(s) and within-subjects factor(s).

$SAGE edge™

SAGE edge offers a robust online environment featuring an impressive array of free tools and resources for review, study, and further exploration, keeping both instructors and students on the cutting edge of teaching and learning.

Access practice quizzes, eFlashcards, video, and multimedia at edge.sagepub.com/priviterarme.

Identify a problem

- Determine an area of interest.
- Review the literature.
- Identify new ideas in your area of interest.
- Develop a research hypothesis.

Develop a research plan

- Define the variables being tested.
- Identify participants or subjects and determine how to sample them.
- Select a research strategy and design.
- Evaluate ethics and obtain institutional approval to conduct research.

Generate more new ideas

- Results support your hypothesis—refine or expand on your ideas.
- Results do not support your hypothesis—reformulate a new idea or start over.

After reading this chapter, you should be able to:

1. Define mixed-methods design.
2. Describe two criteria that determine if use of a mixed-methods design is appropriate.
3. State the three advantages to using a mixed-methods design.
4. Identify three disadvantages of using a mixed-methods design.
5. Identify and describe the three different types of basic mixed-methods designs.
6. Identify and describe three different types of advanced mixed-methods designs.
7. Identify and describe the three important aspects to consider when conducting a mixed-methods design.

Communicate the results

- Method of communication: oral, written, or in a poster.
- Style of communication: APA guidelines are provided to help prepare style and format.

Conduct the study

- Execute the research plan and measure or record the data.

Analyze and evaluate the data

- Analyze and evaluate the data as they relate to the research hypothesis.
- Summarize data and research results.

chapter
fifteen

MIXED-METHODS RESEARCH DESIGNS

So often we hear a phrase that includes the "nature" of the thing you want to know. As an example, a receptionist may ask, "What is the nature of your concern?" In this case, he or she is asking about the "nature" of something, which could be simple or complex depending on the concern in this example. To expand on this example, suppose a teacher wants to know the nature of student study habits. Here we have a broad question from which we could imagine many ways to answer such a question. On one hand, we could quantify "study habits" as the time spent studying per night (in minutes), the amount of work being studied (in number of pages, words, or books read), or the number of breaks taken during a study session. In each case, we quantified studying. While this helps us understand the nature of student study habits, studying is more complex than this. The nature of study habits can be further examined using qualitative analyses as well, for example, such as to record where students study, with whom they study, and what content they are studying. In each case, the variables recorded are now qualitative and further contribute to an understanding of the nature of student study habits.

To this point in the book, we have described research designs in isolation, as unique designs fit to best answer specified research questions. However, as the example given above illustrates, for some questions, using a mix of two or more different types of methods can bolster our understanding of the nature of a behavior—such as the quantitative and qualitative approach taken to understand student study habits. In this chapter, we will therefore discuss the different types of mixed-methods designs, when mixed-methods designs are appropriate, and the process of conducting mixed-methods designs.

15.1 An Overview of Mixed-Methods Research Designs

Mixed-methods designs incorporate quantitative and qualitative data to answer a research question where one type of data is used to inform the other in some way. The two types of data, quantitative and qualitative, are combined in educational settings to understand a variety of questions in education. It combines statistical information gathered from the quantitative part of the study and personal perspectives from the qualitative part of the study. Recall that quantitative designs are interested in evaluating outcomes such as questions about what is effective or the size of the effect expected. Qualitative designs are interested in the processes involved with the outcome such as questions about why something happens or how it happens. By using mixed-methods designs, we can use both perspectives to understand the problem. They are useful when the application of one design is not sufficient to answer the research question.

> A **mixed-methods design** a research design that gathers both quantitative and qualitative data to answer a research question where one type of data informs the other.

Let's take, for example, a question regarding the impact of the Common Core State Standards (CCSS; National Governors Association and Council of Chief State School Officers, 2010). We could look at the impact of student achievement test scores in states that implement CCSS compared to student achievement test scores in states that do not implement CCSS. We could also explore the impact of CCSS for different groups of students such as those with and without disabilities, English language learners, or students who receive free and reduced-price lunches. We may also be interested in examining high school dropout rates of students in states that implement CCSS and those that do not. These are questions suitable for a quantitative design because student achievement test scores and dropout rates are numeric variables. Yet the question of "impact" of implementing the CCSS is more than just differences in tests scores or dropout rates. For example, if we observe differences in student achievement or dropout rates among different groups of students, we may then also want to know how or why the implementation of the CCSS affected student dropout rates in the way we observed using quantitative methods. The impact of the CCSS may also be explored through interviews of students about their educational experiences, where a qualitative design is appropriate. We can use the findings from the qualitative study to explain the findings of the quantitative study. It is these types of questions where a mixed-methods design can be a useful tool.

LEARNING CHECK 1 ✓

1. What is a mixed-methods design?

2. When is a mixed-methods design useful?

Answers: 1. A research study that combines qualitative and quantitative data to answer a research question; 2. It is useful when one method alone is not sufficient to answer the research question.

15.2 When Use of Mixed-Methods Research Designs Is Appropriate

In the above example, we illustrated how a mixed-methods design can be useful, but not all research questions are appropriate for mixed methods. How do we know when we should use a mixed-methods design? There are two core criteria where a mixed-methods design can be useful. First, the question or questions to be examined in a research study should be one(s) in which both methods can be used. When the research questions within a study are solely outcome focused or solely process focused, a study that employs a mixed-methods design would not be suitable. For example, a researcher who asks, "To what extent do high school dropout rates differ among states who adopted CCSS and those that did not?" is asking a strictly quantitative question. An appropriate mixed-methods research question that could incorporate data on dropout rates with other qualitative information to assess the impact of implementing CCSS might be, "What is the impact of implementing CCSS for high school students?"

Second, the study needs to be able to integrate the findings from the two different types of methods. Simply adding qualitative and quantitative measures in the same study, where the information from one measure is not used to inform the other, is not an example of a mixed-methods design. For example, a researcher is interested in the effect of using graphic organizers on acquisition of social studies content. He or she conducts a between-subjects experimental design where students are randomly assigned to the treatment and control groups. Teachers are trained in how to use the graphic organizer in teaching the content. There is a social studies test before and after the graphic organizer intervention to estimate the effect on acquisition of social studies knowledge. This is an experimental, quantitative study. At the end of the study, the researcher asks the teachers during an interview what they liked and did not like about the graphic organizer. This is a qualitative study. The researcher describes the findings of each part of the study separately. The information about what the teachers like and didn't like about the graphic organizer is not used to explain the social studies test results. The results of the social studies test are not used to explain the pattern of likes and dislikes of the intervention. In this way, the data from the two studies are not integrated and thus this would not be considered a study that employs a mixed-methods design.

15.3 Advantages and Disadvantages of Using a Mixed-Methods Research Design

The use of a mixed-methods design has both advantages and disadvantages. One distinct advantage is that this design combines quantitative and qualitative techniques that allow us to examine the research topic from both perspectives. We illustrated how both perspectives could be useful in examining the issue of impact of implementing CCSS. On the other hand, combining the two techniques requires expertise in both areas of research to employ both methodologies in a rigorous fashion. Researchers often align themselves to, and have expertise in, one type of methodology, quantitative or qualitative, so a partnership among researchers is often necessary to obtain the expertise needed for a study that employs a mixed-methods design. The necessity for expertise in both qualitative and quantitative methodologies can be a disadvantage. A second advantage of the mixed-methods design is an increase in the scope of the study than by using one method alone. It incorporates both the breadth advantage of the quantitative design and the depth advantage of the qualitative design. The breadth advantage refers to the ability of a broader generalization of the findings from quantitative studies that have larger sample sizes and employ a random selection of participants or random assignment of participants to groups. The depth advantage refers to the ability of qualitative techniques to delve into the "why" and "how" something happened rather than just "what" happened. The other side to this advantage is that increasing the scope increases the amount of resources needed. These studies may require additional personnel to collect and analyze both the quantitative and qualitative data. These studies also require additional material resources than would be needed by one study alone. Quantitative studies may need valid and reliable instruments and data analysis software, while qualitative studies may need audio equipment to record interviews, transcribing machines, and software to assist in thematic analysis. A study that employs a mixed-methods design would need access to all these resources. A third advantage of the mixed-methods design is that it is useful for complex research questions when one method (either quantitative or qualitative) is not sufficient. Yet, complex questions lead to complex interpretations. Integrating findings and interpreting the findings requires skill to synthesize all the information from mixed-methods studies into meaningful practical implications. Table 15.1 summarizes the advantages and disadvantages of the mixed-methods design.

LEARNING CHECK 2 ✓

1. What are the two criteria used to determine if a mixed-methods design can be appropriate for a study?

2. Name the three advantages and three disadvantages to using mixed-methods designs.

Answers: 1. (1) The research question can be answered using either a qualitative or quantitative design, and (2) both methods can be used to inform the other; 2. Advantages: (1) combines qualitative and quantitative techniques to understand the problem, (2) increases scope and breadth of the study, and (3) useful for complex questions; Disadvantages: (1) requires expertise in both methodologies, (2) increases the resources needed, and (3) complex interpretations that require skill.

Table 15.1 The Advantages and Disadvantages of the Mixed-Methods Design	
Advantage	**Disadvantage**
Combines quantitative and qualitative techniques to understand a problem	Requires expertise in both quantitative and qualitative methodologies
Increases the scope (breadth and depth) of the study	Increases the amount of personnel and material resources needed
Useful for complex research questions	Complex research questions can lead to complex interpretations that require skill to synthesize into meaningful, practical implications

15.4 Types of Mixed-Methods Research Designs

There are three basic mixed-methods research designs and three advanced mixed-methods designs. Most mixed-methods research use one of the three basic designs. The advanced mixed-methods designs apply a basic mixed-methods design in a specific context or situation. The basic designs include the following:

- Explanatory sequential design (QUAN → qual)
- Exploratory sequential design (QUAL → quan)
- Convergent design (QUAN + QUAL)

The three advanced designs include the following:

- Experimental or intervention
- Social justice
- Multistage program evaluation

You notice that after each of the basic mixed-methods designs, there is a lettering system. The capital letters signify which method, quantitative (QUAN) or qualitative (QUAL), is dominant. The arrows indicate that the study is sequential, with one method employed before the other. The + indicates that the two methods were conducted simultaneously.

Basic Mixed-Methods Designs

We will first describe the three basic mixed-methods designs followed by an illustrative example of a published study that used the design. We will then describe each of the three advanced designs and how they relate to the basic designs. Table 15.2 provides individual descriptions of the six mixed-methods designs and summarizes the differences between them.

Explanatory Sequential Design (QUAN → qual)

The **explanatory sequential mixed-methods design** is used to help explain the quantitative information gathered first by using a qualitative technique gathered later. It is a sequential design because the quantitative part of the study will be conducted before the qualitative part of the study. Figure 15.1 illustrates the process of the explanatory sequential mixed design.

> **Explanatory sequential mixed-methods design** is a methodological approach that gathers quantitative and qualitative data, where the qualitative data are used to explain the quantitative data (QUAN → qual), or develop a plan for measuring quantitative data (QUAL → quan).

We begin with an appropriate mixed study design research question. First, we collect the quantitative data and analyze them. The results of the quantitative study are then used to plan the qualitative study. The qualitative study can be used to explain issues that arose during data collection (such as a large number of participants who skipped answering a survey question) or to explain the results themselves. Next we conduct the qualitative portion of the study. The results of both the quantitative and qualitative portions of the study are combined to provide interpretations of the study as a whole. This type of design would be a good technique to explain extreme scores such as participants who do not respond to the treatment.

Howard, Curwen, Howard, and Colon-Muniz (2015) used an explanatory sequential mixed-methods technique to explain the attitudes of underperforming Latino youth toward computer-mediated communication on social networking sites used in education. They justify the use of a mixed-methods design as one that could better explain the findings than the use of one quantitative or qualitative method alone. They first administered a survey (quantitative) about use and comfort level in using the Internet and social networking sites such as Facebook and MySpace. They used the results of the survey to conduct follow-up interviews (qualitative) with a smaller set of randomly selected students. The resulting themes of the interviews were reported and then combined with the survey results to discuss each of the research questions.

> An explanatory mixed-methods design gathers quantitative and qualitative data, where the qualitative data are used to explain the quantitative data (QUAN → qual) or develop a plan for measuring quantitative data (QUAL → quan).

Exploratory Sequential Design (QUAL → quan)

> Exploratory sequential design (QUAL → quant) gathers qualitative then quantitative data where the qualitative data are used to guide the quantitative study.

The **exploratory sequential mixed design** is also used to explore a problem or issue using a qualitative technique before conducting a quantitative study. This problem is usually related

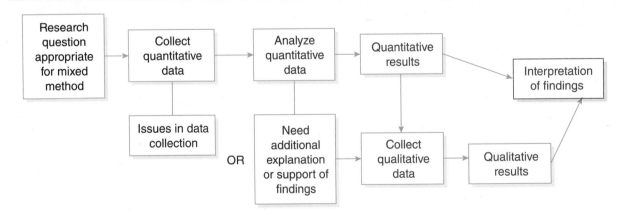

Figure 15.1 Procedure for the Explanatory Sequential Mixed-Methods Design

Source: Adapted from Creswell (2015).

to implementation of an intervention or development of a measurement instrument. It is sequential because the qualitative part of the study is conducted before the quantitative part of the study. This method is typically used when there is not enough information available about the problem or issue to properly plan the quantitative study. The qualitative study can be used to explore the problem or issue to identify or define the key concepts or variables or to formulate potential hypotheses or theory to guide the quantitative study. For example, cyberbullying is a relatively new concept. Researchers could explore issues regarding cyberbullying such as what cyberbullying looks like in different social media formats or how people experience cyberbullying before conducting a quantitative study. Figure 15.2 illustrates the process of the exploratory sequential mixed design. We begin with an appropriate mixed study design research question. First, we collect the qualitative data and analyze them. Then we use this information to develop the intervention or measurement instrument for the quantitative part of the study. The new intervention or measurement tool is then used in the quantitative part of the study. The results of the quantitative study are then generated. Finally, the last step is the interpretation of the findings of the study. The interpretation should include a description of how the results of the qualitative study informed the quantitative study in development of the new intervention or measurement instrument. This type of study could also be used to refine an already developed intervention or measurement instrument. In this case, the interpretation will want to include how the intervention or measurement instrument was improved due to the inclusion of the qualitative portion of the study.

De Nobile, London, and El Baba (2015) used the exploratory sequential mixed-methods design to explore whole schoolwide behavior management approaches (WSBM). They were interested in whether implementation of a WSBM would be associated with lower levels of student problem behavior. The researchers interviewed various school personnel, including teaching staff, educational coordinators, and school administrators regarding their implementation of WSBM. A second question asked the participants to rate

Figure 15.2 Procedure for the Exploratory Sequential Mixed-Methods Design

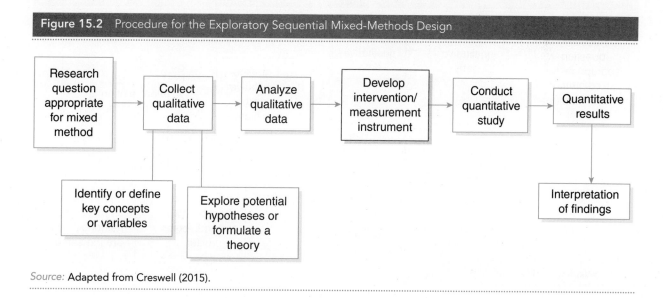

Source: Adapted from Creswell (2015).

the extent of student behavior problems at the school on a scale from 1 (minimal) to 5 (extreme). The qualitative information from the interviews was coded and combined into themes that were used to create a 4-point scale to describe levels of implementation of WSBM ranging from ineffective to very effective. The scale was then used to quantify the level of implementation of WSBM as described in each of the interviews. The researchers then compared the ratings of level of implementation that were created from the interviews to the rating of the extent of the student behavior problems at the school.

An exploratory mixed-methods design gathers qualitative and then quantitative data, where the qualitative data are used to guide the quantitative study.

Convergent Design

A **convergent mixed-methods design** gathers the qualitative and quantitative data at the same time; it is not sequential. In this way, an issue can be examined using both types of information: quantitative information regarding relationships between independent and dependent variables or impact of an independent variable on a dependent variable and the deep, rich qualitative information describing the perspectives of the participants. Figure 15.3 illustrates the process of the convergent mixed-methods design. We begin with an appropriate mixed study design research question. We collect the qualitative and quantitative data at the same time but analyze them separately. Information from both analyses is combined to report the results. The results may report one set of results first and the other second (qualitative and then quantitative or vice versa), or they may be reported together side-by-side to answer each research question. The interpretation brings both pieces together to

A **convergent mixed-methods design** (QUANT + QUAL) a research design that gathers quantitative and qualitative data at the same time to obtain both deep, rich qualitative data and numeric quantitative data to provide a more complete understanding of a problem.

Figure 15.3 Procedure for the Convergent Mixed-Methods Design

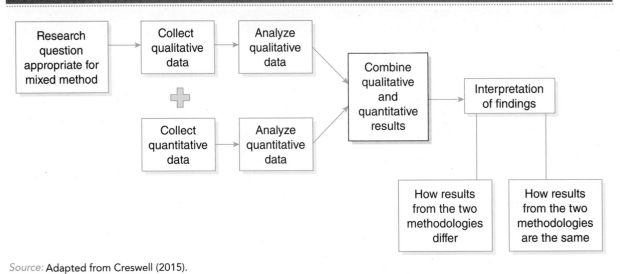

Source: Adapted from Creswell (2015).

describe how the findings from the two different methodologies either support or contradict each other.

Karahan and Roehrig (2014) used a convergent mixed-methods design to explore how learning activities guided by theories of constructionism and social constructivism affect views on environmental awareness and activism of high school students. The researchers designed a series of activities for students to create video projects related to environmental problems. They administered a quantitative pre- and posttest survey on beliefs of environmental problems and collected various types of qualitative data, including writing samples, the video projects, and observations of the students and instructors on the video design process. The survey data were analyzed separately from the qualitative data. The different sources of qualitative data were combined to describe themes related to environmental awareness and activism. In the discussion section, the authors combine the findings from the quantitative and qualitative parts of the study to describe students' environmental awareness and the perceived need for activism.

LEARNING CHECK 3 ✓

1. Describe the procedure for an explanatory mixed-methods design. What is the purpose of this design?

2. Describe the procedure for an exploratory mixed-methods design. What is the purpose of this design?

3. Describe the procedure for a convergent mixed-methods design. What is the purpose of this design?

4. Which basic mixed-methods design is used in the following study description?

   A. A researcher uses information from a database on family and school variables and conducts interviews with parents simultaneously to learn how parents select schools for their children to attend.

   B. A researcher interviews teachers and school- and district-level administrators about what factors affect teacher retention in the local school district. The researcher uses this information to create a survey to disseminate to teachers.

   C. A researcher conducts a nonexperimental study examining the relationship between art integration and mathematics test scores and then asks some students to describe their math class experiences in interviews.

Answers: 1. The QUANT → qual, to explain the quantitative findings; 2. QUAL → quant, to assist in the planning of a quantitative study; 3. QUANT + QUAN, to combine numeric and narrative information in describing a problem; 4. A. convergent mixed methods, B. exploratory mixed methods, C. explanatory mixed methods.

Advanced Mixed-Methods Designs

In addition to the three basic mixed-methods designs, there are three advanced designs. Each of these advanced designs begins with a basic design and frames it within a specific context. The experimental or intervention mixed-methods design uses a mixed-methods design within the context of an experiment evaluating the impact of an intervention. The social justice mixed-methods design uses a mixed-methods design in the context of a social justice framework. The multistage program evaluation mixed-methods design employs a mixed-methods design in the context of a program evaluation.

> An advanced mixed-methods design employs a basic design in a specific context.

Experimental or Intervention Advanced Design

The experimental or intervention advanced mixed-methods design uses one of the three basic mixed-methods designs within the context of an experimental design. Recall from Chapter 14 that an experimental design includes a pre- and/or posttest with assignment to treatment and control groups. The qualitative component may be gathered before the experiment, during the experiment, and/or after the experiment. In each case, the experiment is the primary study, but the qualitative component can be used to supplement the quantitative study. Figure 15.4 illustrates how the experimental advanced design can be embedded in a basic mixed-methods design. An exploratory version of the experimental mixed-methods advanced design embeds the qualitative component before the experiment. The qualitative component prior to the experiment may be used to gather information needed to conduct the experiment. For example, if we are studying the impact of a reading intervention on phonics acquisition, we could conduct a qualitative study prior to the experiment to collect information on potential participants (teachers or students) or aspects of the implementation of the study such as types of phonics instruction already being used, time allotted for reading instruction, or school/district policies on reading instruction. We would then use this information to plan the quantitative study. Employing the qualitative component of the study after the experiment would be an explanatory version of the experimental advanced mixed-methods design. The qualitative component at the end of the experiment can provide additional information regarding the perception of the participants on the intervention. For example, researchers could ask the participants about their thoughts on how well the intervention worked or if the intervention was feasible or usable that could be used to help interpret the results of the experiment. Finally, employing the qualitative component during the experiment would be a convergent version of the experimental advanced mixed-methods design. In this design, the qualitative and quantitative data would be collected together during the implementation of the experiment. The focus of the qualitative component during the course of the study would be on aspects of participating in the study. For example, the researcher could investigate the participants' experiences of engaging in the study or with specific aspects of the intervention. In any case, whether using the explanatory advanced, exploratory advanced, or convergent advanced design, the results of one part of the study are used to inform the other part of the study.

> An experimental or intervention advanced mixed-methods design is a research design that gathers qualitative data in the context of an experiment.

Knaggs, Sondergeld, and Schardt (2015) used an explanatory version of the experimental advanced mixed-methods technique to investigate barriers to college enrollment

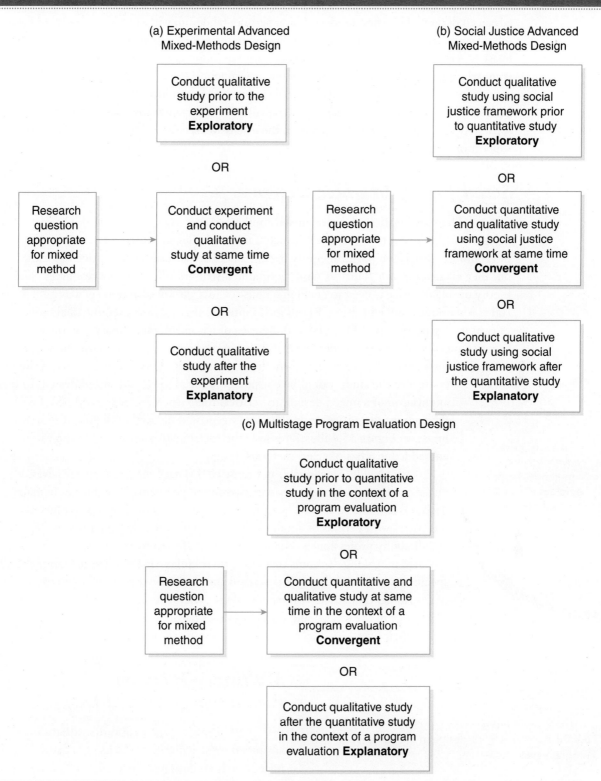

(a) Experimental Advanced Mixed-Methods Design

Conduct qualitative study prior to the experiment **Exploratory**

OR

Research question appropriate for mixed method

Conduct experiment and conduct qualitative study at same time **Convergent**

OR

Conduct qualitative study after the experiment **Explanatory**

(b) Social Justice Advanced Mixed-Methods Design

Conduct qualitative study using social justice framework prior to quantitative study **Exploratory**

OR

Research question appropriate for mixed method

Conduct quantitative and qualitative study using social justice framework at same time **Convergent**

OR

Conduct qualitative study using social justice framework after the quantitative study **Explanatory**

(c) Multistage Program Evaluation Design

Conduct qualitative study prior to quantitative study in the context of a program evaluation **Exploratory**

OR

Research question appropriate for mixed method

Conduct quantitative and qualitative study at same time in the context of a program evaluation **Convergent**

OR

Conduct qualitative study after the quantitative study in the context of a program evaluation **Explanatory**

of students in an urban high school. (NOTE: Although the researchers called this a sequential explanatory design because it is in the context of an experiment, it is an experimental advanced design.) They first used a quasi-experimental design with different cohorts of high school students who had or had not participated in the GEAR UP program. It is considered quasi-experimental because the cohorts were not randomly assigned to the treatment and comparison groups. Upon completion of the experiment (GEAR UP program), three focus group interviews with purposefully selected students were conducted to examine their high school experiences. The results of the qualitative and quantitative data were analyzed separately and then integrated together in the discussion section using the qualitative data to support or contradict the quantitative findings.

Social Justice Advanced Design

The social justice advanced mixed-methods design uses any one of the basic designs within the context of a social justice framework. Social justice refers to a concept of economic, social, and political equity for all. There are several social justice theories, but they all advocate for "fairness" and "equitable distribution" of societal resources. The theory of social justice is used to challenge injustice in a variety of arenas such as human rights, economics, and education. Recall in Chapter 12 that we discussed the qualitative critical theory perspective. These critical theories of feminism, race theory, and queer theory (and others) are used as perspectives to promote social justice of marginalized individuals. Any basic mixed-methods design that uses a critical theory as the context of the study would be considered a social justice advanced design. In this application of a mixed design, the critical theory perspective would be infused throughout the entire study. The findings would be used to highlight sources of injustice. Figure 15.4 illustrates how the social justice advanced design can be embedded in a basic mixed-methods design.

A social justice advanced mixed-methods design employs a mixed-methods basic design in the context of a social justice framework.

McNeilly, Macdonald, and Kelly (2015) used the social justice advanced mixed-methods design to study participation of people with disabilities in making decisions about their lives. They administered a questionnaire and conducted interviews with parents of children with a disability, the children (aged 6–28), and disability professionals. Notice that those affected by the injustice (not being included in making decisions that affect their life) are included in the sample. This specific social justice theory is described and then used to frame the interpretation of the results. The discussion section of the article uses the findings to advocate for change in the way people with disabilities participate in decision making that affects their lives.

A multistage program evaluation advanced mixed-methods design is a research design that employs a basic mixed-methods design in the context of a program evaluation.

Multistage Program Evaluation Advanced Design

The multistage program evaluation advanced mixed-methods design is a basic mixed-methods design in the context of a program evaluation. A program evaluation, as we will see in Chapter 17, is a series of steps to create and assess the merit of a measurement tool or program implemented over a period of time. A program evaluation typically has a formative component to assess the merit during the implementation that is used to refine the program and a summative component at the end of the implementation to evaluate the success of the program. A program evaluation may incorporate a needs assessment, development of the program or measure, implementation of the program or administration of the measure, refinement of the program or measure based on the formative information, and implementation of the final measure or full program. A multistage program evaluation mixed-methods design incorporates both qualitative and quantitative data during the program evaluation process to make decisions of the merit of the program. Figure 15.4 illustrates how the social justice advanced mixed-methods design can be embedded in a basic mixed-methods design.

> **Social justice advanced mixed-methods design** is a research design that employs a mixed-methods basic design in the context of a social justice framework.

Luna, Evans, and Davis (2015) used a multistage program evaluation mixed-methods design to investigate the impact of the Anahuac School and Community Engagement Program (ASCEP), a community-based school dropout prevention program, on ethnic identity and academic aspirations of Latino/Latina high school youth. The authors described how the program and activities and the measurement tool (survey) were developed and piloted tested (i.e., formative assessment). Over 250 students participated in the final ASCEP program. They administered the pre- and posttest questionnaire and conducted postinterviews with a sample of students as summative evaluation measures. The results of the quantitative survey and qualitative interviews were reported separately in the results but were integrated in the discussion section to describe the success of the program.

LEARNING CHECK 4 ✓

1. Describe an experimental (intervention) advanced mixed-methods design.

2. Describe a social justice advanced mixed-methods design.

3. Describe a multistage program evaluation advanced mixed-methods design.

4. Which advanced mixed-methods design is described in the following scenarios?

    A. A research team conducts a needs assessment for technology information for parents, implements a technology workshop, and then assesses the success of the workshop using parent interviews and a survey.

    B. The researchers design a study to examine the efficacy of heterogeneous ability grouping in creating student collaborative learning groups on science test scores. They take field notes on observations of the groups' interaction and engagement during the study.

    C. Researchers conduct a study to examine the racial disparities of school- and district-level administrators using the critical race theory framework.

Answers: 1. An advanced design in the context of an experiment; 2. An advanced design in the context of a social justice framework; 3. An advanced design in the context of a program evaluation; 4. A. a multistage program evaluation design, B. experimental (intervention) mixed-methods design, C. a social justice mixed-methods design.

Table 15.2 A Summary of the Six Mixed-Methods Designs

Mixed-Method Design	Description
Basic designs	
Explanatory sequential design	The quantitative part of the study will be conducted before the qualitative part. The qualitative part of the study is used to explain the findings from the quantitative part of the study.
Exploratory sequential design	The qualitative part of the study is conducted before the quantitative study. The qualitative study is used to explore the issue first because there is not enough information available about the issue to properly plan a quantitative study.
Convergent design	The qualitative and quantitative studies are conducted at the same time. Information from the studies is analyzed separately, then combined to interpret the results.
Advanced designs	
Experimental or intervention	A more specific mixed-methods design where an experimental study is conducted as part of the quantitative portion of one of the three basic mixed-methods designs.
Social justice	A more specific mixed-methods design where a social justice framework is conducted as part of the qualitative portion of one of the three basic mixed-methods designs.
Multistage program evaluation	A more specific mixed-methods design where the mixed-methods study is conducted as part of a program evaluation.

MAKING SENSE—IDENTIFYING A MIXED-METHODS STUDY

There are two ways to identify when a mixed-methods design is used in a research study. The first and easiest way is if the authors specifically say it is a mixed-methods study and provide the type of mixed-methods design used. Second, in the method section of the article, you should find a description of both designs. There is at least one quantitative and one qualitative research question provided in the introduction section of the article with the design used to answer each question in the method section. Since a mixed-methods study combines a quantitative and qualitative approach, you should see a specific design described for each one.

15.5 Conducting Mixed-Methods Research

Conducting a mixed-methods design study that integrates both qualitative and quantitative methodologies requires additional considerations than when conducting just one type of study alone. Researchers need to spend extra time thinking about three important aspects: sampling, study procedures, and data integration. These are the three parts of a study that are most effected by combining the two methodologies into one study.

Recall the different sampling strategies for qualitative and quantitative designs described in Chapter 5. Sampling strategies for qualitative studies are purposeful, and the sample sizes are smaller than quantitative sampling techniques because they seek specific information from specific people. Quantitative sampling strategies are mostly probability-based, random selections with larger sample sizes to generalize to a larger population. In a mixed-methods design, the researcher will need to use two sampling strategies appropriate for each part of the study: one for the qualitative part and one for the quantitative part. Both sampling strategies will need to be employed with equal rigor. The question in mixed-methods studies is how to integrate these two distinctly different sampling strategies since we need both in the same study. Is the sample selected for the two different parts of the study in the same group, is one sample a subset of the other sample, are there two different samples from the same population, or is the sample from two different populations? The answer to this question depends on what type of mixed-methods design is being used. In an explanatory mixed-methods design where the quantitative part of the study is conducted first and the qualitative data are used to explain the quantitative data, the sample for the qualitative part of the study is a subset of the larger sample selected for the quantitative part of the study. To provide information that helps explain the quantitative data, the participants would need to have been a part of the quantitative study. In an exploratory mixed-methods design where the qualitative part of the study is conducted first, the sample for the quantitative part of the study may be from the same population or different population as the participants in the qualitative part of the study. The qualitative part of the study will need a small group of key stakeholders to gather the information needed to conduct the quantitative part of the study. It is not necessary that this group be the exact participants who will participate in the quantitative part of the study. This sample needs to have the information that the researchers need to conduct the quantitative study (e.g., where the participants are potentially located, school/district policy, class schedules). This may include participants from the same population as the participants who will participate in the quantitative part of the study but may also include participants not part of the population who will participate in the study. For example, let's say we are going to conduct a study to implement a teacher-based intervention to improve critical thinking of students in social studies. We may need input from teachers (part of the population) and school administrators and parents (not part of population). The sample for a convergent mixed-methods design where the qualitative and quantitative are conducted simultaneously is ideally the same participants for both parts of the study. This can present a problem, though, since obtaining the amount of qualitative information from a larger sample size needed for the quantitative part of the study may be very large and very cumbersome to analyze. A viable option may be to use a subset of the participants from the quantitative part of the study for the qualitative part. In this case, the researcher should provide justification for the qualitative sampling strategy used to select these participants instead of using all of them.

A second consideration for conducting a study that employs a mixed-methods design is the rigorous application of the procedures associated with each qualitative and quantitative part of the study. The qualitative part of the study will employ a specific qualitative design and all the necessary components of that design as described in Chapters 10, 11, and 12. For example, if the researchers decided to use a narrative inquiry design for the qualitative part of an explanatory mixed-methods design on the impact of implementing the CCSS we described at the beginning of this chapter, then the researchers will need to collect narrative stories of the participants to describe this experience, including the three dimensions of narrative inquiry (i.e., temporality, sociality, and place). The quantitative part of the study will need to employ a specific quantitative design and all the necessary components of that design as described in Chapters 8, 9, 13, and 14. For example, if the researchers decided to use a nonexperimental, survey design for the quantitative part of an explanatory mixed-methods design on the impact of implementing the CCSS, then the researchers will need to create and disseminate the survey using the procedures for survey research. You can see by having two different designs in the same study that the procedures need to be well planned and organized to incorporate all the procedures for both.

The final consideration for conducting a study that employs a mixed-methods design is the integration of the information from the two studies. Integration of the data is how we used information from one part of the study to inform the other part of the study. Recall that this is a requirement for a mixed-methods design. How the data are integrated depends on what type of mixed-methods design is being used. In an exploratory sequential mixed-methods design, the integration occurs by using the information from the qualitative part of the study to design and outline the procedures of the quantitative study. The integration of the two parts of the study will be described in the method section of the research article. In the explanatory sequential mixed-methods design, the qualitative part of the study follows the quantitative part of the study and is used to explain the findings from the quantitative part of the study. The integration of the two parts of the study will occur in the discussion section of the research article. The results may report the quantitative and qualitative findings sequentially with one part described before the other or by merging and discussing the two types of data together. The discussion section will pull the two pieces together and include how the two results support or contradict each other. In the convergent mixed-methods design, the qualitative and quantitative parts of the study take place at the same time. In this case, the method section will describe how the two parts of the study will be combined. The results section will report the data from the two parts of the study either sequentially or combined. The discussion section of the article will pull the two pieces together with a description of how the data support or contradict each other. The integration of data for the advanced designs also depends on at what point in the study the qualitative study is embedded into the quantitative part of the study. If the qualitative part occurs first, then it will be integrated into the method section of the article. If the qualitative part occurs second, then it will be integrated in the results and discussion sections of the article. If the qualitative part occurs at the same time, then it is integrated in the method, results, and discussion sections of the article.

LEARNING CHECK 5 ✓

1. What are the three special considerations when conducting a mixed-methods design?

2. How do these three special considerations apply to the different types of basic designs?

Answers: 1. Sampling, procedures, data integration; 2. Sampling—the participants will vary depending on the type of design, whether they are a subset of the sample of the other part of the study, part of the population from which the sample of the other part of the study was obtained but not a subset, or from a different population; procedures—need to employ rigorous procedures associated with each of the research designs in the study; data integration—depends on which basic design is used, whether information is integrated in the methods (exploratory), results (explanatory), or both (convergent).

CONNECTING TO THE CLASSROOM

An explanatory mixed-methods study is a good way to understand the impact of changes in your teaching practice. A quantitative study can be used to examine any changes in student performance. This is an important indicator of the impact of the change in practice you make but not the only important indicator. It might also be important to understand how the change affected students or how students feel about the change. These questions can be answered by talking with some of the students, which would be a qualitative study. Select students who both appeared to benefit from the change and those who did not to understand how the change affected them. Use the information collected during the quantitative study about how the students performed to develop some interview questions. You can use the information obtained from these interviews to make additional modifications to your initial change in practice to hopefully improve performance even more.

15.6 Ethics in Focus: Minimizing Risk Associated With Qualitative and Quantitative Research

You can now see how choosing a mixed-methods design doubles the difficulty of conducting a study by employing the rigor associated with each methodology and then integrating them together. This also increases the responsibilities of the participants to participate in each part of the study. With the increased difficulty of the study and responsibilities of the participant, the ethical responsibilities of the researcher in minimizing the risk of participating in the study are also increased. It is important that the researcher explain adequately all phases of the study and the participants' role in each phase so that the participants can make an informed decision about whether to participate or not. The risks associated with both types of research methods selected for the mixed-methods design as described in the previous method chapters will apply in a single study that employs a mixed-methods design. In some cases, such as with the exploratory sequential mixed-methods design, the procedures for the second part of the study may not be known at the time of initial consent since consent is given before the study begins. This means that there may need to be separate consents for the two parts of the study to provide the participant with all the information needed to make that informed decision. Mixed-methods researchers need to consider how to minimize the risk associated with each of the two designs in the study when planning the study and how to report this risk to the participants so they can make a truly informed decision about their participation.

CHAPTER SUMMARY

LO 1 Define mixed-methods design.

- A mixed-methods design gathers both quantitative and qualitative data to answer a research question where one type of data informs the other.

LO 2 Describe two criteria that determine if use of a mixed-methods design is appropriate.

- First, the question or questions to be examined in a research study should be one(s) in which both methods can be used.

- Second, the study needs to be able to integrate the findings from the two different types of studies.

LO 3 State the three advantages to using a mixed-methods design.

- Combines quantitative and qualitative techniques to understand a problem

- Increases the scope (breadth and depth) of the study

- Useful for complex research questions

LO 4 Identify three disadvantages of using a mixed-methods design.

- Requires expertise in both quantitative and qualitative methodologies

- Increases the amount of personnel and material resources needed

- Complex research questions can lead to complex interpretations that require skill to synthesize into meaningful, practical implications

LO 5 Identify and describe the three different types of basic mixed-methods designs.

- Explanatory sequential design is used to help explain the quantitative information gathered first using a qualitative technique gathered later.
- Exploratory sequential design gathers qualitative and then quantitative data, where the qualitative data are used to guide the quantitative study.
- Convergent design gathers quantitative and qualitative data at the same time to obtain both deep, rich qualitative data and numeric quantitative data to provide a more complete understanding of a problem.

LO 6 Identify and describe three different types of advanced mixed-methods designs.

- Experimental or intervention advanced mixed-methods design gathers qualitative data in the context of an experiment.
- Social justice advanced mixed-methods design employs a mixed-methods basic design in the context of a social justice framework.
- Multistage program evaluation advanced mixed-methods design employs a basic mixed-methods design in the context of a program evaluation.

LO 7 Identify and describe the three important aspects to consider when conducting a mixed-methods design.

- Sampling—sampling strategies will need to be employed with equal rigor for both the qualitative and quantitative parts of the study. The participants will vary depending on the type of design, whether they are a subset of the sample of the other part of the study, part of the population from which the sample of the other part of the study was obtained but not a subset, or from a different population.
- Study procedures—need to employ rigorous procedures associated with each of the research designs in a single study.
- Data integration—integration depends on which basic design is used; the information will be integrated in the methods (exploratory), results (explanatory), or both (convergent).

KEY TERMS

convergent mixed-methods design 434

experimental (intervention) advanced mixed-methods design 436

explanatory sequential mixed-methods design 431

mixed-methods design 428

multistage program evaluation advanced

mixed-methods design 438

social justice advanced mixed-methods design 439

1. Explain why a researcher might use a mixed-methods design to understand a problem.

2. Which of the following research question(s) is best suited for a mixed-methods design?

   A. How do elementary-aged students perceive their peers with autism?

   B. In what ways do teaching programs affect the decision of alternate route, urban teachers to remain teaching?

   C. What is the relationship between Internet use and body mass index of middle schoolers?

3. A quantitative researcher is interested in conducting a mixed-methods study on the impact of providing reading instruction using text-to-speech software for students who are nonverbal. What extra resources will this researcher need?

4. State the type or types of basic or advanced mixed-methods design(s) that are most closely associated with the following terms:

   A. Needs assessment

   B. Intervention

   C. Critical theory

   D. Sequential

   E. Data integration

5. A researcher is interested in examining the role of district office leaders in the adoption and implementation of the CCSS. She conducts a survey of district leaders across the state, then uses results of the survey to design interview questions and to select specific types of district leaders to interview. What type of mixed-methods design is used in this study? Why?

6. A researcher is interested in understanding how physical activity affects academic achievement. He devised an intervention using fitness trackers and interviewed the participants during the course of the intervention. What type of mixed-methods design is used in this study? Why?

7. A researcher is interested in studying student engagement in virtual schools. She has a theory that students who select the virtual schooling option may have felt marginalized by their traditional public school experience. What type of mixed-methods design is used in this study? Why?

8. Explain how the sampling strategies of quantitative and qualitative designs in exploratory sequential, explanatory sequential, and convergent basic designs are integrated into a mixed-methods study.

9. Explain how quantitative and qualitative designs are integrated into a mixed-methods study.

10. Explain how data from the quantitative and qualitative parts of exploratory sequential, explanatory sequential, and convergent basic designs are integrated into a mixed-methods study.

1. For any of the three following topics, write an appropriate mixed-methods research question and identify a basic or advanced mixed-methods design that could be used to study the topic. Describe why you selected this design.

   A. Differentiated instruction

   B. Collaborative learning groups

   C. Gender differences in learning algebra

   D. Achievement motivation

   E. Inquiry-based teaching

   F. Teacher quality and preservice preparation

   G. Parent-teacher relationships

   H. Social media on student engagement

2. Choose a topic from above and briefly design a study using each one of the mixed-methods designs. Indicate how the information from one part of the study is integrated into the second part of the study.

   A. Explanatory sequential

   B. Exploratory sequential

   C. Convergent

   D. Experimental (will it be exploratory, explanatory or convergent?)

   E. Social justice

   F. Multistage program evaluation

APPLIED RESEARCH DESIGNS

Identify a problem

- Determine an area of interest.
- Review the literature.
- Identify new ideas in your area of interest.
- Develop a research hypothesis.

Develop a research plan

- Define the variables being tested.
- Identify participants or subjects and determine how to sample them.
- Select a research strategy and design.
- Evaluate ethics and obtain institutional approval to conduct research.

Generate more new ideas

- Results support your hypothesis—refine or expand on your ideas.
- Results do not support your hypothesis—reformulate a new idea or start over.

After reading this chapter, you should be able to:

1. Define action research.
2. Identify and describe the differences between traditional and action research.
3. Distinguish between classroom-based and system-based action research.
4. Define practical and participatory action research.
5. Distinguish between proactive and responsive practical action research.
6. Define the seven key features of participatory action research.
7. Identify the differences between practical and participatory action research.
8. Identify and describe the stages of action research.
9. Explain the ethical considerations when conducting action research and what can be done to address them.
10. Describe how to evaluate action research.

Conduct the study

- Execute the research plan and measure or record the data.

Communicate the results

- Method of communication: oral, written, or in a poster.
- Style of communication: APA guidelines are provided to help prepare style and format.

Analyze and evaluate the data

- Analyze and evaluate the data as they relate to the research hypothesis.
- Summarize data and research results.

chapter sixteen

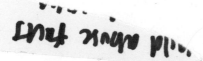

ACTION RESEARCH

While reflecting on her teaching practice, a teacher considers implementing collaborative work groups to increase the individual participation of students in class activities and improve student learning outcomes. As an example, a teacher could implement a research study with the students in her classes to examine the outcomes of implementing the collaborative work groups. A principal wonders if providing transportation to school for parents will increase parental participation in school conferences and other school-based activities. The principal could implement a research study by providing parents with several paid transportation options and monitoring the number of parents who use it. Based on the findings, the teacher might decide to make collaborative student work groups a permanent part of her teaching practice, and the principal might make parent transportation a part of the school budget. By conducting systematic inquiry to evaluate and change educational practice, the teacher and principal are engaging in a form of action research.

You might have the impression that conducting research in the educational context is only for researchers, but this is not true. Action research is an important tool that can be used by teachers and other school and community stakeholders to inform local educational practice. In this chapter, we will examine what action research is, the different types of action research, and the steps and ethical considerations in undertaking an action research project.

> **edge.sagepub.com/priviterarme**
>
> - Take the chapter quiz
> - Review key terms with eFlashcards
> - Explore multimedia links and SAGE articles
>
>

16.1 The Fundamentals of Action Research

Action research is the implementation of systematic inquiry conducted by educational practitioners that is designed to answer questions related to educational practices and student learning outcomes in the context of a specific

> **Action research** is the implementation of systematic inquiry conducted by educational practitioners designed to answer questions related to educational practices and student learning outcomes in the context of a specific educational environment.

educational environment. Action research is an opportunity to evaluate instructional changes in real time within a specific local context. Two terms that can be associated with action research are *progress monitoring* and *data-based decision making*. Progress monitoring is the process of collecting information on student progress repeatedly over a period of time to evaluate the effectiveness of classroom instruction. It can be used for individual students or an entire class. The data can be used to make informed decisions to design instructional remediation based on specific skill deficits based on the data collected. Progress monitoring can be conducted using either teacher-made tools specific to what is being taught in the class or commercially available products that test broader skills that are taught in typical classrooms. *Data-based decisions* is a term used in special education practices to describe the same repeated measurement of student progress over time and using the data to make decisions about the potential need for instructional changes. In this case, the data being collected will be related to a goal in the Individualized Education Plan (IEP). Whatever the term that is used, action research takes the principles of research we have explored in this text and applies them to affect local educational practice.

While both traditional research and action research implement systematic inquiry to address educational issues, there are some distinct differences. Table 16.1 summarizes the differences between traditional research and action research.

Table 16.1   The Differences Between Traditional and Action Research

Characteristic	Action Research	Traditional Research
Researcher role	The researcher is an educational practitioner	The researcher is someone typically outside of the immediate educational context
Reflection	Subjective reflection about self and how the self affects practice	Objective reflection with emphasis to avoid personal, in research process
Relationship between researcher and participant	Participants are seen as equals with a voice in the process	The relationship between researcher and participants is typically hierarchical, with the researcher as the authority
Decision making	Collaborative, democratic decision making among collaborators	The researcher is the decision maker
Impact	Studies local issue within a specific context	Studies educational issues that affect the practice of a larger group
Interpretation	Findings interpreted within the local context	Interested in making generalizable findings
Dissemination	Dissemination is local to colleagues or other interested community stakeholders	Dissemination can be local but is also broad to include publications in journals and presentations at national conferences
Timing of the study	Cyclical within a process of continuous improvement as students and circumstances change	One-shot deal that has a beginning and an end

In traditional research, the researcher is typically someone outside of the educational context where the research is taking place with an expertise in a specific educational issue such as a university professor. In action research, on the other hand, the researcher tends to be a practitioner who is a person actively engaged in education. Anyone can engage in action research, including teachers; school administrators; other school personnel such as media specialists,

> A practitioner is an individual who is engaged in the teaching profession.

counselors, or therapists; or community-based educational stakeholders such as school boards or other local educational action groups. Throughout this chapter, we will refer to this group of action researchers as educational "practitioners." The goal for educational practitioners is to engage systematic inquiry to make decisions about how practice affects students, schools, and/ or themselves. Action research can be conducted by an individual, group of individuals within a school, or group of individuals across different schools. Virtually anyone can reflect and examine their practice to make evidence-based informed pedagogical decisions.

A critical step of action research is the personal self-reflection on past, present, and future practice and the consequences (Schmuck, 1997, 2006). Reflections of past practice and the reactions to it are like a debriefing to understand what happened. This is a necessary antecedent to any change. Reflecting in the present is to think about what is happening

> Reflection is serious thought or consideration regarding the practice of teaching.

right now to change the reactions while the practice is taking place. Future reflection involves planning actions of practice in advance. These reflections help guide the action research study. In contrast, traditional research focuses on objectivity and removing researcher subjectivity from the study to avoid potential bias. To avoid potential bias, the researcher may direct the study and physically remove himself or herself from the process by having other people, such as teachers or graduate assistants, implement the study and collect the data.

In action research, the process is democratic and collaborative, and participants are regarded as collaborators and part of the research team such that they have a voice in the changing practice as it unfolds. In traditional research, the structure is hierarchical, where the researcher is the authority. The teachers who implement the change of practice are also considered participants. Both teachers and student participants are led through the research process by the researcher. The researcher makes all the decisions pertaining to the study.

While traditional research can guide educational practice with illustrations of effective curricular and instructional practices with larger, representative sample sizes that are generalizable to others, the emphasis of action research is to provide direction in understanding how educational practices affect a specific constituency within a specific, local context. Action research is conducted to inform a personal practice; it often does not contain all the elements of high-quality research, and interpretation of results is framed within the local context.

Because action research concentrates on local educational practice issues, is smaller, and does not incorporate all aspects of high-quality traditional research studies, this research is not usually published as journal articles, but it can be. There are journals that specialize in action research such as *Action Learning: Research and Practice* and *Educational Action Research*. Research articles using action research can serve as models on how to implement an action research project or serve as impetus for conducting a research study generalizable to a broader population or vice versa. For example, the teacher interested in collaborative student work groups reads an article about it and wonders whether the strategy described in the article will work for her students. The traditional research study was conducted with similar students, but the teacher wonders if this approach will work within the confines of her classroom with her students and the resources to which she has access. The principal interested in increasing parental participation in school-based activities, for example, reads a research article that increased parent participation by providing transportation to parents and wonders how his community can provide the transportation he needs for parents or how his or her school budget can accommodate this expense. Action research is the way that we can investigate how published research can be implemented in real practice.

Another difference between action research and traditional research is the reflection aspect where the practitioner researcher of action research reflects upon himself or herself and how the personal actions affect personal practice. The intent is to change the self and the practice of the self. In traditional research, reflection often concerns the research process and how to affect the practice of others.

Finally, action research is not a one-shot deal like much of traditional research. In traditional research, the goal is to fill a gap in knowledge. Once a study is completed, the researcher is not likely to conduct the same study again. The next study may be related to the previous one but is likely designed to refine what we know about that gap in knowledge or to fill a different gap in knowledge. Action research is a mind-set of continuous improvement since different students have different needs and their needs change. What worked last year might not work this year with a different set of students. What worked in one school might not work in a different school with different resources or policies. Action research is a pedagogical practice in itself to continuously reflect on personal practices and make informed decisions about how to change practice to meet the needs of students and teachers. This continuous improvement process can be an empowering way to make informed decisions to solve specific problems.

LEARNING CHECK 1 ✓

1. What is the primary purpose of action research?

2. In what ways does action research differ from traditional research?

3. Identify whether the following descriptions are traditional or action research:

   A. A university professor is interested in studying the impact of implementing a social justice perspective into a social studies class on student outcomes with plans to publish the findings in a journal article. She locates several teachers who volunteer to implement her strategy in their classrooms under the professor's direction.

   B. A teacher notices that only a few students participate in class discussions, so she decides to implement a token system to reward participation in her world history class.

C. A media specialist implements a "battle of the books" competition to see if she can increase the number of books students in the school read.

16.2 Types of Action Research

The different types of action research can be classified in two ways. First, we can classify the type of action research by whether it is classroom based or system based. **Classroom-based action research** is conducted at the classroom level to affect a classroom-level issue. This can be research conducted by an individual or a group of teachers designed to affect their own classrooms. Dennis, Knight, and Jerman (2016) employed a classroom-based action research study. One of the authors of this study was a classroom teacher. Using information from previously published traditional research on model drawing to teach solving fraction and percentage word problems, they conducted a study with three students with a learning disability who were having difficulty in solving mathematical word problems in the teacher's classroom. **System-based action research** is conducted within a context larger than just the classroom that considers educational delivery systems or policy. This may be research conducted by a school, school system, or larger community-based group of stakeholders that investigates a systemic issue. Ferrell, Nance, Torres, and Torres (2014) conducted a systems-based action research study within their school regarding a particular problem they were having with students cutting class at the school. They asked other school staff and students why students cut class. They used that information to change school practices and the school attendance policy. Kenner and Ruby (2012) conducted a larger action research study with six schools in London, pairing mainstream schools with "complementary" schools that served Bengali, Somali, and Russian communities to create a syncretic curriculum that was inclusive of the cultural and linguistic knowledge of the students from these different countries living in London. The end result was a shared curriculum that included and supported aspects of each culture.

> **Classroom-based action research** is conducted at the classroom level to affect a classroom-level issue.
>
> **System-based action research** is conducted within a larger context that considers educational delivery systems or policy.

Action research can also be classified by whether it is practical or participatory action research. **Practical action research** is designed to address a localized, classroom-based issue. Participatory action research is a blend of the principles of action research and critical theory (described in Chapter 12) to address educational issues in a broad context of a social sphere in which education is situated. We will discuss each of these in more depth in the next sections.

> **Practical action research** is a planned, systematic inquiry to try out new practices and evaluate the impact of the new practice.

Practical Action Research

Practical action research is very much like the general description of action research in that it is a planned, systematic inquiry to try out new practices and evaluate the impact of the new practice in a local context. It is can involve one practitioner or a small collaborative group of practitioners with an emphasis on changing teacher practices as a localized, classroom issue and subsequent student outcomes. Schmuck (1997, 2006) describes practical action research as something that practitioners need to embed in their everyday practice; it becomes part of the overall pedagogy to reflect and evaluate instructional practices.

Schmuck (1997, 2006) outlines two types of practical action research: proactive and responsive. **Proactive practical action research** is when the practitioner researcher implements a course of action, such as implementing a new instructional practice, and then collects data related to the practice and reflects upon the effects of the new course of action. This is usually an inspirational and creative idea generated by personal reflection. In **responsive practical action research,** the practitioner researcher collects and analyzes data before implementing the new course of action. This is a more conservative, cautious approach to understand the situation before implementing a change in a course of action. Both proactive and responsive action research are a continuous cycle of reflecting, trying new practices, and evaluating the impact of the change.

> **Proactive practical action research** is when the practitioner researcher implements a course of action, such as implementing a new instructional practice, and then collects data related to the practice and reflects on the effects of the new course of action.
>
> **Responsive practical action research** is when the practitioner researcher collects and analyzes data before implementing the new course of action.

As an example of practical action research, let us consider the study by Dennis et al. (2016). They identified a specific problem—the difficulty of solving mathematical word problems for students with learning disabilities. To address that problem, the teacher implemented a model-drawing strategy as a graphic organizer to structure the information contained within the word problem. The teacher conducted a single-case design study with three students to examine the effectiveness of the model-drawing intervention. While the findings indicated that the strategy was effective, because this was an action research study meant to inform one teacher's practice, there were some limitations to the generalizations that could be made for other students. The authors mention the lack of control for other variables that may have contributed to the findings such as student ability level or teacher skill and the lower quality of the single-case procedures by using a simple AB design without staggering participants into the intervention at different times to establish a functional relationship between the intervention and outcome. Because the teacher implemented the change of practice and conducted a study to examine the effects of that change, this would be an example of proactive practical action research. If the teacher had collected information about the students' difficulty prior to implementing the model-drawing intervention, that would have been an example of reactive action research.

> **Participatory action research (PAR)** merges action research and critical theory to critique educational practices and understand how these practices are defined by the social spheres in which education operates.

Participatory action research, known by its acronym PAR, is also called critical action research or critical theory action research. Participatory action research is aligned with the qualitative research critical theory framework but is not necessarily limited to the collection of qualitative data. It merges action research with the critical theory view that education is a social practice that is framed within our political, cultural, economic, ethnic, and gender-related experiences. It evolved from social movements designed to emancipate individuals from the confines of these social spheres. The objective is to critique the practices that operate within these social spheres to understand how our practices are defined by these social spheres and develop a plan to change these practices. It is a collaborative, community-based framework designed to direct change to improve the lives of others, not limited to the field of education. When applied to education, participatory action research seeks to direct change within the educational system.

Kemmis and McTaggart (2005; Kemmis, McTaggart, & Nixon, 2014) describe participatory action research as an iterative process of planning change, implementing change, observing the consequences of the change, and reflecting upon these observations that leads to additional planning, acting, and reflecting in a cyclical pattern. It is a collaborative process undertaken by those who interact with the practice such as teachers, school administrators, students, parents, and other community stakeholders to understand the educational practice and the conditions under which the practice operates in order to exact change on the practice. The participants of participatory action research seek to understand how their personal practice is affected by the practices and structure of the existing social spheres in which the practice operates. In this way, participatory action research is emancipatory, freeing the participants from these social constraints in order to change their personal practice. Kemmis et al. (2014) call these social spheres "practice architectures" that include cultural, economic, and political contexts. They describe seven features of participatory action research:

- It is a *social process* whereby the participants seek to understand the social spheres in which they operate to improve the process of teaching and learning.

- It is *participatory and collaborative* where a group of individuals works together as equals in a democratic mind-set to understand how the social sphere affects their educational practice.

- It is *practical* in that the group examines real practices such as what people do, how they interact, what they mean and value, and how they interpret their world at the present time.

- It is *emancipatory*, where the participants seek to unconstrain themselves from aspects of the social spheres that limit their personal development and contribute to injustice.

- It is *critical* by analytically examining and challenging the practices of the social spheres that constrain their development.

- It is *reflexive*, using a cyclical process of reflection and action.

- It is *transformative* as it seeks to change theory and practice by examining how theory and practice relate to each other to develop insight that can change both.

Table 16.2 Differences Between Practical and Participatory Action Research Approaches

Practical Action Research	Participatory Action Research
Small scale, an individual or small group of individuals	Collaborative group of stakeholders
Emphasis on local impact of changing educational practices	Emphasis on transforming the social spheres in which the educational practice operates
Problem is framed as localized, classroom issue	Problem is framed within a larger societal perspective
The goal is to change teaching practices that affect student outcomes	The goal is to emancipate participants from the constraints hindering their development

While conceptually different, both practical action research and participatory action research aim to improve educational practice. Practical action research is conducted by individuals or a small group of individuals while participatory action research is a larger group of stakeholders with varying perspectives. Using practical action research, the researcher seeks to change teacher practices and student outcomes with a localized classroom frame of reference. Using participatory action research, the researcher seeks change at a broader social level and frees the participants from the constraints of the social spheres. Table 16.2 describes the differences between the two approaches of practical and participatory research.

Ferrell et al. (2014) framed their system-based action research study within the participatory action research framework to change the educational practices of student absenteeism. They formed a "Class Cutting Task Force" to reflect on and study the issue from multiple perspectives (student families, students, school structures, and school personnel), plan changes to practices and policies about student absenteeism at their school, implement the changes, and observe the consequences of the changes. It was a social process in that they examined different social spheres that affected the problem, including families, classrooms, and school policy. Although the research team consisted of only teachers, it was collaborative, participatory, and critical in that other teachers, students, and other stakeholders such as administrators and school resource officers were consulted during the planning stage. It was practical in that absenteeism was a real issue at the time of the study. The process was emancipatory because teachers felt constrained by the current school policy and actions that seemed not to be working to keep students in school. The process included the opportunity to act and reflect on the action. Finally, it was transformative as teacher practice, student behavior, and beliefs about student absenteeism changed with the implementation of the new practice.

LEARNING CHECK 2 ✓

1. What are two ways to classify action research?

2. What are the seven key features of participatory action research?

3. What are the differences between practical and participatory action research?

4. Identify whether each of the following is (a) proactive, practical action research; (b) responsive, practical action research; or (c) participatory action research.

   A. A high school principal brings together a group of teachers, parents, and community leaders to examine why boys of color are more likely to be suspended from school than other students and develop plans to affect the disproportional school suspensions.

   B. Three special education teachers at an elementary school have a problem with students arriving late to class in the morning. They collect data on the students who arrived late, when they arrive, the reasons for being late, and what happens with the other students when these students arrive late. They use this information to plan a course of action to reduce morning tardiness.

MAKING SENSE—PARTICIPATORY ACTION RESEARCH

Participatory action research (PAR) is connected to critical theory as described in Chapter 12. In our previous discussion of critical theory, it was used in the context of qualitative research designs. This theory focuses on life experiences and the struggles of marginalized groups with power, equity, and justice. In a qualitative design, we use the theory to simply understand and describe the struggles. Now with PAR, we use the theory to understand the struggles and devise a plan of action based on what we learned to address the social issues.

Because we first discussed this theory as a qualitative design does not mean that PAR can only be used with qualitative research designs. We can still use the ideas of this theory to gather the information we need to devise plans of action that deal with these struggles in action research studies that gather quantitative data.

16.3 The Process of Conducting Action Research

Whether conducting a practical action research study or a participatory action research study, there is a process involved in conducting action research. Depending on what type of study is being conducted (proactive practical, responsive practical, or participatory action research), the researcher will cycle through the stages in a different order. The process is cyclical so that once one cycle is completed to the results stage, a second cycle begins with reflecting on these results. Figure 16.1 illustrates this cyclical pattern and the following five stages for conducting action research:

- Reflection stage

- Planning stage

- Implementation stage

- Analysis stage

- Results stage

The reflection stage is to identify a need and to reflect on that need. This is a fact-finding process to understand what the problem is and gather as much information about the problem as you can. Depending on the problem, this may involve several activities.

- Introspective reflection into your own practice and how your practice contributes to the problem. Being self-critical can be difficult, but understanding the dynamics between teacher and student is an important aspect to directing change.

- Observation of the target situation to gather information to (a) specifically describe the problem, (b) determine whether there are antecedent conditions associated with the problem, and/or (c) determine the consequences associated with the problem.

Figure 16.1   Action Research Is Conducted in a Cyclical Pattern

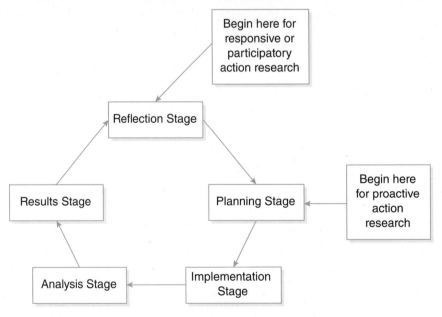

Note: The action researcher will begin the cycle at a different stage depending upon the type of action research used but will cycle through all the different stages.

- Needs assessment to gather information from key stakeholders about the problem. A needs assessment systematically gathers information through surveys, interviews, or focus groups. This can help in determining the scope of the problem and what others already know about it.

The planning stage is to plan a course of action. This step outlines the process of implementing a change in practice (aka the independent variable). This process will involve different activities, depending on the practice being implemented.

- Identify, locate, and secure the resources needed to implement the new practice.

- Inform key stakeholders about the change in practice. In some cases, such as with the change in absenteeism practices, there may need to be some lead time before implementing the change.

- If enlisting a team of practitioners, establish the roles of the different team members, ensuring each has an equal voice.

- Identify the research design to be used and outline the steps involved in that design. If the practice involves a group or classroom, decide if you will have a second control group (nonequivalent groups experimental design) or not (single-group experimental design). Decide if you will have a pretest or not. Decide how to determine which group or class will receive the new practice and which one will not. If the practice involves one individual or only a few individuals, select a single-case design.

- Decide what you will measure and how you will measure change associated with the new practice (aka dependent variable). Decide if you will collect qualitative data, quantitative data, or both. Develop a data collection procedure and appropriate forms to make collection easy and efficient.

The implementation stage is the time to implement the course of action. Follow the action plan you devised and make changes to the plan if you need to. Make sure to describe any changes that you make to the original plan. Also make sure to implement the change of practice long enough to see the change. It may be helpful to implement the change within a natural occurring course of time such as a course unit, grading quarter, or semester.

The analysis stage is to analyze the data once implementation is complete. The analysis should be sufficiently described so that all the stakeholders can understand the findings. Descriptive statistics such as frequency, mean, correlation, or Cohen's d will suffice for most action research analyses, but you may want to look at differences between groups using the t test or analysis of variance (ANOVA). If you do not have access to statistical software, Microsoft Excel can handle most analyses and provide graphs and charts to help to visually describe the data. You may decide to enlist someone with data analysis experience to assist you.

The results stage is a reflection upon the results of the analysis. How well did the course of action address the issue? Are you satisfied with the result? If not, think about what you learned about the issue as a result of going through this process, make some changes, and try again. Action research is a process of reflecting, acting, and reflecting again. Also reflect upon the process itself. Are there things that you would do differently next time? Share your results with others such as fellow teachers, administrators, or other stakeholders. They might also be interested in trying out your new practice. If your result was not satisfactory, they may have ideas on how to modify the practice to be more successful.

LEARNING CHECK 3 ✓

1. Define each stage of the action research process.

2. In what way does this process differ for proactive and responsive action research?

Answers: 1. Reflection stage is to identify and assess the educational need, planning stage plans a course of action, implementation stage implements the course of action, analysis stage conducts the analysis, results stage reflects on the results; 2. Proactive action research begins with the planning stage while responsive action research begins at the reflection stage.

CONNECTING TO THE CLASSROOM

Have an issue in your classroom that you would like to address? You can use action research to evaluate your own practice by using any of the research designs (qualitative, quantitative, or mixed methods) described in previous chapters of this book. If the issue is with a student or a few students not making the expected academic progress, try a single-case design. Perhaps the problem is a little broader, such as dealing with the grief over the death of a classmate. A group experimental design can be helpful.

Make sure to implement the change in practice long enough to see the effect. It is easier to implement changes using the normal structure of the class schedule such as a unit, quarter, or semester. If you don't see an effect to a change in practice where you expected to see some change, it could be that you just didn't implement it long enough.

If you are reluctant to engage in action research because of the statistics involved, you do not need to be a statistician to calculate the results you need. Formulas for mean, standard deviation, frequency, correlation, and t test can be found in Microsoft Excel. Microsoft Excel can create nice graphs and charts to display the data visually. Cohen's d is an easy way to examine progress of students over time or to examine the difference between groups. There are free effect size calculators on the web to help you calculate Cohen's d (e.g., http://www.uccs.edu/~lbecker/, http://www.socscistatistics.com/effectsize/Default3.aspx, or http://www.cem.org/effect-size-calculator).

16.4 Ethics in Focus: Ethical Considerations in Action Research

Conducting action research to inform personal educational practices means that the practitioner action researcher (you) will have a different kind of relationship with the participants than other researchers who are not known to the participants. These participants will likely have a personal relationship with the practitioner action researcher such as the students in the classroom in which the teacher is teaching or parents in the school in which the researcher is the principal. It will be important for the practitioner who is conducting the action research to be able to clearly set boundaries for this dual role. We can do this in several ways, as described in this section.

First, we can restrict the research and the type of information that is collected to be clearly aligned to educational practices under which the action researcher has some control. Asking students about parental discipline styles or family interactions at home is not a good idea. This is a confidentiality issue where the participants may not want you to know certain information about them. If the issue involves personal, out-of-school issues, it would be a better idea to enlist someone with research experience and without the personal relationship to conduct this research for you.

Second, we can establish a collaborative relationship with the research partners where everyone has an equal voice. A research team will need a leader, but this leader should not take an authoritarian role. This is especially important if some of the team members have a supervisory role to other team members such as teachers and students or teachers and principals. Take steps to separate the roles of research team members from their principal roles outside of the research team.

Finally, we can protect participants of action research by avoiding any possible coercion to participate in the action research study. The best way to avoid a sense of coercion is to provide both an informed consent that outlines the study and the time commitment for parents and an assent for the student participants. The informed consent and assent should include how information from the study will be kept confidential and provide an option for the participant to drop out of the study without any repercussions. The action researcher should have both parental consent and student assent in order for the student to be a participant.

When the action research study is being conducted during the normal course of the school day and within the purview of a teacher's normal duties to provide effective instruction, an informed consent or assent may not be needed. For example, if a teacher wants to implement a new strategy to ignore a student who speaks out of turn and positively reinforce the student for raising his or her hand, implement a time delay instructional strategy to teach vocabulary words, or have parents sign a weekly homework log to see if these changes affect student behavior, an informed consent would not be needed. If the action research study involves an activity that does not typically occur in the classroom like the students participating in the survey on absenteeism in the Ferrell et al. (2014) study, the action researcher will want to provide the appropriate informed parental consent and student assent.

16.5 Evaluation of Action Research

Reflection and continuous improvement of local classroom practices are the cornerstones of action research that distinguish it from traditional research. To be reflective and continuously improve, the action research project itself should be evaluated. We can use the phases of action research in the evaluation process. Table 16.3 lists the phases of action research and some evaluation criteria for each phase. When evaluating the phase to reflect and identify the need, make sure the researchers are engaged in a fact-finding mission to describe the educational problem from multiple stakeholder perspectives and the issue is clearly defined. The plan of action should also be clearly described and linked to the facts about the issue gathered in the identification phase. There should be a description of the roles of the research team, and there should be access to the resources needed to address the issue. The implementation of the course of action and any changes that needed to be made to the course of action should also be described. The length of implementation should be long enough to be able to see a change. The time needed to see the change will vary depending on the course of action. We have to use our best judgment and professional expertise to make this call. The data analysis should be sufficiently described and have a direct connection to the problem. For example, if the problem is tardiness, then the data should be centered on tardiness (e.g., arrival time, reason for tardiness, number of times being tardy, consequences of tardiness for the student and classmates). The results should be described in a way that all the key stakeholders can understand them. At the end of the study, there should be a reflection of the result of the change action and some discussion of what other action may be needed to resolve the issue.

There are two disadvantages of action research. First, the process of reflection, planning, and evaluating educational practice does take time, especially when first incorporating it as a part of everyday pedagogical practice. In the long run, however, it can also save time. Using reflection and data to evaluate whether a practice is effective or not

Table 16.3   Criteria for Evaluating the Action Research Project

Phases of Action Research	Evaluation Criteria
Identify and reflect on the need	• The research addresses an issue of educational practice. • Researchers are engaged in adequate fact-finding activities. • The issue is clearly described/defined. • Information is collected from key stakeholders.
Plan a course of action	• The plan of action is clearly described. • The plan of action is linked to the reflection and data are gathered from stakeholders. • Role of the research team is described. • The team accesses the resources it needs.
Implement course of action	• Implementation of the plan of action is described adequately. • Changes to the plan of action are described. • Time was sufficient to see the desired change.
Analyze data	• Analysis is sufficiently described and understandable. • Analysis is connected to the issue to be addressed.
Reflect on results	• The researchers reflect on the results. • Plans for future action are described.

can be seen in a relatively short period of time such as a unit or semester. It is also more time saving than simple trial and error without the thoughtful reflection and collection of data. The second disadvantage of action research is the need for a fundamental understanding of research methods to devise a course of action to evaluate the practice. The practitioner action researcher does not need to be an expert in research methods. A graduate-level course and practicing an action research study in coursework are usually sufficient. There are books on action research in layman's terms to guide the novice action researcher. If additional guidance is needed to get started, a university faculty member in the needed content area can serve as a resource.

LEARNING CHECK 4 ✓

1. What are some ways to protect participants within the dual role of practitioner and researcher?

2. Describe when you would need informed parental consent and student assent.

3. Briefly describe how to evaluate an action research project.

Answers: 1. Restrict the type of information collected from student participants, enlist help from an outside researcher, clearly separate role of teacher and researcher, obtain informed parental consent and student assent; 2. You need consent and assent whenever the research topic or practice is outside of the teacher's normal duties; 3. Make sure that each step of the action research process is thoroughly described.

CHAPTER SUMMARY

LO 1 Define action research.

- Action research is the implementation of systematic inquiry conducted by educational practitioners that is designed to answer questions related to educational practices and student learning outcomes in the context of a specific educational environment.

LO 2 Identify and describe the differences between traditional and action research.

- In traditional research, the researcher is someone typically outside of the immediate educational context. In action research, the researcher is an educational practitioner.

- In traditional research, reflection is objective. In action research, reflection is subjective.

- In traditional research, the relationship between researcher and participants is typically hierarchical, with the researcher as the authority. In action research, the participants are seen as equals with a voice in the process.

- In traditional research, the researcher is the decision maker. In action research, there is collaborative, democratic decision making among collaborators.

- Traditional research studies educational issues that affect a large group. Action research studies local issues within a specific context.

- In traditional research, the findings are generalizable to a larger group. In action research, findings are interpreted within the local context.

- In traditional research, reflection centers on the research process to affect the practice of others. In action research, self-reflection is personal about how the self affects practice.

- In traditional research, dissemination is broad to include publications in journals and presentations at national conferences. In action research, dissemination is local to colleagues or other interested community stakeholders.

- Traditional research is a one-shot deal that has a beginning and an end. Action research is a cyclical process of continuous improvement as students and circumstances change.

LO 3 Distinguish between classroom-based and system-based action research.

- **Classroom-based action research** is conducted at the classroom level to affect a classroom-level issue.

- **System-based action research** is conducted within a larger context that considers educational delivery systems or policy.

LO 4 Define practical and participatory action research.

- **Practical action research** is a planned, systematic inquiry to try out new practices and evaluate the impact of the new practice.

- **Participatory action research** merges action research and critical theory to critique educational practices and understand how these practices are defined by the social spheres in which education operates.

LO 5 Distinguish between proactive and responsive practical action research.

- **Proactive practical action research** is when the practitioner researcher implements a course of action, such as implementing a new instructional practice, and then collects data related to the practice and reflects on the effects of the new course of action.

- **Responsive practical action research** is when the practitioner researcher collects and analyzes data before implementing the new course of action.

LO 6 Define the seven key features of participatory action research.

- It is a *social process* whereby the participants seek to understand the social spheres in which they operate to improve the process of teaching and learning.

- It is *participatory and collaborative*, where a group of individuals works together as equals in a democratic mind-set to understand how the social sphere affects their educational practice.

- It is *practical* in that the group examines real practices such as what people do, how they interact, what they mean and value, and how they interpret their world at the present time.

- It is *emancipatory*, where the participants seek to unconstrain themselves from aspects of the social spheres that limit their personal development and contribute to injustice.

- It is *critical* by analytically examining and challenging the practices of the social spheres that constrain their development.

- It is *reflexive*, using a cyclical process of reflection and action.

- It is *transformative* as it seeks to change theory and practice by examining how theory and practice relate to each other to develop insight that can change both.

LO 7 Identify the differences between practical and participatory action research.

- Practical action research includes individual/small groups while participatory action research includes a collaborative group.

- Practical action research emphasizes changing teacher practice while participatory action research emphasizes changing the social spheres.

- Practical action research investigates a local classroom problem while participatory action research includes a societal perspective of the issue.

- Practical action research emphasizes the impact on student outcomes while participatory action research emphasizes emancipation from social constraints.

LO 8 Identify and describe the stages of action research.

- The reflection stage is to identify a need and to reflect on that need. This is a fact-finding process to understand what the problem is and gather as much information about the problem as you can.

- The planning stage is to plan a course of action. This step outlines the process of implementing a change in practice.

- The implementation stage is to implement the course of action.

- The analysis stage is to analyze the data once implementation is complete.

- The results stage is a reflection on the results of the analysis.

LO 9 Explain the ethical considerations when conducting action research and what can be done to address them.

- The practitioner action researcher will have a personal relationship with the participants compared to other researchers who are not known to the participants. It will be important for the practitioner who is conducting the action research to be able to clearly set boundaries for this dual role.

- Restrict the research and the type of information that is collected to be clearly aligned to educational practices under which the action researcher has some control.

- Establish a collaborative relationship with the research partners where everyone has an equal voice.

- Take steps to separate the roles of research team members from their principal roles outside of the research team.

- Avoid a sense of coercion to provide both an informed consent that outlines the study and the time commitment for parents and an assent for the student participants.

LO 10 Describe how to evaluate action research.

- Each phase of action research can be evaluated based on the clear descriptions of each phase and its connection to the educational issue under investigation.

KEY TERMS

action research 451

classroom-based action research 455

participatory action research (PAR) 456

practical action research 455

practitioner 453

proactive practical action research 456

reflection 453

responsive practical action research 456

systems-based action research 455

REVIEW QUESTIONS

1. What characteristic of the differences between action research and traditional research is reflected in the following scenarios? Does it reflect traditional or action research?
   A. The researcher directs the study.
   B. Findings are interpreted in the context of the classroom where the study took place.
   C. The study is a part of a process of continuous improvement.

2. What is the distinguishing difference between classroom-based and system-based action research?

3. State the type of action research design—(a) practical, (b) participatory (PAR), or (c) both—that is most closely associated with the following terms:
   A. Reflection
   B. Emancipatory
   C. Course of action
   D. Local classroom issue
   E. Social sphere
   F. Practitioner

4. What is the distinguishing difference between proactive practical action research and responsive practical action research?

5. A researcher conducts a PAR project on the use of alternative schools for students who have been removed from traditional schools. Justify how this could be conducted as PAR.

6. Identify the stage of action research in the following descriptions.

    A. The researcher recruits a collaboration team that outlines the research design and how data will be collected.

    B. The team reflects on the findings and how they will act upon them. They share the findings with others.

7. State whether the following statements about the evaluation of an action research project are true or false.

    A. The evaluation plan should examine each phase of the action research process.

    B. Describing changes made to the plan of action is part of the evaluation of the plan, which details the course of action phase.

    C. Evaluation of the action research process is an optional step in the continuous improvement process.

8. A teacher is interested in understanding the extent of cyberbullying among her students. What type of action research can best be used to investigate this issue? Why?

9. A principal has a high turnover rate. She is interested in attracting and retaining highly qualified teachers at her Title I school. What type of action research can be used to investigate this issue? Why?

10. A school board member is concerned about white flight from the public, urban school system in which she lives. What type of action research can be used to investigate this issue? Why?

ACTIVITIES

1. For any of the three following topics, identify an action research design that could be used to study the topic. Describe the steps of the action research study.

    A. High teacher turnover

    B. Low parent involvement

    C. Increase of weapons on school grounds

    D. Impact of direct instruction on reading fluency

    E. Impact of inquiry-based teaching

    F. Effect of peer tutoring

    G. Improving school attendance

    H. Effect of media on student engagement

2. Select an educational problem in your own practice and design an action research study.

   A. What is the educational problem?

   B. What type of information can you gather on the problem?

   C. Design a course of action.

   D. Determine what type of data you will collect.

   E. Describe how you will analyze the data.

   F. Describe how you will reflect upon the results.

3. Select an educational problem in your own practice and reflect. Reflect on your personal pedagogy and gather information from others.

   A. What is the educational problem?

   B. What did you do to reflect on your personal pedagogy?

   C. How did you gather information from others about it?

   D. From whom did you gather information?

$SAGE edge™

SAGE edge offers a robust online environment featuring an impressive array of free tools and resources for review, study, and further exploration, keeping both instructors and students on the cutting edge of teaching and learning.

Access practice quizzes, eFlashcards, video, and multimedia at edge.sagepub.com/priviterarme.

Identify a problem

- Determine an area of interest.
- Review the literature.
- Identify new ideas in your area of interest.
- Develop a research hypothesis.

Develop a research plan

- Define the variables being tested.
- Identify participants or subjects and determine how to sample them.
- Select a research strategy and design.
- Evaluate ethics and obtain institutional approval to conduct research.

Generate more new ideas

- Results support your hypothesis—refine or expand on your ideas.
- Results do not support your hypothesis—reformulate a new idea or start over.

After reading this chapter, you should be able to:

1 Distinguish between merit and worth of an educational program, policy, product, or process.
2 Identify who potential stakeholders are in an evaluation.
3 Distinguish between evaluation and research.
4 Describe the standards that are used to guide evaluations (Joint Committee on Standards for Educational Evaluation).
5 Identify three uses for program evaluations.
6 Describe the limitations of program evaluation.
7 Summarize the ethical responsibilities of the evaluator and how to address them.
8 Distinguish between internal and external evaluation.
9 Distinguish between formative and summative evaluation.
10 Distinguish between expertise-oriented and consumer-oriented evaluation approaches.
11 Distinguish the difference and similarities between the four program-oriented approaches to evaluation (objective-oriented, logic models, theory-based, and goal-free evaluation).
12 Distinguish the difference and similarities between the two approaches to decision-oriented evaluation (the CIPP model and utilization-focused evaluation).
13 Distinguish the difference and similarities between the four approaches to participant-oriented evaluation (responsive, developmental, empowerment, and deliberative democratic). Identify which are practical participatory and transformative participatory.

Conduct the study

- Execute the research plan and measure or record the data.

Communicate the results

- Method of communication: oral, written, or in a poster.
- Style of communication: APA guidelines are provided to help prepare style and format.

Analyze and evaluate the data

- Analyze and evaluate the data as they relate to the research hypothesis.
- Summarize data and research results.

chapter
seventeen

PROGRAM EVALUATION

Suppose that you have set a New Year's resolution to lose weight and improve your overall physical health. After investigating your options, you formulate a plan to join a local fitness club, work with a personal trainer, and use a calorie counter app. To implement your plan, you work out four times per week, meet with a personal trainer once a month, and enter what you eat each day in the calorie counter app to track your calorie intake. Of course, now you need a way to evaluate whether or not your plan is effectively lowering your weight and improving your overall physical health. To measure this, each week you keep a record of your weight, take measurements of your body, count your calories, and keep a diary of how you feel. After 3 months, you review your records and compile all the expenses of your new initiative. You decide that you are happy with your progress. You have lost weight, have greater stamina, and have reduced your total daily calorie count. You decide that your plan is effective and thus is worth the cost.

In this example, you conducted an informal, personal program evaluation. You developed a plan, implemented the plan, and recorded information about the plan you created (e.g., weight, calorie intake, body measurements, and cost) to make a decision about the effectiveness of your plan to lose weight and improve your overall physical health. Similarly, in this chapter, we will introduce program evaluation as a process in educational settings whereby we collect data to use in making decisions about educational programs, policies, products, or processes. Similar to how you evaluated your personal health goals in our example, it is likewise important to evaluate our educational endeavors to maximize the outcomes for students, teachers, administrators, and our communities.

> **edge.sagepub.com/ priviterarme**
>
> - Take the chapter quiz
> - Review key terms with eFlashcards
> - Explore multimedia links and SAGE articles
>
> **$SAGE edge™**

17.1 The Fundamentals of Program Evaluation

The practice of education involves many different programs, policies, products, or processes. Examples of some programs, policies, products, or processes within the practice of education are displayed in Table 17.1. Professionals in education often need to make decisions or judgments about these programs, policies, products, or processes. We often ask questions such as the following: Did the program, policy, process, or product produce the intended outcome? Are there unintended outcomes? Is one program or product more cost-effective than another? What is the feasibility or usability of the program or product? What do people think about how the policy or process is implemented? These are examples of the types of questions we ask in the educational field in which we can use program evaluation.

Program evaluation is the systematic process of gathering information about the merit and worth of something and making a judgment about it in regard to a set of predetermined criteria (Scriven, 1991a).

Merit is the quality of the evaluand in comparison to predetermined criteria or a criterion (Davidson, 2005).

Worth is the value of the evaluand in the specific context in which it is being evaluated (Mathison, 2005).

There are many different kinds of program evaluations, each with their own definition because it is applicable to so many different fields and contexts. We define program evaluation as the systematic process of gathering information about the merit (quality) and worth (value) about something and making a judgment of it in regard to a set of predetermined criteria (Scriven, 1991a). We have chosen the definition provided by Michael Scriven because it encompasses many of the ideas set forth in the many definitions of program

Table 17.1 Examples of Educational Programs, Policies, Products, or Processes

Educational Practices	Examples
Programs	Communities in Schools (CIS)
	Character education
	Drug Alcohol Awareness Education (DARE)
Policies	Attendance
	Discipline
	Testing
Products	Published curricula
	Manipulatives
	Computer equipment
Processes	Special education referrals
	Budgeting
	School improvement

evaluation. This definition is useful when applied to the educational setting since the goal of program evaluation in education often involves the concepts of merit and worth. The distinction between merit and worth is an important one. Merit involves an interpretation of the quality of something compared to a set of predetermined criteria (Davidson, 2005). Rather than simply providing a description of the idea being examined to be interpreted by others as in traditional research, evaluation takes it one step further to evaluate the intrinsic value (basic or essential attributes) of the idea. Worth is the value of the idea within the context in which it is being applied (Mathison, 2005). Figure 17.1 illustrates how it is possible that something has merit but not worth or vice versa.

Figure 17.1 Illustration of the Difference Between Merit and Worth of a Program

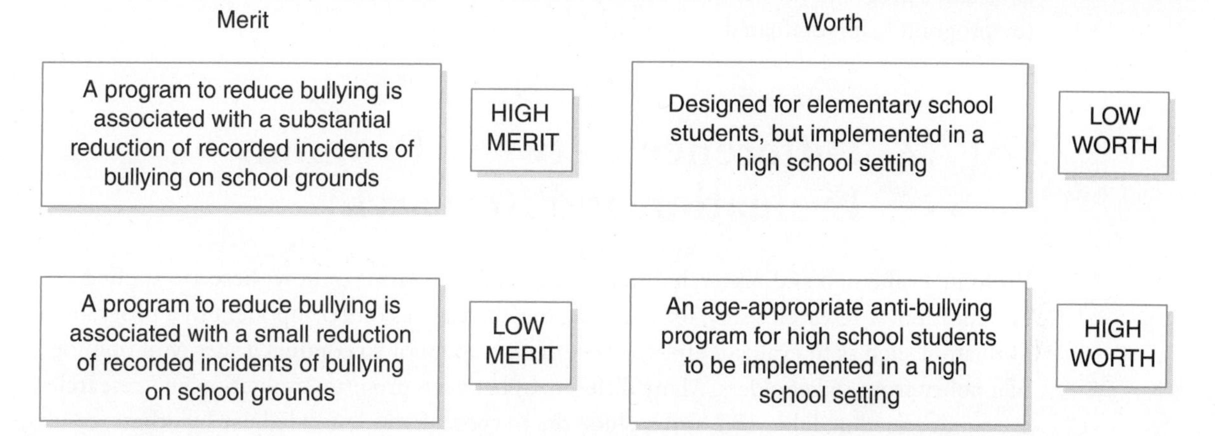

Merit

| A program to reduce bullying is associated with a substantial reduction of recorded incidents of bullying on school grounds | HIGH MERIT |

Worth

| Designed for elementary school students, but implemented in a high school setting | LOW WORTH |

| A program to reduce bullying is associated with a small reduction of recorded incidents of bullying on school grounds | LOW MERIT |

| An age-appropriate anti-bullying program for high school students to be implemented in a high school setting | HIGH WORTH |

CONNECTING TO THE CLASSROOM

A program to reduce bullying is being implemented in a high school. It may have a good record of success in reducing recorded incidents of bullying on school grounds (merit) but is designed for implementation with elementary school students and not high school students with whom it is being implemented (worth). On the other hand, the high school might find an age-appropriate antibullying program for high school students (worth), but it did not reduce incidents of bullying on school grounds (merit).

Program evaluation can be used to evaluate just about anything and with anyone. Instead of using the word *something* as in the Scriven (1991a) definition of program evaluation, the entity being evaluated is often called the **evaluand.** An *evaluand*

Evaluand is a generic term referring to the entity being evaluated. This may be, but is not limited to, a person, product, policy, or idea (Mathison, 2005).

is a generic term to refer to the thing being evaluated, and it can be any program, product, policy, process, or idea.

Stakeholders are an important element in program evaluation. The term stakeholder is the person who has a vested interest in the evaluand. According to Greene (2005), stakeholders can be divided into four groups of people that include (1) those who have the decision authority over the evaluand such as school advisory boards, funding agencies, or education policy makers; (2) those directly responsible for implementing the evaluand, such as school administrators and teachers; (3) those who are the intended beneficiaries or participants of the evaluand, such as parents and students; and (4) those excluded from participating in the evaluand, such as applicants who applied for funding for an alternative program but were not funded or students who applied but were not admitted into the program being evaluated.

> A stakeholder is any person who has a vested interest in the evaluand being evaluated (Greene, 2005).

17.2 Difference Between Program Evaluation and Research

Program evaluation and research differ in many ways in terms of how these are applied to education. A research study, for example, may be used as one component of a program evaluation such as to evaluate effectiveness of a program or to conduct a survey of opinions of a policy from stakeholders. Many differences between program evaluation and research are summarized in Table 17.2 and include the purpose, focus, intended use by others, results, quality criteria, skills required, and dissemination (Fitzpatrick, Sanders, & Worthen, 2011; Mathison, 2007). The purpose of research is to produce generalizable findings that describe relationships or causality between known variables that can be used to develop or refine a theory. It is designed to add knowledge to a field of study. While participants may benefit from implementation of a classroom-based intervention, a larger goal is to advance the theory and develop new knowledge around the intervention so that it may be generalized to others. The purpose of program evaluation is to gather information that describes the merit and value of an evaluand so that it can be used in making a judgment or decision about the evaluand in the specific context in which the evaluation is taking place. There is no intention to generalize the findings to a broader audience.

The foci of research and evaluation also differ. In research, the focus is researcher oriented in that the researcher largely determines the focus, including what research questions to ask and how these questions are best answered. The researcher is considered the expert with the knowledge and skills needed to carry out a study. In program evaluation, the focus is stakeholder oriented. Inclusion of stakeholders in the evaluation process is an important element in program evaluation. A group of stakeholders will often generate the purpose for the evaluation and lead the direction of the evaluation, and a program evaluator may provide input. Additional stakeholders are often included in the evaluation itself to make sure that the evaluation represents the variety of stakeholders affected by the evaluand. Since education is in the public domain, educational program evaluation may often be politically oriented. Diverse political and societal factions have different opinions about public education, and this can affect the priorities of the community and stakeholders in which the evaluation is taking place. Thus, political orientation of the community of stakeholders will affect the focus of the evaluation.

Another difference between research and evaluation is the intended use of the findings by others. In educational research, the researchers will often provide ideas for future research by other researchers to advance the field. They also often provide implications for practitioners to generalize the findings to a broader population than the participants engaged in the actual study. In this way, the impact is delayed and dependent on others to use the information provided by the research. Other researchers may or may not use the suggestions for future research. Practitioners may or may not decide to try to implement the intervention in their classrooms. In fact, the delay for practitioners is quite large with a well-known gap between what we know as a result of research and what is implemented in classrooms. The findings of an evaluation are much quicker than research. The findings are directly linked to and used immediately for making a decision about the evaluand. The findings are intended to be used only by the immediate community of stakeholders and in the specific context in which the evaluation occurred.

The results of research are conclusions made by analyzing and interpreting the data generated by the study. The researchers interpret the findings and compare them to previous research findings. They describe how the results are the same or how they differ from previous work and then make a conclusion about the entity being studied. In program evaluation, the result of the evaluation is the judgment or decision made as a result of the evaluation. Ultimately, the decision may be to continue/not continue to implement the evaluand or modify the evaluand for future use.

Researchers and program evaluators need different skills. Those who conduct research need to have extensive knowledge and expertise in the field of study. Researchers typically follow a specific line or area of research throughout their career. They also need to have knowledge of research methods and data analysis techniques to conduct a research study. Program evaluators do not necessarily need expertise in the area being evaluated as the stakeholders have the expertise. The program evaluator is the collector and organizer of the information. Instead, program evaluators need skills in group dynamics, personnel management, and organizational processes needed to manage a diverse group of stakeholders.

Due to the different purposes of program and evaluation, the products produced and disseminated are different. Research is primarily published as an article in research journals that are readily available to others. Most journals are peer-reviewed, so the work is vetted by others in the field before it is disseminated. Research articles are intended to be read by many people unknown to the researchers. Program evaluations are reports provided to stakeholders. These reports may likely not be available to others outside of the context in which the evaluation took place. While some program evaluations that include a research study may be published, most are not.

The final way that research and evaluation differ is in the criteria used to judge the quality of the research/evaluation. Quality of research is judged by its internal and external validity, replicability, and implementation fidelity. The more rigorous the study to control

Table 17.2 Differences Between Program Evaluation and Research

	Program Evaluation	Research
Purpose	Describe the merit and value Make a judgment or decision Context specific	Produce generalizable findings Describe relationships or causality Develop or refine a theory Add knowledge to a field of study
Focus	Stakeholder oriented Political orientation	Researcher oriented
Intended use by others	Decision making Immediate impact	Ideas for future research Implications for practitioners Delayed impact
Results	The judgment/decision made	Conclusions Compare them to previous research
Skills required	Group dynamics Personnel management Organizational processes	Extensive knowledge in the field Research methods Data analysis techniques
Dissemination	Reports to stakeholders Not widely disseminated	Article in journals Peer-reviewed Publicly available
Quality criteria	Utility Feasibility Propriety Accuracy	Internal and external validity Replicability Implementation fidelity

for threats to internal and external validity, provide a sufficient description so that the study may be replicated, and monitor accurate implementation of the independent variable, the higher the quality of the research. The quality of a program evaluation is judged by its utility, feasibility, propriety, and accuracy (Joint Committee on Standards for Educational Evaluation, 2010). These criteria address quality of a program evaluation based on how it is conducted and used. Let us take a look at these standards.

LEARNING CHECK 1 ✓

1. Define program evaluation.

2. Label each of the following as an illustration of merit or merit.

   A. Laptops purchased for a school at a good price are in good condition.

   B. Laptops purchased for a school are not compatible with the district grading software.

C. A school district offers an alternative program for students who are at risk for dropping out of high school that is available at only some of the high schools.

D. A school district creates an alternative program for students who are at risk for dropping out of high school that has a good record of success.

3. What are seven ways in which research differs from evaluation?

17.3 Program Evaluation Standards

Program Evaluation Standards provided by the Joint Committee on Standards for Educational Evaluation (2010) were developed to guide what a reasonable program evaluation looks like. The Standards are intended to be used by those who conduct program evaluations and consumers of program evaluation and are applicable to a variety of different educational contexts such as in individual schools, school districts, or community agencies that interact with educational settings. There are 30 program evaluation standards in four standard areas: utility, feasibility, propriety, and accuracy. A brief description of the standards with additional details appears in Table 17.3.

Utility is the extent to which the evaluation provides the stakeholders with the information they need in order for the information to be used to make an informed decision. The Standards identify seven utility standards that include stakeholder identification, evaluator credibility, information scope and selection, values identification, report clarity, report timeliness, and evaluation impact. These standards are designed to ensure that the evaluation serves its intended purpose.

Feasibility is the extent to which the evaluation procedures are realistic, diplomatic, and practical given the available time, budget, staff, and stakeholders. The Standards list three feasibility standards that include practical procedures, political viability, and cost-effectiveness. The feasibility standards consider what resources are available because if a program evaluation will seriously disrupt the organizational processes or personnel or exceed the resources available, the organization is not likely to conduct one.

> **Utility** is the extent to which the evaluation provides the stakeholders with the information they need in order for the information to be used to make an informed decision.
>
> **Feasibility** is the extent to which the evaluation procedures are realistic, diplomatic, and practical given the available time, budget, staff, and stakeholders.
>
> **Propriety** is the consideration of the legal and ethical issues that surround the evaluation.

Propriety is the consideration of the legal and ethical issues that surround the evaluation. The Standards provide eight propriety standards that include service orientation, formal agreements, rights of human subjects, human interactions, complete and fair assessment, disclosure of findings, conflict of interest, and fiscal responsibility. There could be serious legal consequences if evaluations did not observe all the legal and ethical obligations for protecting

Table 17.3 Program Evaluation Standards (Joint Committee on Standards for Educational Evaluation, 2010)

Standard Area	Standards	Description
Utility	<ul><li>Stakeholder identification</li><li>Evaluator credibility</li><li>Information scope and selection</li><li>Values identification</li><li>Report clarity</li><li>Report timeliness</li><li>Evaluation impact</li></ul>	<ul><li>Sufficient identification of the relevant stakeholders</li><li>Competence and trustworthiness of the evaluator to perform the evaluation</li><li>Comprehensive scope of the information collected to adequately assess merit and value</li><li>Careful consideration and transparency of the perspectives and rationale used to interpret the findings</li><li>Extent to which the evaluation reports essential information so that it is easily understood</li><li>Dissemination of the findings in a timely fashion so they may be used for the intended purpose</li><li>Amount of influence on the decisions and actions of the stakeholders</li></ul>
Feasibility	<ul><li>Practical procedures</li><li>Political viability</li><li>Cost-effectiveness</li></ul>	<ul><li>Minimal disruptions to collect the needed information</li><li>Fair and equitable consideration of the various stakeholder groups</li><li>Balance of cost and benefit to justify the resource expenditures</li></ul>
Propriety	<ul><li>Service orientation</li><li>Formal agreements</li><li>Rights of human subjects</li><li>Human interactions</li><li>Complete and fair assessment</li><li>Disclosure of findings</li><li>Conflict of interest (COI)</li><li>Fiscal responsibility</li></ul>	<ul><li>Promotion of excellence in the organizations' ability to serve participants and community</li><li>Provision of a formal written agreement that lists all the obligations of evaluator and client</li><li>Adherence to all ethical and legal human rights protections of participants</li><li>Display respect and dignity by evaluators when interacting with clients and stakeholders</li><li>Examination and reporting of strengths and weaknesses</li><li>Access of the evaluation findings to everyone who may be affected by it</li><li>Is disclosed and acted upon so it does not affect the evaluation process or findings</li><li>Prudent and ethical allocation and expenditure of resources</li></ul>
Accuracy	<ul><li>Program documentation</li><li>Context analysis</li><li>Described purposes and procedures</li><li>Defensible information sources</li><li>Valid information</li><li>Reliable information</li></ul>	<ul><li>Complete, clear, and accurate description of the evaluand</li><li>Detailed examination of the context of the evaluand to identify potential influences</li><li>Purposes and procedures of the evaluation are monitored and described in sufficient detail</li><li>Adequate description of the sources of information used in the evaluation</li><li>Information-gathering procedures are developed and then implemented as they are intended</li></ul>

Standard Area	Standards	Description
	• Systematic information • Analysis of quantitative information • Analysis of qualitative information • Justified conclusions • Impartial reporting • Meta-evaluation	• Information-gathering procedures are developed and then implemented to be reliable • Control for possible errors in scoring, coding or filing, etc. • Quantitative analytic methods should be appropriate for the questions being asked and information being analyzed • Qualitative analytic methods should be appropriate for the questions being asked and information being analyzed • Conclusions should be accompanied by all the information necessary to warrant the conclusions • Avoid undue bias or influence by any party that may distort evaluation findings • The program evaluation itself should be scrutinized to make sure it is conducted appropriately

Source: Adapted from the Joint Committee on Standards for Educational Evaluation (2010).

the welfare of the participants, the organization conducting the evaluation, and the evaluator.

> **Accuracy** addresses the technical adequacy of the information contained in the evaluation.

The **accuracy** standard addresses the technical adequacy of the information contained in the evaluation. This is vital to evaluations since they will be used in making decisions of merit and worth. Inaccurate information can lead to inaccurate decisions. The Standards provide 12 accuracy standards. These standards include program documentation, context analysis, described purposes and procedures, defensible information sources, valid information, reliable information, systematic information, analysis of quantitative information, analysis of qualitative information, justified conclusions, impartial reporting, and meta-evaluation.

17.4 Utility and Importance of Program Evaluation

Providing a society with an educated constituency needed for the survival of the society is likely one of the most important tasks of the society, especially a democratic one. A recent poll across eight states ranked the importance of key issues, with education ranked third behind the economy and government spending/debt (Blizzard, 2015). It ranked above concerns about social security, immigration, health care, and taxes. Interestingly, a recent Gallup poll (Saad, 2016) found that although 67% of parents with children currently in K–12 schools are satisfied with their child's education, only 43% of all Americans are satisfied with U.S. education (includes people who do not have children in K–12 schools). The importance of an educated populace and the need to improve satisfaction for K–12 education provide incentives to continuing to improve our educational system. Program evaluation is one tool that we can use to improve educational services.

Think about the number of different programs, products, processes, and policies used in schools and the resources needed to implement them—time, personnel, money, and the other programs, products, processes, and policies we might be able to implement if we were not implementing the ones we now use. We want to make sure that how we spend our resources is effective and efficient. Who would want to spend resources to implement a program or use a product, process, or policy that would not meet or improve some educational outcome? Consider what can be at stake. Some programs are targeted toward equity and social justice ideas such as increasing academic performance, high school graduation rate, or job readiness for marginalized populations. In the end, it will be the students and our society that will pay the price. Program evaluation is extremely important to find what works and eliminate things that do not work.

Notably, the purpose of program evaluation—to provide information that can be used to make decisions about educational programs, products, policies, and processes—is useful for ground-level decision makers within the educational system itself. Ground-level decision makers include school administrators (e.g., superintendents, principals), teachers, parents, and students. Program evaluation is often used to assess the effectiveness of specific programs and products. It can be used to make a decision regarding whether to keep the program or continue to use the product or not. It can also be used for program improvement. Program evaluation can identify program strengths and weaknesses that can be used to make changes to the program to increase its ability to reach the program's goal. Parents and students are also decision makers but in a different sense. They can use the information from a program evaluation to decide whether what program or product is what they want or need.

In addition to providing information to ground-level decision makers, program evaluation can provide important information to policy makers such as boards of education and state and federal legislators. Most broad-based decisions about educational policy are not made by professionals in the field of education. Policy makers make decisions that affect a wide variety of issues like the economy, environment, health care, national security, and immigration. They cannot be experts in everything. It is imperative that policy makers without a deep understanding of the educational system or teaching be provided with the information they need to know to make informed decisions on education policy.

Information from program evaluation is also helpful and may even be a required component for funding for educational initiatives. Funding for educational initiatives is often provided by government agencies such as state departments of education or national agencies such the U.S. Department of Education, National Institutes of Health, or National Science Foundation. These agencies often require an evaluation as part of the grant application. Nongovernmental agencies such as the Bill & Melinda Gates Foundation and Eli and Edythe Broad Foundation also require program evaluations. Funding agencies want to make sure that the monies are being put to good use. Program evaluation as a part of obtaining and maintaining grant funding demonstrates good stewardship of the donated funds.

Importantly, there are also limitations to a program evaluation. Evaluations are confined by the resources available. Organizations, especially smaller ones, may find it difficult to allocate the money, time, and staff needed to conduct a thorough evaluation and might be inclined to cut a few corners. Cutting corners will likely lead to less thorough evaluation and may lead to erroneous findings. Second, sometimes it might be very difficult to identify and quantify all of the potential benefits, costs, and outcomes associated with a program, product, process, or policy. It might even be impossible to identify them all! Let us take, for example, a school conducting a program evaluation on an antibullying program. Some of the costs, benefits, and outcomes are objectives like the cost of professional development for staff or the number of recorded bullying incidents. Yet some of the costs, benefits, and outcomes are subjective and more difficult to measure, such as the feeling of relief or security the school staff and students may feel, or perhaps there is an unintended outcome where the bullies simply move off campus to neighborhoods or cyberspace. Third, it may also be very difficult to determine who all the stakeholders are and whose viewpoints may be needed for the evaluation. In the case of the school antibullying program, in addition to students and school personnel, parents might be identified as stakeholders. Doing so would then also increase the cost of the evaluation. The conditions surrounding the evaluation can also affect the evaluation. The larger the group of stakeholders, the more diverse the views surrounding the evaluand and subsequently the more difficult it will be to arrive at a consensus conclusion or judgment. Finally, program evaluation often has a political element, and this may affect the evaluation. It is important to make sure all the different political factions are taken into consideration so as not to generate a biased evaluation. There is also the possibility that the evaluation results might be misused to gain political favor. It takes an experienced evaluator to be able to negotiate and control these potential limitations.

1. Which of the four Joint Committee on Standards for Educational Evaluation areas is represented in each of the following:

   A. Cost-effectiveness, practical procedures, political viability

   B. Valid information, reliable information, context analysis

   C. Values identification, evaluation impact, evaluator credibility

2. In what ways can program evaluation be useful?

3. What are the limitations to program evaluation?

17.5 Ethics in Focus: Considerations for Protecting the Welfare of Stakeholders

Like researchers who have an ethical responsibility to protect the welfare of participants in their research study, evaluators have the same ethical responsibility to protect the stakeholders who are participating in the evaluation. Recall that researchers are bound to protect participants from harm. This same is true for program evaluators. One protection is from physical or emotional harm. Program evaluators and stakeholders involved in the evaluation must weigh the benefits and risks for the participants who are engaged in or interacting with the evaluand. Given that some stakeholders will be involved with the delivery of the evaluand in some way, such as an administrator or program director, their view of risk and benefit might be seen with a different set of lenses than someone more removed from the evaluand such as a community member or a participant of the evaluand. It is the role of the evaluator to balance the diverse views of the different stakeholders and ensure protection of the participants.

Another protection for participants of an evaluation is confidentiality. There are several considerations to make for protecting confidentiality when conducting an evaluation. One consideration is in how the participant is described. By providing an adequate description of the participant, it may be possible that he or she can be identified by others familiar with the evaluand, even if the individual's name is not used. Another consideration is the relationship between the stakeholders or the relationship between the participants and the stakeholders. In the case of different relationships between stakeholders, it may be that the stakeholder holds some type of authority over others such as student and teacher, teacher and principal, and principal and the board of education. This could be problematic, particularly if the subordinate's views are different from the stakeholder's views. In the case of the relationship between participants and stakeholders, the stakeholders may have access to information about the participants as a result of being involved in the evaluation and the dual role they serve as part of the evaluation that they would ordinarily not be privy to. In both cases, there may be an added sense of coercion or unease due to the release of information that might affect that relationship. The evaluator must be aware of these relationships and what information each stakeholder should have about the others.

The way to negotiate ethical issues is through the consent and assent process. Recall that consent is required for participation in research studies, and this consent is usually through a signed informed consent document. Adults consent for themselves and as parents will provide consent for their children. Minor children are asked to provide assent. This is true for program evaluations, too. All stakeholders should agree to be a stakeholder. If they decline to participate, then there should be assurances that there will not be any repercussions for declining. The consent form should include a thoughtful description of how confidentiality will be maintained and if there are any risks of physical or emotional harm or breach of confidentiality. Using a pseudonym or assigning individuals with a unique identification number and keeping a list of names with pseudonyms/identification numbers in a secure location are two common ways to protect the identity of an individual.

17.6 Models for Program Evaluation

Internal evaluation is an evaluation conducted by an evaluator internal to the evaluand, such as an employee of the organization.

External evaluation is an evaluation conducted by an evaluator not associated with the evaluand.

Program evaluation can be classified in a number of different ways. We can classify evaluation across two dichotomies—internal evaluation versus external evaluation and formative versus summative. Internal evaluation is one in which the program evaluator has some connection to the program. The advantage of using an internal evaluator is that the evaluator will have extensive knowledge needed about the program. This knowledge can be helpful in many ways, such as knowing who the different stakeholders are, understanding how the evaluand operates, and gaining easy access to the information needed. The disadvantage is that internal evaluators may not be as objective as they need to be because they have some stake in the findings or decision that is being made. An external evaluation is an evaluation by an outsider—someone not connected to the evaluand. This outside person will not have the specific knowledge of the evaluand and will need to be provided with the information that the internal evaluator likely already knows, but an outside evaluator will be more objective and may have increased credibility, especially if his or her expertise is program evaluation.

The second dichotomy is the distinction between a formative evaluation and a summative evaluation. A **formative evaluation** is an evaluation that is conducted while the evaluand is being implemented to provide information to improve it. This type of evaluation looks at the evaluand during delivery to make sure it is operating as it was intended and to be able to fix issues as they arise. It may be used over time as a form of continuous improvement. The audience for a formative evaluation is the program personnel themselves. A **summative evaluation** is an evaluation that occurs at the end of a cycle of the implementation of the evaluand to make a final decision regarding merit and worth. The audience for a summative evaluation includes the potential consumers of the evaluand or surrounding community.

> **Formative evaluation** is an evaluation that is conducted while the evaluand is being implemented.
>
> **Summative evaluation** is an evaluation that occurs at the end of the implementation of the evaluand.

Program evaluations can also be classified according to their theoretical orientation or approach. Fitzpatrick et al. (2011) provide four classifications of evaluation approaches that we will use here: (1) expertise and consumer oriented, (2) program oriented, (3) decision oriented, and (4) participant oriented. Many different evaluation approaches fall into these four categories. We will describe some of the more common ones that can be used to examine educational issues.

MAKING SENSE—FORMATIVE AND SUMMATIVE EVALUATION

Educators employ formative and summative evaluations all the time in the natural activities of education. A teacher provides instruction to students (the evaluand). Throughout the instructional period, the teacher collects information about the progress of the students in activities such as homework and progress monitoring. The teacher uses that information to make changes as necessary to the instruction. This is a formative evaluation. At the end of the grading period (quarter, semester, or year), there is a final decision (maybe even a final exam) made about the progress of the student. This final decision is usually a grade. This is a summative evaluation.

Expertise- and Consumer-Oriented Evaluation

The expertise approach is the oldest form of evaluation. Elliot Eisner (1976, 1991) is a significant contributor to expertise-oriented evaluation with his ideas of connoisseurship. A connoisseur is a person who possesses the expertise to make a critical judgment. The expertise-oriented evaluation relies on the professional expertise of each evaluator to judge the quality of the specific evaluand in terms of its summative outcomes. The evaluations in this approach can be (a) formal or informal, (b) conducted in scheduled time periods or ad hoc, or (c) conducted by an established group or individual.

A formal evaluation system has published standards within an established system or organization where the evaluation assesses an organization's adherence to the standards. The most common form of this type of evaluation is accreditation reviews. An example of a formal review evaluation is the accreditation of university education programs that prepare K–12 educators. The Council for the Accreditation of Educator Preparation (CAEP) consolidated two previous accreditation bodies (National Council for Accreditation of Teacher Education [NCATE] and the Teacher Education Accreditation Council [TEAC]) in 2013. It is an independent accreditation organization that provides standards and a formal review process of teacher education programs to make sure they meet the standards. The decision is the awarding of accreditation or not based on the extent to which the program meets the established standards. Some states also have a formal accountability system to evaluate schools to assign them a grade or other rating based on passing rates and/or progress made by students within the schools. Here the decision is not one of accreditation but the grade or rating it is assigned. An informal review system is one where there is not a set of specific, established standards or a specific review schedule. Examples of an informal review system are the peer review of journal articles or faculty theses and dissertation committees that approve the acceptance of an article for publication or thesis/dissertation necessary for awarding a degree. A key feature of formal and informal evaluation systems is that the status of the entity being evaluated can be directly affected by the results. A teacher education program may lose accreditation, an article may not be published, or a school loses enrollment due to the grade or rating it received, for example.

A second distinction of an expertise-oriented evaluation is that it can be conducted at regularly scheduled time periods or as needed (ad hoc). Some expertise-oriented evaluations occur at regular intervals while others occur at irregular intervals prompted by the need for an evaluation. An accreditation review is an example of an expertise-oriented evaluation that is conducted on a regular schedule. Each year, accredited university teacher education programs provide an annual report to CAEP and participate in an onsite visit by a review panel of experts every 8 years. An example of an ad hoc evaluation is a review of the status of a charter school when it has financial difficulties or fails to meet the state accountability standards for student progress. Charter schools often operate under a separate board of directors from the state boards of education. The charter school board would meet to decide the status of a charter school as an issue arises.

The final distinction of expertise-oriented evaluation approaches is whether it is conducted by an established group or individual. An ad hoc

Expertise-oriented evaluation is an evaluation that is conducted by an expert in the field of study.

evaluation might be conducted by an individual with expertise in the area rather than by a group of experts. In this case, the organization hires a consultant to conduct the evaluation. For example, a school district might hire a consultant to review architectural needs for a new school or to review hiring practices. In such cases, there is no need for an expert group; instead, an individual with the expertise will suffice.

Consumer-oriented evaluation approaches are similar to the expertise-oriented approaches to evaluation in that the intent is to judge the value of the evaluand. The difference between the two approaches is in the expertise, methods of evaluation, and audience. In consumer-oriented evaluation approaches, the evaluator is an expert in evaluation and not necessarily in the evaluand. They are an expert on the methods needed to make judgments. As such, the methods used in

> Consumer-oriented evaluation is an evaluation that is conducted by an expert in evaluation to inform the general public.

consumer-oriented approaches are more quantitative, where quality is measured rather than adherence to a set of standards. The audience is generally broader than in expertise-oriented approaches. In expertise-oriented approaches, the audience is the organization seeking accreditation and the consumers of the specific organizations. In consumer-oriented approaches, the audience is the general public and is not specifically known to the evaluator.

Michael Scriven (1974a, 1974b, 1991b) is a major contributor to the ideas of consumer-oriented evaluation. In his consumer-oriented approach to evaluation, evaluation is needs based rather than goal based. His approach begins with a functional needs assessment to identify the criteria that will be used to judge the performance of the evaluand. Data are collected and then synthesized to make a judgment about the evaluand according to the preset criteria. The

> Needs assessment is a systematic process to identify the priorities of an organization or program.

process of the evaluation requires the evaluator to study the evaluand to gain the knowledge needed for the evaluation as opposed to relying on the a priori expertise of the evaluator. This approach is highly dependent on how the evaluand performs. Scriven (1974a) lists 13 criteria for evaluating educational products and programs, 9 of which are related to performance of the product. The 13 criteria for evaluating educational products and programs are as follows:

1. *Need*—there is evidence of the need of the product or program

2. *Market*—there is a mechanism for the product or program to be disseminated

3. *Performance (true field trials)*—evidence of effectiveness in typical settings

4. *Performance (true consumer)*—field trials use all relevant consumers

5. *Performance (critical comparisons)*—product or program is compared to other similar programs or business-as-usual alternatives

6. *Performance (long term)*—effectiveness is maintained over time

7. *Performance (side effects)*—examination of unintended consequences as a result of use of the product or program

8. *Performance (process)*—evidence of feasibility and usability

9. *Performance (causation)*—evidence includes use of appropriate research methodologies

10. *Performance (statistical significance)*—research uses appropriate statistical analysis

11. *Performance (educational significance)*—other assessments of validity and reliability

12. *Cost-effectiveness*—cost analysis includes both monetary and other cost comparisons

13. *Extended support*—system for continuous review of product or program

The consumer-oriented approach to evaluation as described in the work of Scriven (1974a) is seldom used in educational contexts today, although it is still used in comparisons of products and programs in the business world and government agencies such as in *Consumer Reports* comparisons of products or *U.S. News & World Report* rankings of the best high schools, colleges, or hospitals. The What Works Clearinghouse, sponsored by the U.S. Department of Education, Institute for Education Sciences (http://ies.ed.gov/ncee/wwc/), offers comparisons of educational products and programs in a variety of areas, including literacy, mathematics, science, English language learners, and schoolwide programs.

The expertise- and consumer-oriented approaches were influential in the development of other program evaluation approaches that are more often used today to evaluate programs, policies, products, or processes in educational settings. You can find these two approaches in program-oriented and participant-oriented models that are more often used today.

Program-Oriented Evaluation

Program-oriented evaluation focuses on evaluating the key features of the program and using the key features to decide what to evaluate. There are four program-oriented approaches: (1) objective-oriented, (2) logic models, (3) theory-based, and (4) goal-free evaluation.

Program-oriented evaluation approaches focus on evaluating the key features of the program and using the key features to decide what to evaluate. There are four program-oriented approaches: (1) objective oriented, (2) logic models, (3) theory based, and (4) goal-free evaluation. Let us explore each of these evaluation approaches.

Objective-Oriented Evaluation

The key feature of the objective-oriented approach to evaluation is the specification of the objectives of the program, product, policy, or process and then assessing the extent to which these objectives have been met. Ralph Tyler is a prominent developer of the objective-oriented approach to evaluation. He believed that the purpose of educational program evaluation was to appraise the educational objectives (Tyler, 1986). He noted that every subject of an educational curriculum includes the things that a student should learn, and the program should include a plan for student learning. Therefore, program evaluation should identify the objectives, measure the performance of students, and analyze the data in relation to the objectives. The success of the program is the extent to which the program meets these objectives. The difference between the objective and the performance of students could be used for modifying the plan for student learning. While the approach seemed logical and reasonable at the time, today this approach is seen as too simplistic. Education and learning are very dynamic concepts that involve more than simply meeting objectives.

Logic Model Evaluation

Logic models are an extension of the objective-oriented approach to evaluation. They address the criticism that objective-oriented evaluation is too simplistic. Logic models add information in the evaluation process about how the program objectives are achieved. Initially developed by Joseph Wholey (1987), logic models include a graphic representation of the logical relationships between the different elements of the program. Typically, these elements comprise inputs, activities, outputs, and outcomes. Inputs are the resources that are put into the program like money, staff, and equipment. Activities are the actions taken by the program such as professional development or creating materials. Outputs are the things that are produced by the activities like the number of teachers trained or number and length of time of student lessons. Outcomes are the changes that resulted from the implementation of the program, which might be increased knowledge or performance on tests or teacher retention. Outcomes are typically divided into short term, intermediate/medium term, and/or long term. Figure 17.2 illustrates the logic model for an evaluation conducted for development of a district science curriculum (Lawton, Brandon, Cicchinelli, & Kekahio, 2014). The boxes represent the project components and the arrows show the expected relationships between the components. For each element of the model (i.e., resources, activities, outputs, short-term outcomes, mid-term outcomes, long-term outcomes), there is a possible evaluation question. Logic models such as this one are widely used in educational evaluation today.

Theory-Based Evaluation

Theory-based evaluation is closely related to the logic model approach, and sometimes the names are used interchangeably, which can be confusing. Carol Weiss (1972) first introduced the theory-based evaluation model. The distinction of theory-based evaluations is threefold: (1) inclusion of the assumptions about the recipients of the program before they begin the program, (2) the inclusion of the theory of change in the model, and (3) the beliefs about why programs fail to meet their objectives (Bickman, 1987). The theory of change is the reasoning behind why the program will be successful. Both logic models and theory-based approaches will use a graphic depiction to illustrate the relationships of the logic or theory behind the program. The logic model graphic is limited to the resources, activities, outputs, short-term outcomes, mid-term outcomes, and long-term outcomes categories, while the theory-based graphic will illustrate the theory about how something will change.

Coryn, Noakes, Westine, and Schroter (2011) list four potential sources from which a program theory can be developed: existing research and theory, stakeholder theory, observation of the program, and use of exploratory research to examine assumptions in the

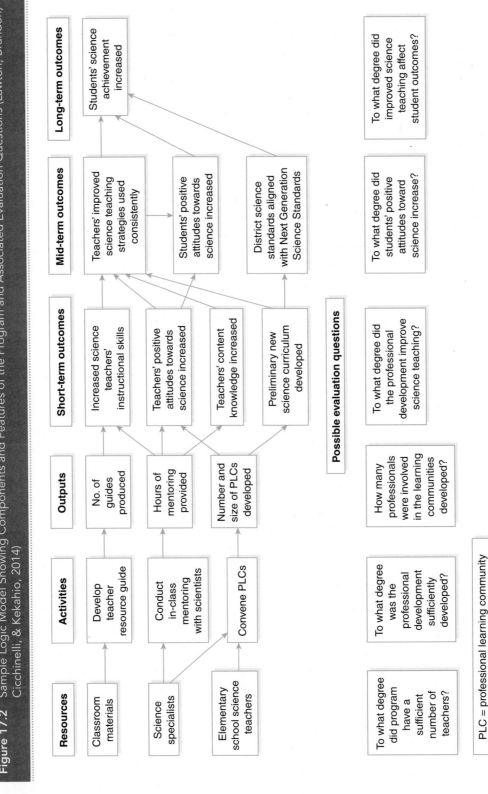

Figure 17.2 Sample Logic Model Showing Components and Features of the Program and Associated Evaluation Questions (Lawton, Brandon, Cicchinelli, & Kekahio, 2014)

Resources	Activities	Outputs	Short-term outcomes	Mid-term outcomes	Long-term outcomes
Classroom materials	Develop teacher resource guide	No. of guides produced	Increased science teachers' instructional skills	Teachers' improved science teaching strategies used consistently	Students' science achievement increased
Science specialists	Conduct in-class mentoring with scientists	Hours of mentoring provided	Teachers' positive attitudes towards science increased	Students' positive attitudes towards science increased	
Elementary school science teachers	Convene PLCs	Number and size of PLCs developed	Teachers' content knowledge increased	District science standards aligned with Next Generation Science Standards	
			Preliminary new science curriculum developed		

Possible evaluation questions

To what degree did program have a sufficient number of teachers?

To what degree was the professional development sufficiently developed?

How many professionals were involved in the learning communities developed?

To what degree did the professional development improve science teaching?

To what degree did students' positive attitudes toward science increase?

To what degree did improved science teaching affect student outcomes?

PLC = professional learning community

program theory. The evaluator works with the stakeholders of the program to build the program theory. To develop this theory, the evaluation should begin with an understanding of the targeted recipients of the program. To produce some change in the recipients as a result of the program, some assumptions need to be made about these individuals. It is important to identify these assumptions as part of the theory of change. Beliefs about why programs may fail were first introduced by Suchman (1967). A program may fail to meet the objectives because either the program was not implemented properly (implementation failure) or, when the implementation was good, the theory behind the program was incorrect (theory failure). These are important distinctions when using the information from the evaluation to improve the program and attain the stated outcomes.

The first phase of a program evaluation using the theory-based approach is to develop the theory of change model with the program stakeholders. Once the model is adequately specified, the second phase of the evaluation is to test the model. To test the theory of change model, the evaluator first examines the implementation of the program to determine if the program is being delivered as it is intended. If the program is not being implemented as it is intended to be, then there is an implementation failure and the evaluator assists the stakeholders to improve implementation. There is no need to assess outcomes until implementation of the program is adequate. Once adequate implementation of the program is achieved, then the evaluator examines the outcomes of the program. If the outcomes do not meet the goals of the program as set out in the model, the theory is rejected; it is regarded as a failure. By using this process, the evaluation examines not only program outcomes but also the underlying mechanisms in which the program operates.

This two-step process perhaps oversimplifies both the development of the program theory and the evaluation of the program theory. Developing a program theory can be a rigorous process. Articulation of the program theory must be clear enough to guide the evaluation that occurs because the theory then drives the evaluation. Specifically, the theory is used to guide the development and prioritization of the evaluation questions, design and execute the evaluation, select measurement tools for examining the processes and outcomes outlined in the theory, and then analyze the outcomes (Coryn et al., 2011). Outcomes of theory-based evaluations include not only program effectiveness but also unintended side effects, as well as the relationship between the constructs in the theory.

Carvalho et al. (2015) used a theory-based evaluation model to examine the Activity Theory-based Model of Serious Games (ATMSG) used in developing electronic, educational games such as *DragonBox*, *GoVenture CEO*, and *Playing History: The Plague*. The theory behind ATSMG is displayed in Figure 17.3. The theory behind these educational games is the premise that there are three activities—the gaming activity, learning activity, and instructional activity. The graphic represents these three activities and the relationship between the activities and the people. The activities share the same person but different motives. The gaming activity motive may be to just have fun, the motive for the learning activity may be to fulfill a course requirement, and the instructional activity motive may be to increase knowledge. The activities share the same tool but have different people. The instructional activity has an intrinsic side that is inside the game and represents how the game supports learning (e.g., help message). The extrinsic side of the instructional activity is conducted outside the game and is performed by the teacher in how the game is used to support

Figure 17.3 The ATMSG Model

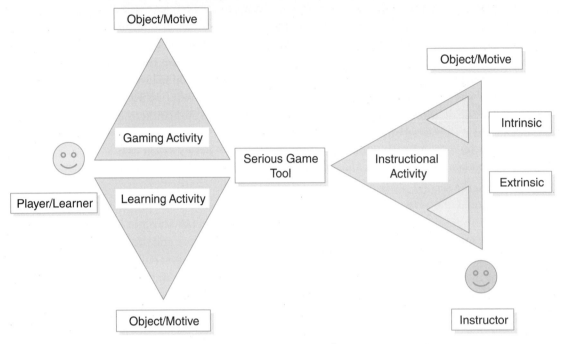

Source: Carvalho et al. (2015).

Note: There are three main activities involved in the use of serious games for education.

instruction before, during, or after the game. You can see how this graphic of theory is more complicated than the graphic of the logic model approach.

The program-oriented approaches to evaluation are an attempt to capture the complexities of educational programs. Yet, they still miss some of the subtleties of educational programs by the orientation toward the objectives or goals of the program. In many instances today, the goals of programs are standards set by agencies overseeing the program such as state departments of education or funding agencies. An attempt to address these criticisms is called goal-free evaluation.

Goal-Free Evaluation

In goal-free evaluation, Scriven (1974b) argues that the evaluator should avoid learning the programs' stated objectives or goals because it causes tunnel vision toward those intended objectives or goals and risks overlooking other unintended positive and negative side effects of the program. The purpose of a goal-free evaluation is to document and measure what the program actually does instead of what it intends to do. The evaluator conducts an independent needs assessment to identify the program goals, then observes and measures the actual processes and outcomes to judge quality of the program and its ability to meet participant needs. In this way, the evaluator can be more objective in evaluating the program; ultimately, evaluation is about what the program actually does rather than what it intends to do. The distinction of goal-free evaluation is in the use of the needs assessment for identifying the goals for the evaluation. In the consumer-oriented approach, the needs assessment was used to identify the specific criteria that will be used to judge the performance of the evaluand. The process of a goal-free evaluation is otherwise the same as with other program-oriented evaluations. It is more of a difference in perspective than a distinct model in that the evaluator identifies the goals of the program rather than using the program's stated goals. Once the evaluator identifies the goals or needs that the program is attempting to fill, the evaluator sets out to measure the performance of the program in relation to these needs just as the other program-oriented program approaches to evaluation.

LEARNING CHECK 3 ✓

1. Identify if the following descriptions are internal or external and formative or summative.

   A. School District A hires an evaluator to assist in the process of gathering stakeholder views to be used to hire the next superintendent.

   B. School District B forms an evaluation team to review the equity of its technology policy.

2. Identify which evaluation approach (expertise oriented or consumer oriented) is being used in the following:

   A. The evaluation team conducts a needs assessment to identify the criteria that will be used to evaluate the performance of the evaluand for the evaluation.

   B. An accreditation team compares the performance of the teacher education program against the formal standards set for awarding accreditation.

3. What are the four types of program-oriented program evaluation?

Answers: 1. A. external, formative, B. internal, summative; 2. A. consumer oriented, B. expertise oriented; 3. Objective oriented, logic models, theory based, and goal-free evaluation.

Decision-Oriented Evaluation

Decision-oriented evaluation approaches are specifically designed to assist decision makers such as program administrators, funding agencies, and policy makers. By serving decision makers, the assumption is that the evaluation is more likely to be used in making a decision and that these approaches will better serve a decision maker's need. There are two approaches to decision-oriented evaluation approaches: the CIPP model and utilization-focused evaluation.

> **Decision-oriented evaluation** is specifically designed to assist decision makers such as program administrators, funding agencies, and policy makers. There are two decision-oriented approaches: the CIPP model and utilization-focused evaluation.

CIPP (CONTEXT, INPUT, PROCESS, PRODUCT) EVALUATION MODEL

Daniel Stufflebeam's CIPP evaluation model is designed specifically for internal evaluations of competing programs or projects such as in making a decision to fund a program among several alternatives. It can be either formative to guide an effort or summative to describe achievement of outcomes. Its core features are the context, input, process, and product evaluation components (Stufflebeam, 2007). A context evaluation is used to assess the needs, assets, and problems to define the programs goals and judging outcomes. An input evaluation assesses alternate approaches and budgets to select a particular program for meeting the identified needs. The process evaluation assesses the implementation of the selected program to determine if it is implemented as intended and if any modifications are needed. The product evaluation measures the outcomes of the program to determine if the needs were met and identify what changes might be needed if the program were to continue.

Additional elements were added to create the CIPP Evaluation Model Checklist (Stufflebeam 2010)—impact, effectiveness, sustainability, transportability, and meta-evaluation. The checklist is publicly available for use in conducting CIPP evaluations. Impact evaluation assesses the program's reach to its target audience by examining whether the program is serving its intended participants and community needs. Effectiveness evaluation assesses the quality and significance of the program outcomes and compares it to alternative programs. Sustainability assesses whether the program initiatives have been (or can be) sustainable over time. Transportability assesses the ability of the program to be implemented under other conditions. The evaluator searches for actual and potential program adopters to seek their judgment regarding the program's ability to be adapted elsewhere. Meta-evaluation is an assessment of the quality of evaluation itself and how well it met the program evaluation standards. The final element is the report that describes the evaluation activities and assessment of the program. Each of the 10 elements lists individual indicators that the evaluator can use to guide the evaluation and check off as having met. It can be used by the evaluation stakeholders as well to guide their participation in the evaluation.

Although the CIPP model is designed to serve decision makers, other relevant stakeholders are involved in the process. Relevant stakeholders should contribute in some way to each of the CIPP components such as assisting in defining the needs and contributing to the collection of information about a program and the outcomes, as well as reaching a conclusion about the program.

Stufflebeam emphasizes that the CIPP model's most important purpose is program improvement. This includes not only improving the performance of a program but also discontinuing programs that do not work. Terminating programs that do not serve the intended purpose frees up funds for other promising programs. Failed efforts can be used as valuable lessons for future efforts.

Tunon, Ramirez, Ryckman, Campbell, and Mlinar (2015) used the CIPP approach to assess the use of digital badges for tracking basic library instructional skills in the Blackboard learning management system. They used the formative CIPP approach as they developed the digital badge system. They counted and reported the number of individual indicators for each element that were met. The context evaluation looked at the needs and the problems with implementing the digital badges within the class structure and in communicating with class instructors. The input evaluation identified that resources needed to implement the digital badges. The process evaluation assessed the implementation of the digital badges and identified issues that affected implementation. The product evaluation examined outcomes, including the technical aspects and student responses to them. The results of this evaluation led to modification of the digital badge system for future implementation.

UTILIZATION-FOCUSED EVALUATION

Developed by Michael Patton, the utilization-focused evaluation approach is based on the idea that an evaluation should be judged by its usefulness to the intended users of the evaluation (Patton, 2008). Therefore, evaluations are judged on their utility or usefulness. Utilization-focused evaluations seek out the intended users of the evaluation and actively engage them in the evaluation process. These intended users of the evaluation are considered the stakeholders. The practice of identifying those people who have a personal interest in the evaluation is called the "personal factor." Like goal-free evaluation, utilization-focused evaluation is not a specific model method; it is just a different perspective. The evaluator guides the intended users of the evaluation through the evaluation process. The result of finding stakeholders who are truly interested in the evaluation and guiding them through the evaluation process so they are the primary decision makers is a decision that they can and will use. Although this view of stakeholders may increase the use of the evaluation results, it also constrains the diversity of views by neglecting other types of stakeholders.

Braun, Billups, and Gable (2013) conducted a utilization-focused program evaluation of the Principal Residency Network (PRN). The mission of this network is to develop principals who can lead innovative schools using equity-oriented leadership practices to improve student achievement. The evaluation was led by a university-affiliated evaluator who partnered with the PRN team (those who were the intended users of the evaluation) to develop an evaluation framework. The PRN team used this as an opportunity to develop a long-term evaluation cycle so program staff could continue the process as continuous program improvement. The evaluator helped the PRN program staff develop additional measures of program outcomes to meet their needs. Once the measures were developed, the evaluation team proceeded to collect and analyze the data according to the short-term and intermediate goals set for participant performance, growth, program completion, and attainment of leadership roles. This example illustrates how the evaluator worked with the intended users of the evaluation and guided them through the evaluation process to reach a decision about the success of the PRN program.

Participant-Oriented Evaluation

Participant-oriented evaluation serves to engage stakeholders in the evaluation process to effect some change, not necessarily to make a decision as in the decision-oriented evaluation approaches. This change may be directed toward individuals, groups, local community, or society at large. The term *participants* replaces the term *stakeholders*. Participants are the program staff and those who receive services of the program. This approach seeks a greater variety of the

> **Participant-oriented evaluation** serves to engage stakeholders, including program participants, in the evaluation process to effect some change.

types of stakeholders involved in the evaluation to consider a greater diversity of perspectives. These approaches have several distinguishing characteristics (King, 2007). First, this approach to program evaluation seeks to engage the individuals who receive services from the program in the evaluation process. The nature and extent of their participation will depend on the type of participant-oriented approach. One end of the participant-oriented continuum is the shared evaluation responsibility between the evaluator and participants, and the other end of the continuum is the participants' complete control of the evaluation. A second distinction is that the evaluator is seen as a facilitator leading the team through the evaluation process and not the decision maker. A final distinction is that participant-oriented evaluations include purposeful activities to engage the stakeholders that increase their ownership over the evaluation results and may lead to increased capacity of the individuals or program staff for conducting program evaluations in the future.

Approaches to participant-oriented evaluation can be classified into two different categories: practical participative evaluations (PPEs) and transformative participatory evaluations (TPEs) (Cousins & Whitmore, 1998). PPE aims to increase the use of the evaluation results by involving the "primary" stakeholders by engaging them in all aspects of the evaluation. "Primary" stakeholders are individuals who are more likely to use the evaluation. It is considered practical in that it is used to make formative decisions but with long-term goals to increase the primary stakeholders' learning about evaluation. There are two PPE approaches to evaluation—responsive and developmental approach. The goal of TPE approaches to participatory-oriented evaluation is to transform or empower the stakeholders through participation in the evaluation process. Participation in the evaluation provides knowledge and skills that can be used for social change. While PPE-oriented evaluations are concerned with empowering primary stakeholders within the program and organization, TPE-oriented evaluations are designed to empower oppressed or less powerful people to bring change to the broader society. There are two TPE approaches to evaluation—empowerment and deliberative democratic approach.

PRACTICAL PARTICIPATIVE EVALUATION MODELS: RESPONSIVE EVALUATION

Responsive evaluation, developed by Robert Stake, draws on personal, subjective experience and stakeholder perception of merit and worth rather than theory or stated goals (Abma & Stake, 2001). Although both quantitative and qualitative research methods may be used in the context of a program evaluation, the evaluation model is qualitatively oriented. The evaluation draws heavily from the specific context and changing needs of the evaluation as it progresses. Judgment of value and worth of the program being evaluated are expressed in how the stakeholders "perceive what is going on." It is distinguished from other models of program evaluation by its flexible, iterative design; acceptance of multiple realities of the stakeholders; and reliance on local knowledge rather than theory (Fitzpatrick et al., 2011). Evaluators using this model of evaluation are in control of the evaluation but will spend considerable time observing and learning about the program to obtain stakeholder views.

Gunn and Lefoe (2013) used a responsive model approach to a formative evaluation during the development of a program that incorporated distributive leadership (shared leadership authority rather than hierarchical or positional authority), individual action-learning plans, and professional networking to develop educational leaders. The responsive evaluation model was selected because it was believed that the evaluation would be a challenge due to the novelty of the distributive leadership idea and use of individual action plans rather than a fixed set of objectives. The responsive model was used to identify a wide variety of stakeholders centered on the activities of the participants in the program. The evaluator observed program activities, administered surveys, and conducted interviews and focus groups to obtain information regarding the perceptions of the program from the stakeholders. The information from these multiple sources was synthesized to describe the perceptions of the different stakeholders regarding the impact of the program.

PRACTICAL PARTICIPATIVE EVALUATION
MODELS: DEVELOPMENTAL EVALUATION

Developmental evaluation was developed by Michael Patton (1994), the same evaluator who developed utilization-focused evaluation. Although developmental evaluation is classified as a participatory model of evaluation, Patton himself describes developmental evaluation not as a model but as a "relationship founded on a shared purpose." This purpose is a long-term partnership for program development and continuous review for improvement of the program. The program evaluator is a part of the program team, instead of program stakeholders being part of an evaluation team. The team includes participants (or potential participants) of the program. The evaluator's role is to facilitate decision making given knowledge of evaluation processes and how to evaluate things engaging stakeholders in the process to achieve their own goals. This model emphasizes the difference between program improvement and program development. It is participatory with the evaluator participating within the program development team and practical in the sense that it is meeting the needs of the participants of the program.

Lam and Shula (2015) used a developmental evaluation approach to create the Assessment Pilot Initiative (API). API was designed to meet the needs of a rapidly expanding teacher education program to develop competencies for classroom assessment. The team devised a logic model for the new course structure that combined core assessment principles, technology, and peer and instructor feedback. The evaluator worked with the teacher candidates in the course and collected information regarding the experiences of the teacher candidates, reporting back to the program team to adjust instruction "on the fly." By working with the teacher candidates during the development of API, their progress and concerns were addressed immediately and were a part of the decision-making process. The evaluator also served as a coach when necessary to share information with the program staff to increase their expertise in technology that could be used with API. This case study description includes key points of developmental evaluation by including program participant participation and the long-term partnership role of the evaluator of the development of the program.

Transformative Practical Evaluation Models: Empowerment Evaluation

The goal of empowerment evaluation is politically motived to emancipate stakeholders, as well as empower them toward self-determination and improvement

(Fetterman, 1994, 2007). Here, self-determination refers to self-determination in evaluation, the ability to self-evaluate. While participants of the program may be included in the evaluation, the evaluator's main role is to guide the program staff to build their capacity to evaluate their own programs. The 10 principles of empowerment evaluation (Fetterman, 2015) are as follows:

Improvement

Community ownership

Inclusion

Democratic participation

Social justice

Community knowledge

Evidence-based strategies

Capacity building

Organizational learning

Accountability

Instead of identifying goals or objectives, collecting evidence to assess the goals, and making a decision, an empowerment evaluation will develop a mission, take stock (examine strengths and weaknesses), and plan for the future. This process, facilitated by an evaluator, creates a "communicative space" whereby stakeholders can be transformed and self-determined.

Charoenchai, Phuseeorn, and Phengsawat (2015) conducted an empowerment evaluation of a program to increase teachers' use of authentic assessment. In their evaluation, they describe three components: developing a mission, taking stock, and planning for the future. Each component is illustrated in Figure 17.4. They defined their mission through surveying learning conditions prior to the program, analyzing learners' strengths and weaknesses, and analyzing the current curriculum. Taking stock included obtaining feedback for teachers and developers in four stages prior to the program being developed, during program planning, during implementation, and then at the end of the program. The evaluation results were then used to plan for the future.

Transformative Practical Evaluation Models: Deliberative Democratic Evaluation

Democratic evaluation was first introduced by MacDonald in 1974 to counter the dominance of power held by bureaucratic and autocratic evaluations where government agencies and agency staff were in control of programmatic decisions (MacDonald & Kushner, 2007). It advocates for evaluation to serve the community with the idea of the public's right to know. The current approach to democratic evaluation is called deliberative democratic evaluation. Deliberative democratic evaluation, an approach developed by House and Howe (2000), is also founded upon the principles of social justice, equity, and empowerment. It seeks to consider all relevant interests and perspectives through inclusion, dialogue, and deliberation (House, 2007). Inclusion refers to not only the inclusion of all relevant stakeholders but also the balance the power among the stakeholders. The role of the evaluator is to ensure that the voices of those with less power are represented in the evaluation. Dialogue is a discovery process by which stakeholder groups determine their real interests by sharing their views and perspectives. This might be in the simple form of a conversation or structured as a debate. The idea is that dialogue helps stakeholders understand their own, real interests, and these interests are shared with the evaluator for use in deliberation. The views of the different stakeholders are then considered by the evaluator to reach a conclusion. The evaluator guides the dialogue and deliberation process of the stakeholders to obtain their views so that a decision can be made regarding the program.

Hreinsdottir and Davidsdottir (2012) used a deliberative democratic evaluation approach to evaluate the quality of preschools. In addition to reviewing preschool curriculum and preschool laws and regulations, the evaluators held dialogues with the preschool children, parents, and staff. The evaluators intentionally sought the views of children as they are considered less powerful and their views may be in contrast to those of parents and preschool staff. Evaluators held small focus groups with children aged 4 and 5 years first and then presented their comments to focus groups of parents and staff. The children's views were considered discussions of educational priorities and services provided in preschools. These views were then also incorporated into the changes in the preschool improvement plans.

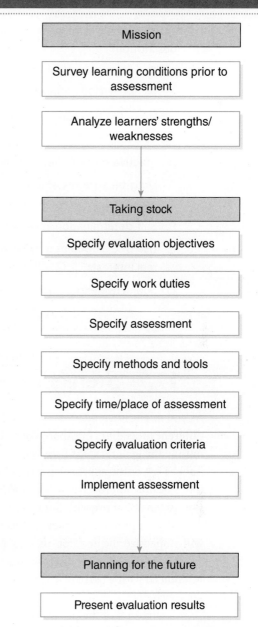

Figure 17.4 An Evaluation of a Program for Teaching Classroom-Authentic Assessment Using the Empowerment Evaluation Approach

Mission

Survey learning conditions prior to assessment

Analyze learners' strengths/weaknesses

Taking stock

Specify evaluation objectives

Specify work duties

Specify assessment

Specify methods and tools

Specify time/place of assessment

Specify evaluation criteria

Implement assessment

Planning for the future

Present evaluation results

Source: Modified from Charoenchai, C., Phuseeorn, S., & Phengsawat, W. (2015). Teachers' development model to authentic assessment by empowerment evaluation approach. *Educational Research and Reviews, 10*(17), 2524–2530. doi: 10.5897/ERR2015.2243. Licensed under CC BY 4.0: https://creativecommons.org/licenses/by/4.0/.

1. What are the two types of decision-oriented evaluation approaches?

2. Which of the two types of decision-oriented evaluation approaches is depicted in this description?

   A. There are several reputable drug awareness programs; the school system evaluation comprises four components (context, input, process, and product).

3. What are the two categories of participant-oriented evaluation?

4. Which of the four types of participative evaluation approaches represents the following perspective (responsive, developmental, empowerment, or deliberative democratic)?

   A. Long-term partnership for program development and continuous review for improvement of the program

   B. Self-determination in evaluation in the ability to self-evaluate

   C. Use of dialogue as a discovery process by which stakeholder groups determine their real interests

   D. Subjective experience and stakeholder perception of merit and worth

Answers: 1. The CIPP model and utilization focused; 2. A. CIPP; 3. Practical participative evaluations and transformative participatory; 4. A. developmental, B. empowerment, C. deliberative democratic, D. responsive.

17.7 Steps in Program Evaluation

As you might imagine, each of the different approaches to program evaluation will have a different procedure, but there are some similarities among the different approaches so we can outline the general steps involved in a program evaluation, as summarized in Table 17.4. Some approaches will follow the general process in a sequential fashion, while more flexible approaches will be more iterative and allow for flexibility for the sequence (e.g., the responsive approach). Some approaches will emphasize one or more steps more than the other steps and the other approaches. For example, the decision-oriented approaches will emphasize the decision-making process, while the participant-oriented approaches will emphasize the identification and selection of stakeholders. It is important to refer to the work referenced with a particular approach before conducting an evaluation using that particular approach.

In each of the program evaluation approaches, an initial step is to identify the relevant stakeholders. The different evaluation approaches define stakeholders differently. Are they the program staff, participants of the program, and/or members of the community? Once the relevant groups of stakeholders are identified, the evaluator seeks out representatives from the stakeholder groups to participate in the evaluation. Setting a focus for the evaluation is the next step. In some evaluation approaches, this will be a list of objectives (e.g., program-oriented approaches). In other approaches, the focus is on program standards (e.g., expertise-oriented approach). In still other approaches, the focus is on empowering the stakeholders (e.g., participant-oriented approaches). Once the focus of the evaluation is established, the evaluation team will design the evaluation. In this step, they need to decide what type of information to gather and how it will be gathered. The information may be qualitative with interviews or focus groups, document reviews, or observations to obtain opinions of stakeholders not a part of the evaluation team. This information may also be quantitative in conducting surveys or a research study. This step also includes determining who will be responsible for different aspects of collecting the data. In many cases, the responsibility for collecting the data will fall on the evaluator, but in the participant-oriented approaches where the focus is on empowering or transforming the program staff and participants of the program, they may become involved in this process as well. Once the evaluation is designed, implementation of the evaluation process begins. This step is likely the one that will take the most time. This is when the interview/focus groups, observations, documents review, survey, or research study will be conducted. Collecting the data will need to be monitored to make sure what is being collected is the information that is needed and that it is collected as intended. Once all the data are collected, they are analyzed. Data are analyzed as appropriate to the type of data collected. Qualitative data will be analyzed to develop themes expressed in the interviews/focus groups. Quantitative data will be analyzed using descriptive or inferential statistics. These data are then used to reach a conclusion. Conclusions may be decisions regarding (a) program improvement, (b) whether to continue a program or not, or (c) which program to implement among the options. Conclusions may also include the future actions that may be needed for program improvement. Finally, the evaluation process, analysis of the data collected, and conclusions are written in a report

Table 17.4 General Steps in Program Evaluation

Step	Description
Identification of stakeholders	Identify the relevant stakeholders that are to be represented in the evaluation process and seek representatives from each stakeholder group to participate in the evaluation.
Set focus for the evaluation	Identify the reasons for the evaluation that may include setting priorities, goals, or objectives.
Design the evaluation process	Identify the types of activities that will be included in the evaluation and outline a process to conduct the evaluation activities.
Conduct the evaluation activities	Carry out and monitor the evaluation activities.
Evaluate the information gathered through the evaluation activities	Analyze the qualitative and/or quantitative data as appropriate for the type of data collected.
Reach a conclusion or decision	Make a conclusion in regard to the focus or priorities set in the focusing step.
Develop and disseminate a report	A report outlining the evaluation process and results is provided to all relevant stakeholders.

and provided to all the relevant stakeholders. This report should be written using language understandable to all the relevant stakeholders.

Program evaluation is an important part of the educational process as a means of program improvement and identification of what things are working to serve the needs of the students, teachers, school administrators, the local community, and the society at large. Research studies are one part of this process and can be used to help with making decisions regarding program effectiveness and school improvement. They can provide objective data to evaluate participant progress and program participant opinion, both of which are vital to programmatic success.

LEARNING CHECK 5 ✓

1. True or false:

    A. Are the steps in the evaluation as listed always conducted in the same sequence?

    B. Can different approaches to evaluation vary in the amount it emphasizes a specific step of the evaluation process?

2. Match the following description to the step in the evaluation process it represents:

    A. Analyze the data

    B. Identify the reasons for the evaluation

    C. Write a report

    D. Carry out and monitor the evaluation activities

Answers: 1. A. false, B. true; 2. A. evaluate the information gathered through the evaluation activities, B. set focus for the evaluation, C. develop and disseminate a report, D. conduct the evaluation activities.

CHAPTER SUMMARY

LO 1 Distinguish between merit and worth of an educational program, policy, product, or process.

- **Merit** is the quality of the characteristics or attributes of something when compared to a set of criteria.

- **Worth** is the value that something has in a specific context.

- An educational program, policy, product, or process can have merit but not worth if the quality is good but does not meet the needs of the people in the specific situation.

- An educational program, policy, product, or process can have worth but not merit if it fits well into the specific context but the quality is not good.

LO 2 Identify who potential stakeholders are in an evaluation.

Potential stakeholders include

- Those who have the decision authority over the evaluand

- Those directly responsible for implementing the evaluand

- Those who are the intended beneficiaries or participants of the evaluand

- Those excluded from participating in the evaluand

LO 3 Distinguish between evaluation and research.

- Research is used to produce generalizable findings that describe relationships or causality between variables that can be used to develop or refine a theory. It is designed to add knowledge to a field of study.

- Program evaluation is used to gather information that describes the merit and value of an evaluand so that it can be used in making a judgment or decision about it in the specific context in which the evaluation is taking place.

LO 4 Describe the standards that are used to guide evaluations (Joint Committee on Standards for Educational Evaluation).

- Utility is the extent to which the evaluation provides the stakeholders with the information they need in order for the information to be used to make an informed decision.

- Feasibility is the extent to which the evaluation procedures are realistic, diplomatic, and practical given the available time, budget, staff, and stakeholders.

- Propriety is the consideration of the legal and ethical issues that surround the evaluation.

- The accuracy standard addresses the technical adequacy of the information contained in the evaluation.

LO 5 Identify three uses for program evaluations.

- Evaluation is useful for ground-level decision makers such as school administrators, teachers, parents, and students to assess the effectiveness of specific programs and products.

- Evaluation can provide important information to policy makers such as boards of education and state and federal legislators that they need to know to make informed decisions on education policy.

- Evaluation is helpful in funding educational initiatives to make sure that the monies are being put to good use.

LO 6 Describe the limitations of program evaluation.

- Evaluations are confined by the resources available.

- It might be very difficult to identify and quantify all of the potential benefits, costs, and outcomes associated with a program.

- It may be difficult to determine who all the stakeholders are and whose viewpoints may be needed for the evaluation.

- There is a political element in identifying all the different political factions and potential political use of the results.

LO 7 Summarize the ethical responsibilities of the evaluator and how to address them.

- Protection is from physical or emotional harm.

- Protection of confidentiality regarding stakeholder descriptions, balancing relationships between the stakeholders, and accessing personal information.

- Provide a signed informed consent document that describes how confidentiality will be maintained and if there are any risks for physical or emotional harm or breach of confidentiality.

LO 8 Distinguish between internal and external evaluation.

- **Internal evaluation** is an evaluation conducted by an evaluator internal to the evaluand, such as an employee of the organization.

- **External evaluation** is in an evaluation conducted by an evaluator not associated with the evaluand.

LO 9 Distinguish between formative and summative evaluation.

- **Formative evaluation** is an evaluation that is conducted while the evaluand is being implemented.

- **Summative evaluation** is an evaluation that occurs at the end of the implementation of the evaluand.

LO 10 Distinguish between expertise-oriented and consumer-oriented evaluation approaches.

- **Expertise-oriented evaluation** is an evaluation that is conducted by an expert in the field of study.

- **Consumer-oriented evaluation** is an evaluation by an expert in evaluation to inform the general public.

LO 11 Distinguish the difference and similarities between the four program-oriented approaches to evaluation (objective-oriented, logic models, theory-based, and goal-free evaluation).

- The key feature of the objectives-oriented approach to evaluation is the specification of the objectives of the program, product, policy, or process and then assessing the extent to which these objectives have been met.

- Logic model evaluations add information in the evaluation process about how the program objectives are achieved through a graphic representation of the logical relationships between the different elements of the program.

- Theory-based evaluation is distinguished by its inclusion of the assumptions about the recipients of the program before they begin the program, a theory of change, and beliefs about why programs fail to meet their objectives.

- In goal-free evaluation, the evaluator avoids learning the programs' stated objectives to measure what the program actually does instead of what it intends to do.

LO 12 Distinguish the difference and similarities between the two approaches to decision-oriented evaluation (the CIPP model and utilization-focused evaluation).

- The CIPP evaluation model is designed specifically for internal evaluations of competing programs or projects such as in making a decision to fund a program among several alternatives.

- The utilization-focused evaluation approach is based on the idea that an evaluation should be judged by its usefulness to the intended users of the evaluation.

LO 13 Distinguish the difference and similarities between the four approaches to participant-oriented evaluation (responsive, developmental, empowerment, and deliberative democratic). Identify which are practical participatory and transformative participatory.

- Responsive evaluation is a practical participatory approach where personal, subjective experience and stakeholder perception define merit and worth. It is a flexible, iterative design that seeks the multiple realities of the stakeholders and relies on local knowledge rather than theory.

- Developmental evaluation is a practical participatory approach where the purpose is a long-term partnership for program development and continuous review for improvement of the program.

- Empowerment evaluation is a transformative participatory approach. The purpose is to emancipate stakeholders and empower them toward self-determination in the ability to self-evaluate.

- Deliberative democratic evaluation is a transformative participatory approach. It is founded upon the principles of social justice, equity, and empowerment and seeks to consider all relevant interests and perspectives through inclusion, dialogue, and deliberation.

accuracy 481

consumer-oriented
evaluation 487

decision-oriented
evaluation 493

evaluand 475

expertise-oriented
evaluation 486

external evaluation 484

feasibility 479

formative evaluation 485

internal evaluation 484

merit 474

needs assessment 487

participant-oriented
evaluation 495

program evaluation 474

program-oriented
evaluation 488

propriety 479

stakeholder 476

summative evaluation 485

utility 479

worth 474

REVIEW QUESTIONS

1. Pick one of the three following topics and describe how it can have worth but not merit, merit but not worth, or both merit and worth.

    A. Process for differentiating instruction

    B. Accreditation of an after-school program

    C. Open-access electronic gradebook for teacher, student, and parents

2. A small group of teachers is investigating the effectiveness of an intervention to improve critical thinking of students. They employ the intervention and data are collected on the students' critical thinking skills. The small group of teachers, principal, and assistant principals uses the results to decide whether to continue the intervention or not throughout the school. The results are shared with other teachers in the school. Is this an example of research or evaluation? Why?

3. Provide examples of the four different types of stakeholders that might be involved in an evaluation of the critical thinking intervention described above.

4. Label each of the following as either research or evaluation:

    A. An investigation of the impact of a book reading club is used to decide to continue it next year.

    B. An investigation of the impact of using a social justice orientation in a social studies course is used to refine theory about social justice instruction.

5. Which of the four areas of the Joint Committee on Standards for Educational Evaluation (2010) are described below?

    A. An evaluation finds that the new attendance policy is not practical. The time and staff necessary are not realistic.

B. An evaluation of a state virtual school program includes all of the relevant information needed to make an informed decision.

6. Name and describe the key distinguishing characteristics of the five types of program evaluation.

7. In what way is a needs assessment used in the consumer-oriented evaluation approach different from the needs evaluation in the goal-free program-oriented approach?

8. Here is an example of a theory of change for the relationship between teacher professional development and student outcomes. What approach to program evaluation uses these graphic depictions for theory of change?

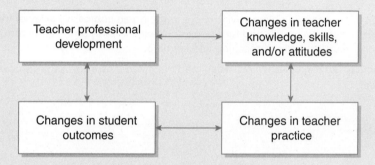

9. Distinguish between the two types of participant-oriented approaches.

10. Look at the general steps in conducting an evaluation.
    A. Which approaches emphasize identification of stakeholders?
    B. How do the four approaches differ in regards to the focus of the evaluation?
    C. What types of conclusions or decisions are made by each of the approaches?

ACTIVITIES

1. Reflect on a school and identify one program, policy, product, and process that could be a target for an evaluation.

2. Identify potential stakeholders for each of the four evaluations. Make sure to use all four kinds of stakeholders in at least one evaluation.

3. Think of one aspect for each of the four evaluation targets (one program, policy, product, and process) that can be evaluated. Form an evaluation question.

4. Identify any possible ethical considerations for each of the four evaluations.

5. Select one evaluation that can be conducted as a summative evaluation and one to be formative. Then select one evaluation that can be conducted internally and one that can be performed externally.

6. Determine which the evaluation approaches (expertise and consumer oriented, program oriented, decision oriented, or participant oriented) can be used for each of the four evaluations.

7. Select one of the four evaluations and determine the steps to follow to conduct the evaluation.

$SAGE edge™

SAGE edge offers a robust online environment featuring an impressive array of free tools and resources for review, study, and further exploration, keeping both instructors and students on the cutting edge of teaching and learning.

Access practice quizzes, eFlashcards, video, and multimedia at edge.sagepub.com/priviterarme.

ANALYZING, INTERPRETING, AND COMMUNICATING RESEARCH DATA

Identify a problem

- Determine an area of interest.
- Review the literature.
- Identify new ideas in your area of interest.
- Develop a research hypothesis.

Develop a research plan

- Define the variables being tested.
- Identify participants or subjects and determine how to sample them.
- Select a research strategy and design.
- Evaluate ethics and obtain institutional approval to conduct research.

Generate more new ideas

- Results support your hypothesis—refine or expand on your ideas.
- Results do not support your hypothesis—reformulate a new idea or start over.

After reading this chapter, you should be able to:

1 State two reasons why it is important to summarize data.

2 Define descriptive statistics and explain how they are used to describe data.

3 Identify and construct tables and graphs for frequency distributions.

4 Identify and describe the different types of frequency distributions.

5 Identify and appropriately use the mean, median, and mode to describe data.

6 Identify and appropriately use the variance and standard deviation to describe data.

7 Define and apply the empirical rule.

8 Identify and construct graphs used to display group means and correlations.

9 Use Cronbach's alpha and Cohen's kappa to estimate reliability.

10 Distinguish between standard scores, z scores, percentile ranks, and age/grade equivalents.

Communicate the results

- Method of communication: oral, written, or in a poster.
- Style of communication: APA guidelines are provided to help prepare style and format.

Conduct the study

- Execute the research plan and measure or record the data.

Analyze and evaluate the data

- Analyze and evaluate the data as they relate to the research hypothesis.
- Summarize data and research results.

ANALYSIS AND INTERPRETATION: EXPOSITION OF DATA

"Crunching the numbers" is a common phrase typically used to describe the large-scale processing or analysis of numeric data. The phrase is often used to imply that by "crunching the numbers," the numbers themselves will make more sense or be values that we can use. For example, sports analysts "crunch the numbers" to create rankings of teams or players based on the large-scale analysis of statistics so that we can more easily see or appreciate how the teams or players rank against each other. While the analysis itself may be complex, the output or result is a simple-to-understand ranking that lists the teams or players in order of how good they are.

In the same way a sports analyst crunches the numbers to make sense of sports data, a scientist crunches the numbers to make sense of data collected during a research study. Typically, researchers make sense of their data by relating them to the hypothesis they are testing. For example, suppose we test the hypothesis that parent attitude toward homework can predict child motivation to complete homework. To test this hypothesis, we can measure the parent attitude toward homework and use statistical analysis to see how this attitude relates to their children's motivation to complete homework. The analysis itself may be complex, but by "crunching the numbers," we can relate the results to our hypothesis. Hence, if the analysis shows support for our hypothesis, then we can state clearly that the pattern of data shows that as parent attitude changes, so does the motivation to complete homework of the children. Hence, the hypothesis is correct.

In this chapter, we will introduce many ways in which researchers summarize data sets using descriptive statistics, which are procedures used to summarize, organize, and make sense of a set of scores, typically presented graphically, in tabular form (in tables), or as summary statistics (single values). Using descriptive statistics, we can "crunch the numbers" to more clearly relate our data to the hypotheses we test.

edge.sagepub.com/ priviterarme

- Take the chapter quiz
- Review key terms with eFlashcards
- Explore multimedia links and SAGE articles

⑤SAGE edge™

18.1 Descriptive Statistics: Why Summarize Data?

Any time you conduct a study, it is important to report the data. To report the data, you typically do not disclose each individual score or measure. Instead, you summarize the data because that is a clearer way to present them. A clear presentation of the data is necessary because it allows the reader to critically evaluate the data you are reporting.

To illustrate the usefulness of summarizing data, Table 18.1a shows hypothetical data for the number of times a student got out of his or her seat for each of 48 participants when a teacher was near or far from where each student was seated. The listing in Table 18.1a is not particularly helpful because you cannot see at a glance how the number of out-of-seat behavior compares between groups (near or far teacher). A more meaningful arrangement of the data is to place them in a summary table that shows the total number of out-of-seat behavior per group. When the data are arranged in this way, as shown in Table 18.1b, you can see at a glance that much more out-of-seat behavior occurred when the teacher was far from the student than when the teacher was near the student. In all, there are two common reasons that we summarize data using descriptive statistics:

- To clarify what patterns were observed in a data set at a glance. It is more meaningful to present data in a way that makes the interpretation of the data clearer.

- To be concise. When publishing an article, many journals have limited space, which requires that the exposition of data be concise. The presentation in Table 18.1b takes up much less space to summarize the same data given in Table 18.1a and is therefore more concise.

Before we summarize data in a figure or table, we often need to explore or review the data to identify possible omissions, errors, or other anomalies (Abelson, 1995; Hoaglin, Mosteller, & Tukey, 1991; Tukey, 1977). We can apply this step as we measure the data for each participant or after all data have been recorded. But this step, if used, must be applied before the data are analyzed statistically or displayed in a figure or table. Figure 18.1 illustrates where this step can be applied in the research process based on the steps of the scientific method first given in Figure 1.1 in Chapter 1.

As an example for applying an exploratory analysis, consider that for the study summarized in Table 18.1, we conducted a time sampling (as described in Chapter 8) and divided the classroom observation time into 10 segments. Therefore, if we found that a value larger than 10 was recorded for a student, then that entry must have been an error and so would have been removed before further analysis. Likewise, we could review the data for missing values and check that values for one group were not mistakenly recorded for another group. The advantage of exploring or reviewing data before reporting them is to make sure

> Descriptive statistics summarize data to make sense or meaning of the measurements we make.

Table 18.1 Arranging Data in a Frequency Distribution

(a)

Out-of-Seat Behavior			
Teacher Far From the Student		Teacher Near the Student	
10	2	0	4
5	2	1	0
3	10	0	2
5	0	4	0
6	2	0	0
0	2	1	0
5	5	2	0
5	3	1	0
4	1	2	3
9	2	0	2
10	0	3	0
10	5	0	0

(b)

Groups	Total Number of Apple Slices Consumed
Far	106
Near	25

Note: A list of the number of times students got out of their seat by 24 participants in each of two groups (a) and a summary table for the total number of times students got out of their seat in each group (b).

that all errors have been removed from the data before further analysis is conducted.

To describe data, we use **descriptive statistics,** which are procedures used to summarize, organize, and make sense of a set of scores, typically presented graphically, in tabular form (in tables), or as summary statistics (single values). Summary statistics include the mean, median, mode, variance, and frequencies. How to calculate and graph these values is described in this chapter. Also, keep in mind that descriptive statistics are used to describe numeric data. Therefore, we can use descriptive statistics only with quantitative but not qualitative research designs. In this chapter, we begin with how to display and summarize frequencies or counts.

Descriptive statistics are procedures used to summarize, organize, and make sense of a set of scores or observations, typically presented graphically, in tabular form (in tables), or as summary statistics (single values).

Figure 18.1 Steps 3 to 5 of the Scientific Method

Step 3: Conduct the study.

Execute the research plan and measure or record the data.

Explore or review the data to identify possible omissions, errors, or other anomalies.

Step 4: Analyze and evaluate the data.

Analyze and evaluate the data as they relate to the research hypothesis.

Step 5: Communicate the results.

1. Method of communication: oral, written, or in a poster.
2. Style of communication: APA guidelines are provided to help prepare style and format.

Note: The box illustrates where data exploration fits in this process. All steps of the scientific method are illustrated in Figure 1.1 in Chapter 1.

LEARNING CHECK 1 ✓

1. What are two common reasons that we summarize data using descriptive statistics?

2. Descriptive statistics make sense of data by presenting them in a table. What are two other ways to present descriptive statistics?

Answers: 1. To clarify what patterns were observed in a data set at a glance and to be concise; 2. Graphically or as summary statistics.

18.2 Frequency Distributions: Tables and Graphs

Suppose you scored 90% on your first research methods exam. How could you determine how well you did in comparison to the rest of the class? One meaningful arrangement to answer this question would be to place the data in a table that lists the ranges of exam scores in one column and the frequency of exam scores for each grade range in a second column. When scores are arranged in this way, as shown in Table 18.2b, it is clear that an exam score of 90% is excellent—only three other students fared as well or better, and most students in the class had lower scores.

Table 18.2 Arranging Data in a Frequency Distribution

(a)

Exam Scores	
90%	80%
59%	72%
64%	84%
77%	87%
88%	60%
78%	66%
94%	78%
96%	73%
65%	81%
79%	55%

(b)

Exam Scores (%)	Frequency
90–99	3
80–89	5
70–79	6
60–69	4
50–59	2

Note: A list of 20 exam scores (a) and a summary of the frequency of scores from that list (b).

A **frequency** is the number of times or how often a category, score, or range of scores occurs. In this section, we will describe the types of tables and graphs used to summarize frequencies. Tables and graphs of frequency data can make the presentation and interpretation of data clearer. In all, this section will help you appropriately construct and accurately interpret many of the tables and graphs used to summarize frequency data in behavioral research.

> A **frequency** is a value that describes the number of times or how often a category, score, or range of scores occurs.
>
> A **frequency distribution table** is a tabular summary display for a distribution of data organized or summarized in terms of how often a category, score, or range of scores occurs

Frequency Distribution Tables

One way to describe frequency data is to count how often a particular score or range of scores occurs using a **frequency distribution table.** In a frequency distribution table, we list each score or range of scores in one column and list the corresponding frequencies for each score or range of scores in a second column. Table 18.3 shows three ways to summarize data in this way.

We can summarize the frequency, stated as $f(x)$, of a continuous variable, a discrete variable, or a categorical variable, and we can summarize the frequency of data that are grouped into intervals or listed as individual scores. To illustrate, Table 18.3a lists continuous data in intervals by summarizing the time in seconds to complete a task (the continuous variable) among a sample of high school

> A frequency distribution table can be used to summarize (1) the frequency of each individual score or category in a distribution or (2) the frequency of scores falling within defined ranges or intervals in a distribution.

students. Table 18.3b lists the frequency of discrete data as individual scores by summarizing quiz scores (the discrete variable) for students in a high school class. Table 18.3c lists the frequency of categorical data by summarizing the number of students in each class year (the categorical variable) at a small school. In each display, the sum of all frequencies (in the right column) equals the total number of observations or counts made.

The type of data measured determines whether to group data into intervals or leave data as individual scores or categories. We group data when many different scores are recorded, as shown in Table 18.3a for the time (in seconds) it took participants to complete a task. When data are grouped, it is recommended that the number of intervals ranges between 5 and 20. Fewer than 5 intervals can provide too little summary; more than 20 intervals can be too confusing.

We leave data as individual scores when only a few possible scores are recorded, as shown in Table 18.3b for quiz scores ranging in whole units from 0 to 4. For data that are categorical, we also identify each individual category, as shown in Table 18.3c for high school year.

> We can summarize the frequency of a continuous variable, a discrete variable, and a categorical variable, either grouped into intervals or listed as individual scores or categories.

Frequency Distribution Graphs

The same information conveyed in a frequency distribution table can also be presented graphically. To present frequency data graphically, we list the categories, scores, or intervals of scores on the *x*-axis (the horizontal axis) and the frequency in each category, for each score, or in each interval on the *y*-axis (the vertical axis) of a graph. The type of graph we use to describe frequency data depends on whether the data are continuous or discrete.

Continuous data are often summarized graphically using a histogram. The histogram is a graph that lists continuous data that are grouped into intervals along the horizontal scale (*x*-axis) and lists the frequency of scores in each interval on the vertical scale (*y*-axis). To illustrate, Figure 18.2 displays a frequency distribution table and a corresponding histogram for the number of student absences over a quarter in an elementary school. Notice that each bar in the histogram represents the frequency of absences made in each interval.

A **histogram** is a graphical display used to summarize the frequency of continuous data that are distributed in numeric intervals using bars connected at the upper limits of each interval.

A **bar chart,** or **bar graph,** is a graphical display used to summarize the frequency of discrete and categorical data using bars to represent each frequency.

A **pie chart** is a graphical display in the shape of a circle that is used to summarize the relative percentage of discrete and categorical data into sectors.

Discrete data are often summarized using a bar chart or a pie chart. A **bar chart** is like a histogram, except that the bars do not touch. The separation between bars reflects the separation or "break" between the whole numbers or categories being summarized. Figure 18.3 displays a bar chart for the number or frequency of high school students who plan to major in psychology, education, or biology in college next year. To summarize these same data as percents, a **pie chart** can be a more effective display (Hollands & Spence, 1992, 1998). Using a pie chart, we split the data into sectors that

Table 18.3 Frequency Distribution Tables for Continuous, Discrete, and Categorical Variables

(a)

Time (in seconds)	f(x)
50–59	4
40–49	9
30–39	12
20–29	13
10–19	7
0–9	5
Total participants	50

(b)

Quiz Scores	f(x)
4	5
3	7
2	8
1	6
0	4
Total participants	30

(c)

High School Year	f(x)
Senior	12
Junior	15
Sophomore	28
Freshman	20
Total participants	75

Note: Continuous data grouped into intervals (a), discrete data listed as individual scores (b), and categorical data given as individual categories (c).

represent the relative proportion of counts in each category. The larger a sector, the larger the percentage of scores in a given category. To illustrate, Figure 18.3 also displays a pie chart for the percentage of students in each of three academic majors. Notice in the pie chart that larger percentages take up a larger portion of the pie.

Continuous data can also be depicted in a line graph or **frequency polygon**. Instead of using bars to illustrate the frequencies, we place a dot at the highest point of the frequency bar and connect the dots with a line. The shape of the distribution can tell us a lot about the scores. We can see the general shape of the distribution, the most and least frequent scores, how spread out the

> A **frequency polygon** is a graphical display using a line to summarize the frequency of continuous data.

scores are, or if there are unusual scores that fall outside of the distribution. Figure 18.4 shows the most common shapes of frequency distributions. Most variables in the population will be normally distributed. This means that the shape of the polygon is symmetrical. If we cut the distribution into half, the right half will mirror the left half. Most of the scores lie in the middle of the distribution and taper off on each side. Some distributions will not be symmetrical, and we

Skewed distribution is a distribution of scores that includes outliers or scores that fall substantially above or below most other scores in a data set.

A negative skew distribution is a distribution where the tail is on the left side or lower end of the x-axis and most of the scores lie at the higher end of the scale.

A positive skew distribution is a distribution where the tail is on the right side or upper end of the x-axis and most of the scores lie at the lower end of the scale.

call them skewed distributions. Skewed distributions can be either negative or positive skew depending on where the tail of the distribution lies. The tail is the lowest end of the distribution. The tail of a negative skew distribution will be on the left side or lower end of the x-axis. This means that most of the scores lie at the higher end of the scale. A frequency distribution of grades in a graduate-level college course and the number of job applications submitted before being hired are examples of variables where the frequency distribution is likely negatively skewed.

The tail of a positive skew distribution will be on the right side or upper end of the x-axis. This means that most of the scores lie at the lower end of the scale. U.S. household income is negatively skewed, with fewer individuals at the higher income levels than lower income levels.

Frequency distributions can also be flat or bimodal. In a flat distribution, there is no marked peak and it can have either no tail or very short tails at both ends. The frequencies are distributed across the x-axis relatively equally. An example of a flat distribution is an average per pupil expenditure variable across schools in a school district if each school received the same per pupil expense. A bimodal frequency distribution has more than one peak. An example of a bimodal distribution would be scores on an exam if students either performed very well (As) or very poorly (Ds). There would be two peaks at grades A and D, with few Bs and Cs.

18.3 Measures of Central Tendency

Measures of central tendency are statistical measures for locating a single score that tends to be near the center of a distribution and is most representative or descriptive of all scores in a distribution.

Descriptive statistics often used to describe behavior are those that measure central tendency. Measures of central tendency are single values that have a "tendency" to be at or near the "center" of a distribution. Although we lose some meaning any time we reduce a set of data to a single score, statistical measures of central tendency ensure that the single score meaningfully represents a data set. In this section, we will introduce three measures of central tendency:

A histogram is used to summarize continuous data. A bar chart or pie chart is used to summarize discrete and categorical data.

- The mean

- The median

- The mode

The Mean

One way to describe behavior is to compute the average score in a distribution, called the *mean*. Because researchers in the behavioral sciences rarely select data from an entire

Figure 18.2 Summarizing Data in a Histogram

Student Absences	Frequency
0–2	3
3–5	6
6–8	4
9–11	3
12–14	2

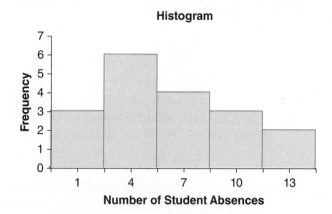

Note: A grouped frequency distribution table (left) and a histogram (right) for the number of student absences over a quarter in an elementary school.

Figure 18.3 Summarizing Data in a Bar Chart and a Pie Chart

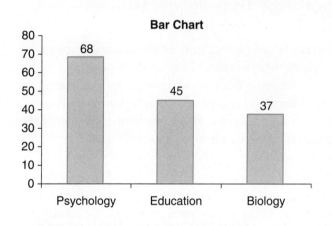

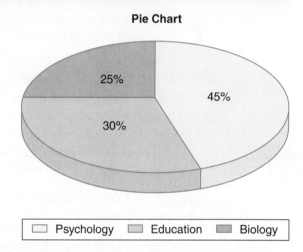

Note: A bar chart (left) giving the frequency of planned college majors of high school students and a pie chart (right) giving the percentage of students in each major. The same data are summarized in each graphical display.

population, we will introduce the **sample mean,** represented as M. To compute a sample mean, we sum all scores in a distribution (Σx) and divide by the number of scores summed (n).

> The **sample mean** is the sum of all scores (Σx) divided by the number of scores summed (n) in a sample or in a subset of scores selected from a larger population.

The sample mean is the balance point of a distribution. The balance point is not always at the exact center of a distribution, as this analogy will demonstrate. Pick up a pen with a cap and remove the cap. Then place the pen sideways on your index finger until it is balanced and parallel with the floor. Once you have steadied the pen, your finger represents the balance point of the distribution of the weight of that pen. In the same way, the mean is the balance point of a distribution of data. Now, put the cap back on the pen and balance it again on your index finger. To balance the pen, you must move your finger toward the side with the cap, right? Now your finger is not at the center of the pen but closer to the cap. In the same way, the mean is not necessarily the middle value; it is the value that balances an entire distribution of numbers.

Using the sample mean as an appropriate measure of central tendency depends largely on the type of distribution and the scale of measurement of the data. The sample mean is typically used to describe data that are normally distributed and measures on an interval or ratio scale. Each is described here.

- The **normal distribution** is a distribution in which half of scores fall above the mean, median, and mode, and half fall below these measures. Hence, the mean, median, and mode are all located at the center of a normal distribution, as illustrated in Figure 18.4. In cases where the mean is approximately equal to all other measures of central tendency, the mean is used to summarize the data. We could choose to summarize a normal distribution with the median or mode, but the mean is most often used because all scores are included in its calculation (i.e., its value is most reflective of all the data).

> **Normal distribution** is a theoretical distribution with data that are symmetrically distributed around the mean, the median, and the mode.

- The mean is used for data that can be described in terms of the *distance* that scores deviate from the mean. After all, the mean balances a distribution of values. For this reason, data that are described by the mean should meaningfully convey differences (or deviations) from the mean. Differences between two scores are meaningfully conveyed for data on an interval or ratio scale only. Hence, the mean is an appropriate measure of central tendency used to describe interval and ratio scale data.

The Median

> The mean is typically used to describe interval and ratio scale data that are normally distributed.

Another measure of central tendency is the **median**, which is the middle value or midpoint of a distribution in which half of all scores fall above and half fall below its value. To explain the need for another measure of central tendency, imagine you measure the following set of scores: 2, 3, 4, 5, 6, 6, and 100. The mean of these scores is 18 (add up the seven scores and divide by 7). Yet, the score of 100 is an outlier in this data set, which causes the mean value to increase so much that the mean fails to reflect most of the data—its value ($M = 18$) is larger than the values of all scores, except one. For these data, the mean can actually be misleading because its value shifts toward the value of that outlier. In this case, the median will be more reflective of all data because it is the middle score of data listed in numeric order. For these data, the median is 5.

> The **median** is the middle value in a distribution of data listed in numeric order.

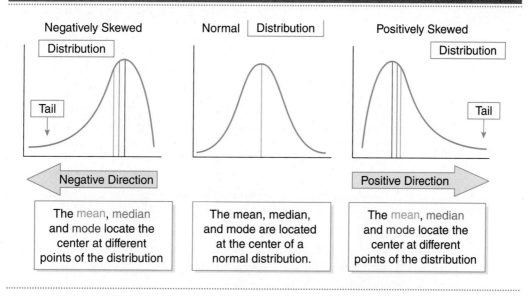

Using the median as an appropriate measure of central tendency also depends largely on the type of distribution and the scale of measurement of the data. The median is typically used to describe data that have a skewed distribution and measures on an ordinal scale. Each is described here.

- Some data can have outliers that skew or distort a data set. As we noted earlier, U.S. household income is skewed, with very few people earning substantially higher incomes than most others in the population. Data that have a skewed distribution will distort the value of a mean, making it a less meaningful measure for describing all data in a distribution. For example, the median (middle) income in the United States is approximately $44,000, whereas the mean income would be much larger than this because the income of billionaires (the outliers) would be included in the calculation. Hence, the median is used to describe skewed data sets because it is most representative of all data for these types of distributions.

- The median is used to describe ranked or ordinal data that convey *direction* only. For example, the fifth person to finish a task took longer than the first person to finish a task; an individual with a bachelor's degree is more educated than an individual with an associate's degree. In both examples, the ordinal data convey direction (greater than or less than) only. For ordinal data, the *distance* (or deviation) of scores from their mean is not meaningful, so the median is used to describe central tendency.

> The median is typically used to describe ordinal data and distributions that are skewed.

The Mode

Another measure of central tendency is the **mode,** which is the value that occurs most often. The mode is a count; no calculations or formulas are necessary to compute a mode. The mode can be used to describe data in any distribution, so long as one or more scores occur most often. However, the mode is rarely used as the sole way to describe data and is typically reported with other measures of central tendency, such as the mean and median. The mode is typically used to describe data in a modal distribution and measures on a nominal scale. Each is described here.

> A **mode** is the value in a data set that occurs most often or most frequently.

- So long as a distribution has a value that occurs most often—that is, a mode—the mode can be used as a measure of central tendency. Modal distributions can have a single mode, such as a normal distribution (the mode and the mean are reported together) or a skewed distribution (the mode and the median are reported together). A distribution can also have two or more modes, in which case each mode is reported either with the mean or with the median.

- The mode is used to describe nominal data that identify something or someone, nothing more. Because a nominal scale value is not a *quantity*, it does not make sense to use the mean or median to describe these data. The mode is used instead. For example, the mean or median season of birth for patients with schizophrenia is not very meaningful or sensible. But describing these nominal data with the mode is meaningful by saying, for example, that most patients with schizophrenia are born in winter months. Any time you see phrases such as *most often*, *typical*, or *common*, the mode is being used to describe these data.

> The mode is typically used to describe nominal data and any distribution with one or more scores that occur most often.

Table 18.4 summarizes the discussion presented here for when it is appropriate to use each measure of central tendency.

Table 18.4 Appropriately Using Measures of Central Tendency

Measure of Central Tendency	Shape of Distribution	Measurement Scale
Mean	Normal	Interval, ratio
Median	Skewed	Ordinal
Mode	Modal	Nominal

Note: Appropriately use each measure of central tendency to describe data based on the shape of the distribution and the measurement scale of the data.

When researchers report the findings of their study, they will begin by describing their data—central tendency and variability. They will not report all three measures of central tendency, just the appropriate one. If the dependent variable is an interval or ratio level of measurement and the distribution of scores is approximately normal, they will use the mean. If the dependent variable is an ordinal level of measurement or the distribution of scores is skewed (even if the level of measurement is interval or ratio), they will report the median. If the dependent variable is a nominal level of measurement, they will report the mode.

18.4 Measures of Variability

Measures of central tendency inform us only of scores that tend to be near the center of a distribution but do not inform us of all other scores in a distribution, as illustrated in Figure 18.5. The most common procedure for locating all other scores is to identify the mean (a measure of central tendency) and then compute the **variability** of scores from the mean. By definition, variability can never be negative: Variability ranges from 0 to $+\infty$. If four students receive the same score of 8, 8, 8, and 8 on an assessment, then their scores do not vary because they are all the same value—the variability is 0. However, if the scores were 8, 8, 8, and 9, then they do vary because at least one score differs from the others. Thus, either scores do not vary (variability is 0), or scores do vary (variability is greater than 0). A negative variability is meaningless. In this section, we will introduce two key measures of variability:

> **Variability** is a measure of the dispersion or spread of scores in a distribution and ranges from 0 to $+\infty$.

- Variance

- Standard deviation

> Variability can be 0 or greater than 0; a negative variability is meaningless.

The Variance

One measure of variability is the **sample variance,** represented as s^2. The variance is a measure of the average squared distance that scores deviate from the mean. A deviation is a measure of distance. For example, if the mean is 10 and you score 15, then your score is a deviation (or distance) of 5 points above the mean. To compute variance, we square this deviation and so would represent the distance of 15 from 10 as $5^2 = 25$ points. The reason we square is that to find the distance that all scores deviate from the mean, we could subtract all scores from the mean and sum up the value. However, using this procedure will always result in a solution equal to 0. For this reason, we square each deviation

> The **sample variance** is a measure of variability for the average squared distance that scores in a sample deviate from the sample mean.

How far do scores in this distribution vary from the mean? How do scores vary in general?

?   **?**

⟵ *Mean* ⟶

Notice that while we know the mean score in this distribution, we know nothing of the remaining scores. By computing measures of variability, we can determine how scores vary around the mean and how scores vary in general.

The **sum of squares** (*SS*) is the sum of the squared deviations of scores from the mean and is the value placed in the numerator of the sample variance formula.

and then sum the squared deviations, which gives the smallest solution greater than 0 for determining the distance that scores deviate from the mean. To avoid a 0 solution, then, researchers square each deviation and then sum, which is represented by the **sum of squares** (*SS*):

$$SS = S(x - M)^2$$

To find the average squared distance of scores from the mean, we then divide by the number of scores subtracted from the mean. However, dividing by the number of scores, or sample size, will underestimate the variance of scores in a population. The solution is to divide by 1 less than the number of scores or deviations summed. Doing so ensures that the sample variance will equal the variance in the population on average. When we subtract 1 from the sample size, the resulting value is called the **degrees of freedom** (*df*) **for sample variance,** which can be represented as follows:

The **degrees of freedom** (*df*) **for sample variance** are 1 less than the sample size, or *n* – 1.

$$df = n - 1.$$

The variance is a measure of the squared distance that scores deviate from the mean.

Hence, the formula for sample variance is the following:

$$S^2 = \frac{SS}{df}.$$

An advantage of the sample variance is that its interpretation is clear: The larger the sample variance, the farther that scores deviate from the mean on average. However, one limitation of the sample variance is that the average distance of scores from the mean is squared. To find the distance, and not the squared distance, of scores from the mean, we need a new measure of variability called the standard deviation.

The Standard Deviation

To find the average distance that scores deviate from the mean, called the *standard deviation*, we take the square root of the variance. Mathematically, square rooting is a correction for having squared each deviation to compute the variance. The formula for the **sample standard deviation (SD)** can be represented as follows:

$$SD = S^2 = \sqrt{\frac{SS}{df}}.$$

> The **sample standard deviation (SD)** is a measure of variability for the average distance that scores in a sample deviate from the sample mean and is computed by taking the square root of the sample variance.

The advantage of using standard deviation is that it provides detailed information about a distribution of scores, particularly for scores in a normal distribution. Using the *Chebyshev theorem*, which is a theorem devised by the Russian mathematician Pafnuty Chebyshev, we can determine that at least 99% of all scores will fall within 10 standard deviations of the mean for any type of distribution with any shape.

The standard deviation is most informative, however, for the normal distribution. For a normal distribution, over 99% of all scores will fall within three standard deviations of the mean. We can use the **empirical rule** to identify the percentage of scores that fall within one, two, and three standard deviations of the mean. The name, *empirical rule*, comes from the word *empiricism*, meaning "to observe," because many of the behaviors that researchers observe are approximately normally distributed. The empirical rule, then, is an approximation—the percentages at each standard deviation are correct, give or take a few fractions of a standard deviation. Nevertheless, this rule is critical because of how specific it is for describing behavior. The empirical rule identifies the following:

> The **empirical rule** is a rule for normally distributed data that states that at least 99.7% of data fall within three standard deviations of the mean, at least 95% of data fall within two standard deviations of the mean, and at least 68% of data fall within one standard deviation of the mean.

- At least 68% of all scores fall within one standard deviation of the mean.

- At least 95% of all scores fall within two standard deviations of the mean.

- At least 99.7% of all scores fall within three standard deviations of the mean.

To illustrate how useful the empirical rule is, consider how we use this principle in education. One value of intelligence and achievement tests is that an individual's score can be compared to his or her peer group and compared to an average score or norm. Most intelligence and achievement tests are created to have a normal distribution with a mean of 100 and a standard deviation of 15. That means at least 68% of scores will fall between 85 and 115, at least 95% of scores falling between 70 and 130, and at least 99.7% of scores falling between 55 and 185. By having both intelligence and achievement tests on the same normal curve, we use the scores from these tests to assist in diagnosing intellectual and learning disabilities. If a child earns a score of 100 on an intelligence test, that would be an average score, and we would expect a comparable score on an achievement test if the child was performing up to his or her potential. If the child's score on an achievement test is 115, one standard deviation above average, then we can say the child is performing above expectations. If the child's score on an achievement test is 85, one standard deviation below average, then we can say the child is performing below expectations and may need further testing for a learning disability. Historically, we have defined the level of intellectual ability based on the number of standard deviations the individual is from the mean. A child might be identified as gifted if the intelligence score is more than one standard deviation from the mean, or a child might be identified with mild, moderate, or severe intellectual disability if the score is two or more standard deviations below the mean.

In educational research, even without knowing the scores for each individual in the sample, by looking at the distribution, we still know a lot about this sample. When the data are normally distributed, we can use the sample mean and standard deviation to identify the distribution of almost all scores in a sample, which makes both measures (*M* and *SD*) very informative when used together.

> For normal distributions, most scores fall within one standard deviation (68%) of the mean, and almost all scores fall within three standard deviations (99.7%) of the mean.

Figure 18.6 The Empirical Rule

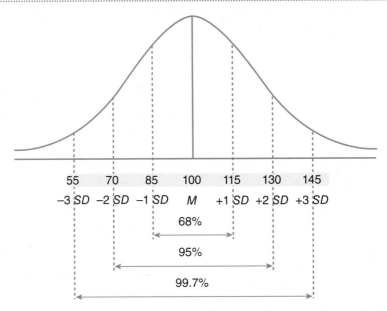

Note: The proportion of scores under a normal curve at each standard deviation above and below the mean. The data are distributed as 100 ± 15 (*M* ± *SD*).

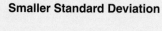

MAKING SENSE—INTERPRETING VARIANCE AND THE STANDARD DEVIATION

Variance and the sum of squares are not directly interpretable. They are important in the calculation of inferential statistics that are described in Chapter 19. Just know that variance is a way to measure how the scores vary around the center point or mean. We use variance of scores only with dependent measures that are interval or ratio when we use a mean.

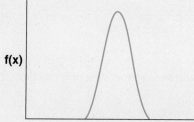

Smaller Standard Deviation

A "thin" curve means that your winrates remain close to the mean average.

A normal distribution with the scores closely around the mean.

Larger Standard Deviation

A "fat" curve means that there is a wider spread of your winrates.

A normal distribution with the scores spread further around the mean.

The standard deviation (*SD*), the average distance that scores deviate from the mean, is very useful. A low *SD* means the scores are closely gathered about the mean, while a high *SD* means the scores are spread further from the mean.

Most of our validated educational measures of achievement and ability use the empirical rule regarding the number of standard deviations from the mean to classify individuals who take these tests. They create tests with a mean of 100 and an *SD* of 15 to classify above- or below-average achievement or intelligence. For example, to operationalize the classification of a gifted student, many schools define gifted as two standard deviations above the mean. For an IQ test, that would mean an IQ score of 130 (100 mean + 30 2 *SD*).

LEARNING CHECK 2 ✓

1. Identify the shapes of the following frequency distributions:

Chapter 18: Analysis and Interpretation: Exposition of Data | 527

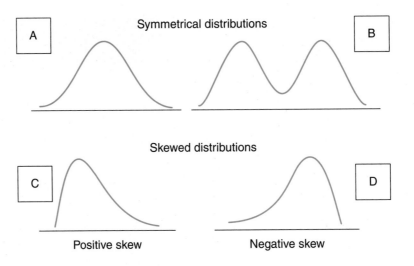

Symmetrical distributions

A

B

Skewed distributions

C

D

Positive skew   Negative skew

2. State whether the mean, median, or mode should be used to describe the data for each of the following examples.

A. The data are skewed.

B. The data have two modes.

C. The data are categorical.

D. The data are on a ratio scale.

E. The data are on an ordinal scale.

F. The mean, median, and mode are equal.

2. Can variability be negative?

3. A researcher measures scores in a sample with a normal distribution of 32 ± 2 ($M \pm SD$). State the cutoffs in this distribution within which each of the following is true:

A. At least 68% of scores lie within this distribution.

B. At least 95% of scores lie within this distribution.

C. At least 99.7% of scores lie within this distribution.

18.5 Graphing Means and Correlations

Graphs can be used to display group means for one or more factors, which is particularly useful when differences in a dependent variable are compared between groups. Graphs also summarize correlational data in which we plot data points for two variables. Graphs for each type of data are introduced in this section.

Graphing Group Means

We can graph a mean for one or more groups using a graph with lines or bars to represent the means. By convention, we use a bar graph when the groups on the *x*-axis (horizontal axis) are represented on a nominal or ordinal scale; we use a line graph when the groups on the *x*-axis are represented on an interval or ratio scale.

To use a bar graph, we list the groups on the *x*-axis and use bars to represent the means along the *y*-axis (vertical axis). As an example of a bar graph to display group means, Figure 18.7a displays the mean time (in seconds) attending to a task among students chewing or not chewing gum. To use a line graph, we similarly list the groups on the *x*-axis and instead use dots connected by a single line to represent the means along the *y*-axis. As an example of a line graph to display group means, Figure 18.7b displays the mean time (in seconds) attending to a task among students aged 3, 4, and 5 years.

We can also use bar graphs and line graphs to summarize the means for two or more factors. For example, in Chapter 19 we will display the means for the levels of two factors (duration and setting) to identify main effects and interactions in Figures 19.3 and 19.4. To construct those graphs, we followed the same rules as described in this section: We listed the groups on the *x*-axis, and in those figures, we used lines to represent the means along the *y*-axis. These same rules can be applied to graph group means for just about any number of groups or factors.

Figure 18.7 A Bar Graph (a) and a Line Graph (b) of Group Means Obtained From Two Hypothetical Studies

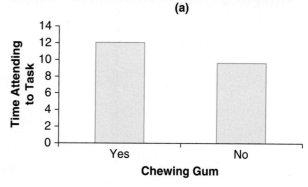

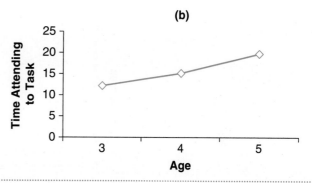

Graphing Correlations

We can graph a correlation using a scatterplot, which is a graphical display of discrete data points (*x*, *y*). To plot a data point, you first move across the *x*-axis and then move up or down the *y*-axis to mark or plot each pair of (*x*, *y*) data points. A *correlation*, introduced in Chapter 9, is a statistic used to measure the strength and the direction of the linear relationship between two factors. The relationship between two factors can be evident by the pattern of data points plotted in a scatterplot.

> A scatterplot is a graphical display of discrete data points (*x*, *y*) used to summarize the relationship between two variables.

When the values of two factors change in the same direction, the two factors have a positive correlation. To illustrate, Figure 18.8a shows a scatterplot of a positive correlation between body image satisfaction and exercise. Notice that as the number of minutes of

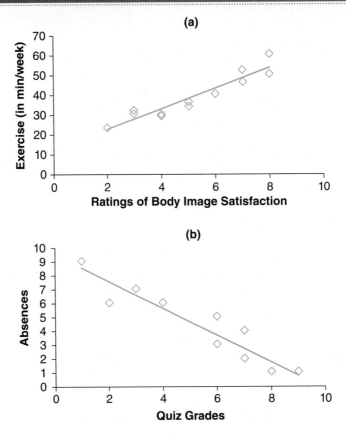

Figure 18.8 A Scatterplot of a Positive Correlation (a) and a Negative Correlation (b) Obtained From Two Hypothetical Studies

Note: The solid lines represent the regression lines.

exercise increases, so do ratings of body image satisfaction; as the minutes of exercise decrease, so do ratings of body image satisfaction. In a scatterplot, the pattern of a positive correlation appears as an ascending line.

When the values of two factors change in the opposite direction, the two factors have a negative correlation. To illustrate, Figure 18.8b shows a scatterplot of a negative correlation between class absences and quiz grades. Notice that as the number of absences increases, quiz grades decrease; as the number of absences decreases, quiz grades increase. In a scatterplot, the pattern of a negative correlation appears as a descending line.

LEARNING CHECK 3 ✓

1. A researcher records the number of dreams that 50 high school freshman students recalled during the night prior to an end-of-year exam. What type of graph or graphs would be appropriate to summarize this frequency distribution? Explain.

Section VI: Analyzing, Interpreting, and Communicating Research Data

Number of Dreams	f(x)
4	16
3	14
2	18
1	7
0	5

2. Which type of graphical display for frequency data is used to summarize continuous data?

3. A researcher reports that cellphone use while driving is negatively correlated with attention to driving tasks. What type of graph should the researcher use to summarize the correlation?

4. For what types of data do we use a bar graph to plot group means? For what types of data do we use a line graph to plot group means?

Answers: 1. A bar chart or pie chart because the data are discrete; 2. A histogram; 3. A scatterplot; 4. We use a bar graph when the groups on the x-axis are represented on a nominal or ordinal scale, and we use a line graph when the groups are represented on an interval or ratio scale.

18.6 Using Correlation to Describe Reliability

We can also describe the consistency of data using a correlation to describe the data. In Section 4.5 of Chapter 4, we introduced three types of reliability for the consistency, stability, or repeatability of one or more measures or observations: test-retest reliability, internal consistency, and interrater reliability. We use a correlational measure to identify the extent to which we have established or demonstrated each type of reliability. In this section, we will specifically describe the correlational measure for internal consistency using Cronbach's alpha and the correlational measure for interrater reliability using Cohen's kappa. The formula and analysis of each reliability measure are introduced in this section.

Cronbach's Alpha (Internal Consistency)

Internal consistency is a measure of reliability used to determine the extent to which multiple items used to measure the same variable are related. This type of measure is useful to analyze, for example, the reliability of a questionnaire or survey that consists of multiple items used to measure the same construct. If participants rated six items that all measure romantic love, then we should expect the responses for each item to be the same or similar because all items measure the same thing. If we then split the items in half (3 and 3), we should expect each half or set of three responses to be related or similar. This type of analysis is computed using **Cronbach's alpha** (Cronbach, 1951), which is used to estimate the average correlation for every possible way that a measure can be split in half. The formula for Cronbach's alpha is as follows:

$$\text{Cronbach's alpha} = \left(\frac{n}{n-1}\right)\left(\frac{\sigma_x^2 - \Sigma\sigma_Y^2}{\sigma_x^2}\right).$$

In the formula, n is the number of items, σ_x^2 is the variance for the total scores across all items, and $\Sigma\sigma_Y^2$ is the sum of the variances for each item calculated one item at a time. Using this formula, Cronbach's alpha is a measure of split-half reliability in that it analyzes the correlation for every possible way to split the test in half. The result is an average correlation for all possible ways to split a measure in half. Cronbach's alpha is like a proportion of variance in that values range between 0 and 1.0, with higher values indicating a stronger correlation or relationship between items on the test.

Cohen's Kappa (Interrater Reliability)

Interrater reliability (IRR) is the extent to which two or more raters of the same behavior or event are in agreement with what they observed. The most straightforward way to measure IRR is to divide the number of agreements between two raters by the total number of observations that were rated. We could then multiply the fraction by 100 to convert it to a percentage. As an example, we could compute the IRR of ratings for the raters described in Table 18.5 as follows:

$$\frac{9 \text{ agreements}}{12 \text{ total observations}} \times 100 = 75\% \text{ agreement.}$$

One limitation of computing IRR this way is that the value could be inflated by chance or error if, for example, the two raters accidentally rated different behaviors but still made similar ratings. A more conservative estimate of IRR that takes the possibility of error into account is **Cohen's kappa** (Cohen, 1961). The following is the formula for Cohen's kappa, in which P_A is the percent agreement and P_E is the percent expected by error:

$$\text{Cohen's kappa} = \frac{P_A - P_E}{1 - P_E}.$$

Table 18.5 The Independent Ratings of Two Raters During 12 Observation Periods

Observation	Rater 1	Rater 2	Agreement?
1	Yes	Yes	√
2	No	No	√
3	Yes	Yes	√
4	No	Yes	—
5	No	No	√
6	No	No	√
7	Yes	No	—
8	Yes	Yes	√
9	Yes	Yes	√
10	Yes	No	—
11	No	No	√
12	Yes	Yes	√

Note: In this example, the two raters agreed on 9 of 12 observation periods. √ indicates agreement.

In the formula, P_E is computed by multiplying the probability of saying yes and no for each rater, then summing each probability. For the ratings shown in Table 18.5, for example, Rater 1 said yes seven times in 12 observation periods ($7 \div 12 = 0.583$); Rater 2 said yes six times in 12 observation periods ($6 \div 12 = 0.500$). The probability, then, that both raters said yes is $(0.583) \times (0.5000) = 0.292$ or 29.2%.

Similarly, Rater 1 said no five times in 12 observation periods ($5 \div 12 = 0.417$); Rater 2 said no six times in 12 observation periods ($6 \div 12 = 0.500$). The probability, then, that both raters said no is $(0.417) \times (0.5000) = 0.209$ or 20.9%. By summing each probability, we obtain the overall probability that two raters agree by chance or error: $P_E = 29.2\% + 20.9\% = 50.1\%$, which makes the following the value of Cohen's kappa:

$$\text{Cohen's kappa} = \frac{75\% - 50.1\%}{1 - 50.1\%} = 50\% \text{ agreement.}$$

18.7 Standard Scores, *z* Scores, Percentile Ranks, and Age/Grade Equivalents

In Chapter 5, we examined norm- and criterion-referenced tests as one way to measure dependent variables such as academic achievement or psychological traits. The raw score

A standard score is one where the raw score is transformed into a normal frequency distribution with a specific mean and standard deviation so that we can compare an individual's score to other scores in the same peer group and make a determination about the relative performance of that individual.

A percentile rank is a standard score that converts the raw score to rank an individual's performance in relation to many other individuals scored at or below that same score.

An age/grade equivalent score is a standard score that compares an individual's score to the average scores of different age groups and represents the same score of an average student of that age or grade.

A z score is a standard score that converts a raw score into a score that tells you how many standard deviations a score is from the mean.

from a norm-referenced test can be transformed into standard scores, percentile ranks, or age/grade equivalents. A standard score is one where the raw score is transformed into a normal frequency distribution with a specific mean and standard deviation. This process is used to create a standardized test so that we can compare an individual's score to other scores in the same peer group and make a determination about the relative performance of that individual. The most common standard score is a z score. A z score has a mean of 0 and a standard deviation of 1. The formula for calculating a z score is

$$z = \frac{\text{raw score} - \text{mean}}{\text{standard deviation}}.$$

Using this formula, every raw score can be transformed into a z score. The z score tells you how many standard deviations a score is from the mean.

A percentile rank is another type of standard score. It uses a frequency distribution to interpret the score of the test in relation to how many other individuals scored at or below that same score. For example, a test score that falls at the 80th percentile rank means that 80% of the individuals taking the test scored at or below that score. Percentile ranks are commonly associated with standard scores. Figure 18.9 illustrates the relationship between z scores and percentile ranks. You can see that each z score is assigned to a specific percentile rank.

Another type of standard score is an age/grade equivalent. Raw scores can be converted to age/grade equivalents. Age/grade equivalent scores compare an individual's score to the average scores of different age groups. It indicates that the individual's score on the test was the same score of an average student of that age or grade. For example, if a sixth grader received an

Figure 18.9 Frequency Distribution of Percentile Ranks and z Scores

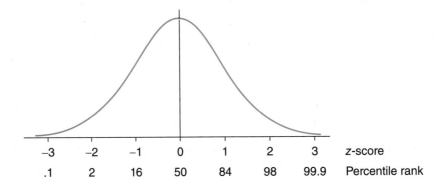

| | −3 | −2 | −1 | 0 | 1 | 2 | 3 | z-score |
| | .1 | 2 | 16 | 50 | 84 | 98 | 99.9 | Percentile rank |

age/grade equivalent score of 4.4 on a reading test, that means he or she received the same score that an average student in the fourth grade, fourth month would receive when taking the same test. It does not mean that the student has the same skills as a fourth grader in the fourth month of school. Age/grade equivalent scores are not considered the most precise way of describing an individual's performance on tests, though. The assigned age/grade equivalent does not mean that the individual has the same skills of someone at that grade or age.

LEARNING CHECK 4 ✓

1. For each of the following descriptions, name the appropriate statistical measure of reliability:

   A. The extent to which multiple items consistently measure the same thing

   B. The extent to which two raters are in agreement

2. State the statistic used to describe each of the following types of reliability:

   A. Interrater reliability

   B. Internal consistency

3. State the type of standard score used for each of the following:

   A. The percentage of individuals who scored at or below that same score

   B. How many standard deviations a score is from the mean

   C. The age or grade that represents the same score of an average student of that age or grade

Answers: 1. A. Cronbach's alpha B. Cohen's kappa 2. A. Cohen's kappa B. Cronbach's alpha 3. A. Percentile rank B. Z score C. Age/grade equivalent

18.8 Ethics in Focus: Deception Due to the Distortion of Data

It was Mark Twain who once said that *there are lies, damned lies, and statistics.* His statement identified that statistics can be deceiving—and so can interpreting them. Descriptive statistics are used to inform us. Therefore, being able to identify statistics and correctly interpret what they mean is an important part of the research process. Presenting data can be an ethical concern when the data are distorted in any way, whether by accident or intentionally. The distortion of data can occur for data presented graphically or as summary statistics. How the presentation of data can be distorted is described in this section.

When a graph is distorted, it can deceive the reader into thinking differences exist, when in truth differences are negligible (Frankfort-Nachmias & Leon-Guerrero, 2006). Three common distortions to look for in graphs are (1) displays with an unlabeled axis, (2) displays with one axis altered in relation to the other axis, and (3) displays in which the vertical axis (*y*-axis) does not begin with 0. As an example of how a graphical display can be distorted, Figure 18.10 displays a line graph (polygon) for hypothetical data of teacher shortage rates for a school district by month. Figure 18.10a displays the data correctly with the *y*-axis starting at 0%; Figure 18.10b displays the same data with the *y*-axis distorted and

Figure 18.10   Two Graphical Displays for the Same Data

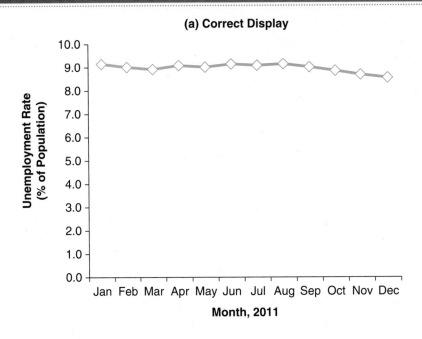

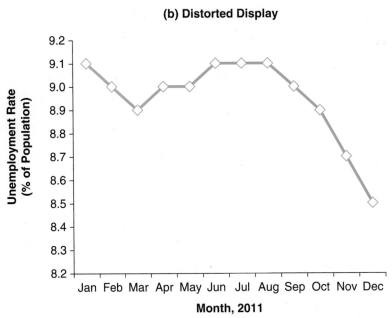

Note: (a) is a correct display and (b) is a display that is distorted because the *y*-axis does not begin at 0%. Data are of hypothetical teacher shortage rates in a school district.

beginning at 8.2%. When the graph is distorted in this way, it can make the slope of the line appear steeper as if unemployment rates are significantly declining, although it is clear from Figure 18.10a that this is not the case—in fact, in 2011, teacher shortage rates were rather stable. To avoid misleading or deceiving readers, pay attention to how data are displayed in graphs to make sure that the data are accurately and appropriately presented.

Distortion can also occur when presenting summary statistics. Two common distortions to look for with summary statistics are when data are omitted or differences are described in a way that gives the impression of larger differences than really are meaningful in the data. It can sometimes be difficult to determine if data are misleading or have been omitted, although some data should naturally be reported together. Means and standard deviations should be reported together; correlations and proportions should be reported with sample size; standard error should be reported any time data are recorded in a sample. When these data are omitted or not reported together, it can lead to erroneous conclusions. For example, if we report that 75% of those surveyed preferred Curriculum A to Curriculum B, you may be inclined to conclude that Curriculum A is a better curriculum. However, if you were also informed that only four people were sampled, then 75% may not seem as convincing. Any time you read a claim about results in a study, it is important to refer to the data to confirm the extent to which the data support the claim being made by the author or authors of a study.

CHAPTER SUMMARY

LO 1 State two reasons why it is important to summarize data.

- It is important to summarize data (1) to clarify what patterns were observed in a data set at a glance and (2) to be concise.

- It is more meaningful to present data in a way that makes the interpretation of the data clearer. Also, when publishing an article, many journals have limited space, which requires that the exposition of data be concise.

LO 2 Define descriptive statistics and explain how they are used to describe data.

- **Descriptive statistics** are procedures used to summarize, organize, and make sense of a set of scores or observations. Descriptive statistics are presented graphically, in tabular form (in tables), or as summary statistics (e.g., mean, median, mode, variance, and standard deviation).

LO 3 Identify and construct tables and graphs for frequency distributions.

- A **frequency distribution table,** which lists scores or categories in one column and the corresponding frequencies in a second column, can be used to summarize (1) the frequency of each individual score or category in a distribution or (2) the frequency of scores falling within defined ranges or intervals in a distribution.

- A frequency distribution table can be presented graphically by listing the categories, scores, or intervals of scores on the x-axis (the horizontal axis) and the frequency in each category, for each score, or in each interval on the y-axis (the vertical axis) of a graph.

- The type of graph we use to describe frequency data depends on whether the factors being summarized are continuous or discrete. Continuous data are displayed in a histogram. Discrete and categorical data are displayed in a bar chart or pie chart. To summarize data as percentages, a pie chart can be a more effective display than a bar chart.

LO 4 Identify and describe the different types of frequency distributions.

- A normal distribution is symmetrical with the peak in the center of the distribution that tapers at each side; when cut in half, one side is a mirror image of the other half.

- A negatively skewed distribution is a distribution where the tail is on the left side or lower end of the x-axis and most of the scores lie at the higher end of the scale.

- A positively skewed distribution is a distribution where the tail is on the right side or upper end of the x-axis and most of the scores lie at the lower end of the scale.

- A bimodal distribution has two peaks rather than one.

LO 5 Identify and appropriately use the mean, median, and mode to describe data.

- The sample mean is the sum of all scores (Σx) divided by the number of scores summed (n) in a sample. The mean is used to describe data that are normally distributed and on an interval or ratio scale of measurement.

- The median is the middle value in a distribution of data listed in numeric order. The median is used to describe data that are skewed and data on an ordinal scale of measurement.

- The mode is the value that occurs most often or at the highest frequency in a distribution. The mode is used to describe distributions with one or more modes and categorical data on a nominal scale of measurement.

LO 6 Identify and appropriately use the variance and standard deviation to describe data.

- The sample variance is a measure of variability for the average squared distance that scores in a sample deviate from the sample mean. The sample variance is associated with $n - 1$ degrees of freedom (df) and is computed by dividing the sum of squares (SS) by df. The larger the sample variance, the farther that scores deviate from the mean, on average. One limitation of sample variance is that the average distance of scores from the mean is squared. To find the deviation or distance of scores from the mean, we take the square root of the variance, called the standard deviation.

LO 7 Define and apply the empirical rule.

- For normal distributions, the empirical rule states that 68% of scores fall within one standard deviation, 95% of scores fall within two standard deviations, and 99.7% of scores fall within three standard deviations of the mean.

LO 8 Identify and construct graphs used to display group means and correlations.

- We can graph a mean for one or more groups using a graph with lines or bars to represent the means. By convention, we use a bar graph when the groups on the x-axis (horizontal axis) are represented on a nominal or ordinal scale; we use a line graph when the groups on the x-axis are represented on an interval or ratio scale.

- We graph correlations using a scatterplot. To plot a data point, you first move across the x-axis and then move up or down the y-axis to mark or plot each pair of (x, y) data points. In a scatterplot, the pattern of a positive correlation appears as an ascending line; the pattern of a negative correlation appears as a descending line.

LO 9 Use Cronbach's alpha and Cohen's kappa to estimate reliability.

- Cronbach's alpha is a measure of internal consistency that estimates the average correlation for every possible way that a measure can be split in half. The higher the value of Cronbach's alpha, the stronger the correlation or relationship between items on the same measure.

- Cohen's kappa is a measure of interrater reliability that measures the level of agreement between two raters while taking into account the probability that the two raters agree by chance or error. The higher the value of Cohen's kappa, the stronger the interrater reliability.

LO 10 Distinguish between standard scores, z scores, percentile ranks, and age/grade equivalents.

- A standard score is one where the raw score is transformed into a normal frequency distribution with a specific mean and standard deviation so that we can compare an individual's score to other scores in the same peer group and make a determination about the relative performance of that individual. The z scores, percentile ranks, and age/grade equivalents are common examples of standard scores.

- A z score converts a raw score into a score that tells you how many standard deviations a score is from the mean.

- A percentile rank converts the raw score to rank an individual's performance in relation to many other individuals scored at or below that same score.

- Age/grade equivalent scores compare an individual's score to the average scores of different age groups to indicate to which age or grade the individual's score is most comparable.

age/grade equivalent
score 534

bar chart 516

bar graph 516

central tendency 518

Cohen's kappa 532

Cronbach's alpha 532

degrees of freedom (*df*)
for sample variance 524

descriptive statistics 513

empirical rule 525

frequency 515

frequency distribution
table 515

frequency polygon 517

histogram 515

median 520

mode 522

negative skew
distribution 518

normal distribution 520

percentile rank 534

pie chart 516

positive skew
distribution 518

sample mean 519

sample standard deviation
(*SD*) 525

sample variance 523

scatterplot 529

skewed distribution 518

standard score 534

sum of squares (*SS*) 524

variability 523

z score 534

REVIEW QUESTIONS

1. Which of the following words best describes descriptive statistics?
   A. Generalize
   B. Summarize
   C. Inference
   D. Decision making

2. In a study on participation in school clubs, 240 middle school students were asked to choose their preference for joining a school club. Create a frequency table of students choosing (1) book club = 35, (2) sport-related club = 98, (3) civic engagement club = 66, or (4) STEM (science, technology, engineering, math) club = 41.

3. The following seasons for participating in sports were recorded for a sample of high school athletes: winter, spring, spring, fall, summer, winter, fall, winter, winter, spring, winter, spring, winter, winter, summer, spring, winter, winter, fall, spring.
   A. Construct a bar chart.
   B. Why is a histogram not appropriate for summarizing these data?

4. The following graphs depict the mean time spent attending to a poster summarizing a new advanced curriculum among education majors from each class year. Which of the following graphs is most appropriate? Why?

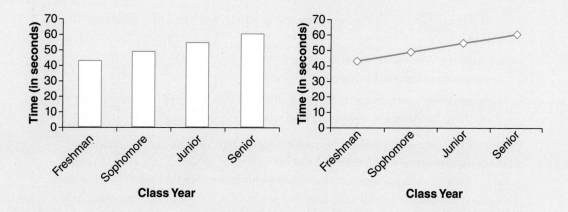

5. Name the type of graph used to describe a correlation.

6. Name the statistic used to identify (a) internal consistency and (b) interrater reliability.

7. Which measure of central tendency, the mean, median, or mode, is most appropriate to describe each of the following variables based on its scale of measurement (as defined in Chapter 4)?

   A. The time, in seconds, it takes participants to complete a graded assignment

   B. The grade received on the assignment (A, B, C, and D)

   C. The ratings of engagement on a scale from 1 to 5

8. State the empirical rule for normally distributed data.

9. Which shape of a frequency distribution is represented in the following descriptions?

   A. Scores on an exam where there were substantially more higher scores than lower scores

   B. Words per minute read correctly where most students scored in the middle and few students scored very high or very low

10. Which of the three types of standard scores is NOT the most precise way of describing an individual's performance on tests?

ACTIVITIES

1. Descriptive statistics are used in science, both in the literature and in the popular media. As an exercise, read through local newspapers, online news sources (e.g., CNN, NBC, or ABC), and popular magazines (e.g., *People*, *Time*, or *National Geographic*). Choose one article from a newspaper, one from an online source, and one from a magazine and then complete the following assignment:

A. Cite the authors, the title or webpage of the article, and the date/year/source of the article.

B. Identify the descriptive statistics included in the article. Were the statistics appropriately described in the article? Explain.

C. Explain if the descriptive statistics used in the article supported the arguments made in it. Were the descriptive statistics misleading? Explain.

2. Pair up with a partner to do the following exercise. You and your partner must independently observe whether or not students are talking during one class. You will make 12 observations. Each observation period should be about 10 seconds. After each observation period, mark *yes* if a student was observed talking during class; mark *no* if a student was not. Create a data sheet with two columns (yes, no) and 12 rows (one for each observation period) and record your observations. Using these data, compute Cohen's kappa to determine the interrater reliability of the observations made.

3. Locate information about the standardized tests used at your school by reading the test manual or a review of the test on the Mental Measurement Yearbook/Tests in Print database on your university library website for large-scale tests or on your state department website for locally created tests of student performance. What types of standard scores are used to interpret individual student performance?

⑤SAGE edge™

SAGE edge offers a robust online environment featuring an impressive array of free tools and resources for review, study, and further exploration, keeping both instructors and students on the cutting edge of teaching and learning.

Access practice quizzes, eFlashcards, video, and multimedia at edge.sagepub.com/priviterarme.

Identify a problem

- Determine an area of interest.
- Review the literature.
- Identify new ideas in your area of interest.
- Develop a research hypothesis.

Develop a research plan

- Define the variables being tested.
- Identify participants or subjects and determine how to sample them.
- Select a research strategy and design.
- Evaluate ethics and obtain institutional approval to conduct research.

Generate more new ideas

- Results support your hypothesis—refine or expand on your ideas.
- Results do not support your hypothesis—reformulate a new idea or start over.

Communicate the results

- Method of communication: oral, written, or in a poster.
- Style of communication: APA guidelines are provided to help prepare style and format.

Conduct the study

- Execute the research plan and measure or record the data.

Analyze and evaluate the data

- Analyze and evaluate the data as they relate to the research hypothesis.
- Summarize data and research results.

After reading this chapter, you should be able to:

1 Define inferential statistics and explain why they are necessary.

2 Describe the process of null hypothesis significance testing (NHST).

3 Distinguish between Type I and Type II errors and define power.

4 Distinguish between parametric and nonparametric tests and choose an appropriate test statistic for research designs with one and two factors.

5 Distinguish between a main effect and an interaction.

6 Identify main effects and interactions in a summary table and in a graph.

7 Distinguish between a chi-square goodness-of-fit test and a chi-square test for independence.

8 Identify and describe the following effect size measures: Cohen's *d*, eta squared, the coefficient of determination, and Cramer's *V*.

9 Distinguish between a point estimate and an interval estimate and explain how estimation relates to the significance and effect size of an outcome.

10 Distinguish between the precision and the certainty of an interval estimate.

ANALYSIS AND INTERPRETATION: MAKING INFERENCES ABOUT DATA

Each day you make conclusions or inferences about what you are experiencing. When you wake up in the morning and smell bacon, you conclude that someone is cooking breakfast; after watching the weather report, you conclude that it is going to be cold enough to wear your jacket; you infer that the guy who is speeding and cut you off in traffic to make a left turn is late to work; you infer that someone is mad by the tone of his or her voice. You make all sorts of conclusions and inferences each day from the little ones described here to more important ones, such as when you infer that a crime is about to happen when you see a person with a mask on holding a gun, or when you see a person staggering out of a bar, you infer that he or she is too drunk to drive. An inference is a conclusion made based on evidence and reasoning.

In science, we systematically record data, and on the basis of these data, we make inferences as well. The inferences we make in science often relate to the populations we are interested in. However, researchers select samples to understand behavior in a population. We therefore must make inferences about populations we are interested in based solely on the data recorded in a sample. To make these decisions, we use inferential statistics, which are statistical procedures that allow us to *infer* or generalize observations made with samples to the larger population from which they were selected. Ultimately, scientists use inferential statistics to be confident that the observations made in a sample will also be observed in the larger population.

edge.sagepub.com/
priviterarme

- Take the chapter quiz
- Review key terms with eFlashcards
- Explore multimedia links and SAGE articles

$SAGE edge™

Throughout this book, we have been introduced to many inferential statistics beginning in Chapter 6. In this chapter, we will take a closer look at how to decide which inferential statistics to use to analyze data based on what we know about a population and the data recorded. We will organize the use of these statistics to better understand why we are using them in various research situations.

19.1 Inferential Statistics: What Are We Making Inferences About?

As illustrated in Figure 19.1, we select a sampling method in Step 2 of the research process to select a portion of all members of a group of interest in a population. In Chapter 6, we explained that researchers select samples because they do not have access to all individuals in a population. For example, in this book, we have tested hypotheses concerning managing classroom disruptive behavior, food selections in the school cafeteria, increasing academic achievement of minority youth, and the relationship between grades and perceptions of teacher effectiveness. In each research study, we did not select all persons in the group of interest. In fact, it would be absurd to consider doing so—you would never select all U.S. residents, for example, to conduct a study.

> Inferential statistics are procedures that allow researchers to *infer* or generalize observations made with samples to the larger population from which they were selected.

> We use inferential statistics to make decisions about characteristics in a population based on data measured in a sample.

In Step 4 of the research process, we often use inferential statistics to analyze and evaluate the data because we are interested in describing the population of interest based on data measured in a sample. To illustrate the usefulness of inferential statistics, suppose we select a sample of students with disruptive classroom behavior to test the hypothesis that a new behavioral therapy is effective. We select a sample of 20 students, conduct the behavioral therapy study, and find that it was effective for the students in our sample. However, we are interested in describing whether this behavioral therapy is effective for *all* students with disruptive behavior and not just those students in our sample. Here, we can use inferential statistics to determine whether the results we observed in our sample are likely to also be observed in the population of *all* students with disruptive behavior. Hence, inferential statistics allow us to use data measured in a sample to draw conclusions about the larger population of interest, which would not otherwise be possible without inferential statistics.

Null Hypothesis Significance Testing (NHST)

Inferential statistics include a diverse set of tests of statistical significance more formally known as *null hypothesis significance testing* (NHST). To begin to understand NHST, let's think of the definition of *null*. Null means nothing or the absence of something. To use

NHST, we begin by stating a **null hypothesis,** which is a statement about a population parameter, such as the population mean, that is assumed to be true but contradicts the research hypothesis. In other words, we begin by assuming we are wrong in our research hypothesis—that there is no difference or relationship. We then conduct a study to

> The **null hypothesis,** stated as the *null,* is a statement about a population parameter, such as the population mean, that is assumed to be true. The null hypothesis is a starting point. We will test whether the value stated in the null hypothesis is likely to be true.

determine if we can reject the null hypothesis, thereby providing support for our own claim.

To illustrate the use of NHST, suppose we state the research hypothesis that a new therapy will reduce symptoms of depression. To use NHST, we begin by stating a null

Figure 19.1 Steps 2 to 4 of the Scientific Method and Why Inferential Statistics Are Needed in This Process

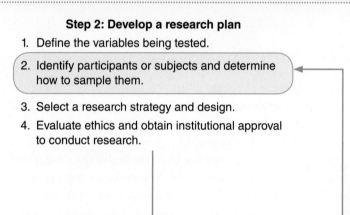

Step 2: Develop a research plan

1. Define the variables being tested.
2. Identify participants or subjects and determine how to sample them.
3. Select a research strategy and design.
4. Evaluate ethics and obtain institutional approval to conduct research.

Step 3: Conduct the study

Execute the research plan and measure or record the data.

Because we select a sampling method in Step 2, we will need inferential statistics in Step 4 to analyze and evaluate the data. Specifically, we use inferential statistics to determine if the results we observed in a sample will also be observed in the larger population from which the sample was selected.

Step 4: Analyze and evaluate the data

Analyze and evaluate the data as they relate to the research hypothesis.

Note: All steps of the scientific method are illustrated in Figure 1.1 in Chapter 1.

hypothesis that the new therapy does *not* reduce symptoms of depression. We then conduct a study to determine if that assumption can be rejected. If we reject the null hypothesis, then we have shown support for the alternative, which is our claim that the behavioral therapy does, in fact, reduce symptoms of depression. At this point, we need a criterion upon which to decide whether to reject or retain the null hypothesis.

The null hypothesis and the criteria used can be applied to an analogy in a criminal courtroom. The prosecutor begins a trial because he or she "hypothesizes" that the defendant is guilty. However, to begin the trial, we do not assume guilt; instead, a jury assumes the defendant is innocent—the assumption of innocence is the null hypothesis. The prosecutor then conducts a trial to show that the null hypothesis should be rejected "beyond reasonable doubt," which is the criterion upon which jurors decide whether a defendant is guilty or not guilty. In a research study, the criterion is a probability value for the likelihood of obtaining the data in a sample if the null hypothesis were true for the population.

> To apply NHST, we state a null hypothesis and then set a criterion upon which we will decide to retain or reject the null hypothesis.

Using the Criterion and Test Statistic to Make a Decision

To establish a criterion for a decision, we state a level of significance for a test. The significance level is the probability of rejecting the null hypothesis when it is actually true. If we reject the null hypothesis, then, we want this probability to be very low. The level of significance for most studies in the education sciences is .05 or 5%. When the likelihood of obtaining a sample outcome is less than 5% if the null hypothesis were true, we reject the null hypothesis because the sample outcome would be unlikely to occur (less than 5% likely). When the likelihood of obtaining a sample outcome is greater than 5% if the null hypothesis were true, we retain the null hypothesis because the sample outcome would be likely to occur (greater than 5% likely).

The level of significance, or significance level, is a criterion of judgment upon which a decision is made regarding the value stated in a null hypothesis. The criterion is based on the probability of obtaining a statistic measured in a sample if the value stated in the null hypothesis were true.

A test statistic is a mathematical formula that allows researchers to determine the likelihood of obtaining sample outcomes if the null hypothesis were true. The value of the test statistic can be used to make a decision regarding the null hypothesis.

A p value is the probability of obtaining a sample outcome if the value stated in the null hypothesis is true. The p value is compared to the level of significance to make a decision about a null hypothesis.

To determine the likelihood or probability of obtaining a sample outcome, if the value stated in the null hypothesis is true, we compute a test statistic. The test statistic is a mathematical formula used to determine how far a sample outcome deviates or varies from the outcome that is assumed to be true in the null hypothesis. Examples of test statistics include those already introduced, such as the correlation coefficient (Chapters 9 and 18), the *t* tests (Chapters 6 and 14), and the analysis of variance tests (Chapter 14). A test statistic is used to find the *p* value, which is the actual probability of obtaining a sample outcome if the null hypothesis is true.

The *p* value is interpreted as error. When differences observed in a sample are attributed to error (or random variation in participant responding), error is large, and the

p value is larger than .05 (the criterion). When $p > .05$, we retain the null hypothesis and state that an effect or difference failed to reach **significance.** When differences observed in a sample are attributed to a manipulation or treatment, error is low, and the p value is less than or equal to .05. When $p \leq .05$, we reject the null hypothesis and state that an effect or difference reached significance.

> **Significance,** or **statistical significance,** describes a decision made concerning a value stated in the null hypothesis. When the null hypothesis is rejected, we reach significance. When the null hypothesis is retained, we fail to reach significance.

19.2 Types of Error and Power

Any time we select a sample from a population, there is some probability of sampling error inasmuch as p is some value greater than 0. Because we are observing a sample and not an entire population, it is certainly possible that a decision made using NHST is wrong. Table 19.1 shows that there are four decision alternatives regarding the truth and falsity of the decision we make about a null hypothesis:

1. The decision to retain the null hypothesis could be correct.

2. The decision to retain the null hypothesis could be incorrect.

3. The decision to reject the null hypothesis could be correct.

4. The decision to reject the null hypothesis could be incorrect.

We investigate each decision alternative in this section. Because we will observe a sample and not a population, it is impossible to know for sure the truth in a population. So for the sake of illustration, we will assume we know this. This assumption is labeled as "Truth in the Population" in Table 19.1.

Decision: Retain the Null Hypothesis

When we decide to retain the null hypothesis, we can be correct or incorrect. The correct decision, called a *null result* or a *null finding*, is to retain a true null hypothesis. This is

Table 19.1	Four Decision Alternatives in NHST	

		Decision	
		Retain the Null	**Reject the Null**
Truth in the Population	True	CORRECT	TYPE I ERROR
	False	TYPE II ERROR	CORRECT **POWER**

Note: A decision can be either correct (correctly reject or retain null hypothesis) or incorrect (incorrectly reject or retain null hypothesis).

usually an uninteresting decision because the decision is to retain what we already assumed: that the value stated in a null hypothesis is correct. For this reason, null results alone are rarely published in behavioral research.

The incorrect decision is to retain a false null hypothesis. This decision is an example of a **Type II error.** With each test we make, there is always some probability that the decision could be a Type II error. In this decision, we decide to retain previous notions of truth that are in fact false. While it is an error, we still changed nothing; we retained the null hypothesis. We can always go back and conduct more studies.

> A Type II error is the probability of retaining a null hypothesis that is actually false. This means the researcher is reporting no effect in the population when in truth there is an effect.

Decision: Reject the Null Hypothesis

When we decide to reject the null hypothesis, we can be correct or incorrect. The incorrect decision is to reject a true null hypothesis, which is a **Type I error.** With each test we make, there is always some probability that our decision is a Type I error. A researcher who makes this error decides to reject previous notions of truth that are in fact true. The goal in NHST is to avoid this error by starting with the assumption that the null hypothesis is correct, thereby placing the burden on the researcher to show evidence that the null hypothesis is indeed false. To demonstrate evidence that leads to a decision to reject the null hypothesis, the research must reach significance ($p < .05$); that is, we must show that the likelihood of committing a Type I error by rejecting the null hypothesis is less than 5%.

> A Type I error is the probability of rejecting a null hypothesis that is actually true. Researchers directly control for the probability of committing this error by stating the level of significance.
>
> The power in hypothesis testing is the probability of rejecting a false null hypothesis. Specifically, power is the probability that we will detect an effect if an effect actually exists in a population.

> A Type I error is when we reject a true null hypothesis.

The correct decision is to reject a false null hypothesis. In other words, we decide that the null hypothesis is false when it is indeed false. This decision is called the **power** of the decision-making process because it is the decision we aim for. Remember that we are testing the null hypothesis because we think it is wrong. Deciding to reject a false null hypothesis, then, is the power, inasmuch as we learn the most about populations when we accurately reject false notions of truth. This decision is the most publishable outcome in behavioral research.

LEARNING CHECK 1 ✓

1. What are the two decisions a researcher can make, each of which could be correct or incorrect?

2. A researcher states that adult supervision during recess significantly reduced aggressive behavior among children in her sample ($p = .12$). Is this conclusion appropriate at a .05 level of significance?

3. Which type of error, Type I or Type II, is associated with a decision to reject the null hypothesis?

4. What is the power of the decision-making process?

19.3 Parametric Tests: Applying the Decision Tree

We apply NHST to analyze a data set in Step 4 of the research process, as illustrated in Chapter 1 and in Figure 19.1 in this chapter. The most common tests of significance are **parametric tests,** which are significance tests used to test hypotheses about parameters in a population in which each of the following is true:

- Data in the population are normally distributed.

- Data in the population are independent of each other.

- Data are measured on an interval or ratio scale of measurement.

> **Parametric tests** are significance tests that are used to test hypotheses about parameters in a population in which the data in the population are normally distributed and measured on an interval or ratio scale of measurement.

Parametric tests are commonly applied to analyze behavioral and educational data because most behavioral and educational phenomena are approximately normally distributed, and most behavioral data can be measured on an interval or ratio scale. Parametric tests are used for interval and ratio data because differences are meaningful on these scales. Therefore, analyzing mean differences between groups is also meaningful—this is the computation made by the test statistics for each parametric test listed in Figure 19.2. Also, many of the physical and behavioral phenomena that educational researchers study are normally distributed, with very few people at the extremes of behavior relative to the general population. For example, if we measure attention span or articulation errors, we can identify that most people will fall within a normal or typical range, a few will have abnormally low levels, and a few will have abnormally high levels; if we measure activity levels, we will identify that most people are moderately active, a few are very active (such as Olympic athletes), and a few are sedentary.

> Parametric tests are used when data in the population are normally distributed and measured on an interval or ratio scale.

If many groups are observed, then to use parametric tests, we must also make the assumption that the variance in the population for each group is approximately the same or equal. Hence, parametric tests require assumptions concerning mean differences between groups, assuming that the variances in each group are about the same. In this section, we will describe how to choose between the following parametric tests in various research situations: the t tests, analyses of variance (ANOVAs), correlation, and regression.

t Tests and ANOVAs

In Chapters 13 and 14, we used group designs with treatment and control (or comparison) groups that differed on the implementation of the independent variable. For these designs, we examine the mean differences between groups on the dependent variables to determine if there was an observed effect for the independent variable. Again, to use parametric tests, we must measure interval/ratio data from populations with data that are normally distributed and have similar variances. If these criteria are met, then parametric tests are appropriate for analyzing the data. Choosing an appropriate parametric test depends largely on how participants were observed (between subjects or within subjects) and how many factors and groups were included in a research design. Figure 19.2 shows how to choose each parametric test for different research situations.

We use parametric tests for any case in which one or more groups or factors are observed to include experiments, quasi-experiments, and nonexperiments. An advantage of using parametric tests to analyze data is that the test statistics provide statistical control of individual error variation that cannot be explained by the levels of a factor. However, also keep in mind that we cannot draw causal conclusions without the methodological control that can only be attained in an experiment—that is, randomization (or control of order effects if the same participants are observed across groups), manipulation (of the levels of an independent variable), and the inclusion of a control or comparison group. Consequently, quasi-experiments and nonexperiments have research designs for which parametric tests can establish statistical control, but because these research designs lack methodological control, they fail to demonstrate cause and effect.

Figure 19.2 A Decision Tree for Choosing Parametric Tests for One and Two Factors

Parametric Tests for One and Two Factors With Interval/Ratio Data

How Many Factors? How Many Groups?	How Are Participants Observed?	Appropriate Parametric Test (chapter covered)
1 → 1		One-Sample t Test (5)
1 → 2	Between-Subjects	Two-Independent-Sample t Test (10)
	Within-Subjects	Related-Samples t Test (11)
1 → 3 or more	Between-Subjects	One-Way Between-Subjects ANOVA (10)
	Within-Subjects	One-Way Within-Subjects ANOVA (11)
2	Between-Subjects	Two-Way Between-Subjects ANOVA (12)
	Within-Subjects	Two-Way Within-Subjects ANOVA (12)
	One Between-Subjects & One Within-Subjects	Two-Way Mixed Factorial ANOVA (12)

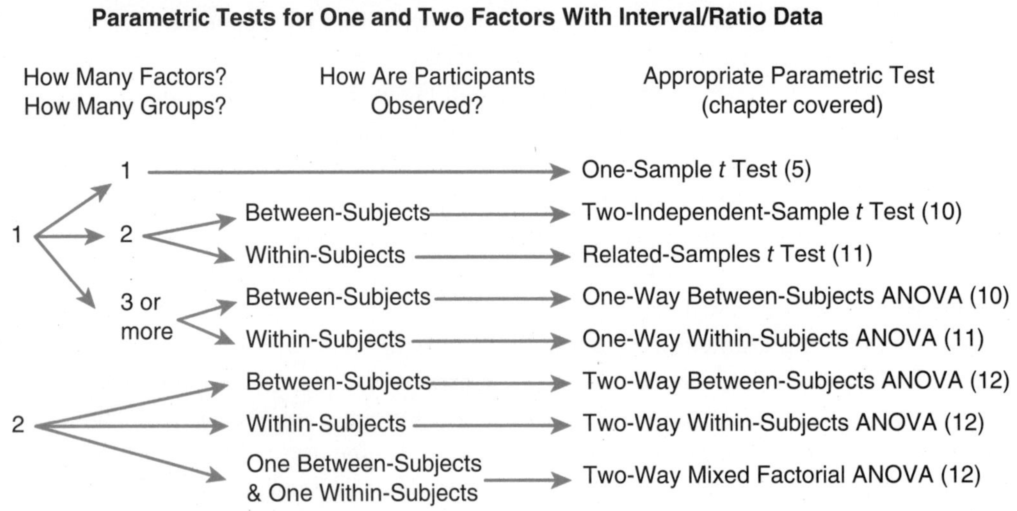

Note: The chapter in which each test was introduced is given in parentheses next to the name for each test.

19.4 Main Effects and Interactions

In this section, we will introduce the factorial design in which the levels of two factors are manipulated, as illustrated in Tables 14.7 and 14.8 from Chapter 14. When the levels of two factors (A and B) are combined to create groups, the design is specifically called a two-way factorial design. Using this design, we can identify three sources of variation:

1. Two main effects (one for Factor A and one for Factor B)

2. One interaction (the combination of levels of Factors A and B)

3. Error variance (variability attributed to individual differences)

We make three independent statistical tests using the two-way factorial design. To show how the sources of variation relate to a research hypothesis, we will work with an example in which we manipulate two factors (studying for a quiz and attending class) and measure quiz scores to answer the following three questions:

> A two-way factorial design is a research design in which participants are observed in groups created by combining or crossing the levels of two factors.

- Did manipulating the levels of Factor A (a main effect) cause differences between groups? Example: Does studying for a quiz result in higher quiz scores? (See Table 14.10.)

- Did manipulating the levels of Factor B (a main effect) cause differences between groups? Example: Does attending class result in higher quiz scores? (See Table 14.10.)

- Did combining the levels of Factor A and Factor B to create groups (the interaction) cause differences between groups? Example: Does the combination of studying for a quiz and attending class result in higher quiz scores? (See Table 14.11.)

In this example, Factor A is whether students studied for a quiz (no, yes), and Factor B is their class attendance (high, low). In this section, we will identify each source of variation and show how measuring each source allows researchers to answer each of the questions identified for each factor.

Main Effects

In a factorial design, we can look at the effects of each factor separately. The extent to which the levels of a single factor cause changes in a dependent variable is called a **main effect.** Using this definition, we also tested for main effects using the one-way ANOVAs earlier in this chapter because we tested for the effects at each level of a single factor.

> A **main effect** is a source of variation associated with mean differences across the levels of a single factor.

For a 2 × 2 factorial design, we can illustrate main effects in the row and column totals of a 2 × 2 table summary. To illustrate, suppose the data in Table 14.10 are quiz scores, where Factor A is whether students studied for a quiz (no, yes), and Factor B is their class attendance (high, low). Table 19.2 identifies each main effect and shows how each would be interpreted, if significant. Notice that we interpret a significant main effect similar to the interpretation of significant results using the one-way ANOVAs.

A significant main effect indicates that group means significantly vary across the levels of one factor, independent of the second factor. In a table summary, such as that given in Table 19.2, we compare the variance of row and column means to interpret the main effects. To compute the test statistic for each main effect, we place the between-groups variance for one factor in the numerator and the error variance in the denominator. Referring to the table summary, the test statistic for the main effect of Factor A is as follows:

$$F = \frac{\text{Variance of column means}}{\text{Variance attributed to error}}.$$

The test statistic for the main effect of Factor B is as follows:

$$F = \frac{\text{Variance of row means}}{\text{Variance attributed to error}}.$$

Table 19.2 Main Effects

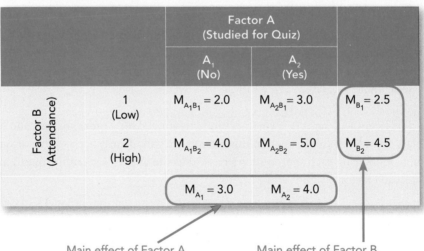

Main effect of Factor A.
If significant, we state that students who studied earned higher quiz scores, regardless of their class attendance.

Main effect of Factor B.
If significant, we state that students with high attendance earned higher quiz scores, regardless of whether they studied for the quiz.

Note: The main effect for each factor reflects the difference between the row and column totals in the table. There are two main effects (one for Factor A and one for Factor B) in a two-way factorial design.

Interactions

In a factorial design, we can also look at the effects of combining the levels of two factors to create groups. The extent to which groups created by combining the levels of two factors cause changes in a dependent variable is called an A × B **interaction.** An interaction is unique to the factorial design in that it allows us to determine if changes in a dependent variable across the levels of one factor depend on the level of the second factor we look at.

For a 2 × 2 factorial design, we can illustrate the interaction in the cells of a 2 × 2 table summary. To illustrate, the quiz data where Factor A is whether students studied for a quiz (no, yes) and Factor B is their class attendance (high, low) are given again in Table 14.11. Table 19.3 identifies two ways to interpret the interaction, if significant. For each interpretation, we look across the levels of one factor at each level of the second factor. Which interpretation we use to describe the interaction depends largely on how we want to describe the data.

A significant interaction indicates that group means significantly vary across the combined levels of two factors. In a table summary, such as that given in Table 19.3, we compare the variance of cell means to interpret an interaction.

> The changes in a dependent variable across the levels of a single factor are called a main effect.

> An **interaction** is a source of variation associated with how the effects of one factor are influenced by, or depend on, the levels of a second factor.

> The change in a dependent variable across the combined levels of two factors is called an interaction.

LEARNING CHECK 2 ✓

1. What are the three effects about which researchers test a hypothesis using the two-way factorial design?

2. Name the statistical procedure used to analyze data for the factorial design with two factors.

3. The variance attributed to error in a factorial design is associated with differences in _____ within each cell.

4. A researcher tests whether the lighting (dull, bright) and background noise (low, high) in a classroom influence student performance on an exam. He conducts a two-way factorial design to analyze the data and finds a significant effect of lighting, with higher scores when the lighting was bright. Is the effect described in this study an example of a main effect or an interaction?

> In a table summary, an interaction is a measure of how cell means at each level of one factor change across the levels of a second factor.

Answers: 1. A main effect of Factor A, a main effect of Factor B, and an A × B interaction; 2. The two-way ANOVA; 3. Participant scores; 4. Main effect.

19.5 Identifying Main Effects and Interactions in a Graph

A main effect and an interaction can be evident when the cell means in a table summary are plotted in a graph. Keep in mind, however, that even if a graph shows a possible main effect

Table 19.3 Interaction

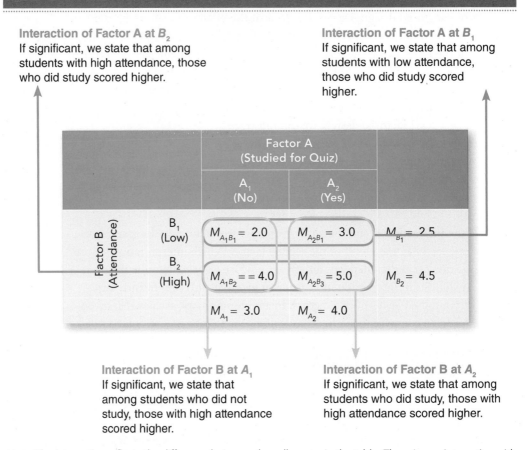

Interaction of Factor A at B_2
If significant, we state that among students with high attendance, those who did study scored higher.

Interaction of Factor A at B_1
If significant, we state that among students with low attendance, those who did study scored higher.

		Factor A (Studied for Quiz)		
		A_1 (No)	A_2 (Yes)	
Factor B (Attendance)	B_1 (Low)	$M_{A_1 B_1} = 2.0$	$M_{A_2 B_1} = 3.0$	$M_{B_1} = 2.5$
	B_2 (High)	$M_{A_1 B_2} = = 4.0$	$M_{A_2 B_3} = 5.0$	$M_{B_2} = 4.5$
		$M_{A_1} = 3.0$	$M_{A_2} = 4.0$	

Interaction of Factor B at A_1
If significant, we state that among students who did not study, those with high attendance scored higher.

Interaction of Factor B at A_2
If significant, we state that among students who did study, those with high attendance scored higher.

Note: The interaction reflects the difference between the cell means in the table. There is one interaction with two ways to interpret it. Each way to interpret the interaction in a two-way factorial design is described in the table.

or interaction, the use of a test statistic is still needed to determine whether a main effect or an interaction is significant. In other words, we use the test statistic to determine if our manipulation of the two factors caused the observed pattern we plotted in a graph. In this section, we look at how three types of outcomes appear graphically for a two-way factorial design.

Graphing Only Main Effects

One possible outcome is to observe only main effects. For the main effects, we would observe changes at the levels of one factor, independent of the changes in a second factor. Consider, for example, a factorial design in which we manipulate whether the setting (familiar, unfamiliar) and the duration (1 hour, 2 hours) of a treatment influence its effectiveness to reduce (lower) school phobia. When the main effects are significant, we look at the row and column means to describe the effect. Figure 19.3 shows how a graph would appear when main

(a) Data showing a main effect of duration only.

		Setting		ROW MEANS
		Familiar	Unfamiliar	
Duration	1 Hour	8	8	8
	2 Hours	4	4	4
	COLUMN MEANS	6	6	

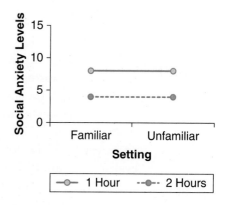

(b) Data showing a main effect of both factors (duration and setting), but no interaction.

		Setting		ROW MEANS
		Familiar	Unfamiliar	
Duration	1 Hour	8	16	12
	2 Hours	4	12	8
	COLUMN MEANS	6	14	

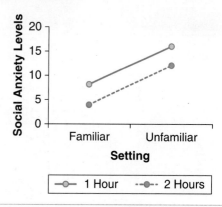

effects are significant: Figure 19.3a depicts a main effect of duration only; Figure 19.3b depicts a main effect of duration and a main effect of setting but no interaction.

Graphing a Main Effect and an Interaction

Another possible outcome is to observe an interaction and also at least one main effect. To identify an interaction, we graph the cell means and look to see if the lines in the graph are parallel. A possible interaction is evident when the lines are not parallel. To illustrate, consider again the example of a factorial design in which we manipulate whether the setting (familiar, unfamiliar) and the duration (1 hour, 2 hours) of a treatment influence its effectiveness to reduce social anxiety. Figure 19.4a depicts a main effect of setting (lower anxiety levels observed in the familiar setting regardless of the duration of the treatment) and an interaction—anxiety levels were lower in the familiar setting for the 2-hour treatment (2 vs. 12) but not for the 1-hour treatment in which anxiety

> The group means in a table summary can be graphed to identify the main effects.

levels were actually the same in each setting (7 vs. 7). Notice in Figure 19.4a that the lines are not parallel, which indicates a possible interaction.

Graphing Only an Interaction

Another possible outcome is to observe only an interaction. For the interaction, we expect to observe that changes in a dependent variable for one factor depend on which level of the second factor we look at. Consider again the example of a factorial design in which we manipulate whether the setting (familiar, unfamiliar) and the duration (1 hour, 2 hours) of a treatment influence its effectiveness to reduce social anxiety. Figure 19.4b depicts an interaction only—the 1-hour treatment resulted in lower social anxiety levels in the unfamiliar setting, whereas the 2-hour treatment resulted in lower social anxiety levels in the familiar setting. No main effects are evident in Figure 19.4b because the row means and column means do not differ. Notice in Figure 19.4b that the lines are not parallel, which indicates a possible interaction.

> The group means in a table summary can be graphed to identify an interaction.

Figure 19.4 The Data and Graph of the Cell Means for One Main Effect and an Interaction (a) and an Interaction but No Main Effects (b)

(a) Data showing a main effect of setting and a Setting × Duration interaction.

		Setting		ROW MEANS
		Familiar	Unfamiliar	
Duration	1 Hour	7	7	7
	2 Hours	2	12	7
	COLUMN MEANS	5	9	

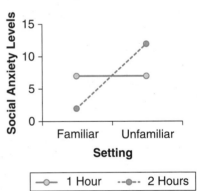

(b) Data showing a Setting × Duration interaction, but no main effects.

		Setting		ROW MEANS
		Familiar	Unfamiliar	
Duration	1 Hour	12	6	9
	2 Hours	6	12	9
	COLUMN MEANS	9	9	

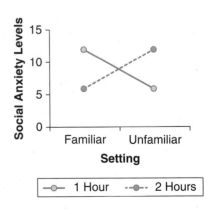

1. Which effect, a main effect or an interaction, can be identified in the row means and column means of a table summary?

2. The following graph summarizes the results of a study that manipulated the caloric density (low, high) and type of food (dessert, snack, meal) consumed in a buffet. Is an interaction evident? If no, then explain your answer.

3. Which effect, a main effect or an interaction, is identified in the cell means of a table summary?

Answers: 1. A main effect; 2. No, because the lines are parallel; 3. An interaction.

19.6 Correlation and Regression

We also introduced in Chapter 9 parametric tests concerning the extent to which two factors are related (correlation) and the extent to which we can use known values of one factor to predict values of a second factor (linear regression). For these tests, we do not manipulate the levels of a factor to create groups; instead we treat each factor like a dependent variable and measure its value for each participant in a study. The correlation coefficient and linear regression do provide statistical control of individual error variation that cannot be explained by the two factors. However, research designs that require these statistics are typically not experimental and so lack the methodological control needed to demonstrate cause and effect.

> The Spearman, point-biserial, and phi correlation coefficients are mathematically equivalent to the Pearson correlation coefficient.

To choose a correlation, we need to know the scale of measurement of the data. For a parametric test, we use the *Pearson correlation coefficient* for data measured on an interval or ratio scale. Other coefficients have been derived from the Pearson correlation coefficient for situations in which at least one factor is not measured on an interval/ratio scale. The *Spearman correlation coefficient* is used to examine the relationship between two factors measured on an ordinal scale; the *phi correlation coefficient* is used to examine the relationship between two factors measured on a nominal scale; the *point-biserial correlation coefficient* is used to examine the relationship between two factors when one factor is dichotomous (nominal) and a second factor is continuous (interval or ratio scale). Each alternative correlation coefficient was mathematically derived from, and therefore equal to, the Pearson formula. For this reason, the Pearson correlation coefficient can be used to analyze data on any scale because its value will equal the value of the other coefficients—with some minor adjustments needed for data on ordinal and nominal scales—adjustments that SPSS will make automatically when you enter the data.

Similarly, choosing an appropriate linear regression model will require that we know the scale of measurement of the data. In addition, we need to know how many predictor variables we will include in the model. For one predictor variable, we use *linear regression*. For two or more predictor variables, we use *multiple regression*. Choosing an appropriate regression model can also depend on whether the research question is exploratory or confirmatory. The details of an exploratory and confirmatory factor analysis, however, go beyond the scope of this book and can be very complex—resources for applying factor analyses using regression models can be found in many upper-level textbooks (see Schumacker & Lomax, 2010; Thompson, 2004; Weisberg, 2005).

LEARNING CHECK 4 ✓

1. State the three assumptions or criteria that must be met to conduct a parametric test for a set of data.

2. In a research study, one group of teachers was asked to rate their school climate on an interval scale measure. State the appropriate parametric test to analyze the data for this hypothetical study.

3. Which correlation coefficient is used to analyze data on an interval or ratio scale?

Answers: 1. Data in the population are normally distributed, data are measured on an interval or ratio scale, and the variance of data in the population for each group is approximately the same or equal when many groups are observed; 2. One-way within-subjects ANOVA; 3. Pearson correlation coefficient.

19.7 Nonparametric Tests: Applying the Decision Tree

Nonparametric tests are significance tests that are used to test hypotheses about data that can have any type of distribution and to analyze data on a nominal or ordinal scale of measurement.

When the distribution in the population is not normally distributed and when data are measured on an ordinal or nominal scale, we apply **nonparametric tests** to analyze data in Step 4 of the research process (see Figure 19.1). Nonparametric tests are tests of significance that can be used to test hypotheses about parameters in a population in which each of the following is true:

Nonparametric tests are used to analyze nominal and ordinal data from populations with any type of distribution.

- Data in the population can have any type of distribution.

- Data are measured on a nominal or ordinal scale of measurement.

Nonparametric tests are often called *distribution-free tests* because the shape of the distribution in the population can be any shape. The reason that the variance and therefore the shape of a distribution in the population does not matter is that a test statistic for nonparametric tests will not measure variance to determine significance. Likewise, because variance is not computed in nonparametric test statistics, these tests can also be used to analyze ordinal and nominal data, which are scales in which the variance is not meaningful. In this section, we will describe how to choose between nonparametric tests for ordinal and nominal data.

Nonparametric tests can also be used with interval- and ratio-level data when the sample size is very small. The rule of thumb is if the sample size is fewer than 30, then the parametric test is likely not appropriate. This is because of the assumption of a normal distribution. When the sample size is so small, the distribution of the sample may not be normal. It is important to check the data to see what shape the frequency distribution is. Another concern with using a parametric test with a small sample size is the lack of power or large Type II error. The size of the sample may be too small to detect what the researcher is looking for in the data. In many cases, when there is a small sample size with interval- or ratio-level data, the most appropriate statistic is likely a nonparametric rather than a parametric test.

Tests for Ordinal Data

Nonparametric tests for ordinal data are used as alternatives to parametric tests, which require that data be measured on an interval or ratio scale. Choosing an appropriate nonparametric test depends largely on how participants were observed (between subjects or within subjects) and the number of groups in the research design. Figure 19.5 shows how to choose each nonparametric test for ordinal data for different research situations.

The structure of the decision tree for choosing an appropriate nonparametric test for ordinal data is similar to that for parametric tests with one factor—note the overlap between Figures 19.2 and 19.5 for one factor. We can require the use of nonparametric tests in two common situations. In the first situation, the data may be on an interval or a ratio scale but are not normally distributed, which is an assumption that must be met for parametric tests. In these situations, we convert the data to ranks (ordinal data) and use the nonparametric alternative test to analyze the data. In the second situation, we record ranked data, in which case the variability of ranks (ordinal data) is not meaningful and so a nonparametric test is required. The specific analysis of each nonparametric test for ordinal data given in Figure 19.5 is beyond the scope of this book (for a full description of the analysis for each test, see Privitera, 2012).

Figure 19.5 A Decision Tree for Choosing Nonparametric Tests for Ordinal Data

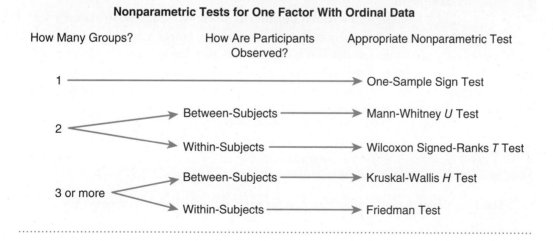

Nonparametric Tests for One Factor With Ordinal Data

How Many Groups?	How Are Participants Observed?	Appropriate Nonparametric Test
1		One-Sample Sign Test
2	Between-Subjects	Mann-Whitney U Test
	Within-Subjects	Wilcoxon Signed-Ranks T Test
3 or more	Between-Subjects	Kruskal-Wallis H Test
	Within-Subjects	Friedman Test

Tests for Nominal (Categorical) Data

Nonparametric tests can also be used to analyze nominal or categorical data. For these research situations, we count the frequency of occurrence in two or more categories for one or two factors. Variance is meaningless in these research situations because it is meaningless to analyze the variance of a single count or frequency in each category—variance cannot be computed for a single value. The nonparametric tests used to analyze nominal (categorical) data are called the *chi-square tests*.

For one categorical factor, we analyze the extent to which frequencies observed fit well with frequencies expected using the chi-square goodness-of-fit test. To illustrate a research situation in which we use this nonparametric test, we will count the frequency of play centers selected in a preschool setting—blocks, books, and water play. If we want to determine if children have a preference for one area, then we begin by assuming that an equal number or proportion of selections will be made for each of the three play centers. If we observe 90 children, then we expect 30 selections in each location. The chi-square goodness-of-fit test is used to determine if the proportion of selections we observe in each location fits well with this expectation. If it fits well, then there is no preference, and the result will not reach significance. If it does not fit well, then there is a preference, and the result will reach significance.

The **chi-square goodness-of-fit test** is a statistical procedure used to determine whether observed frequencies at each level of one categorical variable are similar to or different from frequencies expected.

The **chi-square test for independence** is a statistical procedure used to determine whether frequencies observed at the combination of levels of two categorical variables are similar to or different from frequencies expected.

A chi-square goodness-of-fit test is used to determine how well a set of observed frequencies fits with what was expected.

We can also analyze the extent to which frequencies observed across the levels of two nominal (categorical) factors are related or independent using the chi-square test for independence. When two factors are related, such as activity levels (low, high) and depression (yes, no), the frequencies displayed in a summary table will vary across the cells, as shown in Table 19.4a. When two factors are independent (not related), such as a preference (Coke or Pepsi) and depression (yes, no), the frequencies in a summary table will be the same or similar, as shown in Table 19.4b.

To illustrate a research situation in which we use this nonparametric test, we can test if the play center selection (books, blocks, water play) depended on gender of the child (male, female). If it is independent, then the play center selection will not be related to the gender of the child, and the result will not reach significance. If it is dependent or related, then the play center selection will be related to the gender of the child, and the result will reach significance.

LEARNING CHECK 5 ✓

1. State the nonparametric alternative test for each of the following parametric tests:

   A. One-sample *t* test

B. Two-independent-sample *t* test

C. One-way between-subjects ANOVA

2. State whether a chi-square goodness-of-fit test or a chi-square test for independence is the appropriate nonparametric test for the following example: A health psychologist compares the number of students who are lean, healthy, overweight, and obese at a local school to expected proportions in each category.

3. A researcher makes the decision to reject the null hypothesis using a chi-square test for independence. Does this decision mean that two factors are independent or related?

Table 19.4 A Dependent (a) and an Independent (b) Relationship Between Two Categorical Variables

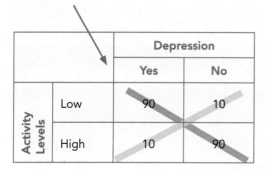

(a) Dependent relationship (two factors are related)

Frequencies do not vary across the cells.

		Depression	
		Yes	No
Activity Levels	Low	90	10
	High	10	90

(b) Independent relationship (two factors are not related)

Frequencies vary across the cells.

		Depression	
		Yes	No
Preference	Coke	50	50
	Pepsi	50	50

19.8 Effect Size: How Big Is an Effect in the Population?

We use NHST to determine if the results observed in a sample are likely to also occur in the population from which that sample was selected. In other words, we use NHST to determine if an effect exists in a population. An **effect** is a term used to describe the mean difference or discrepancy between what

> An **effect** is a mean difference or discrepancy between what was observed in a sample and what was expected to be observed in the population (stated by the null hypothesis).

Effect size is a statistical measure of the size or magnitude of an observed effect in a population, which allows researchers to describe how far scores shifted in a population or the percentage of variance in a dependent variable that can be explained by the levels of a factor.

NHST indicates if an effect exists in a population; effect size indicates the size of an effect in a population.

was observed in a sample and what was expected in the population as stated by the null hypothesis. When we reject a null hypothesis, an effect is significant and therefore does exist in a population; when we retain a null hypothesis, an effect is not significant and therefore does not exist in a population. The decision using NHST, however, only indicates if an effect exists but does not inform us of the size of that effect in the population.

To determine the size of an effect in a population, we compute an estimate called **effect size,** which is a measure of the size of an observed effect in a population. Effect size can describe how far scores shifted in a population, or it can describe the proportion of variance in a dependent variable that can be explained or accounted for by the levels of a factor. Effect size is often reported with many parametric and nonparametric tests for significance. Table 19.5 lists common tests for significance and the corresponding effect size measure reported with each test. The following effect size measures listed in Table 19.5 are described in this section:

- Cohen's d
- Proportion of variance: η^2, R^2
- Proportion of variance: Cramer's V

Table 19.5 Measures of Effect Size That Correspond to Common Tests for Significance

Test for Significance	Effect Size	
	Corresponding Effect Size Measure	Interpretation of Effect Size Measure
t tests	Cohen's d	Its value represents the number of standard deviations that scores shift or fall above or below a value stated in a null hypothesis.
ANOVAs	η^2	Its value represents the proportion of variance in a dependent variable that can be explained by the levels of a factor.
Correlation and regression	R^2	Its value represents the proportion of variance in values of one factor that can be explained by changes in the values of a second factor.
Chi-square test for independence	Cramer's V	Same as R^2

Note: The interpretation is also given for each effect size measure.

Cohen's d

When one or two groups are observed, we can describe effect size as a shift or mean difference between groups in a population using a measure called **Cohen's** *d* (Cohen, 1988). Cohen's *d* estimates the size of a shift in the population as the number of standard deviations that scores shifted. In the formula for Cohen's *d*, the numerator is the sample mean difference—either between two groups or between a sample and a population mean for one group. The denominator is the sample standard deviation for one group or the pooled (averaged) sample standard deviation for two groups. The formula for Cohen's *d* can be represented using the following standard form:

> **Cohen's *d*** is a measure of effect size in terms of the number of standard deviations that mean scores shifted above or below the population mean stated by the null hypothesis. The larger the value of *d*, the larger the effect in the population.

> Cohen's *d* is an effect size measure used with the one-sample, two-independent-sample, and related-samples *t* tests.

$$d = \frac{\text{Sample mean difference}}{\text{Sample standard deviation}}$$

Cohen's *d* is used with the *t* tests. In each case, there is no effect size when $d = 0$, with larger values for *d* indicating a larger effect size in the population. We interpret the value of *d* in terms of standard deviations. The positive or negative sign indicates only the direction of an effect in the population. For example, if $d = +0.36$, then scores shifted 0.36 standard deviations above the value stated in a null hypothesis; if $d = -0.36$, then scores shifted 0.36 standard deviations below the value stated by a null hypothesis.

The size of an effect can be described as small, medium, or large. Conventions for interpreting the size of an effect using Cohen's *d* are identified by **Cohen's conventions,** which are given in Table 19.6 under the *d* column heading. In our example, we would describe $d = \pm 0.36$ as a medium effect size.

> **Cohen's conventions,** or **effect size conventions,** are standard rules for identifying small, medium, and large effects based on typical findings in behavioral research.

CONNECTING TO THE CLASSROOM

Using statistics for your own classroom data does not require an expensive statistical program. You can conduct *t* tests using the Excel formula (f_x) function. When conducting research to inform your own practice, you may not be interested in generalizing to a larger population. If you are only interested in examining the impact of your change in practice for your students, inferential statistics may not be needed. By looking at the mean scores of the different groups, you can see which group performed better. The best way to compare groups, though, is by using Cohen's *d*. There are free effect size calculators using Excel with the formula embedded into the file available on the Internet. All you need is the mean, number of participants, and the standard deviation for each group. Enter these into the effect size calculators and it will calculate Cohen's *d* for you.

Proportion of Variance: η^2, $\mathbf{R}^2$

Proportion of variance is a measure of effect size in terms of the proportion or percentage of variability in a dependent variable that can be explained or accounted for by the levels of a factor or treatment.

Eta squared (η^2) is a measure of proportion of variance used to describe effect size for data analyzed using ANOVA.

When ANOVA is used to analyze data, eta squared is used to estimate effect size.

An alternative measure of effect size is **proportion of variance.** Proportion of variance is a measure of effect size in terms of the proportion or percentage of variability in a dependent variable that can be explained or accounted for by the levels of a factor or treatment. This type of effect size estimate is used when a study includes more than two groups or applies a correlational research design.

To estimate proportion of variance with ANOVA, we compute a measure called **eta squared,** symbolized as η^2. Sometimes, a partial estimate of eta squared is reported for a within-subjects design. The value of eta squared can range between 0 and 1.0 and is interpreted as a proportion or percentage. For example, if $\eta^2 = .04$, then 4% of the variability in a dependent variable can be explained by the levels of a factor. The formula for eta squared can be represented using the following standard form:

$$\eta^2 = \frac{\text{Variability between groups}}{\text{Total variability}}$$

The **coefficient of determination** (R^2) is a measure of proportion of variance used to describe effect size for data analyzed using a correlation coefficient or regression. The coefficient of determination is mathematically equivalent to eta squared.

When a correlation or regression is used to analyze data, the coefficient of determination, R^2, is used to estimate effect size. The coefficient of determination is mathematically equivalent to eta squared: $\eta^2 = R^2$.

The size of an effect for eta squared can be described as trivial, small, medium, or large. Conventions for interpreting the size of an effect using eta squared are given in Table 19.4 under the $\eta^2 = R^2$ column heading. In our example, then, we would describe $\eta^2 = .04$ as a small effect size based on the conventions given in Table 19.6.

A measure of proportion of variance that is used with a correlation or regression analysis is a measure called the **coefficient of determination,** symbolized as R^2. The coefficient of determination is the square of the *correlation coefficient, r,* and its value can range from 0 to 1.0. For example, in Chapter 8, we determined that the correlation between mobile phone use and perceived stress is $r = .54$. Therefore, the coefficient of determination is $R^2 = (.54)^2 = .29$. To interpret R^2, we state that 29% of the variability in perceived stress can be explained by mobile phone use.

The coefficient of determination is mathematically equivalent to eta squared. For this reason, the size of an effect for R^2 can be described as trivial, small, medium, or large using the same conventions given in Table 19.4 under the $\eta^2 = R^2$ column heading. In our example, then, we would describe $R^2 = .29$ as a large effect size based on the conventions given in Table 19.6.

Table 19.6 The Size of an Effect Using Cohen's d, Eta Squared (η^2), and the Coefficient of Determination (R^2)

Description of Effect	d	$\eta^2 = R^2$
Trivial	—	$\eta^2, R^2 < .01$
Small	$d < 0.2$	$.01 < \eta^2, R^2 < .09$
Medium	$0.2 < d < 0.8$	$.09 < \eta^2, R^2 < .25$
Large	$d \geq 0.8$	$\eta^2, R^2 \geq .25$

Note: Eta squared and the coefficient of determination are mathematically equivalent.

Proportion of Variance: Cramer's V

A measure of proportion of variance that is used with a chi-square test for independence is a measure called **Cramer's V**. Its value can range from 0 to 1.0 and is interpreted the same as the coefficient of determination. For example, in Section 19.5, let us say we computed the chi-square test for independence and determined that the play center selection is related to the gender of the student, $\chi^2 = 14.589$. Cramer's V for this example is $V = .16$.

> **Cramer's V** is a measure of proportion of variance that is used as an estimate of effect size for the chi-square test for independence.

To describe the size of the effect as small, medium, or large, we follow the conventions given in Table 19.7. To interpret Cramer's V, we need to identify the factor with the smaller degrees of freedom, $df_{smaller}$. The degrees of freedom for a factor are the number of categories for a factor, minus 1. In our example, there were three categories for each factor (books, blocks, water play). Hence, the smaller degrees of freedom in our example are 2. We can therefore describe $V = .16$ as a small effect size based on the conventions given in Table 19.7.

Table 19.7 Effect Size Conventions for Cramer's V

$df_{smaller}$	Effect Size		
	Small	Medium	Large
1	.10	.30	.50
2	.07	.21	.35
3	.06	.17	.29

Note: Each value represents the smallest value for a given effect size category.

1. _____ is a statistical measure of the size of an observed effect in a population, which allows researchers to describe how far scores shifted in a population or the percentage of variance in a dependent variable that can be explained by the levels of a factor.

2. What measure of proportion of variance is used to estimate effect size when data are analyzed using ANOVA?

3. Eta squared is mathematically equivalent to what other measure of proportion of variance?

4. What test for significance uses Cramer's *V* to estimate effect size?

Answers: 1. Effect size; 2. Eta squared; 3. The coefficient of determination; 4. The chi-square test for independence.

19.9 Estimation: What Are the Possible Values of a Parameter?

As an alternative to NHST, we can also learn more about a parameter (e.g., a population mean) without ever stating a null hypothesis. This approach requires only that we set limits for the possible values of a population parameter within which it is likely to be contained. The goal of this alternative approach, called estimation, is the same as that in significance testing—to learn more about the value of a mean or mean difference in a population of interest. To use estimation, we select a sample, measure a sample mean or mean difference, and then use that sample mean or mean difference to estimate the value of a population parameter.

Estimation is a statistical procedure in which a sample statistic is used to estimate the value of an unknown population parameter. Two types of estimation are point estimation and interval estimation.

A point estimate is a sample statistic (e.g., a sample mean) that is used to estimate a population parameter (e.g., a population mean).

An interval estimate, called the confidence interval (CI), is the interval or range of possible values within which an unknown population parameter is likely to be contained.

Level of confidence is the probability or likelihood that an interval estimate will contain the value of an unknown population parameter (e.g., a population mean).

We measure two types of estimates using estimation: a point estimate and an interval estimate. A point estimate is a sample mean for one group or mean difference between two groups. We use the sample mean (the statistic) to estimate the population mean (the parameter). An interval estimate, called the confidence interval, is the range of possible values for the parameter stated within a given level of confidence, which is the likelihood that a population mean is contained within that given interval.

Interval estimates are reported as a point estimate ± interval estimate. For example, you may read that 53% ± 3% of Americans believe that evolution is true, 34% ± 3% believe in ghosts, or 38% ± 3% believe that professional athletes are good role models for children. The ±3%, called the *margin of error*, is added to and subtracted from the point estimate to find the **confidence limits** of an interval estimate. If we add and subtract 3% from each point estimate, we can be confident that in the population, 50% to 56% of Americans believe evolution is true, 31% to 37%

> **Confidence limits** are the upper and lower boundaries of a confidence interval given within a specified level of confidence.

believe in ghosts, and 35% to 41% believe professional athletes are good role models for children, on average. Exactly how confident we are depends on the level of confidence, which is determined by the researcher. Typical levels of confidence are stated at 80%, 95%, or 99% in behavioral research.

19.10 Confidence Intervals, Significance, and Effect Size

A confidence interval states the range of possible values for a population parameter (e.g., a population mean) at a specified level of confidence. The process of computing a confidence interval is related to the process we used to retain or reject a null hypothesis using NHST. In fact, we can use the information conveyed by a confidence interval to determine the significance of an outcome. We apply the following rules to identify the significance of an outcome:

1. If the null hypothesis were inside a confidence interval, the decision would have been to retain the null hypothesis (not significant).

2. If the null hypothesis were outside the confidence interval, the decision would have been to reject the null hypothesis (significant).

> An interval estimate is reported as the point estimate ± the interval estimate.

We can therefore compare a confidence interval with the decision for a significance test. To illustrate, suppose we conduct a study in which we test if personalized reading selections will increase engagement in reading. We test the null hypothesis that there was no difference in engagement in reading. Hence, if the null hypothesis were true, we would expect a mean difference of 0 engagement. In our study, suppose we make the following conclusion using APA (2009) guidelines to report the result:

The engagement level of students who read personalized books was 4.0 points higher than the students who did not read personalized books.

$$t(9) = 5.48, p < .001, 95\% \text{ CI}[2.35, 5.65]$$

The confidence limits for the 95% confidence interval are 2.35 and 5.65. As expected, we find that the value stated in the null hypothesis (mean difference = 0) falls outside the confidence interval for a test in which we chose to reject the null hypothesis. Hence, a mean difference of 0 is not one of the possible values contained within the confidence interval for the mean difference in the population. We can therefore infer whether the result was significant based on whether or not the value stated in the null is contained within the confidence interval identified. If the value is contained within the confidence interval, then the decision is to retain the null hypothesis; if it is outside the confidence interval, then the decision is to reject the null hypothesis.

We can also interpret effect size using the confidence limits of a confidence interval. The effect size for a confidence interval is a range or interval in which the lower effect size estimate is the difference between the value stated in the null hypothesis and the lower confidence limit; the upper effect size estimate is the difference between the value stated in the null hypothesis and the upper confidence limit. Effect size can then be interpreted in terms of a shift in the population when the value of the null hypothesis is outside a given confidence interval. In our example, we can therefore state effect size as follows: Students in the population were engaged between 2.35 and 5.65 points more when provided with a personalized book to read compared to a nonpersonalized book. This effect size is also illustrated in Figure 19.6.

> The significance and effect size of an outcome can be determined based on the confidence interval identified at a specified level of confidence.

19.11 Issues for Interpretation: Precision and Certainty

When we use estimation to identify a confidence interval, we often refer to the precision and the certainty of the interval. The *precision* of an estimate is determined by the range of the confidence interval: The smaller the range of an interval, the more precise the estimate. The *certainty* of an estimate is determined by the level of confidence: The larger the level

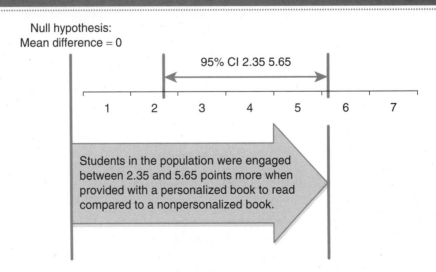

Figure 19.6 The 95% Confidence Interval and Interpretation of Effect Size for the Personalized Reading Engagement Study

Null hypothesis:
Mean difference = 0

95% CI 2.35 5.65

1 2 3 4 5 6 7

Students in the population were engaged between 2.35 and 5.65 points more when provided with a personalized book to read compared to a nonpersonalized book.

of confidence, the more certain the estimate. Therefore, we can use the following rules to identify the precision and certainty of a confidence interval:

1. Decreasing the level of confidence increases the precision of an estimate.

2. Increasing the level of confidence increases the certainty of an estimate.

To illustrate these rules, Figure 19.7 displays the 80% and the 95% level of confidence for the personalized reading engagement study we evaluated in Section 19.10. The upper and lower confidence limits at each level of confidence are given in the figure. Rule 1 indicates that the smaller the level of confidence, the more precise the estimate. The 80% confidence interval is the smaller level of confidence and is also more precise because it estimates the narrowest range within which the mean difference in the population is likely to be contained.

Rule 2 indicates that the larger the level of confidence, the more certain the estimate. The 95% confidence interval is the larger level of confidence and is associated with greater certainty than the 80% confidence interval because we are 95%, compared to 80%, confident that the population mean difference is contained within the confidence interval specified. These rules lead to an important implication regarding the precision and certainty of a confidence interval: To be more certain that an interval contains a population parameter, we typically give up precision. This is usually a sacrifice most researchers are willing to make in that most studies in behavioral research report a 95% or 99% confidence interval in published scientific research journals.

> A confidence interval can be described in terms of the precision and certainty of an interval estimate.

Figure 19.7 The 80% and 95% Confidence Intervals for the Personalized Reading Engagement Study

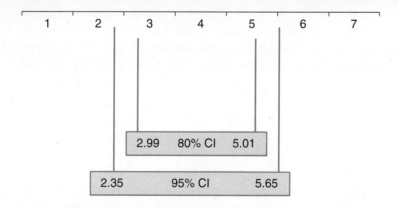

Note: Notice that the lower the level of confidence, the more precise the estimate but the less certain we are that the confidence interval contains the actual population mean.

19.12 Ethics in Focus: Full Disclosure of Data

When reporting statistical results, it is important to report data as thoroughly, yet concisely, as possible. Keep in mind that, as the author, you will have all the data in front of you. However, the reader will not. The reader will only know as much information as you provide. You need to make sure that the data you report in an article are thorough enough that they tell the whole story. For example, suppose you report that a treatment for a behavioral disorder is effective. To support your claim, you provide all significant data, including test statistics and effect size showing that the treatment is effective. However, suppose that your data also show that the treatment is effective for boys but not girls. If you fail to provide all data for this outcome, then your report is misleading because you are selectively omitting data that could indicate limitations in the effectiveness of the treatment.

Evidence of the failure to report all data can be found in the published peer-reviewed literature. Chan, Hróbjartsson, Haahr, Gøtzsche, and Altman (2004), for example, reported in the *Journal of the American Medical Association* that failure to report all data is particularly a problem for clinical trial research in which outcomes reported can mean the difference between life and death for patients. The researchers reviewed over 100 published journal articles and found alarming discrepancies in reporting. They found that many nonsignificant results were not reported, and up to 50% to 65% of trials included outcomes that were incompletely reported in some way, such as missing p values or effect size estimates that could be used in meta-analysis. The researchers suggest that clinical trials research may be biased, and many studies may likely overestimate the benefits of an intervention. This conclusion is important in that it is based on the finding that researchers were not fully reporting data, particularly data that were not significant. To avoid problems in trusting the outcomes reported in a paper, the simple solution is to always fully disclose data.

While this example reports failure of full disclosure of data in the medical field, there is evidence across many fields of study, including education, regarding the failure to report nonstatistical findings that is called the file drawer problem (Rosenthal, 1979). Whether the issue is the deliberate rejection of studies without statistically significant findings by journal editors or that researchers do not submit studies with nonsignificant findings for publication is not known but well documented (e.g., Duryea, Graner, & Becker, 2009; Reese, Thompason Prout, Zirkelback, & Anderson, 2010; Vevea & Woods, 2005). The problem with not reporting nonsignificant findings is we only know about one side of the story. Studies with nonsignificant findings can be just as important in understanding "what works," especially when examining what works for whom and under what conditions. To think that an educational intervention will be effective for everyone under all conditions is simply not likely.

A final thing to consider in the ethics of fully disclosing research findings is inclusion of effect size estimates in addition to hypothesis testing results. The inclusion of effect size estimates is required by both the American Psychological Association (2009) and American Educational Research Association (2006) publications. One reason for this is the fact that the statistics used in hypothesis testing like the t test and ANOVA are highly dependent on sample size. The larger the sample size, the smaller amount of difference that is needed in order for a finding to be statistically significant. It is possible that the same end result of a study with a small sample size may not reach significance but will reach significance if only the sample size is increased (Duryea et al., 2009). The effect size measures the actual difference (whether it is growth over time as in pre- to posttest or the difference between groups). In studies with large sample sizes, a significant finding can be merely a product of the size of the sample and not accurately the actual difference that can be seen by a very small effect size. Another way to avoid problems in trusting the outcomes reported in a paper is to always fully disclose both hypothesis testing and effect size results.

LEARNING CHECK 7 ✓

1. Identify two types of estimates for a population parameter.

2. A researcher compares reading scores in a sample to the general reading score known in the population and reports the following confidence interval: 95% CI −0.69 to 4.09. If the null hypothesis stated that there was no difference in health scores between the sample and the population, then what would the decision likely have been for a significance test? Explain.

3. What is the difference between the precision and the certainty of a confidence interval?

4. True or false: Selectively omitting data can lead to misleading interpretations of data.

Answers: 1. Point estimate and interval estimate; 2. Retain the null hypothesis because the null hypothesis value of a mean difference equal to 0 is contained within the stated confidence interval; 3. The precision of an estimate is determined by the range of the confidence interval, whereas the certainty of an estimate is determined by the level of confidence; 4. True.

CHAPTER SUMMARY

LO 1 Define inferential statistics and explain why they are necessary.

- **Inferential statistics** are procedures that allow researchers to *infer* or generalize observations made with samples to the larger population from which they were selected.

- Inferential statistics allow researchers to use data recorded in a sample to draw conclusions about the larger population of interest—this would not be possible without inferential statistics.

LO 2 Describe the process of null hypothesis significance testing (NHST).

- To use NHST, we begin by stating a **null hypothesis,** which is a statement about a population parameter, such as the population mean, that is assumed to be true but contradicts the research hypothesis. We then state a criterion upon which we will decide to retain or reject the null hypothesis.

- To establish a criterion for a decision, we state a **level of significance** for a test. The level of significance for most studies in behavioral science is .05. To determine the likelihood or probability of obtaining a sample outcome, if the value stated in the null hypothesis is true, we compute a test statistic. A test statistic is used to find the p value, which is the actual probability of obtaining a sample outcome if the null hypothesis is true. We reject the null hypothesis when $p \leq .05$; an effect reached significance. We retain the null hypothesis when $p > .05$; an effect failed to reach significance.

LO 3 Distinguish between Type I and Type II errors and define power.

- A Type I error is the probability of rejecting a null hypothesis that is actually true. Researchers control for this type of error by stating a level of significance, which is typically set at .05. A Type II error is the probability of retaining a null hypothesis that is actually false, meaning that the researcher reports no effect in the population when in truth there is an effect.

- Power is the probability of rejecting a false null hypothesis. Specifically, power is the probability that we will detect an effect if it actually exists in a population.

LO 4 Distinguish between parametric and nonparametric tests and choose an appropriate test statistic for research designs with one and two factors.

- Parametric tests are significance tests that are used to test hypotheses about parameters in a population in which the data are normally distributed and measured on an interval or ratio scale of measurement.

- Nonparametric tests are significance tests that are used to test hypotheses about data that can have any type of distribution and to analyze data on a nominal or ordinal scale of measurement.

- Choosing an appropriate parametric and nonparametric test can depend largely on how participants were observed (between subjects or within subjects), how many factors and groups were included in a research design, and the type of research question being asked.

LO 5 Distinguish between a main effect and an interaction.

- A main effect is a source of variation associated with mean differences across the levels of a single factor. In a two-way factorial design, there are two possible main effects (one for each factor).

- An interaction is a source of variation associated with the variance of group means across the combination of levels of two factors. In a table summary, an interaction is a measure of how cell means at each level of one factor change across the levels of a second factor.

- The test statistic used to analyze the main effects and interactions in a two-way factorial design is the two-way analysis of variance. The two-way ANOVA is used for factorial designs that measure data on an interval or a ratio scale.

LO 6 Identify main effects and interactions in a summary table and in a graph.

- The group means in a table summary can be graphed to identify a main effect, an interaction, or both. A main effect is evident when changes in a dependent variable vary across the levels of a single factor. An interaction is evident when changes in a dependent variable across the levels of one factor depend on which level of the second factor you analyze. Note that even if a graph shows a possible main effect or interaction, only the test statistic can determine if a main effect or an interaction is significant.

LO 7 Distinguish between a chi-square goodness-of-fit test and a chi-square test for independence.

- A **chi-square goodness-of-fit test** is a statistical procedure used to determine whether observed frequencies at each level of one categorical variable are similar to or different from the frequencies we expected at each level of the categorical variable. If frequencies observed fit well with frequencies expected, the decision will be to retain the null hypothesis; if frequencies observed do not fit well with frequencies expected, the decision will be to reject the null hypothesis.

- A **chi-square test for independence** is a statistical procedure used to determine whether frequencies observed at the combination of levels of two categorical variables are similar to frequencies expected. If two factors are independent, the decision will be to retain the null hypothesis; if two factors are related, the decision will be to reject the null hypothesis.

LO 8 Identify and describe the following effect size measures: Cohen's d, eta squared, the coefficient of determination, and Cramer's V.

- **Effect size** is a statistical measure of the size of an observed effect in a population, which allows researchers to describe how far scores shifted in a population or the percentage of variance in a dependent variable that can be explained by the levels of a factor.

- **Cohen's d** is a measure of effect size in terms of the number of standard deviations that mean scores shift above or below a population mean. The larger the value of d, the larger the effect in the population. Cohen's d is an effect size measure used with the one-sample, two-independent-sample, and related-samples t tests.

- When ANOVA is used to analyze data, **eta squared** (η^2) is used to estimate effect size as the proportion of variance in a dependent variable that can be explained or accounted for by the levels of a factor. When a correlation or regression is used to analyze data, the **coefficient of determination** (R^2) is used to estimate effect size. The coefficient of determination is mathematically equivalent to eta squared.

- **Cramer's V** is used to estimate effect size when data are analyzed using the chi-square test for independence and is interpreted the same as the coefficient of determination.

LO 9 Distinguish between a point estimate and an interval estimate and explain how estimation relates to the significance and effect size of an outcome.

- To use estimation, we set limits for the possible values of a population parameter within which the parameter is likely to be contained. Two types of estimates are a point estimate (a sample mean or mean difference) and an interval estimate (the range of possible values for a parameter stated with a given level of confidence).

- An effect would be significant if the value stated in a null hypothesis were outside the limits of a confidence interval; an effect would not be significant if contained within the limits of a confidence interval.

- The effect size for a confidence interval is stated as a range or interval, in which the lower effect size estimate is the difference between the value stated in a null hypothesis and the lower confidence limit; the upper effect size estimate is the difference between the value stated in a null hypothesis and the upper confidence limit. Effect size can then be interpreted in terms of a shift in the population when the value of the null hypothesis is outside a specified confidence interval.

LO 10 Distinguish between the precision and the certainty of an interval estimate.

- The precision of an estimate is determined by the range of the confidence interval. The certainty of an estimate is determined by the level of confidence. To be more certain that an interval contains a population parameter, we typically give up precision.

KEY TERMS

chi-square goodness-of-fit test 562

chi-square test for independence 562

coefficient of determination 566

Cohen's conventions 565

Cohen's d 565

confidence interval 568

confidence limits 569

Cramer's V 567

effect 563

effect size 564

effect size conventions 565

estimation 568

eta squared 566

inferential statistics 546

interaction 555

interval estimate 568

level of confidence 568

level of significance 548

main effect 553

nonparametric tests 560

null hypothesis 547

p value 548

parametric tests 551

point estimate 568

power 550

proportion of variance 566

significance 547

significance level 548

statistical significance 549

test statistic 548

Type I error 550

Type II error 550

1. State whether each of the following describes the use of null hypothesis significance testing (NHST), effect size, or confidence intervals.

    A. The range of values within which a parameter is likely to be contained

    B. An analysis used to determine whether or not an effect exists in the population

    C. The mean shift of scores in the population

2. A study showed that children who snack between meals consumed significantly fewer calories in each meal. If $p = .02$, is this conclusion appropriate for NHST at a .05 level of significance? Explain.

3. State three assumptions or criteria that must be met to conduct a parametric test of significance.

4. A researcher has participants who are experienced or inexperienced with using computers complete a computer task that is either easy or difficult. He records stress levels among participants and finds a significant main effect of experience. He concludes that having experience with using computers causes participants to have lower stress levels compared to those who are inexperienced. Explain why this conclusion is inappropriate.

5. A superintendent is interested in understanding the preference of teachers for different leadership styles of school principals (transactional, transformative, laissez-faire). He asked all teachers to choose the leadership style they prefer. Which chi-square test is appropriate to analyze significance in this study?

6. A researcher reports the following results for a related-samples t test: The results showed that female teachers report similar ratings of job satisfaction, $t(5) = 1.581, p = .175$.

    A. What are the degrees of freedom for this test?

    B. How many participants were observed in this study?

    C. Did the test statistic reach significance? Explain.

7. A researcher finds that the parenting style of a parent is related to the goal orientation of the parent's child, $\chi^2(9) = 16.96, p = .049$.

    A. What are the degrees of freedom for this test?

    B. Is this test a chi-square goodness-of-fit test or a chi-square test for independence?

    C. Did the test statistic reach significance? Explain.

8. A researcher reports that studying increases student confidence ($d = .45$). Using Cohen's conventions, describe the size of this effect as being small, medium, or large.

9. Two professors teach the same class. The mean grade in Teacher G's class is 80% (95% CI 72%, 88%); the mean grade in Teacher P's class is 76% (95% CI 68%, 84%). In which class is the confidence interval more precise? In which class is the confidence interval more certain?

10. What is the decision for a hypothesis test (significant or not significant) if the value stated in a null hypothesis would have been each of the following?
   A. Inside a stated confidence interval
   B. Outside a stated confidence interval

ACTIVITIES

1. Suppose you hypothesize that elementary teachers' sense of self-efficacy to teach math is related to their math pedagogical knowledge.
   A. Choose a research design to test your hypothesis.
   B. What test statistics are appropriate to analyze the data?
   C. Describe the required elements of the statistical statement (e.g., value of t, degrees of freedom, CI, p value).

2. State your own hypothesis in any area of research of interest to you and follow Items A, B, and C from Activity Question 1. Make sure you state a hypothesis that can be tested using one of the many test statistics described in this chapter and throughout this book.

$SAGE edge™

SAGE edge offers a robust online environment featuring an impressive array of free tools and resources for review, study, and further exploration, keeping both instructors and students on the cutting edge of teaching and learning.

Access practice quizzes, eFlashcards, video, and multimedia at edge.sagepub.com/priviterarme.

Identify a problem

- Determine an area of interest.
- Review the literature.
- Identify new ideas in your area of interest.
- Develop a research hypothesis.

Develop a research plan

- Define the variables being tested.
- Identify participants or subjects and determine how to sample them.
- Select a research strategy and design.
- Evaluate ethics and obtain institutional approval to conduct research.

Generate more new ideas

- Results support your hypothesis—refine or expand on your ideas.
- Results do not support your hypothesis—reformulate a new idea or start over.

Conduct the study

- Execute the research plan and measure or record the data.

Communicate the results

- Method of communication: oral, written, or in a poster.
- Style of communication: APA guidelines are provided to help prepare style and format.

Analyze and evaluate the data

- Analyze and evaluate the data as they relate to the research hypothesis.
- Summarize data and research results.

After reading this chapter, you should be able to:

1. State the two general approaches of qualitative data analysis

2. Describe the advantages and disadvantages of the three approaches to recording narrative data.

3. Identify and define the three components of transcription

4. Distinguish between the 11 types of qualitative data analysis

5. Describe the general process of coding qualitative data

6. Distinguish between emic and etic coding

7. Describe how the perspectives of the different types of qualitative research result in a different kind of analysis.

8. Identify the four criteria of trustworthiness

9. Describe the different ways to increase the credibility of a study

ANALYSIS AND INTERPRETATION: MAKING INFERENCES ABOUT QUALITATIVE DATA

In Chapter 19, we introduced the use of data to make inferences or conclusions about our experiences. Let's look at the same examples. When you wake up in the morning and smell bacon, you conclude that someone is cooking breakfast; after watching the weather report, you conclude that it is going to be cold enough to wear your jacket; you infer that the guy who is speeding and cut you off in traffic to make a left turn is late to work; you infer that someone is mad by the tone of his or her voice; you infer that a crime is about to happen when you see a person with a mask on holding a gun; or when you see a person staggering out of a bar, you infer that he or she is too drunk to drive. Recall that an inference is a conclusion made based on evidence and reasoning. We use the scientific method to pose a question, systematically collect data, and analyze the data to reach a conclusion about that question.

In qualitative research, we also systematically record data, and on the basis of the data, we make inferences. When we make inferences using qualitative data, we are less interested in using samples to make inferences about the larger population and more interested in illuminating the meaning of personal experiences and human existence. Such inferences cannot be drawn using inferential statistics; instead, we use specialized coding techniques of the data that we collected through observations, interviews, documents, or visual images.

In this chapter, we will take a closer look at the differences between quantitative and qualitative data analysis, how to organize qualitative data and code qualitative data, and how to evaluate qualitative data and interpretations. We will also look at some of the various qualitative software that can assist in the coding process.

20.1 Qualitative Versus Quantitative Data Analysis

Recall that the aim of qualitative research is to provide rich, detailed descriptions of the phenomena being investigated, while the aim of quantitative research is to produce statistically reliable and generalizable information about the phenomena being investigated. These different aims require different analysis techniques. The quantitative researcher will spend time conducting tabulations using descriptive and inferential statistics. Inferences will be made by null hypothesis significance testing to test the null hypothesis against a predetermined criterion. This criterion is called the level of significance as represented by the p value obtained by employing a test statistic. The interpretation of quantitative data is through either retaining or rejecting the null hypothesis. The analysis and interpretations of qualitative data are not aligned to one process; instead, the researcher will sort and catalog narratives and analyze the data in different ways depending on the nature of the question. The object of qualitative data analysis is to make sense of the large amount of narrative information. The general approach involves developing thick, rich descriptions of the data and then identifying patterns or themes presented in the data. This involves sorting and sifting the information found in the narratives. Flick (2014) describes two major approaches to qualitative data analysis. The first approach is to reduce the amount of data into manageable chunks where the data are classed and grouped based on important elements through a coding process. The second approach is to expand upon the original data to derive meaning from the data. In this approach, the researcher attempts not only to describe the data but to go beyond what the data say to interpret what they mean. Words that have been used to describe this process are *transformation* and *synthesis*. While there is not a formula to apply or one process to follow when analyzing qualitative data, there are guidelines and principles.

20.2 Decisions About How to Record Narrative Data

One of the first decisions to make when collecting and analyzing narrative data is the mode in which the data will be collected. There are three primary options: written notes, audio recording, or video recording. We provided a description and illustration of field notes and expanded field notes in Chapter 10 as a way to record qualitative observations. We also need notes and/or recordings for interviews or focus groups. Here we review the different ways we can take field notes. Written notes can be taken by hand without any special equipment.

The only thing that is needed is a writing utensil and some paper. Written notes can also be taken using a computer or iPad. The difficulties with written notes are the ability to capture everything in writing and the potential for missing something while writing. When writing field notes, the researcher will need to use extensive use of abbreviations and be able to write fast and clearly so the notes can be read later. It is highly unlikely that conversations can be written verbatim. Also, while the researchers are taking notes, that means they are not observing and there is potential that something of value may be missed.

Alternatives to written notes are audio or video recording. Some sophisticated digital audio recorders available allow the researcher to record and store individual interviews in separate files and adjust microphones to capture audio from around a table if conducting a focus group interview. Some of these sophisticated audio recorders may also come with text-to-speech software so the digital files can be converted to a text file and uploaded to a computer. If using an audio recorder without text-to-speech software, then the recordings will need to be transcribed. Transcribing directly from an audio recorder takes a considerable amount of time—starting, stopping, and rewinding to type out exactly what was said. One option to human transcription is the use of transcribing tools. These consist of foot pedals that are connected to the audio device so the individual doing the transcribing can type while operating the audio device with his or her foot. Video recorders have the advantage of capturing more than just what a person says. They are great tools for observations. If the researcher is attempting to capture visual information such a behavior, body language, or facial expressions during an observation, some type of video recording device will be needed. Setting up a camcorder on a tripod may not always be possible or necessary. They are conspicuous, take up a lot of room, and need an outlet close by. Smaller devices such as a handheld camcorder like a Sony Bloggie may be a better fit for the situation. Most cell phones have video-recording capabilities, too. One issue to consider when using video and audio recording is the conspicuousness of the device. Make sure it is okay with the participants to record them. Some participants may not feel comfortable in front of recordable devices.

There are also decisions to be made regarding how to transcribe data recorded from the interviews or observations. These decisions include what to include in the transcriptions. Kowal and O'Connell (2014) provide a description of other important elements of communication that may be needed to answer the research question. First, decide if the transcription incudes only what is said or other features of communication. Other forms of communication may include laughing, crying, pauses, filler words (like *er* or *umm*), body position, proximity, and facial expressions. Of course, the way you recorded the data will determine what type of communication is available to include in the transcription. They describe three components that can be included in transcriptions: the verbal component, prosodic component, and paralinguistic component. The **verbal component** is the words spoken by the participant. The verbal component is transcribed using standard orthography, literary transcription, or eye dialect. Standard orthography transcribes what is said using dictionary spelling of words regardless of how the words were pronounced. Literary transcription records deviations in pronunciation. Eye dialect is similar to literary transcription but includes a phonetic representation of how words are pronounced. Below is an example of a hypothetical statement.

The **verbal component** is the words spoken by the participant.

The eye dialect statement is as it was phonetically pronounced by a hypothetical person. The standard orthography standardizes the statement using words found in the standard dictionary. The literary transcription takes pronunciation into account and allows some deviation from standard orthography as long as the meaning of the word(s) used is known.

Standard Orthography: She is young. It isn't her business.

Literary Transcription: She a young'un, it ain't her business.

Eye Dialect: She a yougin t'ain't her bizness.

The prosodic component is the manner in which words are spoken. These include elements of pitch, loudness, and duration. The pitch is the degree of highness or lowness of the tone of the voice. For example, our pitch becomes higher at the end of a sentence that is a question. This is usually noted by a symbol like + or ? at the end of the word. Loudness is the volume of speech. The person may be whispering or shouting. Transcribers can indicate loudness (often defined as louder than surrounding talk) by using CAPITALS. Duration records the length of the spoken utterances. The time is recorded in tenths of seconds, such as the following:

Joe: She is young. It isn't her business. (2.23)

Sue: Don't you know! (1.12)

The paralinguistic component is the vocal features that occur during speaking that are not words. Laughing and crying are examples of paralinguistic components. These are recorded by including a representation of the sounds made. For example, Sue is laughing:

Joe: She is young. It isn't her business.

Sue: he he he Don't you know! he he he

Figure 20.1 illustrates a transcription using standard orthography notation of an interview with a teacher about teaching reading to students with a developmental disability. The interview questions are noted in bold text. The teacher's responses were transcribed verbatim.

Deciding which type of transcription to use will depend on the type of interpretation the researcher intends to make. Other transcription options include literary transcription and eye dialect. We will revisit this decision in the next section about analysis and interpretation. After the data are transcribed, the researcher can begin to analyze the data. Next we will look at the process of taking a large amount of narrative data and deriving meaning from them.

> The prosodic component is the manner in which words are spoken such as pitch, loudness, and duration.

> The paralinguistic component is the vocal features that occur during speaking that are not words such as laughing and crying.

> Standard orthography transcription records what is said using standard dictionary spelling of words regardless of how the words were pronounced.

> Literary transcription records deviations in the pronunciation of words as long as the meaning of the word used is known.

> Eye dialect transcription includes a true phonetic representation of how words are pronounced.

I offer choices so the students have a chance to get them correct. They're used to typically choosing between anywhere between 2–4 choices and that has 12 on the page, so we're cutting those in half. And then the comprehension questions are much easier this year given the question in the middle with the choices around it. As opposed to last year us reading the question and after we say it the kids have no reference, they just had a whole bunch of words on the page to try to figure out what we wanted them to do. So, I think that's better this year.

Overall, do you feel like there's been an improvement or things need to be changed from the newer version? I think this year is definitely an improvement. There's a few pieces like with the blending that was a little overwhelming for the kids, but it's an easy enough fix that we can adjust it by covering part of the page on the iPad that we don't want them to see.

1. What has been the impact or effect on your students?

I've seen them increase their number of sight words that they know and also with one in particularly, he's improving his comprehension as he's started to actually read the words more himself.

2. What do you see as the benefits of this instruction? What about limitations or problems?

Benefits: It's helping them to learn to read, basically. But it's also a great extension or program to follow up the ELSB which we did not have before. We were going into Reading Mastery which just wasn't really appropriate for our students.

Limitations: Some of the students just aren't as, I guess don't have as good of a knowledge of technology, just the use of the iPad so maybe just some basic training on the iPad needs to be done first before they can understand what to do with the program.

3. What impact has this had on you as a teacher?

I think it's motivated me more as a teacher too, and kind of given me some excitement back. That when I was doing Reading Mastery it was boring for the kid, it was boring for me. This is exciting to use, and it's something that's using technology that the kids are interested in. It's definitely helped me to help them more.

4. What else would you like me to know? (Is there anything else that you would like me to know about your reading programs)?

No.

Semistructured Questions for Teacher Interviews: Video

1. Talk to me about what you saw in the video.

Gabe was doing level 5. He understands really well how to interact with the iPad and probably the technology of it as well as most adults. So it's really easy for him to understand the questions and know what to do, how to respond. He had learned by that point how many times you have to touch that button to get the response you want from it, if it was twice for a letter to move up, the reading bar or not. He was answering most of the letter sounds and first sounds in words correctly. He does really well with sight words in the video.

2. What do you look for on the part of students? Can you point out moments of success? Challenging moments?

I want students to be able to learn the type of interaction they need to be able to have when they're being requested to do something. For some students it's just that they need to stay in their seat and respond by pointing when I ask them a question. Where other students it may be at the point where Grady was at the video where he was actually, I wanted him to read. Because I knew he was at that level where he could comprehend what I was asking him to do more. So really it's just teaching students not only understand the material, but the type of interactions with people.

The letter sounds, the first sounds in words, sight words are a strength for Gabe.

Segmenting is really challenging for Gabe. And it continues to be this year even with the new approach we're taking with that section. So I guess we're going to keep working on that and tweaking it for him.

(Continued)

Figure 20.1 (Continued)

3. What would you do differently?

This year compared to last year, I've changed my set-up of how I have the student sitting at the table. I don't do the iPad on my lap I have it up on the table, with the student either across from me, or kind of right at the corner of the table so I can reach them but they can access the iPad a little better and it's a little sturdier. So that's kind of helped their interaction.

4. What are the strengths or benefits of this instruction?

The strengths—it's a teaching, continuing a lot of the basic skills that we started working on in ELSB, but it's a great continuation or a follow-up to that program. But also it's really moving into teaching the words that the students need to become readers. ELSB kind of was working on all those pieces separately, and now I feel like this is taking those pieces and putting them together so they can really start reading and comprehending what they're reading.

5. How do you measure student achievement?

Data collection. We're really data driven.

What types of data? All kinds depends on what we're doing, I guess.

For specifically in reading, do you have specific sheets you write on for each lesson? Yeah, it's very specific to what they're doing. So we have different sheets for ELSB for story based lessons for writing. I think that's all the ones I do. That are specific to each student's from their IEP goals but then also they're specific to the curriculum that we're working on. So they might have different data sheets for their basic comprehension er, I'm sorry their basic reading from their IEP to their basic reading that we're working on during ELSB or GoTalk.

LEARNING CHECK 1 ✓

1. What is the primary purpose of qualitative analysis?

2. Are the following statements true or false about the general process of qualitative data analysis?

   A. Qualitative data analysis may involve reducing or expanding the data.

   B. There is a specific process to follow in analyzing narrative data.

   C. The object of qualitative data analysis is to make sense of the large amount of narrative information.

3. What type of transcription is being used in the following statement? Which components of transcription are present?

   I think it's motivated me more as a teacher too, and kind of given me some excitement back. That when I was doing Reading Mastery it was boring for the kid, it was BORING for me. Ha ha ha (9.34)

Answers: 1. A. true, B. false, C. true; 2. A. true, B. false, C. true; 3. Standard orthography with prosodic (duration and loudness) and paralinguistic (laughing) components.

20.3 Decisions About Qualitative Data Analysis and Interpretation

As you can imagine by now, qualitative data using narrative descriptions of observations, interviews and focus groups, and documents results in a large amount of data to analyze and interpret. Making sense of this large amount of narrative information might seem overwhelming. As described earlier in this chapter, data analysis occurs in an iterative process during the data collection phase until data are saturated, when no new data are presented or needed to answer the research question. Data are analyzed in relation to the data already gathered to determine if more data are needed. In this section, we will describe the general process of how qualitative researchers analyze the data they have gathered to generate their findings. There are two general goals of data analysis in qualitative research. One goal is to reduce the large amount of information into more manageable chunks. In this approach, the researcher synthesizes all of the narrative data to uncover patterns or themes within the narratives and identify any relationships among these patterns or themes. The large amount of narrative data is reduced to the codes, themes, or patterns that emerge. A second goal of qualitative data analysis is to expand upon the original data to derive meaning or interpret the original data. In this case, the researcher is not only interested in what the person said in the interview but also the meaning or intent of what was said. If the intent is to reduce the amount of information by coding, then standard orthography will suffice. But, if the intent is to expand the original dialog and interpret the meaning, then literary or eye dialect transcription will be used.

There are principles and guidelines on how to analyze qualitative data depending on the qualitative design and theoretical perspective of the study, but the actual process of analysis followed by the researcher will reflect the individual uniqueness of the qualitative study. Patton (2015) provides 10 types of qualitative analysis to which we add one, discourse analysis. These 11 types of qualitative data analysis are not mutually exclusive in that you only select one to use in the analysis of qualitative data. A researcher will likely use several types to analyze the data. For example, a researcher may use content analysis to categorize the content of information relayed in interviews of teachers using inductive (no preconceived set of categories) and emic (using indigenous concepts) perspectives. In this example, the researcher used three types of qualitative analysis: content analysis, inductive analysis, and emic analysis. Table 20.1 (on pp. 590–591), adapted from Patton, summarizes these 11 types of qualitative analysis.

Content Analysis

Content analysis is a general term used for the process of examining text gathered from interview transcripts or documents for the purpose of reducing the amount of information into manageable chunks. This process attempts to summarize or categorize important elements of the text. This process is described and illustrated in Section 20.4.

> **Content analysis** reduces the amount of information into manageable chunks by categorizing important elements.

Case Study

A *case study* is used to tell a story about a case. It is a process of gathering and organizing data to tell a holistic story of the case that is sensitive to the specific context of the case. Data are organized either by themes or in a chronology.

Cross-Case Pattern Analysis

Cross-case pattern analysis is the recursive process to assign a pattern to descriptions across cases that are considered the same thing.

Cross-case pattern analysis groups similar descriptions made by different cases together when these descriptions can be considered the same thing. In the example in Table 20.1, each student is considered a case. Because all three students made a comment about their experience being a person with a disability at school, it is considered a pattern. A pattern is not only when everyone mentions a similar experience; it could just be a subset of the cases. If three of five cases make similar statements, the researcher could also determine that this was a pattern.

Cross-Case Thematic Analysis

Once a pattern is identified, the researcher may decide to interpret the pattern by assigning a name to it in order to summarize and describe what the statements mean. The summary description is called a theme, and the process is called **cross-case thematic analysis.** A theme may be one word or a phrase that best describes the statements. In the example in Table 20.1, these three statements were provided with the theme of "social isolation." Although in different words, each of the statements describes how they are isolated from other students at school. Identifying patterns across cases and assigning them a name to describe the pattern is called cross-case thematic analysis.

Cross-case thematic analysis is the recursive process to assign a theme to the categories in an attempt to provide meaning.

Inductive Analysis

Inductive analysis generates the themes that arise directly from the narratives without any preconceived notions about what the themes may be. Themes are discovered as the researcher analyzes the narratives and is often called open coding. The researcher is open to any and all ideas expressed by the cases in the narratives.

Inductive analysis is when the themes are generated from the narratives without any preconceived ideas.

Deductive analysis is when the researcher has preconceived ideas about what themes may be present in the narratives and seeks to find them.

Deductive Analysis

In **deductive analysis,** the researcher has some expectations or themes that may be present in the narratives and seeks to find these themes. Deductive analysis may be used in two different ways. First, it may be used in concert with inductive analysis as a second step to confirm the themes derived from inductive analysis. The researcher will search other cases' narratives for these identified themes in an attempt to verify it or to find cases that deviate from this theme. It may also be used when the researcher has information from previous studies or from theories about what to expect and seek to confirm these themes as the first step of the analysis.

Indigenous Concept Analysis (Emic)

When the analysis identifies and reports categories and vocabulary specifically used by the case(s), these are indigenous concepts, naturally occurring in a particular place. In addition to identifying keywords and concepts, emic analysis can be used to describe experiences of the cases from their cultural perspective. The idea is to understand the experience as the case sees it. It is also called emic analysis or in vivo coding. In the example in Table 20.1, the researcher uses the words as they were used by the cases to describe their personal, culture-specific experiences.

Analyst-Generated Concepts (Etic)

Analyst-generated concept analysis identifies and reports the experiences of the cases using a researcher or universal perspective. The specific vocabulary used by the cases may be replaced or redefined by the perspective of the world at large. The experiences are interpreted with the outside view instead of an inside one. This type of analysis is also called etic analysis. In the example in Table 20.1, the researcher substitutes the words as they were used by the cases to describe their personal, culture-specific experiences with words and interpretations used more universally.

Indigenous Typologies

Similar to **indigenous concept analysis, indigenous typologies** are intended to reflect the view of the cases and how they classify elements of their world. Once the elements are identified, the researcher seeks to find out the distinguishing characteristics of the elements. For example, the Eskimo language has many words (there seems to be some dispute to how many there are) for snow depending on its consistency (i.e., slushy), location (i.e., on the ground), and form (i.e., drift). In the example in Table 20.1, the case identified four categories of other men in the community.

Analyst-Generated Typologies

Analyst-generated typologies seek to reconstruct the indigenous typologies into analyst-generated terms and interpretations that represent the larger worldview of these categories. The researcher seeks to identify patterns and sort the characteristics so the outside world can understand them. By doing this, though, the researcher risks making interpretations that would not have been made by the cases themselves.

> Emic coding maintains the information in the participants' own words and perspectives.

> Etic coding interprets what the participant says into researcher words using a researcher or more universal perspective.

> **Analyst-generated concept** are concepts, labels, and terms created by the analyst to describe an observed phenomenon
>
> **Indigenous typologies** reflect the perspectives of the case(s) and how they classify elements of their world.
>
> **Analyst-generated typologies** reconstruct the indigenous typologies into analyst-generated terms and interpretations that represent the larger worldview of these categories.

Discourse Analysis

Discourse analysis focuses on the language that is used to describe something. Instead of focusing on just the content of the narrative, the analysis examines the word choice, grammar, and rhetoric used to describe an experience. The example in Table 20.1 illustrates discourse analysis in the differences in how an individual with a disability may be described. The word *retarded*, although once the medical and professional term used to describe an individual with less than average intellectual ability, now has derogatory connotation to most people. Using the words *individual with an intellectual disability* instead recognizes the person as an individual first and has a more respectful connotation.

> **Discourse analysis** focuses on the language used to describe something such as word choice, grammar, and rhetoric used to describe an experience.

Once the narratives have been transcribed and the researchers decide how they plan to analyze the data, the process of analyzing the data can begin. Let's look at the general

Table 20.1 Eleven Types of Qualitative Analysis

Type of Analysis	Definition	Examples
Content analysis	General term for identifying, organizing, and categorizing the content of narrative text	Grouping "three wishes" of students in a Title I school into categories of food, clothing, relationships, etc.
Case study	Qualitative data organized to coherently tell the story or the case (person, organization, community, etc.) that has been purposefully sampled	In-depth study of teachers at one school system to tell their story about implementing the Common Core State Standards
Cross-case pattern analysis	Descriptions of actions, perceptions, experiences, relationships, and behaviors that are similar enough to be considered a manifestation of the same thing	These statements of students with intellectual disabilities are grouped together: "I'd rather be alone," "I am not interested in the same things other kids are," "I only speak to my classmates when they talk to me first."
Cross-case thematic analysis	Interpreting and assigning meaning to a documented pattern by giving it a thematic name, a term that connotes and interprets the implications of the pattern	The statements above are assigned to the theme of "self-imposed isolation."
Inductive analysis	Searching the qualitative data for patterns and themes without entering the analysis with preconceived analytic categories; begin with specific cases, generate general patterns, and discover common themes through cross-case analysis	Patterns and themes to describe teachers' experiences with nutrition education are generated by the narratives of the participants.

Type of Analysis	Definition	Examples
Deductive analysis	Examining the data for illuminating predetermined sensitizing concepts or theoretical relationships	Patterns and themes to describe teachers' experiences with nutrition education are analyzed according to themes identified in previous research.
Indigenous concept analysis (emic)	Identifying and reporting indigenous terminology and concepts; documenting their meanings and interpreting their implications from the perspective of those interviewed	Using the slang words spoken by young, urban males to describe their experience from their perspective using words such as *crib*, *baby mama*, *dis*, or *dawg*; experience is culture specific.
Analyst-generated concepts (etic)	Concepts, labels, and terms created by the analyst to describe an observed phenomenon	Researcher describes the experiences of young, urban males replacing their words from above with *home*, *mother of my child*, *disrespect*, or *loyal friend*; experience is universal.
Indigenous typologies	A continuum made up of contrasting end points that people being studied use to divide some aspect of the world into distinct categories or ideal types	Researcher uses the terms of the young, urban men that they use to categorize people such as *homie*, *blood*, *frenemy*, and *opp*.
Analyst-generated typologies	A continuum or classification system made up by analysts to divide some aspect of the world into distinct categories or ideal types	Researcher describes the people above replacing the words used by the cases with a new interpretation using the descriptions of a close friend, a fellow gang member, a friend that is no longer a friend, and person with whom they do not get along.
Discourse analysis	Focuses on the use of language that is used to describe something; word choice, grammar, and rhetoric that are grounded in culture and context to understand experiences	Researcher looks at word choice and language the case used such as the differences between saying "retarded girl" or "girl with an intellectual disability."

Source: Adapted from Patton (2015). Reproduced with permission.

process of analyzing qualitative, narrative data. Then we will see how the different designs from Chapters 11 and 12 lead to unique interpretations.

LEARNING CHECK 2 ✓

1. Which of the 11 types of qualitative data analysis are represented in the following?

   A. A researcher examines the data for predetermined concepts or relationships.

   B. A classification system is made up by the researcher to divide aspects of the world into distinct categories.

C. A researcher focuses on the use of word choice, grammar, and rhetoric that is used to describe something.

D. A researcher organizes the data to tell a story.

20.4 General Process of Qualitative Data Analysis

The general process of qualitative data analysis is a series of steps to code the narrative and then organize the data in some way to describe the experience. Let's look at how this is done.

Step 1: Coding Narrative Data

Analysis of qualitative data begins with identifying the salient points within the narrative. To do this, the researcher will break the field notes from observations, interview transcriptions, or documents and artifacts into smaller units or chunks called codes. Codes are derived from reading the original words in the narratives. This first step may also be called axial or open coding. While reading through the narratives, the researcher will highlight important words or phrases and assign a few words or a phrase that capture the salient essence of the highlighted words. It is possible to have different codes or important elements within a single participant statement or sentence. The same code can also be applied across different participant narratives (cross-case) when more than one participant mentions the same idea. Figures 20.2 and 20.3 illustrate the data coding process for a transcript in Figure 20.1. In this study, researchers interviewed teachers about how a reading curriculum influenced their reading instruction for students with developmental disability. Notice the color coding and number system in the analysis conducted by hand in Figure 20.2. The researcher underlined the salient points (aka **codes**), then later assigned them to a category by number and color. Each category was assigned a number and different color, as outlined in Figure 20.3. The numbers made it easier to label the category than by writing out the name of the category each time. To more easily find the quotes, a different color of sticky tab was assigned to each category and affixed to the transcript. Figure 20.4 illustrates how Peck et al. (2015) coded their data on how teachers expressed empathy in their preschool classrooms. Notice how they identify the emic codes and then interpret the codes using etic coding. The words in italics are the verbatim words of the participant and labeled as etic coding. The interpretations labeled as etic coding are in the text boxes beneath the quotes.

Codes are words or phrases and assign a few words or a phrase that capture the salient essence of the narrative.

Figure 20.2 Coding the Transcript

choices so the students have a chance to get them correct. They're used to typically choosing between anywhere between 2-4 choices and that has 12 on the page, so we're cutting those in half. And then the comprehension questions are much easier this year given the question in the middle with the choices around it. As opposed to last year us reading the question and after we say it the kids have no reference, they just had a whole bunch of words on the page to try to figure out what we wanted them to do. So, I think that's better this year.

Overall, do you feel like there's been an improvement or things need to be changed from the newer version? I think this year is definitely an improvement. There's a few pieces like with the blending that was a little overwhelming for the kids, but it's an easy enough fix that we can adjust it by covering part of the page on the iPad that we don't want them to see.

d. **What has been the impact or effect on your students?**

I've seen them increase their number of sight words that they know and also with one in particularly, he's improving his comprehension as he's started to actually read the words more himself.   #4

e. **What do you see as the benefits of this instruction? What about limitations or problems?**

Benefits: It's helping them to learn to read basically. But it's also a great extension or program to follow up the ELSB which we did not have before. We were going into Reading Mastery which just wasn't really appropriate for our students.   #8

Limitations: Some of the students just aren't as, I guess don't have as good of a knowledge of technology, just the use of the iPad so maybe just some basic training on the iPad needs   #5
to be done first before they can understand what to do with the program.

4. **What impact has this had on you as a teacher?**

#4 #7
I think it's motivated me more as a teacher too, and kind of given me some excitement back. That when I was doing Reading Mastery it was boring for the kid, it was boring for me. This is exciting to use, and it's something that's using technology that the kids are interested in. It's definitely
#4 helped me to help them more.

5. **What else would you like me to know? (Is there anything else that you would like me to know about your reading programs)?**

No.

Semistructured Questions for Teacher Interviews: Video

1. **Talk to me about what you saw in the video.**

Gabe was doing level 5. He understands really well how to interact with the iPad and the probably
#7 the technology of it as well as most adults. So it's really easy for him to understand the questions

(Continued)

Figure 20.2 (Continued)

and know what to do, how to respond. He had learned by that point how many times you have to touch that button to get the response you want from it, if it was twice for a letter to move up, the reading bar or not. He was answering most of the letter sounds and first sounds in words correctly. He does really well with sight words in the video.

2. **What do you look for on the part of students? Can you point out moments of success? Challenging moments?**

I want students to be able to learn the type of interaction they need to be able to have when they're being requested to do something. For some students it's just that they need to stay in their seat and respond by pointing when I ask them a question. Where other students it may be at the point where Grady was at the video where he was actually, I wanted him to read. Because I knew he was at that level where he could comprehend what I was asking him to do more. So really it's just teaching students not only understand the material, but the type of interactions with people.

The letter sounds, the first sounds in words, sight words are a strength for Grady.

Segmenting is really challenging for Gabe. And it continues to be this year even with the new approach we're taking with that section. So I guess we're going to keep working on that and tweaking it for him.

3. **What would you do differently?**

This year compared to last year, I've changed my set-up of how I have the student sitting at the table. I don't do the iPad on my lap I have it up on the table, with the student either across from me, or kind of right at the corner of the table so I can reach them but they can access the iPad a little better and it's a little sturdier. So that's kind of helped their interaction.

4. **What are the strengths or benefits of this instruction?**

The strengths- its a teaching, continuing a lot of the basic skills that we started working on in ELSB, but it's a great continuation or a follow-up to that program. But also it's really moving into teaching the words that the students need to become readers. ELSB kind of was working on all those pieces separately, and now I feel like this is taking those pieces and putting them together so they can really start reading and comprehending what they're reading.

5. **How do you measure student achievement?**

Data collection. We're really data driven.

What types of data? All kinds depends on what we're doing, I guess.

For specifically in reading, do you have specific sheets you write on for each lesson? Yeah, it's very specific to what they're doing. So we have different sheets for ELSB for story based lessons for writing. I think that's all the ones I do. That are specific to each student's from their IEP goals but then also they're specific to the curriculum that we're working on. So they might have different data sheets for their basic comprehension er, I'm sorry their basic reading from their IEP to their basic reading that we're working on during ELSB or GoTalk.

Figure 20.3 Coding Categories Used to Analyze the Transcript

Code	Description of Code	Sub categories
1. GTP challenges for students	Challenges for students	a. Physical (e.g. hearing, motor skills) b. Behavioral (e.g., attention) c. Segmenting skill *orange* d. Technology e. Teacher adjustments to accommodate students f. Other
2. GTP challenges for teachers	Challenges for teachers	a. Technology b. Script *green* c. Teacher reaction to challenge d. Contextual (e.g. scheduling, space, seating arrangement) e. Other
3. GTP impact on students	Impact on students	a. Interest/engagement b. Skill progress (e.g. skills taught, other learning behaviors) c. Generalization *Yellow* d. Verbalization e. Other
4. GTP impact on teachers	Impact on teachers	a. Having materials b. Using data *pink* c. How to teach phonics d. Effectiveness e. Efficacy (attitudinal/emotional aspects like "amazing") f. Other
5. GTP limitations / weaknesses	Limitations/weaknesses of curriculum	a. Curriculum issues *white*
6. GTP Strengths	Strengths of the curriculum	a. Technology b. Students like it c. Systematic instruction *blue* d. Review/repeat e. Other
7. GTP vs. previous phonics instruction	Comparisons to other curricula	a. Student and teacher impact comparing ERSB to other curricula/instructional methods (like functional) *purple* b. Other
8. Other	Single comments not categorized in 1-7	a. Impact on family b. Impact on other teachers *white*

Figure 20.4 Example of Coding and Identifying an Exemplar

Rosie
Empathy—category
Child—code
Family—code
      Feelings—subcode
      Circumstances—
subcode
Culture—code

Exemplar

I want to do home visits before the beginning of the school year with all my kids. It was such a great time. It meant a lot to the families. It meant a lot to me. I think everyone was a little apprehensive at first. p. 8. [family]. EMIC coding

Memo: empathy focused on **family perspective/feelings**—can tell home visits meant a lot to families. Also shows understanding that there may have been **feelings** of apprehension prior to home visits by families.

[understanding that home visits may cause apprehension for families—but that in the end meant a lot to everyone—influences practice with children/families—she wants to do home visits with all families next year] ETIC coding

We had a child at the beginning of the school year who had just moved here from China and that culture experience was a lot for her to take on. I think it was a lot for the whole family. Dad said, "What we do is we're with the child for the first three days of school. So we want to be here from beginning to end." You have to respect that because you want the child to be successful. But obviously it's something that they both needed. I think he ended up staying for like 5 days. It was working on the individual level of what everyone needs. Parents can always come for lunch or volunteer activities. p. 28. **[child, family, culture]** *EMIC coding*

Memo: Teacher empathy on child, family, culture levels—shows **understanding** in child's and parent's experiences with new culture (**family circumstances, challenge of a new culture**); that respecting family culture is necessary for success of the child but also for the parent. Shows consideration for needs of child and family.

[**Empathy influences teacher's practices** in classroom—accepting family is for the success of the child] ETIC coding

Source: Modified from Peck, Maude, & Brotherson (2015). Reproduced with permission.

It is also possible to identify subcodes within a code. A subcode is a smaller but distinct element of the major code. For example, in Figure 20.4, subcodes for the family code are identified as empathy for the feelings of the family (labeled as feelings) and circumstances of the family (labeled as circumstances). Both of these fall under family but represent different ways a teacher can be empathic with the family.

> Subcode is a smaller element, distinct from a code.

Step 2: Formulating Categories

After coding all of the narrative materials, codes are then combined to form a more manageable set of categories. Codes are grouped together in some logical way with some shared characteristic. Creating categories is a recursive process to capture and assign each code to a category or theme. In this process, the researcher compares and contrasts the codes within a category to support meaning of the categories and the coding scheme. This process is called **constant comparison.** The qualitative researcher will conduct a constant comparison among the codes assigned to a category to develop a category that defines all the codes in a category.

The codes within a category are all elements of the same thing. For example, in the food selection scenario at the beginning of this chapter, codes for a category called "easy to reach" might be "The apple was closer so I grabbed it," "The hamburger was close at the front," or "The fries were right next to the hamburger so I got them, too." Instead of a category, the researcher may decide to provide a theme to describe the codes. In this case, the theme describes or interprets a pattern of responses. For example, "The apple was easy to reach," "Burgers and fries were first in the line and I was in a hurry," and "I couldn't see what was on top" aren't exactly the same thing as "easy to reach," but these comments could be combined together to form a theme about "location." In each case, the comment about the food selection was about where the food was located or not located. In Figure 20.3, for the coding of narratives of teachers about their reading instruction, you can see the name of the code, a description of the code, and the subcodes for each code. There are six subcodes for Code 1, named "challenges for students." In the Peck et al. (2015) study in Figure 20.4, notice that three codes (family, child, and culture) were grouped together under the empathy category with the two subcodes under family.

Step 3: Interpreting Pattern Among the Categories

Finally, the researcher may identify a **pattern** among the categories. A pattern can be formed in many ways, such as how categories are similar or different, how often the categories appear, the sequence of the categories, how they relate to different situations, or whether a category appears to be related to another category. Figure

20.5 illustrates the process of coding, identifying categories, and then forming a pattern among the categories. The theorized pattern from the categories in Figure 20.5 indicates that two of the categories led to the third category, which leads to the fourth category. Figure 20.6 illustrates a pattern of the data from Figure 20.3. In this case, the reading curriculum is believed to lead to changes in teacher behavior where they learned to teach reading to students with developmental disabilities. Learning how to teach reading led to an interplay between fidelity and ownership to modify instruction for individual student needs. This led to changes in student behavior where they learned to respond to reading instruction and generalization of the learning to read into other settings and tasks. This process led to the final block called "self-efficacy," where teachers gained confidence in teaching reading.

Coding is a very subjective process, and it is possible that another researcher may have coded the narratives differently. Therefore, it is important that a qualitative study describe the systematic process of identifying codes, subcodes, categories, and their interpreted pattern or relationship. The codes should come from the data with examples or descriptions of all the codes and subcodes so the reader can understand the researcher's coding process. Notice in Figure 20.5 that quotes that were used to create the codes and subcodes are in italics. Figure 20.7 is a list of the quotes of teachers to be used to illustrate each of the categories.

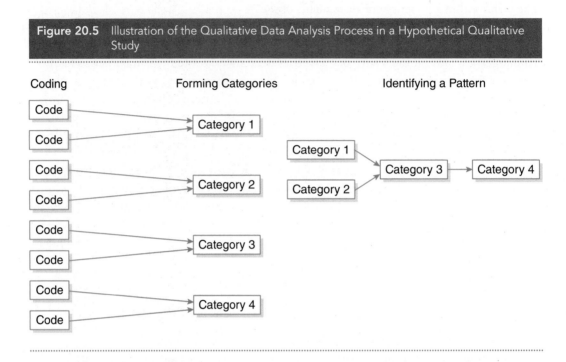

Figure 20.5 Illustration of the Qualitative Data Analysis Process in a Hypothetical Qualitative Study

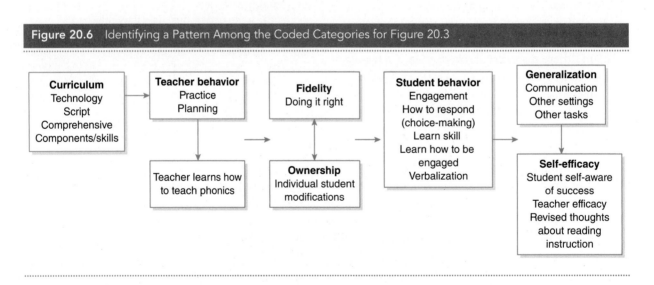

Figure 20.6 Identifying a Pattern Among the Coded Categories for Figure 20.3

Curriculum

#1 – AM, p. 3

#2 – MA, p.3

(BJV p. 2- all in one prog)

(AA p.3- quick, p.4 convenient)

Teacher Adaptations

#3 – BJV, p. 4-5

Follow Script/Maintain Fidelity

#4 – TP, p. 5

#5 – TP, p. 8

Ownership

6 – RB, P. 3 (practicing night b/f)

TP p.9- don't want to do it wrong practice it, it's

yours

Student Behavior

#7 – TP, p. 6

#8 – JBJV, p. 2

#10 – MA, p. 2

#11 – TP, p. 7

#12 – TP, p. 7

#13 – TP, p. 6

#14 – RB, p. 3

#15 – RB, p.4

MA p.3- at first was a cynic…then he did!

Self-Efficacy

#9 – AM, p. 3

#16 – RB, p. 2

#17 – TP, p.10 top

TP p.5-6 (better teacher)

Technology

MA p.2- understands how to use tech

RB p. 2- having iPad… more accessible

21st Century Skills

TP p. 10 (2nd section)

BJV p. 8- (2nd sect) wave of future

Motivating Learners

TP p. 10 2nd section

BJV p 1- enjoyed it, likes tech

AA p 2. Last year amazing. N loves tech

Teacher thoughts on reading instruction

BJV p. 2- before students can't do this, now they

can

RB p. 2-

MAKING SENSE—APPLING QUALITATIVE DATA ANALYSIS

A researcher asks a group of adults with intellectual disabilities to make three wishes. Here are some of their statements:

- My sister got new red shoes and I want some, too.
- I want a girlfriend to kiss.
- Pizza with pepperoni.
- It is getting cold, I need a coat.
- Sex, sex, sex.
- I don't get to have any candy here.
- Cubs gonna win! I wanna jersey!
- I wish I could get married.
- It would be nice to be able to go to Bubba's for dinner.

Let's code the keywords and phrases in each statement. The codes are bolded:

- My sister got new **red shoes** and I want some, too.
- I want a **girlfriend to kiss.**
- **Pizza** with pepperoni.
- It is getting cold, I need a **coat.**
- **Sex,** sex, sex.
- I don't get to have any **candy** here.
- Cubs gonna win! I wanna **jersey!**
- I wish I could get **married.**
- It would be nice to be able to **go to Bubba's for dinner.**

You may have labeled the categories differently, but that is the nature of qualitative research. Each of us has a personal perspective that shapes how we think about things.

Now let's form categories:

Clothing = red shoes, coat, Cubs jersey

Relationship = girlfriend, sex, married

Food = pizza, candy, dinner

The final step is to look for patterns. It appears that these adults want the same things that most people want. One thing that does not appear in these wishes are more generic, ideal wishes like world peace or a clean environment.

20.5 Qualitative Coding Tools

There are a number of ways that qualitative researchers may code their narrative materials. One way is by hand using a printed copy of the narrative and a highlighter to designate the important part of the narrative and writing the codes in the margin of the paper, as illustrated in Figure 20.2. Another way is to use word-processing software by using the highlight function to designate the important part of the narrative and the comment function to label the assigned code. These two ways require the researcher to later compile the list of codes to identify and create categories and manually search for specific codes. Given the large amount of data that qualitative research often generates, this can be cumbersome. There are some computerized tools to help the qualitative researcher in the coding and categorizing process. In general, these tools allow you to upload the content where the researcher can note and label codes, subcodes, and categories. Some color code the different codes so they are easy to see in a narrative. They can also keep track of the codes and categories, provide frequency counts of how often different codes appear, help the researcher locate specific codes in the narratives, work with multiple narratives at once, or create graphics to illustrate the patterns among categories. Figure 20.4 illustrates the use of a computer coding tool.

There are many qualitative computer tools available. The acronyms QDAS (Qualitative Data Analysis Software) or CAQDAS (Computer-Assisted Qualitative Data Analysis) are used to identify this type of software. QDAS is especially helpful when conducting case study and cross-case pattern and thematic analysis. These tools are not as useful for discourse analysis because the researcher is looking for tone, volume, and speed of the narratives and not just content. We only describe four of the more commonly used qualitative coding tools. In all of these tools, transcripts are uploaded into the software. The software is then used to identify and track the use of the codes, subcodes, and categories found in the text. By clicking on a code, subcode, or category, the researcher can locate the places in the transcripts where the codes and subcodes appear. This makes it easy to locate a quote from the transcript to illustrate the code or subcode. Any qualitative coding tool software, such as Hyperresearch by ResearchWare, Inc. (http://www.researchware.com/products/hyperresearch.html) and Atlas.ti from Scientific Software Development (http://atlasti.com/qualitative-software/), can work with audio, video, text, or graphics. Atlas.ti can also incorporate Google Earth screenshots. NVivo by QSR International (http://www.qsrinternational.com/product) can work with these types of materials and also spreadsheets or data from social media. NVivo is the updated version of NUD*IST (Non-numerical Unstructured Data Indexing, Searching and Theorizing). Whichever computerized tool you use, it will save you a lot of time than trying to coding by hand. The tool only helps the researcher keep track of the coding elements. The creativity and rigor are still required by the researcher in the coding process.

1. The following are hypothetical statements made in interviews about why teachers leave the field of teaching. Use the general coding process described above to identify at least one code for each statement. Then identify a category to represent the codes.

   "I don't have the supplies that I need to teach like paper to make copies or dry erase board. I would like to print some things in color for scaffolding ideas."

   "If I had a telephone in my classroom, it would be easier to communicate with students' families."

   "Susan and I have to share our U.S. history textbooks because there are not enough for all of the students."

   "At the beginning of the school year I buy things like Kleenex, hand sanitizer, pencils, and note paper. I also send home a note with my students requesting donations of these types of things."

   "We have one cart of laptops that we have to check out from the media center."

   "The WiFi is inadequate. My classroom is furthest from the modem so whether or not I have access to the Internet depends upon who else is using it at the time."

   "I wish I had a Smartboard."

Answers: 1. Each statement has a code regarding classroom supplies such as paper, dry erase board, telephone, books, Kleenex, hand sanitizer, pencils, laptops, WiFi, and Smartboard. These could be categorized as supplies or resources. You could also have coded the request for donations or low-tech supplies versus high-tech supplies.

20.6 Interpretations Made Using Different Qualitative Designs in the Data Analysis Process

Each of the different qualitative designs is used for a specific purpose that we described in Chapters 11 and 12. Because of the different purposes for which they are used, the interpretations will also be unique. Let's look at how the interpretations for each of the six designs differ.

Phenomenology

Recall that phenomenology is used to describe the essence of a lived experience for a person or people who have lived through a specific phenomenon. Therefore, we can expect the analysis to attempt to provide meaning of this phenomenon from the individual's or individuals' perspective. Patton (2015) describes four steps of phenomenological data analysis as (a) epoch, (b) reduction, (c) imaginative variation, and (d) synthesis. Epoch is not really a step as it is a frame of mind. The researcher must be aware and eliminate personal biases that he or she may have that may interfere with understanding the personal perspectives of the individual(s) in the study. The researcher needs to see the phenomenon from the perspective of the individual and not shaded with his or her own biases and understandings. Reduction is the coding process where key elements of the experience are derived from the data. Imaginative variation is the categorizing of the codes into meaningful clusters that are called "invariant themes." The invariant themes are identified by looking at the data from different perspectives (i.e., imaginative variation). Synthesis is the integration of the themes to describe the meaning and essence of the experience or phenomenon. Given the emphasis on the perspective of the individual's experience, researchers conducting a phenomenological qualitative study are likely to use inductive, indigenous concept (emic), and/or indigenous typology analysis.

Ethnography

Ethnography is used in the study and understanding of culture. This will include extensive observations and interviews with many people over a sustained period of time. It is similar to phenomenology in that it seeks to understand and describe the culture from the perspective of the individual experiences. Because the study of culture involves the study of many people as they experience that culture, ethnographic data analysis will attempt to triangulate the understanding from a variety of different sources. While there is not a series of specific steps in the analysis of ethnographic data, it is likely to use cross-case pattern or thematic analysis, as well as inductive, indigenous concept (emic), and/or indigenous typology analysis.

Grounded Theory

Grounded theory research seeks to construct and verify a theory rather than simply describe an experience like the other qualitative analysis techniques. It will include extensive coding using constant comparison and extensive written notes during the data analysis process. These are called memos. Charmaz (2011) describes using memos on "topics such as the properties of our tentative categories, the conditions when a category is evident, how the category accounts for the data, [and] comparisons between codes and categories" (p. 166). Grounded theory will use inductive, cross-case pattern and/or thematic analysis, indigenous concept or typology (to illustrate the categories) analysis, and analyst-generated concepts or typologies to generate the theory. It may also use discourse analysis.

Narrative

Narrative research is the use of human stories to understand social and cultural phenomena and experiences. This analysis will form general themes to examine the thematic elements of the data, but the intent is to arrive at a holistic understanding of the story. With the focus on telling a story, narrative research will use case study and indigenous concept or typology analysis techniques.

Case Study

Case study research seeks to understand complex social experiences by examining them in-depth through the lens of a case. Recall that a case can be any individual, group, or organization that is bounded by some feature. Analysis of a case study involves identifying key elements of the story and organizing this key information. Interpretation of a case study relies on the description of the key elements of the case. Case study may also include comparing and contrasting different cases. It is very flexible and may use any of the analysis techniques.

Critical Studies

Critical studies examine life experiences as they relate to struggles with power, equity, and justice of marginalized groups. Analysis is focused on identifying the structures of oppression as part of the lived experience with the intent that identification of these structures will be emancipatory. Interpretation will depend on the lens of the critical theory (e.g., feminism, critical race theory, or queer theory). Critical study research will tend to use inductive, cross-case pattern or thematic analysis, indigenous concept or typology analysis techniques, and/or discourse analysis.

The subjectivity of the process of qualitative research and subsequent analysis of narratives of lived experiences make it difficult to evaluate the quality of the study. Recall with quantitative research that we had the concepts of validity and reliability to evaluate the quality of the study. Qualitative research uses different criteria that parallel validity and reliability, called trustworthiness. These techniques increase the confidence that the reader has regarding the integrity of the study and its findings.

20.7 Criteria of Trustworthiness

Indeed, many qualitative researchers flat out reject the notion of validity and reliability because such measures presume that a singular external reality exists, which contradicts the philosophy of a qualitative approach. As an alternative to using validity and reliability, many qualitative researchers instead use four criteria of trustworthiness. The four criteria of trustworthiness are transferability, dependability, confirmability, and credibility. Each criterion is described in Table 20.2 (adapted from Guba & Lincoln, 1989; Lincoln & Guba, 1985). Transferability parallels external validity/generalizability of quantitative studies. It is the extent to which the results can be applied to other participants or situations. Transferability can be demonstrated by the number of the participants included in the study and the number of different situations from which they are drawn. The greater the number of participants and their situations, the more likely the results are transferable to similar participants. Increasing the number of interviews and/or observations of the participants and the time frame from which the data are obtained can

> **Trustworthiness** is based on four criteria: the credibility, transferability, dependability, and confirmability of a qualitative analysis.
>
> **Transferability** (applicability) is the extent to which observed results are useful, applicable, or transferable beyond the setting or context of the research.

Criteria of Trustworthiness	Parallel	Description
Transferability	External validity	Applicability—the extent to which observed results are useful, applicable, or transferable beyond the setting or context of the research.
Dependability	Reliability	Consistency—the extent to which observed results would be similar if similar research were conducted in the same or a similar context.
Confirmability	Objectivity	Neutrality—the extent to which observed results reflect the actual context of participant experiences rather than simply the researcher's perspective.
Credibility	Internal validity	Truthfulness—the extent to which observed results reflect the realities of the participants in such a way that the participants themselves would agree with the research report.

Table 20.2 The Four Criteria of Trustworthiness in Qualitative Research

Source: Adapted from Guba and Lincoln (1989) and Lincoln and Guba (1985).

also increase the transferability. **Dependability** parallels reliability of quantitative studies. Dependability is the extent to which the same results would be achieved if the study were conducted again under similar circumstances. A good way to increase dependability is to thoroughly describe the processes of the study so that another researcher would be able to replicate the process. **Confirmability** parallels the objectivity of quantitative studies. Confirmability reflects the researcher's ability to adequately represent the participant's point of view without influence of his or her own biases and perspectives. Finally, **credibility** parallels internal validity of quantitative studies. It refers to the extent to which the researcher adequately and correctly records and/or describes the realities of the participants in the study. It is important for a qualitative study to embed a process that gives us confidence that the information described is an accurate reflection of what was said or observed. There are a number of different strategies for demonstrating credibility that we describe next.

Dependability (consistency) is the extent to which observed results would be similar if similar research were conducted in the same or a similar context.

Confirmability (neutrality) is the extent to which observed results reflect the actual context of participant experiences rather than simply the researcher's perspective.

Credibility (truthfulness) is the extent to which observed results reflect the realities of the participants in such a way that the participants themselves would agree with the research report.

Although these criteria parallel concepts of validity, reliability, and objectivity, these criteria do not conform well to quantitative research. Without statistical analyses, it is not possible to compare the significance of observed results or generalize beyond the experiences of a few individuals or studies. This makes it difficult to integrate knowledge gained from both perspectives of research. However, qualitative research does provide a unique understanding of behavior from the perspective of the individual. Also, it is a new perspective, compared to quantitative research, and continues to develop and gain recognition in the scientific community.

Developing Credibility

Guba and Lincoln (1989; Lincoln & Guba, 1985) describe some things that a qualitative researcher can do to enhance the credibility of a qualitative study. Readers of qualitative research can use these to evaluate a qualitative study. While a single qualitative study will not use all of these techniques, at least one or more should be referenced in the study. The credibility of a study can be increased by the number of credibility techniques used in the study.

Prolonged Engagement

Prolonged engagement refers to the amount of time spent in the field acquiring the data. This includes time spent to develop rapport with the participants as well as conducting the observations and/or interviews and/or gathering related documents or artifacts. The amount of time spent in developing rapport and gathering data should be sufficient. The definition of *sufficient* depends on the study but should be enough to develop trust of the participants and gain the knowledge necessary to answer the research question. Scarbrough and Allen (2015) observed every class session during the poetry unit 2 to 3 days per week for 90 minutes for 4 weeks. Niland (2015) describes regularly attending the preschool class for 7 months to observe and talk to teachers about their use of singing.

> **Prolonged engagement** is the amount of time to develop trust of the participants and gain the knowledge necessary to answer the research question.

Thick Description

A prolonged engagement should lead to a **thick description** of the details of the study. This includes in-depth descriptions of the context, participants, experiences, and activities involved in the study. The idea here is to provide enough detail about the study to evaluate the transferability of the study to other situations, participants, or settings. It also lends credence to the study in that the researcher was sufficiently and deeply engaged in the study.

> **Thick description** involves extensive description of the context, participants, experiences, and activities involved in the study.

Triangulation

Triangulation refers to using multiple sources in the investigation. Triangulation can be used to ensure that the information is comprehensive to formulate a deep understanding of the topic. This can include multiple participants, observers, or data analysts to obtain multiple ways of comprehending the data. This may also include gathering multiple types of data, including observations, interviews, documents, or even some quantitative data. Different sources of data can add information to the convergent or divergent aspects of the topic. Triangulation may also include gathering information from the same

> **Triangulation** refers to using multiple sources in the investigation such as multiple participants, multiple types of data, or different sources of data.

sources but at different times or places. Triangulation is one of the most common credibility techniques among those we list here.

Member Checking

Member checking involves verifying coding, representations, and/or interpretations of the participants. It is an opportunity for participants to confirm that their views have been adequately portrayed. One way to conduct member checking is to provide the participant with the transcript of the interview or description of the observation to verify accuracy and provide additional clarifying information or correct errors. The researchers may also share their interpretations with the participants, but this can be tricky in case the

> **Member checking** involves verifying coding, representations, and/or interpretations of the participants.

participants and researchers may not agree (recall that many qualitative researchers believe that there can be multiple perspectives of reality). Member checking is also one of the most common credibility techniques among those we list here. Jordan (2015) describes member checking with her participant, a first-grade teacher, three times. She checked with the teacher at the end of the data collection during the final interview and twice during the data analysis phase.

Negative Case Analysis

Negative case analysis, also called *deviant case analysis*, involves searching for contradictory evidence that does not support the identified pattern or interpretation derived from the data. The researchers will specifically look for information that does not support their explanation. This type of analysis lends credence to the analysis because it means that the researcher is making an effort to find evidence that does not support his or her interpretation. The researcher will discuss whether discrepant evidence was found and, if found, will discuss how this contradictory evidence affects the original interpretation. Pasco and Ennis (2015) describe

> **Negative case analysis** involves searching for contradictory evidence that does not support the identified pattern or interpretation derived from the data.

searching for negative cases that may not support the categories generated during data analysis or cases that may provide an alternate interpretation in their study of third graders' understanding of energy expenditure during physical activity.

Peer Debriefing

Peer debriefing involves a review of the data by someone knowledgeable in the area being studied but who was not deeply involved in the study. This is an opportunity to bring another lens to examine the data and lend support (or not) to the interpretations. This process can provide meaningful feedback regarding the coding and categorizing of the data, as well as the identified patterns or interpretations. A different lens may see the data in a different light. This may

> **Peer debriefing** involves a review of the data by someone knowledgeable in the area being studied but who was not deeply involved in the study that can lend support (or not) to the interpretations.

cause the researcher to adjust the original work or lend support to it if the peer debriefer is in agreement. Jordan (2015) also describes regularly using two peer debriefers during data collection and while drafting the manuscript.

External Audit

Like peer debriefing, an external audit involves an outside person knowledgeable in the area being studied to review the process and interpretations of the study. The idea is the same as with peer debriefing—bringing a new set of eyes to examine data and interpretations. The difference is that an external auditor is further removed and unaffiliated with the study.

External audit also involves an outside person knowledgeable in the area being studied to review the process and interpretations of the study, further removed and unaffiliated with the study.

LEARNING CHECK 4 ✓

1. Quantitative research assesses the internal and external validity of a research study. What parallel criteria are assessed for qualitative research?

2. Name the four elements to trustworthiness.

3. Name the seven ways listed in this chapter to establish credibility.

Answers: 1. Trustworthiness; 2. Credibility, transferability, dependability, and confirmability; 3. Prolonged engagement, thick description, triangulation, member checking, negative case analysis, peer debriefing, external audit.

CONNECTING TO THE CLASSROOM

When conducting your own qualitative research, the notion of transferability, the ability of the study to be applied to other participants or situations, is likely of less concern since you are only interested in your own current situation. Issues of dependability (consistency), confirmability (neutrality), and credibility (truthfulness) should be considered when planning a qualitative, action research study. Document the steps you take in your study in detail in such a way that another teacher could follow your steps and conduct the same study and employ as many of the credibility techniques as possible. Conduct the study over time using the natural breaks of the school year such as a quarter or semester. Set aside time each day to record observations and field notes. Then later read over and reflect on these notes and add details as needed. Gather information from other available sources such as attendance records, other teachers, or a gradebook. If the age of the child allows, ask the child to verify your thoughts and seek confirmation or alternative explanations. Other teachers or administrators can serve as peer debriefing or an external audit.

20.8 Ethics in Focus: Confidentiality

The nature of qualitative research and analysis requires deep, rich descriptions of experiences of people. Obtaining and analyzing this kind of personal information can put qualitative researchers in positions where they must balance ethical principles, their need to know certain information, and how to report the findings. Many ethical considerations need to be considered very carefully before conducting a qualitative study. One issue of primary concern is confidentiality. One way to maintain confidentiality of the identity of the participant is the use of a pseudonym to represent the individual in the written narrative without using his or her real name. Yet, even through the use of a pseudonym, individuals might be identifiable to themselves or others by the deep and rich description of their experiences. How will the individual feel if this happens? What might the repercussions be if others recognize the individual through the description? This balance may be even more difficult when working with marginalized individuals who already feel let down by society or may be anxious about the repercussions of being identified. Then there is also the possibility of a researcher becoming aware of potentially harmful situations such as criminal behavior or self-harm.

Negotiating the balance between individual confidentiality, the aim of the research, and how the experience is described relies on the skills of the qualitative researcher. Careful consideration of the possibilities of being identified, how the final descriptions will be written to the satisfaction of the individual, and potential repercussions need to take place before the research begins. The informed consent, in as much as possible, should delineate these and other potential ramifications clearly for the participants to consider in a language that they will understand. Ask if the individuals want to be identified or let them select a pseudonym. Explain how much control over the interpretation, if any, the individuals will have. Clearly define the limits of confidentiality. Once consented, the ability of the qualitative researcher to develop rapport and establish a partnership with the individuals may be needed to negotiate unanticipated confidentiality issues.

CHAPTER SUMMARY

LO 1 State the two general approaches of qualitative data analysis.

- The first approach is to reduce the amount of data into manageable chunks.

- The second approach is to expand upon the original data to derive meaning from them.

LO 2 Describe the advantages and disadvantages of the three approaches to recording narrative data.

- Written notes require no special equipment, but it is hard to capture everything and not likely to be able to record verbatim responses.

- Video recording requires money to purchase special equipment and may be too conspicuous. It can capture more than just what is said.

- Audio recording may also require money to purchase special equipment and may be conspicuous. It can record verbatim responses and other elements of verbal communication. A transcribing machine or text-to-speech software can be used to speed up the transcription process.

LO 3 Identify and define the three components of transcription.

- The **verbal component** is the words spoken by the participant. The verbal component is transcribed using standard orthography, literary transcription, or eye dialect.

- The **prosodic component** is the manner in which words are spoken such as pitch, loudness, and duration.

- The **paralinguistic component** is the vocal features that occur during speaking that are not words such as laughing and crying.

LO 4 Distinguish between the 11 types of qualitative data analysis.

- **Content analysis** is a general term used for the process of reducing the amount of information from narratives into manageable chunks, called codes.

- A **case study** is used to tell a story about a case.

- **Cross-case pattern analysis** groups similar descriptions made by different cases together when these descriptions can be considered the same thing.

- **Cross-case thematic analysis** is the process by which we give a name to it in order to summarize and describe what the statements mean.

- **Inductive analysis** generates the themes that arise directly from the narratives without any preconceived notions about what the themes may be.

- In **deductive analysis,** the researcher has some expectations or themes that may be present in the narratives and seeks to find these themes.

- **Indigenous concept analysis** (emic) identifies and reports categories and vocabulary as it is specifically used by the case(s) as the narratives naturally occur in a particular place.

- **Analyst-generated concept** analysis translates and reports the experiences of the cases using a researcher or universal perspective.

- **Indigenous typologies** reflect the view of the case and how they classify elements of their world.

- **Analyst-generated typologies** reconstruct the indigenous typologies into analyst-generated terms and interpretations that represent the larger worldview of these categories.

- **Discourse analysis** focuses on the language used to describe something such as word choice, grammar, and rhetoric used to describe an experience.

LO 5 Describe the general process of coding qualitative data.

- Code the narrative by highlighting important words or phrases and assign a few words or a phrase that capture the salient essence of the narrative.

- Identify any possible subcodes.

- Formulate categories by combing similar codes together.

- Engage in a recursive process to double check the codes and categories and their meanings (constant comparison).

- Interpret the patterns or themes generated by the coding according to the specific perspective of research design used for the study.

LO 6 Distinguish between emic and etic coding.

- Emic coding contains the information in the participants' own words.

- Etic coding is a code that interprets what the participant says into researcher words.

LO 7 Describe how the perspectives of the different types of qualitative research result in a different kind of analysis.

- A qualitative research design is selected depending on the particular purpose of the study. Each design has a unique perspective that is used in the analysis. It represents the particular lens through which the data will be interpreted. A study will likely use several of the different types of qualitative analyses.

LO 8 Identify the four criteria of trustworthiness.

- Transferability is the extent to which the results can be applied to other participants or situations.

- Dependability is the extent to which the same results would be achieved if the study were conducted again under similar circumstances.

- Confirmability reflects the researcher's ability to adequately represent the participant's point of view without influence of his or her own biases and perspectives.

- Credibility refers to the extent to which the researcher adequately and correctly records and/or describes the realities of the participants in the study.

LO 9 Describe the different ways to increase the credibility of a study.

- Prolonged engagement is the amount of time to develop trust of the participants and gain the knowledge necessary to answer the research question.

- Thick description involves extensive description of the context, participants, experiences, and activities involved in the study.

- Triangulation refers to using multiple sources in the investigation such as multiple participants, multiple types of data, or different sources of data.

- Member checking involves verifying coding, representations, and/or interpretations of the participants.

- Negative case analysis involves searching for contradictory evidence that does not support the identified pattern or interpretation derived from the data.

- **Peer debriefing** involves a review of the data by someone knowledgeable in the area being studied but who was not deeply involved in the study and can lend support (or not) to the interpretations.

- **External audit** also involves an outside person knowledgeable in the area being studied to review the process and interpretations of the study but is further removed and unaffiliated with the study.

KEY TERMS

analyst-generated concepts (etic) 587

analyst-generated typologies 587

codes 592

confirmability 605

constant comparison 597

content analysis 587

credibility 605

cross-case pattern analysis 588

cross-case thematic analysis 588

deductive analysis 588

dependability 605

discourse analysis 590

external audit 608

eye dialect 584

indigenous concept analysis (emic) 589

indigenous typologies 589

inductive analysis 588

literary transcription 584

member checking 607

negative case analysis 607

patterns 597

paralinguistic component 584

peer debriefing 607

prolonged engagement 606

prosodic component 584

standard orthography 584

subcodes 596

thick description 606

transferability 604

triangulation 606

trustworthiness 604

verbal component 583

REVIEW QUESTIONS

1. Distinguish between quantitative and qualitative data analysis.

2. Distinguish between the three different ways to record narrative communication.

3. Identify the types of qualitative data analysis in the following examples:

   A. A researcher describes a group of behaviors that are similar enough to be considered manifestation of the same thing.

   B. Teacher narratives are used to discern patterns and themes of teachers' experiences with the Common Core Standards.

   C. The researcher translates the participant's words into her own words.

4. Describe the general process of qualitative data analysis.

5. In the following codes, identify which one is the code and which ones are the subcodes.

    A. Homelessness, fluency in English, risk factors, truancy, repeating a grade

    B. Scaffolding, instructional strategies, direct instruction, error correction, differentiation

6. How do the different types of research designs influence the type of analysis that will be used?

7. Which of the qualitative designs will interpret participant narratives focusing on identifying the structures of oppression as part of the lived experience of the participant?

8. Which element of trustworthiness parallels external validity/generalizability of quantitative studies?

9. Which form of credibility is described by the following scenario?

    A. The researcher studying the experiences of non-English-speaking immigrant children in public schools gathers information from multiple sources, including teachers, school attendance, grades, and parents.

    B. Once the data are coded and categorized, she asks a colleague who was not a part of the study to review her coding scheme.

10. Name two ways a researcher can protect the confidentiality of a participant in qualitative research.

CHAPTER ACTIVITIES

1. Pick a topic of your choice to conduct a qualitative study. Your study includes interviews, focus groups, and observations. How will you record each of type of data? Why?

2. Now select at least three types of qualitative data analysis that can be used to analyze the data. Why did you select these three types?

3. Code the transcript in Figure 20.1. How does your coding differ from how the researcher coded it?

4. Apply an aspect of transferability, dependability, and confirmability to your study to increase its trustworthiness.

5. Now select three types of credibility to your study and describe how you will apply them to your study.

$SAGE edge™

SAGE edge offers a robust online environment featuring an impressive array of free tools and resources for review, study, and further exploration, keeping both instructors and students on the cutting edge of teaching and learning.

Access practice quizzes, eFlashcards, video, and multimedia at edge.sagepub.com/priviterarme.

Identify a problem
- Determine an area of interest.
- Review the literature.
- Identify new ideas in your area of interest.
- Develop a research hypothesis.

Develop a research plan
- Define the variables being tested.
- Identify participants or subjects and determine how to sample them.
- Select a research strategy and design.
- Evaluate ethics and obtain institutional approval to conduct research.

Conduct the study
- Execute the research plan and measure or record the data.

Analyze and evaluate the data
- Analyze and evaluate the data as they relate to the research hypothesis.
- Summarize data and research results.

Communicate the results
- Method of communication: oral, written, or in a poster.
- Style of communication: APA guidelines are provided to help prepare style and format.

Generate more new ideas
- Results support your hypothesis—refine or expand on your ideas.
- Results do not support your hypothesis—reformulate a new idea or start over.

After reading this chapter, you should be able to:

1 Identify three methods of communication among scientists.

2 Describe three elements of communication.

3 Apply APA writing style and language guidelines for writing a manuscript.

4 Distinguish between the 11 types of qualitative data analysis.

5 Apply APA guidelines for writing and organizing a literature review article.

6 Delineate how results are reported for a qualitative versus a quantitative research design.

7 State APA guidelines for identifying the authorship of published scientific work.

8 Identify guidelines for effectively presenting a poster.

9 Identify guidelines for effectively giving a professional talk.

COMMUNICATING RESEARCH: PREPARING MANUSCRIPTS, POSTERS, AND TALKS

Communicating what was found in a research study is just as important as the finding itself. Albert Einstein said, "If you can't explain it simply, you don't understand it well enough." Being able to communicate what you found, then, is important inasmuch as it not only allows others to understand what you found but also makes clear to others that you understand the finding as well. In this way, your ability to effectively communicate in science can reflect your fundamental credibility as an author.

As a student, you can appreciate fully the value of communicating ideas. In the classroom, you often categorize professors as being good or bad teachers based on how well they could explain or make sense of the material being taught in class. Professors who made sense of difficult material in class often receive higher ratings than professors who are obviously knowledgeable but unable to effectively communicate that knowledge in the classroom. In a similar way, a scientist has the responsibility to make sense of the findings or ideas discovered in a research study. After all, it is of little value to be unable to communicate new knowledge to others. In fact, Einstein himself believed that "any fool can know. The point is to understand." Communicating research findings, then, can be as important as the discovery itself.

In this chapter, we will introduce the methods of communication in research: manuscripts, posters, and talks. Throughout this chapter, we will focus largely on how to effectively communicate ideas using each method and provide tips and strategies to help you in your own work. Following the guidelines described in this chapter can give you the tools you need to effectively appeal your ideas to a diverse audience and allow you to present yourself as an authoritative, credible, and engaging communicator.

21.1 Elements of Communication

Oral and written reports can exist for long periods of time and contribute to a large body of knowledge in education and the sciences. Scientific research is a collaborative effort in which groups of researchers from different universities and institutions across the globe converge to describe their research and interpretations on a topic. Common methods of communication for researchers are in the published peer-reviewed literature and at the many conferences held each year all over the world in which researchers gather to report their most current findings in a poster or introduce their new ideas in a talk. When a peer-reviewed manuscript is published, it is integrated into the accepted scientific body of knowledge and made available for criticism and review by other scientists who accept or reject the ideas presented in that publication. Likewise, a poster or talk can open the lines of communication between scientists in a way that allows them to share ideas to facilitate a more grounded understanding of a topic in the behavioral sciences.

> Three methods of communication among scientists are to publish a manuscript, present a poster, and prepare a talk.

Writing a manuscript for publication, presenting a poster, and preparing a talk are three key methods of communication among scientists. In this chapter, we will introduce the American Psychological Association (APA, 2009) style for formatting and writing manuscripts, as well as provide tips and strategies for presenting a poster and giving a talk. Educational researchers also typically use APA style when writing for publication, presenting a poster, or preparing a talk. First, we introduce three basic elements of communication: the speaker (or author), the audience, and the message. Each element of communication is also summarized in Table 21.1 at the end of this section.

The Speaker or Author

As a speaker or author, you are responsible for mediating a communication. How you communicate will be important in how your message is received by an audience. For a manuscript, it is important to communicate using the following APA guidelines:

1. Use first person and third person appropriately. In APA style, use the first person to discuss research steps rather than anthropomorphizing the work. For example, a study cannot "manipulate" or "hypothesize"; you and your coauthors, however, can (e.g., "We manipulated the levels of the variable . . ." or "We hypothesized that changes would occur . . ."). Also use first-person singular (i.e., "I") if you are a sole author; use first-person plural (i.e., "we") when referring to work you completed with many authors. Use the third person, however, to foreground the research. For example, state, "The results indicate . . ." and *not*

"We found evidence . . ." to report the findings of a study—the study, not the authors, elicits data. The most important suggestion is to be clear and avoid confusion in your writing. For example, "We are facing an autism epidemic . . ." may leave the reader wondering whether *we* refers to the authors of the article, to community members, or to some other group. In these cases, *we* can still be an appropriate referent with a simple rewrite (e.g., "As Americans, *we* are facing an autism epidemic . . ."), or the third person can be used (e.g., "Americans are facing an autism epidemic . . .").

2. Use past, present, and future tense appropriately. To describe previous research, use past tense. For example, state, "The data showed that . . ." or "Previous work demonstrated that . . ." to describe published or completed work. Also use past tense to describe your results for completed work, such as "Scores increased from Time 1 to Time 2" or "The data were significant." In the discussion, you can use present tense to describe current work, such as "To address these concerns, we are conducting several follow-up studies." Use future tense to describe events or work that will occur or be completed at a later time.

3. Use an impersonal writing style. A research manuscript is not a novel, so avoid the use of literary devices beyond what is necessary. For example, avoid using colloquial devices such as "over the top" (in place of "exaggerated") and avoid jargon such as "techy" (in place of "technologically savvy"). Also, use language appropriately. For example, to give a reason for an event or method, use "because" and not "since" (e.g., "male participants were excluded *because* . . .") because "since" indicates the passage of time (e.g., "These studies have not been replicated *since* before 2000"). As another example, to describe something that does not refer to a location, use "in which" and not "where" (e.g., "participants completed a survey *in which* all items pertained to . . .") because "where" indicates a location (e.g., "Participants were situated at the back of a room, *where* a series of items were located").

4. Reduce biased language. The author can use unbiased language in two ways. First, follow APA guidelines for using unbiased language, as discussed in greater detail in Section 21.2, with examples given in Table 21.2 on page 624. For example, people with a disorder should be characterized as a person and not by their disorder using person-first language. To avoid bias, we state "Participants with depression" instead of "Depressed participants," for example. Second, do not use language in a manuscript that would be offensive to others, particularly our colleagues and fellow researchers. For example, to describe the limitations in another study, state, "Gender *was not included* as a factor" instead of "Previous researchers *completely ignored* gender as a factor in their study."

5. Give credit where appropriate. The APA provides specific guidelines for citing sources that are published in the *Publication Manual of the American Psychological Association* (APA, 2009). Any time you cite work that is not your own, make sure you give proper credit to the author of that work using these APA guidelines. Further details for citing sources are given in Section 21.3 in this chapter and also in Appendix A.

6. The perspective of writing using APA style is that the author reports about findings in a research study; the author does not tell about his or her research. In other words, it is the research itself, and not the researcher, that is the focus of the report. The goal of communication is to persuade others based on the methods and findings in a research report and not by catchy literary devices or the actions of the researcher. While this goal also applies to poster presentations and talks, we do make one exception: It is preferred that the speaker uses primarily first person in these forums because posters and talks are interactive. The speaker communicates in real time to other researchers, so using first person more often can be more natural in these settings. Otherwise, the remaining guidelines should be followed to present a poster or give a talk.

The Audience

The audience is any individual or group with whom you intend to communicate. While scientific data may often be completed at a level that is difficult to understand, it is often the case that the audience is more diverse than many authors recognize. For any scientific work, the authors should consider the following audiences who are likely to read their report:

1. Scientists and professionals. Scientists are those who work in universities, laboratory settings, or research-based organizations like The RAND Corporation or the Social Science Research Council. Professionals are those who work in schools or education-related organizations such as Teach for America or the Kahn Academy. These groups are interested in the methods and procedures of your work, as well as in your ideas and interpretations of the outcomes. Scientists and professionals are educated in your field or general discipline. They can also often be among the most critical audiences to evaluate the contributions of your research and ideas because they are often in the best position, in terms of funding and resources, to challenge your results and interpretations, as well as produce their own research to demonstrate the validity of their challenges. Because these groups tend to be the most critical of a research study, most authors tend to write or speak mostly to these groups.

2. College students. It is likely that more students read scientific reports and attend poster sessions and talks each year than those with terminal and professional degrees. Doctoral graduate students, for example, must complete a dissertation and spend many years and endless hours integrating a body of research to develop a research idea and conduct a study worthy of earning a doctoral degree. Undergraduate students often review articles in published works as part of class assignments or attend conferences to gain experience needed for acceptance to graduate programs. College students are likely to be your largest audience and yet they have less background or understanding of the topic being communicated than scientists and professionals. Providing sufficient background of the research

topic and defining or operationalizing key factors in a research study can facilitate an understanding of your work among this group.

3. The general public (laypersons). Many persons in the general public can find and read your work. For example, when parents learn that a member of their family has a behavioral disorder, they can use problem-focused coping strategies to learn more about what is known of a disorder and the potential treatment options for that disorder. In these cases, it is useful to make an effort to communicate data effectively such that this general nonscientific audience can also understand the gist or importance of the findings of a given report.

The audiences with which we share our ideas and works are often larger than we recognize. Consider also that there is a growing popularity in the publication of open-access articles, such as those in open-access peer-reviewed education journals published by Elsevier and Sage Open. Open-access articles are peer-reviewed works that are freely available to scientists, professionals, students, and the general public. The direction of publication, then, is to expand the size of an audience by enhancing how accessible research is, which makes it more pertinent than ever for the author or speaker to effectively communicate to this broader audience.

The Message

The author or speaker communicates the message, which is any information regarding the design, analyses, interpretations, and new ideas contributed by a completed research project or literature review. The message is important inasmuch as an audience understands it. To effectively communicate a message, we should consider the following guidelines:

1. The message should be novel. A novel idea is one that is original or new. You must be able to explain and demonstrate in your work how your ideas add to or build upon the scientific literature. If you can demonstrate what we learn from your ideas, then your ideas are novel.

2. The message should be interesting. An interesting idea can potentially benefit society, test a prediction, or develop areas of research where little is known. Peer-reviewed journals have a readership, and your idea must appeal to those who read that journal if you are to publish your ideas.

3. The message should be informative. An informative message is one that provides a thorough description of a work. For example, the literature should be fully reviewed, the details of research procedures should be fully described, and all data measured in a study should be fully reported. Hence, do not omit information that would be otherwise informative to an audience to determine the extent to which a work is novel and interesting.

For a speaker or author to effectively communicate a message to an audience, it is important to consider the three elements of communication described in this section. The implication of each element suggests that delivering an appropriate, novel, interesting, and informative message to a broad audience will significantly enhance the effectiveness of the communication of a work. Table 21.1 summarizes each element of communication described in this section.

Three elements of communication are the speaker or author, the audience, and the message.

Table 21.1	Three Elements of Communication
Elements of Communication	General Characteristics
The speaker or author	Use appropriate verb tense.
	Use an impersonal writing style.
	Reduce biased language.
	Give credit where appropriate.
The audience	Scientists and professionals
	College students
	The general public (laypeople)
The message	The message should be novel.
	The message should be interesting.
	The message should be informative.

LEARNING CHECK 1 ✓

1. State three methods of communication.

2. State three elements in communication.

3. True or false: Delivering an appropriate, novel, interesting, and informative message to a broad audience will significantly enhance the effectiveness of the communication of a work.

Answers: 1. Publish a manuscript, present, or prepare a talk; 2. The speaker or author, the audience, and the message; 3. True.

21.2 Writing a Manuscript: Writing Style and Language

Peer review is a procedure used by the editors of scientific journals in which a manuscript or work is sent to peers or experts in that area to review the work and determine its scientific value or worth regarding publication.

The most critical method of communication is to publish a work in a peer-reviewed journal, which is any publication that is subjected to a peer review. A peer review is a procedure used by scientific journals in which a manuscript or work is sent to peers or experts in that area to review the work

620 | Section VI: Analyzing, Interpreting, and Communicating Research Data

and determine its scientific value or worth regarding publication. A peer review is often conducted "blind" where the author(s) and reviewer(s) are not revealed to each other. Only upon acceptance from these peer reviewers will a work be published in a peer-reviewed journal. The peer review process is demanding because of the high rejection rates of works submitted to a journal for consideration for publication. Many of these journals reject from 75% to 85% or more of the manuscripts they receive each year. For this reason, publishing a work in a peer-reviewed journal is regarded as a high achievement in the scientific community.

To submit a work for consideration for publication in a peer-reviewed journal, we prepare a document called an **APA-style manuscript.** An APA-style manuscript is a document that is created using the formatting style detailed in the *Publication Manual of the American Psychological Association* (APA, 2009), abbreviated as the *Publication Manual.* APA style is required by over 1,000 research journals worldwide and across disciplines. The *Publication Manual* provides guidelines for writing an APA-style manuscript and should always be referred to when writing a manuscript using this writing style.

> An **APA-style manuscript** is a document that is created using the writing style format detailed in the *Publication Manual of the American Psychological Association,* typically for the purposes of having the work considered for publication in a peer-reviewed journal.

In this section, and in Sections 21.3 and 21.4, we will introduce the writing style described in the *Publication Manual.* This chapter is meant to be an overview of writing using APA style. For a more exhaustive description of this writing style, please refer to the *Publication Manual.* In this section, we introduce four general writing guidelines: Be accurate, be comprehensive yet concise, be conservative, and be appropriate.

> APA-style writing is detailed in the *Publication Manual* and is used worldwide and across disciplines.

Be Accurate

When writing an APA-style manuscript or any type of paper for that matter, the sources you cite, the interpretations you provide, the data you report, and the grammar and writing you present must be accurate. Accuracy in a manuscript is important because it reflects the credibility of the author. Writing a manuscript with even just one error can damage the credibility of the author and, depending on how serious the mistake, lead the audience to question the accuracy of other aspects of the report, even when the other parts of the work are accurate. Keep in mind that to be able to persuade others of the value of a work, the researcher must have credibility with the audience. Losing credibility due to mistakes is often avoidable and seen as the result of sloppy writing and poor revision. To avoid this problem, we can apply a common method: Proofread a paper or manuscript, put it down for a day or two, proofread it again, and then let a friend or colleague proofread it before making final changes. This method can be used to eliminate many errors that may have been otherwise overlooked or ignored.

> Accuracy in a scientific report is important because it reflects the credibility of the author.

Be Comprehensive yet Concise

Being comprehensive means that you include enough information in your report that the reader is able to critically evaluate its contribution to the scientific literature. For a primary research study, for example, this means that the author fully discloses the procedures used and clearly identifies the hypotheses tested and why it was important to test those hypotheses. Being concise means that the author fully discloses his or her study in as few words as possible. It means that the author only makes arguments that are needed to support his or her hypotheses and describes only as many details about the procedures and data so as to allow another author to replicate his or her design. Being comprehensive yet concise is important because it makes the manuscript easier to follow—it provides a full report, while also focusing only on information needed to make arguments and report the procedures and data. The following are four common strategies used to be comprehensive yet concise using APA style:

- Abbreviate where appropriate. Any terms that can be abbreviated or have a common abbreviation should be abbreviated after their first use. For example, to describe participants who exhibit attention-deficit hyperactivity disorder, we spell out attention-deficit hyperactivity disorder on first use with an abbreviation given in parentheses, and all subsequent references to the term can be abbreviated as ADHD. For example, on first use we state, "Only participants exhibiting attention-deficit hyperactivity disorder characteristics (ADHD) were. . . ." On subsequent uses, we only use the abbreviation ADHD. Other common abbreviations include English language learner (ELL), kindergarten through 12th grade (K–12), Individualized Education Plan (IEP), and local education agency (LEA), which are used to make the writing more concise.

- Display data in a figure or table. A figure or table can be particularly helpful when large data sets are reported. For example, to describe participant characteristics, we can report them in the text or in a table. The more characteristics to report, the more concise (and clear) it will be to summarize these characteristics in a table and not in the text. Likewise, any data analyses that are relevant to the hypotheses being tested should be described in a table or figure. In the text, you would only refer the reader to that figure or table. For example, you can state, "The groups all showed a significant increase in responding, as shown in Figure 1." The data for this result would then be given in the figure and not in the text.

- Keep the writing focused. In other words, introduce only those ideas and research needed to persuade the reader of the value of your work or research hypotheses. For example, you may hypothesize that integrating technology in the classroom will improve student grades. In your literature review, then, you should review what we know about classrooms that integrate technology, student learning outcomes related to the use of technology, and how that literature relates to the hypotheses you are testing. You should not introduce any ideas or research other than that directly related to your hypothesis. Likewise, you should only display data in a figure or table that are directly related to your hypothesis and otherwise briefly summarize data that are not directly related to your hypothesis. Focused writing makes it easier for the reader to evaluate the value of your work.

- Do not repeat information. When you read over your own work, ask yourself, Does this sentence add information? If not, then delete it. When you introduce more than one study in a single report, ask yourself, Are the procedures in this study different from those I already introduced? If not, then do not introduce the procedures again; instead, refer the reader to where the procedures were originally introduced. For example, suppose you conduct two experiments using the same research design. In Experiment 1, introduce the full research design; for the second experiment, state, "same as those described for Experiment 1" for all procedures that repeat those already introduced. We avoid repetition in writing to make the writing style more concise. Being comprehensive yet concise is important because the space or the number of pages available in printed peer-reviewed journals is limited. To be published in peer-reviewed journals, then, many journal editors require that a manuscript fully describe a study that was conducted while also taking up as few printed pages as possible.

> An APA-style manuscript should clearly state all essential information in as few words as possible.

Be Conservative

As part of any scientific writing style, it is important to be conservative in your claims and interpretations. In other words, do not generalize beyond the data or overstate your conclusions. For example, suppose we observe that girls were significantly more willing to offer to help another child being bullied than boys. An appropriately conservative conclusion is that girls were more helpful in the experimental situation in our study. That is all we observed: helping behavior. We should not generalize beyond these specific observations. In other words, a statement like "Girls were nicer than boys" is inappropriate. We did not measure *niceness;* we measured *helping.* We can speculate about whether or not our observations indicate that girls are nicer than boys, but make it clear that this is just a speculation and that more research is required. As a general rule, do not make claims about anything that you did not directly measure or observe or that others have not directly measured or observed. Be cautious in your writing. The strengths of your study will be in what you observed, so it is your observations, and not your speculations, that should be the focus of your interpretations in a manuscript.

> Do not generalize your claims or interpretations beyond the data or overstate your conclusions.

Be Appropriate and Unbiased

The *Publication Manual* provides detailed guidelines for using appropriate and unbiased language. Some of the guidelines in the *Publication Manual* are given in Table 21.2. The importance of using appropriate and unbiased language is to ensure that you do not offend those who read your work or those who are the subject of your work. For example, in the sixth row of Table 21.2, we find that it is biased to refer to individuals or groups by their disorder. Hence, it is biased to write "A sample of autistic patients was studied" because we are identifying the group by its disorder. Instead, we should write "A sample of patients with autism was studied." It may seem like a subtle change, but in the first sentence, we identified the group as being defined by its disorder, which could be viewed as offensive. In the revised sentence, we identified autism as one characteristic of this group, which is more appropriate and less biased.

> Follow APA guidelines for using unbiased and appropriate language.

Table 21.2 Examples for Using Unbiased Language

Do Not Use	Instead Use
"homosexuals"	"gay men and lesbians"
"sexual preference"	"sexual orientation"
"men" (referring to all adults)	"men and women"
"black" or "white" (referring to social groups)	"Black" or "White" (capitalized)
ethnic labels (e.g., "Oriental")	geographical labels (e.g., "Asian" or "Asian American")
"victims" or "disordered" (to characterize people)	"People with _____" (e.g., "People with autism")
"case"	"patient"
"sex" (referring to a culture or social role)	"gender"
"gender" (referring to biology)	"sex"
"subjects" (referring to humans)	"participants"
"participants" (referring to animals)	"subjects"

Source: Adapted from the *Publication Manual* (APA, 2009).

LEARNING CHECK 2 ✓

1. What is a peer review?

2. Why is it important to be accurate?

3. State four common strategies used to be comprehensive yet concise using APA style.

4. A researcher measured grades on an exam in two classes and concluded that students in Class 2 scored higher and so must have enjoyed the class more. Is this a conservative conclusion? Explain.

5. Why is it important to use appropriate and unbiased language?

21.3 Elements of an APA-Style Manuscript

Using APA style is as much an editorial style as it is a writing style. The elements of an APA-style manuscript are structured so that the manuscript can be readily typeset and converted to a published document. Having a formatting style that is readily converted to a published document is convenient for editors who, upon acceptance following a peer review, will publish the manuscript in their journal. An APA-style manuscript is organized into the following major sections, each of which is described in this section:

- **Title page.** Title page is always the first page and includes a running head, the title, a list of the author or authors, affiliations, and an author note with the contact information of the primary (contact) author.

- **Abstract.** The abstract is always the second page and provides a brief written summary of the purpose, methods, and results of a work or published document in 150 to 250 words.

- **Main body.** The main body begins on page 3 of a manuscript. The main body is divided into subsections and most often includes the following main subheadings: (1) an introduction section that includes a literature review and identification of research hypotheses; (2) a method section that describes the participants, surveys and materials, procedures, and analyses; (3) a results section that fully discloses the data measured and statistical outcomes observed; and (4) a discussion section that provides an evaluation of the design, the data, and the hypotheses.

- **References.** The references page always follows the main body on a new page. All sources cited in the manuscript are listed in alphabetical order in APA format in this section.

- **Footnotes** (if any). Footnotes are used to provide additional content (such as clarification about a procedure or outcome) or acknowledge copyright permissions. Many manuscripts are written without needing a footnotes section; however, if this section is included in the manuscript, then it should immediately follow the references section.

- **Tables** (if any). Tables can be included, often to summarize participant data or data analyses. Each table is given on a separate page after the references section (or after the footnotes section if included). Table captions are included above or below each table on each page.

- **Figures** (if any). Figures can be included, often to summarize data analyses or illustrate a research procedure. Each figure is given on a separate page following the tables. Figure captions are included above or below each figure on each page.

- **Appendices** (if any). In some cases, there may be supplemental materials, such as surveys, illustrations, or instructions for using complex equipment. Many manuscripts are written without needing an appendix; however, if this section is included, then it should be at the end of the manuscript.

In this section, we will review the sections that are most often included in a manuscript: the title page, abstract, main body (introduction, methods and results, and discussion), and references. As an illustration for each section of an APA manuscript, we will use a manuscript that was recently published in a peer-reviewed journal (Ahlgrim-Delzell et al., 2016). For more detailed APA guidelines including creating margins, page numbers, and running heads, refer to Appendix A.1, which gives a complete copy of a full manuscript that is annotated with instructions for using APA style. In addition, an essential guide for using APA style is given in Appendix A.2.

Title Page

The title page allows an editor to identify the individuals and affiliations of those who have significantly contributed to the work being described in the manuscript. This page is often the only page in which authors identify themselves, which can allow editors at many journals to send out a manuscript for an anonymous peer review by omitting the title page before sending the rest of the manuscript to reviewers. All required parts of a title page are illustrated in Figure 21.1.

The title page includes a running head in all capital letters that is a maximum of 50 characters, and the first page number is aligned to the right. All subsequent pages will also have a running head, but the words *Running head* will be omitted. In addition to a running head, we include the title, author or authors, affiliations, and author note, which are centered on the title page. The title should be no more than 12 words, although it can exceed this total if needed to convey important information to the potential reader. The author note should include the contact information for only one author who is deemed the contact author or the author with whom the editor (and readers of the research, if it is published) will correspond regarding the manuscript.

> The title page is the first page of a manuscript and includes the title, authors, affiliations, and author note.

Abstract

The abstract, shown in Figure 21.2, is the second page and provides a brief written summary of the purpose, methods, and results of a work or published document in 150 to 250 words. The words *Running head* are removed from the header on this page and all other pages

Figure 21.1 APA-Style Title Page

Running head: SYSTEMATIC INSTRUCTION OF PHONICS 1

Systematic Instruction of Phonics Skills Using an iPad for Students with Developmental Disabilities Who Are AAC Users

Lynn Ahlgrim-Delzell[1], Ph.D.

Diane M. Browder[1], Ph.D.

Leah Wood[2], Ph.D.

Carol Stanger[3], M.S.

Angela Preston[1], M.Ed.

Amy Kemp-Inman[1], M.M.

1 University of North Carolina at Charlotte

2 California Polytechnic State University

3 The Attainment Company, Inc.

Author Note

Correspondence concerning this article should be addressed to Dr. Lynn Ahlgrim-Delzell, Department of Educational Leadership, University of North Carolina at Charlotte, 9201 University City Blvd, Charlotte, NC 28223-0001. Contact information: 704-687-8636 (W), laahlgri@uncc.edu.

Support for this research was provided in part by Contract ED-IES-11-C-0027 of the U.S. Department of Education, Institute of Education Sciences, awarded to The Attainment Company. The opinions expressed do not necessarily reflect the position or policy of the Department of Education, and no official endorsement should be inferred.

The running head is all capital letters and appears flush left in a header. It is a maximum of 50 characters.

Manuscript pages are numbered at the top right of every page.

The title, author or authors, and affiliations are centered. The title is a maximum of 12 words if possible.

Author Note is centered, and each paragraph below it is indented.

Source: Ahlgrim-Delzell et al. (2016). Reproduced with permission.

of the manuscript. The structure of an abstract can differ depending on the type of study being described. For APA manuscripts that describe primary research (i.e., the conduct of an experiment or research study), the following components should be described in an abstract:

- An opening sentence of the hypothesis or research problem being tested

- A description of participants (e.g., number, sex, or age) if pertinent to outcomes

- The essential structure or procedures of the research design used

- The basic findings, which can include p values, confidence intervals, or effect sizes

- A one- or two-sentence conclusion indicating the implications or applications of the research outcomes

An abstract can be the most important paragraph in your manuscript because many potential readers, if not interested in your research after reading the abstract, will not be likely to read on. For this reason, make sure you use keywords in your abstract that will appeal to potential readers and words you anticipate that potential readers would use as keywords in online searches. Following these suggestions can help get your work noticed by potential readers.

An abstract is a brief summary of the purpose, methods, and results of a work in 150 to 250 words.

Introduction

The introduction begins on page 3 with the title restated on the first line. On the second line, indent the first paragraph and begin the introduction. An introduction must clearly communicate what makes your ideas novel and interesting in about two to three pages. Your ideas should be novel inasmuch as they build on previous research. Your ideas should be interesting inasmuch as they appeal to the readership of the journal you submit to. The structure of an introduction should use the following organization:

- Introduce the problem and explain why it is important to conduct new research to address the problem. For example:
  - "Learning to read is a cornerstone skill in a literate society. Lack of reading skills and exposure to print, including the knowledge shared in print, can lead to long-term consequences including less developed skills in other academic areas (Lonigan, 2006)." In this first sentence of the introduction illustrated in Figure 21.3, we identified the problem (lack of reading skills and exposure to print, including the knowledge shared in print) and why it is important to conduct research to address this problem (can lead to long-term consequences, including less developed skills in other academic areas).

- Integrate previous research that is relevant to the research you are conducting to address the problem. You must thoroughly review the literature and include any and all research that could affect the validity of your claims and the value of your research. Providing appropriate credit is the responsibility of each author

Figure 21.2 An APA-Style Abstract

SYSTEMATIC INSTRUCTION OF PHONICS   2

"Abstract" is centered
on the top line. The
paragraph below it is
not indented.

Abstract

A phonics-based reading curriculum in which students used an iPad to respond was created for students with developmental disabilities not able to verbally participate in traditional phonics instruction due to their use of augmentative and assistive communication. Evidence-based instructional techniques of time delay and a system of least prompts were used in conjunction with text-to-speech software to enable students to participate in phonics instruction. The instruction included phoneme identification, segmenting and decoding words, sight words, blending, and comprehension after reading a short, decodable passage. Students were randomly assigned to a treatment group who received the phonics instruction using an iPad or a comparison group who received sight word instruction on the iPad. A repeated measures ANOVA found that students who received the iPad-based phonics curriculum outperformed the comparison students on phoneme identification, segmenting and decoding words, sight words, and reading comprehension. HLM analysis supports a two-level model with a time by group membership interaction effect, the inclusion of student-level variables not statistically significant. Implications for practice are provided.

Keywords: phonics, time delay, systematic instruction, autism, developmental disability

The body of the
abstract describes
the hypotheses,
participants,
research design,
basic findings, and
implications in 150
to 250 words.

Italicize and center
a list of 4 to 5
keywords.

Source: Ahlgrim-Delzell et al. (2016). Reproduced with permission.

and contributes to the growth of scientific understanding across studies and disciplines. Also keep in mind the following suggestions:

- Do not review the history of your topic; review only those articles that directly affect your claims and research. Do not describe details of those works that are not pertinent to your work.

- Synthesize previous work to compare and contrast what we know about the topic and what gaps are left by the previous research.

- Cite all sources appropriately. In the text, use *and* to separate the last author; in parentheses, use the ampersand symbol (&).

- Although you must be concise in your writing, make sure that your writing can be clearly understood by the audience to which you are writing.

- State the research questions/statements or hypotheses being tested and state how you plan to address the problem in a way that will build upon (not repeat) the literature. For example:

  - "The purpose of the current study was to build on the recommendations of Connor et al. (2014) and the research of Ahlgrim-Delzell et al. (2014) to develop and evaluate phonics instruction that accommodates students who use AAC. Specifically, our research questions were: (1) What are the effects of a phonics curriculum with systematic instruction and an iPad™ on the identification of phonemes and decoding skills by students with developmental disabilities who use ACC [alternative augmentative communication]? and (2) What student or teacher characteristics mediate the changes in growth between students?" In this sentence, in the last paragraph of the introduction for the manuscript illustrated in Figure 21.3, we identified the research questions (the effects of a phonics curriculum and mediation of reading growth by student or teacher characteristics). We also identified how we will build upon the literature (by using students with developmental disabilities who also use AAC). If a hypothesis is used in place of a research question or statement, the rationale for the hypothesis being tested should also be provided.

An introduction states a problem, reviews pertinent literature, and states why the problem is important and how it will be addressed.

Method and Results

The "Method" section immediately follows the introduction. As shown in Figure 21.4, we bold and center "Method" on the line below the last line of the introduction. On the next line we indent and begin the "Method" section. The "Method" section is divided with many subheadings. The specific subheadings will depend on the design of the study, but all studies should include information on the participants, procedures of the study, data collected, and research design. The major subheadings of the Ahlgrim-Delzell et al. (2016) manuscript—"Participants," "Research Design," "Intervention," "Data Analyses," and "Results"—are described here and illustrated in Figure 21.4.

- The "Participants" subheading is flush left and bold, as shown in Figure 21.4. The "Participants" section should include full details of the participants that are needed in the context of the study, such as age/grade, gender, free and reduced-price lunch status, and ethnicity. The specific characteristics of participants can be listed in a table or in the text. Also, state how participants in the sample compare to the target population of interest and how the total number of participants was determined. In nonexperimental studies, the researchers should state which sampling method was used to select the participants. Notice in this subsection that there are descriptions of both teachers and students with another subheading. A secondary level subheading is indented, bold, and followed by a period. The content of the secondary level subsection begins on the same line as the secondary subheading.

- The "Research Design" subheading follows the "Participants" section and is flush left and bold, as shown in Figure 21.4. This section will include the name and brief description of the research design. Different designs will need to provide different types of information. For example, in experimental studies, this section will include a description of assignment of the participants to conditions (e.g., groups). Studies that do not contain a "Research Design" section will need to have a "Procedures" section instead. The "Procedures" section must describe how participants were treated with enough information so as to allow the reader to fully replicate the procedures. Portions of the procedures can be presented apart from the "Procedures" subheading if it makes the writing more concise and easier to follow.

- The "Intervention" subheading follows the "Research Design" section and is flush left and bold, as shown in Figure 21.4. This section should also describe the experimental manipulation or intervention for each condition (e.g., groups) with enough detail as to allow the reader to fully replicate the manipulation/intervention. This information can include who implemented the manipulation/intervention, any training needed for implementers, the number and duration of the manipulation/intervention sessions, and any incentives.

- The "Data Analyses" subheading follows the "Intervention" section and is flush left and bold, as shown in Figure 21.4. This section is not required using APA style; however, it is required by many journals that use APA-style formatting. If this section is required, then indicate the statistical tests and criterion used for each analysis that will be reported in the "Results" section that follows.

- The "Results" heading follows the "Data Analyses" section and is centered and bold, as shown in Figure 21.4. Fully report all statistical outcomes in this section; however, make sure you place particular emphasis on the results that specifically address the research hypothesis being tested. Report the group means and standard deviations of measured outcomes and the test statistic, significance, effect size, and confidence intervals for statistical outcomes using APA style. Be thorough in the exposition of data, yet provide only enough detail in this section to help the reader understand how the outcomes reported relate to the hypotheses that were tested.

Figure 21.3 Excerpt From an APA-Style Introduction

The introduction begins on page 3 with the running head.

The title is centered beginning on line 1.

The introduction begins on the line below the title and is indented.

Systematic Instruction of Phonics Skills Using an iPad for Students with Developmental Disabilities Who Are AAC Users

Learning to read is a cornerstone skill in a literate society. Lack of reading skills and exposure to print, including the knowledge shared in print, can lead to long-term consequences including less developed skills in other academic areas (Lonigan, 2006). The National Reading Panel (NRP, 2000) recommendations for teaching reading identified five essential components: (a) phonemic awareness, (b) phonics, (c) fluency, (d) vocabulary, and (e) text comprehension. The NRP research review, however, did not include research conducted with students with disabilities. This left a void in understanding what and how to teach reading skills to students with developmental disabilities, especially individuals with intellectual disability and autism spectrum disorder.

In contrast to the NRP recommendations, reading research with students with both intellectual disability and autism spectrum disorder has overly emphasized sight words

AAC. In a single-case multiple-probe design across participants, instruction was provided on three phonics skills (letter-sound correspondence, decoding, and blending) and participants were asked to use the AAC device to demonstrate these skills. All three participants improved their phonics skills using the device. In contrast, the AAC device was restrictive due to its fixed surface size and use of overlays that had to be changed manually as the students' phonics skills evolved. Further investigation is needed for the use of computer-based AT that can incorporate more flexible, digital text and formatting. Portable electronic devices, such as tablet computers, are especially promising for increasing motivation and accessibility to instructional content for students with disabilities (Kagohara et al., 2013; Mechling, 2011).

Students with developmental disabilities can learn to read phonetically. Previous research has not examined outcomes for students with developmental disabilities who also use AAC. The purpose of the current study was to build on the recommendations of Connor et al. (2014) and the research of Ahlgrim-Delzell et al. (2014) to develop and evaluate phonics instruction that accommodates students who use AAC. Specifically, our research questions were: (1) What are the effects of a phonics curriculum with systematic instruction and an iPad™ on the identification of phonemes and decoding skills by students with developmental disabilities who use ACC? and (2) What student or teacher characteristics mediate the changes in growth between students?

Source: Ahlgrim-Delzell et al. (2016). Reproduced with permission.

Note: The beginning of the introduction on page 3 and the last paragraph of the introduction on page 7 are shown in the figure.

Figure 21.4   Excerpts From APA-Style "Method" and "Results" Sections

research questions were: (1) What are the effects of a phonics curriculum with systematic instruction and an iPad™ on the identification of phonemes and decoding skills by students with developmental disabilities who use ACC? and (2) What student or teacher characteristics mediate the changes in growth between students?

Center "Method" in bold on the line below the last line of the introduction (not on a separate page).

Method

Place "Participants," flush left and in bold, on the line below the last line of the "Method" section.

Participants

Teachers were recruited by Exceptional Children Department administrators of two school districts in the southeastern region of the United States. Teachers who agreed

Include a "Procedures" or "Research Design" section, flush left and in bold, below the "Participants" section. If portions can be more clearly presented under their own heading—e.g., a description of surveys or, in this case, a setting— then do so before the "Procedures" section as shown.

Setting

The study was implemented from October 2012 to June 2013. Eight of the 16 schools were located in a large, urban district, and eight schools were located in a rural district. Teacher-delivered instruction primarily occu...

Research Design and Random Assignment

This study utilized a randomized control trial (RCT) design where students were randomly assigned to treatment and control conditions using

Add "Data Analyses," flush left and in bold. It is the final section of the method. This section is optional in some journals.

Data Analyses

In order to answer the first research question regarding the effect of the ERSB, a repeated measures analysis of variance (ANOVA) was used to examine the interaction effects of the ERSB instruction and group membership. Cohen's d, using a pooled standard deviation, was calculated to measure the magnitude of the difference between the treatment and control groups at post-test for each of the individual subtests and the total score.

In order to answer the second research question to investigate possible mediating variables, a three-level Hierarchical Linear Model (HLM) was employed. HLM analysis accounts for the effects of nested, or hierarchical, data. In this study, nesting occurred within the individual students, as repeated measures of student data were collected eight times across the school year and each student data were nested within respective teachers. HLM provides an opportunity to examine the influence of each level of the hierarchy on the outcome measure. Three-level models were examined with measurement occasions at Level 1 (across eight monthly measurements), student group membership (treatment vs control) at Level 2, and student/teacher characteristics at Level 3 with total score as the outcome measure.

"Results" is centered in bold. All statistical outcomes are reported in this section.

Results

Descriptive Statistics and ANOVA Results

Prior to running the analyses, data were screened and assumptions were evaluated for use of the parametric statistics. The assumptions of normal distribution and equal group variances were tenable. For the treatment of

Source: Ahlgrim-Delzell et al. (2016). Reproduced with permission.

Discussion

The "Discussion" heading is centered and bolded on the line below the last line of the "Results" section, as shown in Figure 21.5. On the next line, indent the first paragraph and begin the discussion. In the discussion, you will evaluate and interpret the outcomes in your study. Do not use the discussion to restate points that were already made in the manuscript; instead, use the discussion to build upon or facilitate a stronger interpretation and understanding of the problem that was studied. The structure of a discussion should use the following organization:

- Clearly state whether the findings lend support or nonsupport for the research question/statement or hypothesis that was tested. Briefly explain where in the data the support or nonsupport was observed. For example:
  - In the last sentence of the second paragraph of the discussion in Figure 21.5, the authors state a clear message of support and nonsupport for their research hypothesis: "The current study adds to the evidence for the effectiveness of the iPad for teaching phonics skills through the use of a new app that made it possible to manipulate and voice phonemes."
- Give context for how your findings fit with previously published studies (studies that were likely first described in the introduction). For example:
  - In the first paragraph of the discussion in Figure 21.5, the authors give the following explanation for how their results could fit with previously published studies: "This study attempted to address Connor et al.'s (2014) recommendation. . . . This work extends the work of Ahlgrim-Delzell et al. (2014)."
- Identify potential limitations of your research and methods, imprecision of measures that may have biased the pattern of results observed, and any potential threats to internal or external validity. It is important to be conservative; identify what could be improved to make the reader more confident in the findings you observed. For example:
  - As shown in Figure 21.5, the authors identify several potential limitations for their study, including internal threats for history and instrumentation and external threats for participants and situation.
  - Identify potential areas for future research that build upon the findings of the current study. This section is not required using APA style; however, it may be required by many education journals that use APA-style formatting. If this section is required, then provide suggestions that extend the research by identifying other research that can help fill the gap in knowledge not addressed in the current study.
  - As shown in Figure 21.5, the authors provide three areas for future research that include a more in-depth understanding of prompting strategies, reading comprehension, and technology that can be used to improve student reading outcomes.

The "Method" section of this manuscript is divided into four main subheadings (can be further divided into subheadings): "Participants," "Research Design," "Intervention," and "Data Analyses" (may be optional).

- Include in the discussion a "Implications for Practice" section. This section is also not required using APA style; however, it is often required by many education journals that use APA-style formatting. Implications for practice provide a discussion of how the current study can affect classroom education practices. This section is for education practitioners in an attempt to bridge the gap between what we know from research and what is practiced in classrooms.

- As shown in Figure 21.5, the authors provide four implications for classroom practice that include providing students with intellectual disability, developmental delay, or autism spectrum disorder who use AAC with reading instruction (not just sight word memorization); using explicit and systematic instruction; how long it might take to see student progress; and including reading comprehension in reading instruction.

- Provide a brief summary or commentary on the importance of your findings, as shown in the last subsection of the discussion section in Figure 21.5. In a sentence or two, state how your findings are novel (build upon what is known in the literature) and interesting (to the readership of the journal you are submitting to).

References

The "References" heading begins on a separate page after the "Discussion" section. The word *References* is centered and bolded at the top of the page, and each source that was cited in the manuscript is listed in alphabetical order in this section, as shown in Figure 21.6. The appropriate citation for almost any type of source is provided in the *Publication Manual*. The most common sources cited are journal articles, books, book chapters, ERIC documents, and Internet documents. We will describe the appropriate citation for each type of source in this section. For any other type of source, refer to the *Publication Manual*.

To cite a journal article, list the author or authors, year of publication in parentheses, title of the article, name of the journal in italics, volume number in italics, pages in article, and digital object identifier (doi)—in that order. If a doi or an issue number is not available for an in-print article, then each can be omitted. Include the issue number in parentheses after the volume number only if the volumes of a particular journal are not continuously paginated. The volumes for most journals will be a broken into a series of issues over the course of a year (usually four). The page number of the first issue for the year will begin on page 1. The first page of the remaining issues for the volume will begin where the previous issue ended. For example, if the first issue had 55 pages, the second issue will begin on page 56. This is called continuous pagination. If each issue begins on page 1, then include the issue number after the volume number like this: "*50*(2)." The following citation is an example of a journal article reference:

Ahlgrim-Delzell, L., Browder, D. M., Wood, L., Stanger, C., Preston, A., & Kemp-Inman, A. (2016). Systematic instruction of phonics skills using an iPad for students with developmental disabilities who are AAC users. *Journal of Special Education, 50*, 86–97. doi: 10.1177/0022466915622140

> The "Discussion" section is where the author evaluates and interprets how the outcomes in a study relate to the problem or hypothesis that was tested.

Figure 21.5 Excerpts From an APA-Style "Discussion" Section

Center "Discussion" in bold on the line below the last line of the "Results" section.

Provide commentary on the importance of the research findings.

Describe how findings relate to previously published studies.

Include a statement of support/ nonsupport for the hypothesis tested. If there is no hypothesis, answer the research question.

Identify potential limitations and ideas to extend the research.

Many education journals require a section on "Implications for Practice" that describe how the information learned from the study can be used to improve educational outcomes.

Discussion

This study attempted to address Connor et al.'s (2014) recommendation for a comprehensive literacy program that provides for more frequent and intensive instruction in teaching phonics skills to students with low incidence disabilities who use AAC. Specifically, this research extended the literature on phonics instruction for students with intellectual disability/ developmental delay who use AAC by demonstrating that systematic and explicit instruction and iPad technology that provided accessible receptive and expressive response modes such that students were able to manipulate phonemes to learn to decode words to read connected text and answer comprehension questions. This work extends the work of Ahlgrim-Delzell et al. (2014).

While IQ was not part of the eligibility criteria, 10 of the 12 students who received the ERSB curriculum had moderate-to-severe intellectual disability. Several studies have now demonstrated that students with moderate intellectual disability can acquire phonics skills through explicit instructional strategies (Allor et al., 2010a; Browder et al., 2012; Flores et al., 2004). Kagohara et al.'s (2013) comprehensive review of the use of an iPad to teach students with DD identified 15 studies, but none of these focused on phonics instruction. The current study adds to the evidence for the effectiveness of the iPad for teaching phonics skills through the use of a new app that made it possible to manipulate and voice phonemes.

There are potential threats to internal and external validity in this study. Potential threats to internal validity include history and instrumentation. Differential group instructional interruptions such as illnesses or school/classroom scheduling issues (e.g., Special Olympics) could have impacted the ability of teachers to conduct the daily inst... rem... hist... the ... dep...

Other areas for future research include more in-depth understanding of prompting strategies that may be more effective in teaching phonics to students with intellectual disability or developmental delay. Some of the teachers began to hold up a finger while voicing each sound as a visual signal for each phoneme. With this signal, the students

Implications for Practice

A critical implication is that this population of students can achieve more than only sight word recognition. When given access to a technology-based phonics curriculum, including decodable text, students with intellectual disability, developmental delay, or autism spectrum disorder who use AAC may learn to read and understand connected text. Connor et al. (2014) noted that students with intellectual disability need beginning reading instruction for longer periods of time. Research by Allor et al. (2010b) suggested that students with moderate intellectual disability might need three years of instruction for one year of typical

Source: Ahlgrim-Delzell et al. (2016). Reproduced with permission.

Figure 21.6   APA-Style "References" Section

Center "References" on the top line of a separate page.

Each reference is listed in alphabetical order, and the format for each reference is a hanging indent.

Use lower case a and b to indicate multiple publications by the same authors in the same year.

Always use the ampersand (&) symbol for listing the last author of a multiple-author reference.

Use the *Publication Manual* to find the correct citation for any type of reference. Note that all references shown here are for journal articles.

References

Ahlgrim-Delzell, L., Browder, D. M., & Wood, A. L. (2014). Effects of systematic instruction and an augmentative communication device on phonics skills acquisition for students with moderate intellectual disability who are nonverbal. *Education and Training in Autism and Development Disabilities, 49, 517-534.*

Allor, J. H., Mathes, P. G., Roberts, J., Jones, F. G., & Champlin, T. M. (2010a). Teaching students with moderate intellectual disabilities to read: An experimental examination of a comprehensive reading intervention. *Education and Training in Autism and Developmental Disabilities, 45,* 3-22.

Allor, J. H., Mathes, P. G., Roberts, J., Cheatham, J. P., & Champlin, T. M. (2010b). Comprehensive reading instruction for students with intellectual disabilities: Findings from the first three years of a longitudinal study. *Psychology in the Schools, 47,* 445-466.

Bailey, R. L., Angell, M. E., & Stoner, J. B. (2011). Improving literacy skills in students with complex communication needs who use augmentative/alternative communication systems. *Education and Training in Autism and Developmental Disabilities, 46,* 352-368.

Browder, D. M., Ahlgrim-Delzell, L., Courtade, G., Gibbs, S. L., & Flowers, C. (2008). Evaluation of the effectiveness of an early literacy program for students with significant developmental disabilities using group randomized trial research. *Exceptional Children, 75,* 33-52.

Source: Ahlgrim-Delzell et al. (2016). Reproduced with permission.

Some books have authors and other books have editors. To cite a book with authors, list the author or authors, year of publication, title of the book in italics with edition number in parentheses (if applicable, such as "3rd ed."), city and state of publication, and name of the publisher. For example, the following is an APA reference for the most recent edition of the *Publication Manual;* the second reference is for a book publication that is not published in editions:

American Psychological Association. (2009). *Publication manual of the American Psychological Association* (6th ed.). Washington, DC: Author.

Heritage, M., Walqui, A., Linquanti, R., & Hakuta, K. (2015). *English language learners and the new standards: Developing language, content knowledge, and analytical practices in the classroom*. Cambridge, MA: Harvard Education Press.

The "References" section is an alphabetical list of all sources cited in a manuscript.

Many books are edited and not authored, meaning different authors contribute a chapter to a book that is then edited or assembled by a few of those contributors. For an edited book, then, it is very likely that a specific chapter in that book, and not the entire book, was the source you used. To cite a book chapter, list the author or authors of the book chapter, year of publication in parentheses, name of chapter, name of the editor or editors of the book with "Eds." given in parentheses after all names are listed, title of the book in italics, page range of the book chapter in parentheses, city and state of publication, and name of the publisher. If the book chapter is available electronically, then include the doi or uniform resource locator (URL). As an example, the following is a book chapter reference from an edited book:

Powell, R., Cantrell, S., & Correll, P. (2016). "How are we going to be testing that?": Challenges to implementing culturally responsive literacy instruction. In P. R. Schmidt & A. M. Lazar (Eds.), *Reconceptualizing literacy in the new age of multiculturalism and pluralism* (pp. 425–446). Charlotte, NC: Information Age Publishing.

An ERIC document is a resource found using the ERIC database we discussed in Chapter 2. The ERIC database will provide journal articles, books, and other documents. These other documents can be conference presentations, curricula, or other written works with limited circulation. ERIC documents are distinguished from journal articles by using an ED (i.e., ERIC document) number instead of an EJ (i.e., ERIC journal) number. To cite an ERIC document, provide the name of the author or authors, year of publication in parentheses, title of the document in italics, city and state of the publisher, publisher name, and a "retrieved from" statement with the ED number in parentheses. The following is an example of an ERIC document citation:

Plucker, J. A. (2015). *Common Core and America's high-achieving students*. Washington, DC: Thomas B. Fordham Institute. Retrieved from ERIC database. (ED559992)

The Internet can also be a great resource for information needed for a research study. You will want to make sure that the website from which you find an important resource is an organization that you trust like a professional educational organization or a government-sponsored webpage such as the Institute of Education Sciences (https://ies.ed.gov/). You may find books or published articles on these sites and you will cite them as a book or journal article. An Internet resource is one where the document is only found on the Internet site. To cite an Internet source, provide the author's or authors' name(s), year of publication in parentheses, title of the document in italics, city and state of the publisher, publisher name, and a "retrieved from" statement that includes the URL where the document is located. The publisher is the name of the organization that provided the document on its website. The

URL can be copied and pasted since they can sometimes be very long. The following is an example of an Internet source citation. Notice that the "retrieved from statement" does not include the date it was retrieved. Previous editions of APA did include the date the document was retrieved, but it was eliminated from the most current edition of the APA publication manual. In this example, the author is the publisher. Also notice that when you copy and paste the URL next to the "retrieved from statement," it may automatically fall on the next line if it is too long to fit on the same line as the "retrieved from statement."

> Council for Exceptional Children. (2015). *What every special educator must know: Professional ethics and standards.* Arlington, VA: CEC. Retrieved from http://www.cec.sped.org/~/media/Files/Standards/Professional%20 Ethics%20and%20Practice%20Standards/Code%20of%20Ethics.pdf

LEARNING CHECK 3 ✓

1. What is the maximum number of characters for a running head? What is the maximum number of words for a title?

2. What is the word limit for an abstract?

3. True or false: All manuscripts will have the same heading in the "Method" section.

4. What are the four main sections of the main body of an APA-style manuscript?

5. In what order and with what type of formatting are references listed in a references section?

Answers: 1. The maximum is 50 characters for a running head and 12 words for a title; 2. Between 150 and 250 words; 3. False; 4. Introduction, Methods, Results, and Discussion sections; 5. References are listed in alphabetical order using a hanging indent format.

21.4 Literature Reviews

An APA-style manuscript is typically written to report the findings of primary research, which is research conducted by the authors of a manuscript. However, it is also common to report on a review of literature in the form of a synthesis of previous articles or as a meta-analysis. These types of reports, called **literature review articles,** are often submitted for publication in peer-reviewed journals as well. Because a literature review article follows a different organization from reports of primary research, we will introduce the unique organization of a literature review article in this section.

> A **literature review article** is a written comprehensive report of findings from previously published works about a problem in the form of a synthesis of previous articles or as a meta-analysis.

A literature review article is a written comprehensive report of findings from previously published works in a specified area of research in the form of a synthesis of previous articles or as a meta-analysis. A literature review article can be chosen by research area (e.g., reading comprehension) or by a specific theme in an area of research (e.g., technology-aided interventions and instruction for adolescents with autism spectrum disorder). The goal of a literature review article is to organize, integrate, and evaluate published works about a problem and to consider progress made toward clarifying that problem.

To write a literature review article, we include a title page, an abstract, a literature review (main body), and references. If footnotes, tables, figures, or appendices are included, then we can place them at the end of the manuscript following the references section using the same order introduced in Section 21.3. Two sections in a literature review article that differ from a manuscript or report of primary research are the abstract and the main body. In the abstract, identify the problem and give a synopsis of the evaluations made in the literature review using the same formatting and word count limits identified in Section 21.3. To write the main body, use the following organization:

- Identify the problem and how it will be evaluated. Identify the topic, keywords used to search for articles in that topic, and what search engines you used to find articles. Identify anything in your method of selecting articles that could bias the evaluations made in the literature review.

- Integrate the literature to identify the state of the research. In other words, identify what is known and what is not known. Be clear on how far we have advanced on an understanding of the problem being reviewed.

- Identify how findings and interpretations in the published literature are related or consistent or are inconsistent, contradictory, or flawed. How confident can we be in what is known? For a meta-analysis, report effect sizes for the findings of many studies. Be critical of the samples used, the research designs implemented, and the data and interpretations made to address the problem.

- Consider the progress made in an area of research and potential next steps toward clarifying the problem. Identify what is not known and possible methods or advancements in technology that could be used to clarify the problem further.

A literature review article organizes, integrates, and evaluates published works about a problem and considers progress made toward clarifying that problem.

The main body or literature review is the primary section of a literature review article. The entire review of the literature is contained in this one section. The main body or literature portion of the manuscript can have any headings and subheadings to organize the ideas and evaluations presented in the review. Major headings should be bold and flush left, with the text for that section beginning on the line below the major heading. In all, we can use the analogy of a puzzle to describe a literature review: It is an attempt to fit many puzzle pieces together, with the many articles published in a given area of research being the puzzle pieces in this analogy.

21.5 Reporting Observations in Qualitative Research

In Chapter 10, we introduced the qualitative research design as a method used to make nonnumeric observations, from which conclusions are drawn without the use of statistical analysis. The implication of not using statistical analysis is that the "Results" section in an APA-style manuscript is replaced with an "Analysis" section. A "Results" section in a quantitative study reports the statistical outcomes of the measured data; an "Analysis" section in a qualitative study provides a series of interpretations and contributes a new perspective or generates the possibility that many different perspectives can explain the observations made. For a qualitative analysis, then, the "Analysis" section is written as a narrative and not as a report of statistical outcomes.

Qualitative research is typically not directed by a hypothesis. In other words, researchers do not state a hypothesis and then limit their observations to measure only phenomena that are related to that hypothesis. Instead, qualitative researchers often use interviews, participant observation techniques, and field notes and allow participants to ask their own questions during the time that participants are observed. To analyze observations that are descriptive (i.e., written in words) and often guided by the questions that participants ask, researchers evaluate the *trustworthiness* of their observations, as introduced in Chapter 10 (see Table 10.4). While certainly not an exhaustive list of differences, the following are two key differences in writing an APA-style manuscript for qualitative versus quantitative research:

- The introduction and the "Method" section in a qualitative report argue ways of examining a problem in a way that often leaves open many alternatives that were anticipated or not anticipated by the authors. This is unlike quantitative research in which the introduction narrows in on one or more stated hypotheses upon which the "Method" section outlines what will be observed to test those hypotheses.

- In a qualitative report, a narrative is constructed in an "Analysis" section to describe what was observed. A "Discussion" section, then, evaluates possible explanations for those observations with little effort to generalize beyond the specific observations made. This is unlike quantitative research in which statistical outcomes are reported in a "Results" section, and a "Discussion" section focuses on whether the data showed support or nonsupport for the hypotheses tested.

> The "Results" section in an APA-style manuscript is replaced with an "Analysis" section for qualitative research designs.

For most qualitative research, the goal is to describe the experiences of an individual or a small group. The structure of the manuscript, then, takes the form of a narrative that leaves open many possible explanations and evaluates the extent to which those observations are trustworthy.

21.6 Ethics in Focus: Credit and Authorship

Authorship of a peer-reviewed work is a great achievement. In education, we expect the order of authorship to reflect the relative contributions of those listed as authors. The first author of a manuscript is the individual who contributed the most, with each subsequent author making relatively fewer contributions. Authors listed on the title page of a manuscript should be listed in order of their "relative scientific or professional contributions" (APA, 2009, p. 11) to the work being submitted to an editor or reviewer and not based on their status or institutional position.

The challenges of authorship are in defining what constitutes "relative scientific or professional contributions." Is it the person who conducted the research, wrote the manuscript, developed the research hypothesis, or created the research design? Is it about the relative value of the ideas shared to contribute to the work, or is it in the time spent to complete the work? There is no one answer that can resolve what constitutes more or less "relative scientific or professional contributions." The APA suggests that to resolve any concerns regarding authorship, all potential authors should talk about publication credit as early as possible. Agreeing on the order of authorship prior to completing the work can facilitate less disagreement regarding the order of authorship later in the publication process.

LEARNING CHECK 4 ✓

1. What is the goal of a literature review?

2. What is reported in an "Analysis" section for a qualitative research study?

3. According to the APA, authors listed on the title page of a manuscript should be listed in order of their_____.

Answers: 1. The goal of a literature review is to organize, integrate, and evaluate published works about a problem and to consider progress made toward clarifying that problem; 2. An "Analysis" section in a qualitative study provides, in narrative form, a series of interpretations and contributes or generates a new perspective the possibility that many different perspectives can explain the observations made; 3. relative scientific or professional contributions.

21.7 Presenting a Poster

A **poster** is a concise description of a research study in the form of a display of text boxes, figures, and tables on a single large page.

A **poster session** is a 1- to 4-hour time slot during which many authors stand near their poster ready and open to answer questions or talk about their work with interested attendees.

Aside from writing a manuscript, researchers and professionals often communicate by presenting a poster, which is a concise description of a research study in a display of text boxes, figures, and tables shown on a single large page. A poster is an eye-catching and engaging display that is typically presented during a poster session at a professional conference, such as those held annually by the American Educational Research Association or at smaller venues. A poster session is a 1- to 4-hour time slot during which many authors stand near their poster ready and open to answer questions or talk about their work with interested attendees. To present a poster, you must submit an abstract of your work before the submission deadline of a conference. Upon acceptance of the abstract, you will receive a poster session time to present your poster.

Poster sessions can be exciting because researchers often present their most current work—so current that it has yet to be published in a peer-reviewed journal. For this reason, poster sessions can often give researchers a preview of the type of research that could be published in the coming year and generate many new ideas and directions for advancing research. Although thousands of poster sessions are held each year, the APA does not provide specific guidelines for creating posters. For this reason, the display of posters at conferences and professional meetings can vary quite a bit from poster to poster. Although the APA does not provide specific guidelines, we can identify many strategies you can use to get your poster noticed using the following suggestions adapted, in part, from Becker (2014):

- Keep the title short. The title should clearly identify the topic of your poster and should be the largest font size you use. If needed, shorten the title in order to increase the font size of the title.

- Do not use a small font size, and use a constant font type. The font size should not be smaller than 20-point font, and the font type should be the same for the entire poster (except possibly the title). Larger font size and constant font type is good because it makes a poster easy to read from at least 4 feet away.

- Use colorful figures and borders. A colorful display is eye-catching; however, keep the color simple by using solid colors throughout.

- Display the logo for your school affiliation (optional). Displaying your school logo is a point of pride and a way to advertise to others where the research was conducted.

- Place each text box or section in a logical order. The sections in a poster include the title, the abstract or overview, the method and results, figures and tables, conclusions or implications, and a list of key references. Try to organize each section, moving from left to right, in the same way that it would be presented in an APA-style manuscript.

- Make sure the poster takes less than 5 minutes to read. A poster does not need to be comprehensive; it needs to give enough information such that the reader can understand the gist of what you did and what you found.

- Avoid technical jargon. Do not assume that everyone in the audience is an expert. Avoid using words that are specific to your area of research, or if you do use these words, then define them in your poster. Make the poster accessible to a large audience.

- Always stand near the poster but not directly in front of it. Stay near the poster to let people know that you are available to answer questions or talk about what you did, and stand away from it so that all patrons can clearly see the poster. Also, wait for the audience to address you with questions, and be respectful when you do respond to questions.

- Bring supportive materials, such as reprints or a printed copy of the poster itself, to give to attendees. This gives people something to bring home that will remind them of the poster you presented. Also, bring business cards so people can contact you if they have any follow-up questions after the poster session.

Most authors now use a single slide on Microsoft PowerPoint to create their poster. Directions for using this software to create a poster are given in Appendix A.3. Sample posters that have been presented at professional conferences are also provided in Appendix A.3. Learning how to create a poster and following the suggestions provided in this section can help you make a strong impression at a poster session.

> Researchers can present a poster during a poster session at a conference or professional meeting.

21.8 Giving a Professional Talk

The third method of communication introduced in this chapter is a professional talk. A talk is typically given in a formal setting. Graduate students often present their current work in brown-bag sessions to members of their department. At a doctoral level, researchers can be invited to present their work in a talk at conferences and professional meetings. The advantage of giving a talk is that the presenter is likely the only presenter or one of only a few presenters for the hour or so that the talk is given. In contrast, hundreds or thousands of authors present a poster in a single poster session. For this reason, giving a professional talk can be a great way to reach an engaged audience and promote your research, identify the scientific merits of your research, and even get people excited about your research.

There are many good suggestions for giving a professional talk. The following is a list of eight suggestions for giving an effective talk:

- Arrive early and be prepared. Being on time is the same as being late. You will need time to prepare, practice, and set up any technology, such as Microsoft PowerPoint, needed to give the talk. As a general rule, always arrive about 30 minutes early to make sure everything is prepared so that you can start on time. If the talk is at a conference where your time is immediately after another speaker, arrive before the previous session has ended and wait outside the room until the audience begins to leave. You will typically have 10 to 15 minutes between sessions to prepare.

- Dress appropriately. Be aware of the audience and forum in which you are presenting. Try not to overdress (too formal) or underdress (too informal), but when in doubt, overdress.

- Introduce yourself and any colleagues who are presenting with you. Begin any talk with a brief introduction. State your name(s), affiliation(s), and general area of interest in an effort to relate to the audience and help the listeners understand who you are.

- Begin with an attention-grabber. A great talk captures the attention of an audience. Begin with a story, a short video clip, an exercise, a demonstration, or fun facts that get the audience interested to hear more. For example, if you give a talk on a classroom practice, you could begin by showing a video clip of the practice or by describing how or why you became interested in the practice.

- Use technology to facilitate your talk; do not read from it. Many presentations are given using Microsoft PowerPoint. Do not read the slides verbatim; it reflects poorly on your preparedness and level of understanding of the topic of your talk. Instead, use only a few bulleted words on each slide, talk in your own words, and refer only to the slides as a reference for the order in which you present the topics of your talk. The more you engage the audience (and not the slides), the more effective the talk will be.

- Keep the talk focused. A talk is typically given within a specified time limit that is usually not more than 1 hour. Practice giving your talk often and keep to that script as close as possible during the talk. Stay on topic so that you can stay on time. If an audience member asks an off-topic question or a question that will take too much time to answer, then let him or her know that the question is important to you and that it may be best to answer that question at the end of the talk. This allows you to show respect for the audience member and also allows you to keep the talk on topic and on time.

- Follow through with questions. Many questions can be answered during or immediately after a talk. However, if you do not know an answer to a question or did not get a chance to answer a specific question, then offer to take down the contact information of the person who asked the question so that you can follow up later to answer his or her question. Make sure you follow through.

- Always end with references and acknowledgments. The speaker may have been invited to talk, and many people often help a speaker prepare a talk, so these people should be acknowledged. In addition, any work cited in the talk should be recognized at the end of the talk. If the talk is given using Microsoft PowerPoint slides, then the final slide should list the references and acknowledgments.

The best advice of all is to relax and enjoy the moment. Public speaking tends to be stressful for many people. Breathe deeply, squeeze a stress ball, or tell yourself a joke. Do anything to relax and overcome any anxiety or stress you may be experiencing prior to a talk. For most talks, the audience is voluntary, so by being present at your talk, your listeners have already expressed an interest in your topic. Following the guidelines described in this section, you can give a talk that appeals to your audience and allows you to present yourself as an authoritative, yet engaged, speaker.

1. What is a poster session?

2. What guidelines does the APA provide for creating a poster?

3. What is the advantage of giving a professional talk compared to presenting a poster?

CHAPTER SUMMARY

LO 1 Identify three methods of communication among scientists.

- Three methods of communication among scientists are to publish a manuscript, present a poster, and give a talk.

LO 2 Describe three elements of communication.

- Three elements in communication are the speaker or author, the audience, and the message. The speaker or author uses first person and third person appropriately; uses past, present, and future tense appropriately; uses an impersonal writing style; reduces biased language; and gives credit where appropriate. The audience includes scientists and professionals, college students, and the general public. The message should be novel (contribute new findings or new ideas), interesting (to the readership of the work), and informative.

LO 3 Apply APA writing style and language guidelines for writing a manuscript.

- To submit a work for consideration for publication in a peer-reviewed journal, we prepare an APA-style manuscript using the writing style format described in the *Publication Manual*. Four writing and language guidelines for writing an APA-style manuscript are to be accurate, comprehensive yet concise, conservative, and appropriate. To be comprehensive yet concise, apply the following suggestions: Abbreviate where appropriate, display data in a figure or table, keep the writing focused, and do not repeat information.

LO 4 Apply APA formatting requirements for writing a manuscript.

- An APA-style manuscript is formatted or organized into the following major sections: title page, abstract, main body (includes introduction, methods, results, and discussion), references, footnotes (if any), tables (if any), figures (if any), and appendices (if any).

- A title page is on page 1 and includes the title, authors, affiliations, and author note. On page 2, the abstract provides a brief written summary of the purpose, methods, and results of a work or published document in 150 to 250 words. On page 3, the main body begins with the title on line 1, and the introduction begins on line 2. The introduction states a problem and why it is important to address, reviews the pertinent literature, and states how the problem will be addressed. The "Method" section can be divided into many different subheadings depending on the study, but all manuscripts should contain four main areas: participants, procedures of the study, data collected, and research design. The "Results" section will describe the findings of the study through statistical analyses. The "Discussion" section evaluates and interprets how the outcomes in a study relate to the problem that was tested. The "References" section, which begins on a new page, is an alphabetical list of all sources cited in a manuscript.

LO 5 Apply APA guidelines for writing and organizing a literature review article.

- A literature review article is a written comprehensive report of findings from previously published works about a problem in the form of a synthesis of previous articles or as a meta-analysis. To write the main body of a literature review:
  - Identify the problem and how it will be evaluated.
  - Integrate the literature to identify the state of the research.
  - Identify how findings and interpretations in the published literature are related or consistent or are inconsistent, contradictory, or flawed.
  - Consider the progress made in an area of research and potential next steps toward clarifying the problem.

LO 6 Delineate how results are reported for a qualitative versus a quantitative research design.

- The "Results" section is replaced with an "Analysis" section in a qualitative research study, which provides a series of interpretations and contributes a new perspective or generates the possibility that many different perspectives can explain the observations made. The "Analysis" section is written as a narrative and not as a report of statistical outcomes.

- In a qualitative report, the introduction and the "Method" section argue ways of examining a problem in a way that often leaves open many alternatives that were anticipated or not anticipated by the authors. In the "Analysis" section, a narrative is used to describe what was observed, and the "Discussion" section evaluates possible explanations for those observations with little effort to generalize beyond the specific observations made.

LO 7 State APA guidelines for identifying the authorship of published scientific work.

- According to the APA, authors listed on the title page of a manuscript should be listed in order of their "relative scientific or professional contributions." The APA suggests that to resolve any concerns regarding authorship, all potential authors should talk about publication credit as early as possible.

LO 8 Identify guidelines for effectively presenting a poster.

- A **poster** is a concise description of a research study in the form of a display of text boxes, figures, and tables on a single large page. A poster is presented at a conference or professional meeting in a **poster session,** which is a 1- to 4-hour time slot during which many authors stand near their poster ready and open to answer questions or talk about their work with interested attendees.

- The APA does not provide specific guidelines for creating and presenting posters; however, using the following suggestions is advisable: Keep the title short, do not use small font size and use a constant font type, use colorful figures and borders, display the logo for your school affiliation, place each text box or section in a logical order, make sure the poster takes less than 5 minutes to read, avoid technical jargon, always stand near the poster but not directly in front of it, and bring supportive materials.

LO 9 Identify guidelines for effectively giving a professional talk.

- Giving a professional talk can be a great way to promote your research and get people excited about your work. The following is a list of eight suggestions for giving an effective talk: Arrive early and be prepared, dress appropriately, introduce yourself, begin with an attention-grabber, use technology to facilitate your talk, keep the talk focused, follow through with questions, and always end with references and acknowledgments.

KEY TERMS

APA-style manuscript 621	peer review 620	poster session 642
literature review article 639	poster 642	

REVIEW QUESTIONS

1. State three methods of communication among scientists.

2. State three elements of communication.

3. Scientific journals use a peer review process to determine whether to accept or reject a manuscript for publication. What is peer review?

4. State the writing and language guideline for writing an APA-style manuscript (be accurate, be comprehensive yet concise, be conservative, or be appropriate) that is described by each of the following:

   A. Proofread your manuscript before submitting it.

   B. Abbreviate where appropriate.

   C. Do not generalize beyond the data.

   D. Capitalize the word *Black* or *White* to refer to a social or ethnic group.

5. State the major sections in an APA-style manuscript in order of how each section should appear in the manuscript.

6. A researcher reports that students spent significantly more time attending to a passage given in color than when it was presented in black and white, $t(30) = 4.16, p < .05$. In which section of an APA-style manuscript do we report this outcome?

7. What information is conveyed in the introduction of an APA-style manuscript?

8. What is the goal of a literature review?

9. At what stage in the publication process should potential authors talk about publication credit?

10. How should the sections in a poster be organized, moving from left to right?

ACTIVITIES

1. Conduct a literature search and choose one article that interests you. After reading the article, write a three- to four-page paper that identifies whether each of the following was a strength or weakness in the introduction and discussion of the article, and give an example to support each argument:

   A. Did the introduction: Describe the problem and explain why it is important to conduct new research to address the problem? Integrate previous research that is relevant to the research conducted to address the problem? State the hypotheses being tested and the research design being used to address the problem?

   B. Did the discussion: State whether the findings lend support or nonsupport for the hypothesis that was tested? Give context for how the findings fit with previously published studies? Identify potential limitations of the research and methods, imprecision of measures that may have biased the pattern of results observed, and any potential threats to internal or external validity? Provide a broad summary or commentary on the importance of the findings?

2. Conduct a literature review and find one article that interests you. Create a poster for the study that is described in the article by applying the suggestions introduced for creating posters in Section 21.7.

$\circledS$ SAGE edge™

SAGE edge offers a robust online environment featuring an impressive array of free tools and resources for review, study, and further exploration, keeping both instructors and students on the cutting edge of teaching and learning.

Access practice quizzes, eFlashcards, video, and multimedia at edge.sagepub.com/priviterarme.

APPENDIX A

APA-Style Writing, Sample Manuscript, and Posters

A.1 Essentials for Writing APA-Style Papers

Writing an APA-style manuscript can be challenging and intimidating for many students. Whether submitting a paper for publication or for a class assignment, following APA guidelines is important for helping you to become a better writer. Writing an APA-style manuscript for a class is more than just an assignment—being proficient can help you well beyond the classroom. APA guidelines are widely accepted rules for writing proficiently and are used across disciplines. Understanding and applying these guidelines is therefore a worthwhile endeavor.

APA guidelines provided in the *Publication Manual of the American Psychological Association* (APA, 2009), which we refer to hereafter as the *Publication Manual*, cover many aspects of writing style, and these guidelines are not always conventional. As one example, in the English language, the word *data* can be treated as singular (e.g., the data *is* compelling) or plural (e.g., the data *are* compelling). Although the singular usage of this word is widely used in the United States, the APA treats *data* as the plural of *datum* (as defined in Chapter 1). Keeping up with these many guidelines can be difficult—yes, even for scientists.

This appendix provides a useful guide for following some of the most essential rules provided in the *Publication Manual*. Obviously, you should always refer to the *Publication Manual* if you have any questions, but this guide alone can help you effectively gain points and score better on your APA papers because it summarizes many common issues related to APA writing style and language. This summary is based on feedback from dozens of professors across the country, and it is focused on the areas in writing where students often lose the most points. So please photocopy this guide, highlight it, laminate it, and refer to it as you write your papers.

Note: The information provided in these notes is based on the writing style provided in the *Publication Manual* (APA, 2009). These notes provide the essentials for writing just about any type of research report using the APA writing style format, but they are not a substitute for the *Publication Manual*. If there is any doubt regarding APA writing style, please consult the *Publication Manual*.

Abbreviations

The use of abbreviations is largely the judgment of the author. Overuse can make the text too confusing, and underuse can make the text less concise.

LATIN ABBREVIATIONS

Use abbreviations in parentheses. Use English translations in text. One exception is made for *et al.* (and others) when citing a source (e.g., "Privitera et al. (2013) showed . . . "). Examples with translations include the following:

cf. (compare)	i.e. (that is)	viz. (namely)
e.g. (for example)	vs. (versus)	etc. (and so forth)

UNITS OF MEASUREMENT AND TIME

The following units of time should never be abbreviated: day, week, month, and year. With units of time, abbreviate *hour* (hr), *minute* (min), *millisecond* (ms), *nanosecond* (ns), and *second* (s). Use an abbreviation when a number accompanies a measure (e.g., 5 m) but not without (e.g., "measured in meters"). Report measurements in metric units (e.g., not inches or feet). Do not add *s* for plural units (e.g., 5 meters is 5 m). More examples include the following:

mm (millimeter)	cm (centimeter)	lb (pound)
p.m. (post meridiem)	ml (milliliter)	L (liter)
a.m. (ante meridiem)	g (gram, gravity)	mg (milligram)

Never begin a sentence with a lowercase abbreviation (such as *e.g.*) or a symbol that stands alone (such as α).

Use of Numbers

Use numerals to express the following:

1. Numbers 10 and above and decimals (e.g., 0.25): Use a zero before decimals unless it is a value that cannot be greater than 1 (e.g., correlations and proportions).

2. All numbers in the abstract.

3. Numbers that represent a fractional or decimal quantity, proportion, percentile, or mathematical function (e.g., "8% of students" or "4 times more likely").

4. Time (e.g., 1 hr or 11:00 a.m.), dates (e.g., January 1, 2000), age (e.g., 3-month-olds), scores on a scale (e.g., "mean score was 3 on a 5-point scale"), and exact sums of money (e.g., $4.12).

5. Numbers that indicate a specific row or column in a table (e.g., "row 2 column 1") or that are placed in a numbered series (Figure 1 or rank 1).

6. A list of four or more numbers (e.g., "students viewed 0, 2, 4, or 8 objects").

Use words to express the following:

1. Numbers below 10, except when displayed in a figure or table, or preceding a unit of measurement (e.g., 5 m).

2. Approximations for days, months, and years (e.g., "about two days ago" or "almost three months ago").

3. Common fractions when used as adjectives (e.g., two-thirds majority).

Periods, Commas, and Capitalization

Do not use periods to abbreviate units of measurement, time, routes of administration (e.g., IV indicates intravenous), degree titles (e.g., MA, PhD), or organization titles (e.g., APA).

Do not use commas to separate parts of a measure (e.g., 2 lb 4 oz). Use commas before the final conjunction in lists (e.g., time, money, and resources), with numbers larger than three digits (e.g., 1,000), with a reference citation (e.g., Privitera, 2016), with exact dates (e.g., "March 30, 2015," but not "March 2015"), and for lists within the text (e.g., "choices were (a) low, (b) moderate, and (c) high").

Capitalize nouns preceding a number but not preceding a variable (e.g., Session 1 or session x); capitalize references to specific terms or groups (e.g., write "the control group," but also write "Control Group A," or write "the independent variables," but also write "Independent Variable 1"); capitalize the first word following a colon only if the clause that follows is a complete sentence (e.g., "They identified two potential causes: One cause was environmental, and the second was biological"), and capitalize all words of four letters or more in a heading, subheading, or title (e.g., "Research Methods for the Behavioral Sciences").

Hyphens and Prefixes

Hyphens for compound words (e.g., using *makeover*, *make over*, or *make-over*) and prefixes can be tricky. Refer to the dictionary when in doubt. APA style follows *Webster's Collegiate* in most cases. Also, use the Grammar Guide provided in the study guide that accompanies this book.

The following prefixes will require a hyphen: *all-* (e.g., all-knowing), *ever-* (e.g., ever-present), *quasi-* (e.g., quasi-experimental), *half-* (e.g., half-witted), *ex-* (e.g., ex-girlfriend), and *self-* (e.g., self-fulfilling).

Avoiding Biased Language

The general rule here is to avoid language that may be perceived as offensive. Use a respectful tone (e.g., "Smith et al. did not account for . . .," not "Smith et al. completely ignored . . ."). Use *subjects* when referring to animals observed in a study; use *participants* to refer to humans observed in a study.

Refer to the Guidelines for Unbiased Language at www.apastyle.org/manual/supplement as a more complete guide.

GENDER

Gender is a cultural term referring to social roles; *sex* refers to biology. Avoid sexist bias (e.g., referring to "the nurse" as "she" or using *fireman* instead of *firefighter*).

AGE

Always report an age range (e.g., "17 to 24 years," not "under 24 years"). *Boy* and *girl* are used to refer to persons under the age of 12 years. *Young man* and *young woman* are used to refer to persons aged 13–17 years. *Man* and *woman* are used to refer to adults 18 years or older, and the term *older person* is preferred to *elderly* when referring to persons over 65 years of age.

SEXUALITY

Use *gay men* and *lesbians* or *bisexual individuals*, not *homosexuals*. Use *sexual orientation*, not *sexual preference*.

ETHNICITY

Capitalize *Black* and *White* when referring to social groups. Use geographic locations, not ethnic labels (e.g., use *Asian* or *Asian American*, not *Oriental*). When possible, identify persons by nation of origin (e.g., *Chinese, Japanese, Korean*).

DISABILITIES

Avoid language that objectifies a person's condition (e.g., *autistic, dyslexic, bedridden*). Avoid negative labels (e.g., *disordered*) and slurs (e.g., *retard, cripple*). Place the focus on the individual, not the disability (e.g., say "persons with dyslexia," not "dyslexics").

Data and Statistics

Do not present the equation for a statistic in common use (e.g., a t statistic). If it is uncommon and essential to the paper, then write it in line with the text when possible.

The descriptive statistics (e.g., mean, standard deviation) should enhance the informativeness of the paper—so they should allow a reader to determine the effect size or confidence interval, if possible.

If descriptive statistics are given in a table or figure, do not restate them in the text, but indicate in which table or figure they are given.

Means in the text are reported as M (SD) or $M \pm SD$. Do not use the symbol M in text (e.g., say "the means were . . .," not "the Ms were . . . ").

To report a statistic (e.g., *t* test or *F* test), include enough information for the reader to fully understand the analysis. The information needed varies from statistic to statistic.

The general form for reporting an inferential statistic is "statistic (*df*) = obtained value, *p* value." Always include a space after an arithmetic operator and sign (e.g., =, <, >, +, −).

If the test is one-tailed, then indicate this in parentheses following the *p* value. Include an estimate for effect size when possible for significant effects.

To report a confidence interval, state "([percentage] CI [lower limit, upper limit])"—for example, "(95% CI [1.2, 3.5])." The level of confidence (i.e., the percentage) must be clearly stated.

N typically indicates the total number of subjects or participants in a study, whereas *n* typically indicates the number in each group (or limited portion) of the sample.

Use the symbol for percent when followed by a numeral (e.g., "30% of the variance . . . "); use *percentage* when a number is not given (e.g., "the percentage of time . . . ").

Quotations and Italics

Use double quotation marks (e.g., "text") to

1. Introduce ironic, slang, or coined terms (e.g., It was a "normal" day). However, only use quotation marks the first time the word is used.

2. Include the title of an article or chapter of a book in the text (e.g., The author of the article "Probability Theory" makes some interesting points . . .).

3. Reproduce test material verbatim (e.g., The item was "How often do you _____?").

Use italics to

1. Identify the anchors for a scale (e.g., "Ratings were given from 1 (*not at all*) to 5 (*all the time*)").

2. Cite a linguistic example (e.g., "This study distinguishes between *fair* and *equal* treatment of . . . ").

3. Introduce technical jargon (e.g., "The frequency of *token count* words . . . ").

4. Include the title of a book in the text (e.g., "The author of the book *Research Methods for the Behavioral Sciences* is developing . . . ").

Block quotations are given in a separate paragraph for quotations of 40 or more words. Do not place block quotations in quotation marks. For example:

Privitera (2015) explains the following:

Success is really not something you can easily measure; it is an outcome that is inherent to the dreams and expectations within our mind. What we imagine in our mind as being successful is our own success—no one else can define success for you, except you. (p. 193)

Use single quotation marks (e.g., 'text') within double quotation marks for text that was enclosed in double quotation marks in the original source (e.g., Privitera (2015) believes that "It is important for students to 'become extraordinary' by striving to achieve things they never thought possible" (p. 193)).

Citations in Text

- For a single author, the surname and year must be cited if referencing another work (e.g., "Kelly (2006) found . . ." or "In 2006, Kelly found . . .").

- For two authors, the surname for each author and the year must be stated each time a work is cited in the text (e.g., "Jones and Smith (2010) initiated . . ." or "In 2010, Jones and Smith initiated . . .").

- For three to five authors, the surname for each author and the year must be stated the first time. Any other citation should state the first author followed by *et al.* and the year (e.g., for the first citation state, "Woods, Peters, and Martin (2007) found . . .," and for all remaining citations, state, "Woods et al. (2007) found . . .").

- For six or more authors, all citations give the surname of the first author followed by *et al.* and then the year.

- When multiple first authors are cited in the same parentheses, they should appear in alphabetical order by the first author's surname (not by publication year), in the same way that they appear in the reference list (e.g., " . . . and this hypothesis has support (Albert, 2003; Jonas, 1999; Jones, 2007)").

- Cite two or more works by the same author in order of publication year. Do not restate the author's name for each citation within parentheses (e.g., Walter, 2003, 2007).

- Use alphabetical suffixes (e.g., a, b, c) to differentiate between works published in the same year by the same author (e.g., Douglas 2000a, 2000b).

- For works that have been accepted for publication but not yet published, state "in press" for the publication year.

- To cite a specific portion of a work (e.g., pages, chapter, figure, or table), include the additional information (e.g., Hughes et al., 2006, p. 32).

- To cite a source secondhand (meaning that you got the citation from another source and not the original), make this clear by stating "as cited in" (e.g., "According to Karl Popper (1959), as cited in Platt (1964), there is no such thing as proof in science").

- Cite a personal communication (e.g., e-mail, personal interview, or phone call) in the text only, not in the reference list. Include the name of the communicator and the exact date if possible (e.g., R. J. Smith, personal communication, June 12, 2001).

Note that material that is *reprinted* appears in its exact original form; material that is *adapted* is modified to make it suitable for a new purpose.

Citations in a Reference List

All references cited in the text must be cited in a reference list at the end of a paper or article (except personal communications, because these are regarded as "unrecoverable data").

Reference lists are not numbered and are listed in alphabetical order by letter. For this ordering, a space precedes a letter (e.g., Mann, W. J., precedes Manning, A. J.). Some additional rules include the following:

1. Same-author references are listed by publication year, beginning with the earliest year.

2. When multiple entries have the same first-author surname, one-author references precede multiple-author references (e.g., Gill, T. (2006) precedes Gill, T., & Bond, R. (2002)).

3. Alphabetize group authors (e.g., an institution or agency) by the full official name for the group (e.g., order by American Psychological Association, not APA).

A.2 Grammar, Punctuation, and Spelling (GPS) Writing Guide

American Psychological Association, or APA, writing style is important to learn. In Chapter 15, the use of APA style is described and many tips are provided to help you improve your APA writing. However, without proper grammar, punctuation, and spelling, even the best APA style can appear sloppy. For this reason, we briefly describe the following basic features of writing in this guide that are consistent with the use of APA writing rules:

- Nouns and pronouns
- Verbs
- Adjectives and adverbs
- Prepositions
- Commas
- Colons and semicolons
- Apostrophes
- Quotation marks
- Hyphens
- Sentence structure
- Spelling

Because this guide is written to support the use of APA style, we will focus on aspects of writing that are consistent with APA style. Hence, this writing guide is like your GPS of writing using APA style; that is, it will get your writing where it needs to be—to a college level. This guide is thorough, yet it is also a brief overview of the essentials in writing properly. Using this guide can certainly help you improve your grades on papers, particularly those that require an APA writing style.

Nouns and Pronouns

A noun is used to name or identify a person, place, thing, quality, or action. A pronoun takes the place of a noun, noun phrase, or noun clause. A brief list of rules for using nouns and pronouns appropriately is given here.

USE OF CAPITALIZATION

There are many capitalization rules for nouns and pronouns. Some are straightforward and some vary depending on how words are used in a sentence. The following is a list of fundamental capitalization rules:

Rule 1: Capitalize the first word in a sentence.

- <u>The</u> experiment was a success.

Rule 2: Capitalize the pronoun *I*.

- If only <u>I</u> had considered that alternative.

Rule 3: Capitalize family relationships only when used as proper names.

- She loves her <u>Uncle</u> Bob more than her other <u>uncles</u>.
- He came home to see <u>Father</u>, although his <u>father</u> was not home.

Rule 4: Capitalize proper nouns such as people, places, and organizations.

- Supreme Court, Buffalo Bills, Alcoholics Anonymous, U.S. Marine Corps, Ellicottville Brewing Company, New York City.

Rule 5: Capitalize titles that precede names.

- We asked <u>Sergeant Major</u> Privitera for comment; however, the <u>sergeant major</u> was not available for comment.

Rule 6: Capitalize names of countries and nationalities and capitalize the adjective describing a person from that country or nationality.

- She was born in <u>Canada</u>, which makes her a <u>Canadian</u>.
- There was an <u>Austrian</u> who found refuge in <u>Finland</u>.

Rule 7: Capitalize all words except for short prepositions in books, articles, and songs.

- One of his most significant books was *<u>Beyond Freedom and Dignity.</u>*

Rule 8: Capitalize the names of gods, deities, religious figures, and books, except for nonspecific use of the word *god*.

- His faith called for him to worship only one <u>god</u>, so he prayed to <u>God</u> daily.
- Capitalize religious books such as the <u>Holy Bible</u> or <u>Koran</u> and deities such as <u>Buddha</u> or <u>Jesus Christ</u>.

Rule 9: Capitalize *North*, *South*, *East*, and *West* as regional directions, but not as compass directions.

- A sample was selected at a college in the <u>Northeast</u>.
- The habitat was located a few minutes <u>east</u> of the river.

Rule 10: Capitalize the days of the week, months, and holidays, and capitalize the seasons only when used in a title.

- His favorite season was <u>fall</u>, which is when he enrolled in college for the <u>Fall</u> 2013 semester.

- He did not attend class on <u>Wednesday</u>, which was <u>Halloween</u>. In <u>November</u>, he did not miss a class.

Rule 11: Capitalize historical eras, periods, and events, but not century numbers.

- The <u>Great Depression</u> occurred in the <u>twentieth</u> century and was a difficult time for many <u>Americans</u>.

Rule 12: Capitalize the first word after a colon only when the clause following the colon is a complete sentence.

- The experiment was conducted to learn about human behavior: the outcome.

- The lecturer gave an important lesson: To learn about human behavior means that we advance human understanding.

USE OF PRONOUNS AND PRONOUN CASE

Rule 1: Pronouns should agree in number. In other words, if the pronoun replaces a singular noun, then use a singular pronoun. Note that words such as *everybody*, *anybody*, *anyone*, *someone*, *neither*, *nobody*, and *each* are singular words that take singular pronouns.

- A participant was read an informed consent that <u>he or she</u> signed. (NOT: A participant was read an informed consent that <u>they</u> signed.)

- Everybody had 30 seconds to finish <u>his or her</u> test. (NOT: Everybody had 30 seconds to finish <u>their</u> test.)

Rule 2: Pronouns should agree in person. When you use first person (*I, we*), second person (*you*), or third person (*he, she, they*), be consistent. Don't switch from one person to the other.

- When <u>we</u> are working, <u>we</u> should have time to relax afterward. (NOT: When <u>we</u> are working, <u>you</u> should have time to relax afterward.)

Rule 3: Pronouns should be clearly identified.

- It is important that <u>the executive team</u> gets the decision correct. [NOT: It is important that <u>they</u> get the decision correct. (Who are "they"?)]

- Students completed a test and quiz, then placed <u>the test and quiz</u> face down when they were finished. [NOT: Students completed a test and quiz, then placed <u>it</u> face down when they were finished. (Is "it" referring to the test, the quiz, or both?)]

Here, we will list some additional rules pertaining to pronoun case use. To begin, keep in mind that pronouns have three cases:

Subjective case (pronouns used as subject)

I, you, he, she it, we, they, who

Objective case (pronouns used as objects of verbs or prepositions)

Me, you, him, her, it, us, them, whom

Possessive case (pronouns used to express ownership)

My (mine), your (yours), his/her (his/hers), it (its), our (ours), their (theirs), whose

Rule 4: Some pronouns do not change case or form.

That, these, those, which

Rule 5: Use the subjective and objective case appropriately for formal and informal writing.

Formal writing: In the subjective case, "It is I." In the objective case, "To whom am I speaking?"

Informal writing: In the subjective case, "Who am I speaking with?" In the objective case, "It is me."

Rule 6: When making comparisons, use *than*, *as*, *compared to*, or *versus (vs.)*.

The effect was larger in the experimental group <u>than</u> in the control group. [NOT: The effect was larger in the experimental group. (Larger than what?)]

The effect was larger in the experimental group <u>compared to</u> the control group.

Self-reports were as truthful <u>as</u> possible.

Scores were comparable in the experimental <u>versus</u> the control group.

Verbs

A verb is used to describe an action or occurrence or identify a state of being. A brief list of rules for using verbs appropriately is given here. There are six basic tenses you should be familiar with:

Simple present: We conclude

Present perfect: We have concluded

Simple past: They concluded

Past perfect: They had concluded

Future: They will conclude

Future perfect: They will have concluded

The challenge in sequencing tenses usually occurs with the perfect tenses. Perfect tenses are formed by adding an auxiliary or auxiliaries, which most commonly take the forms of *has, have, had, be, can, do, may, must, ought, shall*, and *will*. We will use the common forms identified here.

Rule 1: Present perfect designates actions that have occurred and are ongoing and consists of a past participle with *has* or *have*.

Simple past: We attended school for four years.

Present perfect: We have attended school for four years.

The simple past implies that "we" are finished attending school; the present perfect implies that "we" are still attending school.

Rule 2: Infinitives also have perfect tense forms when combined with auxiliaries, even when used with verbs that identify the future, such as *hope*, *intend*, *expect*, and *plan*. When the perfect tense is used with verbs that identify the future, the perfect tense sets up the sequence by identifying the action that began and was completed before the action of the main verb.

- The researcher had expected to observe the result. (In this example, the action, "had expected," began and was completed before the action of the main verb, "to observe the result.")

Rule 3: Past perfect indicates an action completed in the past before another action begins.

- Simple past: The scientist developed research protocols and later used them to conduct research.

- Past perfect: The scientist used research protocols that he had developed.

In each example, the research protocols were developed before they were used to conduct research.

- Simple past: The technician fixed the apparatus when the inspector arrived.

- Past perfect: The technician had fixed the apparatus when the inspector arrived.

The simple past indicates that the technician waited until the inspector arrived to fix the apparatus; the past perfect indicates that the technician had already fixed the apparatus by the time the inspector arrived.

Rule 4: Future perfect indicates an action that will have been completed at a specified time in the future.

- Simple future: Friday I will finish my homework.

- Future perfect: By Friday, I will have finished my homework.

The simple future indicates that the homework will be completed specifically on Friday; the future perfect indicates that the homework will be completed at any time leading up to Friday.

IRREGULAR VERBS

Regular verbs consist of the present/root form, the simple past form, and the past participle form. Regular verbs have an ending of -ed added to the present/root form for both the simple past and past participle form. Irregular verbs are identified as verbs that do not follow this pattern.

To help you identify the form of irregular verbs, the list here consists of the present/root form, the simple past form, and the past participle form of 60 irregular verbs.

Present	Past	Past Participle	Present	Past	Past Participle
be	was, were	been	lay	laid	laid
become	became	become	lead	led	led
begin	began	begun	leave	left	left
bring	brought	brought	let	let	let
build	built	built	lie	lay	lain
catch	caught	caught	lose	lost	lost
choose	chose	chosen	make	made	made
come	came	come	meet	met	met
cut	cut	cut	quit	quit	quit
deal	dealt	dealt	read	read	read
do	did	done	ride	rode	ridden
drink	drank	drunk	run	ran	run
eat	ate	eaten	say	said	said
fall	fell	fallen	see	saw	seen
feed	fed	fed	seek	sought	sought
feel	felt	felt	send	sent	sent
find	found	found	sleep	slept	slept
forget	forgot	forgotten	speak	spoke	spoken
forgive	forgave	forgiven	spend	spent	spent
get	got	gotten	stand	stood	stood
give	gave	given	take	took	taken
go	went	gone	teach	taught	taught
grow	grew	grown	tell	told	told
have	had	had	think	thought	thought
hear	heard	heard	throw	threw	thrown

(Continued)

(Continued)

Present	Past	Past Participle	Present	Past	Past Participle
hide	hid	hidden	understand	understood	understood
hold	held	held	wear	wore	worn
keep	kept	kept	win	won	won
know	knew	known	write	wrote	written

Active and Passive Voice

Active voice: Verbs in an active voice show the subject or person acting. The active voice is often a more concise writing style. For this reason, many writers feel that the active voice should be the primary voice of an author.

Passive voice: Verbs in the passive voice show something else acting on the subject or person. This voice is often used only when needed but is usually not the primary voice of an author.

To distinguish between the active and passive voice, we will use two examples for each:

Example 1: Active voice: The graduate student *ended* the study.

Passive voice: The study *was ended* by the graduate student.

Example 2: Active voice: The analysis *showed* significance.

Passive voice: Significance *was shown* in the analysis.

Indicative, Imperative, and Subjective Mood

The **indicative mood** indicates a fact or opinion. Most verbs we use are in the indicative mood.

Examples: The doctor *was* here.

I *am* working late.

She *will bring* her notes.

The **imperative mood** expresses commands or requests. The subject of sentences that use the imperative mood is *you*, although it is not directly stated in the sentence.

Examples: *Be* to class on time.

Turn to page 32 in your book.

Bring your calculator to the exam.

Although it is not directly stated, in each example it is understood that you be to class on time, you turn to page 32 in your book, and you bring your calculator to the exam.

The **subjunctive mood** shows something contrary to fact. To express something that is not principally true, use the past tense or past perfect tense; when using the verb *to be* in the subjunctive mood, always use *were* rather than *was*.

Examples: If the inspector *were* here . . . (Implied: but he is not)

I wish we *had tested* the sample first. (Implied: but we did not)

You would have preferred *to be* in class. (Implied: but you were not)

Adjectives and Adverbs

Adjectives modify nouns in some way. Adverbs modify verbs, adjectives, or other adverbs in some way. A description of each type of modifier with examples is given in this section.

ADJECTIVES

Adjectives modify nouns in some way. For example:

- He was given a survey. (*Survey* is a noun. We know that participants were given the survey; we don't know anything else about the survey.)

- He was given a *brief* survey. (*Survey* is a noun. *Brief* is an adjective. The adjective modifies the noun; we now know the kind of survey completed: a *brief* survey.)

Adjectives can answer the following questions:

- Which? (e.g., "The *third* floor." Which floor? The third floor.)

- How many? (e.g., "*Six* students were absent." How many students? Six students.)

- What kind? (e.g., "The student took a *makeup* exam." What kind of exam? A makeup exam.)

ADVERBS

Adverbs modify verbs, adjectives, or other adverbs in some way. Adverbs most often answer the question: How? For example:

- She *studied quietly*. (*Quietly* is an adverb that modifies the verb *studied*. How did she study? Quietly.)

- The professor was *very* fair. (*Fair* is an adjective that modifies the noun *professor*. *Very* is an adverb that modifies the adjective *fair*. How fair is the professor? Very fair.)

Many adverbs have an *-ly* ending. Some examples: *abruptly, absolutely, beautifully, briskly, brutally, cheerfully, delicately, endlessly, expertly, firmly, lightly, literally, quietly, quickly, randomly, really, slowly, successfully, tremendously, wholeheartedly, willfully, willingly*.

- She was a *tremendously* successful researcher. (*Successful* is an adjective that modifies the noun *researcher*. *Tremendously* is an adverb that modifies the adjective *successful*. How successful was the researcher? Tremendously successful.)

Some adverbs indicate the place or location of an action. Some examples: *everywhere, here, in, inside, out, outside, somewhere, there.*

- The class relocated *upstairs*. (*Upstairs* is an adverb that modifies the verb *relocated*. Where did the class relocate? Upstairs.)

Some adverbs indicate when, how often, or what time an action occurred. Some examples: *always, daily, early, first, last, later, monthly, never, now, often, regularly, usually, weekly.*

- Participants were observed *daily*. (*Daily* is an adverb that modifies the verb *observed*. How often were participants observed? Daily.)

Some adverbs indicate to what extent an action or something was done. Some examples: *almost, also, enough, only, quite, rather, so, too, very.*

- The room was *quite* comfortable. (*Comfortable* is an adjective that modifies the noun *room*. *Quite* is an adverb that modifies the adjective *comfortable*. To what extent was the room comfortable? Quite comfortable.)

A Versus An

Using *a* or *an* in a sentence depends on the phonetic (sound) representation of the first letter in a word, not on the orthographic (written) representation of the letter. If the first letter makes a vowel-like sound, then use *an*; if the first letter makes a consonant-like sound, then use *a*. The following are some basic rules for using *a* or *an*:

Rule 1: *A* goes before a word that begins with a consonant. For example:

- <u>A</u> study
- <u>A</u> replication
- <u>A</u> limitation

Rule 2: *An* goes before a word that begins with a vowel. For example:

- <u>An</u> analysis
- <u>An</u> increase
- <u>An</u> effect

Exception 1: Use *an* before an unsounded *h* in which a vowel follows the first letter. The *h* has no audible sound in its phonetic representation; therefore, we use *an* because the first audible sound is a vowel (e.g., "<u>an</u> honest mistake" or "<u>an</u> honorable life").

Exception 2: Use *a* when *u* makes the same sound as *y* (e.g., "<u>a</u> U.S. sample" or "<u>a</u> united team") or *o* makes the same sound as *w* (e.g., "<u>a</u> one-day trial").

Prepositions

A preposition is a word or phrase typically used before a substantive that indicates the relation of the substantive to a verb, an adjective, or another substantive. A preposition functions as a modifier to a verb, noun, or adjective and generally expresses a spatial, temporal, or other type of relationship. Many forms of prepositions are discussed in this section.

PREPOSITIONS FOR TIME AND PLACE

Prepositions are used to identify **one point in time**.
On is used with days of the week and with a specific calendar day.

- The school week begins *on* Monday.
- My birthday is *on* March 30.

At is used with *noon, night, midnight,* and time of day.

- Class begins *at* noon.
- The stars come out *at* night.
- The deadline is *at* midnight.
- The test will be administered *at* 4:30 p.m.

In is used with *afternoon* and seasons, months, and years.

- He awoke *in* the afternoon.
- The study was conducted *in* spring.
- Snowfall was recorded *in* February.
- He earned his college degree *in* 2012.

Prepositions are used to identify an **extended period of time** using the following prepositions: *since, for, by, from, until, within,* and *during*.

- It has been two years *since* the last cohort was observed.
- Participants were observed *for* two weeks.
- The deadline has been extended *by* two hours.
- The study continued *from* morning *until* night.
- A research protocol must be completed *within* three years.
- I am always focused *during* class.

Prepositions are used to identify a **place**, or refer to a **location relative to a given point**.
To identify a **place**, use *in* to refer to the point itself, use *inside* to indicate something contained, use *on* to indicate a surface, and use *at* to indicate a specific place/location or general vicinity.

- Animal subjects were housed *in* steel cages.

- He placed his notes *inside* the folder.

- The student left his exam *on* the desk.

- Assistance was available *at* the help desk.

To identify a location relative to a given point, use *over* or *above* for a location higher than a point; use *under*, *underneath*, *beneath*, or *below* to identify a location lower than a point; use *near*, *by*, *next to*, *between*, *among*, *behind*, or *opposite* to identify a location close to a point.

- The flask is *above* the cabinet.

- The survey was *beneath* the consent form.

- The child hid *underneath* the table.

- The confederate was *behind* the participant.

- The field was located *between* two oak trees.

PREPOSITIONS FOR DIRECTION OR MOVEMENT

The prepositions *to*, *onto*, and *into* can be used to identify movement toward something. The basic preposition of a direction toward a goal is *to*. When the goal is physical, such as a destination, *to* implies movement toward the goal.

- The mouse ran *to* the cheese.

- The newlyweds flew *to* Paris.

When the goal is not physical, such as an action, *to* marks a verb and is used as an infinitive.

- The student went *to* see her teacher.

- The professor hurried *to* attend the conference.

The preposition *onto* indicates movement toward a surface, whereas the preposition *into* indicates movements toward the interior of a volume.

- The athlete jumped *onto* the platform.

- The solution was poured *into* the container.

Note that *to* can be optional for *onto* and *into* because *on* and *in* can have a directional meaning when used with verbs of motion. The compound preposition (*onto*, *into*) indicates the completion of an action, whereas the simple preposition (*on*, *in*) indicates the position of a subject as a result of that action.

- The shot went *into* the basket OR The shot went *in* the basket.

- The fossils washed up *onto* the shore OR The fossils washed up *on* the shore.

Note that some verbs that indicate direction or movement express the idea that some physical object or subject is situated in a specific place. In these cases, some verbs use only *on*, whereas others can use *on* or *onto*. The following is an example in which *on* and *onto* can be distinguished:

- The pilot landed the aircraft [*on* or *onto*] the runway. (In this case, the pilot lands the aircraft toward a surface, i.e., the runway.)
- The aircraft landed *on* [not *onto*] the runway. (In this case, the plane itself is situated on a specific surface, i.e., on the runway.)

Note also that *to* suggests movement toward a specific destination, whereas *toward* suggests movement in a general direction, without necessarily arriving at a destination.

- The student went *to* the exit during the fire drill. (The exit is the destination; note that *to* implies that the student does not actually go *through* the exit; the exit is the destination.)
- The student went *toward* the exit during the fire drill. (The student was headed in the direction of the exit, but may not have reached or gone through the exit.)

PREPOSITIONS FOR INTRODUCING OBJECTS OF VERBS

Use *of* with *approve* and *consists*.

- She did not approve *of* his behavior.
- The solution consists *of* sugar water.

Use *of* or *about* with *dream* and *think*.

- I dream [*of* or *about*] making the world a better place.
- Can you think [*of* or *about*] a solution to the problem?

Use *at* with *laugh*, *stare*, *smile*, and *look*.

- I had to laugh *at* the joke.
- I tend to stare *at* the screen.
- I saw you smile *at* me.
- I look *at* a map to find directions.

Use *for* with *call*, *hope*, *look*, *wait*, and *watch*.

- I may need you to call *for* help.
- We will hope *for* reliable results with this new test.
- Can we look *for* a solution to the problem?
- Can you wait *for* me to return?
- He must watch *for* the signal before proceeding.

Commas

Using punctuation correctly requires that we distinguish between an independent clause and a dependent clause. An *independent clause* is a passage that is a complete sentence that has a subject and a verb. A *dependent clause* is a passage that also has a subject and a verb, but is an incomplete sentence. In this section, we will identify when it is and is not appropriate to use punctuation with independent and dependent clauses.

The following is a brief list of eight rules for **when to use commas**:

Rule 1: Use commas to separate independent clauses that are joined by coordinating conjunctions (e.g., *and, but, or, nor, so, yet*).

- The study was complete, *but* the data were not analyzed.

- The analysis showed significance, *yet* the results were difficult to interpret.

Note: DO NOT use a comma between the two verbs or verb phrases in a compound predicate.

- The baseball player ran on the bases *and* slid to home. (Do not use a comma because *and* separates two verbs—*ran* [on bases] and *slid* [to home].)

- The researcher explained the expectations and procedures *and* began the study. (Do not use a comma before the last *and* because it separates two verb phrases— *explained the expectations* and *began the study.*)

Rule 2: Use commas after introductory clauses that come before the main clause. The following is a list of common words used to start an introductory clause that should be followed by a comma: *although, after, as, because, if, when, while, since, however, yes, well.*

- *After* a short break, participants had no trouble completing the task.

- *While* the student studied, his roommate was playing loud music.

- *As* stated earlier, human behavior can be understood using the scientific process.

- *Yes*, the findings do support the hypothesis.

Note: DO NOT use a comma if the introductory clause follows the main clause (except for cases of extreme contrast).

- Participants had no trouble completing the task *after* a short break. (Do not use a comma.)

- The student was in a great mood, *although* he failed out of college. (Failing out of college is an extreme contrast to being in a great mood; use a comma.)

Rule 3: Use commas to separate three or more elements or words written in a series.

- The categories of research design are experimental, nonexperimental, and quasi-experimental.

- The food environment was contrived to appear open, hidden, or clustered.
- The researcher gave a participant, who volunteered for the study, who completed all interviews, and who followed all procedures, a debriefing form.

Rule 4: Use commas to enclose clauses, phrases, and words in the middle of a sentence that are not essential to the meaning of the sentence.

- His research, *which was completed many years ago*, was published just this year.
- The verdict, *on the other hand*, did not satisfy the family.
- The patient, *however*, was not ready to be released.

Note: To identify a clause, phrase, or word that is not essential to the meaning of a sentence, follow these three guidelines. Enclose the clause, phrase, or word in commas if:

- It could be omitted and the sentence still makes sense,
- It would otherwise interrupt the flow of words in the original sentence, or
- It could be moved to a different part of the sentence, and the sentence would still make sense.

Rule 5: Use commas to separate two or more coordinate adjectives but not two or more noncoordinate adjectives to describe the same noun.

- Participation in the experimental group required *intense, rigorous* skills. (The sentence uses coordinate adjectives [*intense, rigorous*], so a comma is used.)
- The student wore a *green woolly* sweater. (The sentence uses noncoordinate adjectives [*green, woolly*], so no comma is used.)
- He was prepared for the *cold, chilly, snowy winter* weather. (There are three coordinate adjectives [*cold, chilly, snowy*] with a comma used to separate each, and one noncoordinate adjective [*winter*] with no comma used.)

Note: To identify coordinate adjectives used to describe the same noun, follow these two guidelines. The adjectives are coordinate and a comma is used if:

- The sentence still makes sense when the adjectives are written in reverse order, or
- The sentence still makes sense when *and* is written between the adjectives.

Rule 6: Use a comma near the end of a sentence to indicate a distinct pause or to separate contrasted coordinate elements.

- The study showed evidence of clinical significance, not statistical significance.
- The student seemed frustrated, even angry.
- The research findings were an important advancement, almost landmark.

Rule 7: Use commas to separate geographical names, items in dates (except month and day), titles in names, and addresses (except street number and name).

- The author was raised in East Aurora, New York.

- November 10, 2015, will be the 240th birthday of the U.S. Marine Corps.

- Ivan Pavlov, PhD, was a Noble Prize winner.

- The White House is located at 1600 Pennsylvania Avenue, Washington, DC.

Rule 8: Use a comma to shift between the main discourse and a quotation but not when the quotation is part of the main discourse.

- The parent told his child, "Every moment I am with you is the greatest moment of my life."

- Telling your child to "live every moment as if it is your last" can be inspirational. (No comma is used because the quoted material is part of the main discourse.)

Colons and Semicolons

Colons and semicolons are used to mark a major division in a sentence, typically to bring together two or more ideas into one enumeration. This section describes many rules for appropriately using colons and semicolons.

COLONS

A colon is used to divide the main discourse of a sentence from an elaboration, summation, or general implication of the main discourse. A colon is also used to separate numbers, such as hours and minutes, and a ratio or proportion. The following is a list of five rules for appropriately using colons.

Rule 1: Use a colon before statements that introduce a formal passage or list.

- Three topics are described in this guide: grammar, punctuation, and spelling.

- To do well in this class: Take notes! Read the book! Study often!

Note: DO NOT use a colon after a preposition or linking verb.

- Three topics described in this guide *are* grammar, punctuation, and spelling. (*Are* is a linking verb used in place of the colon.)

- You can do well in this class *by* taking notes, reading the book, and studying often. (*By* is used to link "doing well" with the three criteria listed for doing well.)

Rule 2: Use a colon (in place of a comma) before long or formal direct quotations.

- The German-born American physicist Albert Einstein once *said:* "I am neither especially clever nor especially gifted. I am only very, very curious." (A colon is used to separate the passage from the quoted material; note that a comma can also be used in place of the colon to separate the passage from the quoted material.)

Rule 3: Use a colon before formal appositives.

- Most citizens polled identified the same issue as their main concern: the economy. (A colon introduces an appositive.)

- One class was his favorite in college: psychology. (A colon introduces an appositive.)

Rule 4: Use a colon between independent clauses when the second clause restates or supports the same idea as the preceding clause.

- Scientists are not infallible: On occasion, they can, without intention, misinterpret, mislead, or misrepresent the data they publish. (The second clause expands on and supports the preceding clause.)

- Any idea you develop must be testable: An idea must lead to specific predictions that can be observed under specified conditions. (The second clause expands on and supports the preceding clause.)

Note: To be concise, DO NOT restate the same idea unless it serves to expand on or further illustrate the content in the preceding clause.

Rule 5: Use a colon to separate numbers, such as hours and minutes, and a ratio or proportion.

The deadline was set at *9:00* p.m.

The chances of winning the game were *4:1*. (A ratio can also be stated as *4 to 1* without the colon.)

SEMICOLONS

A semicolon is used to divide the main discourse of a sentence and to balance two contrasted or related ideas. The following is a list of three rules for appropriately using semicolons.

Rule 1: Use a semicolon to separate two independent clauses not connected by a coordinating conjunction.

- Each participant chose the second option; it was the preferred option.

- She finished her exam in one hour; I completed my exam in half that time.

- The laboratory was contrived; it was designed to look like a day care center.

Note: DO NOT overuse semicolons for Rule 1. As a general rule, only apply Rule 1 when using a semicolon in place of a period allows for an easier transition between two complete sentences or independent clauses. As an example, for the sentences below, the transition between the sentences is not made easier by using the semicolon.

- INCORRECT: From a broad view, science is any systematic method of acquiring knowledge apart from ignorance; *from* a stricter view, science is specifically the acquisition of knowledge using the scientific method.

- CORRECT: From a broad view, science is any systematic method of acquiring knowledge apart from ignorance. *From* a stricter view, science is specifically the acquisition of knowledge using the scientific method.

Rule 2: Use a semicolon before a transitional connective or conjunctive adverb that separates two main clauses. Examples of conjunctive adverbs are *consequently*, *besides*, *instead*, *also*, *furthermore*, *therefore*, *however*, *likewise*, *hence*, *nevertheless*, *in addition*, and *moreover*.

- His hypothesis has support; *however*, his statements go beyond the data.

- It was the best product on the market; *yet*, it was overpriced.

- The student was not distracted; *instead*, she was focused.

Note: The same caution applies here regarding the use of semicolons and periods. Only use a semicolon for Rule 2 when using a semicolon in place of a period allows for an easier transition between two complete sentences or independent clauses.

Rule 3: Use semicolons between items that have internal punctuation in a series or sequence.

- The members of the editorial board are William James, editor-in-chief; Ivan Pavlov, associate editor; B. F. Skinner, associate editor; and Chris Thomas, editorial assistant. (A semicolon is used to "break up" the commas used to separate the names from the titles of each editor.)

- Over the next four years, our conference will be held in Buffalo, New York; Chicago, Illinois; Washington, DC; and Seattle, Washington. (A semicolon is used to "break up" the commas used to separate the names of each city and state.)

Apostrophes

An apostrophe is used to form possessives of nouns, to indicate missing letters with contractions, and to show plurals of lowercase letters. Each type of use for an apostrophe is briefly described in this section.

FORMING POSSESSIVES OF NOUNS

An apostrophe is used for the possessive. To see if you need to form the possessive of a noun, make the phrase an "of the" phrase. If the "of the" phrase makes sense, then use an apostrophe—except if the noun after *of* is a building or room, an object, or a piece of furniture.

- The patient's file = the file *of the* patient ("of the" makes sense; apostrophe needed)

- The study's outcome = the outcome *of the* study ("of the" makes sense; apostrophe needed)

- The day's end = the end *of the* day ("of the" makes sense; apostrophe needed)

- The laboratory corridor = the corridor of the laboratory ("of the" makes sense; however, no apostrophe is needed because "the laboratory" is a building or room)

Note: DO NOT use apostrophes with possessive pronouns because possessive pronouns already show possession. For example:

- His lab (NOT: His' lab)
- The team made its quota. (NOT: The team made it's quota. *Its* is a possessive pronoun meaning "belonging to it"; *it's* is a contraction meaning "it is.")

In addition, do not use an apostrophe with units of time. For example:

- The study was two hours long. (NOT: The study was two hours' long.)

The following is a list of five rules for when to use an apostrophe for the possessive:

Rule 1: Add *'s* to the singular form of a word, even if it ends in -*s*.

- The researcher's conclusions
- The student's grade
- James's application

Rule 2: Add *'s* to words in which the plural form does not end in -*s*.

- The nuclei's activity
- The stimuli's presence
- The people's choice

The following is a brief list of words with a plural form that does not end in *s*. Follow Rule 2 for the plural form of these words.

Singular	Plural
Alumna	Alumnae
Alumnus	Alumni
Child	Children
Criterion	Criteria
Curriculum	Curricula
Datum	Data
Dice	Die
Foot	Feet
Focus	Foci
Fungus	Fungi
Man	Men
Mouse	Mice
Nucleus	Nuclei
Person	People
Phenomenon	Phenomena
Stimulus	Stimuli
Woman	Women

Rule 3: Add ' to the end of plural nouns that end in *s*:

- The countries' independence
- The universities' collaboration

Rule 4: Add *'s* to the singular form of compound words and hyphenated nouns.

- The scapegoat's rationale
- The rattlesnake's bite
- The editor-in-chief's decision

Rule 5: Add *'s* to the last noun to show joint possession of an object.

- Tom and Jerry's house
- Denver and Miami's football game

INDICATING MISSING LETTERS WITH CONTRACTIONS

Apostrophes are used in contractions to indicate that letters are missing when two words are combined—for example, *it's* (it is), *don't* (do not), *could've* (could have). However, contractions are NOT used with APA style. For this reason, we will not introduce the use of apostrophes in detail greater than that identified in this paragraph.

SHOWING PLURALS OF LOWERCASE LETTERS

Rule for lowercase letters: Add *'s* to form the plural of lowercase letters.

- Mind your *p's* and *q's*. (Lowercase letters need apostrophe.)
- In sports, it is all about the *w's*. (Lowercase letter needs apostrophe.)

Note: Apostrophes indicating the plural form of capitalized letters, numbers, and symbols are NOT needed. For example:

- Two *MVPs* were selected.
- All students earned *As* and scored in the *90s* on the exam.
- Many *&s* were used in the reference list.

Quotation Marks

Quotation marks are most often used to set off or represent exact spoken or written language, typically from another source. For this reason, using quotation marks correctly is one practical way to avoid plagiarism. Quotations can also be used for other purposes not related to citing other sources. In this section, we will describe many of the rules for quotation mark use.

As a general rule, always open and close quoted material with quotation marks. Hence, quotation marks should always be used in pairs. Quotation marks are used for direct quotations; not indirect quotations. The APA manual provides complete instructions on how to properly cite references in text with and without quotation marks—and therefore for direct and indirect quotation use, respectively.

Keep in mind also that overuse of quotation marks can be poor practice because it gives the impression that the ideas expressed in a paper are not primarily coming from the author or writer. For this reason, make sure to use direct quotations sparingly. If you can simply summarize a work, results, or other details in the text, then paraphrase; that is, use indirect quotations. Only use direct quotations for material or language in which paraphrasing would diminish its importance (e.g., a quote from a famous author or figure such as that given in a speech, a definition for a key term, or an important work or policy).

Note for all examples below that the period or comma punctuation always comes before the final quotation mark. Follow this punctuation rule when using quotation marks.

Rule 1: Capitalize the first letter of a direct quote when the quoted material is a complete sentence.

- The author stated, "A significant outcome is not proof of an effect; a significant outcome indicates evidence of an effect."

- While he did have a viable program of research, it was another researcher who said, "High power may be the most essential factor for a program of research to be viable."

Rule 2: DO NOT capitalize the first letter of a direct quote when the quoted material is a fragment sentence or is integrated as part of an original sentence.

- The students behaved during class because the professor made clear that "self-discipline and control" were important to be successful in his class.

- These findings support the assertion that "it is not all about the calories" when it comes to understanding hunger and fullness.

Rule 3: If the quoted material is a complete sentence and is broken up, then capitalize the first part of the sentence but not the second part.

- "Isolating confounding variables," he said, "is important when conducting an experiment." (Note that two pairs of quotations are used when one quote is broken into two parts.)

Rule 4: Use single quotation marks to enclose quotes within another quotation.

- The participant replied, "He told me that 'I was being too strict' as a parent." (The single quotation marks indicate quotes from a secondary source and not those of the speaker specifically being quoted in double quotation marks.)

Rule 5: You may omit portions of a quote, typically to be more concise, by replacing the omitted words with an ellipsis.

- **Original Quote**: "An experiment with an increased sample size should be able to detect an effect, if one exists, because it is associated with greater power."
- **Revised Quote**: "An experiment with an increased sample size . . . is associated with greater power."

Rule 6: You may add words to quoted material, typically to improve clarity, by enclosing the added words in brackets.

- **Original Quote**: He explained, "At that time, I handed out the survey."
- **Revised Quote**: He explained, "At that time [when participants arrived], I handed out the survey."

Rule 7: Use quotation marks for the definition of a key term if quoted from another source. DO NOT use quotation marks for the key term; instead, use italics or boldface to identify the to-be-defined term.

- *Science* is "the acquisition of knowledge through observation, evaluation, interpretation, and theoretical explanation."

Rule 8: Quotation marks—not used for direct quotes—can indicate words used ironically or even comically.

- It was an awful game at the "Super" Bowl. ("Super" Bowl is an ironic name for the game if the game itself was awful.)
- The sprinter "ran away" from the competition. (This phrase could be construed as funny because "run away" has a double meaning in this context—it relates to winning a competition and the fact that the competition involved running.)

Hyphens

A hyphen can be used to separate words or phrases. The following six rules can be applied and are generally accepted for using hyphens correctly.

Rule 1: Use a hyphen to join two or more words serving as a single adjective that precedes a noun.

- The *well-known* study. (The adjective [*well-known*] precedes the noun [*study*]; use a hyphen to combine the words *well* and *known*.)
- The *clear-headed* researcher. (The adjective [*clear-headed*] precedes the noun [*researcher*]; use a hyphen to combine the words *clear* and *headed*.)

Rule 2: DO NOT use a hyphen to join two or more words serving as a single adjective that follow a noun.

- The study was *well known*. (The adjective [*well known*] follows the noun [*study*]; DO NOT use a hyphen.)

- The researcher was *clear headed*. (The adjective [*clear headed*] follows the noun [*researcher*]; DO NOT use a hyphen.)

Rule 3: Use a hyphen to join letters that may otherwise cause confusion.

- They were asked to *re-sign* the form. (*Re-sign* is "to sign again" whereas *resign* is "to give up" or "to accept as inevitable.")

- We had to *re-cover* the solution. (*Re-cover* is "to cover again" whereas *recover* is "to restore" or "to regain.")

Rule 4: Use a hyphen for prefixes [*ex-* (meaning "former"), *self-*, *all-*, *half-*, *quasi-*]; for suffixes [*-elect*, *-like*, *-typical*]; and between a prefix and a capitalized word (such as a proper noun) or number.

- Prefixes: ex-husband, self-aware, all-knowing, half-asleep, quasi-experimental.

- Suffixes: president-elect, playoff-like atmosphere, schizoid-typical behavior.

- Between a prefix and a capitalized word or number: anti-American, mid-1900s.

Rule 5: Use a hyphen to join multiword compounds (with few exceptions), usually even if the multiword compound precedes or follows the noun.

- His response was *matter-of-fact*.

- The *next-to-last* student was chosen to participate.

Rule 6: Use a hyphen to join compound numbers.

- *Thirty-six* students took the exam.

- A total of *twenty-two* participants dropped out of the study.

Rule 6a: Using APA style, it is necessary to express a number in words when:

- The number is less than 10, except when displayed in a figure or table, or preceding a unit of measurement (e.g., 5 m).

- The number is the first word in a sentence (e.g., Thirty-eight participants were observed), except if the sentence is in the abstract, in which case it is recommended to avoid starting a sentence with a number (all numbers are expressed as numerals in an abstract).

- Approximating days, months, and years (e.g., "about two days ago," or "almost three months went by").

- The number expresses a common fraction when used as an adjective (e.g., two-thirds majority).

Sentence Structure

Sentence structure is the grammatical arrangement of words into sentences. In addition to words, sentences can also include numbers and individual letters or symbols.

Sentence structure is important in that good structure strengthens the flow of ideas in a written work and makes it easier for the reader to correctly understand what is written. In this section, we introduce fundamental rules of sentence structure not yet discussed in this basic writing guide.

SUBJECT-VERB AGREEMENT

Rule 1: Use a plural verb when the subject of a sentence consists of two or more nouns or pronouns connected by *and*; use a singular verb when nouns or pronouns are linked with *or*.

- Jack *and* Jill <u>are</u> in the lab. (Plural)

- His work *or* your work <u>is</u> going to win the prize. (Singular)

Rule 2: When the subject of a sentence consists of two or more nouns or pronouns connected by *or*, the verb must agree with the part of the subject that is closer to the verb in the sentence.

- The graduate students *or* a researcher <u>runs</u> the study. (The "researcher" [singular] is the part of the subject that is closest to the verb *runs*.)

- A researcher *or* the graduate students <u>run</u> the study. (The "graduate students" [plural] are the part of the subject that is closest to the verb *run*.)

Rule 3: A verb must agree with the subject, not with the noun or pronoun in the clause.

- One of the hypotheses <u>is</u> correct. (*One* is singular and is the subject.)

- The hypotheses <u>are</u> both correct. (*Hypotheses* is plural and is the subject.)

- The book, including all appendices, <u>was</u> easy to read. (*Book* is singular and is the subject.)

- The women, even those who did not volunteer, <u>were</u> cooperative. (*Women* is plural and is the subject.)

Rule 4: The following words are singular and require a singular verb: *anybody, anyone, each, everybody, everyone, no one, nobody, somebody,* and *someone*.

- *Each* of the students <u>is</u> responsible.

- *Nobody* <u>is</u> leaving.

- *Everybody* <u>has</u> arrived.

Rule 5: Use a singular verb for nouns that imply more than one person but are considered singular, such as *class, committee, family, group,* and *team*.

- The *group* <u>is</u> ready for therapy.

- The *committee* <u>has</u> made a decision.

Rule 6: Use a singular verb when *either* or *neither* is the subject.

- *Neither* of us <u>was</u> aware of what happened.

- *Either* of them <u>is</u> culpable.

Rule 7: The following expressions do not change the number of the subject or the verb: *with, together with, including, accompanied by, in addition to, along with*, and *as well*.

- The sailor, *along with* his mates, <u>is</u> excited for the trip. (The subject is *the sailor* [singular], so the verb is also singular.)

- The cofounders, *together with* an outside supporter, <u>are</u> pleased with the outcome. (The subject is *the cofounders* [plural], so the verb is also plural.)

Rule 8: The expression *the number* is followed by a singular verb; the expression *a number* is followed by a plural verb.

- *The number* of participants required <u>is</u> substantial. (Singular)

- *A number* of attendees <u>are</u> being honored today. (Plural)

Rule 9: Use a singular verb with sums of money or periods/durations of time.

- The *$20* <u>is</u> for a parking fee.

- *Ten years* <u>is</u> a long time to continue a study.

Rule 10: The verb agrees with what follows *there is, there are, here is*, and *here are* when a sentence begins with one of these terms.

- There <u>is</u> *a question*. (Singular)

- There <u>are</u> *many participants*. (Plural)

- Here <u>is</u> *an example*. (Singular)

- Here <u>are</u> *a few examples*. (Plural)

SENTENCE FRAGMENTS

Sentence fragments are incomplete sentences. Fragments should always be avoided in academic writing, even if the fragment follows clearly from the preceding main clause. For example:

- The study took longer than expected. Which is why we ended it early. (The second sentence is a fragment. If read alone, we are left asking, "What was ended early?")

Possible revisions to make the fragment a complete sentence:

1. The study took longer than expected, which is why we ended it early. (*It* now clearly refers to *the study*.)

2. We ended the study early because it took longer than expected. (*It* now clearly refers to *the study*.)

Many sentence fragments are written as main clauses but lack a main verb or a subject. A sentence fragment with no subject often begins with a preposition. An example for each case is given here. Again, avoid sentence fragments and use only complete sentences in academic writing.

A fragment with **no main verb**:

- A study with three independent variables.

Possible revisions to make the fragment a complete sentence by adding a main verb:

1. A study was conducted with three independent variables.

2. Participants completed a study with three independent variables.

A fragment with **no subject**:

- For making the most of a difficult situation, Jim got promoted.

Possible revisions to make the fragment a complete sentence:

1. Making the most of a difficult situation got Jim promoted. (Removed *for* [the preposition].)

2. Jim got promoted for making the most of a difficult situation. (The sentence was rearranged so that it ends with the prepositional phrase.)

DANGLING MODIFIERS

A dangling modifier is a word or phrase that modifies a word not clearly stated in a sentence. Many strategies can be used to correct sentences with dangling modifiers. The key is to ask *who* did an action. Two examples are given here.

- Dangling modifier: Having completed all preparations, the door was opened. [Who completed all preparations? "Having completed" expresses action, but the doer is not the door (the subject of the main clause): A door does not finish preparations. The phrase before the comma, then, is a dangling modifier.]

To correct the sentence we can name the doer of the action as the subject of the main clause:

- Having completed all preparations, the researcher opened the door. [In this sentence, the doer of the action (completing all preparations) seems logically to be the researcher (identified in the main clause). The sentence is good, and it does not have a dangling modifier.]

Alternatively, we can combine the phrase and main clause into one sentence without a comma:

- The researcher opened the door after completing all preparations. [Again, the doer of the action (completing all preparations) seems logically to be the researcher in this sentence. The sentence is good, and it does not have a dangling modifier.]

Many other strategies can be used to clarify *who* is doing the action. In all, you should be able to clearly identify *who* is doing an action described in a sentence. If the doer of an action is unclear in a sentence, then revise the sentence to make this clear.

PARALLEL SENTENCE STRUCTURE

A parallel structure implies that the sentence uses consistent words and phrases. Here, we give two rules to help you identify and use parallel sentence structure.

Rule 1: Do not mix forms of elements or words in a list, such as elements or words ending in *-ing*, *-ly*, and *-ed*.

- INCORRECT: The athletics test involved throwing, blocking, tackling, and making maneuvers. (Not parallel; the last word changes the *-ing* form.)
- CORRECT: The athletics test involved throwing, blocking, tackling, and maneuvering. (Parallel; all words in the set end in the same *-ing* form.)

Rule 2: A parallel structure that begins with clauses must keep on with clauses.

- INCORRECT: Participants were told to arrive 15 minutes early for the study, to complete all forms, and that they should dress appropriately. (Not parallel; the last underlined clause changes pattern or form.)
- CORRECT: Participants were told to arrive 15 minutes early for the study, to complete all forms, and to dress appropriately. (Parallel; all clauses have the same form or pattern.)

Spelling

In this final section of the guide we will review commonly misspelled words in English. Students often take spelling for granted because Microsoft® Office software includes a spell-check feature. However, many words can be improperly used in a sentence yet be spelled correctly. For example, consider "She was *hosing* around" versus "She was horsing around." In the first sentence, an *r* is missing from the word *horsing*; however, both spellings are a correct word. As another common example consider "He came *form* nowhere" versus "He came *from* nowhere." In the first sentence, the order of *o* and *r* is reversed in the word *from*; the spellings of each word, however, are correct—it is the meaning of each word that is different. Mistakes that are not caught by spell-check also often occur when we drop or forget to add letters to the beginning (e.g., *[un]necessary*, *[mis]used*) or ending (e.g., *common[ly]*, *play[s]*, *grant[ed]*, *no[t]*) of otherwise correctly spelled words. It can be easy to miss or overlook mistakes such as those given as examples here. Make sure you carefully proofread your work before you submit it to try to catch these types of silly and unnecessary mistakes.

Also a concern is misspellings caused by a misunderstanding of the meanings of words used in a sentence. Grammatical and spelling errors often occur because we improperly use words we think are being used correctly. Common examples include *that* versus *which*, *accept* versus *except*, and *then* versus *than*. Mistakes in the use of these words can be difficult to overcome because the author can often "think" the use of these words is correct when in fact it is wrong. To help clarify some of the most common grammatical and spelling errors in English, the following table lists 26 words that are commonly misused. How each word is used in a sentence (as a noun, verb, etc.) and definitions for each word are given, along with examples, if needed, to further clarify the correct meanings and uses of the words.

Words	Meaning
accept/except	*accept:* (verb) to receive something; to join, consent, or enter into agreement
	except: (verb) to exclude or leave out; (preposition) not including; other than
affect/effect	*affect:* (noun) emotion or desire; (verb) to influence or act upon
	effect: (noun) the result of a consequence, action; (verb) to bring about or implement
afterward/afterword	*afterward:* (adverb) at a later time; subsequently
	afterword: (noun) a concluding section in a book or work
already/all ready	*already:* (adverb) by an implied or specified time; now; so soon; e.g., It is break <u>already</u> [by this time].
	all ready: (adjective) completely prepared; e.g., The study was <u>all ready</u> [completely prepared] to begin.
alright/all right	*alright:* (adjective, adverb) to be satisfactory or acceptable; e.g., The evidence is <u>alright</u> [satisfactory].
	all right: (adjective, adverb) without doubt; accurate or acceptable; e.g., The evidence is <u>all right</u> [accurate]. Note: In English, alright is not widely accepted as a word, so avoid its use.
altogether/all together	*altogether:* (adverb) entirely; completely; e.g., The event was <u>altogether</u> [entirely] successful.
	all together: (adverb) collectively; at the same time; e.g., We completed the study <u>all together</u> [collectively].
among/between	*among:* (preposition) surrounded by; being a member in a larger set
	between: (adverb) at, into, or across a space separating two points in position or time
amount/number	*amount:* (noun) a quantity; (verb) a total when added to together
	number: (noun) an arithmetic or countable value; (verb) to comprise or amount to
assure/ensure/insure	*Assure:* (verb) to make secure or certain; to put the mind at rest
	Ensure: (verb) to make secure or certain; to put the mind at rest [assure, ensure: same meanings]
	Insure: (verb) to guarantee persons or property from risk

Words	Meaning
breath/breathe	*breath:* (noun) An ability to inhale and exhale air, oxygen, etc.; exhalation that can be seen, smelled, or heard *breathe:* (verb) to take air into the lungs and exhale it; to be or seem to be alive
can/may	*can:* (verb) has the ability to; be able to; e.g., The analysis <u>can</u> detect effects because it has high statistical power. *may:* (verb) expressing possibility; has permission to; e.g., The institutional review board reported that the researchers <u>may</u> run their study.
cite/site	*cite:* (noun) a citation; (verb) to quote *site:* (noun) a spatial location or position of interest; (verb) to fix or build [something] in a particular location
compliment/complement	*compliment:* (noun) a polite express of praise; (verb) to praise or congratulate *complement:* (noun) something that completes or makes perfect; (verb) to enhance or improve in some way; to make perfect
counsel/council	*counsel:* (noun) advice; (verb) to give [someone] advice *council:* (noun) a body or assembly of persons convened for consultation, deliberation, or advice
everyone/every one	*everyone:* (pronoun) every person [in a group]; e.g., On this day, <u>everyone</u> [every person] agreed. *every one:* (pronoun) each one; The awardee thanked <u>every one</u> [each person] at the ceremony. Note: In English, everyone and everybody can be used interchangeably and mean the same thing.
few/little	*few:* (noun) a minority of people; (adjective) a small number of *little:* (adjective) small in size, amount, or degree; (adverb) to a small extent
its/it's	*its:* (pronoun) forms the possessive case of it; belonging to it, e.g., The board had <u>its</u> meeting. *it's:* contraction of "it is"; Note: Using APA style, always write out "it is."
lose/loose	*lose:* (verb) to be deprived of; cease or fail to retain *loose:* (verb) to set free; release; (adjective) not firmly in place; able to be detached
many/much	*many:* (noun) the majority of people; (adjective) a large number of people *much:* (adverb) to a great extent; (adjective) a large amount [in quantity]
mute/moot	*mute:* (noun) a person who cannot speak; (verb) to reduce or soften sound; (adjective) temporarily speechless *moot:* (verb) to raise or suggest for discussion; (adjective) a subject of debate, dispute, or uncertainty
past/passed	*past:* (noun) a previous time; (adjective) gone by and no longer exists; (adverb) to pass from one side [of something] to another; (preposition) on a further side of [something] *passed:* (verb) move or lie in a specific direction or position

(Continued)

(Continued)

Words	Meaning
principle/principal	*principle:* (noun) a fundamental truth, rule, or belief that governs individual/group behavior *principal:* (noun) person with highest authority or importance; (adjective) most important
that/which	*that:* (pronoun, adjective, adverb, conjunction) used to identify key information about something or someone; e.g., It was in this study <u>that</u> researchers first discovered . . . [*That* allows for a clear transition and flow of key information in the sentence.] *which:* (pronoun) used to specify information related to something previously mentioned or from a definite set; e.g., The landmark study, <u>which</u> was conducted in the 1950s . . . [The information that follows which relates back to the study]; e.g., There are so many classes I like; <u>which</u> do I choose? [*Which* refers to a choice based on a definite set or availability of classes.] Note: Which is usually preceded by a comma; that does not take a comma.
then/than	*then:* (adverb) at a given time; after that; next; soon afterward *than:* (conjunction) introduces a comparison; expresses an exception or contrast
there/they/their/they're	*there:* (adverb) in, at, or to a place or position; e.g., <u>Go there</u> to take your turn. *they:* (pronoun) something or someone previously mentioned or easily identified; e.g., <u>They</u> get a turn. *their:* (adjective) forms the possessive case of *they*; e.g., It is <u>their</u> turn. *they're:* contraction of "they are"; Note: Using APA style, always write out "they are."
who/whose/who's	*who:* (pronoun) used to identify a person or people; introduces a clause that gives greater detail about a person or people; e.g., <u>Who</u> has the next turn?; e.g., The student <u>who</u> went out of turn. *whose:* (adjective) forms the possessive case of *who*; e.g., <u>Whose</u> turn is it? *who's:* contraction of "who is"; Note: Using APA style, always write out "who is."
you/your/you're	*you:* (pronoun) refers to the person who is being addressed; e.g., <u>You</u> have a degree. *your:* (adjective) forms the possessive case of you; e.g., It is <u>your</u> degree. *you're:* contraction of "you are"; Note: Using APA style, always write out "you are."

A.3 Sample APA-Style Manuscript

Writing an APA-style manuscript is unique. The general format for a submitted APA-style manuscript is restated here (from that originally stated in Chapter 21):

- **Title page.** Page 1; includes title, author(s), affiliations, and author note with contact information of primary author.

- **Abstract** (defined in Chapter 2). Page 2; a brief overview of the manuscript no more than 250 words.

- **Main body.** Includes many subheadings beginning on page 3. (1) The introduction section includes a literature review and identification of research hypotheses. (2) The method section includes a description of participants, materials and apparatus, procedures, and analyses. (3) The results section includes a summary of data and the statistical analyses used. (4) The discussion section includes an interpretation and evaluation of the data and how these relate to the research hypotheses.

- **References.** A complete list of all references for each source cited in the manuscript, on a separate page.

- **Footnotes** (if any). Footnotes are used to provide additional content (such as clarification about a procedure or outcome) or acknowledge copyright permissions. Many manuscripts are written without needing a footnotes section; however, if this section is included in the manuscript, then it should immediately follow the references section.

- **Tables** (if any). Each table is given on a separate page following the references. The tables are inserted into the main body upon publication of a manuscript. Table notes are included with each table.

- **Figures** (if any). Each figure is given on a separate page following the tables. The figures are inserted into the main body upon publication of a manuscript. Figure captions are included with each figure. Note: Keep in mind that you are submitting papers for class to your professor and not an editor, so your professor may want you to insert figures and tables in the main body of the text.

- **Appendices** (if any). In some cases, there may be supplemental materials, such as surveys, illustrations, or instructions for using complex equipment. Many manuscripts are written without needing an appendix; however, if this section is included, then it should be at the end of the manuscript.

For multiple experiments, the main body is modified a bit. The order of the main body for multiple experiments is (1) "Introduction" heading; (2) "General Method" heading (for methods common to all experiments); (3) "Experiment 1" heading, with "Method" (specific to only that experiment), "Results," and "Discussion" subheadings; (4) "Experiment 2" heading with the same subheadings, and so on for all experiments; and (5) "General Discussion" heading (this gives an overall summary for all experiments). Using APA style, main headings are centered, whereas subheadings are left aligned on the page. In sum, the only change is in the main body to allow for multiple experiments to be included.

To write an APA-style manuscript, you can refer also to the sample manuscript provided here, which is adapted from a manuscript published in 2015 in the *Journal of Special Education*. The research reported in this sample manuscript was completed at the time by two professors (Dr. Lynn Ahlgrim-Delzell and Dr. Diane Browder) and three undergraduate students (Leah Wood, Angela Preston, and Amy Kemp-Inman). Please feel free to use this sample manuscript to guide your own writing.

The running head
is all capital letters
and appears flush
left in a header. It
is a maximum of
50 characters.

Manuscript pages
are numbered at the
top right of every
page.

Systematic Instruction of Phonics Skills Using an iPad for Students With Developmental Disabilities Who Are AAC Users

Lynn Ahlgrim-Delzell[1], PhD

Diane M. Browder[1], PhD

Leah Wood[2], PhD

Carol Stanger[3], MS

Angela Preston[1], MEd

Amy Kemp-Inman[1], MM

1 University of North Carolina at Charlotte

2 California Polytechnic State University

3 The Attainment Company, Inc.

The title, author
or authors, and
affiliations are
centered. The title
is a maximum of
12 words if possible.

Author Note

Author Note is
centered, and each
paragraph below it is
indented.

Correspondence concerning this article should be addressed to Dr. Lynn Ahlgrim-Delzell, Department of Educational Leadership, University of North Carolina at Charlotte, 9201 University City Blvd, Charlotte, NC 28223-0001. Contact information: 704-687-8636 (W), laahlgri@uncc.edu. Support for this research was provided in part by Contract ED-IES-11-C-0027 of the U.S. Department of Education, Institute of Education Sciences, awarded to The Attainment Company. The opinions expressed do not necessarily reflect the position or policy of the Department of Education, and no official endorsement should be inferred.

"Abstract" is centered on the top line. The paragraph below it is not indented.

Abstract

The body of the abstract describes the hypotheses, participants, research design, basic findings, and implications in 150 to 250 words.

A phonics-based reading curriculum in which students used an iPad to respond was created for students with developmental disabilities not able to verbally participate in traditional phonics instruction due to their use of augmentative and assistive communication. Evidence-based instructional techniques of time delay and a system of least prompts were used in conjunction with text-to-speech software to enable students to participate in phonics instruction. The instruction included phoneme identification, segmenting and decoding words, sight words, blending, and comprehension after reading a short, decodable passage. Students were randomly assigned to a treatment group who received the phonics instruction using an iPad or a comparison group who received sight word instruction on the iPad. A repeated measures ANOVA found that students who received the iPad-based phonics curriculum outperformed the comparison students on phoneme identification, segmenting and decoding words, sight words, and reading comprehension. HLM analysis supports a two-level model with a time by group membership interaction effect, the inclusion of student-level variables not statistically significant. Implications for practice are provided.

Keywords: phonics, time delay, systematic instruction, autism, developmental disability

Italicize and center a list of four to five keywords.

For header: The introduction begins on page 3 with the running head.

Systematic Instruction of Phonics Skills Using an iPad for Students With Developmental Disabilities Who Are AAC Users

The title is centered on line 1.

Learning to read is a cornerstone skill in a literate society. Lack of reading skills and exposure to print, including the knowledge shared in print, can lead to long-term consequences including less developed skills in other academic areas (Lonigan, 2006). The National Reading Panel (NRP, 2000) recommendations for teaching reading identified five essential components: (a) phonemic awareness, (b) phonics, (c) fluency, (d) vocabulary, and (e) text comprehension. The NRP research review, however, did not include research conducted with students with disabilities. This left a void in understanding what and how to teach reading skills to students with developmental disabilities, especially individuals with intellectual disability and autism spectrum disorder.

The introduction begins on line 2 and is indented.

In contrast to the NRP recommendations, reading research with students with both intellectual disability and autism spectrum disorder has overly emphasized sight words with few demonstrations of phonics instruction. In a comprehensive review, Joseph and Seery (2004) found only seven studies targeting code-based strategies for students with intellectual disability. Browder, Wakeman, Spooner, Ahlgrim-Delzell, and Algozzine (2006) identified 128 studies for students with moderate/severe intellectual disability or autism spectrum disorder, but only 17 included phonics instruction. Instead, most studies targeted sight word learning using systematic prompting strategies like time delay. Spector (2011) found similar strategies used to teach sight words to students with autism spectrum disorder. In a review focused specifically on reading for students with autism spectrum disorder, Whalon, Al Otaiba, and Delano (2009) found 11 studies with only 6 that targeted phonics. Given that students with developmental disabilities often struggle with memory capacity, students who are taught to read using a sight word memorization approach will be limited in the amount of text they can read and comprehend (Connor, Alberto, Compton, & O'Connor, 2014). Additionally, students with moderate-to-severe disabilities have not traditionally had access to literacy-rich environments, due at least in part to the assumption that they could not learn or benefit from literacy instruction (Kliewer, 2008).

Studies published since these reviews have provided additional promise that students with developmental disabilities can learn code-focused skills as well as sight words. Browder and colleagues (Browder, Ahlgrim-Delzell, Courtade, Gibbs, & Flowers, 2008; Browder, Ahlgrim-Delzell, Flowers, & Baker, 2012) developed and evaluated a comprehensive reading curriculum using systematic instruction and response prompting for elementary students with moderate-to-severe intellectual disability. They found that students engaged in the curriculum were able to make significant gains in phonological awareness as compared to students in the comparison group. Other researchers (Allor, Mathes, Roberts, Jones, & Champlin, 2010; Allor, Mathes, Roberts, Cheatham, & Champlin, 2010; Chai, Vail, & Ayres, 2015; Flores, Shippen, Alberto, & Crowe, 2004; Lemons, Mrachko, Kostewicz, & Paterra, 2012) have found significant increases in both phonological awareness and phonics skills for elementary students with mild-to-moderate intellectual disability who received systematic instruction in a comprehensive phonics-based program. Similarly, several researchers have shown promise for phonics instruction for students with autism spectrum disorder (Bailey, Angell, & Stoner, 2011; Grindle, Hughes, Seville, Huxley, & Hastings, 2013; Leytham, Pierce, Baker, Miller, & Tandy, 2015; Travers et al., 2011). A common feature of the research for students with intellectual disability and that for students with autism spectrum disorder is the use of explicit instructional strategies like systematic prompting (e.g., Browder et al., 2012) or direct instruction (e.g., Flores et al., 2004). A difference is that more studies for students with autism spectrum disorder have used computer-assisted instruction (Whalon et al., 2009).

Previous works are synthesized by reporting a common finding.

There may be differences in how reading is acquired with subgroups of students with developmental disabilities (e.g., Lemons et al., 2012). One subgroup especially underrepresented in reading research is students who rely on alternative augmentative communication (AAC) and do not have the speech that most reading programs assume in teaching phonics. Almost 40% or 138,000 of the 347,000 children with developmental disabilities below the age of 15 have severe difficulty with speech (U.S. Census Bureau, 2010). The need exists to identify interventions that make it possible for students with developmental disabilities who rely on AAC to participate in phonics instruction.

There is a gap in what we know in teaching reading to this group of students.

Connor et al. (2014) reviewed the results of reading studies funded by the Institute of Education Sciences (IES) and noted the need for more research focused on students with intellectual disability and limited speech. In addition to concluding that students with low-incidence disabilities (e.g., moderate intellectual disability, autism spectrum disorder, and deaf/hard of hearing) benefit from explicit, systematic instruction in phonemic awareness and phonics instruction, Conner et al. recommended that future research include developing comprehensive curricula utilizing systematic instruction for teaching phonics that accommodates students with communication needs who require AAC.

Several researchers have explored ways to teach phonics-related skills to students with communication support needs. Swinehart-Jones and Heller (2009) used a three-step decoding strategy to teach students with cerebral palsy and dysarthritic speech to decode a word; however, demonstration of the skill was indirectly measured through student identification of each word's corresponding picture. Similarly, Copeland and Keefe (2007) provided students with an object or symbol to indicate recognition of letter sounds. Coleman-Martin, Heller, Cihak, and Irvine (2005) used PowerPoint software to present words and phonemes to students with severe speech impairments (one had autism spectrum disorder). In their approach, the teacher asked the student to sound out words "in their head." In contrast, Bailey et al. (2011) had students with autism spectrum disorder who used AAC demonstrate decoding by pointing to pictures for first sounds or for segmented words produced by the interventionist. Chai et al. (2015) used an iPad and constant time delay to teach phonemic awareness by asking students to select pictures that began with the same sound as the target phoneme.

Researchers have used a variety of response options when implementing code-based strategies. Using the *Early Literacy Skills Builder* curriculum (Browder, Gibbs, Ahlgrim-Delzell, Courtade, & Lee, 2007), Browder et al. (2012) provided students with several receptive language response options to indicate their understanding of letters and words such as indicating initial sounds from an array of letters, finding the picture for a segmented word, and indicating pictures with first sounds of words. Coyne, Pisha, Dalton, Zeph, and Smith (2012) used e-books and letter-word recognition games as a part of a comprehensive reading curriculum for students with intellectual disability, including several word attack skills. Although each of these interventions demonstrated some use of letter-sound correspondence, none of them provided a way for students to directly manipulate phonemes (e.g., producing letter sounds, blending or segmenting phonemes), a crucial component of phonics and phonemic awareness instruction (NRP, 2000).

Ahlgrim-Delzell, Browder, and Wood (2014) investigated the use of an AAC device that had the technology to allow students with limited speech to segment and blend speech sounds. The researchers paired the device with systematic and explicit instruction to evaluate the acquisition of phonics skills for students with intellectual disability who used AAC. In a single-case multiple-probe design across participants, instruction was provided on three phonics skills (letter-sound correspondence,

Example of use of &

Use an ampersand (&) to give a reference in parentheses; use the word "and" when a reference is given in the text.

Example of use of *and*

decoding, and blending) and participants were asked to use the AAC device to demonstrate these skills. All three participants improved their phonics skills using the device. In contrast, the AAC device was restrictive due to its fixed surface size and use of overlays that had to be changed manually as the students' phonics skills evolved. Further investigation is needed for the use of computer-based assistive technology that can incorporate more flexible, digital text and formatting. Portable electronic devices, such as tablet computers, are especially promising for increasing motivation and accessibility to instructional content for students with disabilities (Kagohara et al., 2013; Mechling, 2011).

Students with developmental disabilities can learn to read phonetically. Previous research has not examined outcomes for students with developmental disabilities who also use AAC. The purpose of the current study was to build on the recommendations of Connor et al. (2014) and the research of Ahlgrim-Delzell et al. (2014) to develop and evaluate phonics instruction that accommodates students who use AAC. Specifically, our research questions were: (1) What are the effects of a phonics curriculum with systematic instruction and an iPad™ on the identification of phonemes and decoding skills by students with developmental disabilities who use ACC? and (2) What student or teacher characteristics mediate the changes in growth between students?

Research questions are clearly stated.

Method

Center "Method" in bold on the line below the last line of the introduction (not on a separate page).

Participants

Place "Participants," flush left and in bold, on the line below the last line of the "Method" section.

Teachers were recruited by Exceptional Children Department administrators of two school districts in the southeastern region of the United States. Teachers who agreed to participate were asked to identify students who met the eligibility criteria and obtain signed parental consent forms. Student eligibility criteria included (a) use of any AAC system needed to supplement verbal responding during instruction such as a picture system or a technology device, (b) completion or current use of a foundational literacy program or demonstration of competence in identifying at least five letters or sight words, (c) physical capacity to use the iPad2™ by touching response options, (d) inability to decode text, and (e) diagnosed with either intellectual disability or developmental delay by their school system. Researchers observed each student to reconfirm eligibility criteria. An informal assessment of letter identification (e.g., "Which of these letters is the letter *s*?" with four options) and reading of common, simple CVC words such as *mat* (e.g., "Read this word and point to the picture of the word" with four picture options) was used to confirm eligibility for criterion (d) in addition to teacher report of previous student literacy instruction. Teachers also confirmed eligibility criterion (e) by referencing school records.

Students. A prospective power analysis was conducted prior to the study to estimate the number of participants needed based on an estimated effect size (Cohen's $d = 2.65$) from a previous single-case study (Ahlgrim-Delzell et al. 2014), power of .8, with eight repeated measurements using Optimal Design Plus software (Spybrook et al., 2013). The prospective power analysis estimated the need for 40 participants. Thirty-one students in Grades K through 8 met the eligibility criteria and participated in the study. Although it was possible that the study would be underpowered, it was decided to continue with the research because the systematic process would still be useful in developing the curriculum and future research.

Table 1 displays the demographic characteristics of the students by treatment/control group. In addition to a diagnosis of either intellectual disability or developmental delay, 13 students had a diagnosis of autism spectrum disorder. An IQ could not be obtained for three students because they were unable to participate in ability testing. The eligibility criteria included a diagnosis of intellectual disability or developmental delay and not IQ in order to be more inclusive of the kind of students who were ready to learn to read but did

Subheadings are indented, bold, and followed by a period. The content of the subheading begins on the same line.

not have the ability to participate in traditional reading instruction because of the use of

AAC to communicate; this resulted in a wide range of IQs (40–88).

   Teachers. Twenty-two teachers from 16 schools participated in the study. Table 2

displays teacher characteristics by group (treatment, control, or both as described below).

All of the teachers indicated they had some type of literacy or reading training prior to the

study provided by either the school system or completion of a university reading course.

Setting

   The study was implemented from October 2012 to June 2013. Eight of the

16 schools were located in a large, urban district, and 8 schools were located in a rural

district. Teacher-delivered instruction primarily occurred daily at a table or desk in the self-

contained classrooms in which the students were assigned. Individual lessons ranged from

15 to 20 minutes.

   Teachers implemented the interventions after receiving 1 day of training for

both the treatment and control conditions. Training included a theoretical presentation on

the NRP (2000) components of learning to read and principles of systematic instruction,

including time delay and system of least prompts. Demonstrations of the interventions

tailored for both treatment and control groups and practice with the teaching procedures

with fidelity were provided. Each teacher was observed by a researcher and received a

fidelity score of 80% or higher before training ended. Following training, teachers received

ongoing feedback and support for implementation of the intervention and management of

behaviors incompatible with learning through weekly visits, e-mail communications, and

video examples posted online.

Research Design and Random Assignment

The research design outlines the design for the study with a description. Some studies will use a "Procedures" section instead.

   This study utilized a randomized control trial (RCT) design where students were

randomly assigned to treatment and control conditions using simple random assignment

blocked by teacher when multiple students in a classroom were determined eligible to participate. There were nine teachers with both treatment and control students, six teachers with only treatment students, and seven teachers with only control students. Teachers were directed to provide only the instructional condition assigned to individual students. The study began with a pretest followed by implementation of the intervention for 8 months. Eight monthly probes on the dependent variable were collected for each student. The final monthly probe served as the posttest. Independent samples t tests and chi-square analyses were conducted at pretest to identify differences between the randomly assigned treatment and control groups. There were no statistically significant differences on phoneme identification ($t = .903$, $df = 29$, $p = .37$), blending sounds to identify words ($t = .828$, $df = 29$, $p = .41$), decoding for picture word-matching ($t = 1.51$, $df = 29$, $p = .14$), or any of the demographic characteristics as noted in Table 1. There were no statistical differences between the groups of teachers as noted in Table 2.

Treatment Fidelity

Treatment fidelity was assessed each week by a PhD graduate research assistant who observed and video-recorded teachers' implementation of treatment and control group procedures during instruction and completed a procedural fidelity checklist. Fidelity for teachers in both conditions was calculated by dividing the total number of required steps by the total number of steps performed correctly, multiplied by 100. Interrater reliability occurred for 30% of sessions by a second member of the research team who independently scored the fidelity checklist using video recording. Agreement was calculated by dividing the number of possible agreements by the number of agreements reached, multiplied by 100. Mean fidelity for the treatment intervention was 94.8% with means for individual teachers ranging from 88.4% to 98.0%. Interrater reliability was 97.4%. Mean fidelity for the control intervention was 96.8% with means for individual teachers ranging from 75.0% to 100%. Interrater reliability was 100%. Observations of treatment fidelity also offered the opportunity to discern possible treatment diffusion. No instances of treatment diffusion were noted.

Intervention for the Treatment Group

The *Early Reading Skills Builder* (*ERSB*) was the name given to the intervention created for the treatment group. The *ERSB* curriculum blended iPad-based technological speech supports using GoTalk Now (GTN; The Attainment Company, n.d.) and systematic instruction using time delay and shaping/fading of model prompts. The skills to be taught and phoneme sequence were derived from existing curricula (i.e., *Reading Mastery, Corrective Reading, Early Interventions in Reading*). The beginning levels of the *ERSB* were designed to overlap the phonemes and sight words taught in the *Early Literacy Skills Builder* (*ELSB;* Browder et al., 2007) and to serve as the next-step reading curriculum for students who had received this or similar early literacy instruction. Three literacy experts (one general education literacy expert and two experts with expertise in developmental delay/intellectual disability) reviewed the curriculum materials, sequence of skills, and phonemes.

The *ERSB* was divided into eight levels with five lessons per level taught in a 1:1 teacher-student ratio. The skills taught and a description are provided in Table 3. The curriculum presented three new phonemes and a review of three previous phonemes at each level. Target words used in the skill instruction included words that were also in the connected text presented as a story, but also novel words that were not included in the stories. The stories comprised words using phonemes and sight words introduced to that point in the skills training (e.g., Level 6, Lesson 3: I have a pet. The pet is Jed. Jed can be bad.). The comprehension questions were literal and could only be answered through correct reading of the text. To move to the next level in the curriculum, students needed 80% correct answers for two consecutive sessions across all skills.

To indicate their responses, students pressed buttons on the iPad. Phonemes, words, and pictures were programmed into pages on the GTN iPad app. Auditory cueing was activated within the app; this feature allowed students to press buttons on the iPad to voice phonemes or words for review before final selection of their answer. Two unique technological features of the GTN app were that it also included a blending feature, in which students could select a series of individual phonemes to hear the phonemes voiced as a blended word using text-to-speech software, and a quiz feature that would randomize the response options on the page each time the page was accessed. This iPad-based curriculum was designed so that all responses could be made with the device, but verbal approximations of the words were also encouraged, such as "Good using your voice!"

Intervention for the Control Group

The control group received a structured business-as-usual intervention. In order to control for possible confounds of iPad use, systematic instruction, and opportunities to respond, teachers also used the iPad with the GTN app for students in the control group to teach the literacy and/or reading skills that they were already implementing with the same number of response opportunities as the *ERSB*. Teachers were given a list of the target number of responses for each lesson. In this way, these students were considered a control group that did not receive phonics instruction as opposed to a comparison group that received a different, but equivalent, type of phonics instruction. As noted in the review of literature, there is no alternative phonics curriculum for students who require communication support, and sight words have been the most frequently taught alternative. Teachers were trained to use the GTN app and the same systematic instructional procedures (i.e., time delay and system of least prompts) as the treatment intervention and develop materials using the app to teach sight words or to read aloud stories. For instance, teachers programmed sight words into the app and taught the words using constant time delay procedures. They also used the iPads to supplement read-aloud stories using images from the Internet, the GTN image library, or a photo gallery and had students make responses such as identifying vocabulary words or answering questions on the iPad.

Dependent Variables

The dependent variables were created by the researchers from the *ERSB* in a 106-item curriculum-based measure (CBM) that included three *ERSB* skills: (a) phoneme identification (25 items, actual range of scores was 0–25, $\alpha = .90$), (b) blending sounds to identify words (41 items, actual range of scores was 0–41, $\alpha = .87$), and (c) decoding for picture-word matching (40 items, actual range of scores was 2–39, $\alpha = .83$). Subtest-total score correlations ranged from .831 (phoneme identification) to .931 (blending sounds to identify words). A description of each measure is provided in Table 4. Decoding also provided a measure of comprehension where the student had to find a picture that illustrated the meaning of a decodable word.

The items tested in the CBM were similar in format to the *ERSB* curriculum using the GTN app on the iPad but included a mix of trained and untrained items. In this way, the dependent measure was a proximal measure of the intervention. A proximal CBM measure was needed to evaluate the development of the *ERSB* curriculum, which was a primary purpose of the study. The link between the CBM and the curriculum provides support for content validity of the CBM. An extensive search for an accessible distal measure of blending and decoding skills for this population of students was not successful.

Data Analyses

> Add "Data Analyses," flush left and in bold. This section is optional in some journals but required by other journals.

In order to answer the first research question regarding the effect of the *ERSB,* a repeated measures analysis of variance (ANOVA) was used to examine the interaction effects of the *ERSB* instruction and group membership. Cohen's *d,* using a pooled standard deviation, was calculated to measure the magnitude of the difference between the treatment and control groups at posttest for each of the individual subtests and the total score.

In order to answer the second research question to investigate possible mediating variables, a three-level hierarchical linear model (HLM) was employed. HLM analysis accounts for the effects of nested, or hierarchical, data. In this study, nesting occurred within the individual students, as repeated measures of student data were collected eight times across the school year and all student data were nested within respective teachers. HLM provides an opportunity to examine the influence of each level of the hierarchy on the outcome measure.

Three-level models were examined with measurement occasions at Level 1 (across eight monthly measurements), student group membership (treatment vs. control) at Level 2, and student/teacher characteristics at Level 3 with total score as the outcome measure.

"Results" is centered in bold. All statistical outcomes are reported in this section.

Results

Descriptive Statistics and ANOVA Results

Prior to running the analyses, data were screened and assumptions were evaluated for use of the parametric statistics. The assumptions of normal distribution and equal group variances were tenable. For the treatment group, there were two cases of missing data across the eight probes. For the control group, there was one case of missing data across the eight probes. Descriptive statistics for the pretest and posttest for each subtest and total score by group are displayed in Table 5. Cohen's d at posttest was .51 for blending sounds to identify words (moderate effect), .88 (large effect) for decoding for picture-word matching, 1.12 (large effect) for phoneme identification, and .89 (large effect) for the total score. Data were analyzed using a repeated measures ANOVA comparing pretest/posttest scores and treatment/control groups. There were statistically significant interaction effects for three of the four comparisons, including phoneme identification, $F(1, 7) = 3.23$, $p < .01$, $\eta_p^2 = .12$; decoding for picture-word matching, $F(1, 7) = 3.81$, $p < .01$, $\eta_p^2 = .12$; and total score, $F(1, 7) = 7.09$, $p < .01$, $\eta_p^2 = .21$, whereby students in the treatment group outperformed the students in the control condition. Blending sounds to identify words was not statistically significant, $F(1, 7) = .88$, $p = .53$, $\eta_p^2 = .03$. Both groups improved in the ability to blend sounds to identify words. These effects are illustrated by the graphs in Figure 1. The slope of the treatment group is steeper for these three measures, suggesting greater growth.

HLM Results

Three HLMs were tested, including a null model (Model 1), a time + group interaction model (Model 2), and a time + group interaction and other student background model (Model 3). The effect sizes (proportion of variance explained by the models) and the deviance values of these models were used as the comparison between these models. Table 6 provides the parameter estimates of the fixed and random effects of the three models. Since group membership was assigned, a fixed effects model was used. Time was centered at zero at the pretest prior to implementation of the *ERSB*. A sequential increase in numbers of time represented each of the monthly assessments during which the *ERSB* was implemented. An intraclass correlation coefficient of the unconditional model suggests that 81.30% of the variance in scores lies in the growth in time, 18.60% of the variance in scores can be explained by student-level characteristics, and the remaining 0.10% of the variance is attributable to teacher characteristics. Although the variance component at the teacher level is very small, a teacher level was used to account for the nesting of treatment and control group students within teachers. Teacher experience (measured by number of years) in teaching children with special needs was added at the teacher level. Compared with the unconditional model (null model), Model 2 reduced the Level 1 monthly growth variance by 45.20%, student-level variance by 9.59%, and teacher-level variance by 85.31%, whereas Model 3 reduced the Level 1 monthly growth variance by 49.46%, student-level variance by 18.20%, and teacher-level variance by 32.80%.

Using the reduction in the deviance statistics, the group + time interaction model (Model 2) appears to be the best fit. Although Model 3 has more student-level variables and the student's diagnosis of autism is a statistically significant and positive predictor of the monthly rate increase, the change of the deviance scores from Model 2 to Model 3 is not statistically significant, which means that Model 2 is a good fit and parsimonious model. This mixed model is presented as

$$
\begin{aligned}
\text{Total score} = \beta_{000} + \beta_{001} * YRSTEACH_j + \beta_{010} * GROUP_{ij} + \beta_{100} * TIME_{mij} + \\
\beta_{101} * TIME_{mij} * YRSTEACH_j + \beta_{110} * TIME_{mij} * GROUP_{ij} + e_{0ij} + r_{00j} + \varepsilon_{mij}
\end{aligned}
$$

The intercept of the model (34.33) was the initial status (pretest) of control group students. The monthly increase rate of control group students was not statistically significantly different from zero. However, the treatment group students' monthly increase was 2.36 more than that of control group students, and this difference was statistically significant.

Discussion

This study attempted to address Connor et al.'s (2014) recommendation for a comprehensive literacy program that provides for more frequent and intensive instruction in teaching phonics skills to students with low-incidence disabilities who use AAC. Specifically, this research extended the literature on phonics instruction for students with intellectual disability/developmental delay who use AAC by demonstrating that systematic and explicit instruction and iPad technology that provided accessible receptive and expressive response modes such that students were able to manipulate phonemes to learn to decode words to read connected text and answer comprehension questions. This work extends the work of Ahlgrim-Delzell et al. (2014).

While IQ was not part of the eligibility criteria, 10 of the 12 students who received the *ERSB* curriculum had moderate-to-severe intellectual disability. Several studies have now demonstrated that students with moderate intellectual disability can acquire phonics skills through explicit instructional strategies (Allor, Mathes, Roberts, Jones, et al., 2010; Browder et al., 2012; Flores et al., 2004). Kagohara et al.'s (2013) comprehensive review of the use of an iPad to teach students with developmental disability identified 15 studies, but none of these focused on phonics instruction. The current study adds to the evidence for the effectiveness of the iPad for teaching phonics skills through the use of a new app that made it possible to manipulate and voice phonemes.

Research Findings

The first variable for which there was a significant difference between the treatment and comparison groups was phoneme identification. When the teacher stated a phoneme, the student pressed the corresponding printed letter on the iPad. The iPad then provided immediate feedback by repeating the phoneme as the letter was pressed. This pivotal skill of letter-sound correspondence has been one of the stumbling blocks for students who use AAC. In typical phonics instruction, the student practices voicing the phonemes as well as matching them to printed letters. This technology made voicing phonemes possible. Students receiving the typical sight word comparison instruction, in which the iPad voiced the whole word, did not show the same improvement. Systematic instruction of phoneme identification was essential.

The second variable for which there was a significant difference was decoding words and then finding the corresponding picture. This skill was critical because it demonstrated both decoding an entire CVC word and comprehension of that word. Comprehension has often been overlooked in research for students with developmental disabilities (Browder et al., 2006; Chiang & Lin, 2007). For phonics instruction to be meaningful, comprehension needs to be demonstrated from the onset.

Blending sounds to identify a word did not produce a significant difference. In this skill, the teacher voiced three phonemes and the student identified the printed word. This required the student to remember this series of phonemes and then find the correct word. The response options included highly similar distractors (e.g., cat and cot). Some modification in this presentation may have been needed. Students may have needed to select each letter as it was sounded and then use the technology to voice the full word.

Limitations and Recommendations for Future Research

While the ANOVA for two of the three measures from the CBM had a significant interaction effect indicating that the treatment group outperformed the control group, the lack of significant difference for the third measure, blending sounds to identify words, is a limitation of this study. Although it may imply the need for an alternative way to teach students to match a series of phonemes to words, an alternative explanation is that the finding may have been due to insufficient power as there were only 31 students total when 40 students were estimated to be needed. This alternative explanation is supported by the finding of a moderate effect size despite lack of statistical significance. The power analysis was conducted using the total scores by combining scores on the individual three subtests. For small sample sizes, future research may need to consider conducting power analyses on individual subtests rather than one total score.

There are potential threats to internal and external validity in this study. Potential threats to internal validity include history and instrumentation. Differential group instructional interruptions such as illnesses or school/classroom scheduling issues (e.g., Special Olympics) could have impacted the ability of teachers to conduct the daily instruction as designed. Even though the weekly observations/consultations assisted in remediating any potential long-term issues, it is possible that the accumulated short-term history events across the academic year may have differentially affected one group over the other. A second possible internal threat involves the sole use of a researcher-developed dependent variable. Although there is evidence of content validity and internal consistency, more rigorous evidence of structural, concurrent, or predictive validity was not conducted. Potential threats to external validity include participants and situation given that this study was conducted in only two school systems in self-contained classrooms. Students in general education classrooms with full access to the reading curriculum might respond differently to this intervention. For example, they might have more opportunities to generalize their responses. Generalization of these findings to other participants or situations also may be limited, particularly due to the small sample size.

Other areas for future research include more in-depth understanding of prompting strategies that may be more effective in teaching phonics to students with intellectual disability or developmental delay. Some of the teachers began to hold up a finger while voicing each sound as a visual signal for each phoneme. With this signal, the students perhaps realized when the sound was shifting from sound to sound. Future research could examine variations in repetition of prompts. Some phonemes or phoneme combinations may

Identify potential limitations.

Identify potential areas of future research.

require more repetition than others for discrimination learning. The CBM used distractor items with similar sounds/letters that students sometimes selected by mistake (e.g., tan, ton, pan). One consideration for future research might be to measure the number of correct phoneme locations (e.g., "ton" selected for "tan" would be a score of 2/3) and analyze errors (e.g., selecting "o" for "a") to show subtle progress toward skill mastery and areas for remediation. A process of systematically varying phonemes in distractor words, as described by Heller, Fredrick, Tumlin, and Brineman (2002), can be used to identify specific problematic phonemes or errors based on the location of the phonemes (e.g., middle or ending sounds).

Identify potential areas of future research.

Future research also needs to build comprehension into early phonics instruction for students with developmental disabilities. The measure of decoding in this study was created so students read the word and selected a picture representation of the word to demonstrate the ability to sound out words and comprehend the meaning of the words. This is consistent with measures used in prior research for early stages of reading (Browder et al., 2006), including studies on phonics with students who are nonverbal to infer decoding (Browder et al., 2012; Copeland & Keefe, 2007; Swinehart-Jones & Heller, 2009). Even though advances in technology now make it possible for students to demonstrate decoding through electronically voicing the response, the picture-matching response is an essential measure of comprehension. As students progress in their decoding skills, connected text (e.g., short phrases and sentences) should be provided and linked to meaning (e.g., matching to pictures, supplying missing word).

Identify potential areas of future research.

Finally, research is needed on how technology can be used to promote text comprehension. A comprehensive reading program for students with intellectual disability or developmental delay might include a combination of decoding and comprehending decodable text paired with higher levels of comprehension built in through listening to age-appropriate literature read-alouds (Browder et al., 2009).

Implications for Practice

A critical implication is that this population of students can achieve more than only sight word recognition. When given access to a technology-based phonics curriculum, including decodable text, students with intellectual disability, developmental delay, or autism spectrum disorder who use AAC may learn to read and understand connected text. Connor et al. (2014) noted that students with intellectual disability need beginning reading instruction for longer periods of time. Research by Allor, Allor, Mathes, Roberts, Cheatham, et al. (2010) suggested that students with moderate intellectual disability might need 3 years of instruction for 1 year of typical growth in reading. Our results were consistent with this finding in that students using AAC gained acquisition of multiple phonemes but still would need at least 2 more years to master all phonemes. Many of the students in the current study had spent 2 to 3 years mastering skills in an early literacy curriculum. The need for building early literacy skills combined with the time phonics instruction requires means that students with intellectual disability, developmental delay, or autism spectrum disorder may need the opportunity for intensive beginning reading instruction well into the middle school years.

Students with intellectual disability, developmental delay, or autism spectrum disorder who use AAC may benefit from daily phonics instruction that is delivered using explicit and systematic instruction. An iPad, which can allow students to produce and manipulate individual phonemes to blend and segment, might enable students to learn phonics skills, including identifying sounds in words and reading words to find pictures. This program, which included repetitions of phonics skills, sight word reading, and comprehension, may allow students to gain the skills necessary to both read and understand connected text.

Given how long phonics instruction may take, it is essential that it be paired with comprehension in both research and practice. This comprehension can focus on the specific decoded words (e.g., word to picture matching) and early understanding of simple connected text. Since the need for decodable text will limit the literature accessible

Discuss how the research applies to education practice.

Implication that these students can learn to read.

Implication that it may take a long time to see student progress.

Implication that explicit systematic instruction is beneficial.

Implication that reading instruction includes reading comprehension.

through independent reading, students will also need to acquire alternative ways to access age-appropriate literature, for example, by using technology and read-alouds. These alternative modes should also be paired with comprehension measures to promote broad access to literature.

Summarize and provide commentary on the importance of the research findings.

Conclusion

Perhaps the most important implication of this research is that students who use AAC be given the opportunity for phonics instruction through the use of technology. Much more research is needed on how to teach students who use AAC to read, especially as new technology emerges. For example, technology may make it possible for students to receive immediate feedback as they decode words through software that blocks errors. Although progress may be slower for students with developmental disabilities in learning to decode text, being able to do so increases the chance of becoming literate. Literacy is a cornerstone for all academic learning in school and enhances overall quality of life as an adult. With independence in literacy, individuals with developmental disabilities have more opportunities to communicate through social media, access Internet resources, perform jobs, and enjoy leisure resources. The investment of time to teach individuals with intellectual and developmental disabilities to read may be some of the most important hours spent in school.

References

Center "References" on the top line of a separate page.

Each reference is listed in alphabetical order, and the format for each reference is a hanging indent.

Always use the ampersand (&) symbol for listing the last author of a multiple-author reference.

Use the Publication Manual to find the correct citation for any type of reference. Note that most of the references shown here are for journal articles, but you will also find other types of resources such as Internet documents, a government document, software, curricula, and a book.

Ahlgrim-Delzell, L., Browder, D. M., & Wood, A. L. (2014). Effects of systematic instruction and an augmentative communication device on phonics skills acquisition for students with moderate intellectual disability who are nonverbal. *Education and Training in Autism and Development Disabilities, 49,* 517–534.

Allor, J. H., Mathes, P. G., Roberts, J., Jones, F. G., & Champlin, T. M. (2010). Teaching students with moderate intellectual disabilities to read: An experimental examination of a comprehensive reading intervention. *Education and Training in Autism and Developmental Disabilities, 45,* 3–22.

Allor, J. H., Mathes, P. G., Roberts, J., Cheatham, J. P., & Champlin, T. M. (2010). Comprehensive reading instruction for students with intellectual disabilities: Findings from the first three years of a longitudinal study. *Psychology in the Schools, 47,* 445–466.

Bailey, R. L., Angell, M. E., & Stoner, J. B. (2011). Improving literacy skills in students with complex communication needs who use augmentative/alternative communication systems. *Education and Training in Autism and Developmental Disabilities, 46,* 352–368.

Browder, D. M., Ahlgrim-Delzell, L., Courtade, G., Gibbs, S. L., & Flowers, C. (2008). Evaluation of the effectiveness of an early literacy program for students with significant developmental disabilities using group randomized trial research. *Exceptional Children, 75,* 33–52.

Browder, D. M., Ahlgrim-Delzell, L., Flowers, C., & Baker, J. N. (2012). An evaluation of a multicomponent early literacy program for students with severe developmental disabilities. *Remedial and Special Education, 33,* 237–246.

Browder, D. M., Gibbs, S., Ahlgrim-Delzell, L., Courtade, G., & Lee, A. (2007). *Early Literacy Skills Builder (ELSB).* Verona, WI: Attainment Company.

Browder, D., Gibbs, S., Ahlgrim-Delzell, L., Courtade, G., Mraz, M., & Flowers, C. (2009). Literacy for students with severe developmental disabilities: What should we teach and what should we hope to achieve? *Remedial and Special Education, 30,* 269–282.

Browder, D. M., Wakeman, S. Y., Spooner, F., Ahlgrim-Delzell, L., & Algozzine, B. (2006). Research on reading instruction for individuals with significant cognitive disabilities. *Exceptional Children, 72,* 392–408.

Chai, Z., Vail, C O., Ayres, K.M. (2015). Using an iPad application to promote early literacy development in young children with disabilities. *Journal of Special Education, 48,* 268–278.

Chiang, H. M., & Lin, Y. H. (2007). Reading comprehension instruction for students with autism spectrum disorders: A review of the literature. *Focus on Autism and Other Developmental Disabilities, 22,* 259–267.

Coleman-Martin, M. B., Heller, K. W., Cihak, D. F., & Irvine, K. L. (2005). Using computer-assisted instruction and the nonverbal reading approach to teach word identification. *Focus on Autism and Other Developmental Disabilities, 20,* 80–90.

Connor, C. M., Alberto, P. A., Compton, D. L., & O'Connor, R. E. (2014). *Improving reading outcomes for students with or at risk for reading disabilities: A synthesis of the contributions from the Institute of Education Sciences Research Centers* (NCSER 2014-3000). Washington, DC: National Center for Special Education Research, Institute of Education Sciences, U.S. Department of Education. Retrieved from http://ies.ed.gov/

Copeland, S. R., & Keefe, E. B. (2007). *Effective literacy instruction for students with moderate or severe disabilities.* Baltimore, MD: Brookes Publishing Company.

Coyne, P., Pisha, B., Dalton, B., Zeph, L. A., & Smith, N. C. (2012). Literacy by design: A universal design for learning approach for students with significant intellectual disabilities. *Remedial and Special Education, 33,* 162–172.

Flores, M. M., Shippen, M. E., Alberto, P., & Crowe, L. (2004). Teaching letter-sound correspondence to students with moderate intellectual disabilities. *Journal of Direct Instruction, 4*(2), 173–188.

Grindle, C. F., Hughes, J. C., Saville, M., Huxley, K., & Hastings, R. P. (2013). Teaching early reading skills to children with autism using Mimiosprout early reading. *Behavioral Interventions, 28,* 203–224.

Heller, K. W., Fredrick, L. D., Tumlin, J., & Brineman, D. G. (2002). Teaching decoding for generalization using the Nonverbal Reading Approach. *Journal of Developmental and Physical Disabilities, 14,* 19–35.

Joseph, L. M., & Seery, M. E. (2004). Where is the phonics? A review of the literature on the use of phonetic analysis with students with mental retardation. *Remedial and Special Education, 25,* 88–84.

Kagohara, D. M., Van der Meer, L., Ramdoss, S., O'Reilly, M., Lancioni, G. E., Davis, T. N., … & Sigafoos, J. (2013). Using iPods® and iPads® in teaching programs for individuals with developmental disabilities: A systematic review. *Research in Developmental Disabilities, 34,* 147–156. doi: 10.1016/j.ridd.2012.07.027

Kliewer, C. (2008). Joining the literacy flow: Fostering symbol and written language learning in young children with significant developmental disabilities through the four currents of literacy. *Research & Practice for Persons with Severe Disabilities, 33,* 103–121.

Leytham, P. A., Pierce, T., Baker, J., Miller, S., & Tandy, D. (2015). Evaluation of the nonverbal reading approach for two 12 to 13-year-old students with ASD. *Research in Autism Spectrum Disorders, 9,* 68–76.

Lonigan, C. J. (2006). Development, assessment and promotion of preliteracy skills. *Early Education and Development, 17,* 91–114.

Lemons, C. J., Mrachko, A.A., Kostewicz, D. E., & Paterra, M. F. (2012). Effectiveness of decoding and phonological awareness interventions for children with Down syndrome. *Exceptional Children, 79,* 67–90.

Mechling, L. C. (2011). Review of twenty-first century portable electronic devices for persons with moderate intellectual disabilities and autism spectrum disorder. *Education and Training in Autism and Developmental Disabilities, 46,* 479–498.

National Institute of Child Health and Human Development. (2000). *Report of the National Reading Panel. Teaching children to read: An evidence-based assessment of the scientific research literature on reading and its implications for reading instruction: Reports of the subgroups* (NIH Publication No. 00-4754). Washington, DC: Government Printing Office.

Spector, J. (2011). Sight word instruction for students with autism: An evaluation of the evidence base. *Journal of Autism and Developmental Disorders, 41,* 1411–1422.

Spybrook, J., Bloom, H., Congdon, R., Hill, C., Liu, X, Martinez, A., & Raudenbush, S. (2013). *Optimal design plus empirical evidence* (Version 3.01) [Software]. Retrieved from hlmsoft.net/od

Swinehart-Jones, D., & Heller, K. (2009). Teaching students with severe speech and physical impairments a decoding strategy using internal speech and motoric indicators. *Journal of Special Education, 43,* 131–144. doi:10.1177/0022466908314945

The Attainment Company. (n.d.). *GoTalk Now*. Verona, WI: Author.

Travers, J. C., Higgins, K., Pierce, T., Boone, R., Miller, S., & Tandy, R. (2011). Emergent literacy skills of preschool students with autism: A comparison of teacher-led and computer-assisted instruction. *Education and Training in Autism and Developmental Disabilities, 46,* 326–338.

U.S. Census Bureau. (2010). *Prevalence of specific measures of disability among children under 15 years: 2010*. Retrieved May 19, 2004, from https://www.census.gov/people/disability/publications/disab10/table_A4.pdf

Whalon, K. J., Al Otaiba, S., & Delano, M. E. (2009). Evidence-based reading instruction for individuals with autism spectrum disorders. *Focus on Autism and Other Developmental Disabilities, 24,* 3–16.

Table 1

Characteristics of Student Participants at Pretest

Characteristic	Treatment		Control		p
	n	*%*	*n*	*%*	
Gender					.25
Male	14	82.4	9	64.3	
Female	3	17.6	5	35.7	
Ethnicity					.44
African American	6	35.3	5	35.7	
Caucasian	8	47.1	4	28.6	
Asian	1	5.9	1	7.1	
Latino	2	11.8	4	28.6	
Grade					.76
K	2	11.8	1	7.1	
1	3	17.6	3	21.4	
2	2	11.8	1	7.1	
3	1	5.9	4	28.6	
4	1	5.9	0	0	
5	2	11.8	1	7.1	
6	2	11.8	0	0	
7	2	11.8	2	14.3	
8	2	11.8	2	14.3	
Disability					
Autism	8	47.1	5	35.7	.52
Developmental delay	5	29.4	5	35.7	.72
Intellectual disability	12	70.6	9	64.3	.71
Highest level of communication					.42
Verbalize with words	0	0	1	7.1	
Manual signs/AAC	8	47.1	9	64.3	
Picture symbols	6	35.3	3	21.4	
Gestures	3	17.6	1	7.1	
ELSB experience	14	87.5	11	84.6	.82
IQ					.43
IQ 40–55	10	58.8	9	64.3	
IQ 56–70	3	17.6	4	28.6	
IQ 71–85	1	5.9	0	0	
IQ 86–100	0	0	1	7.1	
Unavailable	3	17.6	0	0	
Mean (SD)		50.1 (9.5)		53.4 (12.5)	
Range of scores		40–71		40–88	
Weekly hours in general education					.40
Mean (SD)		2.4 (6.1)		4.7 (8.8)	
Range of scores		4–24		4–28	

Table 2

Characteristics of Teacher Participants at Pretest

Characteristic	Treatment		Control		Both		
	M	*SD*	*M*	*SD*	*M*	*SD*	*p*
No. years teaching	13.3	10.9	14.6	9.4	12.0	7.7	.858
No. years teaching at current school	7.17	9.17	8.4	11.3	6.0	4.9	.853
No. years teaching special education students	13.3	10.9	11.7	10.5	12.0	7.7	.949
No. years teaching students with intellectual disability or autism spectrum disorder	12.7	11.1	10.6	11.0	11.1	7.69	.924
	F	*%*	*F*	*%*	*F*	*%*	
Type of certification							
Regular, standard	4	66.7	7	100	7	77.8	.28
Probationary, temporary	2	33.3	0	—	2	22.2	
Highest level of education							
Bachelor's	4	66.7	4	57.1	5	55.6	.91
Master's	2	33.3	3	42.9	4	44.4	

Table 3

Description of ERSB Skills and Instructional Procedures

Skill	Description	Instructional Procedures
Identify phonemes in isolation	Given a letter sound, select the letter that represents the sound.	Time delay with model prompt and physical guidance if incorrect or no response
Identify phonemes in words	Given a voiced word, select the letter that represents the first sound in the word.	Time delay with model prompt and physical guidance if incorrect or no response
Segment sounds in words	Given a voiced word, select the letters that represent the sounds in the word.	Time delay with model prompt and physical guidance if incorrect or no response
Blend sounds to identify words	Given a stretched word (e.g., ssaamm), select the word.	Time delay with model prompt and physical guidance if incorrect or no response
Decode words to identify a picture	Given a decodable word, read the word and select the picture that represents the word.	Time delay with model prompt and physical guidance if incorrect or no response
Identify sight words	Given a voiced nondecodable[a] word, select the word.	Time delay with model prompt and physical guidance if incorrect or no response
Read connected text	Read a sentence using sight words and decodable[a] words.	Least intrusive prompting with fading of voiced reading of the passage
Answer literal comprehension questions about the text	Given a literal question from the sentence(s) read, select the correct answer.	Least intrusive prompting redirecting student to read the sentence that contains the correct answer and physical guidance

[a]Decodable words were those that could be decoded using the taught phonemes.

Table 4

Description of the CBM Dependent Variable

Skill	Description	Screenshot of Response Options
Phoneme identification	Select the letter to match a voiced phoneme. "What letter says /s/?"	
Blending sounds to identify words	Select a written word to match a voiced word that was stretched. "/r/ /aaag/. Which word am I saying?"	
Decoding for picture-word matching	Read a printed word and select a picture to match the word. "Read the word and find the picture."	

Table 5

Descriptive Statistics for Pre- and Posttests for Treatment and Control Groups

| | Treatment n = 17 | | | | Control n = 14 | | | |
| | Pretest | | Posttest | | Pretest | | Posttest | |
Dependent Variables	Mean	SD	Mean	SD	Mean	SD	Mean	SD
Phoneme identification	11.53	7.25	18.24	5.72	9.36	5.87	11.29	6.81
Blend sounds to identify words	13.94	7.79	19.00	8.28	11.79	6.44	14.79	8.06
Decoding for picture-word matching	8.82	3.73	17.76	7.42	11.71	6.77	11.64	6.33
Total score	34.29	14.50	54.12	18.91	32.86	17.48	37.00	19.60

Table 6

Parameter Estimates of the Fixed and Random Effects of HLMs

Fixed effects	Model 1		Model 2		Model 3	
	Estimate	SE	Estimate	SE	Estimate	SE
Intercept	41.90*	2.37	34.33*	3.87	37.49*	6.08
Time			0.51	0.35	0.04	0.67
Group			1.99	6.54	2.65	7.42
Autism					3.06	6.77
Developmental delay					−0.83	6.70
Intellectual disability					−4.79	5.99
Communicate with AAC					−4.84	3.64
Communicate with picture					−1.62	4.24
Teacher experience			0.25	0.22	0.34	0.18
Time × Group membership			2.36*	0.49	2.28*	0.49
Time × Teacher Experience			< 0.01	0.02	< 0.01	0.02
Time × Primary Autism					1.85*	0.86
Time × Developmental Delay					0.16	0.88
Time × Intellectual Disability					0.51	0.75
Time × Communicate With AAC					0.47	0.51
Time × Communicate With Picture Symbols					−0.98	0.56
Random effects						
Level 1		271.48		245.44		222.06
Level 2		62.10		34.03		31.39
Level 3		0.36		0.05		0.24
Deviance		1,824.61		1,691.81		1,671.34

*Indicates significance at a $p < .05$ level.

Figure 1

Graphs of the Interaction Effects for the *ERSB* Instruction

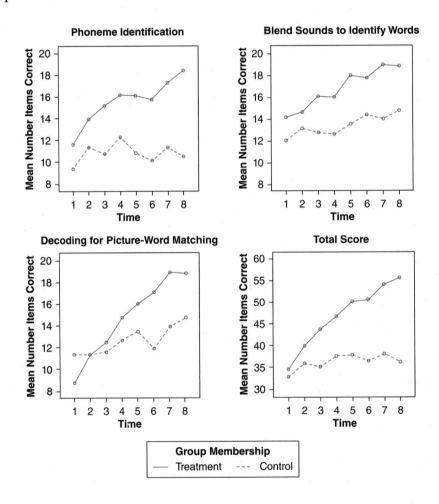

A.4 Poster Template and Sample Posters

As stated in Chapter 15, presenting a poster is one way of communicating research. APA-style posters are typically presented during poster sessions held by professional organizations or local colleges. A poster session is a 1- to 4-hour time slot where many posters are displayed in a room for any person in attendance to observe and ask questions of an author who is standing nearby his or her poster.

One of the most common and professional ways to create a poster is using Microsoft® PowerPoint. This section shows you how to create a poster template using Microsoft PowerPoint (version 2007, 2010). Earlier and more recent versions can, of course, be used to create posters but will require somewhat different selections in the menu bar. To begin, open up Microsoft PowerPoint and follow these directions. In the menu bar, select Design, then Page Setup (for version 2013, select Design, Slide Size, then Custom Slide Size…). These steps will bring up the following dialog box shown here, which should appear basically the same regardless of which version you are using:

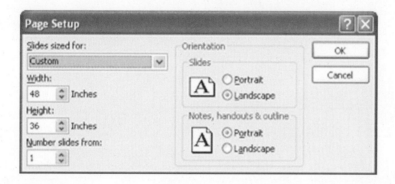

The size of the poster can vary. If you present a poster at an APA conference, then the poster board surface area is 4 feet × 6 feet; full instructions for preparing a poster for the APA conference can be found at http://www.apa.org/convention/poster-instructions.pdf. On this poster board surface, we can choose any number of poster sizes. For our example, we will use the following dimensions: 36 × 48 inches (or 3 feet high × 4 feet wide). To do this, plug in the values shown in the dialog box.

To insert text boxes, go to Insert, then Text Box, in the menu bar (repeat this as often as needed). Each text box can be used to summarize different parts of your study (abstract, methods, deign, results, conclusions, etc.). To align the text boxes, it is useful to use the grid line feature. To do this, go to the menu bar and select View, then check the Gridlines box to superimpose a grid on your slide with 1-inch squares. Make sure you leave 1-inch margins on each side of your poster. When you have completed the poster, simply uncheck the gridlines box and the squares will disappear.

This appendix includes (1) a template for how a poster can be prepared for a class or student research project and (2) two sample posters. One was presented at the Eastern Psychological Association conference and later published in the *Journal of Attention Disorders* in 2015. The second was presented at the Council for Exceptional Children, Division on Career Development and Transition National Conference in 2016. Although posters can have many different looks, one common requirement of a poster is that it is typically organized in chronological order from left to right—the same way a person would read words or sentences on a page to read a story. Hence, start with the abstract or rationale for a study to the left of the poster, then describe the study in order of the research process (from the procedures to the results and discussion), moving to the right of the poster.

Insert the Title Here

Insert Authors Here

Insert the name and location of university or college affiliation

Overview

Insert summary of research project. Do not simply copy and past your abstract....

Methods and Design

Insert summary of methods and design, including the following sections...

Participants:

Research Design:

Materials/Measures:

Procedures:

Statistical Analysis

Insert summary results using statistical values....

- Name the statistical test(s) you used to analyze your data.
- State (in APA format) the test statistic and *p*-value for each test. Each test statistic should have its own bullet.

Results

Insert summary of results without using technical jargon...

*Use a table or figure to make sense of your data.

Just insert the table or figure into this text box and include a figure/table caption.

Summary & Implications

Insert conclusions and implications here....

- Give general conclusions first. Make sure these conclusions relate back to your hypothesis. Don't generalize beyond your data. Use a separate bullet for each conclusion.
- State any major limitations for your study. Briefly (in a sentence or two at most) explain how the limitations influence your conclusions.
- Finally, give a one or two sentence overview for how your results compare with what you expected/what has been shown in the published literature.

References

List key references here...

- References should follow APA format and be in alphabetical order.
- Only list main references here.

Randomized Feedback About Diagnosis Influences Statistical and Clinical Significance of Self-Report ADHD Assessment in Adults

Shelby A. Walters, Jaela E. Agnello, Gregory J. Privitera, and Stacy L. Bender

Overview

- The hypothesis that feedback about an ADHD diagnosis influences how a nonclinical sample scores on the Adult ADHD Self-Report Scale (ASRS) screener
- Participants were a sample of college students ranging in age from 18 to 23 years.
- Participants were given the adult ADHD self-report scale (ASRS)
- In Group Negative ADHD participants were told they exhibited no symptoms of ADHD according to the assessment
- Group Positive ADHD participants were told that they did exhibit symptoms of ADHD according to the assessment
- Group No Feedback, were not given any feedback

Methods and Design

Participants:

- 54 undergraduate university students, both men and women, participated in the study
- Key additional characteristics were 24 women, 30 men; 63% White, 37% Black; and age: $M = 20.4$, $SD = 1.2$ years
- A demographic questionnaire was distributed to participants before the pre-test; those who were clinically diagnosed with ADHD or scored in the ADHD diagnostic range of the ASRS were omitted from the study
- Participants were not clinically diagnosed with ADHD
- The University's Institutional Review Board approved the procedures for this study.

Research Design:

- A between-subjects design was used with 3 groups

Measures:

- The ASRS was used to measure for symptoms of ADHD
- Scoring was based on the frequency of symptoms
- Part A of the ASRS was scored

Procedures:

- Students completed a demographic questionnaire, pre-test of the ASRS, and consent form
- Participants were randomly assigned to one of three manipulation groups in order to decrease likelihood of testing effects
- Group No Feedback, the participants were told nothing. Group Negative was told pretest scores did indicate symptoms of ADHD. Group Positive was told pretest scores indicated symptoms of ADHD
- Post-tests were scored the same as the pre-tests and participants scoring in the ADHD range on the ASRS were recorded
- Once all items were completed, participants were debriefed and dismissed

Statistical Analysis

- The dependent variable was the number of participants exhibiting ADHD after the manipulation
- The independent variable were the groups: positive, negative, and no feedback
- All tests were conducted at a 0.05 level of significance

I. Is clinical significance reliable?

- The Kruskal Wallis H-test was used to assess clinical significance by identifying group differences
  - Tested if the rates of false positives were the same in each group
  - Binomial test was used as post hoc for Kruskal-Wallis H-test to look at group differences

III. Did scores statistically change?

- One-way ANOVA
  - Computed for difference scores in the attentive domain, in the hyperactive/impulsive domain, and the totals for the sum of all 18 items
  - If significant, 95% confidence intervals drawn around the difference scores for each group

Results

Figure 1. 95% confidence intervals by group for differences pretest to posttest on all 18-items of the ASRS (total scores), on the inattentive domain items (sum questions 1-4,7-8), and on the hyperactive/impulsive domain items (sum questions 5-6, 12-18). Difference scores significantly increased for Group Positive for total scores and for scores in the inattentive domain.

- Each group consisted of 18 participants ($n = 18$)
- Distribution of those scoring in the clinical significance range was not equal between groups: Group Negative and Group No Feedback both had a mean rank of 24.00 while Group Positive had a mean rank of 34.50
- The H statistic revealed there was a significant difference between the groups,
  $\chi^2 = 11.805$, $p = 0.003$, $df = 2$.
- There was 1/18 participants that scored in the ADHD range of the ASRS post-test for Group Negative and Group No Feedback in which the binomial test showed that this result matched expected proportions
- Group Positive had 8/18 participants who scored in the ADHD range of the ASRS post-test in which the binomial test showed that this result did not match expected proportions
- ANOVA showed that Group Positive scores significantly increased in the inattentive domain, but not the hyperactive/impulsive domain

Summary & Implications

- When participants received no feedback or were informed that they did not have symptoms consistent with ADHD diagnosis, ASRS scores were consistent in a posttest and the screener met criteria needed to establish test-retest reliability
- When participants were deceived about symptoms consistent with ADHD diagnosis, ASRS scores were unreliable despite scoring below clinical significance in the pretest
- These findings suggest that one possible reason that adults without ADHD can overreport symptoms is that they have self-beliefs regarding their own likelihood of the disorder
- Participants in our study overreported symptoms in the inattentive domain in the posttest, but not in the hyperactive/impulsive domain
- These findings are consistent with studies showing that the inattentive domain is prominent in adults and that hyperactive/impulsive symptoms can decline significantly with age

References

Garnier-Dykstra, L. M., Pinchevsky, G. M., Caldeira, K. M., Vincent, K. B., & Arria, A. M. (2010). Self-reported adult attention-deficit/hyperactivity disorder symptoms among college students. *American College Health, 59(2)*, 133-136.

Kessler, R. C., Adler, L., Ames, M., Demler, O., Faraone, S., Hiripi, E., Howes, M. J., Jin, R., Secnik, K., Spencer, T., Ustun, T. B., & Walters, E. E. (2005). The world health organization adult ADHD self-report scale (ASRS): A short screening scale for use in the general population. *Psychological Medicine, 35*, 245-256. doi: 10.1017/S0033291704002892.

Guyll, M., Madon, S., Prieto, L., & Scherr, K. C. (2010). The potential roles of self-fulfilling prophecies, stigma consciousness, and stereotype threat in linking Latino/a ethnicity and educational outcomes. *Social Issues, 66*, 113-130. doi: 10.1111/j.1540-4560.2009.01636.x

The Effects of Self-Advocacy and Conflict Resolution Instruction to Request and Negotiate Accommodations on High School Seniors with Mild Disabilities

Debra G. Holzberg, Ph.D., David W. Test, Ph.D., and Dana E. Rusher, M.A.
University of North Carolina at Charlotte

Abstract

For students with high-incidence disabilities, the transition from secondary to postsecondary educational settings, poses the additional challenge of acquiring accommodations. Self-advocacy interventions have been identified as important skills for students with disabilities in accessing accommodations. The purpose of this study was to examine the effects of *Self-Advocacy and Conflict Resolution (SACR)* instruction on the ability to request accommodations of four high school seniors with mild disabilities. Results of this multiple probe across participant study indicated a functional relation between *SACR* instruction and the students' ability to request and negotiate academic accommodations in a role-play situation and in-vivo. Implications for practice and suggestions for future research are offered.

Research Questions

1. What are the effects of a self-advocacy and conflict resolution intervention on the demonstration of skills to request and negotiate academic accommodations with high school seniors with mild disabilities in a role-play setting?
2. What are the effects of a self-advocacy and conflict resolution instruction on the students' generalization of accommodations-requesting and negotiating skills to an in-vivo setting?
3. What are the students' perspectives about the effects of the intervention on their use of advocacy and conflict resolution skills and its success in acquiring and negotiating academic accommodations?

Method

Participants:

Student	Age	Race /Ethnicity	GPA	Diagnosis	Requested Accommodation	Postsecondary Goal
Roger	18	Caucasian	3.60	SLD; ADHD	Instructor notes	4-year university
Andy	18	Caucasian	2.90	SLD; ADHD	Extended time	Community college
Bailey	18	Caucasian	3.05	ASD, Level 1; ADHD	Separate setting	4-year university
Jimmy	18	Caucasian	3.28	ASD, Level 1; ADHD	Separate setting	4-year university

Instructional Materials:
- *Self-Advocacy and Conflict Resolution Skills Curriculum (SACR)*
- Scripted Notecards
- Multi-media Presentation

Experimental Design:
- Single-subject, multiple probe across participants design

Intervention:
- *Self-Advocacy and Conflict Resolution (SACR)* Training (Rumrill, Palmer, Roessler, & Brown, 1999)
- Scripted notecards

Dependent Variable:
- **Primary DV**
- The number of correctly demonstrated target behaviors of requesting accommodations and resolving conflicts using the steps in SACR
- **Secondary DV**
- The students' ability to generalize the use of the target behaviors to an in-vivo situation; a meeting with a university professor in order to request his/her accommodations

Part I
Multimedia Presentation

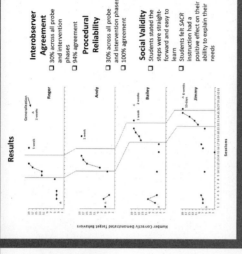

Let's Learn About Postsecondary Education!
KNOW YOUR RIGHTS AND RESPONSIBILITIES

Part II
Self-Advocacy and Conflict Resolution Targeted Behaviors for Requesting and Negotiating Academic Accommodations

1. How would you greet your Instructor at college?
2. What disability do you have?
3. How does your disability affect you in school?
4. What accommodation will help you be successful in a college classroom?
5. What are the benefits of the accommodation you have used in the past?
6. How will this accommodation help you in a college classroom?
7. Who or what will help you with requesting accommodations when you go to college?
8. What will be your responsibility?
9. How will you ask the instructor if the accommodation sounds reasonable?
10. The instructor has expressed concerns with your request. How would you get more information on the situation from the instructor when he/she has expressed concerns regarding how to best accommodate your request?
11. How would you tell the instructor that you do understand his concerns?
12. What would you say to the instructor to make sure he/she understands your needs in the classroom and that he/she wants you to succeed?
13. Since the instructor has concerns about your accommodation, how would you let the instructor know that you have some ideas for fixing the problem?
14. What would you say to the instructor to let him/her know that you have been successful with this accommodation in the past, but are open to new ideas?
15. Summarize all of the solutions that you and the instructor have come up with.
16. How would you ask the instructor which solution he would prefer in his classroom?
17. Restate your accommodation that you have chosen to help you once you are in a college classroom.
18. How will you arrange for the accommodation once you arrive on campus?
19. How will you express your appreciation to the instructor?

Holzberg, Test, & Rusher (2017). Reproduced with permission.

Results

Interobserver Agreement
- 30% across all probe and intervention phases
- 94% agreement

Procedural Reliability
- 30% across all probe and intervention phases
- 100% agreement

Social Validity
- Students stated the steps were straight-forward and easy to learn
- Students felt SACR instruction had a positive effect on their ability to explain their needs

Results

Key Findings:
- Findings indicated a functional relation between SACR instruction and students' ability to request and negotiate academic accommodations
- Three students generalized SACR target behaviors to an in-vivo setting (i.e., meeting with a professor)
- Students with mild disabilities (i.e., SLD, ADHD, ASD – Level 1) were able to learn the steps of SACR instruction in a minimal amount of time (i.e., 4 sessions approximately 30 minutes each)

Limitations:
- Students were from an independent school
- Students were all the same race (i.e., Caucasian); therefore, results may not generalize
- Probe questions were written in a way that did not naturally elicit the target behavior

Suggestions for Future Research:
- Evaluate the effects of SACR instruction on small group settings
- Conducting the study with college students with mild disabilities
- Future studies that enable students to use their notecards in the generalization probe

For Additional Information:

Debra G. Holzberg, Ph.D.
debraholzbergh8@gmail.com

Dana E. Rusher, M.A.
Doctoral Student
Dept. of Special Education & Child Development
derusher@uncc.edu

APPENDIX B

Instructions for Randomizing and Counterbalancing

B.1 Random Numbers Table

Randomization, defined in Chapter 6, is used to ensure that confounding variables operate entirely by chance in a research study. Two strategies of randomization are random sampling and random assignment. Random sampling ensures that all participants are selected to participate for a study at random; random assignment ensures that all participants in a study are assigned to groups or treatments at random. The random number table can be used to accomplish both strategies of randomization. In this brief appendix, we show you how to use the random number table.

Participant Order	Random Number
1	15
2	2
3	33
4	32
5	14
6	1
7	28
8	26
9	7
10	20

Random Sampling

Suppose you have a pool of 10 people from which you select 8 participants to be in your study. To *randomly select* 8 participants from this pool of 10 people, first list all 10 people in any order (participants are listed in numerical order in the table above), then go to the random number table and begin at a random spot in the table. For example, you can drop a coin on the random list of numbers and begin with the number it falls on. Starting with this number, read across or down the list. In the example above, we began with the first number in the upper-left corner and read down. Now a random number has been assigned to each person. Finally, you can choose 8 participants with the lowest number (e.g., Participants 1, 2, 5, 6, 7, 8, 9, 10) or largest number (Participants 1, 3, 4, 5, 7, 8, 9, 10) to be in the sample. Both will produce a random sample of participants from the pool of 10 people.

Random Assignment

To *randomly assign* participants to any number of groups, first list (in any order) all participants in your study (again, participants are listed in numerical order in the table above), and then go to the random number table and begin at a random spot in the table. In this example, we will use the same random list of numbers used in the previous example for random sampling. If we have two groups, then to randomly assign participants to groups, you can assign participants with the lowest five scores to Group 1 (Participants 6, 2, 9, 5, 1) and the highest five scores to Group 2 (Participants 10, 8, 7, 4, 3), or vice versa. For more information about using randomization, visit www.randomizer.org or visit www.random.org.

Table B.1   Random Number Table

15	2	40	24	26	12	32	38	46	46	14	18	9	49	6
2	48	10	21	10	49	10	13	2	25	10	6	1	14	4
33	23	35	43	17	35	4	44	5	45	29	46	31	19	37
32	44	39	44	14	41	36	41	15	47	3	41	43	43	0
14	11	41	30	37	0	47	28	49	13	8	15	26	4	48
1	38	42	17	22	45	27	37	7	1	26	44	16	39	10
28	26	3	34	33	2	33	33	45	28	25	35	2	48	42
26	21	31	13	46	46	44	46	26	15	18	5	18	45	8
7	24	7	7	24	37	16	16	16	38	38	38	8	30	14
20	35	47	14	34	4	29	1	30	39	1	25	4	33	17
8	26	44	20	34	3	10	1	6	7	12	37	8	29	34
48	43	2	7	35	25	30	37	27	36	11	19	14	32	5
41	2	47	9	45	17	16	34	39	8	21	18	11	11	45
43	27	18	19	3	6	41	32	34	22	36	5	1	38	27
28	19	22	42	1	48	22	2	10	3	2	28	2	15	42
21	31	29	27	26	23	42	6	2	1	41	44	38	28	19

47	33	17	11	43	20	35	49	24	39	16	6	48	45	41
20	13	42	24	40	39	23	3	41	19	30	10	24	48	8
14	9	7	45	48	0	9	38	15	44	42	17	47	14	33
39	37	28	21	29	29	31	22	22	35	38	16	6	37	11
15	10	47	1	20	16	25	13	4	30	5	24	7	26	40
31	35	1	48	34	35	36	43	44	9	32	4	28	42	34
22	20	20	2	33	41	41	12	0	7	33	12	47	19	43
26	15	6	40	4	39	44	40	43	12	34	21	27	14	23
40	21	32	39	25	24	47	0	19	48	49	44	10	24	19
6	42	24	10	19	7	7	44	16	44	30	28	48	33	18
10	19	31	47	1	36	12	22	25	39	41	48	5	18	39
16	18	26	20	7	43	17	37	41	46	13	17	13	37	9
28	13	12	22	21	48	38	25	49	15	1	45	2	4	48
46	44	8	32	31	22	18	28	42	49	44	41	4	46	13

31	33	9	42	30	38	45	17	24	15	36	9	28	29	16
30	45	13	48	6	44	4	42	18	19	24	2	7	11	18
43	10	4	0	21	25	26	44	32	13	20	1	4	7	12
32	24	28	23	10	19	11	47	23	42	48	39	8	23	3
16	40	14	20	26	49	44	19	16	47	0	29	37	13	34
37	39	5	49	12	45	16	1	26	16	29	48	1	47	47
26	19	0	18	43	5	40	30	42	20	6	0	38	9	29
39	31	29	32	5	12	33	2	48	37	43	17	36	25	42
23	26	23	26	3	17	28	28	1	4	35	10	47	4	45
10	47	16	3	36	1	21	27	10	29	19	8	21	22	23

40	20	38	26	9	10	33	28	47	25	32	4	18	33	18
42	24	26	14	39	34	49	41	12	23	24	37	41	18	5
38	10	24	12	8	23	16	3	3	38	20	26	14	30	30
37	35	14	23	42	31	30	39	44	29	15	9	37	16	36
46	47	12	19	32	35	36	10	4	42	41	38	19	27	19
43	9	4	46	31	2	7	26	2	24	1	19	4	14	8
5	48	2	33	28	27	48	48	20	47	9	40	1	40	35
11	42	9	37	21	44	21	21	22	43	45	13	22	19	46
27	6	20	34	37	47	47	7	24	31	19	31	30	13	22
6	8	37	6	10	7	24	9	1	28	29	44	38	43	34

44	10	48	37	38	33	45	5	2	15	17	5	12	26	3
17	41	43	6	19	45	35	35	13	3	24	15	8	44	30
41	34	10	1	9	29	23	21	35	28	36	3	15	8	16
30	30	41	38	41	15	29	20	32	18	8	7	9	12	41
19	15	20	40	44	1	14	15	28	39	28	1	34	17	18
38	24	40	14	22	23	28	19	38	26	33	25	49	46	9

2	35	27	8	16	22	49	47	25	4	5	12	19	5	12
40	9	9	17	21	4	17	1	27	14	4	4	42	2	0
7	39	29	13	28	37	27	7	44	47	15	47	0	45	47
26	8	13	47	47	26	6	25	36	21	19	31	21	47	6

13	14	47	35	45	23	17	48	24	18	22	25	47	30	46
5	35	36	34	12	2	19	2	42	42	20	41	9	2	35
31	12	37	46	48	31	9	0	26	10	47	20	34	14	19
43	6	30	18	23	29	28	1	4	49	45	43	35	41	26
39	4	15	11	3	13	35	43	18	47	0	44	15	45	6
35	21	17	42	4	37	48	8	14	36	39	42	17	39	31
40	33	13	12	37	33	37	13	40	27	43	34	26	28	2
29	31	2	45	7	26	6	29	48	14	19	18	24	7	10
48	1	24	10	0	22	41	19	6	8	4	0	43	46	34
6	0	49	22	34	48	27	37	31	26	24	37	44	36	48

31	47	34	10	24	19	47	17	3	15	31	5	24	1	9
38	18	48	9	28	48	7	40	11	9	2	45	20	37	36
42	15	36	49	2	2	20	31	9	31	38	36	31	39	42
28	25	43	31	11	45	22	34	19	21	16	9	38	26	13
29	14	14	39	12	14	2	3	28	19	21	47	6	0	33
6	39	33	46	38	46	38	12	21	18	39	23	5	7	32
16	22	2	48	6	3	15	23	49	12	29	37	13	23	48
36	44	16	34	0	35	0	9	47	3	32	29	21	16	49
8	17	35	42	17	39	44	37	22	36	36	13	39	41	41
10	21	46	32	41	47	36	44	41	43	26	49	1	29	2

41	45	22	49	48	3	40	8	46	16	8	22	18	47	1
36	20	21	17	18	42	3	38	12	49	13	24	12	39	40
17	38	38	13	4	29	27	21	4	42	11	12	9	11	44
9	32	42	3	22	16	14	40	30	19	24	21	5	1	19
42	1	3	22	11	22	15	6	42	6	15	36	2	44	15
24	6	27	37	10	24	45	43	28	31	27	29	17	43	47
35	33	6	38	5	27	43	29	43	11	33	16	34	21	6
30	7	35	47	13	4	17	17	7	37	3	37	40	46	41
6	12	28	30	42	43	26	25	19	3	25	39	29	28	0
26	14	5	31	0	15	25	42	24	33	9	2	33	20	23

16	43	21	13	42	19	30	34	29	18	39	34	29	22	32
49	49	7	10	15	24	18	35	2	49	6	42	30	33	41

Research Methods for Education

2	34	42	46	23	48	13	27	45	40	0	6	1	6	47
0	20	12	34	48	21	37	6	42	22	38	7	18	13	46
11	7	32	3	31	5	35	3	30	14	36	10	22	49	14
35	12	47	37	39	26	45	12	11	17	20	37	16	17	8

44	18	1	33	14	34	38	23	3	9	42	9	47	19	38
6	19	27	35	17	29	6	2	41	30	44	48	42	46	37
37	28	22	26	12	31	42	4	19	34	12	15	44	28	40
32	30	15	29	6	37	29	17	40	45	9	21	38	45	3

30	30	12	28	21	11	1	22	28	27	34	40	34	31	7
37	38	37	31	8	14	9	45	49	20	35	26	33	19	1
4	48	16	11	27	40	8	17	42	9	45	16	40	10	0
1	33	23	14	6	27	41	37	11	8	36	10	36	5	30
8	7	41	45	33	46	46	41	23	10	22	17	23	2	8
23	44	20	4	44	16	48	25	10	37	31	25	13	22	6
25	41	4	22	26	25	35	40	13	14	40	20	44	18	19
2	20	34	19	16	48	7	49	3	28	42	45	14	38	42
24	23	8	5	36	7	17	4	15	3	5	12	4	11	41
35	46	48	18	39	21	12	26	12	22	39	8	21	6	22

38	40	47	42	24	46	32	31	24	7	28	13	28	8	24
16	23	16	27	42	17	31	13	16	10	14	15	14	37	39
29	35	29	43	20	14	23	25	7	32	34	4	41	31	6
33	7	25	21	19	36	40	27	36	46	30	38	9	33	32
35	12	34	45	0	6	38	10	2	25	25	28	36	39	12
43	13	42	18	17	35	9	30	28	29	42	9	19	48	17
9	17	15	22	8	9	48	33	15	47	38	49	45	5	2
32	3	7	5	44	25	43	37	27	27	37	11	17	44	23
1	24	4	44	38	7	8	23	44	2	49	46	38	0	1
40	16	10	2	41	11	18	36	6	18	44	5	10	9	36

B.2 Constructing a Latin Square

In Chapter 11, we introduced the *within-subjects design*, which is a research design in which the same participants are observed in each group.

One drawback of this design is that random assignment is not possible because the same participants are assigned to all groups. Thus, for this design to qualify as an experiment, the researcher must manipulate the levels of an independent variable, include a control or comparison group, and take added measures to control for time-related factors.

A **Latin square** is a matrix design in which a limited number of order sequences are constructed such that (1) the number of order sequences chosen equals the number of treatments, (2) each treatment appears equally often in each position, and (3) each treatment precedes and follows each treatment one time.

One added measure of control for order is *counterbalancing*, which is used to minimize order effects so that the order of presenting treatments, or the order in which participants are assigned to groups, does not systematically vary with the levels of an independent variable.

However, in many cases, the number of groups or treatments in a study is simply too large to fully counterbalance the design. In these cases, it is often best to use partial counterbalancing, which can be accomplished using a **Latin square** (defined here and also in Chapter 11). A Latin square is a partial counterbalancing procedure used to select an unbiased set of order sequences when it is difficult to counterbalance all order sequences in a research design.

An unbiased order sequence is one in which (1) each treatment appears equally often in each position, and (2) each treatment precedes and follows each treatment one time. A Latin square meets both requirements and also ensures that the number of order sequences chosen equals the number of groups or treatments. The following procedures can be used to construct a Latin square with an even and an odd number of groups or treatments (k).

Constructing a Latin Square (When k Is Even)

The following directions are for constructing a Latin square with an even number of groups or treatments (k).

1. Label your treatments alphabetically—so ABCD for four treatments, ABCDEF for six treatments, ABCDEFGH for eight treatments, and so on. We will work through an example for eight groups or treatments. This will make it easier for you to see the overall pattern for ordering.

2. Determine the order sequence for row 1 using the following ordering, in which L is the "last" group or treatment alphabetically:

A, B, L, C, L-1, D, L-2, E

For eight groups or treatments, then, L is Treatment H (the last letter), L-1 is Treatment G (the next-to-last treatment), and L-2 is Treatment F (the third-to-last treatment). These procedures require you to take treatments at the end and insert them into different positions. Hence, with eight treatments, the first row or order sequence is as follows:

Row 1: ABHCGDFE

3. To determine the remaining rows or order sequences, increase one letter at each position of the previous row. The last letter in a row reverts to A because it cannot be increased. In our example, for the second row, A becomes B at the first position, B becomes C at the second position, H becomes A at the third position, and so on:

Row 2: BCADHEGF

For the third row, *B* becomes *C* at the first position, *C* becomes *D* at the second position, *A* becomes *B* at the third position, and so on:

Row 3: CDBEAFHG

Continue this to complete the Latin square with eight rows or order sequences, which is equal to *k* (the number of groups or treatments).

4. Construct the Latin square. In our example, we have eight groups or treatments, so we will have eight rows or order sequences. Hence, the 8 × 8 Latin square for this example is as follows:

A B H C G D F E

B C A D H E G F

C D B E A F H G

D E C F B G A H

E F D G C H B A

F G E H D A C B

G H F A E B D C

H A G B F C E D

The eight rows constitute an unbiased random order sequence for observing participants in each group or treatment. Now you can observe participants in each order sequence to control for order effects.

Constructing a Latin Square (When k *Is Odd)*

With an odd number of groups or treatments (*k*), it is not possible to construct an unbiased order sequence because there will be an odd number of rows. The solution is to basically construct two Latin squares so that the total number of rows or order sequences is even. We will work through an example with five treatments (A, B, C, D, E):

1. Latin Square 1: Follow Steps 1 to 4 given above. This produces the following Latin square (we recommend that you try this on your own):

A B E C D

B C A D E

C D B E A

D E C A B

E A D B C

2. Latin Square 2: Create a second square that reverses the order for each row in the first square. So you will have a total of 10 rows. Here is the first Latin square (top five rows) given with the second Latin square (bottom five rows):

A B E C D

B C A D E

C D B E A

D E C A B

E A D B C

D C E B A

E D A C B

A E B D C

B A C E D

C B D A E

This basically produces a Latin rectangle. The 10 rows constitute an unbiased random order sequence for observing participants in each group or treatment in that each treatment appears equally often in each position, and each treatment precedes and follows each treatment two times. Now you can observe participants in each order sequence to control for order effects.

GLOSSARY

This glossary includes all of the key terms that were defined in each chapter. The number in parentheses following each definition indicates the chapter or appendix where the term was defined.

ABA design   See *reversal design* (13).

Abstract   A brief written summary of the purpose, methods, and results of an article, a chapter, a book, or another published document. The length of an abstract can vary; however, abstracts are usually 250 words or less (2).

Accessible population   The portion of the target population that can be clearly identified and directly sampled from (6).

Action research   is the implementation of systematic inquiry conducted by educational practitioners designed to answer questions related to educational practices and student learning outcomes in the context of a specific educational environment (16).

Accuracy   addresses the technical adequacy of the information contained in an evaluation (17).

Age/grade equivalent score   is a standard score that compares an individual's score to the average scores of different age groups and represents the same score of an average student of that age or grade (18).

Alternating treatment (ABC) design   is a single-case design with a baseline phase followed by a treatment phase. There are at least two different conditions or treatments that are alternated (12).

Analyst-generated concept   Concepts, labels, and terms created by the analyst to describe an observed phenomenon

Analyst-generated typologies   reconstruct the indigenous typologies into analyst-generated terms and interpretations that represent the larger worldview of these categories (20).

Anchors   Adjectives that are given to describe the end points of a rating scale to give the scale greater meaning (5).

Anonymity   A protection of individual identity in which the identity of a participant remains unknown throughout a study, even to those involved in a study (3).

APA-style manuscript   A document that is created using the writing style format detailed in the *Publication Manual of the American Psychological Association*, typically for the purposes of having the work considered for publication in a peer-reviewed journal (21).

Applied research   Uses the scientific method to answer questions concerning practical problems with potential practical solutions (1).

Archival research   A type of existing data design in which events or behaviors are described based on a review and analysis of relevant historical or archival records (8).

Assent   The consent of a minor or other legally incapable person to agree to participate in research only after receiving an appropriate explanation in reasonably understandable language (3).

Attrition   A possible threat to validity in which a participant does not show up for a study at a scheduled time or fails to complete the study (7).

Authority   A method of knowing accepted as fact because it was stated by an expert or respected source in a particular subject area (1).

Autoethnography   is a branch of ethnography where the researcher studies the culture of oneself and how the self is a part of the culture (11).

Bar chart   A graphical display used to summarize the frequency of discrete and categorical data using bars to represent each frequency (18).

Bar graph   See *bar chart* (18).

Baseline phase (A)   A phase in which a treatment or manipulation is absent (13).

Basic research   Uses the scientific method to answer questions that address theoretical issues about fundamental processes and underlying mechanisms related to the behaviors and events being studied (1).

Basic time-series design   A quasi-experimental research design in which a dependent variable is measured at many different points in time in one group before and after a treatment that is manipulated by the researcher is administered (13).

Belmont Report   A published document that recommends three principles for the ethical conduct of research with human participants: respect for persons, beneficence, and justice (3).

Beneficence   An ethical principle listed in the Belmont Report that states that it is the researcher's responsibility to minimize the potential risks and maximize the potential benefits associated with conducting a research study (3).

Between-groups variability   A source of variance in a dependent measure that is caused by or associated with the manipulation of the levels (or groups) of an independent variable (14).

Between-persons variability   A source of variance in a dependent measure that is caused by or associated with individual differences or differences in participant responses across all groups (14).

Between-subjects design   A research design in which different participants are observed one time in each group or at each level of a factor (14).

Between-subjects experimental design   An experimental research design in which the levels of a between-subjects factor are manipulated, and then different participants are randomly assigned to each group or to each level of that factor and observed one time (14).

Between-subjects factor   A type of factor in which different participants are observed in each group or at each level of the factor (14).

Between-subjects factorial design   A research design in which the levels of two or more between-subjects factors are combined to create groups, meaning that different participants are observed in each group (14).

Bipolar scales   Response scales that have points above (positive values) and below (negative values) a zero point (5).

Carryover effects   A threat to internal validity in which participation in one group "carries over" or causes changes in performance in a second group (14).

Case history   An in-depth description of the history and background of the individual, group, or organization observed. A case history can be the only information provided in a case study for situations in which the researcher does not include a manipulation, a treatment, or an intervention (12).

Case study   The qualitative analysis of an individual, a group, an organization, or an event used to illustrate a phenomenon, explore new hypotheses, or compare the observations of many cases (12, 20).

Ceiling effect   A range effect where scores are clustered at the high end of a scale (4).

Central limit theorem   Regardless of the distribution of scores in a population, the sampling distribution of sample means selected at random from that population will approach the shape of a normal distribution, as the number of samples in the sampling distribution increases (18).

Central tendency   Statistical measures for locating a single score that tends to be near the center of a distribution and is most representative or descriptive of all scores in a distribution (18).

Changing-criterion design   A single-case experimental design in which a baseline phase is followed by successive treatment phases in which some criterion or target level of behavior is changed from one treatment phase to the next. The participant must meet the criterion of one treatment phase before the next treatment phase is administered (13).

Checklist   is a list of items from which the respondent selects one or more options (5).

Chi-square goodness-of-fit test   A statistical procedure used to determine whether observed frequencies at each level of one categorical variable are similar to or different from frequencies expected (19).

Chi-square test for independence   A statistical procedure used to determine whether frequencies observed at the combination of levels of two categorical variables are similar to or different from frequencies expected (19).

Citation bias   A misleading approach to citing sources that occurs when an author or authors cite only evidence that supports their view and fail to cite existing evidence that refutes their view (2).

Classroom-based action research   is conducted at the classroom level to affect a classroom-level issue (16).

Closed-ended item   See *restricted item* (5).

Cluster sampling   A method of sampling in which subgroups or clusters of individuals are identified in a population, and then a portion of clusters that are representative of the population is selected such that all individuals in the selected clusters are included in the sample. All clusters that are not selected are omitted from the sample (6).

Codes are words or phrases and assign a few words or phrase that capture the salient essence of the narrative (20).

Coding The procedure of converting a categorical variable to numeric values (4).

Coefficient of determination A measure (R^2) of proportion of variance used to describe effect size for data analyzed using a correlation coefficient or regression. The coefficient of determination is mathematically equivalent to eta squared (19).

Cohen's conventions Standard rules for identifying small, medium, and large effects based on typical findings in behavioral research (19).

Cohen's *d* A measure of effect size in terms of the number of standard deviations that mean scores shifted above or below the population mean stated by the null hypothesis. The larger the value of *d*, the larger the effect in the population (19).

Cohen's kappa A measure of interrater reliability that estimates the level of agreement between two raters while taking into account the probability that the two raters agree by chance or error (18).

Cohort A group of individuals who share common statistical traits or characteristics or experiences within a defined period (13).

Cohort effect A threat to internal validity in which differences in the characteristics of participants in different cohorts or age groups confound or alternatively explain an observed result (13).

Cohort-sequential design A developmental research design that combines longitudinal and cross-sectional techniques by observing different cohorts of participants over time at overlapping times (13).

Collective case study A type of case study used to compare observations of many cases (12).

Comparative design investigates the relationship between one independent and one dependent variable where the independent variable consists of at least two groups (9).

Comparison group is a group that received a different treatment from the experimental or treatment group (14).

Complete counterbalancing A procedure in which all possible order sequences in which participants receive different treatments or participate in different groups are balanced or offset in an experiment (14).

Complete factorial design A factorial design in which each level of one factor is combined or crossed with each level of the other factor, with participants observed in each cell or combination of levels (14).

Completely crossed design See *complete factorial design* (14).

Confidence interval (CI) See *interval estimate* (19).

Confidence limits The upper and lower boundaries of a confidence interval given within a specified level of confidence (19).

Confidentiality A protection of individual identity in which the identity of a participant is not made available to anyone who is not directly involved in a study. Those involved in a study, however, are able to identify participant information (3).

Confirmability (neutrality) The extent to which observed results reflect the actual context of participant experiences rather than simply the researcher's perspective (20).

Confirmational strategy A method of testing a theory or hypothesis in which a positive result confirms the predictions made by that theory or hypothesis (2).

Confound An unanticipated variable not accounted for in a research study that could be causing or associated with observed changes in one or more measured variables (9).

Confound variable See *confound* (9).

Conscious experience is any experience that a person has lived through or performed and can bring to memory in such a way as to recall that experience (11).

Constant comparative method is a process of continually gathering data, analyzing data, and determining what additional data are needed (11, 20).

Constant comparison See *constant comparative method* (20).

Construct A conceptual variable that is known to exist but cannot be directly observed (4).

Construct validity The extent to which an operational definition for a variable or construct is actually measuring that variable or construct (4).

Constructivism is a philosophical view that maintains there are multiple realities, in which people construct their own meaning of the world (10).

Consumer-oriented evaluation is an evaluation that is conducted by an expert in evaluation to inform the general public (17).

Content analysis A type of existing data design in which the content of written or spoken records of the occurrence of specific events or behaviors is described and interpreted. It is a process that reduces the amount of information into manageable chunks by categorizing important elements (8, 20).

Content validity   The extent to which the items or contents of a measure adequately represent all of the features of the construct being measured (4).

Continuous variable   A variable measured along a continuum at any place beyond the decimal point, meaning that it can be measured in whole units or fractional units (4).

Contrived setting   A location or site arranged to mimic the natural setting within which a behavior of interest normally occurs to facilitate the occurrence of that behavior (8).

Control   (a) The manipulation of a variable and (b) holding all other variables constant. When control is low, neither criterion is met; when control is high, both criteria are met (7, 14).

Control by holding constant   A type of restricted random assignment in which we limit which participants are included in a sample based on characteristics they exhibit that may otherwise differ between groups in a study (14).

Control by matching   A type of restricted random assignment in which we assess or measure the characteristic we want to control, group, or categorize participants based on scores on that measure and then use a random procedure to assign participants from each category to a group in the study (14).

Control group   A condition in an experiment in which participants are treated the same as participants in an experimental group, except that the manipulation believed to cause a change in the dependent variable is omitted (14).

Control time-series design   A basic or interrupted time-series quasi-experimental research design that also includes a nonequivalent control group that is observed during the same period of time as a treatment group but does not receive the treatment (13).

Convenience sampling   A method of sampling in which subjects or participants are selected for a research study based on how easy or convenient it is to reach or access them and based on their availability to participate (6).

Convergent mixed methods   (QUANT + QUAL) A research design that gathers quantitative and qualitative data at the same time to obtain both deep, rich qualitative data and numeric quantitative data to provide a more complete understanding of a problem (15).

Correlation coefficient   A statistic used to measure the strength and direction of the linear relationship, or correlation, between two factors. The value of r can range from –1.0 to +1.0 (9).

Correlational research design   The measurement of two or more factors to determine or estimate the extent to which the values for the factors are related or change in an identifiable pattern (9).

Counterbalancing   A procedure in which the order in which participants receive different treatments or participate in different groups is balanced or offset in an experiment. Two types of counterbalancing are complete and partial counterbalancing (14).

Covariance   The extent to which the values of two factors (X and Y) vary together. The closer data points fall to the regression line, the more the values of two factors vary together (9).

Cover story   A false explanation or story intended to prevent research participants from discovering the true purpose of a research study (3).

Covert observation   is when the researcher is a full participant of the activities under investigation, typically observing covertly (10).

Cramer's V   A measure of proportion of variance that is used as an estimate of effect size for the chi-square test for independence (19).

Credibility (truthfulness)   The extent to which observed results reflect the realities of the participants in such a way that the participants themselves would agree with the research report (20).

Criterion sampling   is when the researcher develops a set of predetermined criteria by which to select participants (10).

Criterion variable   The to-be-predicted variable (Y) with unknown values that can be predicted or estimated, given known values of the predictor variable (9).

Criterion-referenced test   is a test that compares one individual's performance on the test to a predetermined level of performance (5).

Criterion-related validity   The extent to which scores obtained on some measure can be used to infer or predict a criterion or expected outcome (4).

Critical case sampling   selects a few essential cases for understanding the issue. The researcher will need to define what characteristics or knowledge the critical case possesses (10).

Critical race theory   is a qualitative design that examines how society and culture intersect with race and power (12).

Critical theory   is a group of philosophical views that contend that reality is defined by social entities such as culture, race, class, politics, and gender (10, 11, 12).

Cronbach's alpha   A measure of internal consistency that estimates the average correlation for every possible way that a measure can be split in half (18).

Cross-case pattern analysis groups   Similar descriptions made by different cases together when these descriptions can be considered the same thing (20).

Cross-case thematic analysis   Interpreting and assigning meaning to a documented pattern by giving it a thematic name, a term that connotes and interprets the implications of the pattern (20).

Cross-sectional design   A developmental research design in which participants are grouped by their age and participant characteristics are measured in each age group (13).

Cross-sectional surveys   administer a questionnaire once to a sample of people to examine attitudes and perceptions as a "snapshot" in time (9).

Data (plural)   Measurements or observations that are typically numeric (1).

Data mining   is when social media posts are perused for keywords or phrases particular for the field under study and copied into files for later use (11).

Data points   The x- and y-coordinates for each plot in a scatterplot (9).

Data saturation   occurs when no new information is derived from the data collection process and all the needed information is obtained (10, 11).

Debriefing   The full disclosure to participants of the true purpose of a study, typically given at the end of a study (3).

Deception   A strategy used by researchers in which participants are deliberately mislead concerning the true purpose and nature of the research being conducted. Deception can be active (deliberately untruthful) or passive (omission of key information) (3).

Decision-oriented   evaluation is specifically designed to assist decision makers such as program administrators, funding agencies, and policy makers. There are two decision-oriented approaches; the CIPP model and utilization-focused evaluation (17).

Deductive analysis   is when the researcher has preconceived ideas about what themes may be present in the narratives and seeks to find them (20).

Deductive reasoning   A "top-down" type of reasoning in which a claim (a hypothesis or theory) is used to generate ideas or predictions and make observations (2, 10).

Degrees of freedom (*df*) **for sample variance**   One less than the sample size, or $n - 1$ (18).

Demand characteristic   Any feature or characteristic of a research setting that may reveal the hypothesis being tested or give the participant a clue regarding how he or she is expected to behave (4).

Dependability   (consistency) the extent to which observed results would be similar if similar research were conducted in the same or a similar context (20).

Dependent sample   See *related sample* (14).

Dependent variable   The variable that is believed to change in the presence of the independent variable. It is the "presumed effect" (4).

Descriptive statistics   Procedures used to summarize, organize, and make sense of a set of scores or observations, typically presented graphically, in tabular form (in tables), or as summary statistics (single values) (18).

Determinism   An assumption in science that all actions in the universe have a cause (10).

Disconfirmational strategy   A method of testing a theory or hypothesis in which a positive result disconfirms the predictions made by that theory or hypothesis (2).

Discourse analysis   focuses on the language used to describe something such as word choice, grammar, and rhetoric used to describe an experience (20).

Discrete variable   A variable measured in whole units or categories that are not distributed along a continuum (4).

Documents   are narrative data and might include such things as newspapers, TV news reports, or minutes of school meetings (5).

Double-barreled items   Survey items that ask participants for one response to two different questions or statements (5).

Double-blind study   A type of research study in which the researcher collecting the data and the participants in the study are unaware of the conditions in which participants are assigned (4).

Duplication   The republication of original data that were previously published (3).

Duration method   A method used to quantify observations made in a study by recording the amount of time or duration that participants engage in a certain behavior during a fixed period of time (8).

Ecological validity   The extent to which results observed in a study will generalize across settings or environments (7).

Effect   A mean difference or discrepancy between what was observed in a sample and what was expected to be observed in the population (stated by the null hypothesis) (19).

Effect size   A statistical measure of the size or magnitude of an observed effect in a population, which allows researchers to describe how far scores shifted in a population, or the percentage of variance in a dependent variable that can be explained by the levels of a factor (8, 19).

Effect size conventions   See *Cohen's conventions* (19).

Emic   coding maintains the information in the participant's own words and perspectives (20).

Empirical rule   A rule for normally distributed data that states that at least 99.7% of data fall within three standard deviations of the mean, at least 95% of data fall within two standard deviations of the mean, and at least 68% of data fall within one standard deviation of the mean (18).

Empiricism   A method of knowing based on one's experiences or observations (1).

Error   A source of variance that cannot be attributed to having different groups or treatments. Two sources of error are between-persons and within-groups variability (14).

Error variance   A numeric measure of the variability in scores that can be attributed to or is caused by the individual differences of participants in each group (14).

Estimation   A statistical procedure in which a sample statistic is used to estimate the value of an unknown population parameter. Two types of estimation are point estimation and interval estimation (19).

Eta squared   A measure (η^2) of proportion of variance used to describe effect size for data analyzed using ANOVA (19).

Etic   coding interprets what the participant says into researcher words using a researcher or more universal perspective (20).

Evaluand   is a generic term referring to the entity being evaluated. This may be, but is not limited to, a person, product, policy, or idea (17; Mathison, 2005).

Evaluation apprehension   A type of participant reactivity in which a participant is overly apprehensive (4).

Event sampling   A strategy used to manage an observation period by splitting a fixed period of time into smaller intervals of time and then recording a different behavior in each time interval (8).

Existing data design   The collection, review, and analysis of any type of existing documents or records, including those that are written or recorded as video, as audio, or in other electronic form (8).

Expectancy effects   Preconceived ideas or expectations regarding how participants should behave or what participants are capable of doing. Expectancy effects can often lead to experimenter bias (4).

Experiment   The methods and procedures used in an experimental research design to specifically control the conditions under which observations are made to isolate cause-and-effect relationships between variables (7).

Experimental (intervention) advanced mixed methods   A research design that gathers qualitative data in the context of an experiment (15).

Experimental group   See *treatment group* (14).

Experimental manipulation   The identification of an independent variable and the creation of two or more groups that constitute the levels of that variable (14).

Experimental mortality   See *attrition* (7).

Experimental research design   The use of methods and procedures to make observations in which the researcher fully controls the conditions and experiences of participants by applying three required elements of control: randomization, manipulation, and comparison/control (7).

Experimenter bias   The extent to which the behavior of a researcher or experimenter intentionally or unintentionally influences the results of a study (4).

Expertise-oriented evaluation   is an evaluation that is conducted by an expert in the field of study (17).

Explanatory sequential mixed-methods design   (QUANT → qual) is used to help explain the quantitative information gathered first using a qualitative technique gathered later (15).

Exploratory case study   A type of case study used to explore or generate hypotheses for later investigation (12).

Explanatory sequential mixed-methods design   is a methodological approach that gathers quantitative and qualitative data, where the qualitative data are used to explain the quantitative data (QUAN → qual), or develop a plan for measuring quantitative data (QUAL → quan).

External audit   involves an outside person knowledgeable in the area being studied to review the process and interpretations of the study, further removed and unaffiliated with the study (20).

External evaluation   is an evaluation conducted by an evaluator not associated with the evaluand (17).

External factor of a construct   An observable behavior or event that is presumed to reflect the construct itself (4).

External validity   The extent to which observations made in a study generalize beyond the specific manipulations or constraints in the study (7).

Extreme case sampling   identifies highly unusual cases (the exception to the rule) as the sample (10).

Eye dialect   transcription includes a true phonetic representation of how words are pronounced (20).

Fabrication   To concoct methods or data that misrepresent aspects of a research study with the intent to deceive others (3).

Face validity   The extent to which a measure for a variable or construct appears to measure what it is purported to measure (4).

Factor   See *independent variable* (7).

Factorial design   A research design in which participants are observed across the combination of levels of two or more factors (14).

Factorial experimental design   A research design in which groups are created by manipulating the levels of two or more factors, then the same or different participants are observed in each group using experimental procedures of randomization (for a between-subjects factor) and using control for timing and order effects (for a within-subjects factor) (14).

Feasibility   is the extent to which the evaluation procedures are realistic, diplomatic, and practical given the available time, budget, staff, and stakeholders (17).

Feminist theory   examines how differential power marginalizes and disadvantages women and defines how they are treated in social settings (12).

Field notes   are notes that are taken during the observation to help the observer recall what was observed (10).

File drawer problem   A type of publication bias in which researchers have a tendency to file away studies that show negative results, knowing that most journals will likely reject them (2).

Floor effect   A range effect where scores are clustered at the low end of a scale (4).

Focus group   is an interview with a small group of about three to eight people where participants interact in response to the question posed by the interviewer (5).

Formative evaluation   is an evaluation that is conducted while the evaluand is being implemented (17).

Frequency   A value that describes the number of times or how often a category, score, or range of scores occurs (18).

Frequency distribution table   A tabular summary display for a distribution of data organized or summarized in terms of how often a category, score, or range of scores occurs (18).

Frequency method   A method used to quantify observations made in a study by counting the number of times a behavior occurs during a fixed or predetermined period of time (8).

Frequency polygon   is a graphical display using a line to summarize the frequency of continuous data (18).

Full-text article   Any article or text that is available in its full or complete published version (2).

Full-text database   Any online database that makes full-text articles available to be downloaded electronically as a PDF or in another electronic format (2).

General inquiry   is an application of a case study where the purpose is to learn about certain cases of interest used to advance general knowledge (12).

Grounded theory   is an empirical, inductive approach for developing a theory from data that are systematically gathered and analyzed (11).

Hawthorne effect   occurs when the participants are selected as part of the treatment group and changes their behavior because they believe they are getting special treatment (7).

Heterogeneous attrition   A possible threat to internal validity in which rates of attrition are different between groups in a study (7).

Higher-order factorial design   A research design in which the levels of more than two factors are combined or crossed to create groups (14).

Higher-order interaction   An interaction for the combination of levels of three or more factors in a factorial design (14).

Histogram   A graphical display used to summarize the frequency of continuous data that are distributed in numeric intervals using bars connected at the upper limits of each interval (18).

History effect   A possible threat to internal validity in which an unanticipated event co-occurs with a treatment or manipulation in a study (7).

Homogeneous attrition   A threat to population validity in which rates of attrition are about the same in each group (7).

Human story   is an in-depth description of actual lived experiences (12).

Hypothesis   A specific, testable claim or prediction about what you expect to observe given a set of circumstances (1, 2).

Hypothetical construct   See *construct* (4).

Illustrative case study   A type of case study used to investigate rare or unknown phenomena (12).

Independent sample   A type of sample in which different participants are independently observed one time in each group (14).

Independent variable   The variable that is manipulated in an experiment. The levels of the variable remain unchanged (or "independent") between groups in an experiment. It is the "presumed cause" (7).

Independent-sample *t* test   See *two-independent-sample* t *test* (14).

Indigenous typologies   reflect the perspectives of the case(s) and how they classify elements of their world (20).

Individual differences   The unique characteristics of participants in a sample that can differ from one participant to another.

Individual sampling   A strategy used to manage an observation period by splitting a fixed period of time into smaller intervals of time and then recording the behaviors of a different participant in each time interval (8).

Inductive analysis   is when the themes are generated from the narratives without any preconceived ideas (20).

Inductive reasoning   A "bottom-up" type of reasoning in which a limited number of observations or measurements (i.e., data) are used to generate ideas and make observations (2).

Inferential statistics   Procedures that allow researchers to *infer* or generalize observations made with samples to the larger population from which they were selected (19).

Informed consent   A signed or verbal agreement in which participants state they are willing to participate in a research study after being informed of all aspects of their role in the study (3).

Institutional review board (IRB)   A review board with at least five members, one of whom comes from outside the institution. These members review for approval research protocols submitted by researchers prior to the conduct of any human participant research. Every institution that receives federal funding must have an IRB (3).

Instrumentation   A possible threat to internal validity in which the measurement of the dependent variable changes due to an error during the course of a research study (5).

Interaction   A source of variation associated with how the effects of one factor are influenced by, or depend on, the levels of a second factor (19).

Internal consistency   A measure of reliability used to determine the extent to which multiple items used to measure the same variable are related (4).

Internal evaluation   is an evaluation conducted by an evaluator internal to the evaluand, such as an employee of the organization (17).

Internal validity   The extent to which a research design includes enough control of the conditions and experiences of participants that it can demonstrate a single unambiguous explanation for a manipulation—that is, cause and effect (7).

Interobserver reliability   See *interrater reliability (IRR)* (4).

Interquartile range (IQR)   The range of values between the third (Q_3) and first (Q_1) quartiles of a data set (18).

Interrater reliability (IRR)   A measure for the extent to which two or more raters of the same behavior or event are in agreement with what they observed (4).

Interrupted time-series design   A quasi-experimental research design in which a dependent variable is measured at many different points in time in one group before and after a treatment that naturally occurred (13).

Interval estimate   The interval or range of possible values within which an unknown population parameter is likely to be contained (19).

Interval method   A method used to quantify observations made in a study by dividing an observational period into equal intervals of time and then recording whether or not certain behaviors occur in each interval (8).

Interval scales   Measurements that have no true zero and are distributed in equal units (4).

Interviews   are used to collect information about the attitude and perceptions of individuals one-on-one or in groups. They can be structured, semi-structured, or unstructured (5).

Interviewer bias   The tendency for the demeanor, words, or expressions of a researcher to influence the responses of a participant when the researcher and the participant are in direct contact (5).

Interviewer effect   Another term for interviewer bias (5).

Intuition   A method of knowing based largely on an individual's hunch or feeling that something is correct (1).

John Henry effect   (compensatory rivalry effect) is when a participant who is assigned to the control group may try harder because he or she was not selected to receive the special treatment (7).

Justice   An ethical principle listed in the Belmont Report that states that all participants should be treated fairly and equitably in terms of receiving the benefits and bearing the risks in research (3).

Justification   is the reason why the study is important along three dimensions: personal, practical, and social (12).

Latency method   A method used to quantify observations made in a study by recording the time or duration between the occurrences of behaviors during a fixed period of time (8).

Latin square   A matrix design in which a limited number of order sequences are constructed such that (1) the number of order sequences equals the number of treatments, (2) each treatment appears equally often in each position, and (3) each treatment precedes and follows each treatment one time (14).

Level of confidence   The probability or likelihood that an interval estimate will contain the value of an unknown population parameter (e.g., a population mean) (19).

Level of significance   A criterion of judgment upon which a decision is made regarding the value stated in a null hypothesis. The criterion is based on the probability of obtaining a statistic measured in a sample if the value stated in the null hypothesis were true (19).

Levels of a factor   The specific conditions or groups created by manipulating that factor (7).

Likert scale   A numeric response scale used to indicate a participant's rating or level of agreement with a question or statement (5).

Linear regression   A statistical procedure used to determine the equation of a regression line to a set of data points and to determine the extent to which the regression equation can be used to predict values of one factor, given known values of a second factor in a population (9).

Literary transcription   records deviations in the pronunciation of words as long as the meaning of the word used is known (20).

Literature review   A systematic search for and recording of information identified in the general body of published scientific knowledge (2).

Literature review article   A written comprehensive report of findings from previously published works about a problem in the form of a synthesis of previous articles or as a meta-analysis (21).

Logistic regression   is a prediction design where the dependent variable(s) is/are dichotomous—pass/fail, case/not case (9).

Longitudinal design   A developmental research design used to study changes across the life span by observing the same participants at different points in time and measuring the same dependent variable at each time (13).

Longitudinal survey   is the same questionnaire administered repeatedly over a period of time to the same participants repeatedly to understand the changes that occur in attitudes and opinions (9).

Magnitude   The size of the change in a dependent measure observed between phases of a design. The larger the magnitude of changes in a dependent measure between each phase, the higher the internal validity of a research design (13).

Main effect   A source of variation associated with mean differences across the levels of a single factor (19).

Manipulation check   A procedure used to check or confirm that a manipulation in a study had the effect that was intended (4).

Matched-samples design   A within-subjects research design in which participants are matched, experimentally or naturally, based on preexisting characteristics or traits that they share (14).

Maturation   A possible threat to internal validity in which a participant's physiological or psychological state changes over time during a study (7).

Maximum variation sampling   maximizes the diversity of the sample by including typical and extreme cases. The individuals selected represent the entire spectrum of possible cases rather than a homogeneous group (10).

Median   The middle value in a distribution of data listed in numeric order (18).

Member checking   involves verifying coding, representations, and/or interpretations of the participants (20).

Merit   is the quality of the evaluand in comparison to predetermined criteria or a criterion (17, Davidson, 2005).

Meta-analysis   A type of existing data design in which data are combined, analyzed, and summarized across a group of related studies to make statistically guided decisions about the strength or reliability of the reported findings in those studies (8).

Mixed factorial design   A research design in which different participants are observed at each level of a between-subjects factor and also repeatedly observed across the levels of the within-subjects factor (14).

Mixed-methods design   A research design that gathers both quantitative and qualitative data to answer a research question where one type of data informs the other (15).

Mode   The value in a data set that occurs most often or most frequently (18).

Multiple regression   is a prediction design with more than one independent variable to predict one dependent variable (9).

Multiple-baseline design   A single-case experimental design in which a treatment is successively administered over time to different participants, for different behaviors, or in different settings (13).

Multistage program evaluation advanced mixed methods   A research design that employs a basic mixed-methods design in the context of a program evaluation (15).

Narrative inquiry   is the use of human stories to understand phenomena and experiences (12).

Narratives (or narrative data)   are words collected via interviews or documents that are used for analysis (10).

Natural setting   A location or site where a behavior of interest normally occurs (8).

Naturalistic observation   The observation of behavior in the natural setting where it is expected to occur, with limited or no attempt to overtly manipulate the conditions of the environment where the observations are made (8).

Needs assessment   is systematic process to identify the priorities of an organization or program (17).

Negative (disconfirming) case sampling   seeks to find individuals who do not fit into the emerging patterns identified in the analysis (10).

Negative case analysis   involves searching for contradictory evidence that does not support the identified pattern or interpretation derived from the data (20).

Negative correlation   A negative value of r that indicates that the values of two factors change in different directions, meaning that as the values of one factor increase, values of the second factor decrease (9).

Negative skew distribution   is a distribution where the tail is on the left side or lower end of the x-axis and most of the scores lie at the higher end of the scale (18).

Netnography   is a branch of ethnography that uses social media to examine the culture of the online world by examining computer-mediated social interaction (11).

Nominal scale   Measurement in which a number is assigned to represent something or someone. Numbers on a nominal scale are often coded values (4).

Nonequivalent control group   A control group that is matched upon certain preexisting characteristics similar to those observed in a treatment group but to which participants are not randomly assigned. In a quasi-experiment, a dependent variable measured in a treatment group is compared to that in the nonequivalent control group (13).

Nonequivalent control group posttest-only design   A quasi-experimental research design in which a dependent variable is measured following a treatment in one group and also in a nonequivalent control group that does not receive the treatment (13).

Nonequivalent control group pretest-posttest design   A quasi-experimental research design in which a dependent variable is measured in one group of participants before (pretest) and after (posttest) a treatment and that same dependent variable is also measured at pretest and posttest in another nonequivalent control group that does not receive the treatment (13).

Nonexperimental research design   The use of methods and procedures to make observations in which the behavior or event is observed "as is" or without an intervention from the researcher (7).

Nonprobability sampling   A category of sampling in which a sample is selected from the accessible population. Nonprobability sampling methods are used when it is not possible to select individuals directly from the target population (6).

Nonparametric tests   Significance tests that are used to test hypotheses about data that can have any type of distribution and to analyze data on a nominal or ordinal scale of measurement (19).

Nonresponse bias   A bias in sampling in which a number of participants in one or more groups choose not to respond to a survey or request to participate in a research study (6).

Norm-referenced test   is a test that compares one individual's performance on the test to other individuals' performance on the same test (5).

Normal distribution   A theoretical distribution with data that are symmetrically distributed around the mean, the median, and the mode (18).

Null See *null hypothesis* (19).

Null hypothesis A statement about a population parameter, such as the population mean, that is assumed to be true. The null hypothesis is a starting point. We will test whether the value stated in the null hypothesis is likely to be true (19).

Nuremberg Code The first international code for ethical conduct in research consisting of 10 directives aimed at the protection of human participants (3).

Objects of awareness are those things that bring an experience to memory or consciousness (11).

Observer is a research role where the observer is neither seen nor heard. The researcher is as unobtrusive as possible in the situation being observed and the participants may not even know that they are being observed (10).

Observer as participant is a qualitative researcher who is primarily an observer but will have limited interaction with the participants (10).

One-group posttest-only design A quasi-experimental research design in which a dependent variable is measured for one group of participants following a treatment (13).

One-group pretest-posttest design A quasi-experimental research design in which the same dependent variable is measured in one group of participants before (pretest) and after (posttest) a treatment is administered (13).

One-sample *t* test A statistical procedure used to test hypotheses concerning the mean of interval or ratio data in a single population with an unknown variance (18).

One-way between-subjects ANOVA A statistical procedure used to test hypotheses for one factor with two or more levels concerning the variance among group means. This test is used when different participants are observed at each level of a factor and the variance in a given population is unknown (14).

One-way within-subjects ANOVA A statistical procedure used to test hypotheses for one factor with two or more levels concerning the variance among group means. This test is used when the same participants are observed at each level of a factor and the variance in a given population is unknown (14).

Open-ended item A question or statement in a survey that allows the respondent to give any response in his or her own words, without restriction (5).

Operational definition A description of some observable event in terms of the specific process or manner by which it was observed or measured (1).

Opportunistic sampling obtains participants serendipitously to take advantage of circumstances or new events as they arise (10).

Order effects A threat to internal validity in which the order in which participants receive different treatments or participate in different groups causes changes in a dependent variable (14).

Ordinal scale Measurement that conveys order or rank only (4).

Outcome validity The extent to which the results or outcomes observed in a study will generalize across different but related dependent variables (7).

Outlier A score that falls substantially above or below most other scores in a data set (9).

Overt observation is when the researcher takes an active role in the activities under investigation, typically by assuming the role being studied (10).

***p* value** The probability of obtaining a sample outcome if the value stated in the null hypothesis is true. The *p* value is compared to the level of significance to make a decision about a null hypothesis (19).

Paired-samples *t* test See *related samples* t *test* (14).

Pairwise comparison A statistical comparison for the difference between two group means. A post hoc test evaluates all possible pairwise comparisons for an ANOVA with any number of groups (14).

Paralinguistic component is the vocal features that occur during speaking that are not words such as laughing and crying when transcribing an interview (20).

Parametric tests Significance tests that are used to test hypotheses about parameters in a population in which the data are normally distributed and measured on an interval or ratio scale of measurement (19).

Parsimony A canon of science that states that, all else being equal, simpler explanations should be preferred to more complex ones (2).

Partial counterbalancing A procedure in which some, but not all, possible order sequences in which participants receive different treatments or participate in different groups are balanced or offset in an experiment (14).

Partially open-ended item A question or statement in a survey that includes a few restricted answer options and then a last one that allows participants to respond in their own words in case the few restricted options do not fit with the answer they want to give (5).

Participant A term used to describe a human who volunteers to be subjected to the procedures in a research study (6, 10).

Participant as observer is when the researcher is engaged with the participants of the study and may be viewed as a friend or colleague. The participants know that this person is the researcher (10).

Participant expectancy A type of participant reactivity in which a participant is overly cooperative (4).

Participant fatigue A state of physical or psychological exhaustion resulting from intense research demands typically due to observing participants too often or requiring participants to engage in research activities that are too demanding (14).

Participant reactivity The reaction or response participants have when they know they are being observed or measured (4).

Participant reluctance A type of participant reactivity in which a participant is overly antagonistic (4).

Participant variable A quasi-independent or preexisting variable that is related to or characteristic of the personal attributes of a participant (13).

Participatory action research (PAR) merges action research and critical theory to critique educational practices and understand how these practices are defined by the social spheres in which education operates (16).

Participant-oriented evaluation serves to engage stakeholders, including program participants, in the evaluation process to effect some change (17).

Pattern analysis is the recursive process to assign a pattern to descriptions across cases that are considered to be the same thing (20).

Patterns among categories can be based on how they are similar or different, how often they appear, sequence of the categories, how they relate to different situations, or whether a category appears to cause or influence another category (20).

Pearson correlation coefficient A coefficient used to measure the direction and strength of the linear relationship of two factors in which the data for both factors are on an interval or a ratio scale of measurement (9).

Peer debriefing involves a review of the data by someone knowledgeable in the area being studied but who was not deeply involved in the study that can lend support (or not) to the interpretations (20).

Peer review A procedure used by the editors of scientific journals in which a manuscript or work is sent to peers or experts in that area to review the work and determine its scientific value or worth regarding publication (3, 21).

Peer-reviewed journal A type of publication that specifically publishes scientific articles, reviews, or commentaries only after the work has been reviewed by peers or scientific experts who determine its scientific value or worth regarding publication. Only after acceptance from peer reviewers will a work be published (2).

Percentile rank is a standard score that converts the raw score to rank an individual's performance in relation to many other individuals scored at or below that same score (18).

Phase A series of trials or observations made in one condition (13).

Phenomenon A situation or a person's perception of the experience; it refers to what the inquiry is about (12).

Phenomenology The qualitative analysis of the conscious experiences of phenomena from the first-person point of view of the participant (11).

Pie chart A graphical display in the shape of a circle that is used to summarize the relative percentage of discrete and categorical data into sectors (18).

Pilot study A small preliminary study used to determine the extent to which a manipulation or measure will show an effect of interest (4).

Place recognizes that human stories take place somewhere, in some concrete space (12).

Plagiarism An individual's use of someone else's ideas or work that is represented as the individual's own ideas or work (3).

Point estimate A sample statistic (e.g., a sample mean) that is used to estimate a population parameter (e.g., a population mean) (19).

Political/governmental context is a self-description that includes current political and legal issues that affect an individual (11).

Population A set of *all* individuals, items, or data of interest about which scientists will generalize (1).

Population validity The extent to which results observed in a study will generalize to the population from which a sample was selected (7).

Positioning is the comparison of the narrative inquiry with other research conducted on the topic (12).

Positive correlation A positive value of *r* that indicates that the values of two factors change in the same direction: As the values of one factor increase, values of the second factor also increase; as the values of one factor decrease, values of the second factor also decrease (9).

Positive skew distribution is a distribution where the tail is on the right side or upper end of the *x*-axis and most of the scores lie at the lower end of the scale (18).

Positivism/postpositivism is a philosophical view shared by both quantitative and qualitative researchers where the belief is that there is one reality that can be studied using a structured scientific method, verified, understood, and tested as theories (10).

Post hoc test A statistical procedure computed following a significant ANOVA to determine which pair or pairs of group means significantly differ. These tests are needed with more than two groups because multiple comparisons must be made (14).

Poster A concise description of a research study in the form of a display of text boxes, figures, and tables on a single large page (21).

Poster session A 1- to 4-hour time slot during which many authors stand near their poster ready and open to answer questions or talk about their work with interested attendees (21).

Power The probability in hypothesis testing of rejecting a false null hypothesis. Specifically, power is the probability that we will detect an effect if an effect actually exists in a population (8, 19).

Practical action research is a planned, systematic inquiry to try out new practices and evaluate the impact of the new practice (16).

Practitioner is an individual who is engaged in the teaching profession (16).

Prediction design uses one independent variable to predict the later occurrence of the dependent variable (9).

Predictor variable The variable (X) with values that are known and can be used to predict values of another variable (9).

Primary source Any publication in which the works, ideas, or observations are those of the author (2).

Proactive practical action research is when the practitioner researcher implements a course of action, such as implementing a new instructional practice, and then collects data related to the practice and reflects on the effects of the new course of action (16).

Probability sampling A category of sampling in which a sample is selected directly from the target population. Probability sampling methods are used when the probability of selecting each individual in a population is known and every member of the population has an equal chance of being selected (6).

Program evaluation is the systematic process of gathering information about the merit and worth of something and making a judgment about it in regard to a set of predetermined criteria (17).

Program-oriented evaluation focuses on evaluating the key features of the program and using the key features to decide what to evaluate. There are four program-oriented approaches: (1) objective-oriented, (2) logic models, (3) theory-based, and (4) goal-free evaluation (17).

Prolonged engagement is the amount of time to develop trust of the participants and gain the knowledge necessary to answer the research question (20).

Proportion of variance A measure of effect size in terms of the proportion or percentage of variability in a dependent variable that can be explained or accounted for by the levels of a factor or treatment (19).

Proportionate quota sampling A type of quota sampling used when the proportions of certain characteristics in a target population are known. Using this type of quota sampling, subjects or participants are selected such that the known characteristics or demographics are proportionately represented in the sample (5).

Proportionate stratified random sampling A type of stratified sampling in which a proportionate number of participants are sampled from each subgroup such that the sample resembles proportions in the population of interest (5).

Propriety is the consideration of the legal and ethical issues that surround the evaluation (17).

Prosodic component is the manner in which words are spoken such as pitch, loudness, and duration when transcribing an interview (20).

Pseudoscience A set of procedures that are not scientific, and it is part of a system or set of beliefs that try to deceptively create the impression that the knowledge gained represents the "final say" or most reliable knowledge on its subject matter (1).

Publication bias The tendency for editors of peer-reviewed journals to preferentially accept articles that show positive results and reject those that show only negative results (2).

Qualitative research Uses the scientific method to make nonnumeric observations, from which conclusions are drawn without the use of statistical analysis (1, 7).

Qualitative research design See *qualitative research* (1, 7).

Qualitative variable Varies by class. A qualitative variable is often a category or label for the behaviors and events researchers observe and so describes nonnumeric aspects of phenomena (4).

Quantitative research Uses the scientific method to record observations as numeric data. Most research conducted in the behavioral sciences is quantitative (1).

Quantitative variable Varies by amount. A quantitative variable is measured as a numeric value and is often collected by measuring or counting (4).

Quasi-experimental research design The use of methods and procedures to make observations in a study that is structured similar to an experiment, but the conditions and experiences of participants lack some control because the study lacks random assignment, includes a preexisting factor (i.e., a variable that is not manipulated), or does not include a comparison/control group (7, 13).

Quasi-independent variable A variable with levels to which participants are not randomly assigned and that differentiates the groups or conditions being compared in a research study. Because the levels of the variable are preexisting, it is not possible to randomly assign participants to groups (7, 13).

Queer theory examines how social construction of knowledge, organization of society, and societal practices privilege some and discriminate against others based on sexual orientation or other odd behavior (12).

Questionnaire is an instrument to measure a predetermined, standard set of items about attitudes or perceptions of the participant (5).

Quota sampling A method of sampling in which subjects or participants are selected based on known or unknown criteria or characteristics in the target population (6).

Random assignment A random procedure used to ensure that participants in a study have an equal chance of being assigned to a particular group or condition (7).

Randomization The use of methods for selecting individuals to participate in a study and assigning them to groups such that each individual has an equal chance of being selected to participate and assigned to a group (7).

Range The difference between the largest (*L*) value and the smallest (*S*) value in a data set (18).

Range effect A limitation in the range of data measured in which scores are clustered to one extreme (4).

Rank order scale is a scale to order the options in a sequence such as preference, priority, or desire (5).

Rapport A relationship in which people understand the feelings and ideas of others and communicate them well (5).

Ratio scale Measurement that has a true zero and is equidistant (4).

Rationalism A method of knowing that requires the use of reasoning and logic (1).

Raw score A single measurement or observation (1).

Reactivity is when the participants alter their behavior in some way because they know they are being studied (10, 11).

Reflection is serious thought or consideration regarding the practice of teaching (16).

Regression See *linear regression* (9).

Regression line The best-fitting straight line to a set of data points. A best-fitting line is the line that minimizes the distance that all data points fall from it (9).

Regression toward the mean A change or shift in a participant's performance toward a level or score that is closer to or more typical of his or her true potential or mean ability on some measure, after previously scoring unusually high or low on the same measure (7).

Related sample A type of sample in which the same or matched participants are observed in each group (14).

Related-samples *t* test A statistical procedure used to test hypotheses concerning the difference in interval or ratio scale data for two related samples in which the variance in one population is unknown (14).

Reliability The consistency, stability, or repeatability of one or more measures or observations (4).

Repeated measures design See *within-subjects design* (14).

Replication The reproduction of research procedures under identical conditions for the purposes of observing the same phenomenon (3).

Research design The specific methods and procedures used to answer a research question (7).

Research ethics Identifies the actions that researchers must take to conduct responsible and moral research (3).

Research hypothesis A specific, testable claim or prediction about what you expect to observe given a set of circumstances (1).

Research method See *scientific method* (1).

Research protocol A proposal, submitted by a researcher to an IRB, outlining the details of a study he or she wishes to complete and how he or she will address potential ethical concerns. Only upon approval by an IRB is a researcher allowed to conduct his or her study, and all researchers are bound to follow the protocol once it is approved (3).

Resentful demoralization is when a participant assigned to the control group may instead feel demoralized or resentful because he or she was not selected for the treatment group (7).

Respect for persons An ethical principle listed in the Belmont Report that states that participants in a research study must be autonomous agents capable of making informed decisions concerning whether to participate in research (3).

Response bias occurs whenever the individuals who respond to a survey respond differently than those who do not (9).

Response rate The portion of participants who agree to complete a survey among all individuals who were asked to complete the survey (9).

Response set   The tendency for participants to respond the same way to all items in a survey when the direction of ratings is the same for all items in the survey (5).

Responsive practical action research   is when the practitioner researcher collects and analyzes data before implementing the new course of action (16).

Restricted item   A question or statement in a survey that includes a restricted number of answer options to which participants must respond (5).

Restricted random assignment   A method of controlling differences in participant characteristics between groups in a study by first restricting a sample based on known participant characteristics, then using a random procedure to assign participants to each group. Two strategies of restricted random assignment are control by matching and control by holding constant (14).

Restriction of range   A problem that arises when the range of data for one or both correlated factors in a sample is limited or restricted, compared with the range of data in the population from which the sample was selected (9).

Reversal design   A single-case experimental design in which a single participant is observed before (A), during (B), and after (A) a treatment or manipulation (13).

Reverse causality   A problem that arises when the direction of causality between two factors can be in either direction (9).

Reverse-coded item   An item that is phrased in the semantically opposite direction of most other items in a survey and is scored by coding or entering responses for the item in reverse order from how they are listed (5).

Risk-benefit analysis   A type of analysis in which the researcher anticipates or weighs the risks and benefits in a study (3).

Sample   A set of *selected* individuals, items, or data taken from a population of interest (1).

Sample mean   The sum of all scores (Σx) divided by the number of scores summed (n) in a sample or in a subset of scores selected from a larger population (18).

Sample standard deviation (SD)   A measure of variability for the average distance that scores in a sample deviate from the sample mean and is computed by taking the square root of the sample variance (18).

Sample variance   A measure of variability for the average squared distance that scores in a sample deviate from the sample mean (18).

Sampling bias   A bias in sampling in which the sampling procedures employed in a study favor certain individuals or groups over others (6).

Sampling error   The extent to which sample means selected from the same population differ from one another. This difference, which occurs by chance, is measured by the standard error of the mean (5).

Sampling frame   See *accessible population* (6).

Sampling with replacement   A strategy used with simple random sampling in which each individual selected is replaced before the next selection to ensure that the probability of selecting each individual is always the same (6).

Sampling without replacement   A nonrandom sampling strategy most often used by behavioral researchers in which each individual selected is not replaced before the next selection (6).

Scales of measurement   Rules for how the properties of numbers can change with different uses (4).

Scatter diagram   See *scatterplot* (9).

Scattergram   See *scatterplot* (9).

Scatterplot   A graphical display of discrete data points (x, y) used to summarize the relationship between two factors (9, 18).

Science   The acquisition of knowledge through observation, evaluation, interpretation, and theoretical explanation (1).

Scientific integrity   The extent to which a researcher is honest and truthful in his or her actions, values, methods, measures, and dissemination of research (3).

Scientific method   A set of systematic techniques used to acquire, modify, and integrate knowledge concerning observable and measurable phenomena (1).

Score   A single measurement or observation; see also *data* (1).

Secondary source   Any publication that refers to works, ideas, or observations that are not those of the author (2).

Selection differences   Any differences, which are not controlled by the researcher, between individuals who are selected from preexisting groups or groups to which the researcher does not randomly assign participants (13).

Selective coding   involves organizing the categories or themes that articulate a theory (11).

Selective deposit   The process by which existing records are selectively recorded or deposited into document files that can be accessed for analysis (8).

Selective survival The process by which existing records survive or are excluded/decay over time (8).

Self-report measure A type of measurement in which participants respond to one or more questions or statements to indicate their actual or perceived experiences, attitudes, or opinions (5).

Semi-structured interview is an interview with a set of questions that is presented to all the individuals being interviewed but the responses are open-ended (5).

Sensitivity of a measure The extent to which a measure can change or be different in the presence of a manipulation (4).

Significance Describes a decision made concerning a value stated in the null hypothesis. When the null hypothesis is rejected, we reach significance. When the null hypothesis is retained, we fail to reach significance (19).

Significance level See *level of significance* (19).

Simple correlation design examines the relationship between one independent and one dependent variable at one point in time. The information for both variables is gathered at the same time (9).

Simple quota sampling A type of quota sampling used when little is known about the characteristics of a target population. Using this type of quota sampling, an equal number of subjects or participants are selected for a given characteristic or demographic (6).

Simple random sampling A method of sampling subjects and participants such that all individuals in a population have an equal chance of being selected and are selected using sampling with replacement (6).

Simple stratified random sampling A type of stratified random sampling that involves selecting an equal number of participants in each subgroup (6).

Single-case experimental design An experimental research design in which a participant serves as his or her own control and the dependent variable measured is analyzed for each individual participant and is not averaged across groups or across participants (13).

Skewed distribution A distribution of scores that includes outliers or scores that fall substantially above or below most other scores in a data set (18).

Snowball sampling begins with one or two participants who can provide information about the topic under investigation. The researcher will ask these participants if they know someone else who can provide additional information. These new participants are also asked if they know someone else. The sample becomes larger as the study continues like making a snowball and rolling it through the snow (10).

Social desirability is when the participants change their behavior to put themselves in the best light. They respond in ways that are not true to themselves but in a way that they think would be more socially desirable (7).

Social justice advanced mixed methods design A research design that employs a mixed-methods basic design in the context of a social justice framework (15).

Sociality is a dimension of narrative inquiry that includes the personal, social, and relationship with the researcher (12).

Solomon four-group design An experimental research design in which different participants are assigned to each of four groups in such a way that comparisons can be made to (1) determine if a treatment causes changes in posttest measure and (2) control for possible confounds or extraneous factors related to giving a pretest measure and observing participants over time (14).

Stability The consistency in the pattern of change in a dependent measure in each phase of a design. The more stable or consistent changes in a dependent measure are in each phase, the higher the internal validity of a research design (13).

Stakeholder is any person who has a vested interest in the evaluand being evaluated (17; Greene, 2005).

Standard error of the mean The standard deviation of a sampling distribution of sample means. It is the standard error or distance that sample mean values can deviate from the value of the population mean (6).

Standard orthography transcription records what is said using standard dictionary spelling of words regardless of how the words were pronounced (20).

Standard score is one where the raw score is transformed into a normal frequency distribution with a specific mean and standard deviation so that we can compare an individual's score to other scores in the same peer group and make a determination about the relative performance of that individual (18).

Standardized achievement test measures current learned skills associated with different age or grade levels (5).

Standardized aptitude test measures the potential of an individual to learn and is used to predict future performance (5).

Standardized personality test measures an individual's affective traits or psychological makeup (5).

Statistical power The likelihood that data in a sample can detect or discover an effect in a population, assuming that the effect does exist in the population of interest (8).

Statistical significance See *significance* (19).

Stratified random sampling   A method of sampling in which a population is divided into subgroups or strata; participants are then selected from each subgroup using simple random sampling and are combined into one overall sample (6).

Structured interview   is an interview with a specific set of questions and response options (5).

Structured setting   See *contrived setting* (8).

Subcode   is a smaller element, distinct from a code (20).

Subject   A term used to describe a nonhuman that is subjected to procedures in a research study and to identify the names of research designs (6).

Sum of squares (*SS*)   The sum of the squared deviations of scores from the mean and is the value placed in the numerator of the sample variance formula (18).

Summative evaluation   is an evaluation that occurs at the end of the implementation of the evaluand (17).

Survey   is the systematic process used to administer a questionnaire (8).

Survey research design   The use of a survey, administered either in written form or orally, to quantify, describe, or characterize an individual or a group (9).

Systematic sampling   A method of sampling in which the first participant is selected using simple random sampling, and then every nth person is systematically selected until all participants have been selected (6).

System-based action research   is conducted within a larger context that considers educational delivery systems or policy (16).

Target population   All members of a group of interest to a researcher (6).

Temporal validity   The extent to which results observed in a study will generalize across time and at different points in time (7).

Temporality   is a dimension of narrative inquiry to understand that events have a past, present, and future (12).

Tenacity   A method of knowing based largely on habit or superstition (1).

Test   is a predetermined, standard set of items designed to measure a characteristic or skill (5).

Test statistic   A mathematical formula that allows researchers to determine the likelihood of obtaining sample outcomes if the null hypothesis were true. The value of the test statistic can be used to make a decision regarding the null hypothesis. The test statistic also allows researchers to determine the extent to which differences observed between groups can be attributed to the manipulation used to create the different groups (19).

Testing effect   The improved performance on a test or measure the second time it is taken due to the experience of taking the test (7).

Test-retest reliability   The extent to which a measure or observation is consistent or stable at two points in time (4).

Thematic analysis   is the recursive process to assign a theme to the categories in an attempt to provide meaning (20).

Theoretical sampling   is the use of personal experience and professional immersion into the field of study to be able to give meaning to the data (11).

Theoretical sensitivity   is the use of personal experience and professional immersion into the field of study to be able to give meaning to the data collected (11).

Theory   A broad statement used to account for an existing body of knowledge and also provide unique predictions to extend that body of knowledge. A theory is not necessarily correct; instead, it is a generally accepted explanation for evidence, as it is understood (2).

Theory development   is an application of case study where the researchers state hypotheses to develop new theories or to test existing theories (12).

Thick description   involves extensive description of the context, participants, experiences, and activities involved in the study (20).

Time sampling   A strategy used to manage an observation period by splitting a fixed period of time into smaller intervals of time and then making observations during alternating intervals until the full observation period has ended (8).

Transferability (applicability)   The extent to which observed results are useful, applicable, or transferable beyond the setting or context of the research (20).

Treatment group   A condition in an experiment in which participants are treated or exposed to a manipulation or level of the independent variable that is believed to cause a change in the dependent variable (14).

Treatment validity   is the extent to which the treatment can be generalized, whether the treatment can be implemented as it is conceptualized to other individuals (7).

Triangulation   refers to using multiple sources in the investigation such as multiple participants, multiple types of data, or different sources of data (20).

True zero The value 0 truly indicates nothing on a scale of measurement (4).

Trustworthiness is based on four criteria: the credibility, transferability, dependability, and confirmability of a qualitative analysis (20).

Two-independent-sample *t* test A statistical procedure used to test hypotheses concerning the difference in interval or ratio scale data between two group means, in which the variance in the population is unknown (14).

Type I error A "false-positive" finding. It is the probability of rejecting a null hypothesis that is actually true. Researchers directly control for this error by stating the level of significance (19).

Type II error A "false-negative" finding. It is the probability of retaining a null hypothesis that is actually false. This means the researcher is reporting no effect in the population when in truth there is an effect (19).

Typical case sampling selects individuals who are average or representative of the issue being investigated (10).

Unbiased estimator Any sample statistic obtained from a randomly selected sample that equals the value of its respective population parameter on average (18).

Uniqueness is a consideration of narrative inquiry that refers to what new information is provided by the study (12).

Unobtrusive observation A technique used by an observer to record or observe behavior in a way that does not interfere with or change a participant's behavior in a research setting (5).

Unstructured interview is an interview where there is no predetermined set of questions (5).

Utility is the extent to which the evaluation provides the stakeholders with the information they need in order for the information to be used to make an informed decision (17).

Validity The extent to which a measurement for a variable or construct measures what it is purported or intended to measure (4).

Variability A measure of the dispersion or spread of scores in a distribution and ranges from 0 to $+\infty$ (18).

Variable Any value or characteristic that can change or vary from one person to another or from one situation to another (1, 4).

Verbal component is the words spoken by the participant when transcribing an interview (20).

Within-groups variability A source of variance in a dependent measure that is caused by or associated with observing different participants within each group (14).

Within-subjects design A research design in which the same participants are observed one time in each group of a research study (14).

Within-subjects experimental design An experimental research design in which the levels of a within-subjects factor are manipulated, and then the same participants are observed in each group or at each level of the factor. To qualify as an experiment, the researcher must (1) manipulate the levels of the factor and include a comparison/control group and (2) make added efforts to control for order and time-related factors (14).

Within-subjects factor A type of factor in which the same participants are observed in each group or at each level of the factor (14).

Within-subjects factorial design A research design in which the levels of two or more within-subjects factors are combined to create groups, meaning that the same participants are observed in each group (14).

Worth is the value of the evaluand in the specific context in which it is being evaluated (17; Mathison, 2005).

z **score** is a standard score that converts a raw score into a score that tells you how many standard deviations a score is from the mean (18).

REFERENCES

Abelson, R. P. (1995). *Statistics as principled argument.* Hillsdale, NJ: Lawrence Erlbaum.

Abma, T. A., & Stake, R. E. (2001). Stake's responsive evaluation: Core Ideas and evolution. New *Directions for Evaluation, 92,* 7–21.

Achinstein, B., Curry, M. W., & Ogawa, R. T. (2015). (Re)labeling social status: Promises and tensions in developing a college-going culture for Latina/o youth in an urban high school. *American Journal of Education, 121,* 311–345.

Ahlgrim-Delzell, L., Browder, D., Stanger, C., Wood, L., Kemp-Inman, A., & Preston, A. (2016). Systematic instruction of phonics skills using an iPad for students with developmental disabilities who are AAC users. *The Journal of Special Education, 50,* 86–97.

Ahlgrim-Delzell, L., & Rivera, C. (2015). A content comparison of literacy lessons from 2004 and 2010 for students with moderate and severe intellectual disability. *Exceptionality, 23,* 258–269.

AIMSweb. (2014). Retrieved from http://www.pearsonassessments.com/learningassessments/products/100000519/aimsweb.html

Albert, U., Salvi, V., Saracco, P., Bogetto, P., & Maina, G. (2007). Health-related quality of life among first-degree relatives of patients with obsessive-compulsive disorder in Italy. *Psychiatric Services, 58,* 970–976. doi:10.1176/appi.ps.58.7.970

Al-Dujaily, A., Kim, J., & Ryu, H. (2013). Am I extravert or introvert? Considering the personality effect toward e-learning system. *Educational Technology & Society, 16,* 14–27.

Allor, J. H., Mathes, P. G., Roberts, J. K., Jones, F. G., & Champlin, T. M. (2010). Teaching students with moderate intellectual disabilities to read: An experimental examination of a comprehensive reading intervention. *Education and Training in Autism and Developmental Disabilities, 45,* 3–22.

American Educational Research Association (AERA). (2006). Standards for reporting on empirical social science research in AERA publications. *Educational Researcher, 35,* 33–40.

American Educational Research Association (AERA). (2011). *Code of ethics.* Washington, DC: Author.

American Psychological Association (APA). (1953). *Ethical principles of psychologists.* Washington DC: Author.

American Psychological Association (APA). (2009). *Publication manual of the American Psychological Association* (6th ed.). Washington, DC: Author.

American Psychological Association (APA). (2012). *Guidelines for ethical conduct in the care and use of nonhuman animals in research.* Washington DC: Author. Retrieved from http://www.apa.org/science/leadership/care/guidelines.aspx

American Psychological Association (APA). (2013a). *APA databases: PsycARTICLES.* Retrieved from http://www.apa.org/pubs/databases/psycarticles/index.aspx

American Psychological Association (APA). (2013b). *APA databases: PsycINFO.* Retrieved from http://www.apa.org/psycinfo/

Anderson, E. A. (1976). The chivalrous treatment of the female offender in the arms of the criminal justice system. *Social Problems, 23,* 349–357.

Antonietti, A., Cocomazzi, D., & Iannello, P. (2009). Looking at the audience improves music appreciation. *Journal of Nonverbal Behavior, 33,* 89–106. doi:10.1007/s10919-008-0062-x

Appelt, L. (2015). Review of dual language instruction from A to Z: Practical guidance for teachers and administrators. *International Journal of Bilingual Education and Bilingualism, 18,* 355–357.

Asef-Vaziri, A. (2015). The flipped classroom of operations management: A not-for-cost-reduction platform. *Decision Sciences Journal of Innovation Education, 13.*

Association of Internet Researchers. (2012). Ethical decision-making and Internet research recommendations from the AoIR Ethics Working Committee (Version 2.0). Retrieved from http://www.aoir.org/reports/ethics2.pdf

Aviles de Bradley, A. (2015). Homeless educational policy: Exploring a racialized discourse through a critical race theory lens. *Urban Education, 50,* 839–869.

Badanes, L. S., Dmitrieva, J., & Watamura, S. E. (2012). Understanding cortisol reactivity across the day at child care: The potential buffering role of secure attachments to caregivers. *Early Childhood Research Quarterly, 27,* 156–165. doi:10.1016/j.ecresq.2011.05.005

Baker, M. T., & Taub, H. A. (1983). Readability of informed consent forms for research in a Veterans Administration medical center. *Journal of American Medical Association, 250,* 2646–2648. doi:10.1001/jama.1983.03340190048030

Balk, D. E., Walker, A. C., & Baker, A. (2010). Prevalence and severity of college student bereavement examined in a randomly selected sample. *Death Studies, 34,* 459–468. doi:10.1080/07481180903251810

Bar-Eli, M., Azar, O. H., Ritov, I., Keidar-Levin, Y., & Schein, G. (2007). Action bias among elite soccer goalkeepers: The case of penalty kicks. *Journal of Economic Psychology, 28*, 606–621. doi:10.1016/j.joep.2006.12.001

Baruch, Y. (1999). Response rate in academic studies: A comparative analysis. *Human Relations, 52*, 421–438. doi:10.1177/001872679905200401

Baruch, Y., & Holtom, B. C. (2008). Survey response rate levels and trends in organizational research. *Human Relations, 61*(8), 1139–1160. doi:10.1177/0018726708094863

Beard, K. S. (2012). Making the case for the outlier: Researcher reflections of an African-American female deputy superintendent who decided to close the achievement gap. *International Journal of Qualitative Studies in Education*, 25, 59–71.

Becker, L. M. (2014). *Presenting your research: Conferences, symposiums, poster presentations and beyond.* Thousand Oaks, CA: Sage.

Bell, E. E. (2014). Graduating Black males: A generic qualitative study. *The Qualitative Report, 19*, 1–10.

Berenhaus, M., Oakhill, J., & Rusted, J. (2015). When kids act out: A comparison of embodied methods to improve children's memory for a story. *Journal of Research in Reading, 38*, 331–343. doi:10.1111/1467-9817.12039

Betz, N. E., Klein, K. L., & Taylor, K. M. (1996). Evaluation of a short form of the career decision-making self-efficacy scale. *Journal of Career Assessment, 4*, 47–57. doi:10.1177/106907279600400103

Bickman, L. (Ed.). (1987). *Using program theory in evaluation: New Directions for program evaluation.* San Francisco, CA: Jossey-Bass.

Blair, E., & Zinkhan, G. M. (2006). Nonresponse and generalizability in academic research. *Journal of the Academy of Marketing Science, 34*, 4–7. doi:10.1177/0092070305283778

Blatt, B., & Kaplan, F. (1974). *Christmas in purgatory: A photographic essay on mental retardation.* Syracuse, NY: Human Policy Press.

Bleakley, A., Hennessy, M., Fishbein, M., & Jordan, A. (2009). How sources of sexual information relate to adolescents' beliefs about sex. *American Journal of Health Behavior, 33*, 37–48.

Bleiler, S. K. (2015). Increasing awareness of practice through interaction across communities: The lived experiences of a mathematician and mathematics teacher educator. *Journal of Mathematics Teacher Education, 18*, 231–252.

Bliss, S. L. (2014). Review of the Early Reading Assessment. *Mental Measurement Yearbook, 20.*

Blizzard, R. (2015). *Communities in Schools election poll.* Retrieved from https://www.communitiesinschools.org/media/filer_public/fa/b4/fab46054-39e3-4dac-a83f-afcaa5822d2b/education-election_poll_executive_summary_memo.pdf

Bradley, M. M., & Lang, P. J. (1994). Measuring emotion: The Self-Assessment Manikin and the semantic differential. *Journal of Behavior Therapy & Experimental Psychiatry, 25*, 49–59. doi:10.1016/0005-7916(94)90063-9

Braun, D., Billups, F. D., & Gable, R. K. (2013). *Transforming successful principals.* Palo Alto, CA: Stanford Educational Leadership Institute.

Brezsnyak, M., & Whisman, M. A. (2004). Sexual desire and relationship functioning: The effects of marital satisfaction and power. *Journal of Sex and Marital Therapy, 30*, 199–218. doi:10.1080/00926230490262393

Browder, D. M., Wakeman, S., Spooner, F., Ahlgrim-Delzell, L., & Algozzine, R. (2006). Research on reading instruction for individuals with significant cognitive disabilities. *Exceptional Children, 72*, 392–408.

Bublitz, B., Philipich, K., & Blatz, R. (2015). An example of the use of research methods and findings as an experiential learning exercise in an accounting theory course. *Journal of Instructional Pedagogies, 16*, 1–11.

Byrnes, V. (2009). Getting a feel for the market: The use of privatized school management in Philadelphia. *American Journal of Education, 115*, 437–455.

Calnan, M., Smith, D., & Sterne, J. A. C. (2006). The publication process itself was the major cause of publication bias in genetic epidemiology. *Journal of Clinical Epidemiology, 59*, 1312–1318. doi:10.1016/j.jclinepi.2006.05.002

Campbell, D. T., & Stanley, J. C. (1966). *Experimental and quasi-experimental designs for research.* Chicago, IL: Rand McNally.

Capaldi, E. D., & Privitera, G. J. (2008). Decreasing dislike for sour and bitter in children and adults. *Appetite, 50*(1), 139–145. doi:10.1016/j.appet.2007.06.008

Carr, J. M. (2012). Does math achievement h'APP'en when iPads and game-based learning are incorporated into fifth-grade mathematics instruction? *Journal of Information and Technology Education: Research, 11*, 269–286.

Carvalho, M. B., Bellotti F., Berta R., De Gloria A., Sedano C. I., Hauge J. B., Hu J., & Rauterberg, M. (2015). An activity theory-based model for serious games analysis and conceptual design. *Computers & Education, 87*, 166–181.

Centers for Disease Control and Prevention. (2011). *U.S. Public Health Service Syphilis Study at Tuskegee: The Tuskegee timeline.* Atlanta, GA: Author. Retrieved from http://www.cdc.gov/tuskegee/timeline.htm

Chan, A.-W., Hróbjartsson, A., Haahr, M. T., Gøtzsche, P. C., & Altman, D. G. (2004). Empirical evidence for selective reporting of outcomes in randomized trials: Comparison of protocols to published articles. *Journal of the American Medical Association, 291*, 2457–2465. doi:10.1001/jama.291.20.2457

Chan, K. C., Lam, S., & Covault, J. M. (2009). White American pre-service teachers' judgments of Anglo and Hispanic student behaviors. *Intercultural Education, 20*, 61–70.

Charmaz, K. (2011). A constructivist grounded theory analysis of losing and regaining a valued self. In F. J. Wertz, K. Charmaz, L. M. McMullen, R. Josselson, R. Anderson, & E. McSpadden (Eds.), *Five ways of doing qualitative analysis* (pp. 165–204). New York, NY: Guilford.

Charoenchai, C., Phuseeorn, S., & Phensawat, W. (2015). Teachers' development model to authentic assessment by empowerment evaluation approach. *Educational Research and Reviews, 17*, 2524–2530.

Chen, J.-Q., McCray, J., Adams, M., & Leow, C. (2014). A survey study of early childhood teachers' beliefs and confidence about teaching early math. *Early Childhood Education Journal, 42*, 367–377.

Chen, X.-L., Dai, X.-Y., & Dong, Q. (2008). A research of Aitken Procrastination Inventory applied to Chinese college students. *Chinese Journal of Clinical Psychology, 16*, 22–23. doi:10.1016/j.paid.2010.02.025

Choo, P., Levine, T., & Hatfield, E. (1996). Gender, love schemas, and reactions to romantic breakups. *Journal of Social Behavior and Personality, 11*, 143–160. doi:10.1207/S15327957PSPR0601_1

Chouinard, R., & Roy, N. (2008). Changes in high-school students' competence beliefs, utility value and achievement goals in mathematics. *British Journal of Educational Psychology, 78*, 31–50.

Christensen, L. (1988). Deception in psychological research: When is its use justified? *Personality and Social Psychology Bulletin, 14,* 664–675. doi:10.1177/0146167288144002

Christon, L. M., Arnold, C. C., & Myers, B. J. (2015). Professionals' reported provision and recommendation of psychosocial interventions for youth with autism spectrum disorder. *Behavior Therapy, 46,* 68–82.

Clandinin, D. J., Pushor, D., & Orr, A. M. (2007). Navigating sites for narrative inquiry. *Journal of Teacher Education, 58,* 21–35.

Clark, M. H., & Shadish, W. R. (2008). Solomon Four Group Design. In P. J. Lavrakas (Ed.), *Encyclopedia of survey research methods* (pp. 830–831). Thousand Oaks, CA: Sage.

Cohen, J. (1961). A coefficient of agreement for nominal scales. *Educational and Psychological Measurement, 20,* 37–46. doi:10.1177/001316446002000104

Cohen, J. (1988). Statistical power analysis for the behavioral sciences. Hillsdale, NJ: Lawrence Erlbaum.

Cohn, M. A., Fredrickson, B. L., Brown, S. L., Mikels, J. A., & Conway, A. M. (2009). Happiness unpacked: Positive emotions increase life satisfaction by building resilience. *Emotion, 9,* 361–368. doi:10.1037/a0015952

Connelly, F. M., & Clandinin, D. J. (2006). Narrative inquiry. In J. L. Green, G. Camilli, & P. Elmore (Eds.), *Handbook of complementary methods in education research* (3rd ed., pp. 477–487). Mahwah, NJ: Lawrence Erlbaum.

Cooper, H., & Rosenthal, R. (1980). Statistical versus traditional procedures for summarizing research findings. *Psychological Bulletin, 87,* 442–449. doi:10.1037/0033-2909.87.3.442

Coryn, C. L. S., Noakes, L. A., Westine, C. D., & Schroter, D. C. (2011). A systematic review of theory-driven evaluation practice for 1990 to 2009. *American Journal of Evaluation, 32,* 199–226.

Cousins, J. B., & Whitmore, E. (1998). Framing participatory evaluation. In E. Whitmore (Ed.), *Understanding and practicing participatory evaluation* (New Directions in Evaluation, No. 80, (pp. 3–23). San Francisco, CA: Jossey Bass.

Cronbach, L. J. (1951). Coefficient alpha and the internal structure of tests. *Psychometrika, 16,* 297–334.

Curry, S. J., Mermelstein, R. J., & Sporer, A. K. (2009). Therapy for specific problems: Youth tobacco cessation. *Annual Review of Psychology, 60,* 229–255. doi:10.1146/annurev.psych.60.110707.163659

Daniulaityte, R., Falck, R., Li, L., Nahhas, R. W., & Carlson, R. G. (2012). Respondent-driven sampling to recruit young adult non-medical users of pharmaceutical opioid: Problems and solutions. *Drug and Alcohol Dependence, 121,* 23–29. doi:10.1016/j.drugalcdep.2011.08.005

Davidson, J. (2005). Merit. In S. Mathison (Ed.), *Encyclopedia of evaluation* (p. 247). Thousand Oaks, CA: Sage.

De Nobile, J., London, T., & El Baba, M. (2015). Whole school behaviour management and perceptions of behavior problems in Australian primary schools. *Management in Education, 29,* 164–171. doi:10.1177/0892020615589135

Dennis, M. S., Knight, J., & Jerman, O. (2016). Teaching high school students with learning disabilities to use model drawing strategy to solve fraction and percentage word problems. *Preventing School Failure: Alternative Education for Children and Youth, 60,* 10–21. doi:10.1080/1045988X.2014.954514

Denzin, N. K., & Lincoln, Y. S. (2011). Introduction: The discipline and practice of qualitative research. In N. K. Denzin & Y. S. Lincoln, *The SAGE book of qualitative research* (4th ed., pp. 1–20). Thousand Oaks, CA: Sage.

DePaolis, K., & Williford, A. (2015). The nature and prevalence of cyber victimization among elementary school children. *Child Youth Care Forum, 44,* 377–393.

Derlega, V. J., Metts, S., Petronio, S., & Margulis, S. T. (1993). *Self-disclosure.* Newbury Park, CA: Sage.

Dickens, R. H., & Meisinger, E. B. (2016). Examining the effects of skill level and reading modality on reading comprehension. *Reading Psychology, 37,* 318–337. doi:10.1080/02702711.2015.1055869

Dickersin, K. (1990). The existence of publication bias and risk factors for its occurrence. *Journal of the American Medical Association, 263,* 1385–1389. doi:10.1001/jama.1990.03440100097014

Dillman, D. A. (2000). *Mail and Internet surveys: The tailored design method* (2nd ed.). New York, NY: John Wiley.

Dillman, D. A., Smyth, J. A. & Christian, L. M. (2014). *Internet, phone, mail, and mixed-mode surveys: The tailored design method.* Hoboken, NJ: John Wiley.

Donaldson, S. I. (2007). *Program theory-driven evaluation science: Strategies and applications.* New York, NY: Lawrence Erlbaum.

Dukes, E., & McGuire, B. E. (2009). Enhancing capacity to make sexuality-related decisions in people with an intellectual disability. *Journal of Intellectual Disability Research, 53,* 727–734. doi:10.1111/j.1365-2788.2009.01186.x

Dunn, L. M. (1979). *Peabody picture vocabulary test.* Minneapolis, MN: American Guidance Service.

Dunn, R., & Dunn, K. (1978). Teaching students through their individual learning styles: A practical approach. Reston, VA: Reston.

Durden, T., Escalante, E., & Blitch, K. (2014, September). *Culture matters—Strategies to support young children's social and cultural development* (NebGuide G2241). Lincoln: University of Nebraska–Lincoln Extension, Institute of Agriculture and Natural Resources.

Duryea, E., Graner, S. P., & Becker, J. (2009). Methodological issues related to the use of p < 0.05 in health behavior research. *American Journal of Health Education, 40,* 120–125. doi:10.1080/19325037.2009.10599086

Duong, J., & Bradshaw, C. P. (2013). Using the extended parallel process model to examine teachers' likelihood of intervening in bullying. *Journal of School Health, 83,* 422–429.

EBSCO Industries. (2015). *EBSCOhost.* Retrieved from https://www.ebscohost.com/.

Educational Resource Information Center. (n.d.). *About the ERIC collection.* Retrieved from http://www.eric.ed.gov/ERICWebPortal/resources/html/collection/about_collection.html

Eisner, E. (1976). Educational connoisseurship and criticism: Their form and function in educational evaluation. *Journal of Aesthetic Education, 10,* 135–150.

Eisner, E. (1991). Taking a second look: Educational connoisseurship revisited. In M. W. McLaughlin & D. C. Phillips (Eds.), *Evaluation and education: At quarter century. Ninetieth Yearbook of the National Society for the Study of Education, Part II* (pp. 9169–9187). Chicago, IL: University of Chicago Press.

Errami, M., & Garner, H. (2008). A tale of two citations. *Nature, 451,* 397–399.

Ersoy, A. F. (2014). Active and democratic citizenship education and its challenges in social studies classrooms. *Eurasian Journal of Educational Research, 55,* 1–20.

Evans, A. D., & Lee, K. (2011). Verbal deception from late childhood to middle adolescence and its relation to executive functioning skills. *Developmental Psychology, 47*, 1108–1116.

Falloon, G. (2015). What's the difference? Learning collaboratively using iPads in conventional classrooms. *Computers & Education, 84*, 62–77.

Ferguson, C. J. (2010). Blazing angels or resident evil? Can violent video games be a force for good? *Review of General Psychology, 14*, 68–81. doi:10.1037/a0018941

Ferrell, E. W., Nance, C. N., Torres, A. L., & Torres, S. M. (2014). Using participatory action research to address absenteeism. *Action Learning: Research and Practice, 11*, 201–214. doi:10.1080/14767333.2014.909184

Festinger, D. S., Marlowe, D. B., Croft, J. R., Dugosh, K. L., Arabia, P. L., & Benasutti, K. M. (2009). Monetary incentives improve recall of research consent information: It pays to remember. *Experimental and Clinical Psychopharmacology, 17*, 99–104. doi:10.1037/a0015421

Fetterman, D. M. (1994). Presidential address: Empowerment evaluation. *Evaluation Practice, 15*, 1–15.

Fetterman, D. M. (2007). Empowerment evaluation: Yesterday, today, and tomorrow. *American Journal of Evaluation, 28*, 179–198.

Fetterman, D. M. (2015). Empowerment evaluation: Theories, principles, concepts, and steps. In D. M. Fetterman, S. J. Kaftarian, & A. Wandersman (Eds.), *Empowerment evaluation: Knowledge and tolls for self-assessment, evaluation capacity building, and accountability* (pp. 20–42). Thousand Oaks, CA: Sage.

Feuerborn, L., Tyre, A., & King, J. (2015). The Staff Perceptions of Behavior and Discipline (SPBD) Survey: A tool to help achieve systemic change through schoolwide positive behavior support. *Journal of Positive Behavior Interventions, 17*, 116–126.

Fischer, K., & Jungermann, H. (1996). Rarely occurring headaches and rarely occurring blindness: Is rarely = rarely? *Journal of Behavioral Decision Making, 9*, 153–172. doi:10.1002/(SICI) 1099-0771(199609)9:3<153::AID-BDM222>3.0.CO;2-W

Fisher, R. A. (1925). *Statistical methods for research workers.* Edinburgh, Scotland: Oliver & Boyd.

Fisher, R. A. (1935). *The design of experiments.* Edinburgh, Scotland: Oliver & Boyd.

Fitzpatrick, J. L., Sanders, J. R., & Worthen, B. R. (2011). *Program evaluation: Alternative approaches and practical guidelines.* Boston, MA: Pearson.

Flick, U. (2014). Mapping the field. In U. Flick (Ed.), *The Sage handbook of qualitative research* (pp. 3–18). Thousand Oaks, CA: Sage.

Flory, J., & Emanuel, E. (2004). Interventions to improve research participants' understanding in informed consent for research: A systematic review. *Journal of the American Medical Association, 292*, 1593–1601. doi:10.1001/jama.292.13.1593

Frampton, M. (2014). Spirituality, health and ageing. In D. Lyons (Eds.), *The Evergreen guide: Helping people to survive and thrive in later years* (pp. 117–128). Hauppauge, NY: Nova Science Publishers.

Frank, R. H. (1988). *Passions within reason: The strategic role of the emotions.* New York, NY: Norton.

Frank, R. H. (2001). Cooperation through emotional commitment. In R. M. Nesse (Ed.), *Evaluation and the capacity for commitment* (pp. 57–76). New York, NY: Russell Sage.

Frank, S., Laharnar, N., Kullmann, S., Veit, R., Canova, C., Hegner, Y. L., . . . Preissl, H. (2010). Processing of food pictures: Influence of hunger, gender and calorie content. *Brain Research, 1350*, 159–166. doi:10.1016/j.brainres.2010.04.030

Frankfort-Nachmias, C., & Leon-Guerrero, A. (2006). *Social statistics for a diverse society.* Thousand Oaks, CA: Pine Forge Press.

Galvan, J. (2006). Writing literature reviews: A guide for students of the behavioral sciences (3rd ed.). Glendale, CA: Pyrczak.

Garbarski, D., Schaeffer, N. C., & Dykema, J. (2015). The effects of response option order and question order on self-rated health. *Quality of Life Research, 24*, 1443–1453.

Garcia, J., Kimeldorf, D. J., & Koelling, R. A. (1955). A conditioned aversion toward saccharin resulting from exposure to gamma radiation. *Science, 122*, 157–158.

Gardner, M. (1957). *Fads and fallacies in the name of science.* New York, NY: Dover. (Expanded version of his *In the name of science,* 1952.)

Gier, V. S., Kreiner, D. S., & Natz-Gonzalez, A. (2009). Harmful effects of preexisting inappropriate highlighting on reading comprehension and metacognitive accuracy. *The Journal of General Psychology, 136*, 287–300.

Glaser, B. G. (1978). Theoretical sensitivity: Advances in the methodology of grounded theory. Mill Valley, CA: Sociology Press.

Goldkamp, J. S. (2008). Missing the target and missing the point: "Successful" random assignment but misleading results. *Journal of Experimental Criminology, 4*, 83–115. doi:10.1007/s11292-008-9052-6

Good, P. I., & Hardin, J. W. (2003). *Common errors in statistics (and how to avoid them).* New York, NY: John Wiley.

Good, R. H., & Kaminski, R. A. (2011). *DIBELS Next.* Eugene, OR: Dynamic Measurement Group. Retrieved from https://dibels.org/

Gottfried, M. A., & Harven, A. (2014). The effect of having classmates with emotional and behavioral disorders and the protective nature of peer gender. *The Journal of Educational Research, 108*, 45–61.

Gourman, J. (1997). *Princeton review: Gourman report of graduate programs* (8th ed.). Princeton, NJ: The Princeton Review.

Greene, J. C. (2005). Stakeholders. In S. Mathison (Ed.), *Encyclopedia of evaluation* (pp. 397–398). Thousand Oaks, CA: Sage.

Grove, N. (2014). Personal oral narratives in a special school curriculum: An analysis of key documents. *British Journal of Special Education, 41*, 6–24.

Guba, E. G., & Lincoln, Y. S. (1989). *Fourth generation evaluation.* Thousand Oaks, CA: Sage.

Gunn, C., & Lefoe, G. (2013). Evaluating action-learning and professional networking as a framework for educational leadership capacity development. *International Journal for Academic Development, 18*, 45–59.

Gurley, D. K., Anast-May, L., & Lee, H. T. (2015). Developing instructional leaders through Assistant Principals' Academy: A partnership for success. *Education and Urban Society, 47*, 207–241.

Hadfield, G., Howse, R., & Trebilcock, M. J. (1998). Information-based principles: Biotechnology is influenced not only by their perceptions about the magnitude for rethinking consumer protection policy. *Journal of Consumer Policy, 21*, 131–169.

Hains-Wesson, R., & Young, K. (2017). A collaborative autoethnography study to inform the teaching of reflective practice in STEM. *Higher Education Research & Development, 36*, 297–310. doi:10.1080/07294360.2016.1196653

Hammill, D. O., Pearson, N. A., Hresko, W. P., & Hoover, J. J. (2012). *Early reading assessment.* Austin, TX: Hammill Institute on Disabilities.

Hampton, J. (1998). Between-subjects versus within-subjects designs. In J. Nunn (Ed.), *Laboratory psychology: A beginner's guide* (pp. 15–38). Hove, England: Psychology Press/Erlbaum (UK) Taylor & Francis.

Han, S. (2014). School mobility and students' academic and behavioral outcomes. *International Journal of Education Policy & Leadership, 9*, 1–14.

Haney, C., & Zimbardo, P. G. (1977). The socialization into criminality: On becoming a prisoner and a guard. In J. L. Tapp & T. L. Levine (Eds.), *Law, justice, and the individual in society: Psychological and legal issues* (pp. 198–223). New York, NY: Holt, Rinehart & Winston.

Hannover, B., & Kühnen, U. (2002). "The clothing makes the self" via knowledge activation. *Journal of Applied Social Psychology, 32*(12), 2513–2525. doi:10.1111/j.1559-1816.2002.tb02754.x

Hansson, S. O. (2015). *The Stanford encyclopedia of philosophy: Science and pseudoscience.* Retrieved from http://plato.stanford.edu/entries/pseudo-science/

Harcourt Educational Measurement. (2002). *Stanford Achievement Test* (10th ed.). San Antonio, TX: Author.

Hartford, K., Carey, R., & Mendonca, J. (2007). Sampling bias in an international Internet survey of diversion programs in the criminal justice system. *Evaluation & the Health Professions, 30*, 35–46. doi:10.1177/0163278706297344

Haueter, J. A., Macan, T. H., & Winter, J. (2003). Measurement of newcomer socialization: Construct validation of a multidimensional scale. *Journal of Vocational Behavior, 63*, 20–39. doi:10.1016/S0001-8791(02)00017-9

Hayes, S. C. (1981). Single-case research designs and empirical clinical practice. *Journal of Consulting & Clinical Psychology, 49*, 193–211.

Hayes-Moore, S. (2015). Trading spaces: An educator's ethnographic exploration of adolescents' digital role-play. *Journal of Language & Literacy Education, 11*, 34–46.

Hellström, Å. (2003). Comparison is not just subtraction: Effects of time- and space-order on subjective stimulus difference. *Perception & Psychophysics, 65*, 1161–1177.

Hoaglin, D. C., Mosteller, F., & Tukey, J. W. (1991). *Fundamentals of exploratory analysis of variance.* New York, NY: John Wiley.

Hobson v. Hansen, 269 F. Supp. 401 (D.C. 1967).

Hoffman, H. F., Quittner, A. L., & Cejas, I. (2015). Comparisons of social competence in young children with and without hearing loss: A dynamic systems framework. *Journal of Deaf Studies and Deaf Education, 20*, 115–124.

Hoglund, W. L., Jones, S. M., Brown, J. L., & Aber, J. L. (2015). The evocative influence of child academic and social-emotional adjustment on parent involvement in inner-city schools. *Journal of Educational Psychology, 107*, 517–532.

Holfeld, B., & Leadbeater, B. J. (2015). The nature and frequency of cyberbullying behaviors and victimization experiences in young Canadian children. *Canadian Journal of School Psychology, 30*, 116–135.

Hollands, J. G., & Spence, I. (1992). Judgments of change and proportion in graphical perception. *Human Factors, 34*, 313–334.

Hollands, J. G., & Spence, I. (1998). Judging proportions with graphs: The summation model. *Applied Cognitive Psychology, 12*, 173–190. doi:10.1002/(SICI)1099-0720(199804)12:2<173:: AID-ACP499>3.0.CO;2-K

Holman, E. W. (1975). Immediate and delayed reinforcers for flavor preferences in rats. *Animal Learning & Behavior, 6*, 91–100.

Hondagneu-Sotelo, P. (2002). Families on the frontier: From *braceros* in the fields to *braceras* in the home. In M. M. Suarez-Orozco & M. M. Paez (Eds.), *Latinos: Remaking America* (pp. 259–273). Berkeley: University of California Press.

Horne, J. A. (1988). Why we sleep: The functions of sleep in humans and other mammals. Oxford, England: Oxford University Press.

Horner, R. H., Swaminathan, H., Sugai, G., & Smolkowski, K. (2012). Considerations for the systematic analysis and use of single-case research. *Education & Treatment of Children, 35*, 269–290.

House, E. R. (2007). Deliberative democratic evaluation. In S. Mathison (Ed.), *Encyclopedia of evaluation* (pp. 104–108). Thousand Oaks, CA: Sage.

House, E. R., & Howe, K. R. (2000). Deliberative democratic evaluation. In K. E. Ryan & L. DeStafano (Eds.), *Evaluation as a democratic process: Promoting inclusion, dialogue, and deliberation* (pp. 3–12). San Francisco, CA: Jossey-Bass.

Howard, G. S., Lau, M. Y., Maxwell, S. E., Venter, A., Lundy, R., & Sweeny, R. M. (2009). Do research literatures give correct answers? *Review of General Psychology, 13*, 116–121. doi:10.1037/a0015468

Howard, G. S., Hill, T. L., Maxwell, M. H., Baptista, T. M., Farias, M. H., Coelho, C., . . . Coulter-Kern, R. (2009). What's wrong with research literatures? And how to make them right. *Review of General Psychology, 13*, 146–166. doi:10.1037/a0015319

Howard, K. E., Curwen, M. S., Howard, N. R., & Colon-Muniz, A. (2015). Attitudes toward using social networking sites in educational settings with underperforming Latino youth: A mixed methods study. *Urban Education, 50*, 989–1018. doi:10.1177/0042085914537000

Howard W. Odom Institute for Research in Social Science. (2011). *Odum Institute Dataverse Network.* Retrieved from http://www.irss.unc.edu/odum/contentSubpage.jsp?nodeid=586

Hreinsdottir, A. M., & Davidsdottir, S. (2012). Deliberative democratic evaluation in preschools. *Scandinavian Journal of Educational Research, 56*, 519–537.

Hume, L. E., Lonigan, C. J., & McQueen, J. D. (2012). Children's literacy interest and its relation to parents' literacy-promoting practices. *Journal of Research in Reading, 38*, 172–193.

ITHAKA. (2013). *JSTOR.* Retrieved from http://www.jstor.org/

Jeynes, W. H. (2015). A meta-analysis: The relationship between father involvement and student academic achievement. *Urban Education, 50*, 387–423.

Jha, V., Quinton, N. D., Bekker, H. L., & Roberts, T. E. (2009). What educators and students really think about using patients as teachers in medical education: A qualitative study. *Medical Education, 43*, 449–456. doi:10.1111/j.1365-2923.2009.03355.x

Joint Committee on Standards for Educational Evaluation. (2010). *The program evaluation standards* (3rd ed.). Thousand Oaks, CA: Sage.

Jordan, M. E. (2015). Extra! Extra! Read all about it: Teacher scaffolds interactive read-alouds of a dynamic text. *The Elementary School Journal, 115*, 358–383.

Kaptchuk, T. J. (1998). Powerful placebo: The dark side of the randomized controlled trial. *Lancet, 351*, 1722–1725.

Karahan, E., & Roehrig, G. (2014). Constructing media artifacts in a social constructivist environment to enhance students' environmental awareness and activism. *Journal of Science, Education and Technology, 24*, 103–118. doi:10.1007/s10956-014-9525-5

Kazdin, A. E. (2011). *Single-case research designs.* New York, NY: Oxford University Press.

Kemmis, S., & McTaggart, R. (2005). Participatory action research: Communicative action and the public sphere. In N. K. Denzin & Y. S. Lincoln (Eds.), *The SAGE handbook of qualitative research* (3rd ed., pp. 559–604). Thousand Oaks, CA: Sage.

Kemmis, S., McTaggart, R., & Nixon, R. (2014). *The action research planner: Doing critical participatory action research*. New York, NY: Springer.

Kennedy, C. H. (1993). *Sexual consent and education assessment*. Philadelphia, PA: Drexel University Press.

Kennedy-Lewis, B. L., Murphy, A. A., & Grosland, T. J. (2016). Using narrative inquiry to understand persistently disciplined middle school students. *International Journal of Qualitative Studies in Education, 29*, 1–28.

Kenner, C., & Ruby, M. (2012). Connecting children's worlds: Creating a multilingual syncretic curriculum through partnership between complementary and mainstream schools. *Journal of Early Childhood Literacy, 13*, 395–417. doi:0.1177/1468798412466404

King, J. A. (2007). Making sense of participatory evaluation. *New Directions for Evaluation, 114*, 83–105. doi:10.1002/ev.226

Klar, H., & Brewer, C. (2013). Successful leadership in high-needs schools: An examination of core leadership practices enacted in challenging contexts. *Educational Administration Quarterly, 49*, 768–808.

Kline, R. B. (2008). *Becoming a behavioral science researcher: A guide to producing research that matters*. New York, NY: Guilford.

Knaggs, C. M., Sondergeld, T. A., & Schardt, B. (2015). Overcoming barriers to college enrollment, persistence, and perceptions for urban high school students in a college preparatory program. *Journal of Mixed Methods Research, 9*, 7–30. doi:10.1177/1558689813497260

Komorita, S. S., & Graham, W. K. (1965). Number of scale points and the reliability of scales. *Educational and Psychological Measurement, 25*, 987–995.

Kowal, S., & O'Connell, D. C. (2014). Transcription as a crucial step in qualitative research. In U. Flick (Ed.), *The Sage handbook of qualitative research* (pp. 64–78). Thousand Oaks, CA: Sage.

Kozinets, R. V. (2010). Netnography. In *Doing ethnographic research online*. Thousand Oaks, CA: Sage.

Krefting, L. (1991). Rigor in qualitative research: The assessment of trustworthiness. *The American Journal of Occupational Therapy, 45*, 214–222. doi:10.5014/ajot.45.3.214

LaFollette, M. C. (2000). The evolution of the "scientific misconduct" issue: A historical overview. *Proceedings of the Society for Experimental Biology and Medicine, 224*, 211–215. doi:10.1111/j.1525-1373.2000.22423.x

Lam, C. Y., & Shula, L. M. (2015). Insights on using developmental evaluation for innovating: A case study on the cocreation of an innovative program. *American Journal of Evaluation, 36*, 358–374.

Lange, K. W., Reichl, S., Lange, K, M., Tucha, L, & Tucha, O. (2010). The history of attention deficit hyperactivity disorder. *Attention Deficit Hyperactivity Disorders, 2*, 241–255.

Langlois, J. H., Kalakanis, L., Rubenstein, A. J., Larson, A., Hallam, M., & Smoot, M. (2000). Maxims or myths of beauty? A meta-analytic and theoretical review. *Psychological Bulletin, 126*, 390–423. doi:10.1037//0033-2909.126.3.390

Lapointe, A. A. (2015). Standing "straight" up to homophobia: Straight allies' involvement in GSAs. *Journal of LGBT Youth, 12*, 144–169. doi:10.1080/19361653.2014.969867

Larry P. v. Riles, 793 F.2d 969 (9th Cir. 1979).

Lawton, B., Brandon, P. R., Cicchinelli, L., & Kekahio, W. (2014). *Logic models: A tool for designing and monitoring program evaluations* (REL 2014-007). Washington, DC: U.S. Department of Education, Institute of Education Sciences, National Center for Education Evaluation and Regional Assistance, Regional Educational Laboratory Pacific. Retrieved from http://ies.ed.gov/ncee/edlabs

Liesegang, T. J., Albert, D. M., & Schachat, A. P. (2008). Not for your eyes: Information concealed through publication bias. *American Journal of Ophthalmology, 146*, 638–640. doi:10.1016/j.ajo.2008.07.034

Likert, R. (1932). A technique for the measurement of attitude. *Archives of Psychology, 140*, 55.

Lincoln, Y. S., & Guba, E. G. (1985). *Naturalistic inquiry*. Beverly Hills, CA: Sage.

Liou, D. D., Martinez, A. N., & Rotheram-Fuller, E. (2015). "Don't give up on me": Critical mentoring pedagogy for the classroom building students' community cultural wealth. *International Journal of Qualitative Studies in Education, 29*, 104–129.

Lipkus, I. M. (2007). Numeric, verbal and visual formats of conveying health risks: Suggested best practices and future recommendations. *Medical Decision Making, 27*, 696–713. doi:10.1177/ 0272989X07307271

Long, T. C., Errami, M., George, A. C., Sun, Z., & Garner, H. R. (2009). Responding to possible plagiarism. *Science, 323*, 1293–1294. doi:10.1126/science.1167408

Lovett, M. W., Lacerenza, L., DePalma, M., & Frijters, J. C. (2012). Evaluating the efficacy of remediation for struggling readers in high school. *Journal of Learning Disabilities, 45*, 151–169.

Luna, N., Evans, W. P., & Davis, B. (2015). Indigenous Mexican culture, identity and academic aspirations: Results from a community-based curriculum project for Latina/Latino students. *Race, Ethnicity and Education, 18*, 341–362. doi:10.1080/13613324.2012.759922

Lynch, M. (2015). Guys and dolls: A qualitative study of teachers' views of gendered play in kindergarten. *Early Childhood Development and Care, 18*, 679–693.

MacDonald, B., & Kushner, S. (2007). Democratic evaluation. In S. Mathison (Ed.), *Encyclopedia of evaluation* (pp. 109–113). Thousand Oaks, CA: Sage.

Machin, D., & Thornborrow, J. (2003). Branding and discourse: The case of *Cosmopolitan. Discourse & Society, 14*, 453–471. doi:10.1177/0957926503014004003

Madsen, K. A., Hicks, K., & Thompson, H. (2011). Physical activity and positive youth development: impact of a school-based program. *Journal of School Health, 81*, 462–470.

Magazine Publishers of America. (2013). *Consumer marketing*. Retrieved from http://www.magazine.org/insights-resources/research-publications/guides-studies

Mahner, M. (2007). Demarcating science from non-science. In T. Kuipers (Ed.), *Handbook of the philosophy of science: General philosophy of science—focal issues* (pp. 515–575). Amsterdam, the Netherlands: Elsevier.

Mann, M. J., Smith, M. L., & Kristjansson, A. L. (2015). Improving academic self-efficacy, school connectedness, and identity in struggling middle school girls: A preliminary study of the REAL Girls program. *Health Education & Behavior, 42*, 117–126.

Martin, M. O., & Mullis, I. V. (2011). *Methods and procedures in TIMSS and PIRLS 2011.* Boston, MA: International Study Center, Lynch School of Education, Boston College. Retrieved from http://timssandpirls.bc.edu/methods/t-sample-design.html

Marwick, C. (2003). US doctor warns of misuse of prescribed stimulants. *BMJ, 326,* 67. doi:10.1136/bmj.326.7380.67

Masters, E. A. (2013). Research misconduct in National Science Foundation funded research: A mixed-methods analysis of 2007–2011 research awards (Doctoral dissertation). Retrieved from ProQuestLLC. (ED550845)

Matell, M. S., & Jacoby, J. (1971). Is there an optimal number of alternatives for Likert scale items? Study 1: Reliability and validity. *Educational and Psychological Measurement, 31,* 657–674. doi:10.1177/001316447103100307

Mathison, S. (Ed.). (2005). *Encyclopedia of evaluation.* Thousand Oaks, CA: Sage.

Mathison, S. (2007). What is the difference between evaluation and research—and why do we care? In N. L. Smith & P. R. Brandon (Eds.), *Fundamental issues in evaluation* (pp. 183–196). New York, NY: Guilford.

Maynard, B. R., Kjellstrand, E. K., & Thompson, A. M. (2014). Effects of check and connect on attendance, behavior, and academics: A randomized effectiveness trial. *Research on Social Work Practice, 24,* 296–309.

Mazur, D. J., & Merz, J. F. (1994). How age, outcome severity, and scale influence general medicine clinic patients' interpretations of verbal probability terms. *Journal of General Internal Medicine, 9,* 268–271. doi:10.1007/BF02599654

McCaleb, K. N., Andersen, A., & Hueston, H. (2008, December). An investigation of school violence and pre-service teachers. *Current Issues in Education, 10.* Retrieved from http://cie.ed.asu.edu/volume10/number3/

McCallum, J. M., Arekere, D. M., Green, B. L., Katz, R. V., & Rivers, B. M. (2006). Awareness and knowledge of the U.S. Public Health Service syphilis study at Tuskegee: Implications for biomedical research. *Journal of Health Care for the Poor and Underserved, 17,* 716–733. doi:10.1353/hpu.2006.0130

McCambridge, J. (2007). A case study of publication bias in an influential series of reviews of drug education. *Drug and Alcohol Review, 26,* 463–468. doi:10.1080/09595230701494366

McCormick, A., Schmidt, K., & Clifton, E. (2015). Gay-straight alliances: Understanding their impact on the academic and social experiences of lesbian, gay, bisexual, transgender, and questioning high school students. *Children & Schools, 37,* 71–77.

McLaughlin, K. (2003). Agency, resilience, and empowerment: The dangers posed by a therapeutic culture. *Practice, 15,* 45–58. doi: 10.1080/09503150308416918

McNeilly, P., Macdonald, G., & Kelly, B. (2015). The participation of disabled children and young people: A social justice perspective. *Child Care in Practice, 21,* 266–286. doi:10.1080/13575279.2015.1014468

McNemar, Q. (1946). Opinion-attitude methodology. *Psychological Bulletin, 43,* 289–374.

Mellor, J. M., Rapoport, R. B., & Maliniak, D. (2008). The impact of child obesity on active parental consent in school-based survey research on healthy eating and physical activity. *Evaluation Review, 32,* 298–312. doi:10.1177/0193841X07312682

Milgram, S. (1963). Behavioral study of obedience. *Journal of Abnormal Social Psychology, 67,* 371–378. doi:10.1037/ h0040525

Miller, F. G., Wendler, D., & Swartzman, L. C. (2005). Deception in research on the placebo effect. *PLoS Medicine, 2,* e262. doi:10.1371/journal.pmed.0020262

Milman, N. B., Carlson-Bancroft, A., & Boogart, A. V. (2014). Examining differentiation and utilization of iPads across content areas in an independent, preK–4th grade elementary school. *Computers in the Schools: Interdisciplinary Journal of Practice, Theory, and Applied Research, 31,* 119–133.

Mishna, F., Schwan, K. J., Lefebvre, R., Bhole, P., & Johnston, D. (2014). Students in distress: Unanticipated findings in a cyberbullying study. *Children and Youth Services Review, 44,* 341–348.

Morgan, E. S., Umberson, K., & Hertzog, C. (2014). Construct validation of self-reported stress scales. *Psychological Assessment, 26,* 90–99. doi:10.1037/a0034714

Morse, R. (2015, May 11). How states compare in the 2015 best high school rankings. *U.S. News & World Report.* Retrieved from http://www.usnews.com/education/best-high-schools/articles/how-states-compare

Muliira, J. K., Nalwanga, P. B., Muliira, R. S., & Nankinga, Z. (2012). Knowledge, perceived risks and barriers to testicular self-examination among male university students in Uganda. *Journal of Men's Health, 9,* 36–44. doi:10.1016/j.jomh.2011.11.004

Muthersbaugh, D., Kern, A., & Charvoz, R. (2014). Impact through images: Exploring student understanding of environmental science through integrated place-based lessons in the elementary classroom. *Journal of Research in Childhood Education, 28,* 313–326.

National Commission for the Protection of Human Subjects of Biomedical and Behavioral Research. (1979, April 18). *The Belmont Report: Ethical principles and guidelines for the protection of human subjects of research.* Retrieved from http://www.hhs.gov/ohrp/humansubjects/guidance/belmont.html

National Early Literacy Panel. (2008). *Developing early literacy: Report of the National Early Literacy Panel.* Washington, DC: National Institute for Literacy. Retrieved from http://lincs.ed.gov/publications/pdf/NELPSummary.pdf

National Governors Association and Council of Chief State School Officers. (2010). *Common core state standards for English language arts.* Washington, DC: Author.

National Reading Panel. (2000). Teaching children to read: An evidence-based assessment of the scientific research literature on reading and its implications for reading instruction (NIH Pub. No. 00-4754). Washington, DC: U.S. Department of Health and Human Services.

Newman, D., Finney, P. B., Bell, S., Turner, H., Jaciw, A. P., Zacamy, J. L., & Feagans Gould, L. (2012). *Evaluation of the effectiveness of the Alabama Math, Science, and Technology Initiative* (AMSTI) (NCEE 2012–4008). Washington, DC: National Center for Education Evaluation and Regional Assistance, Institute of Education Sciences, U.S. Department of Education.

Niland, A. (2015). "Row, row, row your boat": Singing, identity and belonging in a nursery. *International Journal of Early Years Education, 23,* 4–16.

No Child Left Behind Act of 2001, Pub. L. No. 107–110, 115 Stat.1425 (2002).

Office of Research Integrity. (2011a). *Avoiding plagiarism, self-plagiarism, and other questionable writing practices: A guide to ethical writing.* Retrieved from http://ori.dhhs.gov/education/products/plagiarism/plagiarism.pdf

Office of Research Integrity. (2011b). *Handling misconduct.* Retrieved from http://ori.dhhs.gov/misconduct/cases

Olson, C. M., Rennie, D., Cook, D., Dickersin, K., Flanagin, A., Hogan, J. W., . . . Pace, B. (2002). Publication bias in editorial decision making. *Journal of the American Medical Association, 287*, 2825–2828. doi:10.1001/jama.287.21.2825

Ottenbacher, K. J. (1993). The interpretation of averages in health professions research. *Evaluation & the Health Professions, 16*, 333–341. doi:10.1177/016327879301600306

Parascandola, M., Hawkins, J., & Danis, M. (2002). Patient autonomy and the challenge of clinical uncertainty. *Kennedy Institute of Ethics Journal, 12*, 245–264. doi:10.1353/ken.2002.0018

Parker, I. (2005). *Qualitative psychology: Introducing radical research.* New York, NY: Open University Press.

Pasco, D., & Ennis, C. D. (2015). Third-grade students' mental models of energy expenditure during exercise. *Physical Education and Sport Pedagogy, 20*, 131–143.

Patton, M. Q. (1994). Utility tests. In S. Mathison (Ed.), *Encyclopedia of evaluation* (pp. 428–429). Thousand Oaks, CA: Sage.

Patton, M. Q. (2008). *Utilization-focused evaluation.* Thousand Oaks, CA: Sage.

Patton, M. Q. (2015). *Qualitative research & evaluation methods* (4th ed.). Thousand Oaks, CA: Sage.

Peck, N. F., Maude, S. P., & Brotherson, M. J. (2015). Understanding preschool teachers' perspectives on empathy: A qualitative inquiry. *Early Childhood Education Journal, 43*, 169–179.

Pillay, J., Dunbar-Krige, H., & Mostert, J. (2013). Learners with behavioral, emotional and social difficulties' experiences of reintegrating into mainstream education. *Emotional and Behavioral Difficulties, 18*, 310–326.

Platt, J. R. (1964). Strong inference: Certain systematic methods of scientific thinking may produce much more rapid progress than others. *Science, 146*, 347–353.

Plavnick, J. (2012). A practical strategy for teaching a child with autism to attend to and imitate a portable video model. *Research and Practice for Persons With Severe Disabilities, 37*, 263–270.

Pliner, P. (1982). The effects of mere exposure on liking for edible substances. *Appetite, 3*, 283–290.

Pollak, O. (1950). *The criminality of women.* Philadelphia: University of Pennsylvania Press.

Popper, K. R. (1959). *The logic of scientific discovery.* New York, NY: Basic Books.

Porowski, A., & Pasa, A. (2011). The effect of communities in schools on high school dropout and graduation rates: Results from a multi-year, school-level quasi-experimental study. *Journal of Education for Students Placed at Risk, 16*, 24–37.

Privitera, G. J. (2008a, February). Decreasing dislike for sour and bitter in children and adults. *The International Fruit & Vegetable Alliance (IFAVA) Scientific Newsletter*, p. 4.

Privitera, G. J. (2008b). *The psychological dieter: It's not all about the calories.* Lanham, MD: University Press of America.

Privitera, G. J. (2012). *Statistics for the behavioral sciences.* Thousand Oaks, CA: Sage.

Privitera, G. J., Agnello, J. E., Walters, S. A., & Bender, S. L. (2015). Randomized feedback about diagnosis influences statistical and clinical significance of self-report ADHD assessment in adults. *Journal of Attention Disorders, 19*, 447–451. doi:10.1177/1087054712461178

Privitera, G. J., Cooper, K. C., & Cosco, A. R. (2012). The influence of eating rate on satiety and intake among participants exhibiting high dietary restraint. *Food & Nutrition Research, 56*, 10202. doi:10.3402/fnr.v56i0.10202

Privitera, G. J., & Freeman, C. S. (2012). Validity and reliability of an estimated daily intake scale for fat. *Global Journal of Health Science, 4*(2), 36–41. doi:10.5539/gjhs.v4n2p36

Privitera, G. J., Phillips, T., Zuraikat, F., & Paque, R. (2015) Emolabeling increases healthy food choices among grade school children in a structured grocery aisle setting. *Appetite, 92*, 173–177. doi:10.1016/j.appet.2015.05.024

Rader-Brown, L., & Howley, A. (2014). Predictors of the instructional strategies that elementary school teachers use with English language learners. *Teachers College Record, 116*, 1–19.

Rasinski, K. A., Lee, L., & Krishnamurty, P. (2012). Question order effects. In H. Cooper, P. M. Canic, D. L. Long, A. T. Painter, D. Rindskopf, & K. J. Sher (Eds.), *APA handbook of research methods in psychology: Foundations, planning, measures, and psychometrics* (Vol. 1, pp. 229–248). Washington, DC: American Psychological Association.

Rector, T. S. (2008). How should we communicate the likelihood of risks to inform decisions about consent? *IRB: Ethics & Human Research, 30*, 15–18.

Reddy, L. A., Fabiano, G., Dudek, C. M., & Hsu, L. (2013). Development and construct validity of the Classroom Strategies Scale—Observer Form. *School Psychology Quarterly, 28*, 317–341.

Reese, H. W. (1997). Counterbalancing and other uses of repeated-measures Latin-square designs: Analyses and interpretations. *Journal of Experimental Child Psychology, 64*, 137–158. doi:10.1006/jecp.1996.2333

Reese, R. J., Thompason Prout, H., Zirkelback, E. A., & Anderson, C. R. (2010). Effectiveness of school-based psychotherapy: A meta-analysis of dissertation research. *Psychology in the Schools, 47*, 1035–1045.

Reid, E. E., Barody, A. J., & Purpura, D. J. (2015). Assessing young children's number magnitude representation: A comparison between novel and conventional tasks. *Journal of Cognition and Development, 16*, 759–779.

Resnick, J. H., & Schwartz, T. (1973). Ethical standards as an independent variable in psychological research. *American Psychologist, 28*, 134–139.

Reynolds-Keefer, L., Johnson, R., Dickenson, T., & McFadden, L. (2009). Validity issues in the use of pictorial Likert scales. *Studies in Learning, Evaluation, Innovation and Development, 6*, 15–24.

Ridgers, N. D., Saint-Maurice, P. F., Welk, G. J., Siahpush, M., & Huberty, J. L. (2014). Non-overweight and overweight children's physical activity during school recess. *Health Education Journal, 73*, 129–136.

Robinson-Cimpian, J. P. (2014). Inaccurate estimation of disparities due to mischievous responders: Several suggestions to assess conclusions. *Educational Researcher, 43*, 171–185. doi:10.3102/0013189X14534297

Rosenthal, R. (1984). *Meta-analytic procedures for social research* (Applied Social Research Methods, Vol. 6). Beverly Hills, CA: Sage.

Rouder, J. N., & Geary, D. C. (2014). Children's cognitive representation of the mathematical number line. *Developmental Science, 17*, 525–536.

Ruppar, A. L., Gaffney, J. S., & Dymond, S. K. (2015). Influences on teachers' decisions about literacy for secondary students with severe disabilities. *Exceptional Children, 81*, 209–226.

Rutledge, S. A., Cohen-Vogel, L., Osborne-Lampkin, L., & Roberts, R. L. (2015). Understanding effective high schools: Evidence for personalization for academic and social emotional learning. *American Educational Research Journal, 52,* 1060–1092.

Saad, L. (2016). *U.S. education ratings show record political polarization.* Retrieved from http://www.gallup.com/poll/194675/education-ratings-show-record-political-polarization.aspx?g_source=CATEGORY_EDUCATION&g_medium=topic&g_campaign=tiles

Saleh, M., Lazonder, A. W., & de Tong, T. (2006). Structuring collaboration in mixed-ability groups to promote verbal interaction, learning, and motivation of average-ability students. *Contemporary Educational Psychology, 32,* 314–331.

Scarbrough, B., & Allen, A. (2015). Writing workshop revisited: Confronting communicative dilemmas through spoken word poetry in a high school English classroom. *Journal of Literacy Research, 46,* 475–505.

Scheiter, K., Schubert, C., Gerjets, P., & Stalbovs, K. (2015). Does a strategy training foster students' ability to learn from multimedia? *Journal of Experimental Education, 83,* 266–289.

Schmuck, R. A. (1997). *Practical action research for change.* Arlington Heights, IL: IRI/Skylight Training and Publishing.

Schmuck, R. A. (2006). *Practical action research for change* (2nd ed.). Thousand Oaks, CA: Corwin Press.

Schocker, J. B., & Woyshner, C. (2013): Representing African American women in U.S. history textbooks. *The Social Studies, 104,* 23–31.

Schredl, M., Fricke-Oerkermann, L., Mitschke, A., Wiater, A., & Lehmkuhl, G. (2009). Longitudinal study of nightmares in children: Stability and effect of emotional symptoms. *Child Psychiatry & Human Development, 40,* 439–449. doi:10.1007/s10578-009-0136-y

Schumacker, R. E., & Lomax, R. G. (2010). *A beginner's guide to structural equation modeling* (3rd ed.). New York, NY: Routledge.

Scott, C. K., Sonis, J., Creamer, M., & Dennis, M. L. (2006). Maximizing follow-up in longitudinal studies of traumatized populations. *Journal of Traumatic Stress, 19,* 757–769. doi:10.1002/jts.20186

Scriven, M. (1974a). Checklist for the evaluation of products, producers, and proposals. In W. J. Popham (Ed.), *Evaluation in education* (pp. 7–33). Berkeley, CA: McCutchan.

Scriven, M. (1974b). Prose and cons about goal-free evaluation. In W. J. Popham (Ed.), *Evaluation in education: Current applications* (pp. 34–67). Berkeley, CA: McCutchan.

Scriven, M. (1991a). Beyond formative and summative evaluation. In M. W. McLaughlin & D. C. Phillips (Eds.), *Evaluation and education: At quarter century. Ninetieth Yearbook of the National Society for the Study of Education, Part II* (pp. 19–64). Chicago, IL: University of Chicago Press.

Scriven, M. (1991b). *Evaluation thesaurus* (4th ed.). Newbury Park, CA: Sage.

Seong, Y., Wehmeyer, M. L., Palmer, S. B., & Little, T. D. (2015). Effects of the self-directed individualized education program on self-determination and transition of adolescents with disabilities. *Career Development and Transition for Exceptional Individuals, 38,* 32–141. doi:10.1177/2165143414544359

Shih, T., & Fan, X. (2008). Comparing response rates from web and mail surveys: A meta-analysis. *Field Methods, 20*(3), 249–271. doi:10.1177/1525822X08317085

Shulman, E. (1967). *Evaluative research.* Beverly Hills, CA: Sage.

Sieber, J. E. (2007). Respect for persons and informed consent: A moving target. *Journal of Empirical Research on Human Research Ethics, 2,* 1–2. doi:10.1525/jer.2007.2.3.1

Siebers, R., & Holt, S. (2000). Accuracy of references in five leading medical journals. *The Lancet, 356,* 1445. doi:10.1016/S0140-6736(05)74090-3

Sim, M. G., Hulse, G., & Khong, E. (2004). When the child with ADHD grows up. *Australian Family Physician, 33,* 615–618.

Singh, S., Sylvia, M. R., & Ridzi, F. (2015). Exploring the literacy practices of refugee families enrolled in a book distribution program and an intergenerational family literacy program. *Early Childhood Education Journal, 43,* 37–45.

Sprecher, S., & Cate, R. M. (2004). Sexual satisfaction and sexual expression as predictors of relationship satisfaction and stability. In J. H. Harvey, A. Wenzel, & S. Sprecher (Eds.), *Handbook of sexuality in close relationships* (pp. 235–256). Mahwah, NJ: Lawrence Erlbaum.

Stevens, S. S. (1946). On the theory of scales of measurement. *Science, 103,* 677–680.

Stewart, A. E., & St. Peter, C. C. (2004). Driving and riding avoidance following motor vehicle crashes in a non-clinical sample: Psychometric properties of a new measure. *Behaviour Research and Therapy, 42,* 859–879.

Stipek, D., Newton, S., & Chudgar, A. (2010). Learning-related behaviors and literacy achievement in elementary school-aged children. *Early Childhood Research Quarterly, 25,* 385–395.

Strauss, A., & Corbin, J. (1994). Grounded theory methodology. In N. K. Denzin & Y. S. Lincoln (Eds.), *Handbook of qualitative research* (pp. 217–285). Thousand Oaks, CA: Sage.

Stufflebeam, D. (2007). CIPP model (context, input, process, product). In S. Mathison (Ed.), *Encyclopedia of evaluation* (pp. 60–65). Thousand Oaks, CA: Sage.

Stufflebeam, D. (2010). CIPP evaluation model checklist: A tool for applying the CIPP model to assess projects and programs. San Francisco, CA: Jossey-Bass.

Suchman, E. (1967). *Evaluative research: Principles and practice in public service and social action programs.* New York, NY: Russell Sage.

Sutherland, S., Stuhr, P. T., & Ayvazo, S. (2014). Learning to teach: Pedagogical content knowledge in adventure-based learning. *Physical Education and Sport Pedagogy, 21,* 233–248.

Tarman, B., & Kuran, B. (2015). Examination of the cognitive level of questions in social studies textbooks and the views of teachers based on Bloom Taxonomy. *Educational Sciences: Theory & Practice, 15,* 213–222.

Taylor, D. (2002). The appropriate use of references in a scientific research paper. *Emergency Medicine, 14,* 166–170. doi:10.1046/j.1442-2026.2002.00312.x

Taylor, J. E. (2008). Driving phobia consequent to motor vehicle collisions. In M. P. Duckworth, T. Iezzi, & W. T. O'Donohue (Eds.), *Motor vehicle collisions: Medical, psychosocial, and legal consequences* (pp. 389–416). New York, NY: Elsevier.

Thompson, B. (2014). Exploratory and confirmatory factor analysis: Understanding concepts and applications. Washington, DC: American Psychological Association.

Trials of war criminals before the Nuremberg military tribunals under Control Council Law No. 10 (Vol. 2). (1949). Washington, DC: Government Printing Office.

Tubin, D. (2015). School success as a process of structuration. *Educational Administration Quarterly, 51,* 640–674.

Tukey, J. W. (1977). *Exploratory data analysis.* Reading, MA: Addison-Wesley.

Tunon, J., Ramirez, L. L., Ryckman, B., Campbell, L., & Mlinar, C. (2015). Creating an information literacy badges program in Blackboard: A formative program evaluation. *Journal of Library & Information Services in Distant Learning, 9,* 157–169.

Tyler, R. (1986). Changing concepts of educational evaluation. *International Journal of Educational Research, 10,* 1–113.

Unrau, N., Ragusa, G., & Bowers, E. (2015). Teachers focus on motivation for reading: "It's all about knowing the relationship." *Reading Psychology, 36,* 105–144.

U.S. Bureau of Labor Statistics. (2013). *Databases, tables & calculators by subject.* Retrieved from http://data.bls.gov/timeseries/LNS14000000

U.S. Department of Education. (2010). *What Works Clearinghouse procedures and standards handbook.* Retrieved from http://ies.ed.gov/ncee/wwc/)

U.S. Department of Health and Human Services. (2007). *Guidance on reviewing and reporting unanticipated problems involving risks to subjects or others and adverse events.* Retrieved from http://www.hhs.gov/ohrp/policy/advevntguid.html

U.S. National Library of Medicine. (2013). *Databases, resources & APIs.* Retrieved from http://wwwcf2.nlm.nih.gov/nlm_eresources/eresources/search_database.cfm

Varghese, A. L., & Nilsen, E. (2013). Incentives improve the clarity of school-age children's referential statements. *Cognitive Development, 28,* 364–373.

Vevea, J. I., & Woods, C. M. (2005). Publication bias in research synthesis: Sensitivity analysis using a priori weight functions. *Psychological Methods, 10,* 428–443.

Villa, E. Q., & Baptiste, H. P. (2014). Creating an equitable classroom environment: A case study of a preservice elementary teacher learning what it means to "do inquiry." *Multicultural Education, 21,* 25–32.

Wakefield, A. J., Murch, S. H., Anthony, A., Linnell, J., Casson, D. M., Malik, M., . . . Walker-Smith, J. A. (1998). Ileal-lymphoid-nodular hyperplasia, non-specific colitis, and pervasive developmental disorder in children. *The Lancet, 351,* 637–641.

Wansink, B., & Kim, J. (2005). Bad popcorn in big buckets: Portion size can influence intake as much as taste. *Journal of Nutrition Education and Behavior, 37,* 242–245.

Weisberg, S. (2005). *Applied linear regression.* Hoboken, NJ: John Wiley.

Weiss, C. H. (1972). *Evaluation research: Methods for assessing program effectiveness.* Englewood Cliffs, NJ: Prentice-Hall.

White, J. M., Wampler, R. S., & Winn, K. I. (1998). In identity style inventory: A revision with a sixth-grade reading level (ISI-6G). *Journal of Adolescent Research, 13,* 223–245. doi:10.1177/0743554898132007

Wholey, J. S. (1987). Evaluability assessment: Developing program theory. In L. Bickman (Ed.), *Using program theory in evaluation: New directions for program evaluation* (pp. 77–92). San Francisco, CA: Jossey-Bass.

Williams, D. (2008). Exercise, affect, and adherence: An integrated model and a case for self-paced exercise. *Journal of Sport and Exercise Psychology, 30,* 471–496.

Willson, V. L. (1981). Time and the external validity of experiments. *Evaluation and Program Planning, 4,* 229–238. doi:10.1016/0149-7189(81)90024-0

Wolf, M., Sedway, J., Bulik, C. M., & Kordy, H. (2007). Linguistic analyses of nature written language: Unobtrusive assessment of cognitive style in eating disorders. *International Journal of Eating Disorders, 40*(8), 711–717. doi:10.1002/eat. 20445

Wu, C., & Chiang, C. (2014). The developmental sequence of social-communicative skills in young children with autism: A longitudinal study. *Autism, 18,* 385–392.

Yakubova, G., & Bouck, F. C. (2014). Not all created equally: Exploring calculator use by students with mild intellectual disability. *Education and Training in Autism and Developmental Disabilities, 49,* 111–126.

Young, M. M., Wohl, M. J. A., Matheson, K., Baumann, S., & Anisman, H. (2008). The desire to gamble: The influence of outcomes on the priming effects of a gambling episode. *Journal of Gambling Studies, 24,* 275–293. doi:10.1007/s10899-008-9093-9

Zigmond, M. J., & Fischer, B. A. (2002). Beyond fabrication and plagiarism: The little murders of everyday science: Commentary on "Six Domains of Research Ethics" (K. D. Pimple). *Science and Engineering Ethics, 8,* 229–234.

Zimbardo, P. G. (1975). On transforming experimental research into advocacy for social change. In M. Deutsch & H. Hornstein (Eds.), *Applying social psychology: Implications for research, practice, and training* (pp. 33–66). Hillsdale, NJ: Lawrence Erlbaum.

Zöllner, F. (1860). On a new kind of pseudoscopy and its relation to the phenomena of motion described by Plateau and Oppel. *Annals of Physics, 186,* 500–525.

INDEX

Research Methods for Education